The IDG Books Bible Advantage

The *Multimedia Producer's Bible* is part of the Bible series brought to you by IDG Books Worldwide. We designed Bibles to meet your growing need for quick access to the most complete and accurate computer information available.

Bibles work the way you do: They focus on accomplishing tasks — not learning random functions. These books are not long-winded manuals or dry reference tomes. In Bibles, expert authors tell you exactly what you can do and how to do it. Easy to follow, step-by-step sections; comprehensive coverage; and convenient access in language and design — it's all here.

The authors of Bibles are uniquely qualified to give you expert advice as well as insightful tips and techniques not found anywhere else. Our authors maintain close contact with end users through feedback from articles, training sessions, e-mail exchanges, user group participation, and consulting work. Because our authors know the realities of daily computer use and are directly tied to the reader, our Bibles have a strategic advantage.

Bible authors have the experience to approach a topic in the most efficient manner, and we know that you, the reader, will benefit from a "one-on-one" relationship with the author. Our research shows that readers make computer book purchases because they want expert advice on a product. Readers want to benefit from the author's experience, so the author's voice is always present in a Bible series book.

In addition, the author is free to include or recommend useful software in a Bible. The software that accompanies a Bible is not intended to be casual filler but is linked to the content, theme, or procedures of the book. We know that you will benefit from the included software.

You will find what you need in this book whether you read it from cover to cover, section by section, or simply one topic at a time. As a computer user, you deserve a comprehensive resource of answers. We at IDG Books Worldwide are proud to deliver that resource with the *Multimedia Producer's Bible.*

Brenda McLaughlin
Senior Vice President and Group Publisher

MULTIMEDIA PRODUCER'S BIBLE

MULTIMEDIA PRODUCER'S BIBLE

by Ron Goldberg

IDG Books Worldwide, Inc.
An International Data Group Company

Foster City, CA ♦ Chicago, IL ♦ Indianapolis, IN ♦ Southlake, TX

Multimedia Producer's Bible

Published by
IDG Books Worldwide, Inc.
An International Data Group Company
919 E. Hillsdale Blvd.
Suite 400
Foster City, CA 94404

Library of Congress Catalog Card No.: 96-76352

ISBN: 0-7645-3002-X

Printed in the United States of America

10 9 8 7 6 5 4 3 2 1

1B/QX/RQ/ZW/IN

Distributed in the United States by IDG Books Worldwide, Inc.

Distributed by Macmillan Canada for Canada; by Contemporanea de Ediciones for Venezuela; by Distribuidora Cuspide for Argentina; by CITEC for Brazil; by Ediciones ZETA S.C.R. Ltda. for Peru; by Editorial Limusa SA for Mexico; by Transworld Publishers Limited in the United Kingdom and Europe; by Academic Bookshop for Egypt; by Levant Distributors S.A.R.L. for Lebanon; by Al Jassim for Saudi Arabia; by Simron Pty. Ltd. for South Africa; by Pustak Mahal for India; by The Computer Bookshop for India; by Toppan Company Ltd. for Japan; by Addison Wesley Publishing Company for Korea; by Longman Singapore Publishers Ltd. for Singapore, Malaysia, Thailand, and Indonesia; by Unalis Corporation for Taiwan; by WS Computer Publishing Company, Inc. for the Philippines; by WoodsLane Pty. Ltd. for Australia; by WoodsLane Enterprises Ltd. for New Zealand. Authorized Sales Agent: Anthony Rudkin Associates for the Middle East and North Africa.

For general information on IDG Books Worldwide's books in the U.S., please call our Consumer Customer Service department at 800-762-2974. For reseller information, including discounts and premium sales, please call our Reseller Customer Service department at 800-434-3422.

For information on where to purchase IDG Books Worldwide's books outside the U.S., please contact our International Sales department at 415-655-3172 or fax 415-655-3295.

For information on foreign language translations, please contact our Foreign & Subsidiary Rights department at 415-655-3021 or fax 415-655-3281.

For sales inquiries and special prices for bulk quantities, please contact our Sales department at 415-655-3200 or write to the address above.

For information on using IDG Books Worldwide's books in the classroom or for ordering examination copies, please contact our Educational Sales department at 800-434-2086 or fax 817-251-8174.

For authorization to photocopy items for corporate, personal, or educational use, please contact Copyright Clearance Center, 222 Rosewood Drive, Danvers, MA 01923, or fax 508-750-4470.

About the Author

Ron Goldberg is the technical director of E/Town (`http://www.e-town.com`), a Web site dedicated to consumer electronics. He has written about emerging technologies for many publications, including *New York Newsday, Los Angeles Times, Popular Science, InterActivity,* and *Premiere.*

ABOUT IDG BOOKS WORLDWIDE

Welcome to the world of IDG Books Worldwide.

IDG Books Worldwide, Inc., is a subsidiary of International Data Group, the world's largest publisher of computer-related information and the leading global provider of information services on information technology. IDG was founded more than 25 years ago and now employs more than 8,500 people worldwide. IDG publishes more than 270 computer publications in over 75 countries (see listing below). More than 90 million people read one or more IDG publications each month.

Launched in 1990, IDG Books Worldwide is today the #1 publisher of best-selling computer books in the United States. We are proud to have received eight awards from the Computer Press Association in recognition of editorial excellence and three from *Computer Currents*' First Annual Readers' Choice Awards. Our best-selling *...For Dummies*® series has more than 25 million copies in print with translations in 30 languages. IDG Books Worldwide, through a joint venture with IDG's Hi-Tech Beijing, became the first U.S. publisher to publish a computer book in the People's Republic of China. In record time, IDG Books Worldwide has become the first choice for millions of readers around the world who want to learn how to better manage their businesses.

Our mission is simple: Every one of our books is designed to bring extra value and skill-building instructions to the reader. Our books are written by experts who understand and care about our readers. The knowledge base of our editorial staff comes from years of experience in publishing, education, and journalism — experience which we use to produce books for the '90s. In short, we care about books, so we attract the best people. We devote special attention to details such as audience, interior design, use of icons, and illustrations. And because we use an efficient process of authoring, editing, and desktop publishing our books electronically, we can spend more time ensuring superior content and spend less time on the technicalities of making books.

You can count on our commitment to deliver high-quality books at competitive prices on topics you want to read about. At IDG Books Worldwide, we continue in the IDG tradition of delivering quality for more than 25 years. You'll find no better book on a subject than one from IDG Books Worldwide.

John Kilcullen
President and CEO
IDG Books Worldwide, Inc.

VIII
WINNER
Eighth Annual
Computer Press
Awards 1992

IX
WINNER
Ninth Annual
Computer Press
Awards 1993

IDG BOOKS WORLDWIDE™

Acknowledgments

To research this codification of essential knowledge for the multimedia producer, I've spoken with many people and have seen many things over the better course of a decade. I've attended so many trade shows that by now, I must have seen the "future" more times than anyone since Nostradamus. I exchanged views with industry optimists and pessimists; often one would become the other as their company's fortunes rose or fell. I spoke with producers of great projects that failed and modest projects that succeeded — and vice versa. I watched as tiny Web design groups made up of a handful of twentysomethings became hot Silicon Alley agencies, and as mighty consumer electronics giants lost millions placing chips on the wrong next big thing. These and many other voices and experiences were all vital to the compilation of this book, but several voices were of particular importance, and I'd like to take a moment to thank them here:

James Berry: Jim is a producer at the interactive division of New York's Segal & Gale. He and I met some time ago on one of the proverbial "projects from hell," where his deft blend of technical skill and Zen-like unflappability saw the project through. Jim's insights and experiences were especially helpful in preparing the chapter on product testing.

Howard Blumenthal: Having had his hands in just about every permutation of multimedia dating back to the 1970s, Peabody Award-winner Howard has always been a prototypical "multimedia producer" and an inspirational figure to me personally. His experiences in producing everything from online services to CD-ROMs to traditional and emerging forms of broadcast and print media were invaluable to this book's perspectives on marketing, publishing, careers and the business aspect in general.

Jennifer Kramer: As a Webmaster dating back to the Web's earliest commercial days, Jennifer qualifies as a wizened veteran of the cyberworld. Her observations about technical execution, user interaction, customer support and the nature of the Web in general were indispensable to this book's chapters and perspectives on the World Wide Web.

Richard Lainhart: In addition to being an accomplished 3D artist and animator, a recorded MIDI composer, and all-around swell guy, Richard is one of New York's finest Macintosh gurus. I've seen him fix an errant machine by simply glaring at it. Richard's thorough understanding of multimedia tools and techniques was essential to the chapter on multimedia hardware and software.

Caroline Meyers: Caroline is a digital artist who has seen desktop multimedia from its earliest days — she's the first person I ever saw who handed her resume around on a HyperCard stack. These days, she keeps busy with artwork for a variety of interactive projects. Her design style is characterized by clarity and elegance, as evidenced by the illustrations I was privileged to include in the chapter on interface design.

In addition to the contributions of the above individuals, without which this book would have been impossible, many thanks are in order to **my partners at E/Town** for giving me the time off to write; to **Henry Bar-Levav** of Oven Digital (`www.oven.com`); **Adeo Ressi, Steve Turoff** ,and **Filip Stoj** of the Myriad Agency (`www.myriadagency.com`); numerous editorial gurus, including **Joseph Gelmis, Ted Greenwald, Larry Henchey, Glenn Kenny** and **David Laskin**; **Patricia Pane** of Adobe, **Suzanne Porta** of Macromedia, **Dave Pohle** of Equilibrium systems, **Kerri Walker** and **Doedy Hunter** at Apple Computer; and of course, **my family and friends**.

Ron Goldberg

(The Publisher would like to give special thanks to Patrick J. McGovern, without whom this book would not have been possible.)

Credits

Senior Vice President and Group Publisher
Brenda McLaughlin

Acquisitions Manager
Greg S. Croy

Acquisitions Editor
Ellen Camm

Software Acquisitions Editor
Tracy Lehman Cramer

Marketing Manager
Melisa M. Duffy

Managing Editor
Andy Cummings

Administrative Assistant
Laura J. Moss

Editorial Assistant
Tim Borek

Production Director
Beth Jenkins

Supervisor of Project Coordination
Cindy L. Phipps

Supervisor of Page Layout
Kathie S. Shutte

Supervisor of Graphics and Design
Shelley Lea

Media Archive Coordination
Debbie J. Gates

Development Editor
Pat O'Brien

Copy Edit Coordinator
Barry Childs-Helton

Copy Editor
Susan Christopherson

Technical Reviewer
Sean Lee

Project Coordinator
Sherry Gomoll

Layout and Graphics
Linda M. Boyer
Maridee V. Ennis
Angela F. Hunckler
J. Tyler Connor
Drew R. Moore
Mark C. Owens
Brent Savage
Gina Scott
Michael Sullivan

Proofreader
Jennifer K. Overmyer
Rachel Garvey
Dwight Ramsey
Robert Springer
Karen York

Indexer
Anne Leach

Production Administration
Tony Augsburger
Todd Klemme
Jason Marcuson
Jacalyn L. Pennywell
Leslie Popplewell
Patricia R. Reynolds
Theresa Sánchez-Baker
Melissa Stauffer
Bryan Stephenson

Contents at a Glance

Table of Contents

Prologue

The idea behind this book is daunting, both for the writer and readers. Any compendium claiming to be total knowledge — a "Bible," no less — for the multimedia producer is doomed to inadequacy. Size and timeliness are the issues. There could never be a single book big enough to contain all the knowledge a successful multimedia producer would want. And even if there could be, by the time it was done, much of its subject material would have changed by the time it was published — multimedia moves too quickly for printed books.

So why try to write one? Because the industry is so new that people who wouldn't ordinarily think of themselves as being "multimedia producers" find that they already are. Or would like to be. The vast enticements that the multimedia industry offers, especially at this early stage, have made a lot of people excited about being a part of it, especially as a producer.

A successful multimedia producer is someone who understands both generalities and specialties. While many of today's best producers have come from one area of specialization — design, programming, marketing, or even another medium like film or TV — specialists don't necessarily understand other specialties. But if they want to make it as a successful producer in this business, they need to.

This book was undertaken as an effort to provide a field guide to the uncountable issues a multimedia producer needs to be conversant with in order to prevail in this business. For the novice, it serves as an overview of how a project flows, from conception through execution, distribution and support. For the specialist who suddenly finds him or herself a generalist, it provides concise catch-up reading on other important areas of specialization. For the outsider, it's an overview of who, what, when, where, how and why a production comes alive.

Let's get started!

In the Beginning

PART I

In This Part

CHAPTER 1

Background

- It's 1965. An auditorium is full of sales managers watching a projected presentation at a large convention center. The presentation consists of filmstrips, synchronized tape recorders, and overlapping slide projectors. The presentation is called "Multimedia."
- It's 1975. Two teenagers are sitting around an electronic console at the local shopping mall. To the sounds of various boops and beeps, they furiously twirl an electronic game paddle, which in turn slams a tiny electronic ball across a video playing field. Their game is advertised as multimedia.
- It's 1985. Pop artist Laurie Anderson is performing a concert in which computers not only generate the music but also control the lighting and accompanying video. As she plays her violin, her bow sends digital signals that trigger the computers. The performance is described as multimedia.
- It's 1995. The Joneses are home, but each is busy in a different room. Dad is at the home office, plugging digital pictures into a business presentation. Mom is learning a second language from an interactive software program. Upstairs, the kids are on their own computers. While one cruises the Internet for help with an essay on Melville, the other is reenacting her favorite Disney movie from an interactive CD-ROM. For the Joneses, multimedia is now a part of their everyday life, even if they don't always call it by the M-word.

These examples aren't just indicators of how that elusive word, *multimedia,* has evolved, though they're an apt reminder of how much and how fast things have changed. They also show how elastic the term has always been, still is, and is likely to remain.

Multimedia. What does it mean? Often, it means nothing more than whatever the person saying it wants it to mean. Multimedia has been used to describe everything from elaborate new interactive art forms to an occasional colored spotlight running through a rock concert. The very word, by virtue of overuse and the speed of technological change, has already begun to engender a backlash: when they talk about this medium to people who aren't in the business, producers often refer to it as "the M word." Though multimedia is a real medium, and one that refuses to live inside an easily boxed definition, the word itself can be as vague today as "digital" and "iron-fortified" were when they had their heyday as buzzwords.

Without too much of a stretch, we can accept the definition of multimedia by simply deconstructing the compound word: a collection (hence the *multi*) of informative or entertaining experiences, presented through some combination of media pertaining to our experience of the world, primarily through sight and sound. In most cases, this collection resides on a single delivery medium, perhaps a CD-ROM or a Web site. In others, the delivery is more or less free form, with the sights and sounds coming from a series of devices, sometimes even controlled by the active participation of the audience or single user.

But multimedia is more than a method of expression. It's an art form and an industry, a new perceptual paradigm that will undoubtedly be as important to human communication as the printing press was more than 500 years ago. It has already changed the way we learn and understand, and altered our insights into ourselves and each other. As the 20th century speeds toward its conclusion, we have no way of knowing just how profound an effect that multimedia — and its eventual outgrowths, such as virtual reality — will have on our society in the 21st century. But for now, we have the exciting opportunity of being on the ground floor of something truly remarkable. An age of discovery, if you will.

Being Multimedia

This book is meant as a guide for people who want to accept the challenge of being part of the multimedia industry. That industry is a complex, eclectic world filled with paradoxes, offering open-ended creative opportunities that are based on the heartless rigidity of mathematics and computer code. It's an environment in which specialists depend on generalists. It's a billion-dollar industry in which it's often hard to make a buck.

The multimedia industry is richly detailed with different talents and skills. The most successful participants are the ones who are familiar with many of them and excel at one or more. Many of these skills intersect. For example, a successful graphic designer is aware of how long the 3D artist will need for rendering the ideas, who knows that the animator needs small file sizes that run smoothly with the sound designer's audio cues that the legal team is rushing to get cleared, so that the packaging team can meet the plant's deadline and the distributor's holiday order.

The ultimate goal of all these efforts, usually combined with many others, is a worthwhile product, be it a game, a reference work, a Web site, or a new experience that can't be named. The successful multimedia producer is involved in many different aspects of bringing that product to life. With so much going on, even the most seasoned multimedia producers can barely keep up with everything they would like to know. Technology changes so quickly, and so many disparate new talents enter this industry every year, that the state of the art is constantly evolving. Last year's killer interface idea becomes this year's cliché; new ways replace the old in negotiating rights and properties; six months of intensive content programming for an online service can quickly go down the tubes when the online service changes its business model from proprietary code to HTML and the World Wide Web.

This book covers the process, the individuals, the problems, and the rewards that come with a life in multimedia. Obviously, no one book on a subject this broad can hope to be comprehensive. In the time that it has taken to write this manuscript, dozens of new software programs and updates have hit the market, laws have changed, computer hardware has gone through a cycle of improvement, and the balance of power in the digital Wild West of the Internet has swung like a pendulum. In an industry that changes so quickly, no compendium of knowledge that's committed to paper and ink can be regarded as completely timely.

Further, the world of multimedia is many worlds put together. Each of these worlds — acquisitions, design, programming, testing, marketing, promotion, and so on is a specialty unto itself, even though the people who excel at them are often skilled in another aspect of the multimedia process that's separate from their field of expertise. A truly comprehensive source of knowledge on all these subjects would overfill a bookshelf, much less a single manuscript folio.

Rather, this book is meant as a sort of "scout's handbook" for people who want to be part of the multimedia phenomenon. In it, I discuss what this business is and which people do what to make it happen. I cover aspects of the following issues:

- ✦ Initiating and designing a project
- ✦ Taking the project through the production process
- ✦ Testing the product
- ✦ Marketing the product
- ✦ Supporting the customers who use the product

I also suggest ways to find work in this industry: what you need to know, who you meet, where you meet them, and what it might be like to work with them. I discuss how to position a title for market success, which is a process that begins long before a single line of code is written. Finally, I finish with a list of sources for more information and services. Bundled with this book is a CD-ROM containing software demonstrations of powerful multimedia tools, as well as examples of digital creativity that you can analyze and emulate through the knowledge you'll acquire here.

Anyone who aspires to be a multimedia producer will want to be familiar, if not fluent with, virtually all the material in this book. If you want to specialize in a particular discipline in the multimedia world, you'll find the basics here, along with guideposts to related information. If you want to get into this industry as an employee or an entrepreneur, and the idea of conceiving, creating, executing, or selling multimedia sounds like a great thing to do for a living, you've come to the right place.

The Emergence of a Multimedia Industry

Even in 1996, you often hear multimedia described by cynics as a "zero-billion dollar industry." The joke is not only old, it's inaccurate: billions of dollars are in fact exchanged each year in multimedia products and services. Profits are a different matter, of course, and are no more predictable than they are in any industry that, at its core, is based on creative intellectual property.

But it isn't fair to call multimedia an "industry" on its own. Multimedia is really more of a subset of other, related industries, such as motion pictures, the music industry, and traditional print publishing. The biggest players in the multimedia world are the names you would easily associate with other entertainment and reference media: Disney, Warner, Paramount, Grolier, Virgin, and many others. At the time of this writing, independent companies that are solely dedicated to the creation of multimedia are still the exceptions rather than the rule. The reasons for this are simple.

For one thing, multimedia can be an expensive medium to work with, especially when a project is lavish and meant for mass market acceptance. Budgets on elaborate multimedia projects can range in the millions, and because people still don't spend as much money on CD-ROMs as they do on records, books, arcade games, and video rentals, profit returns can be slow — much too slow for a small company to stay afloat for very long. The big studios can have a dominating presence in this industry because they can afford to leverage slow returns against other, more immediately profitable media.

To a certain extent, that situation is changing. As better hardware and tools become ever more accessible, and as ways to distribute titles become more immediate, independent multimedia studios are becoming more commonplace and profitable. The mega-selling CD-ROM title *Myst* was largely the work of two brothers, and its success has spawned scores of hopeful startups looking to recreate the idea of an "indie" project becoming a boffo seller. The World Wide Web — the "television" subset of the Internet — has dropped the requirements even further. A huge Web site such as HotWired or c\net can have dozens of people staffing it. But the Web has some extremely successful sites that are created, fed, and maintained by fewer than a handful of individuals. As the industry and the medium continue to evolve, the possibilities for successful independent multimedia ventures look wide open. For now, though, the most consistent success stories usually come from the major multimedia production companies.

Video games planted the seed

Despite the recent proliferation of CD-ROMs and sites on the Web, the video game industry, spearheaded today by powerhouses such as Sega, Nintendo, Atari, Sony, and others, probably comes the closest to exemplifying a truly sizable and self-contained multimedia industry.

These companies just mentioned develop both hardware and software for interactive entertainment, either in the home or in a video arcade. Certainly, nobody would dare put the zero tag on the video game business: total revenues for 1995 were 3.8 billion dollars according to the IDSA (International Digital Software Association), and they are expected to grow to $4.3 billion this year.

Things weren't always this rosy, and the early success of the video game business came out of a decade-long struggle. When a young Nolan Bushnell began selling an electronic tennis game called "Pong" in 1972, he had stiff competition from pinball machines, the game of choice in amusement parlors at that time — those parlors being the seed for what would eventually become the video arcade. Many hand-built prototypes, anxious sales meetings, and long car rides took place before people even agreed to take a "Pong" table into their saloons, much less mass produce it.

Suffice it to say that Pong became a hit, and in the years following, it spawned an entirely new sector of the amusement industry, based on elaborate arcade games that ate many of the quarters of preadolescent Americans. Those early hits, such as "Space Invaders," "Battle Zone," "Asteroids," and many others whose names would probably elicit a tinge of nostalgia for some of you, eventually made the video game business into a huge entity. By 1981, the industry was pulling in more than $5 billion a year. But things began to go sour through the mid-'80s as a glut of half-hearted games flooded the market in an effort to capitalize on the fad. A precipitous drop ensued, and by 1984, total revenues of home video games dropped to less than $1 billion.

Though video games have rebounded in a spectacular way here in the mid-1990s, the reason for the initial bust of the mid-'80s has been the cause of much after-the-fact speculation. One good reason was that many toy dealers (the major retail point for video games) were unable or unwilling to keep up with multiple inventories for all the competing game systems. Those days saw quite a few: Intellivision from Mattel, ColecoVision from Coleco, BallyVision from Bally, the Magnavox Odyssey, and others. At $30 – $40 per cartridge game, keeping a stock of dozens, if not hundreds of titles became impossible for all but the largest dealers.

Other parties blamed the fall on a dearth of interesting game titles, which may well have been true. It's been said that most video games fall under one of a few headings. Some are the "shoot-'em-up" type, in which you destroy the enemy before it destroys you. Some are the "maze" type, in which players run from interlopers through single or multiple environments. Finally, you can play the "puzzle" game, in which you either fill or unfill the screen with data before time or another enemy ends the game. With only a few notable exceptions, these variations continue to dominate the world of game design.

Undoubtedly, the downfall was also a matter of technological limitation. The elaborate color graphics taken for granted on today's inexpensive home gaming consoles were barely being achieved on expensive, dedicated arcade machines back then, and were unthinkable for a home unit. Besides, around this time, wary consumers were already looking at another new technology. They were about to discover the personal computer.

The PC takes over

1994 was the first year that home computers actually outsold television sets for a single year. But that success, which in reality was only the tip of the iceberg, was based on yet another decade-long struggle. The first wave of personal computers, which had hit the market in the early 1980s, were limited machines that hinted at unlimited potential. One of the first big sellers, the TRS-80 from Tandy, featured a mere 4 kilobytes of memory, with no color, no sound and no disk drive. Programs, such as they were, were loaded from a cassette tape. All this power cost about $1,000, which today would buy a 486-based machine with 4 megabytes of internal memory, one or two floppy drives, a sizable hard drive, and color graphics.

In those early days, multimedia on the PC was a distant dream. Most hardware was retained in business offices, where plain monochrome text displays were more than sufficient to run the database and word processing tasks for which they were invariably used. The emerging force that would come to dominate personal computing, the MS-DOS operating system from Microsoft, was constricted by an upper limit of 640 kilobytes of random-access memory (RAM). In addition, graphics capability on these machines was minimal, when actually available, and sound capability was restricted to a few assorted warning beeps through a tiny internal speaker.

By the mid-1980s, the technology had advanced to the point at which color was no longer an anomaly, and so began the first tentative steps toward multimedia on the PC. By this time, Apple Computer had released its new vision of the computing future, the Macintosh. Based on a new input device called the *mouse,* which Apple had learned about at Xerox's Palo Alto Research Center (PARC), the Macintosh offered point-and-click simplicity for people who wanted to use computers without learning how to use one.

By this time, many competitors showed up in what was shaping up to be the tip of a boom market. Atari, which had seen its game console business drop to a fraction of its glory days, got into the PC business, as did newcomers called Osborne, Kaypro, Compaq, and more established names such as IBM and NEC. Although all these machines fell short of the sight-and-sound experience offered by dedicated arcade games, each was an incremental step forward in power and operability.

Goaded by the explosive growth of the PC, people were realizing that computer literacy was going to be a key skill in the coming years. The interactivity and immediacy of learning through computers led to a strong push for computers in the classroom. The technology was still too expensive to realize the educator's dream of "a PC on every desk," but districts that could afford them installed personal computer "labs" in schools. The early systems taught students the fundamentals of file creation and management, database structure, and ASCII characters.

Around this time, businesses began turning to the PC for what would eventually come to be known as computer-based training, or CBT — a large part of today's multimedia market. A typical CBT presentation was a custom-designed application built around "if/and" or "what-if" scenarios, to which trainees would respond and be graded. The elaborate training programs that we take for granted today were still a long way off, and what few were produced were often realized through a dedicated hardware medium, such as interactive laserdisc. But the advantages of CBT were obvious, and despite the considerable expense and bother that the primitive technology incurred, the PC had found another major beachhead.

The PC grows up

A typical personal computer from the first wave of commercially available products between 1980 – 1985 consisted of less than a megabyte of random access memory, one or two low-density, $5^1/_4$-inch floppy drives, a monochrome monitor, and a keyboard. Even these configurations, virtually unusable by today's standards, might cost several thousand dollars, ensuring that only businesses and privileged individuals could work with them in those days.

A theory in the personal computer business, called Moore's Law, states that processor power will double every 18 months. Over the past ten years, that law has shown remarkable consistency. Back in the mid-'80s, such a theory would not only have made manufacturers blanche with fear but might have stopped many of them from getting into the business. Progress was much slower then, due to the softer demands of a smaller market and less competition amongst PC makers.

The breakthrough came with the introduction of the Intel 80286 chip in 1987, which facilitated faster computations and, typically, the ability to produce color graphics on a usable scale. Fixed hard drives began to appear as a regular feature on home computers. Today, a 20MB hard drive is considered somewhat pitiful, but back then, it represented digital storage space equal to some 60 floppy disks, and the consumer market jumped. As the hard drives became bigger, so did the floppy disks. The old $5\frac{1}{4}$-inch standard floppy, named for its thin, bendable makeup, could hold 360 kilobytes of information. These soon gave way to the smaller $3\frac{1}{2}$-inch floppy, which doubled the storage capacity to 700 kilobytes; and soon, through higher-density magnetic technology, the storage doubled again to about a megabyte and a half. Simultaneously, hardware prices began to drop and the PC boom was in full swing.

CD-ROM and other goodies

When the compact disc was introduced in 1981, its developers envisioned it as a versatile storage medium. Mostly for commercial reasons, the first implementation was to store high-quality, digitized music in this medium. But Sony and Philips, the two companies responsible for the birth of the CD, saw other uses for the small silver platter. Because it could hold digital data of any sort, and in generous amounts — up to 660 megabytes without compression — companies developed several variations of the CD. One variation was called CD-ROM, for read-only memory.

The CD-ROM's developers envisioned it as a substitute for many floppy disks. Companies could hold an entire year's worth of data on a single disc; libraries could store the equivalent of 250,000 pages of text. But a few pioneering companies, among the Lewis and Clarkes of the digital world, foresaw that the CD-ROM could present more than just data. It could be a potent new medium for interactive entertainment, much as the laserdisc had been in an earlier incarnation.

CD-ROM drives were a rarity until the early 1990s. Voyager, one of the first companies to utilize the new medium for creative works, introduced a series called "CD Companion" in 1990. The first such project was a compact-disc-based critical guide to Beethoven's *Ninth Symphony,* with accompanying notes by musicologist Robert Winters. Created for the Macintosh platform, which had always been a few steps ahead in terms of multimedia capability, the title piqued the interest of both the public and the press. A second title soon followed: Stravinsky's *Rite of Spring,* which was also based on the Macintosh's HyperCard multimedia capabilities.

Titles such as these required better sound capabilities than most PCs could deliver. The Macintosh had always been equipped with sound potential, but typical Intel-based machines had to be retrofitted with a stereo sound card in order to take advantage of these new titles. Consumers didn't mind, though, and despite the often maddening task of installing and configuring sound cards, the market for these components took off. Here in the mid-'90s, a PC without stereo capability is an anomaly.

Soon, the software became advanced enough to push the limitations of the hardware. The rotational speed and data throughput of early CD-ROM technology was insufficient for much more than text and rudimentary graphics. These early drives, now called single-speed drives, poured data into the computer at the rate of 150 kilobytes per second. That number was soon exceeded by the new double-speed, or 2X, drives, which doubled the throughput to 300 Kbps. These days, triple, quadruple, and even sextuple (6X) drives are common, with corresponding improvements in speed and performance.

Faster, more powerful hardware became necessary when CD-ROM developers began toying with the idea of putting video on a disc. Because of the tremendous demands that it puts on the PC, video is notoriously hard to reproduce in the digital domain. A single frame of digitized, uncompressed video takes up almost an entire megabyte. Multiply that by the 30 frames per second that you need for moving pictures, and you end up with a real technical challenge.

Software and hardware developers came up with a variety of solutions. Most were based on the idea of compression, which is a technique that reduces the amount of information present in any given datastream. Along with compression, developers began using slower frame rates (less than the standard 30 frames per second that full-motion video uses), and smaller screen sizes, both of which substantially cut down on processor requirements. Even in these compromised forms, the public was very receptive to the idea of video clips on CD-ROM. It was now possible to offer a single medium that could handle text, sound, pictures, and video. Multimedia was being born.

Chicken or egg?

Not everyone predicted that the personal computer would become an everyday household item. For any product to reach the kind of critical mass that the PC is approaching, people need a compelling reason to buy one.

The advent of multimedia titles, facilitated mainly though more the more powerful hardware that was becoming commonplace, helped spur PC sales to new levels by the beginning of the 1990s. In 1990, a council was formed to establish a hardware standard for the playback of multimedia material. Called the MPC standard (Multimedia PC), it called for at least a 386-based processor, a stereo sound card, SVGA graphic capability, and a double-speed CD-ROM drive. With the user base standard thus established, software developers began to churn out more titles. With more titles flooding the market each week, consumers bought more and more PCs.

Pretty soon, people started to get the idea that not only could they enjoy prerecorded multimedia content, they might like making it themselves. Until this time, development for multimedia was handled by dedicated programming languages, many of which are still in use today; I discuss them later in the book. Through simple presentation programs such as PowerPoint and Persuasion, ordinary users could make something that leaned toward multimedia, but without animation, sound, or any of the other compelling features of a true multimedia experience.

Rolling their own

Two advances led to the idea that ordinary people (read: nonprogrammers) could and should produce their own multimedia. The first was the market introduction of self-contained "authoring" programs that allowed for easy assembly of multimedia elements. Programs such as Macromind (now Macromedia) Director and Q-Media for Windows put a user-friendly "shell" around the more complex vagaries of making multimedia content. Although these applications made the creation of multimedia more egalitarian, they did nothing to alleviate the problem of distribution. Just how does a sizable multimedia entity get passed around? If the presentation were small enough, a floppy might occasionally suffice, but this was rarely a usable solution. Removable media, such as SyQuest drives, were costly and bulky. Affordable CD-ROM "burners" were still a gleam in the public's eye, and disc replication was still expensive enough to preclude mass distribution by small companies.

The early 1990s brought a widespread digital solution. The rise of online activity, with data being shared over telephone and computer networks, allowed for a true movement of content. Commercial online services such as America Online, CompuServe, Prodigy, and Delphi were only the beginning. The real movement came from the Internet, a vast, worldwide network of computer systems originally built in the 1960s as an information safeguard in the event of war. Educational and research facilities had been using the Internet for years, but in 1991, a graphical subset of the Internet called the World Wide Web popularized the Net in the same way that CD-ROM popularized multimedia-capable PCs.

By this time, CD-ROM software had become widespread and accessible enough to replace the floppy disk as a primary mode of information distribution. Catalogs and resumes began appearing on ROMs because a big enough user base existed to make such efforts worthwhile. Between CD-ROM and the Web, the power of multimedia had finally reached the masses. And it is here that I return to the present.

The Real Multimedia

As I've already noted, multimedia is a slippery term with many possible interpretations. For the purposes of the multimedia producer, coming up with a working definition of both words would be useful. First, the easy one.

Multimedia, as I use it to define the cool new medium that I've been going on about, is the combination of audio/visual media elements with interactivity. The audio/visual media elements that are being controlled in some way through interactivity can vary. A typical multimedia title might include any combination of text, pictures, computer graphics, animation, audio, and video. Interactivity is another one of those slippery words; technically speaking, anything that requires you to do something is interactive, even a phone call. But true interactivity as it pertains to multimedia requires that someone — the user — change some aspect of the audio/visual elements by a deliberate or nondeliberate action.

For example, when you use an automatic teller machine at the bank, you are controlling the transaction through interactivity. Your input determines whether you make a deposit or withdrawal and what the dollar amount will be. Contrast this with the opposite of interactivity: a passive experience. When you watch a movie on your VCR from beginning to end without changing anything, you are involved in a passive experience. Listening to a record is a passive experience. But jumping through the various songs on the record while you listen is an interactive experience. Interactivity demands some level of user participation.

That participation can take any number of forms through a variety of delivery systems. In fact, probably the most tangible evidence of how deeply multimedia is already ingrained in the public consciousness is the number of different settings in which you'll find it.

Delivery Systems

The three pillars of the multimedia experience are hardware, software, and user participation. All three can exist on many different platforms, depending on the multimedia producer's goals. I cover the most common ones at the time of this writing in the following sections.

CD-ROM

As discussed earlier, a CD-ROM is a compact disc that can hold 660MB of digital data. Presenting multimedia in this form has many advantages, which explains the explosive growth of this medium. Some of these advantages include:

- ✦ CD-ROM is inexpensive to duplicate; depending on volume, the per-unit cost of a disc can be less than a dollar.
- ✦ CD-ROM is easy to distribute, with the format having found a home in many types of retail environments: book stores, record stores, software stores, mail-order houses, and so on.
- ✦ CD-ROM has an enormous user base. At the time of this writing, approximately 17 million CD-ROM drives are in use here in the U.S. The vast majority of new desktop computers now being sold feature a CD-ROM drive, which for now and the future ensures a sizable target audience for CD-ROM content.

✦ That content can be of several types. The most common incarnation is that of a consumer product — a title that is meant to be bought and used on the merits of its content. That includes games, entertainment titles, reference works, clip art collections, how-to discs, and whatever else might be successful subject material for a CD-ROM production.

Another increasingly popular use of CD-ROM is that of the promotional disc. Typically, these are distributed free of charge, because the point of them is to promote or sell something else. Typical uses of this kind of CD-ROM include a multimedia demonstration of products or services, a sampler of a game or a software application, or a companion disc to a larger service. Good examples of this last type of approach come from the online world. The major commercial online services all distribute a companion CD-ROM that features tours and accessory artwork meant to work in tandem with online time.

A third use of CD-ROM that is just becoming popular is the CD-ROM catalog. More economical to produce and distribute than a traditional paper-printed catalog, CD-ROM catalogs also offer the advantage of multimedia presentation. Selling an album is much easier if you let the audience hear a bit of it; selling real estate is easier when you can give the customer a visual tour of the prospective property.

The online world

As I discussed previously, the world of online communications has been a tremendous avenue for multimedia content. Both the commercial online services and the Web are rich with graphics and sound, and getting richer. Unfortunately, the technology for presenting *dynamic* multimedia — information that changes over time such as animation, video, and sound — has been constricted through the online medium.

The reason for this is mostly a question of bandwidth, but other technical problems exist as well. Bandwidth is the common term for how much digital information can travel over a transmission standard at any given time. In the case of the online world, bandwidth is almost always limited to the capabilities of standard copper telephone wire. At present, that translates into 28.8 kilobits per second, a fairly leisurely rate of transfer that stymies any convincing sense of motion over the phone line. Dedicated transmission mediums do exist that are optimized for online use, such as ISDN and T-1 phone lines, and I discuss them later in this book. But the audience with these kinds of capabilities is still very small.

Another problem with presenting multimedia over online systems is that, thus far, no real standard exists for the playback of dynamic media. Sound was the first to appear online, but in terms of the commercial services, sound is actually stored on the user's hard drive rather than generated in real time. The friendly chirps and catch phrases commonly heard during an America Online session are good examples of these canned sound effects.

On the World Wide Web, progress has been a bit more interesting, at least in terms of sound. Though still in their infancy, technologies exist that successfully produce "streamed" audio in real time. Audio fidelity is still poor, but you can expect that to change in short order.

Other dynamic media, such as animation and video, haven't fared as well. Through the early part of 1996, no real standard existed for playing these media online and in real time. When dynamic media was actually available, it was presented as a self-contained file that needed to be downloaded; that is, the user had to transfer the multimedia file from the online environment down to his or her computer, where it would be played back later. The size of multimedia files, coupled with the low bandwidth of copper phone lines, made this process tedious, if not completely impractical.

That, too, should change. At the time of this writing, developers are working on a new technology for the Web that will allow animations and video to play in real time, without a download session. This technology, being developed by companies such as Sun Microcomputer and Macromedia, should arrive on the Web before the end of the year. Proponents believe that these technologies will not only revolutionize the Web but establish it as the premiere medium for multimedia content of all kinds. Further, you should see significant changes in the hardware delivery systems for online content; the copper phone wire may soon go the way of the rooftop TV antenna. In the coming months, the world will see modems that work much faster through coaxial wires such as those on a cable TV. These "cable modems" will have bandwidth and speeds far beyond what even the best twisted-pair technology can offer. In addition, other delivery media, such as direct-broadcast satellite systems and fiber-optic connectivity, are moving off the drawing boards into real plans for widespread implementation.

Corporate communications and CBT

Multimedia can be a powerful medium for persuasion and, as such, has found a comfortable home as a tool for in-house business communication and training. Interestingly, multimedia finds its most varied implementations within the corporate sector.

For example, private industry has been the biggest market for multimedia titles that run on proprietary systems, as opposed to standard CD-ROM or floppy-disk presentations. Since the mid-1980s, companies have been using dedicated multimedia machines such as Philips' Compact Disc-Interactive (CD-I) system, as well as interactive laserdiscs and other self-contained players for the aforementioned CBT (computer-based training). The advantage to this approach is financial: putting a $300 CD-I machine on everyone's desk is cheaper than a $1,500 PC.

The corporate world offers outstanding opportunities for multimedia development. In many ways, the revenues generated there kept the industry going through the lean years when there wasn't much of a consumer base. Although the titles aren't usually as elaborate or sexy as games and other consumer titles, the market is steady, and a successful product can be measured by its quality and effectiveness rather than the vagaries of the consumer market.

Museums and other institutions

A museum seems like an unlikely place for interactive multimedia, but it is where the medium has its longest-standing presence. People go to a museum — whether dedicated to art, science, or a specific subject — to see and hear, to find out more. A multimedia presentation is hardly a substitute for seeing a great painting or a dinosaur fossil, but it can be an excellent tool to flesh out the presentation, providing detailed information without requiring a specialized individual to give it out.

In the museum world, multimedia is usually delivered by way of an interactive kiosk. A *kiosk* is a self-contained stand with a video screen, some kind of user input device, and a source delivery medium, such as a laserdisc or a CD-ROM. Producing content for these kiosks is generally simpler than producing content for widespread distribution, because the technical specifications are limited to a single delivery system, which has often been optimized for one particular multimedia presentation.

Sales presentations

Because of its persuasive abilities, multimedia has become a popular way to make a sales pitch. These presentations, developed either in-house by the company or by independent contractors, can be distributed via CD-ROM or other fixed media, through online services, or, more typically, through a real-time demonstration held between salesperson and prospective customer.

The trouble with this last method is that portability becomes an issue. A salesperson can't count on the target customer having the specialized hardware to play back the multimedia presentation. Presentations to large groups require even more specialized equipment such as video projectors.

As a result, most multimedia sales presentations are made to small groups, delivered from a portable computer. In this way, the salesperson has complete control over the playback environment.

Video games

Without question the most popular form of multimedia, video games have captured the world's imagination for more than twenty years.

Their initial implementation was in the laboratories of academia, where students of the computer science departments wrote their own rudimentary games from scratch. Some of these later found expression in the way of dedicated arcade consoles, which first appeared on the scene in the mid-1970s and have been with us ever since. These consoles have been the proving ground for many a new multimedia technology, and, typically, a successful arcade game finds expression through other multimedia formats meant for mass distribution.

The most popular of these is the home-based game console; the fierce hardware wars of the 1980s have whittled down, Darwin-style, to a handful of competing formats. The major players in this market are Nintendo and Sega, both of which got their start in arcade technology; and Sony, which introduced its competing PlayStation in 1995. Several other companies, such as Atari, Philips, and 3DO, have held a tenuous position in this lucrative market, though their market penetration is nowhere near that of their larger rivals.

Most video games for home use come on either a proprietary cartridge or a CD. The former has been with us since the beginning, and even though they are more expensive and difficult to produce than disc-based games, they are widespread (and lucrative) enough to have continued on through today. They also offer a significant advantage to the user in that game play is substantially faster from a cartridge than it is from an optical disc such as a CD-ROM. This, plus a relatively high price tag, has allowed the major game makers to easily keep this older technology in the sales loop. Discs for dedicated game consoles first began appearing on the market in 1992, and although they represent substantial improvements in ease and cost of replication, the sluggish gameplay has kept them from being the dominant medium in the video game console business. This has resulted in a slower growth curve for these games than might otherwise have been expected.

Disc-based video games aren't just for game consoles, however; they exist in huge numbers as CD-ROMs. Because so many households already have PCs with CD-ROM drives, game developers can now tap into a huge market, consisting particularly of families who have no small children and, hence, no game console.

A multimedia video game represents the most lucrative opportunity for the multimedia producer: a successful game can easily sell millions of copies. The stakes are considerably higher here than any other area of multimedia development, however. A video game must be extremely compelling, original, or lucky to catch on with the fickle youth market. Such criteria lead to high research, production, and marketing costs. Still, video games are to multimedia what rock and roll is to music: a huge staple that helps keeps the rest of the industry solvent.

Future technologies

Most of the multimedia incarnations I've discussed so far are experiences for individuals or small groups. Other forms of multimedia are more large-scale in nature, such as the simulations that you'll find in Las Vegas or at Disneyland. These big-budget arenas are where many of the more cutting-edge technologies are first unveiled, and they serve as a source for much "trickle-down" technology.

Among the more interesting is virtual reality, a much-hyped medium that could very well be to the 21st century what cinema was to the 20th. Virtual reality is an artificially created environment that operates in three dimensions. Participants (or players) interact with this environment or with each other by way of controllers, such as joysticks or even body wear. Although virtual reality's foreseen future remains a long way off, you can see its first cautious steps in dedicated environments throughout the country. This includes arcades, amusement parks, and research facilities.

The near future will likely bring us multimedia in many new forms. One of the most interesting possibilities lies in the still-embryonic field of interactive television. Although this proposed medium lends itself to almost as many hype-laden visions as multimedia itself, the broadcast, cable, and telecommunications industries are now devoting billions of dollars to making ITV the face of the future.

In that future, consumers will have movies and other entertainment on demand simply by pressing a few buttons on their remote controls. Game aficionados will be able to play against opponents in another city or another state. The electronic voting booth envisioned by politicians may well turn out to be a reality, along with video telephony and other "futuretech" ideas that are actually decades old. Research on these technologies has yielded some fascinating results, but implementation has so far been sketchy.

Why? It's a nice dream, but so far, that's all it is. By now, interactive TV has been tried in one form or another for almost 20 years. The problems aren't just technological, although, to be sure, the technology to pull this kind of medium off just doesn't exist in a reliable form yet. Whether people actually want this level of interactivity from their television sets is not yet clear. TV has earned its reputation as the passive media of choice around the world. Will users want to compose their own entertainment through their TV sets, or prefer to be entertained by professional storytellers and infomerchants? So far, the answer leans toward the latter. That may change as practical technologies such as small direct-broadcast satellite dishes and cable modems bring forth a quantum leap in bandwidth and usability. But for now, the main opportunities in the medium of interactive television are in the fields of research and development.

What Makes Multimedia Run?

For the multimedia producer, taking a project from inception to completion involves innumerable challenges. But none may be so daunting as the process of identifying the proper home for the content. Many different platforms exist for multimedia playback, and projects intended for any of them are usually shaped from the beginning to work within the guidelines of that platform.

The most commonplace environment for multimedia is the personal computer. Unfortunately, that covers a lot of ground. Two major PC platforms spread across America: the IBM compatibles and the Apple Macintosh. Neither is completely compatible with the other, although, to a certain extent, sharing information and disks between the two platforms is possible. The IBM-compatible camp, alternately known as Intel-based, Windows-based, or "Wintel" machines, comprises about 90 percent of the PC market here in the U.S. The Macintosh clocks in at about 8 percent, with the remainder spread throughout high-end machines such as those from Silicon Graphics and Sun, as well as low-end machines from the likes of Commodore and Atari.

This presents the multimedia producer with a bit of a quandary. In terms of overall customer base, 90 percent is a good number to target. Unfortunately, that percentage declines somewhat when multimedia is the application. For example, in terms of CD-ROM penetration, the percentage of Macintosh users jumps to almost 15 percent, with an even larger jump on the Web and still a bigger jump among multimedia professionals. Leaving out this sizable and dedicated sector of the market can be a costly mistake, but more and more developers are leaning toward this scenario in an effort to cut production and marketing costs.

For now, most producers get around the problem in a clunky but effective way, by offering two versions of the same title, one for each platform. In some cases, they produce "hybrid" titles that will run on either the PC or the Macintosh, but because even a CD-ROM has storage limitations, the possibilities here are a bit more constricted. One of numerous proposed solutions to this situation is having "open" operating systems that don't care which machine they're running on. For now, however, the Web is the only multimedia environment that is not platform specific in that it works almost the same way on both PCs and Macs.

Dedicated kiosks are a more focused environment for the multimedia producer. Because the playback station is a known quantity, little of the usual compromise and confusion arise when producers are trying to produce content for the largest possible market. Even the kiosk world, however, contains differing platforms with varying capabilities. As a result, production that's intended for a kiosk is always composed specifically with those capabilities in mind.

Who Makes Multimedia?

Some pages back, I said that the meaning of the term *multimedia producer* was slippery. I seem to have come up with an acceptable definition of multimedia, and even interactivity. But just who is a producer?

Many people wear the name with pride, though they don't necessarily all do the same thing. In the most literal terms, a "producer" is anyone who is responsible for the creation of content. But that creation involves much more than what the target audience will finally see. A producer can be a creative or an administrative figure.

Typically, the multimedia producer is both. Multimedia is usually a highly collaborative medium, although successful titles have been accomplished by one talented individual with vision and persistence. The size and scope of the project determine how many people are really needed to bring a title to life. In most cases, a team of individuals is responsible for a successful multimedia foray. Who are these people, and what do they bring to the table? I discuss many of the roles open to multimedia professionals in Chapter 10. But for now, I look at some of the major forces behind the creation of a multimedia production, without going too deeply into specific job titles.

Project creation

The project creator(s) is the person (or persons) who has envisioned a successful multimedia project. The project creator has added up the variables of potential financing, marketing, technical feasibility, and creative implementation, and with luck, has come up with a winner. In many ways, the project creator has the easiest job of all: being creative. In other ways, it's the most thankless task in the multimedia world, because between conception and realization lie thousands of potential pitfalls.

The project creator can come from any one of many different disciplines. Indeed, one of multimedia's most striking qualities is that the creative impetus can originate from almost anywhere — the visual arts, mass communications, literature, music, academia, and so on. After the project creator has committed his or her vision to a form that can be shared with other individuals, the work really begins.

Project management

Between the fantasy of a universally lauded multimedia project and the reality of getting it to market lies the work of the project manager. This individual is responsible for bringing together the administrative, creative, and technical people who will bring the project to life.

Although the role sounds like a purely administrative one, nothing could be further from the truth. In addition to the quantifiable administrative tasks such as making sure that the accountant pays the bills and the printing plant delivers the packaging's artwork in time, the project manager deals with the creative team that will actually create the multimedia title. That in itself is a multifaceted skill requiring someone with the patience of a diplomat, the doggedness of an attorney, the picky temperament of an accountant, the eyes of a painter, the mind of a salesperson, and the soul of an artist. Naturally, people like this are rare, though they are becoming less so as multimedia becomes more widespread.

Project promotion

Unless a project is conceived solely as a self-contained work of art, the world of commerce is always involved in a multimedia project. Somewhere along the line, someone must be convinced to part with money in order to make the project real. This may be as simple as getting a backer to finance the title or as difficult as getting a nation of finicky adolescents to think your title is the coolest thing ever to come down the pike.

The promoter is the one who convinces the outside world that it wants the product. This can be as simple as making a sales pitch to a small company or institute, or as elaborate as a multimillion-dollar marketing campaign conducted through the media. Without the promoter, nobody is interested in the project except its makers, and perhaps the bank.

Producer is a big word

George Lucas, the creator of *Star Wars*, is a producer. So are perennial Grammy winner Quincy Jones, "Saturday Night Live" creator Lorne Michaels, and a thousand people that few (besides their friends and families) have heard of. I've already defined the producer as someone who's responsible for the creation of content, so now I discuss how the multimedia producer fits the bill.

A feature motion picture usually involves more than one producer. The executive producer is typically the person who has procured the financing and major creative forces for the creation of the film, including the most basic property, the script. The individual(s) credited with being the producer of a motion picture is mostly akin to what I've called the multimedia project manager.

On the other hand, a record producer is usually responsible for the creative end of a project, choosing the engineer, the session musicians, and sometimes even the arrangements. A TV producer is often the creative impetus behind a hit show, whereas a producer of industrial videos will commission the creative talent.

The multimedia producer shares similarities with all these figures. To be successful, the multimedia producer knows both the administrative and creative factions on the project, and is conversant with the issues and challenges that both sides incur. Additionally, a multimedia production usually shares some kind of creative affinity with one of the more traditional entertainment forms that I've just outlined. This affinity explains why the early "stars" of the multimedia industry were actually refugees from these other disciplines, enticed by the lure of an exciting new medium.

That situation, however, is changing. Though some multimedia productions may be conceptually similar to, say, a TV show — sometimes even based on one — true interactive multimedia is a specific medium unto itself, with its own specific guidelines. For the multimedia producer, possessing a background in any of the more usual creative fields isn't a hindrance, but neither is it a necessity anymore.

Contract or in-house

Who makes multimedia? In the case of a large company such as Sega or Microsoft, multimedia development is often handled on an *in-house* basis. This means that the producer and his or her staff are employees of the company that is responsible for the financing and development of the multimedia project. For situations in which the production is carried out in-house, the assigning company is in the driver's seat. Unless otherwise specified, it owns the project in all its tangible and intangible forms, as well as the right to market and otherwise exploit the creative property.

On the other hand, many multimedia productions are handled on a *contract* basis, meaning that the producer is an independent contractor and is responsible for delivering goods and/or services in accordance with the terms of the contract agreed upon by both the producer and the client who has commissioned the project.

In this second scenario, the relationship between producer and client is highly malleable, and depending on the deal that's struck, either party can retain certain rights to the intellectual property contained within the multimedia production. The typical flow of work in these situations begins with a job description that clearly states what the producer is expected to deliver to the client, when, and for how much. An acceptance period follows, during which any questions of responsibilities and rights are negotiated before a contract is signed. The contract also states the payment schedule and spells out any future rights or royalties that the contracted producer might retain to the project.

Naturally, both ways of working have pros and cons. Working as you are in an uncertain field, you'll find some security in knowing that you are on staff at a solvent (you hope) company, and that the paychecks will be issued on time. Knowing that other parties are responsible for whatever details are not assigned to the in-house producer also helps. Of course, being the employee of any company brings a type of insecurity as well, because a job is a job, a boss is a boss, and relationships between the two are rarely permanent.

The contract producer has much more leeway but also much more responsibility. The costs of negotiating a legal agreement are borne by the independent contractor, as are all necessary expenses in seeing the project through to fruition. Crashed hard drives, flaky employees, blizzards — these problems keep the independent multimedia producer awake at night. But the producer also has the satisfaction of being independent and able to take advantage of the fast-moving opportunities that are an everyday fact in the world of multimedia.

You've now completed a brief tour of what the world of multimedia is and how the multimedia producer fits into it. This world has much to be learned — almost too much. Contracts and intellectual property issues, new software and production techniques. Design, programming, testing, marketing, and after-market support. This book guides you through various phases of the project, taking you from conceptualization and acquisitions all the way through your celebratory bottle of champagne. In these pages, you'll see many people that you recognize, maybe even yourself. But it never hurts to learn more than you already know, especially in a field as complex and constantly shifting as multimedia. So, I begin at the beginning, with the inception of the multimedia project described in the next chapter.

Creating the Product

P A R T

II

In This Part

CHAPTER 2

Before the Production Starts

✦ Preproduction is the process of intelligently mapping out a cohesive strategy for the entire multimedia project, including content, technical execution, and marketing.

✦ Adequate preproduction planning is the only thing resembling an insurance policy that the rest of the project enjoys, but even this is no guarantee of smooth sailing. Preproduction goals must sometimes be flexible.

✦ Preproduction entails a collaborative effort, just as the rest of the production does. Not all of the talent involved in preproduction need stay the course for the entire the project, however.

✦ Every hour spent on effective preproduction eventually pays for itself in increased productivity for the entire production team, thereby multiplying its monetary/time value exponentially.

The process of making multimedia begins with an idea. The idea, often referred to in these hype-laden times as "the vision," is a conceptual starting point. Ironically, that starting point is actually a visualization of the ending point — the multimedia experience that the targeted end-user will have. The multimedia producer can't begin to assemble the resources and talent to pull off a finished product without a clear vision of who's going to use it, what hardware they'll be using it with, whether market conditions are ripe for the product, and whether distributors will carry the title. In a sense, the conceptual process is a collaboration between the person with the idea and the imagined user who might like it.

These variables are the intellectual clay with which the multimedia producer works to fashion a concept. The concept then turns into a proposal, then a plan, then a prototype, and then, if all goes well, an actual production. But these aren't the only variables by any means. Even projects that are thought out well and targeted to a receptive audience can falter at any time during the production. The pitfalls are numerous. Time and money are two of the biggest: many a production has fallen prey to the vissicitudes of capitalization and missed deadlines. Even if all goes right, a peculiar kind of irresistible force is at work in the world of multimedia. The technology and the user market change so quickly in this industry that today's great plan may be yesterday's old and boring news by tomorrow.

Predicting these forces can be as pointless as predicting the weather. One day, a major computer supplier may decide that 8X CD-ROM drives and built-in MPEG video cards should be standard gear for that supplier's model season. Other manufacturers rush to catch up, soon followed by the big and small clone makers. In a matter of months, often much less time than it takes to develop a multimedia production, the prevailing market conditions can change. By the time it's released, your hip and groovy production, which took none of these potential (unknowable, really) variables into account, is now, by some standards, outdated.

Of course, unstable conditions in the multimedia world are a fact of life. They shouldn't deter you from undertaking a production, unless all the data you collect during preproduction tells you that the odds are stacked against your project's success. Obviously, if that's the case, you might want to reconsider at least some aspects of your planned title or site. But these same unstable conditions can work in the multimedia producer's favor. For example, early work in a developing technology can mean that you're first on the shelf with finished work when that technology hits critical consumer mass. One hit title in a particular genre can have a positive fallout effect on many other titles that are conceptually similar. The success of one title such as *Myst* spurs the success of many "wandering mystery" games. The success of one HTML technique on a Web site spurs countless iterations across the entire Web, faster than you can say "appropriated code." Unknown waters never stopped a true explorer. And no matter how well planned or market researched, any multimedia undertaking is a bit of an exploration.

Starting Off on the Right Foot

I have already mentioned that conceptualization is an imagined collaboration between the developer and the target audience. Only one side of this partnership actually has a voice — and it's the end user. In most multimedia projects, virtually every conceptual decision made by the producer is a reaction to that voice. Sometimes, a third party is involved who has conceived some or all of the project already and assigned it to your company. Unfortunately, that third party, whether it's a publisher looking for projects, a company commissioning a computer-based training presentation, or a client requesting an online "presence," may not have partaken in this collaborative vein.

When projects like these are originated outside the creative team that will develop them, a new kind of that aforementioned irresistible force enters the picture. The Acme Widget company probably didn't know or care what an MPEG card was when it asked you or your company to design a CD-ROM title featuring full-screen, completely interactive video clips. Nor did that company care that UNIX programmers can be more expensive than Director programmers, or that most of Acme's "great ideas" for interactive examples infringe on copyrighted likenesses and other protected intellectual properties. It just knows what it wants, and it wants your company to make it.

Just by these tip-of-the-iceberg examples, you can easily see that the more conceptualizing the development team does duing preproduction, the better. Although having outside ideas and perspectives is always good and usually necessary, the collaboration process is always best undertaken when a control factor exists. That control factor is best defined as understanding. Part of the multimedia producer's job is to apply this understanding, whether it's to a commissioning client or to a game plan that will bring off a title that people will like and can use.

What kinds of ideas make sense?

No matter who ultimately takes credit for the idea for a project, that idea usually adheres to the basic structure of any market-driven initiative. A need or desire exists, and people develop a product to (they hope) fill it. In the multimedia world, that idea can come from any number of places. It can develop on its own as a solitary flash of inspiration, or it can be an obvious product that either harkens back to an existing similar product or predicts a new one that will still feel familiar to users. Virtually no limit exists concerning the kinds of content that can be developed as multimedia. But unless someone undertakes the project strictly as a labor of love, with no commercial considerations, you'll usually find an economically valid reason for developing the project. Considering the time and financial budgets that some projects consume, the more valid these reasons are judged to be at the outpost, the better.

Getting an assignment from a company. . .

Until the explosive commercial growth of the Internet and the World Wide Web, most company-assigned multimedia projects fell under one of two categories: corporate communications or training. The first of these has already, in a few short years, turned from a novelty to an expected aspect of many companies' communications strategies. The second has actually been a pillar in the development of a multimedia industry, and continues to be a vital source of new projects for producers everywhere. The Web has changed all that. In many cases, companies develop Web sites to combine these and many other content items: catalogs, promotion, contests, and hype sheets. A company has plenty of work to do to have an up-to-date multimedia presence. It needs people to do it. You or your company may be the ones for the job.

But because multimedia in general has experienced such rapid popular acceptance, the rush has been on for all sorts of multimedia projects from assigning parties, many of them far outside the corporate sector. This increase in projects has resulted in a gold rush for developers, with many projects assigned and undertaken because multimedia seems so universally "necessary" to these assigning entities. In many ways, what's been a boon for developers has actually been a hindrance for these companies to adequately get their points across. In the rush to "be multimedia," many companies commission multimedia projects that, truth be told, are unnecessary and often less effective for the people who are supposed to use them than paper, video, or any of the other old ways through which these companies communicated. A speech from a corporate director with a couple of pie charts may be an easy project to undertake for a CD-ROM, but for the people who need to see it, is booting a CD-ROM really a better idea than a traditional corporate video? Maybe not, and in many cases, definitely not.

. . .And sometimes refusing an assignment

In situations such as these, the multimedia producer is in a bit of a quandary. For example, I was recently offered an assignment to create a CD-ROM for a foreign government's Trade Office. The idea behind the content was to entice potential investors to enter the local economy. Traditionally, that sales pitch had been distributed on videocassette to these potential investors. The tapes featured lots of footage of gorgeous beaches and palm trees, smiling financial types extolling the virtues of the robust local economy and enthusiastic workforce, followed by addresses and phone numbers for information.

The agency for the Trade Office had decided, however, that videocassettes were passé, and in order to be perceived as being up to-the-minute, the agency wanted a CD-ROM. Not a bad idea, in theory. When I pressed the people there for the details, though, I saw that the agency that was commissioning the project had no idea of the interactive potential of multimedia, and, frankly, no desire to incorporate it into the presentation. The preproduction team and I saw great possibilities and benefits to the end user: the ability to search specific information on the CD-ROM, or to tailor user questions to a particular investor profile. But the assigning agency simply wanted an exact duplicate of its traditional video presentations — linear, passive information — on a CD-ROM. Rather than keep a simple, inexpensively produced project that would enjoy a universal delivery system (a VCR), the company wanted to graft the information and experience onto an inhospitable medium.

That grafting would require expensive video compression, with the attendant degradation of the footage, as well as the assumption that all the potential targets for the presentation would have a CD-ROM drive. Worse, the company expected that these CD-ROMs would be appropriate for group presentations, running from a traveling salesman's laptop computer onto a video projector to entice groups of potential investors — again, a linear presentation with no interactivity. Clearly, the agency didn't understand how CD-ROMs work; in all probability, that agency had never even used one. But someone there had decided to have "a multimedia."

For the producer, these situations are deceptively tempting. I could have produced the CD-ROM that this agency wanted, but I could not have made the final project be what the agency had envisioned. The people there had no idea of development expenses, target hardware, or even interactivity, and they didn't realize that the medium they were already using, videocassette, was actually more appropriate and cost-effective than going multimedia. In situations like these, the producer has several choices.

For better or worse, some producers take advantage of an unsophisticated client, accepting the work and the money. Some will try to convince the client of the superiority of doing the presentation in a different way, moving the client toward a project that's closer to the client's real aims. Some producers will simply turn down the work, because satisfying clients who don't know what they want is often an impossible task. In my case, I managed to convince the people at this agency that unless they wanted to take advantage of the CD-ROM medium, the presentation that they envisioned was better served on videocassette. Rather than foster bad blood on a project that neither party would be proud of, I chose to decline, and was able to pass the job along to a video producer I know. That producer will no doubt return the favor one day, because good networking is an essential ingredient of the multimedia business, as you'll see in a later chapter.

Granted, no multimedia producer wants to turn down work. But sometimes it's the best way. Not only does doing so free more time for better projects, but honesty with a client is a compelling reason for that client to return to you when the next project comes up.

Kinds of Assignments

Getting work or a solicitation of work from an outside client is proof that you or your company has arrived in the multimedia business. But the project can be one or more of many types, sometimes in an area in which your company is inexperienced. The only way to get more experience is to produce the assignment. But what kinds of assignments might you get from outside clients? Here are a few:

- ✦ Interactive communications
- ✦ Corporate-based training endeavors
- ✦ Public exhibitions (for example, trade shows)
- ✦ Educational assignments (schools, museums, others)
- ✦ An original idea of yours that interests a client enough to want to see it developed

The following sections take a closer look at the nature of these assignments.

Interactive communications

One of the biggest booms in multimedia has come in the way of multimedia communications. These projects go under many names: interactive press kits, multimedia company profiles, and now, the ubiquitous "Web presence." The range of sophistication of these assignments is extremely wide. One company might put up a Web site that effectively duplicates and even surpasses what its entire sales team has been trying to express all year. I've known other companies to waste 99 percent of a CD-ROM's capacity by sticking a few text-based press releases onto a disc.

For the producer, these communications projects, when they are performed as fixed (as opposed to online) media, can be highly profitable and a lot of fun to do, mainly because the amount of work (and budget!) that goes into them is limited. For online work, the assignment is different — very different. Building a Web site for a company's communications strategy can be as simple or as complex as the client demands, not to mention the continuing job of Webmastering and filling the site with content. At some point in that situation, the multimedia producer and client must agree on what is actually being done: constructing a site or building and maintaining a site. These are not nearly the same job, and you neeed to make this clear in no uncertain terms to a client who may not know better.

Some producers would rather spend a long time working on one project, but for most production companies, a succession of smaller projects is the way to keep the bills paid and the staff hard at work. "Easy" projects are a much sought-after prize for the multimedia producer, and after your company gets a reputation for being able to produce these projects — on time and on budget, of course — you may find more work out there than your company can handle.

Corporate training

Computer-based training, or CBT, is a mainstay of multimedia development, and in many ways has been responsible for opening the eyes of corporate America when it comes to the potential value of multimedia. Interactive courseware can be the most effective way of teaching individual or groups of workers about new techniques, plans, and other crucial information that they need to be aware of to do their job properly.

In many cases, companies that assign productions relating to CBT already have a model in mind. That might be existing courseware, whether taught by an individual or by other audio/visual materials such as video and audio tapes. In some cases, the commissioning client will ask the multimedia producer to duplicate the existing experience as closely as possible within a new medium. In others, the gamut of possibilities that interactive media offers will be the focus of the production.

CBT presentations are typically more difficult to produce than most multimedia projects. This difficulty arises from the fact that the material is always highly customized to the specific needs of the client, and in many cases, to specific dedicated hardware such as laserdisc or CD-I (Compact Disc-Interactive). Further, courseware is almost always meticulous in answering every possible query that a trainee might have, making for an elaborate interactive branching structure on the design end. Typically, CBT assignments range from expensive to very expensive, and the producer and the commissioning company undertake a close, continuing collaboration.

Public exhibitions

The multimedia producer can find work in the field of multimedia exhibits, which is a catchall expression for everything from public kiosks to trade show exhibits. The multimedia project will be used by many people at one location rather than by people at varying locations using many widely distributed copies. As a result, you can develop these kinds of projects with a more specific focus than you can with a production that is meant for wide distribution. This stronger focus has implications for both the design and the target hardware.

In terms of design, these projects can actually be simpler to execute than most other types of multimedia projects. Typically, a public multimedia exhibit is a controlled experience for the user: click here, see this, click there, see that. Because the idea is to let many people use the multimedia, you can assume that you won't want any one person using it for very long; others will be waiting in line.

Typical iterations of this kind of presentation are through an interactive kiosk with a touch screen, a CD-ROM set up on single or multiple computer stations, or sometimes, in a situation in which picture and sound need to be of the highest possible quality: an interactive laserdisc. To their advantage, these kinds of projects are usually easy to design and highly visible. On the negative side, many institutions don't have particularly big budgets to work with; museums and cultural institutions, some of the prime commissioners of these kinds of works, are rarely in a position to be financially extravagant.

Educational assignments

Schools and other educational institutions such as libraries are extremely fertile areas for multimedia development, and many production companies can rightfully call them bread-and-butter clients. These kinds of projects can range from community outreach programs to courseware for students. The market is a lucrative but by no means a simple one, from either a technical or marketing perspective.

Many schools are now wiring the classrooms with either PC stations or PC "laboratories" in which students perform their own research on CD-ROMs or Web sites. In fact, many schools now allow and even encourage their students to actually develop their own multimedia productions. The possibilities here for the professional multimedia developer are numerous: CD-ROMs, Web sites, hypertext-based courseware, and interactive learning games for young students.

This market is in a constant state of expansion. New course materials are developed every year, and older materials must be updated, often by the producers who developed the original materials. A project successfully sold to one school district might easily mushroom into numerous districts, thereby making one project many times more profitable to the producer.

Materials for schools, however, are usually held to rigorous sets of technical, financial, and content requirments. School districts are public institutions bound by local and federal statutes. These institutions rigorously control the content for these multimedia presentations, and they expect the content to live up to established standards. Further, they have tightly controlled budgets. In most cases, the producer will have no flexibility with the assigned budget and schedule. In other words, this is a market with great possibility, but the work is exacting and often subject to many different opinions, sometimes by people who don't know a thing about multimedia. Still, much work and money is available to the multimedia producer in the educational sector. Don't ignore this market.

Your own idea

Of course, having an outside company solicit your talent to help that company realize its plans for multimedia is a wonderful thing, boosting both the bank account and your own company's prestige. But many multimedia producers don't want to wait for work to come to them. They're interested in developing their own ideas for a commercial or educational project.

One thing that most people in the multimedia industry don't lack is a surplus of good ideas. This industry attracts some of the most creative and imaginative people in the world, from all walks of life and professional disciplines. But good ideas are nothing more than that unless they can stand up to many tests, including the ultimate test: market receptivity. Having a good idea for a multimedia project is only a first step, the visualization. To take the vision to the next step requires significantly more work than the original conception sketched on a napkin or imagined while staring at the ceiling in the middle of the night. Each successive step between idea and realization means even more work. But the rewards here can go beyond adjectives. The satisfaction of conceiving, developing, and marketing a successful multimedia project is a singular experience with potentially lifelong rewards for the team that did it. But how do you do it?

Who's "Publishing" This?

After the initial visualization discussed earlier in this chapter, the next step is Important Decision #1: Who will publish this project? Publishing means different things in the multimedia world, and the word *publisher* probably has as many slippery definitions as the word *producer,* as I discussed previously. For the sake of simplicity, I define the publisher as the individual or company who will be responsible for the public dissemination of the multimedia project. This might be through retail or corporate distribution, or through an online presence with the publisher's name as the titular head of the online entity.

A relationship with a publisher is important, and for many multimedia producers, indispensable. But many other producers prefer to publish themselves, and one of the great egalitarianisms of multimedia is that doing so is entirely possible, especially online. Some multimedia producers, working independently, will work to produce final "gold-disk" masters of their multimedia titles; in other words, a finished product that has been tested and is ready for duplication and marketing. Others will already have an agreement with a publisher before starting production on the title, knowing that a larger entity will be responsible for distributing that title. Still others prefer no outside publisher at all, thereby not only retaining all rights and benefits, but also exercising total control over every aspect of the production. Clearly, this last method is financially risky and scarier than having a larger company behind your multimedia efforts. But you can do it, and in many cases, an outside publisher will actually pay more to distribute a finished independent title than it might for a work still under progress or even conception.

Studying the Marketplace

Regardless of who publishes the finished multimedia entity, the initial challenge is to predict what kind of title will have a chance at popular acceptance. That holy grail, unfortunately, often has little relation to a title's ingenuity, originality, or finished quality. Predicting the market is an art in itself, a process that lives up to the chestnut of 90 percent perspiration and 10 percent inspiration. What makes this process so difficult is that it involves a sober look at past, present, and future, a scrutiny that involves your own company (or team), the entire multimedia industry, and the outside market for your product.

The past as a guideline

One obvious way that marketing professionals determine the potential for a future product is to study how other products that are conceptually similar have been received in the past. If the public rushed in droves to see movies about dinosaurs, you can bet that they will do it again for another movie about dinosaurs. "Me, too" products are a staple of any market economy, as professionals who are paid big bucks to divine consumer trends know. They base their assumptions partly on what has worked in the past.

In the multimedia world, this kind of thinking is effective, but only to a point. In fact, it's a much smaller point than virtually any other industry you can compare it to. The two main reasons for this are technology and the target audience.

Technology

Technology is the great unknown here. In the time that I spent writing this book, the standard technology of home PCs changed from a typical 90MHz Pentium processor to a typical 133MHz processor. The usual size of a hard drive is now one gigabyte or more, a size that would have meant additional money just a few months ago. The modem sold with these computers when I started (if they were bundled at all) was usually 14.4 baud; in the intervening months, the average speed has doubled. And PCs aren't alone. Software has changed, too. When this book was in preproduction, Java (a programming language for the Web and beyond) was an experimental toy that Sun Microsystems hadn't yet released to the larger computing world. Now you see Java code in even the most low-budget, personal home pages. Technological change happens so quickly in the multimedia world that you need to be at least remotely aware of what market conditions might be like when the project is finished.

Audience

The other great drawback to basing your future plans on past examples is that the audience for multimedia is growing exponentially. For example, at the time when work on this book began, the best market estimates discerned that almost 90 percent of the people on the World Wide Web in the U.S. were male. Just months later, that number has slipped to less than 70 percent, and with the continuing evolution of popular commercial online services such as America Online, CompuServe, and Prodigy toward the Web, that number will change these figures even more. The audience for multimedia projects can change drastically over the course of a production, and sometimes, the more fickle whims of a target audience can turn against last week's trend faster than you can say "Atari." When you develop your project, you find an awareness of the past to be essential knowledge. Relying upon it, though, is a big mistake.

The present as a guideline

The present is a much better guideline to base your development assumptions on, simply because the present usually has the benefit of at least the most recent shift in technology. It is by no means a perfect measuring stick, however: again, the technology will shift between the time the production begins and ends. You can glean key ideas from carefully observing and researching present market conditions and the multimedia products that either fill them or leave gaps.

Filling the gaps

These gaps are probably the best place to start conceiving a successful multimedia title. Some of the greatest success stories in this industry came from simple ideas that filled market holes. The immensely popular arcade game *PacMan* is a great example. Market research had shown that the shoot-'em-up and search-and-destroy arcade games of the time (1980) were being used primarily by young boys, and not girls. Someone reasoned that girls might have just as many quarters as boys, and wouldn't mind spending them if they found a game that was less violent and stereotypically masculine. *PacMan* not only hit the target market dead on but spawned several successful sequel games targeted even more directly to the female audience, including *Ms. PacMan* and *Baby PacMan.* Even in high tech, stereotypes persist.

Market gaps are still a clear and present opportunity in the multimedia world, at least at the time of this writing. Even with tens of thousands of multimedia titles and even more Web sites online, the market is still not adequately served in many areas. Part of this comes from the same "me, too" mentality that I mentioned previously. But some of these gaps aren't so much a matter of finding something different — but not too different. They're a matter of finding needs that aren't being filled at all. Why? Because, on the surface, these "needs" aren't as sexy to work on as a slick interactive general interest title, or don't have the same boffo box office potential as a killer game title or a useful medical reference work.

Finding the gaps to fill

Innumerable opportunities exist for title development that have more modest goals than big box office. One of the great advantages of this medium, especially in an online venture, is that you can cater to a niche rather than mass market.

Identifying these niches through market research will yield a superb collection of possibilities for multimedia development. Remember, every megahit such as *The 7th Guest* creates dozens of interactive ROMs that try to do close to the same thing and are met with market indifference. But how many titles such as *The Oregon Trail* and *Who Built America?* get developed every year? Maybe their uniqueness explains why these titles are successful sellers as individual purchases and bundled software, and tons of game developers are grumbling that no money is there to be made in multimedia. This business has no shortage of mogul wannabes. But you should remember that many multimedia success stories exist that never get covered in *Wired* or *Business Week.* Those are stories worth a sequel.

The future as a guideline

As I said at the outset of this chapter, the process of conceiving a multimedia title is a predictive one. Part of making good predictions is knowing where the market is going, not only in terms of popular content but also in terms of technology. The methodology here is mostly a matter of research. But that research is extraordinarily broad, and must cover what's both possible and likely.

In many ways, that situation is less fluid for fixed media such as CD-ROM than for online media such as a Web site. At least with CD-ROM, a user base and set of standards are already established. Most CD-ROM drives are quad-speed or better, most people use Windows (with some Mac), most people know how to use a CD-ROM. In the online environment, the issues change almost weekly. Popular Web-browsing software adds new enhancements all the time; frequently, a new test version becomes available before the previous version has even begun to penetrate the market in any significant way. New technologies happen all the time on the Web, not only on the software side but the hardware side as well.

The changing of the wires

At the time of this writing, the cyber-elite use ISDN or T1 telephone lines for quick data transmission. Both are orders of magnitude faster than the common 14.4 or 28.8 modems available to most consumers. By the time this book comes out, both of those technologies will begin to be surpassed by the new cable modems that use coaxial cable wires rather than the telephone-oriented "twisted pair" wires. This will allow the use of much bigger, more elaborate graphics on the Web, with much faster data rates. And by the time cable modems become popular, new transmission technologies such as direct-satellite broadcast may well be arriving. It's a guessing game at which only the most dedicated can hope to succeed.

The successful multimedia producer keeps abreast of trends in the industry: past, present and future. People who succeed in this business are voracious consumers of information, constantly scanning trade journals, special-interest publications, Web sites, and online newsgroups for the latest buzz. Nobody can predict the future, especially the future of an industry as fluid as multimedia. But being prepared for change — and change is inevitable here — is a way to lay a solid foundation for the integrity and eventual success of your title.

A Short Course in Intellectual Property

Probably the most profound changes that have occurred during the multimedia revolution have been in the area of intellectual properties. Even the seismic shifts of technological change pale in comparison to a world in which protected intellectual properties can be perfectly duplicated and transmitted all over the world in a matter of seconds. The legal profession is approaching this issue as one of its greatest challenges as we head into the 21st century. The laws as written and practiced up to now have been woefully inadequate within these changing tides. A new generation of legal specialists is trying to come to grips with the immense set of legal issues ushered in by the information age. I don't exaggerate in saying that legal rather than technological or even market issues are the most volatile aspect of the multimedia business.

So, what is legal and what isn't? This is an industry based on information and entertainment. How are "properties" of this sort protected? One of the Internet's philosophical clichés tells us that "information wants to be free." That may be true, but the people who create it don't always want it to be free. If it's not free — and the Web serves up an entire universe of information that is — are fees allocated? Who is entitled to them? The writers? The programmers? The publisher? All of the above? What constitutes "fair use" of this information? Private use only? Public but not-for-profit use? Commercial use?

A word to the wise: see a lawyer

Nobody, repeat, nobody can answer these questions with the certainty that you want except for a qualified legal expert. When you use any materials that you or your team has not created from scratch from an original idea, you need the advice and counsel of an experienced lawyer. Going forward without one should be unthinkable. The guidance presented here is intended only as a primer on essential issues of intellectual property. Ownership of protected intellectual property can be so complex, and its use in multimedia (often referred to in existing legal contracts as the vague "media yet to be invented") so fraught with subtleties, that you should always consult a lawyer regarding all outside content and performances brought in for the project.

What is an intellectual property?

Simply put, intellectual property is a product of human imagination and skill that can be awarded a monetary value. Obviously, a multimedia production falls under this heading, as do many other kinds of creative endeavors such as music, books, films, photographs, and computer software. According to U.S. law, intellectual property is property in the most literal sense of the word, in that it can bought, sold, and licensed just like a tangible physical property such as a car or a house.

Intellectual property is protected by several different kinds of laws. In multimedia, which is considered computer software, these laws include copyrights, trade secrets, patents, and trademarks. The laws afford the final multimedia entity, such as a CD-ROM, protection as intellectual property. But multimedia productions can include aspects of other media inside the final work of intellectual property. Therefore, the laws governing this new medium are complex and still evolving.

The following sections take a quick look at some basic legal concepts.

What is a copyright?

A copyright is the vehicle of legal protection for an intellectual property. These rights give the work's creator, the author, legal control over how that property is used. Copyrights can be transferred and sold in the same way that an intellectual property can. Copyrights are a kind of "virtual" property under the law. The owner of the copyright on a work of intellectual property has the right to exploit the work in any way he or she sees fit. This can take the form of performance rights, distribution rights, reproduction rights, and the right to adapt the intellectual property to another intellectual property.

The first person to own the copyright to an intellectual property is the author, and under the law, the author is granted an immediate copyright on the work as soon as it's created. But not in all cases is the author in the legal sense also the author in the creative sense. The law stipulates four different ways to become an author:

- ✦ Be the person who created the work in the first place.
- ✦ Be an employer who paid an employee to create the work, as "work for hire."

- Be the commissioning agent for an intellectual property created by an independent contractor.
- Be part of a collaboration that creates the intellectual property, making you a joint author.

As you can see, the word *author* can have as many slippery definitions as *"producer"* in the multimedia world. But in the legal definition, the author is the impetus behind the intellectual property, not necessarily the hands that physically created it.

What qualifies for copyright protection?

To be granted a copyright, an intellectual work must live up to three basic requirements:

- It must be original.
- It must be in a form that is fixed and tangible.
- It must meet the legalese stipulation of "minimal creativity."

Each of these requirements deserves a closer look.

Originality

In this context, *original* means that the idea of the work originated with the author who applies for copyright protection. Originality in the sense of being unique or novel is not a requirement for copyright law, though it helps, of course. Independent creation is the issue here, which means that even if an existing copyrighted work is already similar to the one just created, the new authors are still protected under copyright law.

Fixed and tangible

This can be as simple as a typed page or as elaborate as a finished multimedia production. An idea can be copyrighted only if it can be experienced by others via one of the five senses. An idea that exists in the author's head but hasn't been fixed in some tangible form is not eligible for copyright protection.

"Minimal creativity"

The last legal qualification that must be satisfied is a slippery term called *minimal creativity.* This stipulates that the author put in at least a minimal amount of creative and intellectual effort to produce the property. Simply recording the sounds of a street corner, for example, cannot result in a copyrightable recording. If the same author records that scene and edits, processes, or otherwise manipulates the audio, that work satisfies minimal creativity requirements and is now copyrightable.

A second word to the wise

Understanding these basic legal concepts at the start of production is important. Fluency here not only protects the producer's finished product but also gives the team an insight into the possibility of bringing outside creative material into the production. Knowing the values and other attachments to existing intellectual properties that might be brought into the title, such as existing music, pictures from movies, and text from books, is crucial. Without an understanding of them, the production budget can quickly spiral out of control. In a worst-case scenario, you might even have to halt the project's distribution and order it destroyed to protect an existing copyright or intellectual property.

Multimedia and the Law

Multimedia is a difficult medium from a legal standpoint. Original materials created in-house by a multimedia developer or team are protected under copyright law. Likewise, an outside contractor who produces multimedia content for the assigning author usually transfers all rights to the original intellectual property over to the author. But not all multimedia is created as original work, and the nature of bringing in outside creative materials and talents almost always involves the subtleties of ownership and copyrights in the preproduction process. You can have problems here — major problems. These usually fall under one of two headings: permissions and privacy issues. Permissions relate to the process of negotiating the right to use previously copyrighted material. Privacy issues relate to possible infringements of the rights of other individuals or copyright holders to control physical likenesses, such as photographs or audio recordings of famous people.

Situations in which the producers don't control the copyrights to intellectual property being used in the production make permissions necessary. Negotiating these rights can be complicated, especially if the authors or copyright holders are no longer in business or even alive. Producers who are unable to locate copyright holders within "reasonable" limits of time and money are actually afforded some measure of protection under the law. But the decision to go ahead and use copyrighted material without permission can be dangerous. In many cases, such as the ones in which the copyright holders are not found, the repercussions, if any, may be slight. But with a more blatant offense or a troublesome copyright holder, you could risk theft charges, which is what copyright infringement is, in simpler language. Legal actions, litigation for damages and compensations, and, naturally, big legal fees are just a sample of what might occur.

What materials can you use without permission?

With legal trouble as a good incentive to play on the right side of the tracks, the producer may well ask what materials are considered fair game. Some intellectual properties cannot be copyrighted. For example, individual words are part of the public domain, as are short phrases and names, as long as they don't signify a specific product or service. Likewise, facts cannot be copyrighted, nor can works created by U.S. government employees as part of their jobs. But the producer might encounter other situations in which he or she will want to use preexisting intellectual property without permission. The law affords the right to do that in some cases.

Public domain

In the U.S., a piece of intellectual property that is not protected by copyright, either because it was never copyrighted or because the copyright has run out under the law, is considered to be public property; that is, property in the public domain. Public domain materials need no permissions for use, and nobody can copyright or otherwise claim title to the work again. Because copyright protection lasts only for 75 years, copyrights do run out, at which point previously "owned" work becomes part of the public domain.

Another time limit to be aware of when you consider public domain materials is that some copyrighted materials published before 1964 and not copyright-renewed are now in the public domain. Those materials were originally copyright protected for 28 years, with an option for another 47-year renewal when the copyright laws were changed. If the copyrights on those properties were not renewed in their 28th year (1964), they became part of the public domain in the 29th year after publication.

Just because a work is in the public domain doesn't mean that the multimedia developer has totally free access to it, and in the electronic age, this can be slippery territory. For example, Beethoven's *Ninth Symphony,* having been written in the early 19th century, is clearly in the public domain. But the sheet music that describes the orchestration isn't, and a sound recording of the symphony is most definitely protected. The artists, conductor, and publisher all have rights here. Likewise, an object or invention might be in the public domain but owned by an individual or company who has the right to restrict access to its likeness. This is why Microsoft has been so active over the past few years in buying up the rights to classic images and artwork. In cases like these, you can expect fees for the use of even these public domain materials.

Fair use

Another situation in which you can use protected material without permissions is the very elusive concept of "fair use." Under the reigning definition of fair use, an author is permitted to make use fair use of existing intellectual material if some educational, scientific, cultural, or other "useful" purpose is demonstrable. Fair use laws were instituted to advance knowledge so that important ideas and writings could be disseminated without lengthy diversions into the questions of ownership and licenses.

The very phrase *fair use* has been a battleground of sorts in the evolving field of intellectual property law in the electronic age. In 1989, the rap group 2-Live Crew was sued for copyright infrigement over its parody of the Roy Orbison song, "Pretty Woman." The case was decided in the group's favor, with the U.S. Supreme Court ruling that parody and satire are valid examples of fair use. Just two years later, however, the California-based audio collage ensemble Negativland was successfully halted from distributing a recording called "U-2," which featured CD packaging that looked suspiciously like a new album from a certain Irish rock group, and vocal samples from radio star Casey Kasem, who objected to his likeness being used without permission. Even though Negativland's recording was clearly satirical, Island records, the company that controlled the rights to the group U2's music, was able to halt distribution and call for the destruction of all existing copies of the work.

Fair use is often decided by the amount of copyrighted material that's included in the new work. No concrete guidelines exist as to how much is too much. A paragraph of text from a book may be considered fair use, but a paragraph from a short essay may not be. Likewise, the content of the appropriated material is also of some importance. Even a short snippet from a book or recording can be considered off limits for fair use, if the material is the essence of the protected work. I have seen cases in which something as short as a digitally-sampled snare drum hit has been grist for the legal mill, with charges that the 0.5 seconds of material on that sample was the essence of the offended drummer's sound. One way to minimize the ill effects of a dicey fair use call is to ensure proper attribution to all creative parties.

Licensing rights

When a work is copyright protected, the author is afforded certain rights and privileges under the law. Those rights are exclusive and include the right to reproduce, distribute, perform, or create adaptations to that work. If the production decides that these copyrighted materials are essential to the project, the producer must negotiate a license fee for their use. Not only does this mean monetary compensation for the author but also permission for the multimedia producer to use the work in some or all of the ways that the author has the right to use them.

Some agencies specialize in licensing works of intellectual materials, such as stock photo, video, and music houses. These agencies typically charge a flat fee for commercial usage. With printed material, the first step is to contact the permissions department of the publisher. If doing so is not possible because the publisher is out of business or otherwise unavailable, the author or other copyright holder must be located before the work can be used in a legally righteous sense. Some agencies will search copyrights for you for a fee; see the list of sources in Chapter 12 for company information.

The best way to avoid hassles with rights and permissions on a multimedia project is to create original content. This might seem overly obvious, but doing so is not always possible, and sometimes it is actually more cost- or creatively effective to include materials that have permissions issues attached. I can't give you any hard and fast rules here, other than to make sure that everything going into the production is legally clear, either through original effort or duly-acquired permissions. Without this assurance, which in some cases is guaranteed by an actual insurance contract (typically called "Errors and Omissions"), the production is in trouble. Maybe not today or even tomorrow, but, quite possibly, one day out of the blue.

Budgeting and Prototypes

As you can see, the process of conceiving a multimedia title is nowhere nearly as simple as having a good idea and then executing it. A business as volatile as this one always presents issues to contend with, right up until the time the product finally makes it into the user's homes, and even thereafter. But probably the biggest issue, after the good ideas and careful preparation are laid down on paper or in a spreadsheet, is the issue of money. All sorts of issues: money in, money out, money when? Without money to pay for production and marketing (never mind food and shelter), the project becomes something other than a commercial venture. It becomes a labor of love.

Not all that glitters brings gold

This labor of love is not nearly as uncommon as you might believe. Lots of people do multimedia just for the fun of it. In the world of fixed media, big projects are impractical as a labor of love because not many people will spend tens or hundreds of thousands of dollars with no possibility of financial return. Some people pass around hypercard stacks and funny little interactive movies for their friends. Others do CD-ROMs as a portfolio or resume, which is an investment, not a commercial endeavor.

In the online world, however, where having your own Web site can be as inexpensive as $15 a month and a bit of your time, the situation is very different. Many people design their own multimedia for the Web just for the sake of doing it. Because the Web medium is largely free of cost to the end user, no one expects a financial return from these sites. They are created because the developer wants it done.

Why? Why not? Not every work of creative skill is intended as a profit-making venture. Thousands of sites on the WWW are nothing more than interactive "post cards" from individuals such as John and Jane Doe. Some are much more elaborate than you would think, with 3D graphics, Java scripts, Shockwave animations, and elaborate design. What's the motivation here? Could be anything. Can anyone quantify and accurately explain human creative endeavor? Perhaps the page is composed by a designer wanting to learn HTML skills or do some self promotion. Maybe a teenager creates one who just loves the idea of being his or her own "TV station" on the Internet.

Perhaps the page exists as a public service, or a fan club, or an advanced form of graffitti that says "I exist." Why these sites exist isn't the point. That they do exist is the point, and if all you have in mind for your multimedia project is a final entity that is, in itself, its own reward, you might as well skip the rest of this chapter and move on to the actual making of your project.

Multimedia as commercial venture

Even in view of the sea of noncommercial Web sites, most multimedia projects, whether fixed or online, are meant as commercial endeavors. They are developed so that they can be sold or sponsored and enjoyed, and so that the production company can receive (it hopes) enough revenues not only to do the next project, but also to pay the staff and even make a little profit. Sometimes the profit may even be big, though this is more exceptional than optimistic souls would like to believe.

Even though multimedia is a creative skill and the final product is an intellectual property, the arrangements of financing and budgeting a production are very much as they are in other creative industries, such as film and television. You'll set guidelines as to what the project is, how long it will take to produce, and what the anticipated return might be, from a purely speculative viewpoint. You'll arrange financing to allow all these factors to move along a schedule. If the plan goes off without hitches and the predictions have been largely accurate, the investors (whether outside parties or the development team) will receive their rewards.

Note

The basic phases of the commercial multimedia outreach are probably all that can be even remotely compared to more traditional and established media forms. The process of making multimedia (depending on the nature of the project, of course) can be so fraught with variables, even for the most seasoned producer, that the process of accurately predicting things such as budgets is little more than educated guesswork.

I've already discussed some of the variables involved in a multimedia production, but I'll do some review before I give you a look at the budgeting process. The expenses that will be incurred during a multimedia production can be divided into "hard" and "soft" expenses, as the following sections discuss.

Hard costs

Hard costs are outgoing monies that can be adequately quantified, whether through fixed expenses or known escalations of expenses. In a mulitmedia production, hard costs include (but aren't limited to) the following:

- ✦ The basic costs of equipment (whether rental or purchase)
- ✦ Office expenses (rent, utilities, and so on)
- ✦ Salaries; software purchases; consulting fees; production fees such as disc pressing; duplication fees; packaging costs; duties and tariffs; licensing fees; studio costs; and anything else deemed a necessary expense for the production of the project

The hard costs make up the bulk of the production expenses, but these can be brought down in numerous ways, as they are on most projects. One way that is, unfortunately, rather common in this industry is to defer salaries, at least for the people who run the company. Many a hit project has benefitted from the dedication of the people who make it and manage to pay their bills while receiving little or no compensation from the project. An entrepreneurial adventure, which is what many multimedia projects are, is often funded with little more than sweat equity: the energy of the parties who have the vision. The cliché that you hear about two folks working out of their garage in their spare time to make a project happen is a cliché for a reason. It happens all the time.

Of course, not all salaries can be deferred, nor can the expenses incurred by the vendors involved. Expecting other people to work on your project for free is unreasonable unless they have some compelling reason to do so, such as a financial interest in the ultimate success of the production. In that case, the relationship between employer and employee, author and work-for-hire becomes exceedingly blurred. People who work for part of the action are closer to partners than they are to employees, and the relationship must be clearly understood by all parties before they proceed along these lines. Anything less than absolute clarity on these issues is a sure bet for trouble down the road — at the very least, ill feelings; and possibly litigation.

Minimizing hard costs

You can reduce the pain of hard costs in several ways:

✦ **Lease it rather than buy it.** One less painful way to minimize hard costs is by leasing rather than purchasing. With hardware, you must make a decision as to whether a sizable purchase makes sense not only in the present (is there enough money in the budget for that cool new workstation or a larger monitor?) but also for the long term. Hardware becomes outdated quickly these days, and unless the purchase makes sense for the long run, keeping the team's cash closer to the vest, parsing out just enough to get the job done, is usually best.

✦ **Barter for services.** Bartering is an exceptionally useful tool for bringing down hard costs. For multimedia companies already engaged in work-for-hire projects, especially on the Web, making barter arrangements with suppliers is actually a fairly easy process. Many vendors don't already have a Web presence, and those that do don't always keep them supplied with new technology or programming. More than one office has been set up with equipment, new or used, from a supplier that has traded these goods for services such as a Web page, scanning, a CD-ROM test pressing, or other jobs that are fairly easy for a multimedia team to supply.

✦ **Resource sharing.** If you can find a way to share resources, you can cut down on two serious hard costs: equipment and office space. In many cities that feature a vibrant multimedia developer community, such as San Francisco, New York, and Seattle, entire neighborhoods are dominated by small production companies. Simple math reveals that several parties sharing an office spend less than just one would. Sharing equipment also has advantages because most offices don't need more than one copier, scanner, digital camera, or other key piece of gear. In New York's Silicon Alley, for example, entire office building floors often act as small "incubator" spaces, housing several small production companies that share facilities and a receptionist. Naturally, these kinds of relationships can be as unstable as any "roommate" situation, but for companies just starting off or on a tight budget, sharing space and gear sometimes makes sense.

Soft costs

The vague but somehow always bigger-than-you-think "soft costs" can be characterized as expenses that are known, but not always quantifiable, in advance. These expenses often seem minor and just a normal part of doing business. In reality, they are, but they can quickly escalate out of control and become a significant financial drain. The soft cost of telephone expenses is a good example of an otherwise small cost that can quickly become a monster. A few coast-to-coast calls a day, to a distributor or home-office employee, can purge hundreds of dollars from the monthly balance sheet.

Caution

Legal expenses are a notorious soft cost, because you can't predict with certainty how long a legal action, no matter how simple, will take. For example, even the process of a nondisclosure agreement (a simple document saying that what one party shows or says to another party should be kept confidential between the involved parties) can turn into a nightmare if each party has a different NDA that they use as a matter of course.

Getting a handle on soft costs is largely a matter of discipline. This discipline, however, is needed throughout the rest of the production, into the hard costs and all the way through a marketing effort. Many successes in this business have hype and flashiness to thank, of course, and those usually cost money. But an element of frugality is always an advantage, even when bigger projects come along that afford bigger budgets.

Budgeting the production

The process of deciding how much producing your multimedia title will cost is a mystical art. Some multimedia projects cost virtually nothing to produce, outside of the time they take to make and the initial hardware and software application expenditures. On the other hand, the average budget for a high-profile CD-ROM game, with pretensions to box office acceptance, now routinely runs over a million dollars, with a marketing budget that can be equivalent or higher.

Note

No one formula holds water as an absolute guideline for a multimedia budget. There are some financial and creative ideas that you can quantify from the beginning, of course. But a single change in design or marketing approach can have a domino effect on the rest of the budget. A key employee can come down with the flu two weeks before the product's final ship date, thereby setting everything back and creating another domino effect of time and money. A power outage can ruin key files; an inexpensive, easy-to-procure license might take weeks longer and many legal bills deeper than originally thought.

Top-selling games such as *Myst, Total Distortion,* and *The Deadalus Encounter* were created on production budgets that averaged between $700,000 and $1.5 million dollars. On the other hand, equally successful titles such as *Who Killed Sam Ruppert* and *The Journeyman Project* cost $100,000 or less. Corporate training presentations adhere to these same kinds of wild budget ranges, although educational titles are usually a bit more controlled in terms of cost because of the nature of the market.

And that's just for fixed media. A Web site such as Paul Allen's successful *c\net* or *Wired* magazine's cutting-edge *HotWired* site are staffed by dozens of full-time employees. Each needs a salary, health benefits, a desk, a computer, a phone line, and enough other equipment and support material to get his or her job done. Compare this to a typical small-business Web site run by a core of perhaps two or three individuals, who may be running a nicely profitable business out of a home office with virtually no overhead. Both are successful ventures. So, how do you glean a budget plan for one by looking at the other? Obviously, you don't. What do you do? Clearly, you need to have an idea of how much your production will cost in terms of time, money, and other resources. You can begin to formulate some ideas by making some intelligent guesses and having a nimble finger on your spreadsheet program when you answer the following questions:

1. **How long will the project take to produce?**

   Because multimedia is a labor-intensive industry, the greatest expense in creating it is the time put in by the talent pool. Development time for a Web site can be as short as a month, even weeks. Development time on huge CD-ROM projects such as *The 7th Guest* or *Jump Raven* is calculated in years. And remember, multimedia is an industry in which a 9-to-5 workday is almost unheard of. The work week of a multimedia company consists of far more than 40 man hours.

   Quantifying the employee expenses is the first place to start in coming up with a reasonable dollar figure for developing your multimedia title. Although many multimedia professionals put far more hours in on a project than they receive payment for, compensating them in a mutually agreeable way at the project's inception is the beginning of a workable budget. Making an intelligent guess as to how much compensation is a matter of creating a development schedule, which I discuss in the next section.

2. **What are the potential difficulties?**

   Presumably, the talent assembled to create the multimedia project is up to the job in terms of competence and experience. But every project has its own bugaboos, whether technical, legal, or marketing oriented. An essential part of the preproduction process involves quantifying these risks to the best of your ability, and building the resources to transcend them into the budget.

Take, for an easy example, a new authoring program, which your development team has decided to use because it promises more power and productivity. In theory, both of these promised features sound like time savers, and if they prove to be so, they'll easily justify the additional hard cost of buying the software. A new program creates its own domino effect, however. You'll have to allow for a learning curve for at least one person, which sets back the schedule in two ways: one by spending needed production time acclimating the development team to the program; the other by stealing those learning hours from the actual project development. Add in the potential nightmares of getting to know new tech support personnel and finding your way around the inevitable bugs and foibles of a new program, and suddenly, something that you thought would save money has ended up costing a lot more than you bargained for.

To understand just how a seemingly minor technical decision can affect the production, remember that technical support is also incumbent upon the producer after the project is released. If you're building a Web site and decide to incorporate all the latest fads — frames, tables, Shockwave, Java scripts — you run the risk of delivering your product to people who may not be able to use them the way you intended. Your use of these technologies might freeze their computers, or worse, cause a serious crash. You must be prepared for these scenarios, which means that your product testing period is extended, which means more time and, of course, more money.

As you can see, the difficulty of the project, both in terms of development and support, are critical aspects of a project's budgetary costs. A more difficult project means more hours, more trial and error, more testing, and more bug fixes. Can you afford them? You need to know in advance.

3. Is there a rush?

Between 30 – 40 percent of all CD-ROM titles are sold during the Christmas holiday season. Therefore, to have a fighting chance in the best selling period, your title must be on the retailer's shelf by September. Your project must therefore be tested and ready for duplication by August. You'll have to time the production to meet these deadlines. If the production has started without adequate foresight into these dates, that means a rush, which translates into more money.

The situation can be even more harried for a Web site, as companies rush to establish a presence on the Internet. Although you can put up a small site quickly, you must allow time to adequately debug it. Many Web developers expect this debugging period to take place after the actual release date, but a paying client is interested in cutting a check only for the final result of a bullet-proof site. Naturally, this circumstance moves the release schedule up, with the attendant extra man-hours and money that doing so entails. Although clients may expect to pay extra for a "rush" job, you must spell out this timetable in advance so that you can compensate for it adequately in the schedule and the budget. You'll find a big difference between a relaxed month of normal work and a crazed month of overtime, sleeplessness, and ill-feeling.

Unfortunately, no foolproof method exists for figuring out how much your production will cost. Sometimes the costs are whatever the financing allows for; a sudden infusion of investor cash at just the right time can inflict all sorts of changes in expenses across the board! But in other cases (many other cases), the idea is to spend as little as possible while yet producing a project that remains reasonably close to your initial vision. Remember that every aspect of multimedia is a trade-off between what's desirable and what's possible. After you've reached those compromises, you'll have a basic idea of what you're setting out to make. And only then can you know how much it will cost to make it.

The schedule

After you decide what financial resources are available for the multimedia project, your next step is to come up with a schedule that will take it from planning through production, testing, marketing, and aftermarket support. The goal here is to stay on target for the actual ship date, moving resources around in whatever way is feasible to adhere to that deadline.

Caution Delays in the schedule have a profound impact across the entire production. The impact can be as minor as having to keep your personnel on for an extra week or two. It can be as major as jeopardizing your relationship with the assigning client, or even as disastrous as missing a major retailing season.

Developing a schedule is, again, the art of understanding the relationship between the desirable and the possible. The former pertains directly to the original vision for the project, which by now has been tempered by additional input from the marketing and technical teams, and by an awareness of final distribution plans when the project is finished. The second aspect of the relationship is what's possible given the resources available, pertaining to the ship date. A multimedia production can go on indefinitely: revisions, fixes, and enhancements can be added at almost any time if resources allow. With a Web site, this never-ending quality is part of the process because most Web sites are in a constant state of update, whether for content or technical improvements.

But most projects do come to an end at some point. They are deemed complete so that they can be used by the target audience. To propose an ending date — the ship date — for the project, you need to ask serious questions at the outset, come up with the best possible answers, and be realistic and flexible when it looks as if the answers aren't the right ones. The following are a few important questions to consider when making up a schedule:

1. **Has the team ever successfully developed a project like this?**

   A positive answer to this question actually answers many questions, all of them in a positive way. For example, if the new project is conceptually similar to a previously developed project, all sorts of preexisting resources may be available. Foremost among them are the experiences that the development team gained on that last project. Knowing how to do something is usually a function of having done it successfully in the past, and a smooth work dynamic is always easier to attain when the team has already worked together before. Along with this prior experience, you may also be able to salvage code, backgrounds, and technical routines from an earlier project and seamlessly resurrect these elements in the new one. Many a Web designer has come up with a set of good templates and scripts that gets re-used on a number of projects. This is not self plagiarism. This is intelligent recycling of resources. Hollywood does this with fancy sets. Take a close look at *Invaders from Mars* (the original) and you'll see sets from *Gone With the Wind.* Reinventing the wheel is costly and time consuming, which, in multimedia, are the same thing.

2. **Is the schedule realistic or just optimistic?**

   Herein lies a major judgment call, one that requires the producers to be aware not only of available and expected resources but also of that "digital force majeure" that I discussed earlier. A rule in multimedia production, called the "Two-Times" rule, seems, much to the chagrin of developers and financiers alike, to hold true: any given task can take two times longer and cost twice as much to accomplish as expected. Experienced developers modulate this (with a bit of bravado) by simply building an extra time/money contingency into the budget and the schedule (not necessarily double). When a seasoned producer develops the schedule, he or she will be aware of the need for this contingency. So many things can happen that predicting why or when is nearly impossible. The service bureau upon which you depend for color repro may be unexpectedly closed for vacation or a funeral. Your Internet connection can go down for the night, eliminating the possibility of getting a file for an important finance meeting. Unexpected hindrances are a fact of life here, and they can range from annoying to catastrophic. The only way to get a handle on them is to expect them and build the time and schedule so that you can compensate adequately for them when and if they do happen. If they don't happen (a rare occurrence), you win anyway: the project comes in on time and under budget.

Dealing with delays

Because of the inevitable unforeseen circumstances, the schedule will have delays of one sort or another. These delays can be isolated (the good scenario) or symbiotic (the bad scenario). Either type can be a problem, though the former type is less destructive than the latter.

An isolated delay can be optimistically regarded as a one-time or one-event problem. A miscommunication between team members that results in a programming or aesthetic error is an isolated delay: fix the problem and the delay is gone. You can usually solve isolated delays with a minimum of disasterous impact. You should expect and compensate for them by contingency allotments in the budget and schedule.

Symbiotic delays are much more troublesome. With this kind of delay, one problem directly or indirectly creates consequences down the line, thereby multiplying the delay exponentially. A good example is your art director coming down sick with the flu. On the surface, it's an isolated delay: when he or she is up and around again, problem solved, right? Wrong. Without that person in the loop doing his or her work, the rest of the art department is typically at a standstill. Associated artwork cannot be approved, or more cautiously, even generated. Programmers cannot continue to apply code to the graphics because no graphics exist. Because the programmer can't work efficiently, the schedule gets moved back. With the schedule moved back, the ship date might change, and so on.

No one can provide set rules for dealing with these delays because they are by nature unpredictable. There are solutions, however:

- **Find out whether you can simply reprioritize the aspect of the production that's being affected by the delay.** If the task isn't of immediate or lasting importance, the producer may have to make this compromise.
- **Call on outside resources to help accomplish the task.** Many production teams will more than occasionally resort to extra freelance help in a crunch. Extra help is part of the contingency that you prepare for during the budgeting and rescheduling process.
- **Split workloads and responsibilities among other parties.** Although dividing the work may not be ideal, especially in a small, already overworked team, having this kind of talent backup can at least ensure that delays are only annoying rather than potentially debilitating to the entire project.

Financing the Prototype

In most cases, even an experienced multimedia producer will develop a prototype (a demonstration version) of the project before going on to create the working version. There are many reasons for doing this. For one thing, the prototype gives you a working model of what the project might look like, which will get people interested in working on it. It gives you a chance to do some preliminary test marketing; feedback from these initial impressions can be as good as gold. It gives you an idea of what the overall desirability for your product might be in the marketplace. Most important, a prototype serves to get publishers or other financial parties interested in you project. Without financing, most projects simply won't come to pass.

Who should pay for the prototype? You'll find two schools of thought here:

- One school supports self-financing, and the advantage of retaining as much of the project as possible for as long as possible.
- The other school looks for outside financing from the get-go, and is willing to give up some control in return for adequate capital.

Adherents to either side usually stake their positions on their own previous experiences in multimedia development. Although that approach makes perfect sense on the surface, the past isn't always a good indicator as to what the future holds. The multimedia world is extremely volatile in many ways, but none so profound as the financial aspects. Last year's top CD-ROM publisher might decide that CD-ROMs are out and the Web is in, hence few new projects in fixed media — or none at all. A trusted venture capital group decides technology is more important than content to its immediate goals, and suddenly, that group is investing in networks rather than multimedia projects. A distributor goes out of business; a major chain decides that it has less shelf space for new titles; a publisher gets swallowed up by another publisher who's not interested in outside projects. As you can see, what happened last year in multimedia might as well have happened last decade.

Still, someone must decide who's going to put up the money for making the project, and the two schools of thought, even considering all the variables I just discussed and a million other possibilities, both have valid arguments.

Self-financed prototypes

This is the easy one. A developer who puts up the money to produce a prototype of a multimedia project protects the most important idea in the multimedia world: ownership of content. Although many of these self-financed prototypes will eventually blossom into a full-fledged production that is actually financed by an outside publisher, the producer approaches that situation from a position of strength. Because the publisher can get a "sneak preview" of what the title does and what it looks like, it will generally be more receptive to at least considering the title for publication; with the prototype already developed, the publisher need spend no money on making the decision. In these situations, the dialectic between creator and marketer is at its simplest.

Because a prototype can be as simple as a digital "sketch" version of the proposed finished title, authoring one doesn't have to be expensive. The real creative capital — the potential — is what's behind the prototype. The purpose of the prototype is to demonstrate this potential in no uncertain terms. Self financing the prototype allows the production team to demonstrate to outside parties such as investors and publishers that the team has a legitimate project, the talent to develop it, and a certain amount of "sweat equity" already dedicated to it. Financial people like to see all these things.

Where can you obtain financing?

All the hype on the nightly news about how multimedia, the Internet, and all things digital are supremely tempting to anyone with money to invest in these industries might give you the impression that if you simply "build it, they will come." That might have been true in the first heady years of this business, but it is most certainly not the case anymore. On a high level, Wall Street has a much more circumspect attitude toward anything high tech than it did the day that it made Netscape Communications the most successful initial public offering in the history of the American stock market.

This industry has so much silicon snake oil in this industry that even successful companies with visionary products sometimes have a hard time getting the financing they need. On a lower level, financing a multimedia project is like financing any other creative endeavor, such as a film or an album. Sure, the project could turn out to be wildly successful and return the investments many times over. But more often, the project isn't a smash hit. Estimates concerning the record industry indicate that 25 percent of all recordings brings in enough money to "subsidize" the other 75 percent of everything that the major labels release. In multimedia, the figures are even more dire. Of course, this is still a young industry with much financial potential. In the meantime, however, projects that lose money are still much more commonplace than projects turning a significant profit. Most investors are all too aware of this. But you still need money, and there's still money to be had. Where do you get it?

Love money

Although perhaps not the sexiest way to finance a project, many a creative endeavor has been financed by love money: money that's gathered from friends, family, and other parties who have a mostly personal, but also financial, interest in seeing that your project gets off the ground.

Love money need not come from outside people, either. Even if the principals who develop the prototype (or even the finished project) are already devoting sweat equity (which, in a better world, would be real money as opposed to virtual money), hard work and good intentions aren't enough. The principals almost always put in some of their own money. This can come from anywhere: second mortgages, stock liquidation, even credit card debits. But these sources usually aren't enough, and the producers must go elsewhere for more.

When they are contributing love money, individuals and corporations close to the producers go through a similar process, dipping into personal or otherwise closely held finances in order to make an investment in the project. The particulars of these financial arrangements vary greatly; you can usually get away with paying off your parents more slowly than you can with American Express or MasterCard. The advantages here are simple. Love money is usually more procurable than bank money for a multimedia project; a bank might view multimedia as a potentially unsound investment. But if you decide to go this route, be aware of the baggage that can come with love money. If something disastrous happens and the project never comes off, you'll feel really bad when you can't repay investments to your friends and family.

Angels

A financial angel is a source of capital that's closer to a patron than an investor, though money from here is rarely a matter of pure patronage: usually, strings are attached. Financial angels are of the same species as love money, but they're better for the producer because they are usually better capitalized and more experienced in investment than are friends and family. Finding an angel is work in itself — so much so that some agencies and individuals actually specialize in finding such angels for intellectual properties. But many a great production, whether in the arts, science, or scholarship, owes its very existence to the often anonymous angels that gave it the initial break.

It would be nice if every aspiring multimedia producer had a rich Uncle Arnold who just happens to have tens or hundreds of thousands of dollars to invest on speculative projects. Angels can often fulfill the same role. Many funding agencies and foundations specialize in helping creative projects, especially if the project is going to some worthy cause. *Worthy cause* is a nebulous term here because each of these agencies has its own company mandate as to what is worthy of funding. Some will fund projects that are geared toward the educational sector, some support only the arts or a specific category of the arts, some are geared to projects that help the physically challenged or specific ethnic groups. Some support a variety of worthwhile endeavors.

Many of these agencies are geared toward the nonprofit sector, which means that if your project is simply a commercial venture, they probably won't be interested in helping you out. But if your project will ultimately benefit any of the categories just named, you might find a highly receptive audience here. Agencies such as the National Endowment for the Arts are government supported and have a mandate to fund projects to the limit of an allocated annual budget. Others are private foundations that operate under a similar "must-fund" mandate, though the available funds from these agencies are typically smaller.

In either case, if your project is actually oriented toward a worthy cause that fits under these angels' funding guidelines, a bit of research to see whether your angel might give your project wings is worthwhile. The best place to start looking for these public angels is at your local library, which should have the guidelines that these granting agencies require of a funding request. For the most essential information, the ground-zero of information on these agencies is The Foundation Center at 79 5th Avenue, New York, NY, 10011; (212) 620-4230.

Venture capital

When a large amount of money must be raised, either to build a project or build a company, many multimedia developers begin to dream of venture capital. A venture capital company is an agency that serves as an angel on steroids. You'll encounter a few limitations in dealing with a VC group. How much money you're seeking doesn't matter, because to a good VC agency, the amount of money is almost immaterial. Serving the public well being or a sector of the public that isn't being well-served are not stipulations as they are with a public funding agency. The VC group is interested in only one thing: Does enough potential exist for long-term profitability?

For a single title, the answer is almost invariably no, which is why so few VC companies invest in multimedia titles. A multimedia producer securing VC funding for a project is not unheard of by any means. But the mathematics of this industry, at least for individual titles, simply don't add up to something that interests most VC companies. These companies typically are looking for returns on investment of at least 30 percent. That's a lot of titles sold for a startup, especially when distribution and a track record aren't already part of the mix. For the Web, a proven financial model isn't in place, so the situation is even more dire. Further, multimedia titles, whether fixed or online, are something that the public can judge — and reject. A superb title isn't necessarily a popular one, as many producers can attest. The fickle nature of public tastes, along with the precarious position that many multimedia companies are in as they develop their products, leave most VC companies cold.

If you decide to follow this avenue for potential funding, understand that a venture capital group isn't interested in much beyond strict numbers. Also understand that all the hype and enthusiasm you can muster isn't an effective sales pitch. A venture capital group requires a thorough business plan, with realistic projections that don't make the group laugh. Above all, venture capitalists are interested in controlled, not predictive, risks. A venture group will be more likely to invest in a risk of execution — can your company survive, can it meet schedules, and so on — than in risks of taste — that is, the consumer market. You'll spend months working a deal with a VC group, weeks to prepare your business plan for the VC group's perusal, and days to hear a rejection. Unless you're absolutely convinced that you have something to make a venture capital group salivate, you might as well save your energy for more productive endeavors.

Publisher financing

Because most independent multimedia producers don't have the resources to be competitive with titles that are completely self-financed, self-published, and self-marketed, most developers of commercial titles eventually seek the assistance and collaboration of a publisher. This relationship can happen at any point in the project's genesis. A relationship with a publisher from the outset often means that the prototype and production will be paid for through advance funding. The relationship, when the project is finished, is typically an exchange of capital and services, in which the developer supplies the "product" and the publisher supplies the financing and marketing to make it into a hit. For most commercial multimedia projects, a relationship with a publisher is a given. But the nature of the relationship can vary.

Unless the project is being done in-house by the publisher, essentially making you and/or your team company employees, an arrangement in which the publisher finances your title is considered a work-for-hire agreement. In such a relationship, the publisher ultimately will own the lion's share of the spoils, most typically the copyright and the bulk of the revenues, if any. Granted, this is probably not the pot of gold you had in mind when you first started sketching out your ideas for a great multimedia title. But wait, it gets worse. When the publisher funds development of the title, the deal for the developer usually breaks down in one of two ways:

✦ **The publisher pays you for costs and advances you a fixed amount as the "profit" from the project.** This model assumes no ongoing profit to the developers. The publisher pays for the direct costs of the project and an agreed amount for overhead and expenses. On top of these monies, the developers receive a fixed payment (considered the profit) in advance of actually selling any copies of the title. This profit, which can be compared to a restaurant that automatically tacks on a 15 percent gratuity for the waiters, is usually fixed between 10 to 20 percent of the overall budget. In other words, the publisher pays for everything (within reason), provides enough profit so that the developers make at least a little bit of money, and that's the end of the deal. The good news for the developer is that the production and personnel will be paid for, and that no matter what the title actually ends up doing on the market, the developer makes a profit. The bad news is that if the title actually turns out to be highly successful, no direct profit ensues for the developer beyond the initial allotment. It's not a great deal, but for producers and companies without a track record, it's much better than going it alone, without a publisher.

✦ **The publisher advances monies against future royalties**. This model is more typical and tantalizing, but also riskier. In this situation, the publisher provides finance to the developers The publisher can recoup these monies (check the publishing contract to see just how much) against the percentage of royalties that the publisher and the developer agree on. Royalties typically range from 5 percent of net wholesale revenues to around 20 percent, depending on the track record of the developer and the specific deal that you strike. The good news with this model (for the developer) is the incentive here. If the title has a chance of doing really well, and the company producing it has a financial stake in the success, a much greater incentive exists to put out a superb title. An "evergreen" title, one that continues to sell well years after its initial release, can bring money into the company on an ongoing quarterly or annual basis.

The drawback for the developer under the second model is that advances aren't always enough to cover production expenses and overhead. Although some advances from a capable publisher can exceed a million dollars for a high-profile title, even that sum isn't always enough to get a company going, especially if the developers are robbing Peter to pay Paul with every week's payroll. In a worst-case scenario, the producers take the advance and still have to find additional funding. That means parsing out additional shares of the profits to third parties, a potential accounting nightmare and lessening of eventual profits.

Let's Make a Deal

Regardless of who developed the prototype, when it is completed and seems to have prospects for financial success, many multimedia producers begin to look for a partner. That partnership might be as simple as a basic distribution agreement with a publisher, along the lines that I just discussed. Or it could be a partnership in only the loosest sense of the word, and the developer is an "equal" party in name only. Regardless of the specifics, a strategic partner, most typically a multimedia publisher, is probably the best choice for an independent multimedia company. This is a competitive business with many different areas of professional specialty. Having the combined talents of many different financial, editorial, and marketing specialists, as you would have with a publisher as partner, is an inestimable benefit.

This benefit applies to a Web site as often it is does to a CD-ROM title. Although a partnership with an online publisher isn't as crucial as it is to the CD-ROM producers and their publishers, the relationship brings the same kind of benefits — just expressed in a different medium. Although an independent site might have "distribution" on the Web in the most literal sense of the word, getting the distribution that really counts — which is visitation — is not so easy. The kind of distribution that a publisher can offer comes in the way of reprints or linkage; that is, getting the site or material from it noticed by surfers who might not ordinarily have come across it on their own.

A development deal

When the publisher is convinced that the project has merit, based on a working prototype (or sometimes less!), it may decide to offer the producers a development deal. In the case of a CD-ROM title, the publisher usually funds the project and retains all or most of the rights. The funding typically comes as an advance against future royalties in the range of 5 to 25 percent of net wholesale price of the title. With an online title, the publisher usually funds the development of the site or content area in return for revenues brought in by subscriptions, fees, advertisements or whatever other method the publisher uses to bring in money.

These kinds of situations clearly put you in a true partnership with a publisher, regardless of how generous or draconian the terms are. Both parties have a vested interest in making sure that the project is successful, therefore you are partners. But partnerships of any stripe are involved relationships that must be carefully chosen. Finding a publisher isn't particularly hard, if you have a good title. Finding the *right* publisher is another question.

The right partners

Finding the right publisher is substantially more difficult. The right publisher is the one who is most interested in *your* kind of content and can best help advance that content to the target audience.

With a CD-ROM publisher, you need a company that has clout with distributors and retail channels, and who knows how to run a successful marketing and sales initiative. Other advantages that come with a good CD-ROM publisher, such as technical support and services and outstanding packaging teams, are important, too. But nobody cares unless your title gets to market. When you're considering a relationship with an online publisher for your online project, the right partner is a publisher that not only has ample traffic in its own right (distribution), but also places from which it can direct that traffic to your site or content area. An online environment usually doesn't have a retail channel; the process of "selling" your multimedia online is a matter of distribution and marketing.

Devising an agreement

When both the multimedia producer and the publisher agree to work together, the next step is to form a development contract. This is a legal document that lays out the terms of what is expected from both parties during and after the production. Through this agreement, the producer provides the publisher with a schedule of *deliverables* — fixed deadlines by which certain materials must be remitted to the publisher for approval. When the project is finished, the deliverables switch to the side of the publisher, who must send regular accountings to the producer of how the project was marketed and sold. The deliverables here also include royalty statements (and checks!) from the publisher.

Note The key points of an agreement should be carefully considered by a lawyer.

The agreement consists of the following key points:

- ✦ Definitions
- ✦ Deliverables
- ✦ Texting and acceptance
- ✦ Intellectual property rights
- ✦ Credits

- Warranties
- Progress payments
- Terms and terminations

I discuss each of these points in the following sections.

Definitions

In plain English, the definitions consist of a detailed description of what both the producer and the publisher agree on as the basic framework of the product and the joint venture. On the producer's side, the definitions in the agreement include an overview of the title, what it is intended to accomplish when it is finished, who will be able to use it, how it will be built, how it will run (hardware issues), and what schedule the project is expected to adhere to. On the publisher's side, the definitions should clearly state all responsibilities — financial, technical, and support — that the publisher is contracting to provide.

Making these definitions as specific as possible (on both sides) is extremely important, particularly as they pertain to deliverable dates and monies. Both the producer and the publisher must understand, however, that schedules and sometimes even product specifications can change from the time the project is initiated to the time of its completion (I discuss this in more detail shortly).

In this part of the agreement, the producer provides whatever support materials the publisher asks for in terms of being able to quantify and describe the workings of the project. That means a script, storyboards, a flowchart of interactivity, a general description of the interface, a list of content that needs to be licensed, a plan for product testing, a schedule of deliverables, and, of course, the budget.

Deliverables

These producer's deadlines (some optimistically call them "goals") are the overriding challenge that the multimedia producers battle every day. Meeting deliverables ensures two important things:

- The production is moving along according to schedule.
- The publisher is confident that your team can fulfill its end of the agreement.

Defining the deliverables and their related due dates is one of the most important parts of a development agreement, and here is where you'll really find out what your relationship with the publisher is like. Unless the specifics of the deliverables are clearly laid out in the agreement, trouble can spring up, even when the deadlines are met. For example, the producers may submit deliverables that are clearly in keeping with the spirit of the contract, while the publishers may accept them and demand that changes be instituted so that the deliverables live up to their expectations. This can wreak havoc on the rest of the production. A change in already-submitted deliverables not only means that "finished" work needs to be changed, but also that the effort to change them takes away time and resources from the rest of the workflow.

Note Not only is specifically defining the nature of the deliverables in the agreement imperative, but defining what constitutes a "reasonable" change in the deliverables, either from the producer or publishers, is imperative as well. On deadline day, the producers might submit something that's almost — but not quite — what the contract calls for. If you're lucky, the publisher will understand and remain patient until the next deliverable date. On the other hand, the publisher might accept the deliverables and ask for revisions that were not specifically agreed to in the contract.

Again, the idea is to get everything down in writing as comprehensively as possible. Whatever latitude either party is granted to make changes in the deliverables must be agreed upon in advance, or the spectre of trouble will always loom in the background.

Testing and acceptance

A development agreement should clearly state a minimum level of technical specifications for all deliverable materials. This area can be difficult to nail down, especially when the project is being developed from source code rather than an authoring tool. To make sure that the deliverables live up to the publisher's expectations, the publisher must be able to view the submitted materials. These materials may not be easy to "play" outside of the authoring environment, especially before the project is completed.

Regardless, the publisher will want to see physical evidence of the project's progress, and know that, upon final delivery, the project lives up to the spirit and letter of the development agreeement. The producer can help this process along by assembling demonstration screens and interactive segments to assure the publisher that it's getting what it paid for. At the end of the production, the final project must live up to at least the minimum technical standards agreed to in the development deal. Any of the inevitable changes that happen during the production, no matter how seemingly insignificant, should be agreed to by the publisher before the producer goes too far off in a direction that might be deemed unacceptable.

Intellectual property rights

The development agreement should clearly state which nonoriginal materials are intended for use within the production. More important, this agreement needs to state who will be paying for any required licensing and who will incur the legal fees for ensuring safe use of these materials. Again, clarity is an important point. Sketching an agreement in which the producer says that the production will include licensable materials is not enough, because unless the exact cost and availability of those materials can be quantified in advance, the budget and schedule can go haywire. In many cases, the publisher will have an easier time licensing outside materials, and some publishers not only have access (and rights) to material of this type, but also a legal team that can be a big help in getting other materials.

Credits

The issue of authorship is almost always a sticky one when you're working with an established publisher as a partner. Under the terms of most development deals, the publisher becomes the author — the owner of the intellectual property — and, in some unfortunate cases, the developer is left out in the cold in terms of getting any return on his or her work outside of money. In this business, you're only as good as your last project, and the more successful credits that you can build for yourself and your company, the better chance you'll have getting financed for your next project. Therefore, ensuring that you and your team receive appropriate production credits somwhere on the title is imperative.

In the case of a CD-ROM, the credits are usually displayed on a screen that the user can access either from the help button ("About The Production" is a popular label) or through a splash screen that comes up as the user is quitting the program. With an online project, the developers of the site are often linked somewhere where the user can click to find out more about who built the title.

Note Many publishers are loathe to credit the developers on a Web site. They want the end user to believe that the publisher is the party that came up with such a good title. In that situation, the online credit is worth fighting for.

The home page of a Web site can include either a text credit or even a link from the credit to the developer's home page. Getting this placement is worth some legal negotiations, because this credit becomes your company's calling card. Some publishers will allow this credit on their site for a fixed amount of time, perhaps 60 to 90 days. If the publisher is adamant about refusing credits to the developers on the site (rare, but it happens), your team needs to make a value judgment. In the multimedia world, a good reputation is worth more than money.

Warranties

A *warranty* is a promise of the intended quality or quantity of the product that is being developed. With a physical product such as a toaster, the warranty is easy to define: if the toaster does not live up to expectations, the customer has a legitimate right to remedy the situation. In the case of something that doesn't exist yet, such as a multimedia production that's being developed, the rules are a bit more elastic, though warranties are still part of the agreement.

Two different kinds of warranties pertain to a multimedia development deal:

- ✦ **Express Warranty.** A literal guarantee that the product will live up to agreed-upon standards and will work properly according to those standards.
- ✦ **Implied Warranty.** A legal clause asserting that certain rights and responsibilities are inherent in the agreement, even if they are not specifically stated. Some typical implied warranties are the warranty of free-and-clear title (no infringement on other copyrighted materials), warranty of merchantability (the product is of sufficient quality for the publisher to sell), and warranty of compatibility, which states that the product will work under existing standards of hardware and software operability.

Note Because so many warranties and representations are implied in a development agreement, the producer would be well advised to include a disclaimer in the actual contract. This disclaimer typically states that the publisher (or other client) allows the developer to disclaim any other warranties that aren't specifically set down in the agreement. This boilerplate legal language might seem like so much filler to the untrained eye, but it serves an important purpose in case of disagreements between parties. Make sure that this disclaimer is in your contract.

Progress payments

The payments due to the producers in a development deal are usually tied to the schedule of deliverables. Typically, the process is initiated by the publisher forwarding the first advance payment upon signing the development agreement. Other payments are tied to milestones in the production schedule as agreed upon by both producer and publisher. The number of milestones and payments is a matter of negotiation between both parties.

The publisher typically offers a good faith payment when the agreement is signed. Witholding a certain percentage of the final amount at the end of the process is also typical, however. Doing so ensures that the project satisifies the publisher's expectations. With a CD-ROM, this isn't usually a problem, because the testing process is usually of fixed duration and sometimes even undertaken by the publisher. If you have an online project, particularly a Web site, the situation may be more involved. Because a Web site is usually an ongoing project, debugging and instituting new features and functionalities take longer than they do with fixed media. Both parties of the partnership must agree on what constitutes a finished project. Reaching an agreement as to when production leaves off and maintenance (that is, the process of upkeeping and improving an online project) begins is also essential.

Terms and terminations

The term of the agreement is usually simple. It runs from the date that the agreement is signed until all aspects of the agreement have been performed to the satisfaction of both parties. But in most development contracts, both parties will have the right to terminate the agreement if certain standards have not been lived up to. This is called a *termination.*

Termination from the publisher's viewpoint is invoked when the producers fail to produce according to the terms of the agreement. This is called a *breach of contract.* Different kinds of breaches exist. A *Material* breach is one in which clear warrants have not been satisfied. The breach could consist of a missed deadline, a product feature that is omitted or doesn't work properly, or any other major change in the project implementation. Generally, the termination clause allows for a set amount of time for the producer to make good on these breaches. Sixty days is typical.

From the producer's standpoint, the typical breach comes when the publisher does not make payments according to the agreement, although the breach can also extend into marketing and distribution. If such occurs, the producer has certain legal avenues through which to correct the breach. But if the project is in mid-development, complications can occur.

Note: For the producer's protection, a clear statement in the termination clause pertaining to who is the owner of the copyrights to the project in the event of a breach of contract is essential. Ideally, the developer retains all rights to the material until the publisher fulfills its end of the contract.

As you can see, even a so-called clear agreement between a producer and a publisher can be fraught with intricate legalisms that must be understood before you undertake the project. I can't say it too often: The help of an experienced attorney is absolutely crucial before signing any contracts. I wrote this section to give you, the producer, a basic familiarity with the contract process. But before you sign anything, spend the money necessary to get the advice of someone who truly understands legal contracts, and better yet, has experience with multimedia or software agreements.

Devising a Technical Plan

After the contract is signed, the preproduction process is technically at an end. Now begins the production process. Before they begin generating any materials, however, the producers have a bit more planning to do. Although most of these plans will have been discussed with the publisher before anyone signs a contract, some publishers are less sophisticated with inherent multimedia technical issues than the developer will be. Therefore, the developer is the one who should assume responsibility for coming up with a technical plan that will address the needs of the production and the needs of the end user. This is where the framework for the multimedia assumes its final shape before pictures are drawn, sounds are recorded, and code is written.

Minimum technical specifications

Clearly, the first major decision is how the end user will experience the project. Through a CD-ROM? Over the Internet? Using a floppy disk? Some combination of all of these? Each delivery system has its own foibles and performance characteristics, which, in many cases, are beyond the producer's ability to predict with much accuracy. You have no real way of knowing how fast your target audience's modems are, or how much hard-drive space the users have available for your title's installation and other support files. But as the producer, you must make an intelligent guess and build a product that will perform well under the conditions that you specify. Those conditions are called the *system requirements,* and they are useful to both the end user and the producer. In the following sections, I discuss some of the issues relating to system requirements.

Screen requirements

Not all computer monitors have the same capability regarding color performance and graphic resolution. Some monitors are capable of displaying 256 colors (8-bit video), whereas others can display thousands or millions of colors. Some monitors have a coarser resolution (dot pitch) than others, which has an effect on text with small point sizes and graphics that rely on high-resolution displays.

The typical home PC, at the time of this writing, includes a 13" to 15" color monitor that is capable (at least) of 640-x-480 resolution in 256 colors. Even though these are not particularly impressive performance characteristics, they're common enough to give the producer a safe target at which to aim the project. In fact, some authoring programs are actually limited to this kind of resolution, with the knowledge that productions developed at this level will enjoy wide user compatibility.

If the development team wants to undertake higher quality images at better video resolution, it should know that not everyone will be able to enjoy the work. This has implications for graphic file formats. Concerning a CD-ROM production, most developers author for 256 colors and include a help screen that alerts users to switch their system to that screen resolution. With an online production such as a Web site, the developers usually end up developing for fewer colors anyway, because using fewer colors results in faster download times.

CD-ROM speed

At the time of this writing, the typical CD-ROM drive built into PCs is called an 8X drive, which means that the rotational rate is four times faster than the original CD-ROM drives that came out in the late 1980s. That data rate was 150 kilobytes per second. An 8X drive can pour data at a rate of 1200 Kilobytes per second. Many other kinds of drives are already in circulation. Just a year ago, 2X drives were the standard, and already many people have 6X drives and even 8X drives.

The advantage of a faster drive is that the data from the actual CD-ROM can be poured into the computer at a much higher rate than with a slower drive. This increased speed is especially critical for video, as you'll see in a later chapter. Authoring multimedia that absolutely depends on state-of-the-art CD-ROM playback doesn't make sense, however, for several reasons. Besides the obvious one that not everyone will be using this technology, the more subtle reason is that the state of the art changes all the time. What you work extra hard for today may be pointless tomorrow. The rule of thumb here is to author for the lowest expected level of user hardware and stick to it. That way, better systems will perform better, but lesser systems will still be able to see your work.

Memory requirements

Every home PC has a set level of random-access memory (RAM) available to the user. In the very early days of home computing, this might have been as low as 4K of RAM! As Microsoft began to popularize its DOS (disk operating system) scheme to the home computing market, the upper level of RAM was set at 640K. As the Apple Macintosh became popular, RAM allocations began to creep upwards to one megabyte and even more, because the system was not tied to DOS's upper limit of 640K. As the price of memory dropped over the years, and as operating systems such as Windows became more popular, the RAM requirements became more elaborate.

Today's typical PC ships with at least 8MB of RAM, and even this is a bare minimum for machines with the Windows 95 or Macintosh System 7.5 operating systems. Depending on how the user has his or her machine configured, the operating system alone can consume 8MB or more. At the time of this writing, PCs equipped with 16MB of RAM are starting to show up on the shelves at CompUSA and other major retailers. Someday we may look at 16MB of RAM with the same smiling disdain we now reserve for those prehistoric DOS machines and their 640K RAM limit.

In the meantime, the producer should be aware of how much RAM a user will need to adequately experience the multimedia title. Obviously, the more RAM the user has, the better the performance will be. But because most people don't have more RAM than they think they need, or more than came with the computer from the factory, the producers should approach RAM requirements in the same way as ROM speed requirements. In other words, author for the lowest hardware requirements that you believe are necessary to run the title in a way that's adequate.

Hard disk requirements

Many multimedia titles can run in a self-contained mode. That is, users can run a CD-ROM from the CD-ROM itself without having to install anything on their PC's hard drive. On a Web site, that means that all the content is viewable without the need for a user download, which, again, necessitates the use of the user's hard drive.

Although these kinds of self-contained titles are common, they're not always typical. Many CD-ROM projects need to be installed on the user's hard drive. The application and other support files needed to run the program are therefore actually on the user's hard drive. These files send commands to the CD-ROM, which then delivers the materials that the hard drive requests. A Web or other online project can also make use of the user's hard drive. Some sites allow for downloadable material that users can save onto their machine — for example, text, pictures, and animations.

Either way, the producer must make a value judgment as to how much hard drive space is necessary to require of the user. Some huge programs require as much as 20MB of hard drive space or more. This is a lot to ask of the user, especially considering that most PCs more than a year old have hard drives with less than 500MB in the first place, and much of this space will have been allocated to programs and files that the user accumulated long before seeing your project.

The rule of thumb here is to make the installation and other files that have to go to the user's hard drive fit into as little space as possible. For an elaborate productivity application, a user will understand having to free up enough hard drive space for the program to work. But for a multimedia title, which presumably doesn't warrant daily use, asking that perhaps 10 percent or more of the user's hard drive be allocated to your title is nervy and undesirable.

Modem speeds

Because online multimedia travels over telephone lines, it is beholden to the limitations of that technology. In other words, online multimedia can be used only as quickly as the medium that translates them — the hardware "pipeline" — can allow. At the time of this writing, the limited bandwidth of twisted-pair phone lines is the single most debilitating quality of online multimedia. This will change quickly with the advent of new technologies such as cable modems, fiber optic lines, and other transmission advancements. In the meantime, you've got to work with what exists.

Typically, that leaves you with a modem speed of 14.4 or 28.8 kilobits per second. Compare this to a 4X CD-ROM drive, which has a data rate of 600 kilobits per second, and you can see how online multimedia is crippled by these low data rates.

Obviously, the producer must compensate for these limitations when designing a technical specification for the project. This translates into making sure that file sizes for pictures and text are kept to minimum. Most online producers keep their pictures to file sizes of 50K or less. These can usually be downloaded in less than 30 seconds, which as of this writing is considered adequate speed for the Web. With the advent of Shockwave and other methods of dynamic media for the Web, these rules are being bent every day, and many Shockwave animations are 100K or even 200K in size. Clearly, the producer needs to make a value judgment here. If you think that the materials you're asking the user to wait for will be worth the wait, go for it. But understand that Web surfers can be an impatient bunch, and if they have to wait too long to see what you've got, they only need to click the mouse to travel somewhere else.

Web browsers

Unlike a CD-ROM, an online multimedia project depends on an external piece of software for the user to experience it. If you're using a commercial online service, the software for America Online, CompuServe, or any of the others serves as the software. On a Web site, the software program that you use to look at content is called a *browser.* The browser is, in large part, responsible for the quality of the experience that the user will have. The capabilities of the browser are of prime importance to the multimedia developer, because not all features work with all browsers and not all browsers are popular enough to ensure a wide target audience.

The two most popular browsers in use on the World Wide Web are Netscape Navigator and Microsoft Explorer. As of this writing, both programs are due out in version 3.0. Although they both offer different strengths and capabilities, they are largely similar in their capability to play the vast majority of Web-authored multimedia. Other browsers, such as Mosaic, Global Network Navigator, and the proprietary browsers found in services such as America Online are generally not as full-featured as the two major browsers from Netscape and Microsoft.

Note

When a producer is developing for the Web or any online medium, picking a target browser or browsers and constantly testing the developing product to make sure that it plays well under that software are essential activities. No one can predict which new features will be implemented in these browsers at any given time. Tests of "beta" versions of Navigator and Explorer are in constant circulation on the Web, but developing for standards that have not yet gained popular acceptance can be dangerous, resulting in features that don't work from one browser to another.

When the plan is in place, the target market established, the contracts signed, and the technical specifications decided, the preproduction process is at an end. Now is the time to start actually designing the multimedia project, after which it will be produced, tested, and marketed. Even though you've already done lots of work, you are still at the beginning of the production. You've already seen how to bring a multimedia project to conception. The next step is to start building it.

CHAPTER 3

Interface Design

✦ The interface design is the most important aspect of the production that can rightfully be regarded as completely under the production team's control.

✦ Effective interface design is often a predictive process; design goals are developed in relation to what the producers feel the user wants or needs.

✦ The art of designing an interface is a composite of technical, artistic, and psychological skills — both sides of the brain are required.

✦ A good interface is easy and enjoyable to use, which means the design must accommodate the limitations of the playback hardware.

In his intriguing book *The Society of Mind,* digital-age patriarch Marvin Minsky puts forth the idea that the mind, whether human or artificial intelligence, is made up of a connected string of otherwise simple agents. When they are organized into a whole, these agents are capable of the fathomless complexities that we know as thoughts and feelings, which translate into human experience.

Multimedia in all its many aspects — conception, financing, design, production, and the rest — is a medium that clearly follows this theory. In the realities of putting out a title, a variety of otherwise unconnected thoughts and acts are connected and manipulated to make the project happen. Keeping these agents (which in reality aren't so simple — humans never are) working toward a unified goal is one of the key challenges of the production process. Unless everything moves in sync during production and post production, the title simply doesn't get out. But because the title obviously must get out (otherwise, why waste the time working on it?), an even more important example of Minsky's theory can be applied to multimedia, and that's the cardinal point of relationship between multimedia and the user: the user interface.

Much of the challenge of creating a good interface for multimedia is weaving some very different agents (some of them not so simple) into a cohesive experience. This is true on both a physical and conceptual level. In the physical sense, numerous talents, skills, and sensibilities are combined to form the actual content that the user will see. Ideally, the user interface reflects the sum of these parts, rather than the parts themselves. If the title is meant to showcase or convey many different ideas, the user interface becomes the central point of access and interaction to all of them. If the multimedia title is meant to convey or showcase only one idea, the interface must place all elements of the production in the service of that one goal.

The Interface Is the Window

Successful interface design, from Minsky's holistic point of view, also relies on much more subtle agents than mere pictures or sounds. The real variables are the level of expectation that both the user and the multimedia itself (that is, the computer) bring to the table. These expectations inform every aspect of the communication between the user and the machine, to which I refer as a combination of software and hardware. Of course, machines such as personal computers can have only so many of these preconceptions in their limited memory. They can be painfully simple and unforgiving; minimum hardware requirements for a multimedia title are a good example of a limited, machine-oriented "expectation."

Great expectations

One obvious preconception that the machine might bring to the dialogue with the user is a fixed determination of how much time a human user will realistically wait for a computer action to occur, such as the time limits imposed on the machine during a PC chess match. Another example of machine preconception is the breadth of possible branches that a human user would take through a multimedia title, or the integration of separate ideas or actions embedded in software "choices" for the user. Because we design computers to work with humans rather than with other machines, we often prefer focused, interactive possibilities to unlimited ones.

Much more important to the human-to-machine dialogue is the level of expectation that the user brings to the table and good multimedia design. Good multimedia design prioritizes the user's obvious expectations in its choice of content. A user who buys a disc on the Italian Renaissance expects to see examples of the art and music (photos and audio clips) at the very least. But interface design is much more than catering to this superficial standard.

User preconceptions

Design is also a matter of taking educated guesses at more primal cultural and cognitive user preconceptions. For example, when a person sees a red button on the screen, what does the color red signify? Does it mean "pay attention to me"? Does it mean "stop"?

A user seeing an on-screen arrow pointing to the right will assume (perhaps wrongly) that the button navigates onward; that is, to the next page, next idea, and so on. Conversely, an arrow pointing to the left usually signifies a backward movement, to the previous page, for example. Because we read from left to right (in Western languages, anyway) this assumption is natural; our eyes move rightward to take in more information. But what meaning does an arrow have when it points up or down? Does it say the same thing to most users? Does the on-screen content make the meaning evident, or does it need to be amplified by a label or even a help button?

The ability to answer the many other questions that arise from similar considerations is the domain of the interface designer, the perceptual science officer of the multimedia team. From the artistic, technical, and sometimes even commercial standpoints, the interface design is probably the most crucial decision of the entire project.

What Is the Ideal Interface?

The ideal interface is many different things to many different producers and productions. In other words, the *ideal* interface doesn't exist. For the purposes of the target audience, however, you must make the best choice possible, given the important role it plays as the visual/cognitive doors to and through the multimedia creation. The user interface is the place where the content makes its initial and continuing impression upon the people who are interacting with it. The user interface comprises the look and feel of the entire production, and further, the look and feel of the talents that have produced it. It's so important that it can easily mean the difference between a fun game and a tedious one, a useful reference work or a shelf potato. A project with great content but an unattractive or clumsy interface is still a failure. On the other hand, a compelling interface can make mediocre content seem much more enjoyable than it really is.

The interface takes up the lion's share of the user's multimedia experience. How will you organize this experience? Will its organization be logical, such that the interactivity is laid out in clearly understandable, cause-and-effect terms? Or will it be more freeform, encouraging the user to explore? Will the interface be conspicuous, meant to be part of the experience? Or will it be so transparent that the user concentrates solely on the content? You'll see examples of such interface-design issues in this chapter.

These decisions are the kernel from which the rest of the production grows, and they are decided in advance of everything. Because multimedia is, in essence, computer programming, the process of interface design doesn't lend itself well to improvisation. Unlike any of the single elements that go into it — video, text, audio, and graphics, an assembled multimedia production cannot be easily altered in "post" the way you can re-edit a video or remix some music. The interface, no matter what it's supposed to do or feel like, is the road map for the producer as well as for the user. But with so many different possibilities, how do you pick one? Obviously, you must base your answer to that question on the specific goals and challenges of each project, resolving them to give the end users the experience that you originally intended for them.

Cause & Effect = Challenge & Solution

Because multimedia is always created for an audience of some kind, that audience's expectations are the most important factors to consider in designing a user interface. This level of the planning process is one-half market awareness and one-half creative imagination. For better or worse, the realities of the market are usually a big factor. This is true not only for the actual production phase (what does the budget allow?) but for the product's afterlife as well (how easily and affectionately will the audience relate to what you're trying to get across?). Throughout any multimedia title's creation, the two halves of this equation — market awareness and creative imagination — coexist in a constantly shifting, symbiotic relationship of cause and effect.

It's instructive to think of the tension between those two halves as challenge and solution, two opposite poles of any multimedia project, that in the end will somehow intersect. Throughout the entire project, and particularly during the process of designing the interface, both the challenges and the solutions branch and subdivide themselves into smaller challenges and solutions. This process is as basic as the laws of physics, even though here they extend to creative and economic decisions as well: every action results in an equal and opposite reaction. These reactions are expressed as the results of the actions (decisions) that are either conceived by the multimedia team or levied upon it as a limitation (such as budget or technology). It sounds complicated, but in reality, it's pretty simple. When you make a creative decision, you dictate certain assumptions of technology, project capitalization (human and monetary resource), and market reaction. These in turn usually subdivide into a crop of smaller issues with accompanying decisions to be made.

I've called the causes challenges and the effects solutions even though, by definition, the words seem self-contradictory. After all, a cause (action) really seems closer to a solution than an effect. In many cases throughout the production, it will be. But these words have been chosen purposefully, to better reflect the "mirror-image" relationship of the concepts. The importance of each subdivision of cause and effect rises and falls with each successful solution to a challenge. Like a game of chess, each move that you make in a multimedia production engenders at least one countermove that you must eventually deal with successfully. When you have met all the challenges and overcome all the obstacles, you've reached the goal. Checkmate. (Figure 3-1 provides an overview of this process.)

What Does Your Audience Want?

The challenge/solution hierarchy is shaped like an inverted pyramid, with the most important ideas at the top of the list, and the details coming in ever-increasing numbers as you move further down the project. Challenge number one always lies in the most basic idea behind the creation of a multimedia title: successfully predicting what your audience will appreciate. Who will be using this product, if I may call it that for the moment? Who, exactly, is the typical user? Is there one? And if you can target one, how can you tailor a project so that as many users as possible will like it?

Answering this basic question gives the project its starting point, at least on a technical level. In fact, the answer to this initial question is usually the reason that multimedia titles are conceived in the first place; after all, most multimedia is made for a consumer society. To be sure, some multimedia projects are more dedicated to preserving a specific individual or group vision, the market be damned. But because multimedia creation is still a relatively expensive proposition (compared to a paper and pencil, anyway), projects such as these are the exception.

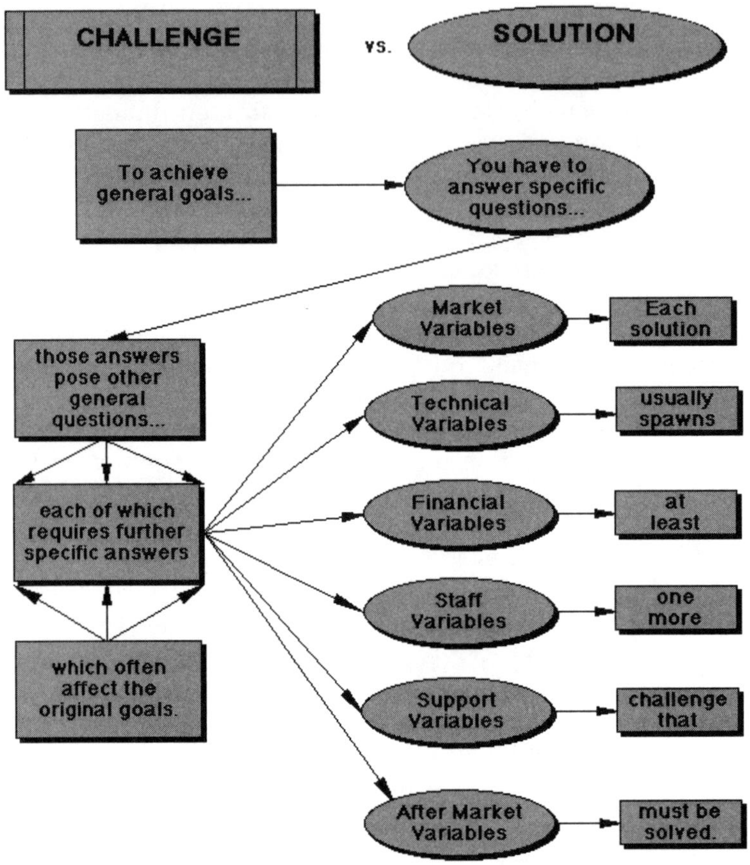

Figure 3-1: Creative challenges require creative solutions. The cause and effect relationship between the two is consistent throughout the life of the project.

Because multimedia titles are conceived for an audience, the mechanisms by which that multimedia will reach the audience become the foremost challenge requiring a solution. Aside from hardware considerations (though they are of course important), you must also assess the level of experience, intelligence, and computer sophistication that your audience brings to the table. A project conceived for a mass audience must live with very different limitations than a project for jaded teenaged gamers.

This decision is obviously crucial to the design aspect, but you should keep in mind that consumer expectations also extend to content. And the content is always the second great influence on the design. For example, if the target audience is already familiar with the content, such as a collector looking at a

CD-ROM about postage stamps, you're safe to assume a certain level of expectation; for example, you should probably include pictures of postage stamps. That implicit expectation must influence your decisions concerning interface design. When the multimedia is about lots of rectangular pictures — such as postage stamps — the interface design must successfully absorb that visual "given" into its presentation.

Conversely, if the target audience is coming to the multimedia title without clear preconceptions as to the content's presentation, the interface designer would seem to be working with fewer limitations. On a base level, that's true. In reality, however, this more open challenge (how to shape a user experience when no perceptual road map is implied) demands another solution in itself. In this example, the interface designer isn't catering to an expectation; rather, the expectation is being formed as the user goes through the multimedia experience.

Still, there begs the question of the most immediate first challenge — who is the target audience? A successful answer to this first challenge solves important problems right off the bat. Obviously, the answer has immediate implications for the rest of the production — marketing, design, and programming, just to name a few. More important, however, this first answer also clearly demonstrates the interactive give-and-take between challenges and solutions. By visualizing the target audience, you've already made certain decisions that will have to be serviced eventually with creative solutions. Those new solutions will themselves invariably give birth to new challenges. In multimedia, as in nature, every action causes a reaction, except that, unlike the scientific dictum, the reaction may not be equal and opposite. It could either be minor or utterly chaotic.

I've created a sample project for you to follow to see some of the bumps and grinds between challenge and solution. I've picked an easy one. The first project is a CD-ROM on cooking. In a later chapter, you'll look into "porting" your cooking title over to the World Wide Web.

A CD-ROM Interface

Although cooking certainly isn't a topic that is easily pigeonholed, for the purposes of your CD-ROM, that's a good thing. You're looking for something wide ranging so that you can pick and choose between several interface structures and their attendant technical challenges. In a multimedia production whose subject material is as general as this, the producer can pursue innumerable directions. One option is to offer a shallow overview of a broad topic; another is a focused look at one or more aspects of the topic. The interface designer has to follow suit, and the look and feel of the interface must accurately reflect the direction that the producer has chosen. Because I've chosen something so general (imagine all the CD-ROMs that you could do on cooking), I make decisions throughout the rest of this chapter that reflect my desire to illustrate concepts to you, the reader, rather than make focused and perhaps more "correct" decisions that should in reality be based on market research and many other factors that would apply to the imagined audience.

Your first big, if arbitrary, decision is that you want to put out a slick product. So, your initial plans for your cooking title, which I call "Good Eating" for neutrality's sake, are for something that includes narration, photographs, how-to videos, and even a way for the users to create and save their own recipe books. Because of this elemental decision, you already have certain assumptions in place concerning the conceptualization, development, and marketability of your product. This is the first example of the challenge and solution symbiosis.

Take a look at the multileveled "ripple" effect that your initial decision engenders. You're going with a broad topic, so you stand a good chance of your product finding favor with a large general audience. Obviously, though, not every computer being used by the general public will be able to adequately reproduce your fancy audio and video clips, which you've made part of the equation by agreeing on a technically sophisticated product.

You need to find a compromise here, a gray zone between what the audience wants and what your multimedia team can deliver. With intelligent compromise on your side, you can probably have the best of both worlds — an advanced CD-ROM that plays well on many, if not most, computers.

Where in the middle to meet?

The process of deciding and creating the interface for your cool cooking disc will organically grow from the same two directions that have already been outlined: challenge and solution. Your first challenge has already been decided for you: you want this thing to look and sound dynamic, rather than be a boring, static presentation of recipes and cooking information. Such halfhearted titles are often referred to as "shovelware," having been quickly shoveled to market with little concern for look, feel, and usability. Such uncaring work not only insults the user but reflects badly on the company that markets it, virtually guaranteeing a "once burned, twice shy" attitude by any potential customer who has used the shovelware. With those types of titles, niceties such as good interface design play only a small part in the product considerations, if they play any part at all.

You don't want to do that. Because you have a rich multimedia feel in mind for your CD-ROM, you can put that down as your first challenge: to develop a technically sophisticated product. As you can see from Figure 3-2, that single challenge has veered you toward a simple set of solutions. But those solutions have, in turn, spawned several more challenges. All of these challenges need their own solutions if the project is to be developed and completed with the original goal in mind. Predicting the fallout from each decision and being prepared to cope with it is the essence of the multimedia producer's craft.

Sometimes, the sheer number of challenges spawned by the opening solution are enough to make the producer go back to the drawing board and reconsider the opening solution. In this case, you've seen that the challenge of making your CD-ROM as technically sophisticated as possible has already brought with it some potential headaches, as follows:

- ✦ Does the budget allow hiring a professional video company to provide you with your clips?
- ✦ Can you afford to license those clips?
- ✦ Do you know any professional narrators, or can you find one or afford one?

You've decided that you want to let the user save information onto the hard drive. More questions:

- ✦ Do the authoring tools that you're using allow for that option?
- ✦ Does your programming team know how to do it?
- ✦ Are you inviting financial, technical, and timetable problems by insisting on this feature?

Note One hour of inexpensive constructive thought is worth many hours of expensive production time.

Even at this early point in the preproduction process, the time has already come to take stock of your options. As your diagrams show, every decision in the production chain, especially when you're talking about interface design, comes saddled with consequences. The question now, in your CD-ROM on cooking, is whether plowing ahead with the original plan makes sense, or should you begin to make the first of the many compromises that any multimedia production entails.

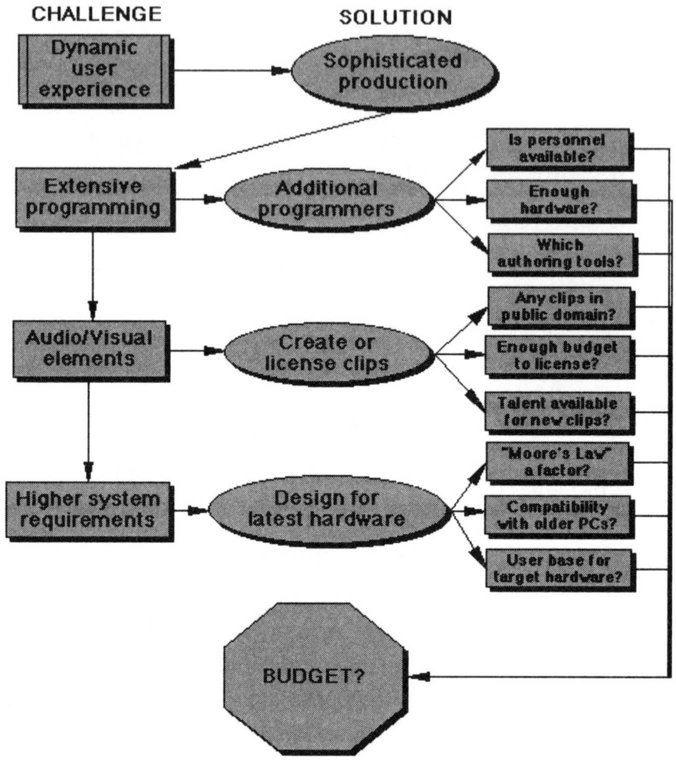

Figure 3-2: A general decision always leads to a series of macro- and micro-decisions, some of which will be based on factors out of the producer's control.

You've already established your primary desire, which is to have a full-featured CD-ROM with all the bells and whistles. You've seen the basic problems that follow from that decision, and now you're considering your options. What's the most sensible direction to follow? Go with the original instinct, or back down now in favor of pragmatism?

Taking Stock of Resources

As with every human enterprise, multimedia production presents a chasm between what you want to do and what you're capable of doing. The original visualization of the ideal, finished multimedia title is often very different from what actually turns into computer code and gets marketed. Although most of the give-and-take compromises will be decided at varying points of the production, the major ones that you're talking about now — what's desirable versus what's possible — must be decided in the beginning, during preproduction.

In this case, because you're at that elemental stage of planning, when major decisions are made more easily than they are later, you'll base your decision on sensible, "first-consideration" criteria. In a way, this opening conceptualization process is the pencil sketch for the rest of the multimedia production. It's here that decisions can be changed quickly, because the project hasn't really materialized yet. It's obviously much easier — and most desirable — to get the big philosophical questions out of the way before human and monetary resources have actually been expended. Still, in addition to the instincts of the producer and creative team, outside factors must guide the project's conceptual pillars.

The first one to consider is one of the most elemental questions that the producer and the designer have to answer comfortably before they embark on a plan to actualize their multimedia concept. That is, what are the project's available resources?

I must state here, with less than a grain of salt, that in the world of multimedia production, money can solve most problems, and time can solve many more. If the project can, without strain, add additional funds to the budget when needed, many otherwise pressing problems simply go away, to become issues of time rather than possibility. And if time isn't an issue — that is, the title isn't focused on temporal subject material, or you don't have a real need to make marketing deadlines such as holiday retail orders — the producer has the extreme luxury of honing the project until everyone is convinced that it's as perfect as possible. But in real life, virtually no project has unlimited funds, and even a production with a generous opening budget must somehow make that funding last across that entire process, all the way through marketing, advertising, and ongoing customer support, perhaps years after the product's release.

With that in mind, accepting what your team really has at its disposal will be based on a more general heading than budget or personnel. I call this available resources, which is not the same as available money. Money helps, but it can't always buy what you need to get the job done. Other vital resources must be given equal weight, including available tools, production talent, programming skill, licenses, and time. None of them comes cheaply, and in the case of time, money can't buy it.

Goals ÷ resources = production plan

You should base your decision of how to allocate resources of both time and money to the multimedia design largely on controllable criteria, which is an advantage that, unfortunately, rarely exists throughout the rest of the production and post-production process, after the design decisions have already been reached. When a team is already at work on a project, no matter how soon into the production, shifting content or execution ideas in any significant way is a real effort. Invariably, major changes in direction after the production has begun weakens the productivity and morale of other persons working on the project. Not only have you lost time, but you'll lose more time as the team regroups and (you hope) gets back up to speed. In other words, the more ideas that you can "lock in" at this early stage, the smoother everything else will run for the rest of the production. Early decisiveness is an advantage that keeps on paying.

Left-brain issues

As I said earlier, the interface designer brings a dual perspective (at least) to the multimedia project. The realities of the commercial marketplace demand an acute awareness of the resources I've been discussing. But you should never think of these resources as merely a matter of allowable budget or the lack of it. Some of the situations that will be equally formidable in terms of neat solutions to the designer's challenges come from external, and therefore uncontrollable, situations.

For example, certain technological realities in the marketplace must be acknowledged for good design decisions to be made. Audio is an obvious one. How can you best present your lovingly recorded multimedia music tracks when most target computers can play only constricted 8-bit sound from cheesy multimedia speakers? Does it make sense to try? If the music is so important, would it make more sense to do an "Enhanced CD" rather than a CD-ROM, so that it plays through the user's stereo rather than PC audio system? How important is the music to the title's success? Questions such as these inform basic design decisions on how to bring audio into the user's experience.

When composing for the Web, the interface designer has even more left-brain issues to deal with. Many of the desired enhancements that jazz up a site, such as animation, are dependent not only on the users' computers but on the speed of their modems, their choice of browser, and their access to the associated plug-in features that allow for things such as real-time multimedia on the Web. It's delusional to expect that all the target users will have the correct combination of hardware and software for the ideal design, especially when new technology arrives weekly. I get into these issues further in the chapter on the Web.

Technical issues, both present and future, are far from the only noncreative issues of which the creative interface designer must be aware. Legal issues, for example, are almost always more complicated than they appear, even after agreements are contracted and signed. In the current unstable climate of intellectual property and copyright protections, with new media appearing every year, legal issues seem to exist in a sort of digital Bermuda Triangle.

Even the best legal specialists are still adapting to these evolving laws. Although it's a stretch to think that an interface designer must be fluent with these issues, they are yet another left brain tax. For example, say that you decided to incorporate some video commentary from a world-renowned cooking expert for your culinary CD-ROM. Agreements were reached, contracts were signed, video was shot and edited. One month later, with your CD-ROM still in production, the cooking expert signs a deal with a major publisher, who now holds exclusive worldwide rights to the expert's public appearances, live or recorded. Does this affect your own CD-ROM in any way? If you think the answer is a flat-out no, maybe you had better review the previous chapter.

Although keeping track of all these (and many more) variables is technically the job of the producer, not the interface designer, the effect that these variables can have, now or later, should inform the choice of the interface design. It's not desirable to force alterations in the design choices after they've begun to be implemented. Even so, the design should be strong enough in its vision to survive the invariable changes and revisions that will accompany it throughout the production process. A good design will still be a good design, even within the limitations of available resources.

Right-brain issues

By now, it should be understood that material limitations are always going to be with us in the multimedia process. But even though these are real considerations, they certainly don't receive the main emphasis during user interface design. This interface is a realm in which imagination is worth more than money, and the slickest production values can be pulled off by cleverness rather than budget. The place to start looking at your production is one where dollars can't touch you — the creative realm.

The look and feel of the design

The style of your multimedia title — or (to use a phrase popularized during Apple's prolonged plagiarism suit against Microsoft) the "look and feel" of the title — is of paramount importance to both the designer and the user.

Think of the multimedia title as a theatrical play. The audience isn't interested in the trouble the set designer went through, or how many rehearsals it took to get the blocking down just right. The audience sees only the finished play — and the success of the play is based on how much the audience enjoyed what it got to see. In multimedia, the interface is what the audience gets to see.

Because that audience interacts so directly with the art and design of the interface, making good decisions up front sets the tone for the rest of the multimedia title. Along with the producer, those decisions are made by the interface designer, a unique new media figure that, in the best cases, combines the aesthetic sense of a visual artist, the showmanship of a filmmaker, the poise of a tour guide, and the precision of a computer programmer.

Consistency

Working closely with the client and/or executive producer, the designer seeks to create an attractive, functional, and, most important, a unified multimedia experience for the user. The designer takes the expectations, preconceptions, and limitations handed to him or her from the producer and the outside world, and makes sense of them. The designer is the one who translates all the elements of the production — the content as well as the style — into a cohesive tool on which the user can count for consistency throughout the duration of the multimedia experience.

Many reasons exist to insist upon this consistency as a guiding force throughout the interface, and a good interface designer will be mindful of all of them. Obviously, a unified look is desirable. Even if the multimedia is meant to showcase a number of different looks, by way of branches to different subjects or sections, the main user interface has to be the consistently recognizable doorway to all of them. No matter what the user views, he or she must navigate all of the title's interactivity from the interface, which, in one form or another, is present throughout the entire experience. Any glitches in consistency will confuse the user and instantly dent the overall functionality of the title.

Form follows function

Even though a world of possibility exists for producing innovative visuals for the interface, a unified feel is important for the same reasons that a magazine layout, or the functionality of a PC application, is important. When interacting with this material, the user must be able to make intelligent choices in order to enjoy the experience or find it useful. When a user discovers that a pull-down menu, for example, is the navigational tool to make a certain choice, it's confusing and frustrating to apply that same discovery elsewhere in the title, only to find that it no longer applies in the new section. The established cognitive paradigms are the models to follow.

These paradigms include reading, which goes from top to bottom and left to right (in English, anyway); the Windows or Macintosh desktop, whose menu bars pull down with expected results; or even the telephone, which has a dial tone followed by keystrokes, a connection, and a conversation. This is not to say that the interface designer can't do wild and creative things from within these paradigms. But in interface design, form should always follow function. And it's worth keeping in mind that when the designer establishes a function for the user, the user expects that function to be consistent throughout the multimedia experience.

Fundamentals of Screen Design

Designing an interface is like working with a blank canvas. But every artist is prepared with a palette of colors, brushes, and ideas before starting to work. Multimedia is no exception. The process of interface design begins with the creation of a master list of all the visual and aural elements that will be used throughout the title. In many cases, these elements must be created from scratch by artists and technicians. For now, paper and pencil will do, or better yet, some assistive software, which I discuss shortly.

Getting organized

It's time to take a first shot at designing a front end for your cooking CD-ROM. You'll start by assembling the list of available elements, both on hand and to be created. Your goal now is to organize these elements into a series of connections and branches that will emulate the interactive experience that the user will have after these elements are assembled.

For this purpose, some kind of project management software can be a real help. Numerous packages are available, ranging from the creation of simple flowcharts to elaborate charts that can track the entire production process in terms of time, responsibility, and money. Some of the better-known packages include *Visio* and *Inspiration,* both of which feature enough versatility to be useful to the art directors, programmers, and marketing team, as well as the interface designer.

Back to your cooking CD-ROM. You can use a simple flowchart, created with even simpler charting software, to lay out your basic navigation. Lots of designers like to work with even bigger "screens," using magic markers on wall charts or whiteboards. Whichever tools you use, allow yourself lots patience. Sometimes, a navigational philosophy that seems simple can actually be quite complicated by the time you implement it.

Even though you've previously decided that your CD-ROM will be technically sophisticated, that doesn't mean that using the CD-ROM should be a complicated experience. A simple, logical design can be ornamented with snazzy features, and because you plan to have lots of different branches and topics on your cooking title, you want the navigation — the user's interactive experience — to be straightforward.

The splash screen

The first thing the user sees with any fixed multimedia title, after any necessary installation, of course, is called the *splash screen* (Figure 3-3). This image is analogous to the cover of a book — it's a visual come-on to get the user excited about the experience that he or she is about to have inside. The splash screen is also the starting point for the rest of the title, and must either contain the main menu or offer a simple gateway to it.

In online terms, the splash screen may also be referred to as the home page, although a Web site's home page often includes some or all of the main menu. The technical parameters are very different for fixed media, such as a CD-ROM, than they are for media delivered in real time, such as a Web site. For example, with a CD-ROM, the graphic possibilities are more plentiful because you don't need to wait for graphics to slowly download over a telephone line, as you do with a Web site. Also, users often pay for online multimedia by the hour, and longer download times mean frustration and a potential user turn-off.

Figures 3-4 and 3-5 provide alternative examples of how a splash screen can accomplish its two primary goals: to convey a feel for what the rest of the production will be like, and to offer the user a navigational front door. In some cases, the splash screen is used to give a bit of information about the company that designed the multimedia title, whereas in others, the splash screen is a throwaway graphic — an intermediary and temporary step that happens between the time the user starts the multimedia program and actually gets to use it.

Figure 3-3: A splash screen doesn't have to be complicated or even precise. It can be a welcome mat to the user's experience.

Figure 3-4: A simple design.

Figure 3-5: An even simpler alternative.

The main menu

If the splash screen is the welcome mat of the multimedia title, the main menu is the lobby. Here, the user chooses where to take the interactivity, both now and later in the disc. I can't overstate the importance of designing and executing a functional and attractive main menu: this is the one place to which the user will return repeatedly. I'll show you how to play around with a few designs for "Good Eating" to give you some possibilities for approaching your main menu.

In the first example (see Figure 3-6), you've given the user a completely straightforward way of navigating the CD-ROM. Everything the user needs to get to is right here: the different categories, an option for getting user help, and, of course, the one addition that every main menu needs but no producer really wants to implement — the exit option. A single click on any of these options should take the user directly to the chosen section (as shown in Figure 3-7). Any extraneous steps between this mouse click and the desired information would be most unwelcome — at least on a CD-ROM. For a Web site, that rule is a lot more flexible, but you'll get to that in the chapter on marketing.

To be sure, you'll find titles that don't allow a simple one-click exit out of the program. When the user clicks on the exit, a dialog box will come up, asking whether the user is sure that he or she wants to leave. The reasons for this are simple: you give users the choice of changing their mind and re-entering the title. Why would you want to do this? First, nobody likes to see the audience leave the theater. But you could argue for an altruistic motive here, too. If the exit button is placed too close to other navigational options, users might exit by mistake. Giving them the option to change their minds is a useful feature.

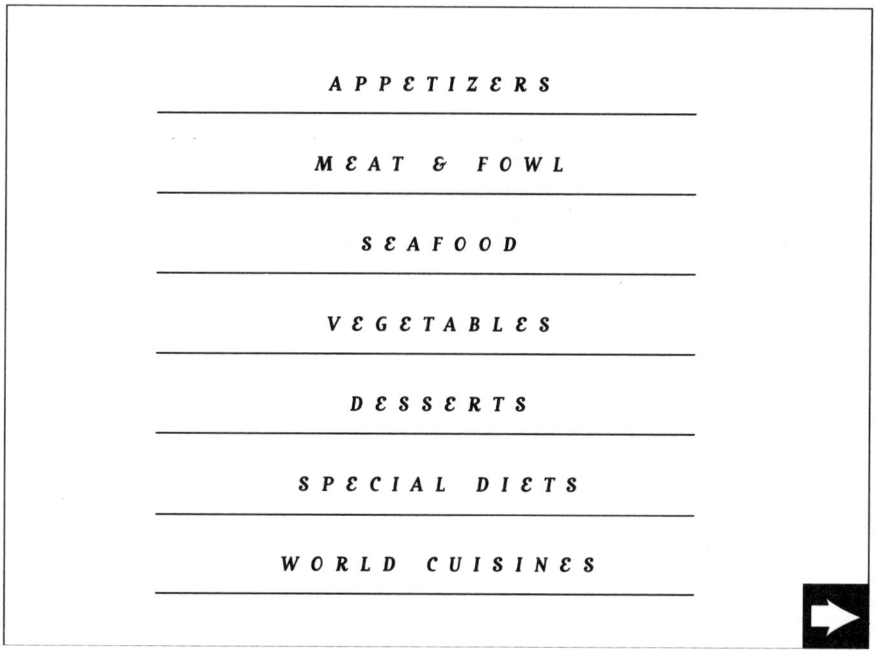

Figure 3-6: Unlike the splash screen, the main menu should be intuitive and allow the user instant access to important features of the production.

Your First Critique

Even though nothing is wrong per se with your first example, it isn't particularly attractive. You've used text as an informative and logical way for the user to find his or her way around. Text is informative, but too much text is boring, especially if too many options are present, as you have here. Further, because you have to stick fast to your rule about a uniform design through the interface, each time the user goes another level deep into the program, there will be more text, perhaps even more densely arranged than it is in the main menu (see Figure 3-7). A dependence on text in the main menu may very well drive you down a cul-de-sac that will be difficult to escape later in the presentation, as you'll see in just a little while.

Again, for now, I must stress that this example is based on a CD-ROM model. Text has a completely different and much more viable function in the online environment. Because most of the information online must be downloaded over the telephone line at the time of request, the smaller the requested file, the less time the download takes. Text takes up very little space in comparison to graphics, especially color graphics. In the online world, it's an issue. But for now, we're talking CD-ROM, so I'll move on to pictures and get back to your main menu sketches.

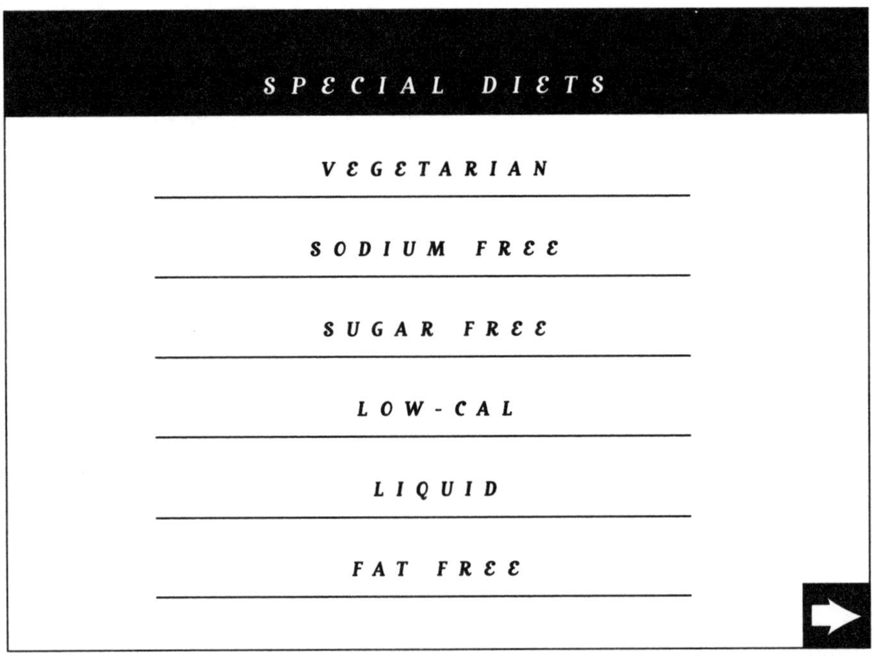

Figure 3-7: This submenu has followed the same logic as the main menu. As you can see, the main menu heading has been highlighted so users know where they are.

As you can see in Figure 3-8, your main menu approach has changed completely, substituting graphics for the text. As you can see, the main menu is much more attractive and has a real multimedia feel, in comparison to the text-based version. But is it functional? What do these pictures really tell you about your navigational options? Will they get the same point across to every different user? And, as before with the text example, do you lead yourself down a dead end when you use a purely pictorial approach for your secondary menus?

The process of creating the main menu that you really want, that will accomplish everything necessary, ultimately brings you back to the challenge/solution map. You've seen that text works, but it's ugly, and that graphics work, but they're too vague. What's the answer? How about a combination of the two? The most widespread method of accomplishing this is via the icon — a small, pictorial representation that owes more to mnemonics than to literal interpretation. In the real world, icons are used all the time to quickly and wordlessly represent ideas to people.

Figure 3-8: Changing the main menu to a graphical (rather than text-based) interface gives the production a more entertaining feel.

You can start by laying out your CD-ROM's main menu with icons (Figure 3-9). As you can see, the graphics give your screen a much more attractive look, but including a text label has eliminated the graphical ambiguity. Besides accomplishing your primary goal of making the layout functional yet attractive, you've now created another advantage for your production that will help you down the line.

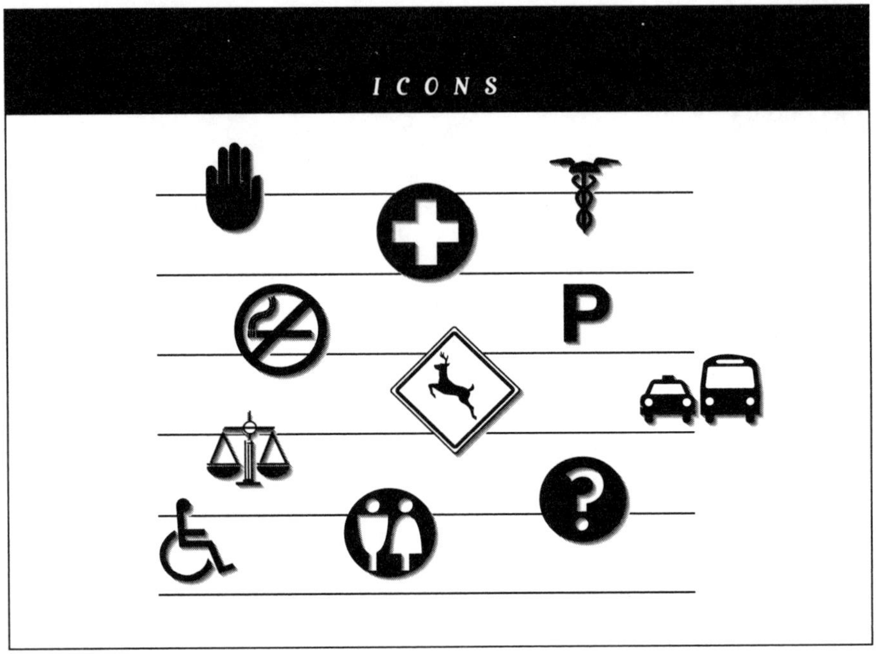

Figure 3-9: Icons are visual shorthand for important ideas that can be expressed without language.

Your icons will be repeated throughout the production (as in Figures 3-10 and 3-11) always signifying the same things to the user in a sort of cognitive shorthand. This repetition conforms to the mandate for consistency in the interface design, even if it means teaching the user a new concept to begin with. The first time the user sees icons, their meaning might be vague or misunderstood, unless, of course, they're labeled with text. After all, not everyone interprets pictures in the same way. But after the user has interacted through these icons, the icon's meaning is set for the rest of the program. In other words, giving users something new to learn is okay, as long as the knowledge is useful later in the title.

Secondary Menus, Branching, and Beyond

I've already described the main menu as the lobby for the multimedia production, so it would be fair the describe the secondary, tertiary, and deeper menus as the actual guest rooms. Each of these rooms should always have at least two doors — one to get back to the previous room (screen) and another to return to the main menu, in case users want to go to other rooms that aren't directly connected to the room they're in now.

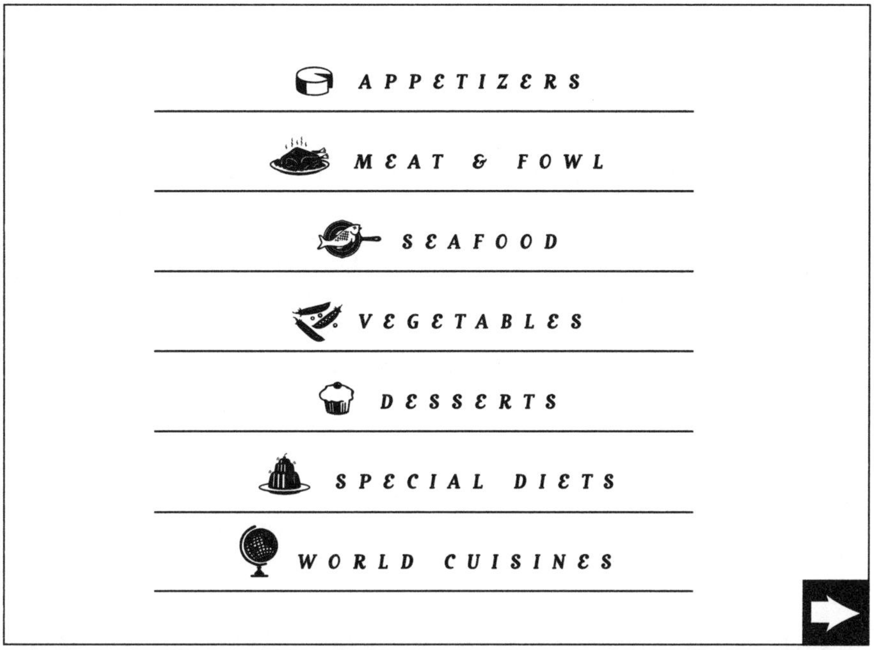

Figure 3-10: A combination of text and icons is not only clearly understandable, but defines the icons well enough to use them later in the production without text labels.

Figure 3-11: Note the consistent use of text and icons, linking the submenu visually to the main menu.

Figures 3-12 through 3-14 show how the branches for "Good Eating" develop from main menu through secondary and tertiary environments. Here you'll confront the next challenge, which is to decide how you want to interconnect the various menus.

Branching, which is the name for the navigational connections between content points, is the essence of the interactive experience. When a user makes an on-screen choice that takes the user from one place in the multimedia to another, this connection is called a *branch*. Branching is the foremost challenge for the interface designer, because here is where the road map for the user is laid out in rigid computer code. This is not to say that branching need be rigid; you'll find CD-ROM titles whose interactive branching is completely open, meaning that the user can jump at will from any one place in the title to any other place. Naturally, other titles exist whose branching is more constricted, because the producers want the user to have a more controlled experience. Neither method, nor all the variations in between, is the "correct" one. It's all a matter of context — choosing the appropriate interactivity for each individual title.

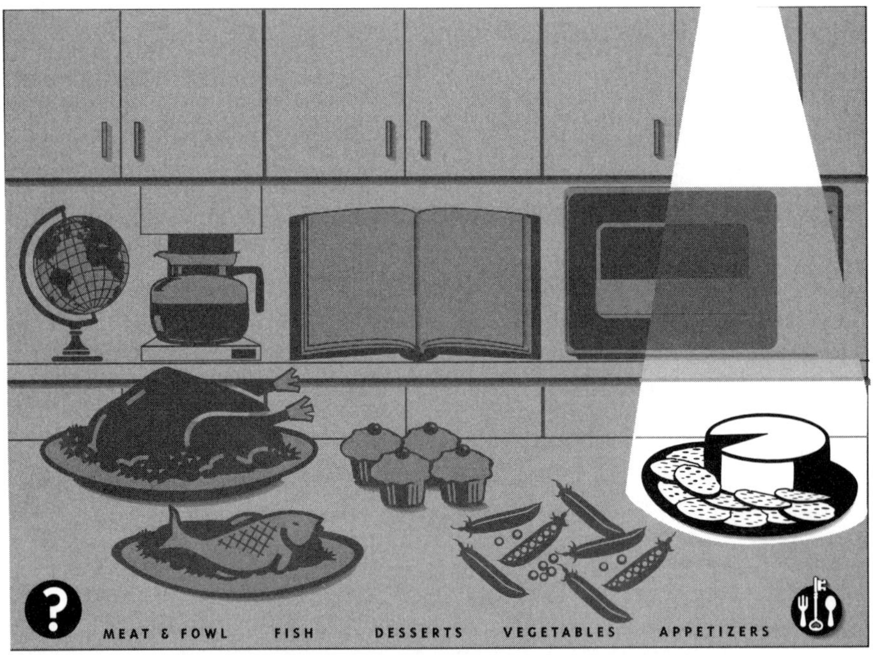

Figure 3-12: In an interface designed with unidirectional branching, each user move is followed by logical, linear steps to the next level of the production.

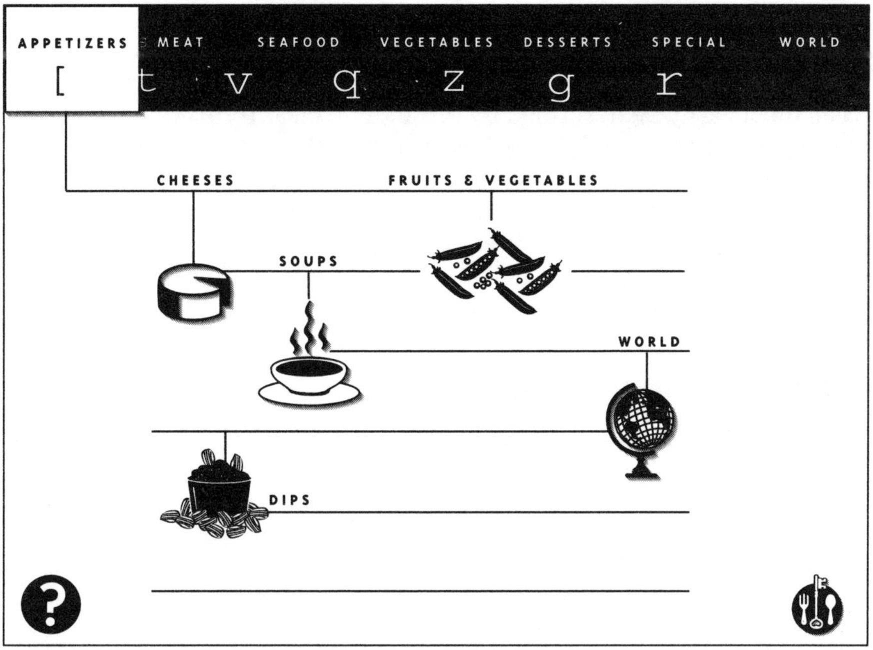

Figure 3-13: Note the continuity of the icons and text from the main menu.

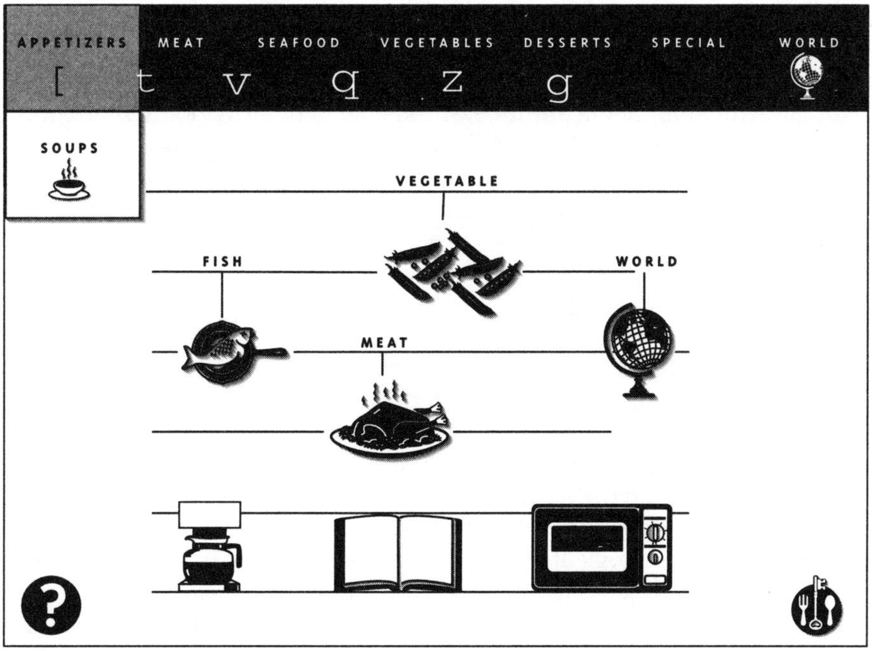

Figure 3-14: Further continuity at the submenu level.

Branching comes in three flavors: *unidirectional, multidirectional,* and *omnidirectional.* These patterns have been called many things by many experts of interface design and cognitive communication, but their patterns can most easily be described by these three clear terms that best depict the navigational options. Each of these three methods has a place in a fixed multimedia environment such as a CD-ROM, and sometimes they're used in combination with each other. In an online multimedia environment, the possibilities are similar but the drawbacks are a bit more problematic. I take a look at online branching in a later chapter. For now, you can see how your CD-ROM branches to its various content areas.

Unidirectional branching

The most basic and easily understood user interfaces work with a *unidirectional* branching pattern. In this simple scheme, each branch followed by the user progresses in a direction that has been predetermined by the authors.

Referring back to Figures 3-12 through 3-14, you can see that each specific section of the main menu leads directly to a specific section in the secondary menu. The connections are mostly linear; this is a good interface for getting tasks accomplished quickly, such as for a bank withdrawal at an ATM or a product look-up in a multimedia catalog. Even if the practical objective of the multimedia isn't so goal-oriented, unidirectional branching is sometimes all that's necessary, and it's simple enough for a child to use. Unidirectional branching implies a very logical cause-and-effect paradigm, and working with this kind of built-in control offers undeniable advantages, both for the user and for the multimedia author. For the user, a unidirectional branching structure requires making only a minimal number of decisions regarding navigation: click on point A and you'll go to point B. It might seem overly limited, given the range of possibilities, but in a unidirectional structure, such limitation is a plus. The user can always access the requested information or entertainment in a completely logical, straightforward, cause-and-effect way.

Not only does the user benefit from this simplicity, the author does, too. One of the key challenges in an open interface design, such as the multidirectional and omnidirectional examples that I explore shortly, is that you have no real way of predicting where a user will navigate at any particular point in the multimedia. Unlike the multimedia producers, the end user has no preconceptions of how the content should be viewed. Hence, what seems to the producers to be a logical course to navigate — point A to point B to point C, and so on, won't necessarily be the path chosen by the end user, who might jump around the multimedia in a completely capricious or freeform way.

Of course, in many cases, the producer will want to encourage the user to unstructured exploration. But those cases would be better served by a different kind of interface branching. For more cut-and-dried goals, especially for multimedia titles that have lots of different content on one disc or site, letting the user walk through the program in a controlled way makes much more sense, with the producer predetermining as much of the interactivity as possible. By narrowing the user's choices, such as through a unidirectional navigation path, the multimedia producer has made life simpler not only for the user but for the interface author as well.

Multidirectional branching

In many situations, a unidirectional branching pattern is unneccesarily cumbersome — it'll take users to the right place, but too much work is involved in getting there. If point A always leads to point B, arrival at point G or H means that extra keystrokes and unwanted screens will always be part of the equation. The next level in opening up the interface to more user choices is called *multidirectional branching*. It's a more open-ended structure that retains much of the control of unidirectional branching, but provides the ease and opportunity for the user to tailor the multimedia experience in a more individual way.

Figures 3-15 to 3-17 give you an idea of how you might lay out your cooking title with multidirectional branching. Essentially, you've connected several of your "rooms" via a hallway. The object is to group associated ideas in a logical way to encourage the user to explore them. This kind of interface design is useful when you have a lot of content, but you don't want freeform access to that content because authoring such a design would be difficult. Remember that, no matter what kind of interface you choose, access between any two given points of the multimedia must be bidirectional. If you have the user go from point A to point B, you must always provide a way for the user to jump back from B to A.

This sounds like an obvious concept, but when you've gotten into a fully free-form branching structure, the links between navigated paths become blurred. After several exploratory mouse clicks, the user may decide to return to the last place of extended interest, and if he/she has jumped to an area that isn't directly connected to the desired point of return, frustration quickly sets in. Of course, authoring multimedia in which each of the areas is connected to all the other areas is possible, but this is not only impractical for titles with a great deal of content, it's also a lot of extra programming work, which means extra money and time.

Figure 3-15: As the user continues through the interface path, the desired information should always be logically accessible, no matter where the path begins (note the different location of the highlighting).

Multidirectional branching is a good choice for titles whose multimedia can easily be divided amongst several major ideas or areas. The advantages are simple. Not only does the user get more choices, but the producer can tailor these choices in an intelligent way that encourages an experience that the user might not have chosen. The process of understanding how people will interact with your multimedia is largely predictive. For example, the producers and interface designers can make intelligent guesses as to how the user will jump around the title, or, in the case of unidirectional branching, the designers can actually close off the user options.

Sometimes, this overfocus can actually be a detriment. In multidirectional branching, you offer the user a choice of where to go, and the user, when confronted with these choices, might inadvertently make an unwanted choice. In this way, the interactivity is actually closer to "surfing" than to a focused, linear experience.

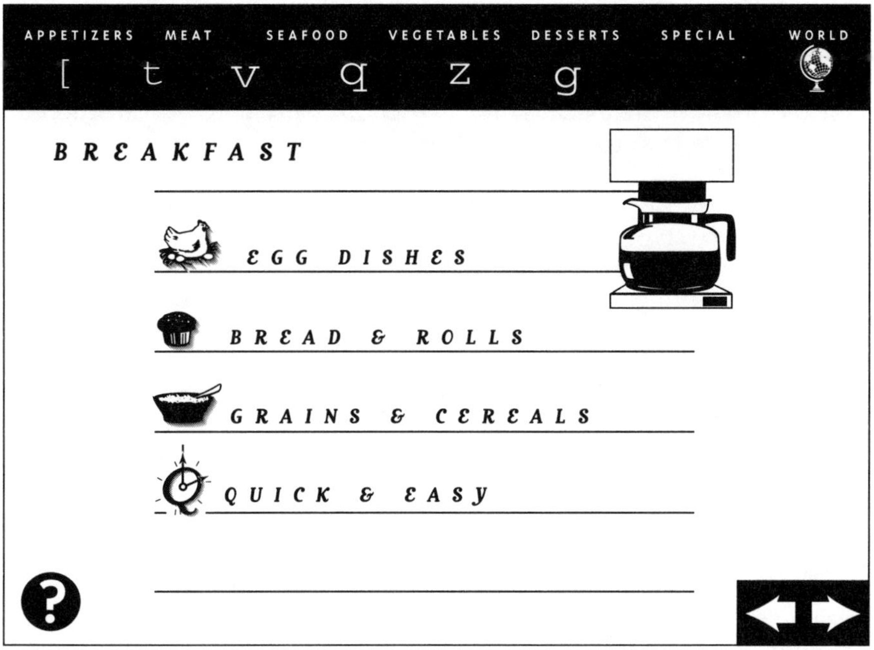

Figure 3-16: As before, secondary and tertiary screens guide the user through the path begun in the primary screen; note the different icons.

But that can be a real boon, on the other hand. If your title has enough interesting content, you want to encourage the user to explore all of it. Allowing users to react in a more freeform way will make the title more fun, and in most cases, ensure that more of the content is actually reached by the user.

In the "Good Eating" example, you can easily see how to offer the user a simplified yet versatile experience with multidirectional branching. People might be seeking a specific dish or cooking technique, but if they are presented with the possibility of exploring other things — offered as a choice through multidirectional branching — those choices might catch their interest as well, encouraging them to look into their previously desired information later. Multidirectional branching is probably the best interface choice for this title, but before you settle here, look at one more way of doing things.

Omnidirectional branching

As its name implies, an omnidirectional branching structure is one that allows the user to go any place in the title at any time. This can even extend to a random approach, which, through clever programming on the part of the design team, allows users' selections to take them to undetermined places in the content. Fully omnidirectional branching is the most difficult interface design to program, but ironically, it can be the easiest interface for the user to navigate, because no restrictions exist as to the direction the user must navigate to get where he or she wants to go.

Going back to your cooking CD-ROM (see Figures 3-17 and 3-18) , you can see that you have so many content possibilities, allowing unfettered access from every point to every other point would be cumbersome and confusing. There's something to be said for freedom of choice, but when the user is presented with too many choices, the title become unusable.

What would be a good context for omnidirectional branching? Clearly, a situation in which all the content is interrelated is ripe for this approach. For example, a real estate agency might develop a CD-ROM whose numerous properties are being offered to a potential buyer. In this case, you want the buyer to be able to see any of the properties, easily comparing one to the other. An omnidirectional structure would provide the fastest way of doing that — as long as there aren't too many properties on the disc. Now, take the same example and substitute your cooking content, which is loaded with recipes, techniques, and multimedia annotations. Because the possibilities are so much more varied, omnidirectionality would quickly bury the user with choices, and that's not what you want.

Omnidirectional branching is a less developed technique than either unidirectional or multidirectional. This is primarily because most interactive titles have a finite amount of content, due to the storage restrictions of the CD-ROM or other fixed format. Even at 660 megabytes, a CD-ROM can be quickly filled by video and audio clips, which is why many of the more elaborate game titles are coming out on two and even three separate discs. Needless to say, a situation in which the user is forced to switch discs in order to fulfill a branching choice is an example of poor programming. This slows down the action and makes for a cumbersome user experience, which is the last thing you want.

As new technologies develop, many of these restrictions are melting away. For example, at the time of this writing, a new optical disc format called DVD-ROM is only months away from a market debut. Rather than the relatively paltry 660MB of storage, a DVD-ROM can hold 4.7 gigabytes of compressed information — a quantum leap forward. Moreover, because of this efficient data compression, the new format allows for the inclusion of smooth, full-screen video clips far beyond what today's CD-ROMs are capable of

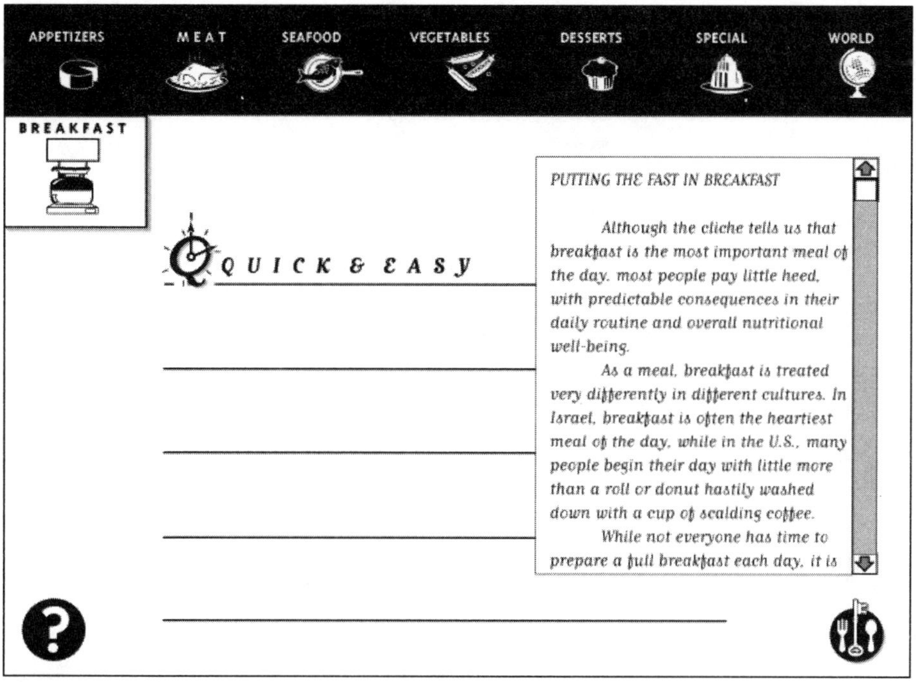

Figure 3-17: The cookbook layout shown here lends some organization to an extensive list of choices.

delivering. Clearly, with new advances such as these, interface designers will be better able to take advantage of heretofore impractical techniques such as unrestricted omnidirectional branching, as well as other design/content criteria that are difficult to present

Navigation — Global and Otherwise

No matter which branching method you choose for a multimedia production, two factors remain constant. One is that the user will need some kind of physical contact with the computer or game system in order to access the multimedia. The other is that users don't always have the time, patience, or desire to follow the presentation in the ideal way that the authors intended. Both these factors have an important impact on the title's usability quotient. One is dealt with in advance of design; the other is implemented as part of the design.

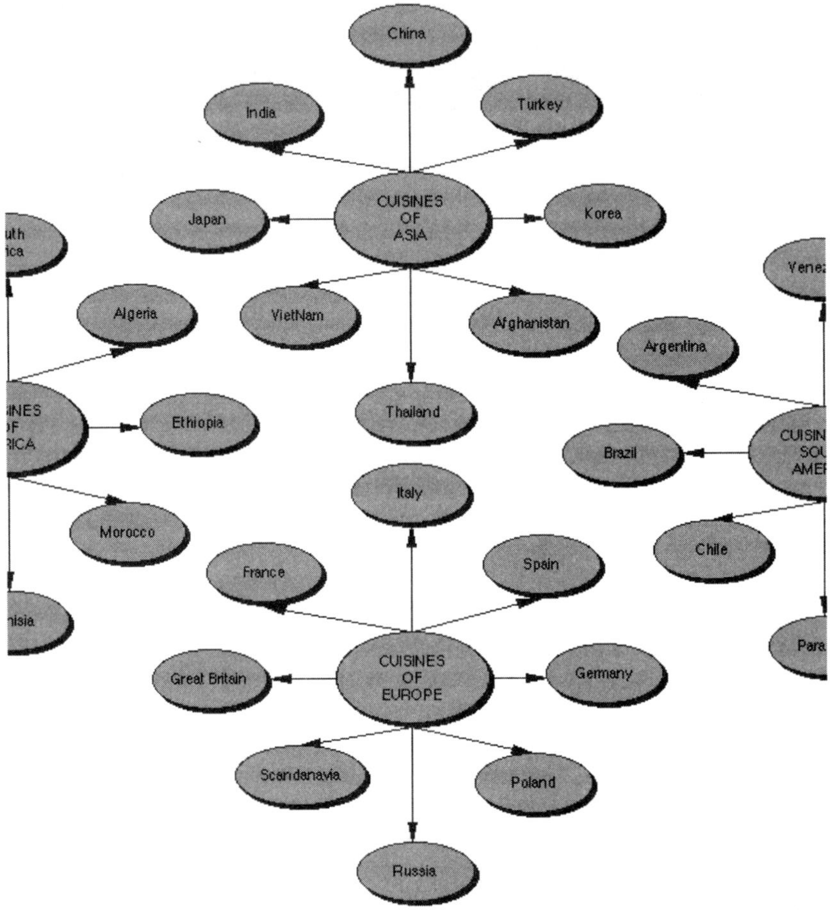

Figure 3-18: This diagram demonstrates how unlimited branching among many ideas would be overwhelming for the user.

The first factor begs the question: by what mechanism will the user make all these choices? Will it be through a mouse? A joystick? A touch-screen? Each choice will have an influence on interface design. For example, if the main input device is a mouse, which is by far the most typical case for either CD-ROMs or Web sites, you must take into account how much the mouse has to move in order to ensure a usable experience. Having often-accessed navigational icons placed at opposite corners of the screen may look appealing and balanced, but it means that the user will have a lot of extra arm work in making choices. The less on-screen "real estate" between frequently accessed points, the better, at least as far as the mouse is concerned.

For titles such as games, for which a joystick is the probable input device, the interface designer needs a clear idea of how sophisticated those user joysticks are likely to be. Most current joysticks are capable of at least eight points of access — the four compass points, plus the midpoints between them. With this in mind, it makes sense to group logically related ideas together, so that when, for example, the user moves the joystick from the nine o'clock position (pure west) to the six o'clock position (pure south), the southwest position that the user will always pass through to get there should be utilized in an intelligent way. If the user should accidentally or spontaneously decide to stop at the eight o'clock position (southwest), the corresponding multimedia link should be at least peripherally related to both the ideas attached to pure south and pure west.

Regardless of which device the user employs to access the multimedia content, two key navigational elements are a must in any interface: a way to return to the main menu and a way to exit the program. These are called "global" navigation links because they are always included in a multimedia title and exist independently of content. Although these links can be built into the interface in any number of ways, access to them must always be simple and straightforward. Nothing is more frustrating to the user than trying to do something simple and being forced to go through hoops for satisfaction.

Access to the main menu is something that might well be offered on virtually every screen of the title, so that users can always return to this crucial spot with a minimum of effort. The main menu is often used as a selection of last resort: when users are confused as to where to go next, they always have the comforting terrain of the main menu to guide them to a next step. In some cases, the functions of the main menu can be duplicated in design throughout the rest of the title, which eliminates the need for the user to actually navigate back to the "official" main menu. This, of course, doesn't eliminate the need for a main menu — the user still needs to see one at the beginning of the presentation to make the first choices of navigation. But situations that call for the functionality of the main menu to be built into other content screens — called *redundancy* — don't necessitate offering the user a full-fledged button to return to the original main menu.

The exit button can also be a continuous offering, though many producers prefer to keep the exit located in the main menu, thereby reducing the user's temptation to leave the program. It's a self-serving but quite commonplace design. Note that the exit button can serve more functions than simply letting the user quit the multimedia program. Most PC users already understand that pressing Ctrl+Q or Option+Q lets them quit the program they're running, and if they really want to exit your multimedia title, that's usually what they'll hit. But a dedicated exit button can do more than quit. It can bring the user to a splash screen that offers additional information about the company or the producers; it can advise users of other titles; and it can offer food for thought that actually brings the users back into the multimedia, even after they've made the conscious decision to leave it. Of course, the splash screen conjured up by clicking the exit button should always give the user the chance to change his or her mind and reenter the content. Simply having the program exit when the exit button is clicked is a waste of opportunity. Think of the exit splash screen as the last message you'll be able to give the user before he or she packs your title back onto the shelf. Make good use of the opportunity.

Because you've now discovered at least one element, and maybe more, that will probably have to be on-screen at all times, you should start looking at the design possibilities. I've skated around the issue, but now you can see, if you haven't already, that a multidirectional interface is probably the best choice for your "Good Eating" CD-ROM. You know that a unidirectional structure is probably too limited for such a broad topic, and that a freeform omnidirectional structure could quickly devolve into chaos. You've made a sensible choice with a multidirectional approach, so now you can start to lay out your title.

Working with Elements

The components that the designer uses to express the interface can come from varying sources. Many of these source elements will be digitally created, whereas others will be digitized files of nondigital media such as printed photographs, audio, and video. Each of these elements can serve multiple purposes, and their selective use is the key to understanding the designer's art.

Using text

Of all the ways that humans communicate, words are the most basic and most specific tools. This fact makes text a major player in just about every multimedia title, even when it's often deliberately overshadowed by more dynamic multimedia elements. For a reference work, text is a given. But even the most kinetic and wordless game title needs (at least) the occasional label on important icons and navigation paths.

Even though text is "only words," it's actually one of the most versatile players in the production. Examples of different kinds of text that are used for different situations are the following:

✦ **Display text:** Meant as a label or a link

✦ **Button text:** Serves an identifying function for other multimedia elements

✦ **Body text:** Contains all the text passages that are longer than a single phrase

Each type of text has its own set of opportunities and requirements. Display text is the easiest to work with, requiring the least stringent technical requirements. Display text can be any size that's attractive and functional, any color that complements the interface design, and, for technical or aesthetic purposes, it can even be converted to a graphical representation of text. Figure 3-20 shows various uses of text.

Figure 3-20: Different uses of text on one screen.

Font considerations

Using a graphical representation of text is an important idea to consider. In order for the end user to play back text exactly the way the author intended, the end user needs to have the intended font (typeface) on his or her computer. Some CD-ROM producers, feeling that their choice of font is especially important, actually include the font on the finished disc, which end users will install into their system. This step is cumbersome but is the only way to ensure that what you want is what they get. In cases like these, the producers acquire a license for the font from the particular releasing company that created it. Obviously, this adds extra steps and expense to the production, as well as the hassles that users will encounter in installing these new fonts — which, after all, do take up space on both the hard drive and in the system directory.

In the Web environment, specific font requirements are complicated somewhat by the user's choice of Web browser. Browsers such as Netscape Navigator allow the user to choose both a display (scalable) font and a fixed (stationary) font. But again, these choices are limited to the fonts that are already in the user's computer. When it is asked to display a font that isn't in the system, the target computer will automatically substitute a different — perhaps very different — font. This can lead to problems with spacing between words, and leading, which is the space between text characters. The lack of real predictability is an issue with almost all screen elements across the world of multimedia, and text is certainly no exception. Commonplace fonts (such as those typically preloaded in Windows and the Mac OS) are always a safe, if not particularly exciting, choice. If those choices are, for whatever reason, unacceptable to the producer, the only real alternative is to make text into graphics.

The graphic alternative

Changing on-screen fonts into bitmapped graphics is a time-tested compromise that not only gives the designer the freedom of font choice but also shields the user from having to own or install the designer's chosen fonts. This conversion, which essentially takes a "picture" of the text and turns it into a graphic representation, is accomplished through either a dedicated graphics package or, in some cases, multimedia authoring tools. In this way, words are actually transformed into pictures of words, sort of the way a fax machine works. To be sure, you'll pay a price with this method — another solution that engenders another challenge (we can't seem to get away from this dialectic, can we?). In the digital realm, pictures take up much more memory — both RAM and hard-drive space — than text. By running up an interface screen with lots of true text, it's a fairly sure bet that the user's PC won't be choked by extensive processor requirements. This isn't always true of bitmapped text, especially if the text is large or ample. But if it's intelligently arranged, the bitmapped text method is quite workable, and often is the only way to ensure predictable font results with all end users.

Other text issues

Even though text presents fewer problems for the producer than other multimedia elements, you still must be aware of some issues when you're using it. These are mostly creative issues, which are the best kind of problems to have. But some technical and perceptual caveats are worth discussing.

For example, the issue of font size is an important one. Many multimedia authoring programs have constricted control over text, but most will at least allow you the choice of sizes. For display fonts, aesthetic issues should be the guide. But for body text, readability has to be the paramount concern. At screen resolution, the typical home computer system can display only 72 to 80 dots per inch, or dpi. That means that if the text is too small, it becomes illegible. Fonts are measured by "point" sizes: the higher the point size, the bigger the text. At screen resolution, few fonts can be displayed at smaller than 12-point, and even then, some fonts are so delicate that they lose legibility. The fonts that suffer most from this malady are referred to as *serif* fonts. A serif is an ornament that's designed to make large blocks of text more readable. This is usually expressed as tiny knobs or posts attached to the stems of letters, and with small-point text, these ornaments really help with readability. Obviously, then, a *san-serif* font is one that has no serifs. Large blocks of san-serif text are perceptibly more difficult to read, which is why newspapers and textbooks are almost always printed with serif fonts.

Choosing the proper font for screen resolution is obviously more difficult, because a computer monitor, at 72 dpi, has much less apparent resolution than a printed page, which usually starts at 300 dpi for even the cheapest fanzine publication. Experimentation is a worthwhile pursuit here, keeping in mind a good rule of thumb: if you have to look closer at the monitor to comfortably read text, the font size is too small.

Text can be made more comfortable to read when it's enclosed within borders or specific backgrounds. Obviously, color plays a part here — black text on dark backgrounds is an obvious no-no. Conversely, white text on a dark "button" or color swatch can often be highly legible, even at smaller sizes than would normally be considered appropriate. Experimentation will show what's usable and what's not.

For situations that have a lot of text, such as some of your recipes for "Good Eating," you have a choice: to scroll or not to scroll? Scrolling happens when you have too much text to fit on a single screen. Text appears in a box (which can take up the entire screen) with a universally understood scrollbar that allows the user to go back and forth within the text. Scroll boxes are a useful tool, but are they always necessary?

Figure 3-21 shows a typical way of graphically representing what would ordinarily be a text-heavy section of your presentation. If we listed all these world regions in text, we'd probably need to use at least one scroll box. That solution would seem easy for the author, but it requires the user to do some work. In the case of a recipe, which people like to have right in front of them (presented, for example, on an index card), a scroll box is not necessarily the best solution. If you arrange your text information so it all fits on one screen, as the map has accomplished, you've put your point across with great economy. Of course, not every scenario lends itself well to this approach, but it's one way to provide an alternative to the scroll box. Why avoid the scroll box? Because whenever you can save the user some small hassle (such as extra mouse clicks or scrolls), you want to oblige.

Graphics and Video

Visual elements are the keystone of any multimedia title — the aspects that people remember after they've turned the power off. I don't need to stress here how important attractive graphic design is; the producer and designer are already well aware of this. But using still photos involves some technical issues, especially with video, that you must take into account as part of the framework of limitations within which.

Using color

The first issue to consider is color. Here in the mid-1990s, you can safely assume that virtually everyone using your multimedia offering is using a color-capable computer or game console. Exceptions exist and, in some cases, taking those exceptions into account may be worthwhile. But even though it's ubiquitous, color is not the same from one host machine to another.

When colors are displayed on a computer, they are picked from a *palette* of available hues that stays resident in the computer's display system. Not every computer has the same available palette. For example, some displays can work only with *8-bit* color, which develops full-color pictures from a palette of 256 colors. This is by far the most commonplace color capability,

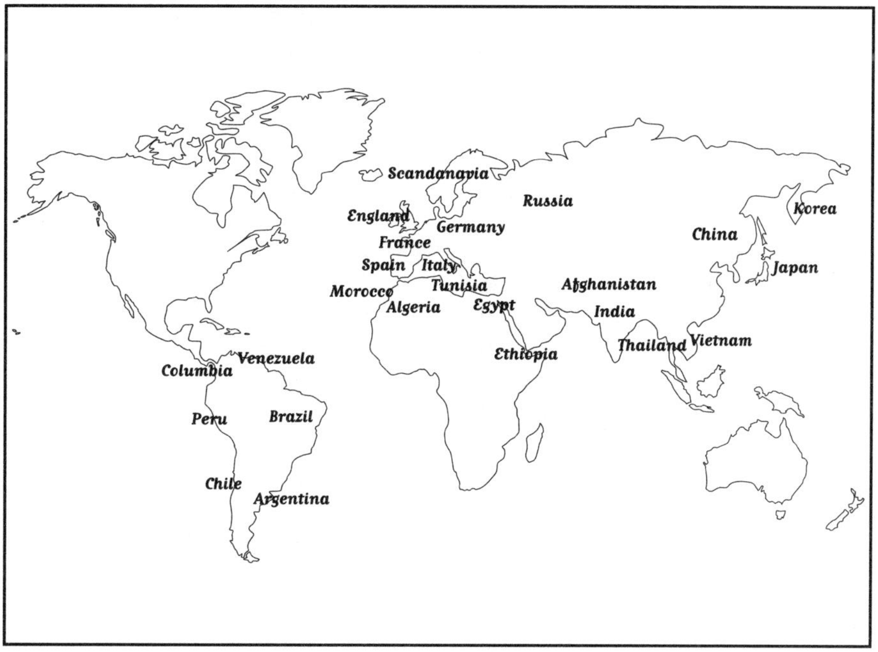

Figure 3-21: This map gets the point across efficiently.

and most multimedia titles, even those with highly elaborate graphics, will be optimized for use on this basic configuration. Other popular (though less so) color capabilities — also known as *bit depths* — include *16-bit color* (a palette of over 65,000 colors) and *24-bit color*, which offers a palette of millions of colors. The companion CD-ROM bundled with this book shows examples of how color palettes affect picture quality.

Working with file size

After color, the most crucial aspect of a graphic multimedia element is its size — file size, to be specific. The actual dimensions of the graphic are obviously up to the designer, within the parameters of good layout. But the size of the graphic file itself — the number of kilobytes or even megabytes that the graphic assumes in memory, is in fact a key issue. The reasons for this is simple: large files take up more RAM, they take longer to "draw" on screen, and, if they're large enough, they rob enough processing and display power from the host machine to slow down or even crash the presentation.

Good answers to these issues can be found. Intelligent bit depth is an obvious one. Keeping the physical dimensions of the graphics smaller (which keeps the file size smaller) is another, and data compression is a third. I discuss compression more in Chapter 6 on software tools.

Video

Moving pictures are, at the time of this writing, something of a holy grail for the multimedia developer. To be sure, lots of CD-ROM titles, and now, the occasional online venue, offer motion video as an annotation or integral part of the presentation. But video presents the most formidable technical demands in all of multimedia, which is why so much effort is being undertaken by so many parties to find new ways of presenting it.

The problem of storage

Full-motion video works in a similar way to film, in that a series of moving pictures flashes by so quickly that the eye perceives the separate pictures as continuous motion. Whereas film runs at 24 frames (pictures) per second, video moves at 30 frames per second. Each frame of video, when digitized for multimedia use, takes up almost an entire megabyte of memory storage. Multiply that by 30 frames per second that you need for moving pictures, and suddenly you need about 18,000 megabytes of storage, or the capacity of more than 20 CD-ROMs, to represent one minute of full-screen, full-motion, uncompressed video.

This is why video quality is typically so poor in multimedia titles. Even after the video is compressed — which, at the time of this writing, is the only effective way to put video into a multimedia title — the memory requirements are still daunting. To keep things manageable from a technical standpoint, most video "windows" in a multimedia production are not full screen, and are often far from it.

This is not to say that video can't be an effective part of the multimedia title. It must be efficiently integrated into the rest of the presentation, however, and the fallout from its technical demands must be answered throughout the rest of the authoring stage. Moreover, the limitations of video playback in the multimedia environment needn't be crippling or even particularly noticeable.

Using compressed video

For example, many multimedia video clips run at only 15 frames per second or less. This doesn't represent motion as fluidly as the full 30 fps, but it's enough to get the idea across, and if the video footage is of something stationary such as a single talking head, the perceptual difference is easily forgiven by the audience. The same goes for the size of the video window.

Although full-screen video certainly has impact, it's often overkill for a simple annotative clip. Typical video windows are sized at 320 pixels across by 240 pixels high — also called quarter screen — and are often half that size.

The art of making compressed video look good is one that's still being perfected, as new techniques and technologies become available. But one idea to keep in mind is that video compression has an easier time with stationary objects than it does with fast-moving action. By and large, video compression uses a perceptual coding scheme that predicts the difference between one picture and the next. Picture data that remains the same in both shots is largely eliminated, and only the differences between picture A and picture B are actually recorded — *encoded* — when the video is being digitized. This results in smaller, more usable files. In other words, video footage of a single narrator talking from in front of a plain, solid-colored background, is much easier to efficiently compress than the same scene with moving details in the background. When you are preparing to shoot video for a multimedia title, details such as backgrounds, lighting, and exposure should be carefully considered, taking the eventual compression artifacts into account.

Navigational Controls

Interface design is a two-way medium. The producer and the designers have presented the users with content and options to other content. The users meet them halfway by moving around this content — navigating it — through a series of interactive gestures. Designers provide many options to the user for navigation. Some are so simple that the user doesn't even notice them. Some are so dense as to be submerged in a larger design goal. But some basic navigational tools serve as an essential "grammar" of multimedia production, no matter what the design. They are elementary concepts that can be taken to ever more complex levels, depending on what the programmer decides to do.

Buttons

I've already discussed text, pictures, and icons as ways of signifying navigation through a multimedia title. But all of these elements serve as metaphors for the real idea that you're trying to convey — the idea of buttons. Buttons are direct-access tools for the user to initiate interactivity in a multimedia environment. Buttons in multimedia serve the same function as they do in any piece of technology, be it a toaster or a cockpit. When you push one, something happens. In the "grammar" of interactive media, buttons are the most basic cognitive element.

You have many different kinds of buttons from which to choose, as you can see in Figure 3-22. Buttons straddle the line between the literal directness of text navigation and the intuitive directness of icon-based navigation. Typically, a button is given a label, whether through words or by association to a graphic element already inherent in the multimedia. In some cases, interface designers opt for a less literal approach, but that aesthetic decision should not be taken lightly. For example, forward and backward are two key navigational options for which buttons might be used.

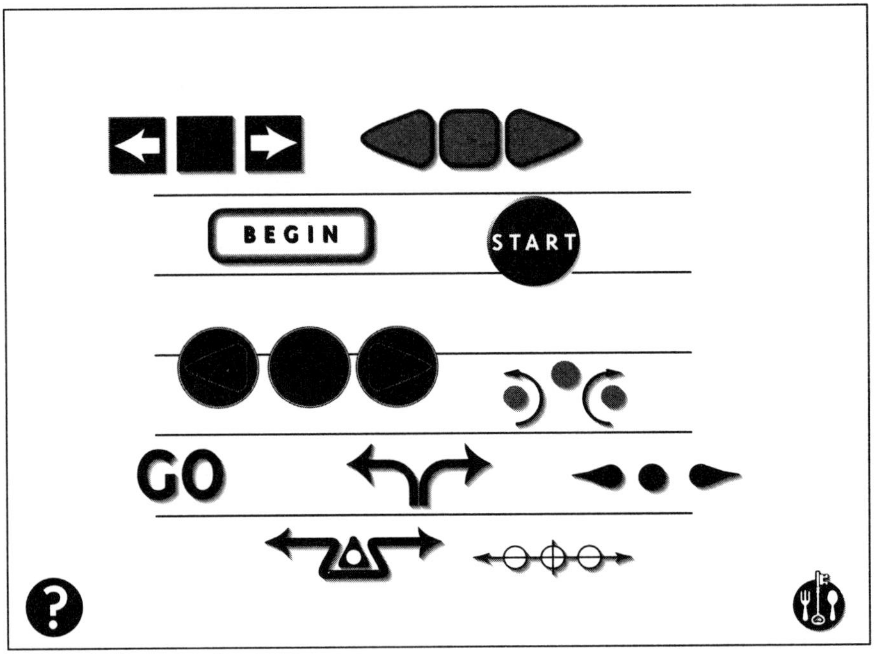

Figure 3-22: Types of buttons.

How do you represent that idea without words? The common answer is a right-pointing arrow for forward and a left-pointing arrow for backward. Why this setup? As mentioned previously, English is read from left to right. Something you haven't read will be to the right, and something you've already read is to the left. It's a bit of a stretch, and probably not as valid for multimedia titles meant for non-English speaking markets. Some apologists claim that these "directional" buttons mimic the buttons found on a tape deck. That may be valid, but it's somewhat short-sighted. Not everyone who uses multimedia is experienced with a tape deck.

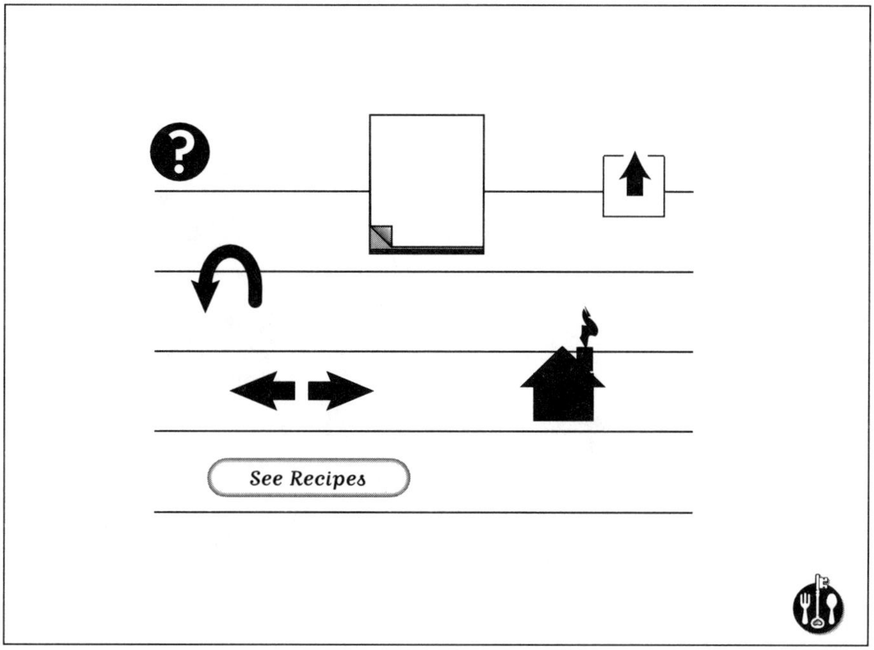

Figure 3-23: Regardless of visual style, buttons are usually explicit in their meaning, sometimes so much so as to include text.

No matter what function is attached to it, button design can be approached from one of three directions. The most common type is the direct button — click it, and the appropriate task attached to that button is accomplished (refer to Figure 3-23). Another type of button is called a selectable button. Selectable means that when the button is clicked, it's actually highlighted, thereby enabling another action or set of actions to occur, as shown in Figures 3-24 to 3-25.

The last major type of button is the *rollover* button. A rollover button (see Figure 3-26) occupies an on-screen hotspot. When the user moves the mouse or joystick over the rollover button, the hotspot alerts the user that an action can be initiated, typically by "lighting up" the hotspot area.

Although all three button choices are valid and commonly used, being mindful of other interface design characteristics makes sense. For example, too many rollover buttons with illuminated hotspots placed too closely together will confuse the user as to the actual functions. If a selectable button brings up a list of other buttons, that selectable button must always be distinguishable from the new buttons it engenders.

Figure 3-24: Direct buttons such as the microwave-oven button execute a clearly understood interaction, but need not be literal in their presentation.

Figure 3-25: The microwave oven is a selectable button with a hotspot. Here the user has clicked on the on the hotspot, enabling a second set of choices.

Figure 3-26: In this figure, the dotted lines reveal how various hotspots are arranged throughout the interface.

Menus

Ever since the advent of home computing, the menu has been the primary mode of discourse between machine and user. As its name implies, it's a list of choices, just like a restaurant menu. The difference is that a waiter isn't around to act as a messenger. When the user chooses something from a computer menu, something has to happen, whether it's an action being enacted or a user preference being set.

Because virtually everyone working on a PC is already used to the idea of menus, taking advantage of them whenever necessary makes sense. As with buttons, several different menu archetypes exist, all of which can be extremely useful depending on the context.

Pull-down menus

The pull-down menu is a list of choices that resides under a single specific heading. For example, calling up the File menu on an application in either Windows or the Macintosh operating systems will bring up a pull-down menu that allows for file management — Open, Close, Save, Save As, and so on. Pull-down menus can be activated either by holding down the mouse or controller over the heading, or via a "sticky" pull-down menu that pulls itself down automatically whenever the user brings the controller over the hotspot — which, in this case, is the pull-down menu's heading.

Pull-down menus are a great way to give the user many choices in just a little bit of screen real estate. The only text that needs to clutter up the screen at any one time is the heading. Because the user options in the pull-down will disappear from the screen as soon as a choice is implemented, this is an elegant, efficient way of offering the user choices. The disadvantage to a pull-down menu is that it's a linear mode of expression: look at a list of choices, pick one. In order to make another choice, the user must return to the pull-down menu, which isn't always the most direct method of interactivity. For situations in which more choices are necessary, it's best to look at other menu options.

Hierarchical menus

In this menu scheme, the user is once again presented with a list of choices emanating from a single menu option. Like the pull-down menu, the user approaches the hierarchical menu for a single idea. But instead of a linear list of choices, a hierarchical menu offers a visual road map of choices, sometimes even interconnected to other menu options. The advantage here is that the user has more freedom to explore other interactive avenues that may not have been the original intended destination.

As Figures 3-27 and 3-28 show, you can graphically see the advantages and disadvantages of using pull-down and hierarchical menus for your "Good Eating" title. Your user wants to look up recipes. If you employ the pull-down option, you'll give your users a direct list of what kind of recipes to peruse. But as this example shows, your information on recipes may be too varied or elaborate for a single menu to hold comfortably. This is when a hierarchical menu might come into play.

Pop-up menus

One of the most underused but effective menu designs is the pop-up menu. In this scheme, the user clicks on either a main menu heading or an on-screen hotspot, and receives what initially looks like a single choice. This choice is the option that is currently being used by the program. But if the user holds down the mouse on this choice, something interesting happens — another list of choices "pops up." From there, the user moves the cursor over the desired menu choice and releases the mouse, thereby choosing the new menu option.

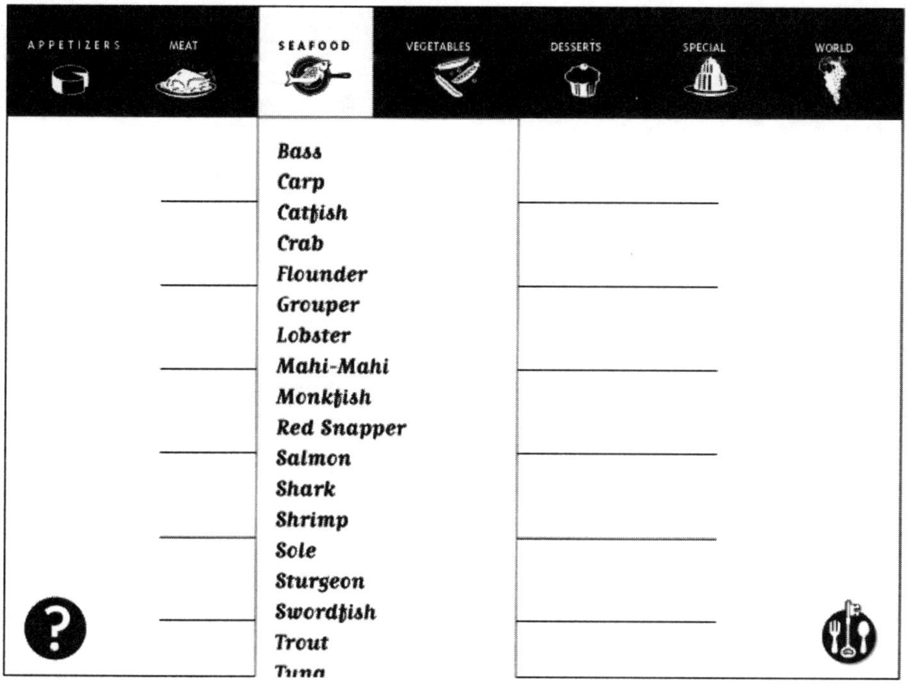

Figure 3-27: A pull-down menu is intuitive and often useful, but will cover a lot of screen area when in use, especially if it offers many menu choices.

Pop-up menus are so useful because they accomplish two important tasks. The first one is to allow the interface designer the same screen economy as a pull-down menu — only one main menu choice need be on the screen until the user needs to see the rest of the options. That's a big advantage when you have to offer the user a lot of different options. But just as important, a pop-up menu tells the user where he or she is right now. As soon as the user invokes a pop-up menu, a defaulted menu setting is already in place — the setting that the audience is currently using. When using a pop-up menu, the user not only gets to choose what to do next, but can see, in clear terms, how that choice is different from the present setting.

As a way of moving from one section of an interactive title to another, this design accomplishment is not a big deal — all you have to do is watch the screen and you can see the difference. But for more subtle interactive changes, the pop-up menu can be a star. For example, most operational preferences — the sound volume, the font choices, large video window versus small, are all handled best by a pop-up menu because those choices present the user with a comparative change, which will stay in place as the default setting until the user returns to the pop-up menu.

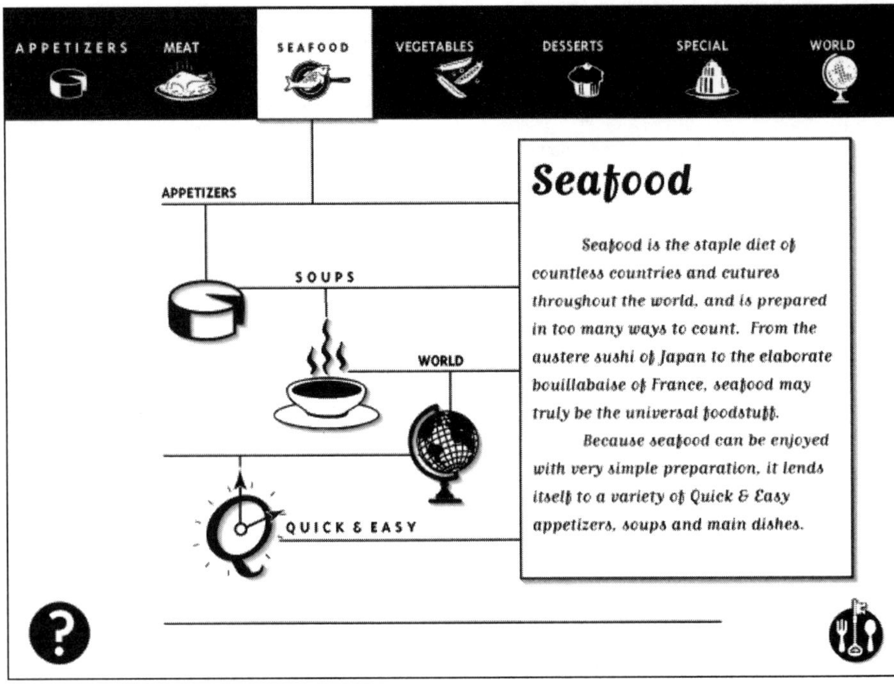

Figure 3-28: Here the next level down the hierarchy is easily understandable by the user, allowing more intuitive navigation.

Help screens

No matter how carefully you design a title, no matter how simple and intuitive it seems to the designers, and no matter how smoothly the whole thing runs after it's finished, some user — someone, somewhere — will have trouble or questions. Unless the content is so simple that help is unnecessary (which is almost never the case) or the designers are flat-out inconsiderate, almost every multimedia title is well served by a system of user help.

Help screens typically do one or more of three things. First, they explain how the program works. It may seem elementary to the designers that a right arrow means forward and a left arrow backward, but here again, it's always important that the multimedia producer sit in the potential audience's shoes for a while. A brief help explanation, either through text, menus, narration, or video, of the basic functions of the program is almost always necessary in a mainstream multimedia title. This is true even if the accompanying documentation already says the same thing.

Besides explaining how the program works, a help screen may offer a global list of various ideas within your multimedia title. It can also offer a search function for more specific ideas about which users may have questions. In the case of "Good Eating," a global help screen might explain to the user how to search for a particular recipe or cooking technique. A more focused help screen might allow the user to choose from a list of help topics, or, in some cases, allow a direct query for help be entered and searched.

Context-sensitive help

The interface designer has several options to consider regarding a help screen for users. By far, the most typical one is to offer a help icon that's strategically located for easy access — often in the main menu, and sometimes even throughout the entire presentation. But a more subtle and direct way of offering the same thing comes from context-sensitive help, which affords the user specific answers to specific questions.

Context-sensitive help, as its name implies, relies on a particular on-screen context in order to work. For example, if you came across a cooking technique with which you weren't familiar, you could easily look it up in a global help section. But that would be tedious, involving numerous steps of help access, subject look-up, and, finally, help. Usually, the user will be impatient for more direct satisfaction.

That's where context-sensitive help comes in. In this technique, the user typically moves the mouse over into a general help section and chooses context-sensitive help, or presses a specially programmed key or button over the area requiring help — in other words, the context. At that point, the cursor might turn into a question mark, or some other symbol that denotes help. Clicking again on the requested subject automatically brings up context-sensitive help. The user gets what he or she wants quickly, and more important, can return to the presentation quickly.

Multimedia Hybrids – New Directions

Throughout this chapter, I've spotlighted interface designs for pretty mainstream media. CD-ROM drives are standard issue on virtually all new PCs, and the same is almost true for modems. But technology advances itself so quickly that even before these two technologies have reached total consumer penetration, newer ways of delivering multimedia content are starting to emerge.

Many of these new delivery systems are the result of major commercial interests from entertainment companies, broadcast companies, telecom companies, computer makers, and other parties that see multimedia as the "next big thing." Because technology usually moves faster when it's spurred on by visions of profit, it's not surprising that all these parties converge, trying to devise efficient and profitable ways of expanding the capabilities and delivery of multimedia content.

Many of these emerging technologies will do away with the technical limitations inherent in CD-ROM and twisted-pair modem delivery. CD-ROM is a notoriously slow delivery medium, able to pour only so much data to the computer's processor at a time because of the physical limitations of how fast the disc can spin and be "read." Modem delivery is even weaker, with slow modem transmission speeds — even for digital phone lines — making truly dynamic multimedia such as full-screen video and full-fidelity audio impossible.

In the very near future, technologies such as cable modems, which are capable of many times the speed of today's typical analog modems, will speed online content into the home, perhaps to a PC screen, perhaps to a television set, or perhaps both. Fiber-optic lines will also allow for much higher bandwidth, as will direct-broadcast satellite technologies, which are already in development for multimedia use. CD-ROM discs will soon be superseded by DVD (Digital Video Discs), which will offer video, audio, and graphic performance many times more capable than today's limited media. Designing for these new media will be a challenge. For now, these are futuristic technologies, but they ask some valid questions regarding the present — namely, how much of the multimedia team's resources will be put to the task of adapting these new tools as they become available?

Online CD-ROM hybrids

One clever way that this gap is being bridged today is by content that exists in both online and fixed CD-ROM form simultaneously. The early pioneers of this technique have been the commercial online services, and their methodology is simple: use the CD-ROM to connect to the online material, and have the online material reference the CD-ROM.

As typified by commercial online carriers such as America Online, CompuServe, Prodigy, and WOW!, a CD-ROM-online hybrid uses a metaphor that's similar to the relationship between a computer's hard drive (storage memory) and RAM (random access memory). To provide users with an aesthetically attractive and satisfyingly dynamic online experience, many graphics have to go to the screen. As you've seen, many graphics means lots of download time in the online environment. Sending too many to the user creates a slow and boring experience that won't soon be repeated.

Big graphics and sounds aren't a problem for CD-ROMs, but after they've been "burned" with all their content on board, CD-ROM discs are completely fixed; new material and updated content is impossible, unless the producer is willing to go back and re-press the actual discs.

Clearly, these two media can coexist, and they often do in the commercial online world. Of course, the user must have both a CD-ROM drive and a modem to play, but that's becoming a commonplace situation. The user boots the CD-ROM as he or she would any other multimedia title. Appropriate graphics are poured onto the screen; design here follows the same rules that I've already laid out for other CD-ROM titles. But there's a difference. The user can click on a button and launch into the online service.

Most online services, commercial or otherwise, are booted from software that is installed on the user's hard drive. In this case, the CD-ROM is merely a substitute for the hard drive, and the online service is accessed in the same way — click and you log on to the service. But now, instead of the online server having to send graphics and other weighty material over the phone line, it can simply send minute control commands back to the user's host computer, which then references the graphics on the CD-ROM disc. This results in an easier job for the technologies and a more fluid experience for the user.

The possibilities can go even further. In this technological context, having key sections of the online service already programmed as buttons in the CD-ROM's multimedia content would be possible. The user would simply click on them and go directly to chosen places online. You could even go further and have intelligent queries sent by the CD-ROM over to the online service, requesting new or updated information, which is then downloaded onto the user's hard drive — all automatically. Clearly, this hybrid approach has intriguing potential. The primary reason that it has not become commonplace is that few online sites require enough available data to warrant development of a companion CD-ROM. You'll find exceptions, of course, besides the commercial online services. Their numbers will grow in the coming years, as producers devise new ways of delivering faster, bigger, and more dynamic multimedia content.

CHAPTER 4

Production

- ✦ Job titles, roles, and skill sets have evolved to reflect the complexities of multimedia production.
- ✦ You can find the people for your production team in various parts of the country and diverse working situations.
- ✦ Tailor your production team's working arrangements and labor relations to fit the needs and realities of your project.
- ✦ Knowledge of — and respect for — intellectual property and copyright are crucial to your project's success.

From the time that a multimedia title is conceived to the time that it's delivered, dozens of jobs and schedules must be successfully navigated, often simultaneously. But the one job that usually takes the most time and effort is that of laying out the vision in digital computer code and making the project spring to life. This is the *production* process. Production is everything that happens after the initial planning (preproduction) stage and up to the final release version. It's the process of assembling the product.

Production is such a varied and unclassifiable process that no way exists for making fool-proof production schemes that will be valid for every project. A simple multimedia production, created solely with original content, can actually be created by a single individual. This is by no means a typical scenario; more likely, the multimedia title will have several, if not many, people working on the production. But this scenario is not rare, either. Individuals who gravitate toward the hallowed mantle of Multimedia Producer are often skilled at one or more aspects of the production process, be it graphic design, project flow, or even programming. Furthermore, many of today's multimedia authoring tools are simple enough for nonprogrammers to understand and manipulate. Individuals such as these can literally sit down in front of a computer and, using one or several software programs, create a finished multimedia title.

But should they? You've already come to understand that multimedia requires a multitude of talents. Even though it may be cheaper and more expedient to adopt a DIY approach to production, rare is the individual who is sufficiently skilled in every production aspect that's necessary for a professional production. This caveat obviously goes beyond just production. If you can find an individual who's a skilled programmer, has a great eye for design, knows audio, video, and animation backward and forward, can negotiate intellectual property rights, knows how to troubleshoot, has great marketing ideas, and can work well with a team and a deadline, hire that person immediately and make him or her promise to never leave. If that doesn't describe anyone you know or can find — and it probably won't — accept the inevitable. A multimedia project is almost always best served by a team of creative individuals who may well have a wide range of skills and interests, but have expertise in *at least* one important area.

Roles and Skills of the Production Team

Who are these people and what do they do? The digital age has produced some amusing new job descriptions such as "infopreneur," "digitalogist," "listmaster," and "virtualist." Business-card collecting at a multimedia trade show almost always yields some entertaining moments. Not that all of it is entirely whimsical. In an evolving industry such as multimedia, roles, titles, and responsibilities are evolving, too. The skills that most multimedia professionals bring to this young industry have traditionally been acquired in other related media, such as print publishing, television, film, radio, and video games. That will certainly change as rapidly as everything else in this industry.

Because a varied set of interests is characteristic of a multimedia worker, thinking in terms of roles rather than actual job titles is probably more sensible. When you assemble a team, you should ensure that these roles are clearly understood by the individuals who fill them. Although having a graphic designer who understands the requirements of audio and a production coordinator who knows marketing is desirable, bear in mind that responsibility is not the same as talent. To keep the production from devolving into chaos and the work crew from quickly descending into frustration, knowing who's doing what and who answers to whom are essential.

The producer

The most overused title in the multimedia world is also the most misunderstood and least easily pigeonholed. After all, a multimedia production has a lot of producers. But the actual "producer" of a multimedia title is one person or group of persons who assumes responsibility for the development of the project. That could mean gathering the forces to create it, or supervising the hands-on work that builds it. It could mean conceptualizing the project in the first place, or commissioning it. Often, it means all of these things. But it always means that the Producer — with a capital *P* — is most responsible for getting the project off a cocktail napkin and onto an audience's display screen. The responsibility sounds big because it is.

Many skills are necessary to pull off even several of these jobs, much less all of them. For that reason, the multimedia producer has to be a special kind of person. Management skills are probably at the top of the list in importance. In most cases, numerous different people will come in and out of the production, and the producer must be able to interface well with most of them. Even if the workgroup is small, superior management skills are necessary to deal with budgets, schedules, and the inevitable crises.

After management skills, vision is the next essential quality of a good multimedia producer. Until the visualization of the multimedia production is written down and finalized, the vision of how it looks and feels is the producer's responsibility. The producer must be able to communicate this vision to the appropriate parties who will develop the plan to execute that vision. During the actual production process, the producer is very much like the captain of an ocean-going ship. Imagine a map, a planned route, a vehicle, and a crew. The producer is the one who knows where everyone is going, and how to get there most efficiently. The producer's vision of the final destination must be firm enough for the crew to pitch in together with confidence, despite the fact that the horizon shows no sign of land.

Beyond the job skills that can be described on a resume, a successful multimedia producer is someone with a golden temperament. Rare is the production in which everything goes completely smoothly. How well the producer deals with adversity and unpredictability has a telling effect on how the production ultimately comes off. Other creative people, with all the personality dynamics that can come with creativity, will come into contact with the production. A good producer is someone who inspires them to do good work. Although everyone has his or her own style of inspiration with collaborators and employees, most people will tend to rally around someone they like more readily than someone they fear.

What qualifications can one have for this multileveled position? Aside from the aforementioned qualities, a multimedia producer often brings a background in more traditional media to the party. Multimedia as an industry is so new that people who've cut their production teeth here are in relatively short supply. Large companies who invest sizable sums into ambitious multimedia enterprises are often loathe to pin their hopes on an individual that can't claim many years of experience. This is a bit of a Catch-22 because multimedia is young enough that even the most wizened veterans can claim only a handful of years in the business.

Therefore, most of today's multimedia producers have a background in more traditional media forms. In the online world, many multimedia producers have migrated from television or radio, both mediums bearing some similarity to the immediacy of online. In CD-ROM work, a producer often brings a background from print publishing, graphic design, or computer-based training (CBT). These situations undoubtedly ease as more people become qualified to be multimedia producers simply through more cumulative experience in multimedia. Multimedia may resemble some other forms, but online is not television and CD-ROMs are not books. The new media is its own animal, and sometimes the preconceptions brought in by a broadcast or print veteran can actually work against the project. This is something that the good multimedia producer will always have in mind and be receptive to when other members of the team remind him or her.

In short, the producer is the head of the entire multimedia production. Although a good one won't get bogged down in the complex minutiae of the workflow, a good one will be aware of what's happening everywhere, and will be able to speak cogently to the inevitable problems that arise during the development of a multimedia title.

Project manager

Although this title is usually held by the producer, project management is a large enough job by itself to often warrant a specialized individual (or individuals) to assume this responsibility. Using a print analogy, the *project manager* is much like a periodical's production manager; in the film world, this person is called a line producer. No matter what you call them, project managers are responsible for the day-to-day supervision of the production.

The primary responsibility here is to ensure that the directives of the producer are carried out by the rest of the crew. Therefore, the project manager becomes the master sergeant working under the general's (producer's) orders. As the main interface between the poles of "what's desirable" and "what's possible," a project manager's most vital talent has to be communication. Each goal, deadline, or query must be clearly articulated to everyone concerned, so that the team is absolutely aware of what is expected and when. Further, a good project manager has to have a sense of foresight. An intelligent, proactive response to a potential problem keeps small crises from becoming big crises, which will necessitate the producer's involvement and slow down the production.

Being an overseer on a complex project with numerous creative individuals at work isn't particularly fun, except for certain kinds of personality types. A bit of cold-hearted efficiency is in order at all times for the project manager, who may be the one exception to the rule that people will respond better to inspiration than fear. If the producer is the good cop, the project manager often plays the bad one. Well, somebody's got to do it!

Associate producer

When dealing with a sizable project, the producer might need a second set of hands to make sure that everything gets done. Although a smaller production sometimes farms these responsibilities out to a low-level assistant or intern, a more fully realized work group often includes an *associate producer*.

As far as the rest of the team is concerned, the associate producer is an extension of the producer, and is often the one directly supervising the action when the producer is away or indisposed with another problem. The associate producer might be a producer in training, getting on-the-job exposure to the many challenges and hazards that he or she will face when moved up to the producer's chair. The position is precarious, offering great insights and many responsibilities by such inside exposure to the production. But in many ways, the associate producer is also the fall guy, more often having to accept responsibility for things gone wrong than credit for things gone right.

For newcomers to the field, an associate producer position is one to be highly prized. In many ways, it's a matter of being a glorified gopher, but by the end of a project or two, a good associate will be ready for more responsibility. This is the training ground for the multimedia producers of tomorrow.

Writer

Although text may or may not be an emphasized aspect of the multimedia project, at some point or another, words are important, even if only in the user help screens. Anyone with a command of the English language can write, but in the context of a multimedia production, an experienced writer — one who has written for this medium — is always a boon to the production and, in some cases, an essential cog.

Even the most graphically oriented project has many documents for someone to write, from the beginning of the production to the end. These include request forms for permissions, work orders to go to vendors and production team members, promotional materials to be composed, scripts to be written, project updates to be submitted to the controlling parties. And, oh yes: what about text material in the finished production itself?

In the multimedia world, words have an important place, although prose doesn't get the emphasis that it does in any other reading material such as a book or periodical. For example, a CD-ROM benefits greatly from crisp, concise writing that expresses what needs to be expressed in as few words as possible — taking up less screen space and less time away from the user's actual multimedia experience. When people "read" material from a CD-ROM, they're doing one of two things. They may be absorbing reference material or instructions, in which case, full prose is appropriate. More likely, however, they're reading words so that they know where the experience is going and can control it through interactivity. A good multimedia writer can pare down the verbiage to the bare essentials, which is appropriate for a CD-ROM. The writer's work becomes the literary equivalent of icons.

In the Web world, text takes on a different meaning; for many Web sites, text is the *raison d'être*. Obviously, a site whose text information is the reason that customers are visiting is an appropriate venue for at least one professional writer, perhaps more.

Writing for online is a specialized skill that is reflective of larger evolutions (some might say de-evolutions) of language. The traditional grammatical skills of effective prose are not necessarily germane in the online world, where the emphasis is on economy, clarity, and, occasionally, wit. A writer who will succeed in this medium need not be a published author. Someone with superior communication skills and experience in online writing — especially in terms of message boards and e-mail — would, however, be an extremely valuable addition to a multimedia team.

Interface designer

Although I've already given you an overview of what goes into the art of interface design, I haven't discussed the kind of individual or individuals who might have expertise in this evolving area. The *interface designer* is typically a strange bird — part artist, part scientist, part psychologist.

More so than visuals, text, or any other readily grasped aspect of a multimedia production, the interface designer should be a student of human cognition. This is the science of how people perceive, understand, and react. This is something of an inexact science because everyone reacts to stimuli in different ways. But a successful interface designer understands that people interact with machines, especially computers, in preconceived ways. The interface designer's goals should be to either work within the guidelines of those preconceptions or bring in other preconceptions that will further the project without disorienting or frustrating the user.

Where do these preconceptions come from, and how can an interface designer learn them well enough to manipulate them for the goals of the production? In many cases, those preconceptions are learned from other media that saturate everyday American life. In television, we understand that a blackout leads to a commercial. In film, we intuitively understand that a fade-out takes the story to another time, and a dissolve often takes it to another place. In a newspaper, we expect to read an article in vertical columns that begin at the top and end at the bottom. The interface designer not only understands these cognitive starting points, but can extend them and their implied conventions into the multimedia arena.

That being said, the most important skill for an interface designer is a sense of empathy. One person is asked to design an interface that will be seen and used by many different people. How will those people react? Will they be overwhelmed by a lot of screen elements, or impressed? Will they follow the same kind of interactive flow logic that the producers intended, or will they feel free to explore? If they do explore, what branches might they take from any given point?

The interface designer is charged with the job of taking these differing perceptions into account and creating a front end that will satisfy as many people as possible. The ability to see within different parties — the intelligence and curiosity of the end user, the talents of the art director, the chops of the programmer — and to make them mesh is the interface designer's stock in trade. This field doesn't have many experts just yet. But it will. The interface designer is really the auteur of the multimedia production.

Art director

The *art director* is responsible for the visual appeal of the multimedia project. This consists of literally everything that the user will see — colors, icons, textures, and shapes, as well as dynamic media such as photographs, video, and audio. Although the art director may not actually create these elements, he or she must still assume final responsibility for the look of all of them and, while they're at it, the look of the entire production.

The art director is first brought into the project during the conception stage. Many of the creative and technical decisions will have to be made with either the art director's input or tacit approval because the actual execution of the project will always be reflective of the art director's vision. During this initial phase, the art director has the greatest input that he or she will have during the rest of the production. After the art design and production is under way, the job becomes largely supervisory, consisting of overseeing the accomplishments of the art team and making corrections as they become necessary. By the time the project is programmed and ready for testing, the art director's job is largely finished, although last-minute corrections are a frequent occupational hazard in this business.

A multimedia art director's background usually reflects traditional print or, to a lesser extent, broadcast skills. Training in graphic design, illustration, painting, or the like is extremely useful, as is some experience with production techniques such as color separations and typography. Unfortunately, although such backgrounds are helpful, these skills won't necessarily translate seamlessly to the multimedia environment. Multimedia is collaborative not only in terms of personnel but from a technical standpoint as well. A beautifully designed screen is only a well-designed screen when it takes into account the various needs and limitations of hardware, software, and user sophistication. In other words, someone who can design beautiful work that's impractical for multimedia use is not an effective art director for this medium.

In essence, then, the most useful skill for a multimedia art director is teamwork. Art design is traditionally a discipline in which an individual works alone to come up with a compelling vision. In multimedia, this solitary approach rarely works. Therefore, the art director must learn to separate him or herself from the mindset of solitary inspiration. A collaborative medium holds room for many creative individuals. But no individual's work stands alone in a multimedia production.

Associate designers and artists

The art director on a multimedia production typically has a staff of individuals to execute his or her creative decisions. Because effective multimedia art direction is one-half creative and one-half technical, dividing these responsibilities among two specialists is common. Both do similar work, but the designer's job is to regard the bottle as half empty, whereas the artist must see it as half full. In other words, the art director assigns the technical caveats to the designer — an individual whose job is to execute the art director's goals on a technical level — and the creative challenges to the artist who is charged with executing the art director's aesthetic decisions.

As with producers and associate producers, the designers and artists are often apprenticing on a production. To be sure, they have set goals and responsibilities, and in many cases, they are specialists in their respective fields with little interest in moving beyond them. But as the multimedia world grows older, the medium will eventually grow its own star art directors and creative heads, who will no doubt graduate from these associate roles.

Animation director

Animation is a compelling feature of virtually all fixed multimedia presentations, and a growing component of online multimedia. Animation is the surest way to introduce dynamism to a project; nothing says "Multimedia!" in such loud capital letters as animated images.

Animation is the process of turning a series of static images into fluidly moving graphics. The discovery of animation goes all the way back to the 19th century, with the experimental photographs of Edward Muybridge and the French invention of the kinescope. Humankind discovered that if a series of changing pictures was flashed by the human eye fast enough, the brain would perceive the changing information as one continuous motion. Years later, with the advent of motion pictures, someone discovered that 24 frames, or pictures, per second was enough to convey fluid motion. Today's films still use 24 fps, whereas video actually ups the rate to 30 fps.

The animation director's job is to develop the artwork and storyboards that will bring these lifeless frames into motion. Two kinds of animation typically show up in a multimedia project: 2-D and 3-D animation. Both aim for the same goal of making things move on the screen. But 2-D (two-dimensional) animation is grounded in traditional cel animation techniques learned from motion pictures, whereas 3-D animation is a new digital discipline that's still in an evolutionary and expensive state.

The difference between the two, as far as personnel is concerned, is that although both 2-D and 3-D animators usually have traditional flat animation skills, a 3-D animator typically has access to more powerful equipment. Two-dimensional animation can be accomplished by a number of easily accessible animation software packages, and can be used on most garden-variety PCs. Three-dimensional animation, however, is hardware intensive, meaning that powerful computers are necessary for serious work. Objects that are animated in 3-D are first *modeled* as opposed to drawn — figures begin life as a series of wire-frame skeletons. They are then *rendered* through a 3-D software package that taps the power of a loaded PC or even a workstation such as an SGI or a Sun, often for hours or days at a time, to produce the finished animation. The costs for 3-D work, in terms of both hours and money, are substantially greater than 2-D work. But 3-D work is significantly more attention getting than 2-D work, and often pays for itself in impact: 3-D animation is now a staple of big-budget TV commercials as well as Hollywood features.

As a result of the hardware requirements, most multimedia teams farm out 3-D work to a specialist, who either owns the necessary equipment or has ready access to it. Although you can bring such a person and such machines into the team proper, you might find deferring that expense to be best. After all, technology gets more powerful and less expensive every year. The longer you wait for the zippiest new techniques, the less they will cost. Of course, that won't satisfy a client who's clamoring for the newest-latest, so each case should be decided on its individual merits — and budget.

3-D modeler

Because 3-D work is such an elaborate process, several specialties have arisen among the people who do it. I've already covered the 3-D animator, but before the graphics can be rendered in 3-D, they must first be modeled. In some cases, the modeling is the bulk of the 3-D appeal, especially when original "characters" are being created for the multimedia project.

The *3-D modeler* is an artist who begins the work of 3-D animation by creating the artwork as a series of storyboards. These storyboards include directions on such otherwise arcane details as which direction the light and shadows are coming from, which angle the "camera" is shooting from, and which direction the animation will be moving in. From there, the modeler will construct a series of digital "drawings" based on wire-frames — a skeletal representation of the insides of the 3-D artwork. The computer uses these skeletons as a reference point for how to fill in the rest of the artwork, which, as I've pointed out, is rendered in another process altogether.

This rendering process can take hours or even days for a computer to calculate, depending on what technique is used to render the 3-D objects and how elaborate the objects are. One of the key skills for a 3-D modeler or animator is patience, because a lot of time is spent waiting for computers to execute creative decisions.

As technology moves forward, more and more affordable software and hardware packages are available that can do 3-D work on a professional scale. At the time of this writing, the complexity of the required software and hardware for 3-D work more or less guarantees that well-paid specialists will be the ones doing 3-D work on a multimedia production. But that's rapidly changing, and although the software available for a PC or a Mac won't win any Clio awards for best special effects (at least not yet), these products are rapidly rising to the point at which they're an acceptable, sometimes even equivalent, substitute for the fabled "render farms" used by Hollywood studios.

Sound designer

Audio is almost always an integral part of a multimedia title, at least for fixed media such as CD-ROM. In the online world, audio exists in a somewhat primitive state, but it's rapidly becoming indispensable at the best Web sites. A specialist who understands the intricacies of quality audio work is always welcome on the set. This person is the *sound designer.*

Audio for multimedia almost always exists in digital form, meaning that sound data has been digitized and stored on a hard drive or CD-ROM. This takes the traditional process of sound design — microphone, tape, editing, mastering — one step further and with one more set of pitfalls. When the end user listens to the audio that the sound designer has captured, it's usually through a small, tinny-sounding set of multimedia speakers, sometimes even through the computer's built-in speakers. These speakers are incapable of playing back sound with full fidelity, and the sound designer must compose his or her work to conform to the limitations of this typical playback gear.

A specialized sound designer has a background in audio recording, obviously, but a background in music is useful, too; knowing the sonic character of instruments is a great help in recording them properly for multimedia playback. Beyond the traditional knowledge of microphones and tape decks, a multimedia sound designer must be familiar with digital audio tools. Essentially, these are hardware/software packages that accept a sound source such as a tape deck or microphone, run them through an input into the computer, digitize them onto a hard drive, and process them so that they can be used in different ways. The audio editing and processing techniques that were traditionally done with outboard processing devices and razor blades are now done in the digital domain. The sound designer must be adept not only at utilizing these tools but at optimizing the finished sound for the context in which it will be used through the multimedia content. The sound designer therefore needs a working knowledge of sample rates, file formats, bit depths, and other technical qualities that I discuss in the next chapter.

In a way, the sound designer has one of the easier jobs on the multimedia set. The tools for digital audio are more mature and evolved than many other multimedia software programs, and unlike more recent disciplines such as 3-D and digital video, the techniques for recording good sound are well established. Many software tools are available for the novice to create audio for multimedia. But capturing good sound is an art. If good sound is important to the production, a talented sound designer is a must.

The lead programmer

Also called the software engineer or chief technology officer, the *lead programmer* is, after the producer, the most important individual on the multimedia set. All the executive, financial, and creative decisions amount to nothing unless the project can be physically developed so that others can use it. If the producer is the architect of the multimedia title, the lead programmer is the chief contractor. Without this individual, no project exists.

The lead programmer enters the project when it has already moved from concept through storyboard and is now ready for actual development. The lead programmer's first responsibility is to choose the proper authoring tools with which to create the production. This is not just a matter of choosing technology. The authoring tools chosen will have a direct effect on the budget, the personnel, and the schedule. Choosing simple tools makes life easier for the rest of the crew and opens up possibilities if personnel members don't make it through the entire project — it's always easier to find emergency or fill-in help for widespread tools than it is for exotic ones. But simplified tools usually carry associated technical limitations that may crimp the intended vision of the project. More elaborate tools — meaning actual computer-language programming versus authoring — are usually more robust and able to carry off more sophisticated projects. But fewer individuals are skilled in this kind of programming, which means higher pay rates and longer personnel searches to find qualified workers.

After this crucial decision is reached, the lead programmer must ensure that the directives of the other members of the creative team can be carried out in software. That means keeping up with the most recent software revisions and versions, confirming that all of the other programmers have the right hardware/software to perform their jobs. The lead programmer also supervises their work so that the combined efforts of the programming team can mesh smoothly. Part of the challenge here is to estimate time budgets for the completion of the programming. Because different programmers have different levels of skills — especially when they're asked to work on tools that aren't completely familiar "first languages," schedules can rapidly disintegrate. The lead programmer is responsible for laying down firm foundations for expected technical goals, and making sure that they're met.

Such an individual encompasses many talents and, as a result, good lead programmers are a valuable commodity. They must be not only crack programmers themselves, but also effective communicators with the other creative forces on the team. They must be bastions of calm throughout the production process, which is more difficult than it sounds because the execution of the entire project is resting on their shoulders.

Typically, the lead programmer, as the name implies, has a group of programmers working under him or her. Although that group is often responsible for the actual number crunching, the lead programmer assumes responsibility for their work. It's a hard job but an essential one.

QA manager

Quality assurance is an important job no matter what the product, but in multimedia, this job can go on long after the public has begun using the product. For this reason, a multimedia *QA manager* is often a staff position rather than a one-shot temporary job. This is especially true in the case of an online project, in which revisions and updates happen all the time.

Quality assurance in the multimedia world takes on increased importance because a poor-quality product is not only a disappointment but can actually mess up an end-user's computer by changing around components of the computer's display, sound, or even the operating system. Rendering a user's PC useless through a flawed CD-ROM or online download process will cast a poor reflection on the project and the company that produced it. It could also result in angry phone calls at the very least — and perhaps even a lawsuit. Effective QA for a multimedia project is most essential.

The QA manager is brought into the project during the product planning. Depending on the scope of the title, the QA manager offers insights on how long effective testing on the finished product will take. A CD-ROM may take as much time to test on multiple platforms as it did to program it in the first place. For a Web site, the stakes are even higher: debugging, especially on elaborate sites with built-in databases and search engines, can go on for months, during what is called an *alpha* version and then a *beta* version. Both of these test periods are discussed in detail in Chapter 7.

The QA manager is responsible not only for supervising and testing all these versions, but also for compiling reports from the field done by other testers. This period of testing can be flexible or rigid, depending on the initial test schedule that was agreed upon earlier in the production. The "bug reports" that are compiled during this period are kept as detailed databases of known problems, and here the QA tester learns to work closely with the lead programmer.

Because the QA manager's main job is to find things that are wrong with a product, you need a certain type of individual to be effective in this position. Tenacity — with a willingness to put off satisfaction until every conceivable rock is overturned, looking for flaws — is a key quality. The second qualification is patience, because few things in life are as unappealing as an angry call from an end user who can't get the product (or his or her computer) to work. Third, good QA managers must be able to stick to their guns. Theirs is the voice that must tell the rest of the team that the work isn't ready yet — and they must stand by their conviction until the work is done.

Office manager

This isn't the sexiest job in the multimedia world. A good *office manager,* however, is not only a necessity but a godsend in this harried environment. The office manager performs the multitude of little tasks in the background that go unnoticed — until a day comes when those tasks don't get done. Then, look out.

What are these small-but-important tasks? The list that follows covers a few.

- Making sure that the programmers have enough floppy disks to pass around their work
- Knowing who to throw off of a print queue when an important printing job has to be done
- Supervising the e-mail system in and out of the office — the lifeline to the outside world
- Keeping office supplies stocked
- Coordinating messenger deliveries and courier pickups
- Keeping everyone who's working on the project, including those who aren't physically in the main work setting or office, in the loop with the proper updates that they need to get their jobs done

The office manager has a never-ending, seemingly thankless job. When you find the right office manager, marry the person — or do anything possible to keep him or her there.

An office manager typically brings in similar skills from another work environment. Many of the supervisory tasks translate well from other industries and businesses. But the particulars of multimedia production — the harried schedules, the "unique" people, the variety of required information and supplies, typically create a "ramp-up" period of acclimation for office managers from other industries. Patience is a virtue here for the rest of the team.

The two key qualities for a good multimedia office manager are organizational skills and, in the best cases, a sense of humor. Keeping on top of innumerable details is demanding work and not for the organizationally challenged. An office manager is not a receptionist, not a gopher, and not a babysitter, though this person often must play all these roles and more. In a hectic environment, the office manager's voice must be one of sanity and composure, which is why a sense of humor comes in handy.

That's nice, but we're low-budget here. . .

The roles that I've just described are fairly typical job descriptions on a fairly typical multimedia production. In a perfect world, lots of money would exist to hire lots of talented people so that the production could include all of them. But in the real world, these jobs are often combined, with two, three, or even more of them performed by the same individual. The reasons for this don't all have to do with money. And, of course, combining jobs has its pros and cons.

One reason that several of these jobs are assumed by one person is that multimedia professionals can be a multitalented lot. People with real multimedia experience in one area are usually familiar with the other areas that directly affect their main area of expertise. For example, those familiar with digital 3-D design are almost certain to have experience in traditional 2-D graphics because their new skill is actually drawn from the old. A video expert is almost certainly fluent (though not necessarily expert) in audio techniques. A C++ programming expert almost always knows something about other operating-level computer languages.

How to take advantage of these multiple skill sets is something for the multimedia producer to consider carefully. Obviously, one person doing two jobs is less expensive than two people. (At least on the surface.) But is it over the course of a long production? Tight deadlines mean pressure, and when an individual has more than one concurrent deadline, trouble is never far away. Justifying these budgetary savings at the beginning of the production may be easy, but come crunch time when the lead programmer is stuck re-sampling the audio clips instead of fixing bugs, the rest of the workflow can come to a crashing halt.

In general terms, my best advice is that you hire as many specialists as the budget and trust level allow. The budget might be a bit top-heavy at the beginning of the project, and you might have more organizational work throughout the course of the production. But many talented people can do better work than just a few, and with a release date looming, the production is almost always better off with a larger workgroup. The key people aren't overloaded with responsibility (they can occasionally even be rested and nonstressed), and unforeseen responsibilities can be assigned without placing an unfair burden on too few people.

Finding the People

Multimedia professionals truly are an uncommon breed, and more and more of them are entering the marketplace each year. This is only natural: as the industry grows, more people have access to the tools, hence more people learn the skills of their respective trades. And as the business end continues its exponential rise, the demand for these professionals rises proportionately. But who are these people and where do you find them?

The search for qualified, talented people can be a simultaneously exhilarating and frustrating process. Ironically, the pros are the same as the cons. Because multimedia skills can be learned in private, many people throughout the country (and the world) have made themselves into talented graphic designers, programmers, engineers, and so on, more or less on their own. They're everywhere: urban centers and the suburbs, college campuses, even high schools. They have no median age group; some of the best programmers are middle-aged people who have been downsized out of the corporate technology sector, whereas others are whiz kids straight out of school or even still there.

In most industries, a demonstrable professional track record is a necessity. In the multimedia world, which is still so new, many of the most talented individuals are just getting into the business. For example, some of the best graphics designers have come from the print media industry, but others who have a profound understanding of digital graphics don't have a single hard-copy credit to their name. Similarly, someone who has worked with MIDI and digital audio on a home studio/desktop setup may be more savvy in the multimedia environment than a studio engineer with years of experience on outdated analog systems.

This is not to say that you shouldn't want experience on your multimedia team. It's just a reminder that experience and skills come in all flavors in this new industry, and keeping an open mind concerning someone's potential is a key aspect of finding talent. In fact, many of the more elaborate online ventures, laden with big budgets and bigger aspirations, have actually sunk their own boats by choosing team members based on their experiences in more traditional media — television, print, radio, and so on. A TV producer might have a fine track record of successful shows, and know how to pick a team and work with it. But multimedia is a new medium, and many of the old paradigms simply don't translate as well as skills developed and honed specifically in an older and less fluid environment.

The network

As is true with so many industries, the best way to find good multimedia people is through networking. Creative types usually mingle with like-minded individuals, and in this field, even more of an "in crowd" aesthetic exists than with most.

In an industry so new as the online industry, physical and electronic gatherings are without a doubt the place to find potential collaborators. This ranges from the people you'll meet on an existing project to the "new media" gatherings now being held in virtually every U.S. city with pretentions to a new media industry presence. Online SIGs (special interest groups) and trade conventions are other good spots. The magnetism of this industry is quite striking. Besides multimedia professionals, these forums attract the curious from all other media industries, as well as writers, photographers, designers, and all manner of potential multimedia professionals. Multimedia is the buzzword of the '90s, and everyone's curious about it.

O.P.P. (Other People's Projects)

No place better exists to meet good multimedia professionals than in the obvious place of a multimedia project. Multimedia is a fluid industry in that workers aren't always on staff and are often free to pursue other opportunities when the project is finished. Even the people who are engaged on a full-time basis with a regular employer are often fluid in their approach to long-term employment. This isn't quite as mercenary as it sounds. Talented multimedia professionals are usually in big demand, depending on the geographical market, and more advantageous offers from competing ventures are unavoidable. Fortunately, the pool of entering professionals manages to fill the void, and these new workers themselves will often turn around after a few projects or months with a client. High employee turnover is characteristic of this industry.

While they are on a project, multimedia professionals are often "making their bones" — building up a portfolio of creative accomplishments that can be used for later professional advancement. Aside from some exceptions, naturally, this mindset is accepted and understood by most employers in the industry. The onus is on the employers to offer conditions and incentives that will keep good people in their workplace — quite a turnaround from the traditional model of "lifetime employment" in which the worker expects to rise in the company through merit or seniority. In this context, a worker's rise is often through multiple employers.

Therefore, when you work on a multimedia project, remember that the associates of today are the producers of tomorrow. The poor grunt whose job is to successfully debug thousands of lines of code will be a head programmer before too long, and the graphics person who's stuck compressing other people's artwork will one day grow up to be a full-fledged graphic designer (sooner rather than later, if he or she is good at it). The old cliché about being nice to the people you meet on the way up is truer here than in almost any other industry.

Becoming friendly with this core base of people is a key networking skill. Events move so quickly in the multimedia industry that, based on the success of a single project, today's small-team operation might be tomorrow's full-blown creative team. Literally. In this regard, timing is an especially important issue. Finding that small, energetic company with hungry workers is the best possible scenario.

Geography

Industrial centers of the old school are often based on fortuitous geography. Old-time power plants are usually located near rivers and waterfalls; granaries are located within easy shipping distance from farms; manufacturing plants are located where labor is cheap and plentiful. As an industry that depends on intellectual products rather than raw materials, multimedia is less reliant on geographical advantages than other industries are. In its few short years of existence, however, the multimedia industry has managed to polarize itself in a few select geographical areas. All of them are rich with multimedia projects and talent. But some are more developed than others.

As in many creative industries here in the U.S., the cardinal points of the multimedia industry are divided between a West coast hub and an East coast hub. Both are well stocked with multimedia activity. Both serve in leadership roles for their particular emphasis, whether it's technology, marketing, licensing, or pure research. But some places are more fertile grounds than others for specific multimedia disciplines, as you'll see. What follows here is a set of gross geographical generalizations. By no means are the cities mentioned below locked into a particular part of the multimedia industry. Still, even though you'll find exceptions to the rules, the following cities have built reputations for being strong in a particular area of multimedia, both in terms of business and personnel.

San Francisco Bay area

The main hub of the multimedia industry in the United States is undoubtedly the area between San Francisco Bay and San Jose, California. Here is where the phrase "Silicon Valley" was first tagged, and here is where you'll find the widest, most advanced pool of multimedia talent and activity in the world. If you want to find some of the best programmers, software engineers, interface designers, and multimedia visionaries, look no further than this area. The companies and individuals represented, especially from the software industry, read like a *Who's Who* of everything digital.

Why San Francisco? Two factors have contributed to its rise as a multimedia power, one tangible, one intangible. For the former, the entrepreneurs of Silicon Valley have made their home in this area, and as the PC business has grown, the talent pool from all over the world has gravitated here where the action is. But the intangible is that this area of central California is home to an exceptional population of individualistic, creative people — a heady mix that perfectly complements the entrepreneurs looking for forward-thinking people.

Because the multimedia industry is so entrenched here, the surrounding support networks are impressive. Many of the top universities in the area offer courses and even majors in multimedia and the digital disciplines. Innumerable workshops are held all over the Bay area each week, offering educational opportunities as well as networking opportunities. Several of the industry's most important trade shows are held in this area, including Intermedia, Multimedia Expo, and MacWorld, along with many trade shows for the online industry that need a presence in this geographical area.

New York

If San Francisco is the technological and design pole of the U.S. multimedia industry, New York is the place with the content. Many good reasons exist for this, not the least of which is that New York has a population of almost ten times the size of San Francisco. But history plays a part here as well.

New York is the hub of the publishing industry: books, magazines, and custom publishing projects. Virtually all these traditional media outlets now have at least an arm, and sometimes entire divisions, devoted to multimedia and online publishing. Until fairly recently, New York was also the hub of the television industry, and it retains a strong presence in the film and radio industries. Oh yes — it's also the financial capital of the country; Wall Street has enough money to fund many multimedia projects, especially if they're business oriented.

For these reasons, a sizable new media industry has quickly sprung up in the Big Apple, and in a kind of tribute to its California precedent, the part of Manhattan that has become home to multimedia business is called "Silicon Alley." The city of New York is making a significant investment in the multimedia industry, renovating old buildings with fiber-optic wiring and state-of-the-art communications, and offering these spaces at a discount to multimedia businesses. The city estimates that, by the end of the century, multimedia will be as important to the city's economy as the television industry.

Because New York is also a major cultural center, with museums and galleries that attract visitors from all over the world, it is also home to innumerable artists of every stripe. Naturally, many of them have turned to multimedia as an exciting new medium in which to work, although San Francisco has more designers per capita than New York. Although New York has an ample pool of talented programmers, designers, and engineers in New York by dint of sheer numbers, the strength of this multimedia market is still content and the mechanisms by which to acquire, license, and distribute it.

Los Angeles

Los Angeles is the capital of every trend imaginable, and therefore lays claim to a fast-growing multimedia industry. Because the city's economy is so deeply entrenched in the entertainment business — film, music, and television — a major movement is afoot in LA to find ways to re-purpose that content for the new media. San Francisco may have the technicians and New York may have the marketing/distribution, but Los Angeles has the properties.

Because so much established entertainment content already exists in the vaults of the Los Angeles entertainment industry, the major players in this business (the Disneys, Paramounts, Universals, and the rest) have all begun interactive divisions in an effort to capitalize on the commercial possibilities of multimedia. Trying to put themselves on the cutting edge of multimedia development, the Los Angeles entertainment industries have made numerous outreaches to the technical teams centered in San Francisco. This melding of Hollywood and Silicon Valley has been a problematic relationship. The long hours spent with caffeine and cold pizza in the darkened rooms of Silicon Valley are miles away from the swimming pools and long lunches of Beverly Hills, and no small measure of misunderstanding and sometimes even mistrust has arisen between the two industries. But that situation is already settling itself. Each side has something the other wants.

Seattle/Portland

The three-hour drive between Portland and Seattle is peppered with many digital industries, and multimedia production is no exception. Seattle and the surrounding suburban area is dominated by industry giant Microsoft, which a few years ago began in-house development of its own multimedia content, instead of simply licensing and distributing titles from other makers. A bit further south, in Ashland, you'll find game-maker Trilobyte; and in Portland, software manufacturers like Now Software. Because the population is young and technologically aware, the local school systems are a fine training ground for future multimedia professionals, and many independent production companies are located in this Pacific Northwest corridor. The talent pool is smaller than the aforementioned cities, but in terms of qualified designers, programmers, and online experts, this part of the country is well stocked.

Boston

Although Boston was the east coast hub in the early days of the PC business, it hasn't really kept up with the growth of the multimedia industry. This is puzzling, considering that some of the most talented computer professionals in the country were trained there, courtesy of places such as M.I.T. and the Ivy schools. One of the last great holdovers from the old days (less than a decade ago) is the MacWorld convention, which is still held annually in the city. Other than that and a few online companies such as BBN and Delphi, action isn't particularly swinging. At the time of this writing, and in terms of actual multimedia production, Boston is still a place you come from, not a place you end up.

Washington

Our nation's capital is the birthplace of the Internet and, historically, has been host to some of the country's finest minds in science and technology. Here you'll find one of the largest multimedia clients in the world: the U.S. government. Virtually every important government office, from the Library of Congress to the Internal Revenue Service, has multimedia or online development either already implemented or on the way. Washington is also host to some of the most cutting-edge research and development in the digital sciences.

Other areas

To be fair to the rest of the country, smaller pockets of multimedia activity are spread throughout the U.S. The area around Austin, Texas, always a creative hub, has a presence both as an academic outreach and as a neighbor of Apple Computer. A few hours drive away, Dallas is making a name for itself by hosting a goodly amount of digital research and development; companies such as nearby Texas Instruments are making that possible. In the Southeast, Atlanta is a blossoming center for content and multimedia development, courtesy of Ted Turner's media empire and the IBM Multimedia studio. Activity is also spread around the country in urban centers and the surrounding suburbs in cities such as Chicago, Minneapolis, New Orleans, and Las Vegas. In fact, you could probably find multimedia production going on in just about every sizable city in the U.S. But for the purposes of finding personnel and projects, you want to go where the markets are, and that means the population centers I've already discussed.

Finding people through the Internet

When you're looking for multimedia talent, you'll derive the most immediate satisfaction from meeting people. You know their work, you see their presentation, you get a feel for whether you can work together. But FTF (face to face) meetings are a constricted way of reaching out into a potential talent pool. The latest spin, and one that's been particularly effective for people doing multimedia online, is to find people through the Internet, especially the Web.

According to people whose job is to find multimedia professionals, going through the traditional channels of locating qualified employees, such as an ad in the Sunday newspaper, has little value. Adeo Ressi, CEO of the Myriad Agency, a Web design group in New York, put it succinctly: "You put an ad in the Times. You get a bunch of snail mail and faxes, which immediately tells me that the respondees aren't the people I'm looking for. I'm in the online business, I expect something electronic. How about a URL? I've never hired anyone who hasn't sent me a URL, either as their own home page or as an example of their work."

True, unless you're in a major multimedia development center such as San Francisco or New York, you're unlikely to see Help Wanted ads calling for page designers and 3-D animators. But all over the Web are literally millions of designers and animators. How do you find them?

One way to do it, cumbersome and time consuming as it may be, is rich with almost infinite possibility. That way is to simply canvas the Web. You follow links and go to various "Cool Site" listings until you find someone who seems to have the skills you're seeking. Canvassing the Web opens up the potential talent pool exponentially. In the vast majority of cases, you'll see a way to contact the talent that has put together the material that impressed you. From there, it's a matter of making the first e-mail contact, and after that's done, the ball is rolling.

Obviously, not everyone who contributes to a striking multimedia Web site will be personally represented by an e-mail address for direct contact. You'll have to apply some rudimentary investigative skills. For example, if a site has great-looking 3-D graphics that make you think you might be interested in the modeler, but no artist is listed, you can make intelligent guesses as to how to get in touch. Looking at the site's URL and service provider will give you good hints.

On a personal page, the domain name of the URL will usually be followed by a directory that denotes some kind of user identification, such as a slash and a tilde, followed by a username, as follows:

```
http://www.interport.net/~rgold/
```

A URL from a commercial service provider listed in this way usually implies that the directory belongs to "rgold" (the hint is in the squiggly symbol, the tilde, that proceeds the username). A bit of common sense and an educated guess tells you that if you simply take the username and flip the expression around, you might have a shot at an e-mail address — in this case, `rgold@interport.net`. Even if you don't have an easy e-mail address available, figuring it out is often just a matter of scratching the surface by one or two steps.

Why reach out over the Internet for talent in this way? Much of the reason has to do with the geography-related issues I just discussed. If you're in New York and you're looking for a programmer, you'll probably have some options, but not nearly as many as if you were looking in the San Francisco Bay area. Why not look there, too?

A multimedia want ad

Obviously, combing the Web for interesting multimedia talent is a painstaking, proactive process. It requires time and effort, and although it does afford the opportunity to be somewhat selective, the approach is somewhat haphazard. Obviously, not all the talent is on the Web, and even more obviously, searching every nook and cranny of cyberspace for potential collaborators would be impossible.

Another way to find multimedia people is by an online want ad. These are often best performed over a commercial online service, such as America Online, CompuServe, or Prodigy, because these services provide a common gathering place for online individuals, and the mechanisms for message boarding and special interest groups are already in place. A call for portfolios or resumes left in a well-visited online area can yield hundreds of responses. That's the good news. The bad news is that many of the most talented multimedia people are also the most advanced, and the most advanced multimedia people don't necessarily use commercial online services for their e-mail and Web access the way that beginners might. This method of searching reveals a large pool of prospects, but quantity isn't the same as quality.

Naturally, local organizations that do business in cities with a large multimedia presence are also a good place to scout multimedia talent, either through a Web site or a proprietary local bulletin board. For example, San Francisco has the Bay Area Multimedia Technology Alliance, which can be accessed at

```
http://mlds/www.arc.nasa.gov/form
```

Of a less specific local nature, you'll find a huge site on the Web called the "Monster Board," which can be accessed at

```
http://www.monster.com/
```

Evaluating Responses and Choosing Prospects

With any luck, a posted employment notice will generate a usable number of potential multimedia workers. These responses may not be as immediate as a want ad placed through traditional channels such as a newspaper. Not everyone checks the online postings every day, so allocating at least two weeks for response time makes sense before you make the assumption that no more responses are coming in.

The next step, of course, is e-mail contact with the potential employee. You can't assume that every multimedia professional is a capable writer, or that people express themselves best through e-mail, but this is where you'll begin to get a basic idea of whether this person is intelligent, articulate, and eager about the possibility of working on your project. Several e-mails are usually necessary before a face-to-face meeting is a good idea. In the meantime, the employer will have time to evaluate the applicant's work and make a preliminary decision as to whether that person might be an asset or a liability to the team.

What kind of person is best for a multimedia project? Obviously, talent plays a part; a designer with a good eye and a programmer with meticulous habits are always people you want on your team. But multimedia is such an unpredictable process that it takes a certain kind of person to fit in with the other certain kinds of persons who will be populating the project. I've already discussed the key qualities to seek in the different titles among multimedia professionals. But there are more.

When they are asked which quality they look for most in an aspiring employee, most producers will give you an answer that, no matter what the synonym, translates into hunger: the hunger to succeed. In most cases, multimedia is not an easy 9-to-5 job with weekends free and generous holiday time, as you'll see in just a few pages. In fact, it's not so much a job as a lifestyle, and not everyone will be up to the task, which can be daunting, especially as deadlines approach. A sense of excitement, a sense of eagerness, a sense of confidence in their own skills and confidence in their ability to intelligently improvise outside of those skills — these are what multimedia producers are looking for in potential workers. That's why so many multimedia professionals, especially in the Web business, are young people. They realize that they're forging a new medium and are eager to make their mark in it. They usually don't have families who will wonder where they are at odd hours of the night and, for better or worse, they usually don't have mortgage payments that require a fixed level of employment stability. The medium is fluid, and the people who work best in this medium are able to adapt with enthusiasm.

How can you get a sense of this from e-mail? You can't. All you can do is set the stage, as best you can, by posing good questions through the electronic correspondence. When that's done, the face-to-face interview begins. From there it's a question of the applicant's qualifications and the producer's hiring smarts.

Candidate, résumé, and portfolio: the anti-rules

Innumerable books exist on the subject of how to conduct a job interview, and many of the time-tested rules apply here as they do in other businesses. But the multimedia industry doesn't have special rules of the interview so much as it has "anti-rules." That's because this is not only a new industry, but in many ways, it represents a new paradigm in employee-worker relations and all the formalities that one associates with them. Many traditional ideas about personal appearance, work history, and portfolio offerings simply aren't valid in the multimedia world. Rather than go over the obvious qualities you want to judge (for example, whether someone bathes regularly), I take you through some of the "anti-rules" to be aware of in evaluating potential workers and their work.

Appearance

Undoubtedly, you've heard the cliché about how ties have been outlawed in Silicon Valley. As with all clichés, this has an element of truth. Many multimedia companies are headed by members of the baby boom generation who hold traditional formalities such as suits, high heels, and neckties in utter contempt. Unless the applicant will be in the public eye in the form of sales meetings and continual client contact, the multimedia business generally accepts business attire as being whatever keeps you comfortable enough to do the job. Limits exist, of course, and an employer should look askance at an applicant who seems inconversant with ideas such as clean laundry. But one of the happy new anti-rules of the multimedia business environment is that individualism is celebrated rather than looked on with suspicion. Unless an applicant's appearance sets off an alarm, or will plainly be uncomfortable for more conservative clients to deal with, appearance should not be a big issue.

Work history

Time was when an employee who skipped around various companies throughout his or her work history was viewed as unreliable, untalented, or otherwise professionally tainted. In a job market in which downsizing is viewed as a positive occurrence, these ideas are losing credibility. More important, they have little relevance in the multimedia world.

People expect talented multimedia professionals to have a wide range of credits, and almost without exception, a substantial list of former employers comes along with those credits. This is probably anti-rule #1: a lengthy client list is actually a plus rather than a minus. Naturally, spending time at the interview recounting those numerous work experiences makes sense. But here, the emphasis should be on what those relationships were like as opposed to how many there were. Can the applicant get along with other people? What sorts of personal habits (phone calls, music, smoking) might be a problem with the other members of the team? Were those prior relationships terminated because the project was finished, or for some less agreeable reason?

Training/education

Many industries expect a college degree of incoming job applicants. In some industries, the prestige of the college attended or the level of degree attained carries a special status, which, though it may be irrelevant to the day-to-day tasks of business, will still have meaning to an employer.

Unlike many industries, multimedia is a business in which a worker can be prodigiously talented and admirably experienced without formal training. As I've said before, anyone with a computer, some software, and talent can become a successful multimedia professional, so harping on formal academic achievement (still a rarity in this discipline, anyway) doesn't make sense.

If the candidate does come with formal training in multimedia, be aware that the independent academies such as art schools, technical institutes, and the like are often far more adept at putting out qualified people than traditional colleges, many of which only touch upon multimedia as part of their art or computer sciences departments. Therefore, you should look on a degree or certification from one of these schools as a plus, not a minus. Also, in many cases, these independent learning institutes specialize in a particular skill or technical application. For example, you can probably feel confident with a programmer who's been trained at M.I.T. and a designer from the Parsons School of Design, to name two of many possible superior multimedia training grounds.

The portfolio

Employers in traditional media such as magazine publishing judge a designer or artist's skills by the attractiveness of the applicant's portfolio — a collection of work that serves as a demo of the artist's talents. Factors such as an aesthetic sense, a sense of style, and a personal stamp are qualities that employers seek. But with multimedia, art doesn't stand alone. It's a backdrop for the work of numerous other talents, many of which are far removed from the simple creativity of graphic design.

Most important, employers scrutinize how an artist's style — as represented by the portfolio they display — can translate to the digital medium (specifically, the digital project they want to develop). Naturally, the best scenario is for artists to submit digital examples of their work. But if the only samples they have are in traditional media, the employer must make an intelligent judgment on how that work will translate to digital form. For example, an artist who relies on tiny brushstrokes and minute details may make a tremendous impression on paper. But will those subtleties translate to a cheap 13-inch monitor with poor resolution? An artist whose work depends on gradient shades may be working at a disadvantage in the digital realm, in which colors are often constricted to 256 shades.

Therefore, the anti-rule of portfolio evaluation is as follows: *See the work not for what it is, but for what it could be.*

Reasonable Hiring Practices and Working Conditions

One pervasive (if somewhat ugly) joke in the business goes something like this: "Multimedia is a 9-to-5 job. It starts at 9:00 on Monday and goes until 5:00 on Sunday." If this sounds a bit daunting, it probably should. When a production is in full swing, life can become rather hectic for the people working on it. A deadline is a deadline, and although most multimedia production companies are somewhat looser with worker schedules than other, more traditional businesses, that should in no way imply that the workload is casual. In fact, reality is quite the opposite. Multimedia — particularly Web business — is one of the most labor-intensive endeavors in the professional world.

You've heard the clichés about the programming jocks who live glued to their monitor screens, subsisting on Twinkies and Jolt cola, venturing out into the real world just long enough to get some sleep and some laundry done, relating to the outside world via e-mail and the occasional sticky note. Although you'll find these characters (called Cybergeeks, Microserfs, Digitheads, Otaku, and many other less savory names) in Generation X novels and between the pages of *Wired,* they do in fact exist. By no means are they typical of the larger multimedia workforce, though many employers probably wouldn't mind that. But they are indicative of the larger idea, which is that multimedia is a profession in which you've got to stay the course until the job is done. And, in this business, with all the revisions, updates, and new products always on the horizon, the job is rarely done.

According to U.S. labor laws, 40 hours is an agreed-upon standard for weekly work effort performed by a full-time staff employee. Exceeding this schedule brings, theoretically, overtime compensation into play. In the multimedia world, such timetables are nothing short of laughable. What really happens is that everyone works until the project is completed. Whatever that takes. People who employ multimedia professionals expect this. Aspiring multimedia professionals should expect it, too. Sixty and seventy hours per week is not uncommon when deadlines are approaching. Evenings and weekends free? In many cases, these are quaint notions.

How, then, do you motivate an employee who's looking at an indefinite workload? With luck, during the hiring phase you established an understanding of the realities of the day-to-day work environment. At that time, the new employee displayed a willingness to go along with the schedule when the situation calls for it. Still, when the realities of a day-into-night workload become more than occasional, keeping the employees motivated and comfortable is essential, even under these hectic conditions. How can you do this, aside from the obvious carrot of more money, which in many cases is unavailable, and in many other cases cannot possibly compensate for robbing a person of his or her life for an indefinite period of time?

One way to keep multimedia workers happy as they toil around the monitor is to be aware that their current project is consuming the bulk of their waking life. This is a time to apply what is known as the "rubber rule." That is, realize that your employees need to attend to some semblance of a life outside of the project, so cut them some slack to do that.

In a typical white-collar office, an employee is expected to put in a typical eight-hour work day. Of those eight hours, though, the actual productivity time is probably closer to five or six hours. Where does the rest of the time go? Lunch breaks, coffee breaks, cigarette breaks, personal phone calls, water cooler klatches, and the like. No employer likes to admit it, but this lost productivity is a given — part of the daily fabric of office work. In the multimedia world, the same eight hours per day are expected. But to get a true eight hours from an employee, a typical work day at the office is actually closer to 10 hours. The same breaks happen within the course of the day, but in multimedia, the clock typically doesn't stop at 5 p.m.

Even if you use the "rubber rule" and allow people to take care of their personal business while they're stuck at the office for 10 to 12 hours per day, you still have the issue of keeping them motivated and excited about this draconian schedule. How do you do it? Mostly by creating an environment that's friendly and inclusive, one that understands that people need a life, even if they don't have one during a heavy project workload.

Some ways in which many multimedia employers create such an environment include niceties that the rest of corporate America might do well to emulate. The physical environment receives primary attention: the atmosphere gets attention with ergonomic chairs and desks, appropriate lighting, and adequate equipment that allow the employees to get their jobs done without fighting physiology or technology. In addition, nurturing the collegial atmosphere of the office proper is essential. Whenever creative people are gathered together under one roof, especially in this business, you're bound to discover an element of like-mindedness and, occasionally, an element of friendly competition. This is a potentially exciting environment in which to work, and building on this is one way to get people excited about staying at the office for half of the physical day.

Ironically, in this way the cumulative several hours per day that the employees aren't performing specific work tasks become productivity of a different kind. More often than not, these hours are actually learning periods. The workers are not only learning how their co-workers operate but also are picking up tips from other skilled people. A ten-minute break spent between the art director and the animator is rarely a simple gab fest. One is watching the other, picking up information and indirect experience that helps current and future projects move along. A quick insight from one person to the other, passed as casual information during a coffee break, can easily turn into a labor-saving technique or problem work-around that passes from one department to the other. More often than not, the employer is actually the beneficiary of these casual "off" moments, both in terms of worker morale and enhanced teamwork.

Negotiating fair rates

One of the, if not *the,* most important morale builders for employees is money, which should go without saying. In this field, skilled labor, especially in the fields of programming and 3-D production, can command hundreds of dollars per hour when it's farmed out to an independent contractor. Of course, staff employees won't be making these rates, but in most cases, they know that they could be if they were working independently. How, then, do you figure out a pay scale that will be affordable to the employer and fair to the employee, something that will keep the company properly solvent and keep the workers motivated?

Before I begin to answer that question, take a look at a dilemma that faces the employer who's going to have to make these financial decisions. On the one hand, an employer wants workers who come to the project not only with talent but with experience. On the other hand, experience commands a commensurate salary. Given a choice between the two, many independent multimedia producers make a compromise, using young, hungry (read: less expensive) talent wherever possible, and experienced (read: more expensive) talent in key positions. This blend gives the employer the most range and the most options.

For example, simply by being involved in the project, a young employee, ready to build a resume/portfolio, is going to be compensated over and above the paycheck by on-the-job training. That may not be enough to keep someone motivated for the long term, but in the beginning, even a somewhat underpaid employee will understand this value. The company makes an investment of time, training, and materials to bring these young people up to a higher level of professionalism. That investment must be acknowledged, and is in large part responsible for what some industries and some employees might consider an arrangement in which talented people are not necessarily rewarded with fair market value.

Other incentives

There's no art in finding hungry people who'll work cheaply — for a time. But there is an art to keeping them reasonably contented. It's often the small incentives that help here. A few gestures of corporate good will go a long way when the hours are long and the pay is low. These needn't be grand; even something as simple as a good-quality mousepad can actually make a meaningful difference.

The thing that makes gestures such as this really work is the understanding that everyone is here because each is excited about multimedia and being a part of its creation. Anything that helps that along is a welcome addition for everyone.

For example, some employers will send their workers to trade shows and conventions as an incentive. It's a great one for workers who've just come into the field, because these shows are the best place to network and meet other people and other projects. But this incentive helps the employer, too, because the attendees will be gathering intelligence to be brought back to the office, which helps with new ideas, new products, and new contacts.

Small bonuses, at strategic points, are always welcome, and can often mean more as a gesture than as a significant renumeration. But when bonuses are small, they're sometimes better presented almost as "gifts" than they are a salary enhancement. Some of these niceties, such as a RAM upgrade, or a detachable keyboard, or a new graphics tablet, or any number of gestures such as these can have a positive affect on attitude and productivity that's well out of proportion to their relatively low cost. Like the trade show incentive, these "gifts" serve both the employer and the employee.

Even smaller in cost, but hardest to achieve and most rewarding to accomplish, is a group-wide tone of supportiveness and positive feedback. With the pressures of schedules and the nitpicky nature of what is, after all, computer programming, the tendency exists for day-to-day work assessment to be critical rather than laudatory. "Fixes" have to be made, which implies that things are somehow broken. Honest criticism of work is necessary in the flow of the project, but all too often, the accomplishments are regarded as met expectations and nothing more. It's important to let people know when they're doing a good job. It usually gives them at least the incentive to keep doing a good job, and the incentive to do even better work.

Job titles

Obviously, job titles do have meaning in the multimedia world, because responsibility for specific tasks usually resides with one or several specific individuals. But in many small-group multimedia situations, people wear a lot of hats. To the outside world, someone might be a Webmaster. But inside the site, that Webmaster is often also the graphic designer, HTML programmer, promotions director, and business contact. In the strange world of DIY multimedia, job descriptions and job titles are often relative.

In smaller situations such as these — and many of them exist — the job title is a convenient tag that depends on context, sort of a "virtual" title. The only parties who need to understand a multimedia person by these titles are potential contacts. It's understood that many Web sites and production teams are small operations with less than five people. The people inside those teams know who's responsible for what. How they present themselves to the outside world is almost completely up to them, as long as it accurately reflects their skills and/or aspirations. This is why you see a lot of business cards at multimedia trade conventions with titles such as "Digital Guru," "WebMeister," and "Programmus Maximus."

In a more populated work situation, job titles are often grown into rather than hired at the outset. Multimedia teams of middle size — a team of less than two dozen — often have creative talent that spills over from one skill to another. For example, graphic designers for the Web are often, out of necessity, skilled HTML programmers. If they come into a work environment and excel at one or the other, they may gravitate toward one title or the other. Or, if they excel at both, they may become a project supervisor. If they excel at more jobs than just these, they may become an associate or even a full producer. You need this kind of flexibility in regarding job titles with a team this size. The whole art of multimedia is to be many faceted, and perceiving people by their title can be very misleading.

Only in the larger environments will you find strict adherence to fixed job titles. That's because only a large-scale project can afford the luxury of specialists. In this context, the workers share in this luxury, by being able to ply their chosen (or hired) skill full time. It's nice if they're interested in skills outside of their responsibilities. But though they may be talented there, too, their primary job description will take up most of their day.

Employees, partners, or contractors?

Multimedia companies that develop commercial products are always hoping that they'll hit it big with their product. It can happen. In today's hyperspeed industry, tiny cottage businesses can quickly become entertainment powerhouses. Even if the firm is less dramatically profitable, you have still the question of how the profits are to be parsed out to the people that make the project possible. Will it be just a matter of a weekly or monthly salary compensation? A piece of the action? A work for hire?

Obviously, every multimedia business is different, and the people who populate it have their own individual circumstances and arrangements regarding business relationships. These need to be clearly defined whenever possible. This makes for clear expectations and responsibilities, and at least begins to defuse any possibility of misunderstandings regarding who will share the spoils in what way.

Staff employees are workers who are full or part timers who are collecting regular wages for regular work performed per the ongoing company directives. Depending on the hours they work, they are entitled to compensation that corresponds to federal and state labor laws, including tax considerations. If employee benefits such as health and dental insurance, investment plans, stock options, and the like are part of the package that the employer uses to entice or reward potential workers, the staff employees will share in this bounty.

In most cases, the designation of "employee" is enough to set forward the mindset of being solely a paid regular worker. In theory, this worker has little interest in the profitability of his/her company, outside of natural curiosity that the company is doing well enough to be successful and pay continuing wages. That means that any profit sharing, which is not a typical compensation for "mere" employees, is offered only through the largesse of the employer.

When the group is relatively small, it's not uncommon for the multimedia collaborators to share in the eventual profits from their labor. This implies that the work relation is a partnership, though the legal expression of the arrangement may be different. All kinds of partnerships and corporations work well in the multimedia industry (see Chapter 11), some geared toward long-term business associations, some merely set up for the sake of a single collaborative project. The rules of the partnership can vary greatly, depending on the relationship between the parties, the goals of the association, the inclusion of responsibilities to outside parties, and other highly variable factors. No matter what the arrangement, the basic rules should always be laid out in a legal operating agreement, which serves as the business framework for the partnership and proof of intent in case of future disputes between partners.

If partnerships are the most attached relationships in the work environment, independent contractors are the most detached. Outside multimedia talent can be hired strictly by the job, the clock, or the calendar. Though they may be hired often enough to be thought of as staff people, independent contractors are actually outside businesses that have been hired by the project. Those businesses, even if they're just one individual, are responsible for their own financial wherewithal, including tax payments.

One thing that both the producer and the workers need to be aware of while they negotiate these relationships is the question of intellectual property. So much of multimedia production is unquantifiable intellectual capital. If a staff employee comes up with a great original idea while working on an in-house project, who owns the rights to it? The person who came up with it, or the production company who was paying that person to be there to come up with such great ideas?

In these days in which copyright laws and intellectual property issues are undergoing such rapid and fundamental change, it's difficult to answer the example except in general terms. Typically, an independent contractor owns his or her intellectual capital, unless specifically signed away as part of a product or service to a client. A staff employee is assumed to be contributing intellectual capital in exchange for a job — here, the production company can make a strong case for ownership of specific intellectual properties contributed while the staffer was at work. I delve a bit deeper into these issues later in this chapter.

Working as a team

Although many arts are involved in a multimedia production, and many of the people who work on one are artists, the collaborative process of making multimedia is in many ways the antithesis of any other artform. Many of the skills may resemble the traditional model of artist as solitary creator. But even though the workers are usually performing their tasks in front of a computer monitor — usually a highly solitary, one-on-one experience — the process of multimedia is collaborative in the most unique sense of the word. It's a collaboration that is completely interactive and interdependent. Even though jobs may be happening out of chronological "sync," everything must somehow mesh in the end.

That being said, the concept of teamwork is absolutely critical to the success of any multimedia production. The people that make up the team may be very different individuals, and more attuned to the man/machine relationship in the workplace, but for the sake of the project, they have to be highly cognizant of the others around them, to coordinate work and meet the goal: the deadlines. A strong cause-and-effect relationship is at work here, and in a multimedia team environment, nobody's work is an island. In this situation, the producer is much like an orchestral conductor, and is charged with the responsibility of keeping the team synchronized and productive.

That being said, how does one pick the team? Obviously, individuals are chosen for their particular skills, and key skill sets need to co-exist in any multimedia workflow. But getting a team project to flow smoothly is much more than simply putting the right talents in the room. Consider the psychology involved: During the project, the team is more like family than officemates, and, at times, team members might even feel as if they are living together. The long hours that approach deadline days mean much time spent together. It has to be smooth.

In many cases, these teams aren't so much assigned as formed organically. Certainly, the separate talents will be brought together by the producer. But like-minded individuals who are at similar levels of expertise often will naturally gravitate toward each other. In many of these smaller workgroup situations, the team actually forms itself.

Integration and inclusion

Although everyone working on the multimedia project will have his or her own individual or small-group deadlines, these deadlines are travelstops along the way to the real goal: the project's delivery date. Not everyone needs to be intimately involved in his or her co-workers' deadlines, but a general awareness of where people are is helpful because it affects their own timetable. That's because of the interactive quality I mentioned earlier — for example, the programmer can't insert animations into the title when they don't exist yet, so completion of the programmer's deadlines is often dependent on someone else's timely delivery of deadline material.

In this context, the key responsibility for the producer, along with the project manager, is to coordinate the workflow so that all involved are on schedule — and pleased with their work. Attracting talented people is important, but making sure that they're performing to the best of their abilities is just as important. The way to do this is a deft good-cop/bad-cop routine, in which the producer is not only aware of everyone else's deadlines, but able to juggle them perfectly. The three main factors to consider in making these judgments are workload, skill sets, and personalities.

Workload

Most multimedia situations will have at least one individual whose skills are so strong that the producer would like to get as much work as possible from this direction. Ironically, the sense of appreciation that this individual gets from the production team can often inspire that person to take on additional work, because it's agreed that his or her work is the best in the house. This is a mistake for both the producer and the worker.

An overburdened workload for any one individual can quickly degrade both the quality of the work and the likelihood of reaching the deadline. When faced with multiple responsibilities, the hours get longer, the attitude gets more jaded, and the producer must exert more effort in order to get quality work; the point of diminishing returns arrives quickly when the burden of responsibility seems insurmountable or never ending.

Skill sets

Because one of the producer's big responsibilities is to attract talent to projects time and time again, it makes sense that the producer should be the one to determine where on the projects those talents should be placed. Obviously, the size, scope, and budget of the production will have great influence on who's necessary to carry it out. But in the close quarters of a small production team, it's more than a matter of who can do what. It's also a matter of how well those skills will complement the other skills that will orbit the rest of the project.

In theory, skill sets should be an absolute factor, and choosing people to fill certain responsibilities based solely on their skill sets would be an easy and effortless way to manage a project. But different strengths and weaknesses are magnified in the context of a multimedia workgroup, and these factors must be considered by the producer before choosing up teams. For example, an interface designer whose forte is the flexibility of his/her designs — users can interact with them in several different ways — is a plus for the team, except when paired with other workers who have a more fixed approach to their work, with a signature style of graphic or layout design. Together, the results might be great work, but at what cost in misunderstanding and time lost? Skill sets are like people: in order to work together smoothly, there must be a complementary quality, which is something the producer must assess before assembling the team. This is "soft" science, to be sure, but it's essential.

Personalities

The scene is a corporate board room where a large client is making final negotiations with a hot young Web design firm. The client representative is a corporate lifer with a grey flannel suit who's used to vendors that feature the requisite 3-martini lunches and a get-to-know-you at the local golf course. The design firm's client contact is a tatooed GenX'er with a pierced septum and a torn "Eat The Rich" T-shirt. The possibility always exists that these two parties can work well together, but in general terms, the relationship has already started out on the wrong foot.

The same is true within the actual workplace. Because the project brings together the workers for such an intensive period, the cramped quarters of the work environment — no matter how large it is in physical terms — will invariably bring out a certain amount of tension, both good and bad. Personality plays a big part here, because until the project is done, co-workers are more like family than anything else. And families fight. Here, the producer delves into a judgment role that's tinged with psychology and, actually, a bit of paternalism. Pairing someone slow and methodical with someone whose best work comes in creative spurts will serve only to alienate both parties from each other. Likewise, a chatty co-worker might be a pleasant diversion to one party but a miserable daily distraction to another. It's hard for the producer to make these assessments with new personnel, but, ultimately, he or she must assume responsibility for making correct decisions, and taking action to rectify incorrect ones before they begin to degrade the workflow.

Where to work?

One of the great shifts in employment trends throughout the 1990s has been the advent of the home-based worker. Most multimedia artists have at least a workable computer setup at home, and many of them actually have full-blown rigs that are superior to what they'll find in an office because they've been upgraded and customized to specifically fit their owner's area of expertise. With the possibility of work delivery and easy professional correspondence through modem and e-mail, where should everyone work? Is an office really necessary? No, but it's a good idea.

The case for a single office

A single, centralized office has many advantages that not only make the producers feel better about the project being under control, but actually help move the workflow along. In a centralized office, it's possible to keep continual tabs on workflow and problems that arise on the fly, so that they can be defused before they become even bigger problems. A question of clarity in an office is a matter of getting up from a chair, walking over to another chair, asking the question, and (with luck) getting an answer. The same question posed from a remote location can mean a busy signal on the phone, a crossed or nondeliverable e-mail, a long file transfer over a modem as opposed to immediate producer assessment, and the possibility that the communication won't happen in a timely fashion — or at all.

When everyone is concentrated at a single location, inestimable advantages in speed, communication, and comaraderie exist. The producer has the advantage of immediate gratification to questions, attention to problems, and one-to-one dialog with the individuals in the workgroup. The workers have the advantage of daily interaction with the other cogs in the multimedia machine, which gives them a better idea of where they stand in the deadline tree and what they need to do to keep on schedule. The clients have the advantage of one-stop communication, and can get a hold of whichever individual they need to speak to in order to diffuse problems or otherwise help ensure the commissioning client's satisfaction.

Of course, not everyone chooses to work this way, especially in a Web-oriented business, in which the workers are often miles away from each other. A single office is, of course, a substantial additional expense that must be assumed by the producer. Aside from the expense, the office must become a place of refuge during the course of the project, and so the office manager should expect long-distance phone calls, empty pizza boxes, courier deliveries, and a hundred other unexpected events and moments that tinge the office with the feel of a dorm room. If you expect people to live at the office, which they often do during a production, you have to expect that their personal lives and habits will intrude upon the office environment.

The case for virtual commuting

As this book is being written, I'm sitting in a home office in lower Manhattan. The editor is reviewing materials in Indianapolis. Researchers are at work in Pennsylvania and New Jersey, and a graphic contributor lives down the street. All of us have coordinated our work through the telephone and through modem transfers. I've never met my publisher, who's half a country away, in a face-to-face encounter. Yet we've put together a project of this size without daily supervision or interaction. Can't the same be done with multimedia?

Of course it can, and it often is. Multimedia is such a new business that the people who have experience at it have often learned their craft while working at home — in the same solitary, one-on-one paradigm that defines digital productivity of any kind. It's possible to coordinate a multimedia project from disparate points, and there are advantages to doing so.

For one thing, many multimedia professionals are better equipped to work at home than they'll ever be at an office. A 3-D specialist, for example, will invariably own or lease the powerful hardware that's necessary for professional-level production. Not many employers will make that kind of investment, at least not on a multiple scale; that is, more than one 3-D animator. This is one reason that independent contractors can command the wages that they do. They have the gear.

For another thing, home office workers will have total access to software and reference materials that are necessary to their craft. It's already on their machine and configured in such a way as to make them as productive as possible. Finally, home office workers are comfortable in their work surroundings. They have a routine that's already in place and a schedule that they've adapted to, and breaking that routine in order to try to duplicate it at a separate office location can be time-consuming at best and impossible at worst.

That being said, does it make sense to allow the workers to "phone" their work in? The only answer here must be based on two qualifications: trust and experience. The producer needs to trust in the worker's productivity without daily, hands-on supervision, and trust like that rarely happens without prior experience. It shouldn't surprise the employer that the workers would rather be at home, especially in the case of an independent contractor. But on the other hand, it shouldn't surprise the worker that the employer would prefer — or insist — that the worker come in every day to the office. I can't give you a correct answer here; you'll have to decide every case on individual merit and context.

Hiring performers

Although a multimedia production depends on a core group of talented individuals working as a team, it's often desirable or necessary to bring additional talent into the mix. Some obvious examples include voice-over talent, musicians, and on-screen personalities for video. In most cases, these performers are hired on a per-job basis, though in situations in which a company has continual productions on the schedule, a staffer with talent in one or more of these areas is a good investment.

The rules for hiring performers are very different than they are for staff employees and independent multimedia contractors. For one thing, you've got legal issues to consider when someone's likeness is involved. For another, union rules exist for professionals within specific categories, such as the Screen Actors Guild, the Writer's Guild of America, the American Federation of Musicians, and many others. The rules of renumeration are already set in stone by these unions, and any ongoing compensation for the performers in the way of royalties must be carefully considered and legally bound.

How much do you pay?

Big-name movie stars, though they're usually entitled to extremely high salaries or royalty considerations, will often work for a fraction of their usual rate if they like the project enough. This can be the case for multimedia talent, too, but it isn't typical by any means. This is a new medium that only now is starting to reach out to established artistic talent taken from other media, such as film, television, and radio. The newcomers are usually looking for another revenue stream, not a magnanimous artistic statement.

What exactly are these rates? Because the medium is so new, no set rules can be used to deal specifically with multimedia, so existing rules from the other media usually apply. But this can be extremely impractical for a multimedia production. For example, experienced voice-over talent can command fees as high as $500 per hour. For a big-budget beer commercial, that's not an outlandish sum; recording a thirty-second spot doesn't take all that long.

On the other hand, a narrator on a multimedia title may have to recite and rerecord dozens or hundreds of lines of dialog, to correspond with the many different interactive branches that the title can take. At these premium prices, it's easy to see how the budget can quickly go to pot. How, then, does the producer come to a fair compensation arrangement with outside performers?

If they're sticking with the union, so are you

If the multimedia production is wealthy or ambitious enough to consider using performers that are advanced in their careers and, hence, members of a performer's union, you have no choice here; the producer must abide by the rules of the union. You need to be aware of two main unions relevant to artists. AFTRA is the American Federation of Television and Radio Artists; SAG is the Screen Actor's Guild. The primary difference between these two organizations is that the former mainly represents on-screen or on-air performing talent, whereas the latter mainly represents talent from behind the camera or console — engineers, recordists, camerapersons, and so on. There is a bit of blur between the two unions, but for the most part, the multimedia producer deals with one or the other, depending on the talent hired.

Because the multimedia industry is so new, both of these unions have come up with working arrangements for work in this new medium. These arrangements are a bit sketchy at this point in history, because a reliable working paradigm for multimedia has yet to be formulated; the medium, especially with the explosion of online multimedia, is far too fluid for fixed laws. Still, a mechanism is in place from both of these unions for their members who are involved in multimedia productions. The multimedia producer and the production's legal team have to be aware of them at the time of hiring.

One-time or ongoing use of talent

The simplest arrangement that these two unions provide for use of talent in a multimedia production, characterized by both unions as an "interactive media agreement," is an agreement for one-time or otherwise limited use of talent. This is called a "one production only," or OPO, agreement. The agreement specifies that the union-represented talent will be compensated according to union wage scales, and that the arrangement with the multimedia producer/production is limited by the number of productions for which that talent is employed. Under current OPO rules, a union member can be used in up to three separate productions at the rates specified in the OPO agreement. After that number has been passed, the producer agrees to compensate the union talent by the terms of an ongoing contract, which typically extends a guarantee of these wages to the performer for a period of several years.

Those rates, which are in flux at the time of this writing, correspond roughly to the following formulas: An AFTRA or SAG performer gets just over $500 for an eight-hour day, with extras receiving just over $100 for the same hours. Rates are charged by the half-day or full day, regardless of how much actual work is performed within that time frame. In exchange for this compensation, the multimedia producer typically receives the right to distribute the work on all existing platforms and future platforms yet to be devised. A significant exception is made for online delivery, as media titles that are distributed this way are at risk for unauthorized copying and distribution. Both unions ask for an additional payment for distribution through online or video-on-demand. Plus, the addition of the contracted performance in an additional multimedia title outside of the contracted title entails another payment, according to union rules. In addition, if a producer uses union talent in an ongoing way, the producer is required to contribute to AFTRA's or SAG's member health benefits program, which at present is almost 13 percent of the gross compensation due each performer.

The terminology here can admittedly be slippery: if a CD-ROM title spawns a sequel in which the same performer footage is used again, is it considered a new title? Similarly, what happens when a production retains its original title, yet has undergone such a radical revision that, for all intents and purposes, it's a new production? Which rules apply? When dealing with performer unions, the producer has to be aware that he or she really isn't in a position of power. Union rules must be obeyed religiously; if not, eventual trouble is sure to arise. This is why so many producers choose to rely on nonunion talent, which may be less well-known but much more controllable.

Rights and Properties

The subject of intellectual property and the corresponding copyright laws that apply to them are, at the time of this writing, very much in flux. In the age of digital media, it's possible to alter, transfer, duplicate or otherwise distribute intellectual property at the click of a button. Naturally, this has caused widespread havoc among the publishing and legal communities. All too often, it's the producers who have taken the brunt of the draconian and sometimes overly expedient rules that governing legal agencies have instituted to deal with the situation. In other words, the producer should be extremely careful in securing rights, not only for intended overt use but for future considerations as well.

Of all the laws that apply to intellectual property, the most important one to the multimedia developer is the Copyright Act. This law is intended to protect multimedia creations from unauthorized use, and affords the multimedia producer several important rights regarding the duplication and distribution of copyrighted work; the rights to prepare and distribute variations or new works based on the copyrighted material; certain performance and display rights pertaining to the work; and, of course, the right to market the work to the public.

The question here, as with any copyright issue, is ownership. Who, exactly, "owns" a piece of intellectual property? If a production team staff member comes up with the property, does it belong to the individual or to the company? What if an independent contractor comes up with the same?

Multimedia employers usually deal with potential problems such as these by including language in an initial employment contract that clearly specifies a transference of all rights to intellectual property created when "on the job." That agreement mainly applies to independent contractors, whose work is considered as "work for hire." The differences here are compelling. Under copyright law, the creator of an intellectual property work is the sole owner of that work, provided that the rights to that work have not been signed away to the hiring party. In other words, the one who created the property owns it unless he or she specifically signs the rights away. Many hiring parties will insist on an agreement such as this with independent contractors, although the specifics, as with any contract, are negotiable.

In many cases, the line between a staff employee and an independent contractor will be blurry on a multimedia production. Someone might actually come into the office every day, perform a daily workload, get paid every week, and still be only an independent contractor. What does the law say about this? Many things, unfortunately, and although the laws regarding these situations are an important thing for the multimedia producer to gain fluency in, a detailed discussion of these topics is outside the purview of this book. As the copyright and intellectual property laws continue to develop, and as more and more multimedia producers come up against situations concerning ownership and rights, guides to the legal world of multimedia will be necessary. For right now, I recommend two good books: *Software Development: A Legal Guide* by Stephen Fishman, and *The Business of Multimedia* by Nina Schulyer. Of course, no single tome is a substitute for a knowledgeable attorney, whose services are essential for any serious multimedia endeavor.

Requirements for copyright protection

Before a copyright can be claimed on any work, several qualifications must be observed before the law will recognize such a copyright claim. This is true of any type of intellectual property — film, novel, musical work, and yes, a multimedia title.

First, the work must exist in some fixed form. An idea, orally expressed, is not tangible proof of the idea's existence, and so in order to receive copyright protection, the idea must be demonstrable to a third party. In the case of a CD-ROM, this isn't a problem: after the intellectual property is committed to computer code or pressed to a disc, the idea is fixed and tangible. In the case of a Web site, the act of committing it to a hard drive should be sufficient — as long as the idea can be communicated through mechanical, as opposed to discoursive, means, the idea is fixed and, therefore, copyrightable.

Naturally, in order to receive a valid copyright, the work must be original. By that, I mean that the work may not be plagiarized or otherwise infringe upon the rights of other intellectual property holders. This can be extremely slippery territory. For example, even though "creative originality" or newness is not a requirement for a copyright, one cannot produce a work of intellectual property that's based on facts or information that exists as free information — information that's in the public domain. Simply reproducing a list of known information, such as geographical data, for example, is not an original creation, and therefore can't be copyrighted. What you might be able to copyright, however, is the presentation of the idea — what the law refers to as "independent creation doctrine." Again, these issues are highly complex, and an experienced legal mind is your best guide to navigating them successfully.

The third important qualification to be met, if a work is to be protected under copyright law, is that the work must fall under one of the categories of copyrightable materials as defined by the Copyright Act. Under this heading, you'll find the traditional intellectual materials — sound recordings, literature, motion pictures, audiovisual works, and other tangible expressions of intellectual property. The multimedia content that's under consideration for copyright protection must fall somewhere within these guidelines. Fortunately, in virtually all cases, it will.

These copyright protections extend to all those who own intellectual property. This is why multimedia producers are learning a single, effective mantra for the '90s: "make original content." Obviously, the creator of original content is, in fact, the copyright holder, and even if it always costs more in time and intellectual capital to develop original content, as opposed to buying or licensing it, the advantage is clear in the long run. In cases of using intellectual properties in a multimedia production, the rights to which clearly belong to another copyright holder, negotiations for licensing are appropriate and necessary.

Using preexisting material

U.S. copyright law does, in fact, allow for exceptions to the use of preexisting intellectual property owned by outside parties. This doctrine is called *fair use*, which is one of the stickiest concepts in all of legaldom. Fair use doctrine states that copyrighted material may be used as long as four elements of the intended use are satisfied by law.

One is the amount and sustainability of the work used; in other words, how much of the copyrighted work is ending up in the multimedia project? One recurrent example of how this law is treated can be heard in just about any rap or hip-hop record on the radio. The use of taking digital samples of other records is de rigeur here, and if only a tiny snippet is used, this might fall neatly under fair use law. But then again, it may not. A "signature" sample that clearly states to the listener who the original owner is — a famous guitar riff, a line of dialogue from a movie — may not fall under fair use. Again, this area is extremely vague under the law.

Another area that the law looks for is the nature of the previously copyrighted work — whether it can fulfill conditions stated by existing copyright law. For example, including a section of a previously published intellectual property in the multimedia production may be considered fair use as long as the courts are satisfied that this doesn't infringe upon the actual or potential copyrights of other parties. In other words, appropriating a sample from an existing hit song is clearly a question for fair use, but a sample from an unpublished song that is not yet protected under copyright laws may not be even this cut and dried.

A third area of fair use judgment is the intended use of the actual appropriated material. In other words, is the point of the appropriated material to further a commercial aim, or to offer commentary on the material itself? Satire, scholarship, and criticism are legitimate areas of fair use, whereas simply appropriating existing content for commercial gain is not. Again, this is a slippery issue, and each question is best regarded by an experienced legal counsel.

Finally, the law looks upon the effect that the re-use of the existing material will have on the marketplace for the material's original use. Simply put, if you include video footage on a CD-ROM that exists on another CD-ROM and is owned by a second party, will widespread distribution of the re-used material inhibit the chances of commercial success for the orignial copyright holder? The law tends to be strict in protecting the rights of the original owner, which is just one more reason to not only carefully consider any use of existing copyrighted material, but to repeat the mantra: make original content.

CHAPTER 5

Webmastering

✦ The World Wide Web is the most dynamic, new digital medium of all, on or off the Internet, and presents unique challenges to the multimedia designer.

✦ As opposed to fixed media delivery systems, the WWW is fluid, interactive and subject to constant change at the hands of its many "authors."

✦ True multimedia capabilities are still rudimentary, but innovative programming and new technology will steadily improve the standard of integrated, real time play.

✦ A Web site is an ongoing process, not a finished project — one that will demand some regular commitment from its Webmaster.

✦ ✦ ✦ ✦

Welcome to Infotopia?

By now, the World Wide Web (WWW) has gotten enough mass media attention that the average American has likely heard the phrase without knowing the experience. (Of course, you could say the same thing about a lot of people who actually have their own Web sites, but more about that later. . .) It has been touted as everything from the replacement for all existing communications methods to the ultimate tool for demographically segmented direct marketing. It's either the birth of something as big as television, or something as fleeting as the CB radio craze of the 1970s. At the time of this writing, the truth lies somewhere in between.

Despite all the hype, the Web is not for everyone. As a collection of stored information and as a social reality, it can do more than post your billboard ad on the Information Superhighway, and its users are savvy enough to demand more . . . and more! But a certain commitment is required of a Webmaster that has no counterpart in CD-ROM or kiosk production. Many aspects of the WWW mold this reality, and they will be considered in detail later in this chapter.

What Is the Web?

The WWW is commonly referred to as the "graphical portion" of the Internet. What's really being described is that subset of computer servers and terminals hooked up to the rest of the Internet that store and/or access files coded in the HTML format. HTML, which stands for HyperText Markup Language, is a very accessible programming language that allows hypertextual links between files on one server or many, which the browser can call up at the click of a mouse button.

Graphics are not the sole identifying aspect of the Web, although they make the experience of browsing — also called "surfing" and "cruising" — more appealing than in older Net protocols, such as Gopher and Usenet. Actually, some users access Web documents using only a text-based browser, such as Lynx. They cannot fully take advantage of the multimedia elements displayed on the over 30 million documents currently known as the Web, but much of the Web's content is information (read: text) based, and graphics don't always matter much to some sites.

What truly sets the Web apart from all other online protocols is not any one newfangled multimedia property, but rather its hypertext feature. All media elements are present, and generally of higher quality, in fixed forms of interactive multimedia. However, the global aspect of the Web's indigenous HTTP/HTML programming link-ups makes the Web at any time a sprawling but singular document, produced by a multitude of blinkered authors, each only partially aware of all the others. This takes the ease of a self-contained, hypertexted CD-ROM product and marries it to a real-world, global context — which, in many ways, is not completely knowable. The HTTP referred to here stands for HyperText Transfer Protocol, the overriding code format for linked information.

Why a Web Site?

One of the best parts of producing for the Web comes from being able to know, through automatic reports and direct communications with site visitors, how your message is getting across to your users. This usage, particular to the Web, plays a role in the continuing experience of being a Webmaster — the individual(s) who actually run the site. Accesses by users are broken down into "hits" by the number-crunchers, on a day-to-day basis. The issue, however, is not merely that your site is being visited by any number of people, but also that you need to know their reactions. Organic "growth" metaphors are hard to resist in trying to describe this incremental process. You must take into account that people who install Web home pages add to and adapt their material according to the response they get. Their sites can eventually incorporate material donated by total strangers; they can shift focus in response to feedback, or deliberately link up with a series of other Web pages to form a "ring," separate from all other hypertextual round-robins. Finally, during the overall development of their home pages, some can leave the dominating constraints of time, budget and even organizing theme of fixed multimedia presentations behind in some fit of inspiration. So, building a Web site is a lot like yard work: sometimes your crabgrass can overpower your hydrangeas, or vice versa. After your home page becomes a multidocument exhibit, keeping track of your links in and out and the freshness of your material can take time, energy, and a sharp set of pruning shears.

Too Much Is Not Enough

A critical textbook on hypertextual document production was written by a database specialist named James Martin, and his background is not extraneous to the Web's imperative. "Shovelware," that *bête noir* of CD-ROM publishing, has its counterpart on the Web. This blight of unimaginative, dead-end textual sites is one extreme of the scale of WWW documents. The other ends in the database programmers' nightmare of "spaghetti code": hypertext for hypertext's sake. Without the defining limits of a simple and complete project, a post-urban sprawl of virtual back alleyways and dead-ends can threaten to exhaust and finally defeat the interest of any surfer. If you haven't been on the Web, imagine at least the hypertext in a CD-ROM. You wouldn't like pressing a link and getting nowhere, or winding up at an inappropriate document, or getting a list of links that all lead to other lists of links without any content whatsoever! These outcomes are not only possible but quite common on the Web, a useless bore to anyone with slow Internet connections, which is to say, most everyone. The recent innovation of global search mechanisms, which can pinpoint any word or phrase you choose out of the vast array of URL (Uniform Resource Locator) addresses, can ease the pain of searching for appropriate material. However, they cannot alleviate the fundamental burden of documents that are either empty, misleadingly titled, or just not coherently interlinked with any others.

Should You Do a Web Site?

Two camps of opinion are divided along the lines of appropriateness: should pre-existing publications be repurposed for the Web, and if so, how and why? Web purists not only want available content to be exclusively online, but also to have live, interactive collaboration between Webmasters and users as a future possibility. The Web then will not only link itself, but will, in a way, create itself as well. More realistic (or unimaginative, if you want to be uncharitable) folks recognize that everyone, outside of the chosen few who set indigenous WWW codes and standards, will all have different backgrounds and preferences determined by their familiarity with older means of communications. Hypertexting a linear project poses an aesthetic dilemma: Will the translation take? Will the effort be worth it? Who's to judge?

You may well wonder what all this has to do with online multimedia. The short answer is: everything. Right now multimedia is not so *multi* on the Web. It is instead spotty, unreliable, not accessible by a wide audience, and often dispensed in uncoordinated, byte-sized pictorial and sonic chunks. When and if this situation changes into something that resembles classic multimedia, that event may be cataclysmically sudden or agonizingly slow. Not even the experts can predict it.

Those involved in laying out the superstructure of online media are involved in their own long-distance jam session with other free spirits who have their own ideas. At the same time, the means of delivery is a slowly evolving infrastructure shepherded by giant telecommunications conglomerates, as well as individual entrepreneurs, working in tandem or in competition. Unless you are funded by a major corporation and your target audience is made up of those with fast Pentium machines and T-1 access lines, you will have to make do with an abbreviated version of your dream site. Can you still make it worth the work and wait, for any and all visitors? Will you just be taking a shot in the dark? Or will others take potshots at you?

The bad news first

"Lost in Hyperspace" is not just a theme song for Web surfers anymore, who click around from site to site and suddenly realize they no longer know in what countries their last two host sites were located. Web fever has also taken its toll on the first wave of infatuated users and pioneering content providers. Webmasters — those who tend to the day-to-day operations of maintaining a site — may have felt slowly alienated by the steady stream of random accesses made by haphazard curiosity-seekers. They can also see mutually exclusive versions of their same type of site appear worldwide. The depressing question is, "If I can't tell these sites apart, can any of my visitors tell mine apart from the rest?"

Jennifer Kramer, the main provider and designer of online content for a small virtual video store called "The Picture Palace" (or PicPal for short), admits to having burned out just in time to greet a sea change in the makeup of online visitors and correspondents. She spent a year and a half watching prospective content providers in her husband's circle of professional contacts, one after another, decide to post online video mailorder catalogs of their own and become retailers in their spare time.

Just when she felt the most despondent about her site's ability to hold its own against an onslaught of interchangeably generic-looking and ill-prepared competition, she noticed an increase in the number and quality of spontaneous submissions by interested users. She fielded the sort of offers she had hoped for all along. By mid-'96, she began planning a live Webcast between a Brazilian film director and surfers accessing her server in Rhode Island, as well as the integration of a university student's architectural design thesis involving the renovation of old movie houses. A literature teacher even volunteered material for PicPal's weekly Newsreel, a front-page feature. Her lampoon of Disney adapting *Crime and Punishment* as a musical found an appreciative audience, and Jennifer got to take a week off from writing that particular column. However more hopeful this all made her feel, the fact remains that her workload and responsibilities will only increase as her content becomes more tailored and high-tech. PicPal will approach its second anniversary with limited multimedia capabilities, dictated by the amount of server space rented by its proprietors.

Ray E. Danen of the Los Alamos National Laboratory, on the other hand, found himself at the same time still waiting for inspiration to strike regarding his personal home page housed at New Mexico State University. He began the page as a lark, with a text-based presentation. Then he read somewhere that the key to successful online presentations is unique content. So he marched up a local mountainside to capture the Hyakutake comet on film as it passed overhead one night. Soon after, while the comet itself was still news, he found his page garnering 800 "hits" a day. (A typical image appears in Figure 5-1.) Seeing himself favorably reviewed by a Web search engine called "Webcrawler" was a pleasant surprise. However, when a link to his site was removed from a prominent spot on Yahoo!'s "what's new" list, overall response rate declined. Now Danen does not feel particularly motivated to capture a new audience or reclaim the old one, though he remains open to suggestions.

Figure 5-1: Ray Danen's own photos of the Hyakutake comet attracted lots of attention (http://web.nmsu.edu/~rdanen/).

Andrew Tokeley of New Zealand had been travelling abroad for three years when he returned home to news of the exciting new prospects of Web programming. During that passing moment of euphoria, he set up his own home page; an image from it appears in Figure 5-2. In the long run he has decided that the technology is best used for research purposes, by businesses and universities. Aside from that, he cannot see that anyone has found a use for it aside from passing entertainment. In his mind (and in many others!), the Web is an invention in search of a need to fulfill. He prefers to think that a demand should be felt before technology is marshalled to address it, but in the absence of that, he feels the Net's huge potential is bound to remain dormant for quite a while.

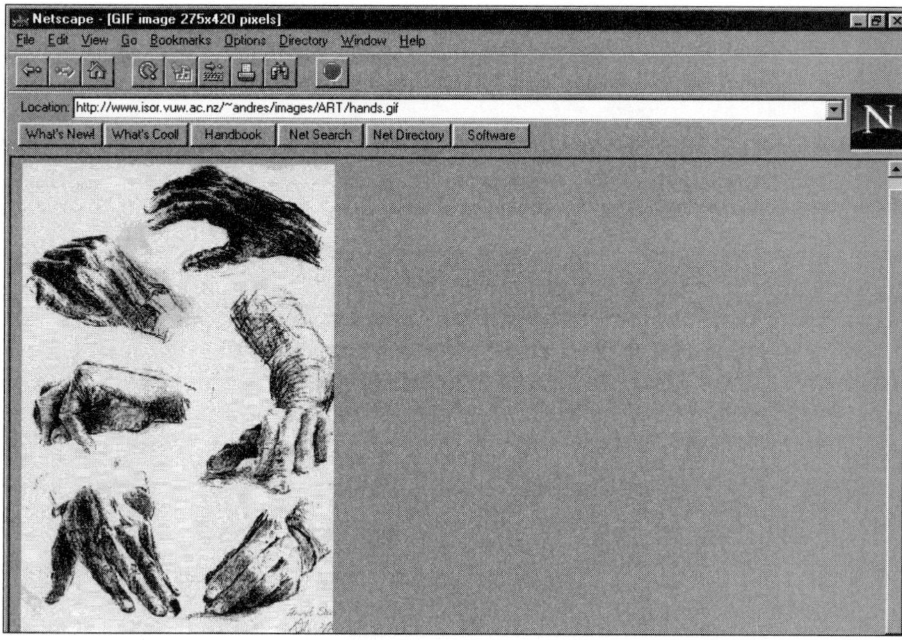

Figure 5-2: Andrew Tokeley stores his artwork in a small online gallery (http://www.isor.vuw.ac.nz/~andres/contents.html).

Even John Faherty, a multimedia bigwig at perhaps the most aggressive new technology corporation, Digital Equipment Corporation, has felt a little of the wind go out of his sails. He and his family hooked into the Net in the very early '90s. John himself began to surf the Web with version 1 of the earliest graphics-capable browser, known as Mosaic. When he first set up the Faherty family Web site (Figure 5-3), John considered it a model for other families, especially those working part-time and on a budget. There were still interesting things to do within a limited application of software and hardware, and visitors did respond positively to the family's leadership. John admits the first incarnation of their site was very amateurish, but he felt more concerned with giving the visitor a sense of a family "persona" and an inspirational experience. Surfers popped by and asked for nontechnical advice on how to set up their own pages, and John was happy to respond. Now, as his older kids have ventured off into real-life experiences such as dating, high school, and sports, the Web site has been placed in lower social priority.

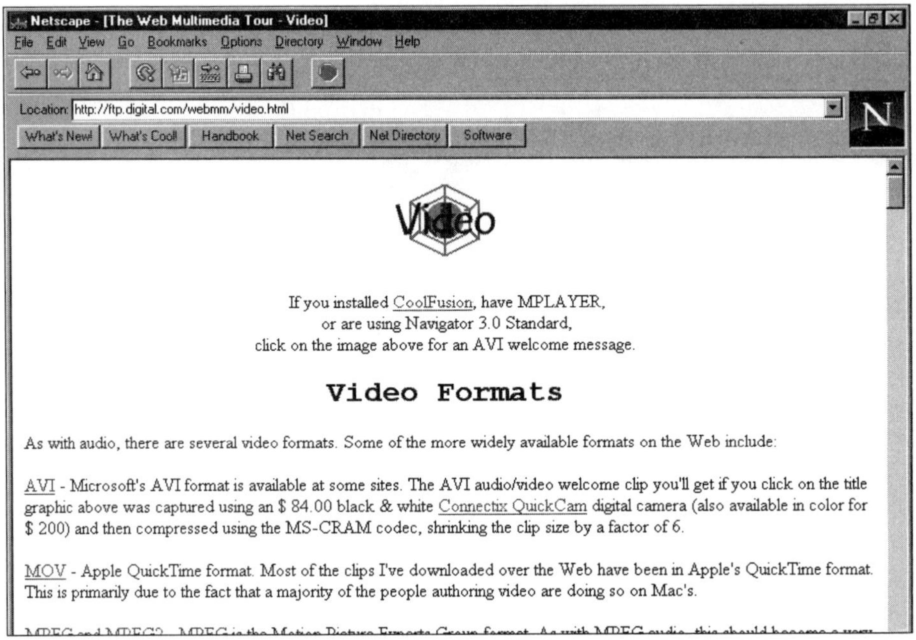

Figure 5-3: John Faherty's Multimedia Tour covers late-breaking news like the video streaming package Cool Fusion. (http://ftp.digital.com/webmm/fbegin.html).

Meanwhile, the Net no longer resembles the level playing field or integrated community in the rosy dreams of its pioneers: The Web is becoming more segmented by cliques and SIGs (special interest groups), as well as large traditional media companies bent on remaking the Web in their image. Although the Faherty's were featured in a *Newsweek* article on family involvement in the WWW, John writes this experience off as a fluke — not indicative of a strong upward trend in nonprofessional access or content provision.

Inevitably, anonymous marketers have noticed this overall sense of exhaustion and seen fit to exploit it. One mass mailing that may land in a Webmaster's e-mail box contains an apparently chatty message. The purported sender, with an AOL (America Online) address, decries the eroding sense of community on the WWW and promises to trade links as long as the recipient visits the URL address given. What greets the visitor is a three-page ad with only one link out, to another business site. In the wake of such blatant manipulation of the system and people on it, cynicism may beget cynicism from now on. The Tragedy of the Commons may strike the way it did on Usenet — that e-mail-based section of the Net now overrun by commercial cross-postings and petty flame wars. Many sites posted in the early '90s are now dormant or abandoned or dismantled; though you may find this trend hard to detect amid the thousands of new pages popping up daily.

Therein lies the lesson for a prospective Webmaster, especially if you propose to take on responsibility for the most volatile and time-consuming activity in Webdom: multimedia content provision. The basic thematic issues become more pressing when you must ask yourself not only why you try something in the first place, but whether you want to develop or improve it indefinitely. When enough Web sites appear that have all the impact and value of Burma Shave signs along the Information Superhighway, a saturation point may be reached that will permanently hobble the Web's development as a form of communications. If you do not give yourself a long-term purpose beyond an immediate goal, you risk not only alienating your visitors, but disillusioning yourself, all to the detriment of this new medium.

Now . . . the good news

Okay, you're a little bit bummed after reading these caveats. But don't plunk this book down in despair! Considering how heavy it is, you might just hurt yourself.

Not all of your visitors will be looking for a massive, perfectly rendered showboat of a site. Those may get all the press coverage, but you never hear a word about their traffic unless they break the 1-million-hits-a-day mark or make the mistake of uploading photos of some naked starlet. The Web is perfect for experimental work, or the sort of material you can't get anyone to pay you to make. You can also marshall your talents to promote a cause dear to your heart, or post information that would otherwise not be widely available. An online portfolio can double as an art gallery and interactive resume. You might even get lucky enough to land a job setting up a site for some other Webmaster so that you can have all the fun and none of the housework! If you're a neophyte, you can set up a framework and fill it in slowly, as long as you don't insult visitors' intelligence by devoting entire pages to messages such as, "I'll do blah-blah here when I get around to it." You can even put together some combination of the above as you see fit.

A happy medium is in the works at the IPL, or Internet Public Library (Figure 5-4). The hosts are a series of library science students who take a certain class pertaining to information storage. You may have heard the comparison of the entire Internet to a library, which irks the folks at IPL. To their standards, what sets apart a real library from any old rummage sale pile of books is the intelligent design of information retrieval. That takes more than arranging volumes according to the Dewey Decimal System. On the Net, this requires even more forethought. The IPL began as almost pure text, but the arrangement of pages was already broken down into the sections planned for development. In the works was a children's section with weekly stories and science lessons. An information desk would field general questions. A lounge would be reserved for library science specialists and discussion of problems specific to online information systems design.

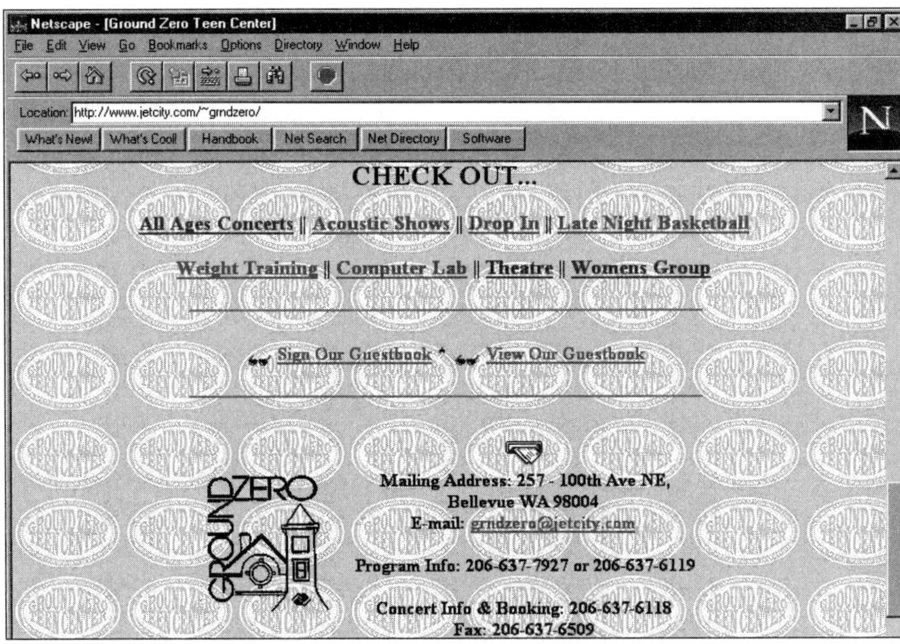

Figure 5-4: The Internet Public Library has presented online collaborations with museum sites (http://www.ipl.org/exhibit/kelsey/gallery.html).

Soon enough, the front page began to resemble a real life lobby, with gray and pink granite-textured navigational icons. A gallery began to house exhibits that supported artwork with historical background and supplemental material, with subjects ranging from American railroads to fake Egyptian artifacts. As space and funding allows, the IPL will integrate other media as long as the material is justified as an educational tool and the overall presentation keeps to the style chosen by the original designers.

Webmasters are Everywhere and Everyone

An example of a Webmaster who really lives the role is provided by fourteen-year-old Greg Morris of The Puget Sound Community School in the Pacific Northwest (whose Ground Zero site appears in Figure 5-5). The school, founded by Andrew Smallman, is run by three paid staff members and about three dozen volunteers. The school has no fixed address, and it is organized according to the principles of the homeschooling movement. Students are not required to take any particular group of subjects and they are not given grades. Children are registered as if they are taking lessons at home, but they are supervised by state-licensed educators in various settings. "Career Day" is every day, so kids are encouraged to investigate subjects that interest them and may serve them well in the future. Computers and technology are among many options, but Greg Morris, in particular, seems at home with the Net and its array of features. Spaces in three cities around the area are donated by "building coordinators," various businesses who then receive a free Web page in return, designed by the students. Morris began providing this service under Smallman's tutelage, but soon outstripped his mentor's knowledge. Eventually he even volunteered for a training session at a senior citizen home, to help the folks learn e-mail and all that newfangled stuff.

Even educational sites take on an extracurricular flavor, if the chosen site administrator has a skill or obsession he or she is willing to share. Mikael Marklund of Sweden, who is otherwise preoccupied with teaching and also with writing a book on mathematics, maintains a flyfishing site (`http://www.skelleftea.se/utb/balder/personal/ba-mma/flyfish.html`). Not only his own students but avid flyfishers around the globe have seen his pages on how to make your own lures, rodbuilding and other arcane subjects. These areas are in English, but Marklund has a separate area in Swedish devoted to writer/photographer Hans Lindman, who wrote eloquently about the sport. Visitors from as far away as Japan, Australia, and the U.S. have sent compliments and questions. Fellow fishermen also link to his site from theirs.

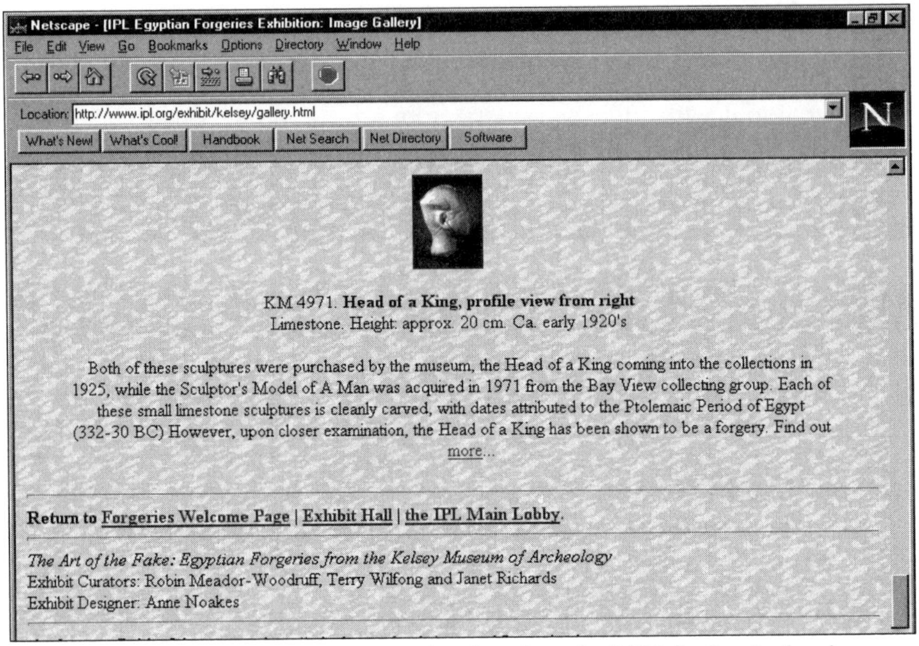

Figure 5-5: Puget Sound Community School students build Web sites for local organizations like Ground Zero Teen Center (http://www.pscs.org/~gmorris/team/).

Stepping In

The real benefit to getting your own page up and running, even before anyone solicits your expertise, is that it provides the best overall training, and provides an impetus for you to keep on your toes. Scouting the Web for new ideas or object lessons in good or bad design, scoping out the competition, and getting to test authoring software before it hits the market, will give you an edge.

Producers and developers whose experience is limited to venues not subject to limitations that are particular to current Web standards tend to make the sort of Webmasters that don't care if their site's front page takes ten minutes to download. Matt Schultz and John Boshears are two high school students who decided over lunch one day to take advantage of the 2MB of space allotted to them as subscribers to their Internet provider. They read a few books and picked up WebEdit (for HTML), PaintShop Pro (for graphics) and Internet Explorer (to test pages) for free, online. The pair have linked sites with wacky lists of purported quotes from insurance claims forms, information about Web site security issues and other material that interests them (Figure 5-6). John has reported his share of crank e-mail, but one visitor from Texas found him randomly with the Webcrawler Roulette. It turned out she is the same age and shares his interests, and they have gotten along famously since.

Playing the Skin Game

Self-publishing means self-promotion. No matter how many people you can get involved in contributing to your Web site you must remember that only the originator can determine the site's overall personality. To that end, the Webmaster picks up the slack and gets everything to gel into a coherent, predetermined design. This ongoing process of re-orientation and minor adjustments has become even more crucial during the recent spate of growth on the Web. Unless your site can be immediately identified by key visual elements standard to every page, you will risk letting people on and off

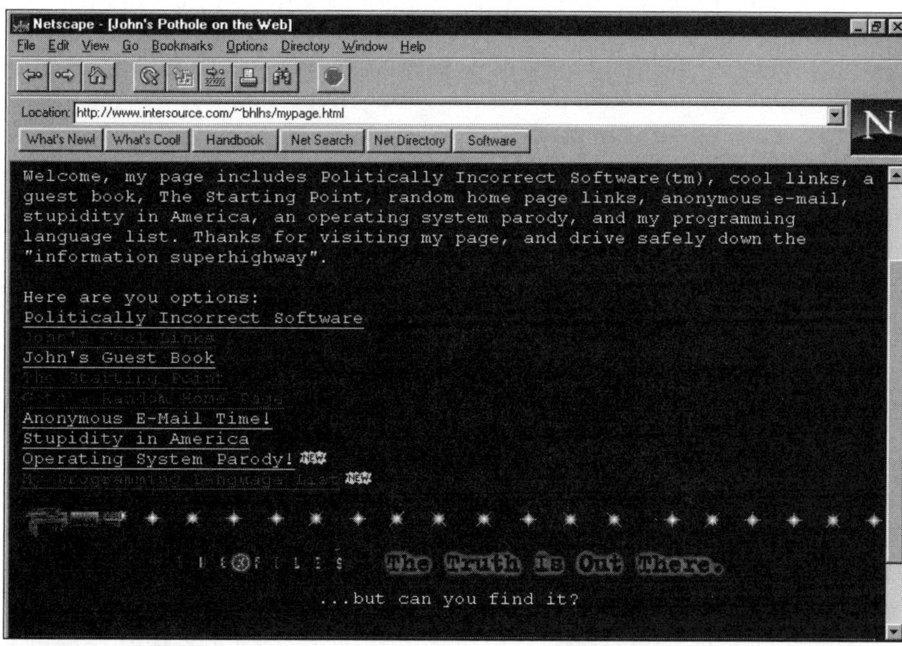

Figure 5-6: John Boshears' site warehouses his own scripts for various Web page gadgets (http://www.intersource.com/~bhlhs/mypage.html).

your server space without them ever knowing who their host was. The dirty details will follow, of course, but no collection of rules you might follow will do the work of sitting down and figuring out how you think you would best appear — and appeal — to total strangers that might have just stumbled across you and your work by accident.

There really is no precedent for this kind of encounter. It may seem like bumping into someone on the subway, but it might best be described as dialing a wrong number and finding yourself having a conversation with a total stranger. Because the Net is all connected by phone lines calling each other, it's quite literally true! Of course, you can't show yourself with all your warts highlighted in sequential thumbnail-sized pictures (just don't put it past some Webmasters). In a way, you have to reinvent yourself as your own brand name. Craven as it sounds, this is less a matter of commercialism than a repercussion of what the technology allows. You can package your most private thoughts for public consumption — whether anyone wants to see your dream diary. So, how do you want your confessions to go over in the wide awake world?

Opening yourself to feedback, maintaining some basic netiquette, and encouraging visitors to identify or empathize with you and your message may be a juggling act for you. Yet for every anonymous crank e-mail or personal diatribe that lands in your lap, there may be a new opportunity to learn about the world. If the glum opening of this chapter was meant to show anything, it was to give some hint as to the number of surfers who are a little defeated or jaded, but not quite ready to surrender. A flame may be just someone's way of testing to see whether your mail-to form is attached to a robot. Send the flamer something that doesn't look like a form letter and see what reaction you get! Threshold levels are different for everyone, so you may learn only that your material is too strong for some when you field a complaint. Do everything you can to prevent someone from landing on one of your back pages and into a nasty surprise. Then play it as it lays from there.

Your Site Is Your Brand

David Ogilvy is a name commonly invoked in relation to this issue of the new soft-sell. As the founder of the legendary marketing firm of Ogilvy & Mather, he revolutionized the way American business pursued a relationship with consumers. From its start in the post-War years, Ogilvy & Mather grew at a fabulous pace into the multinational network it is today. Of course, they have their own Web site. And, of course, it houses a selection of judicious pronouncements that apply as much to the traffic on the WWW right now as it ever did to print and television advertising. Ogilvy always said that people don't buy from clowns, and his distinctive reserve is sorely missed in an environment that now breeds self-indulgence, rude gestures and excess attitude. He always said not to treat consumers as if they're morons. And after all, we are consumers as well as producers (via HTML) and promoters (via hypertext) on the Web; should we not take the same consideration to heart?

Yet even Ogilvy admits he didn't come up with his best idea. He further confesses that he did not believe in the concept of "brand name personality" when he first ran across it in *Harvard Business Review.* Ogilvy was actually, in his youth, a slash and burn direct-mail type promoter, who cared only about immediate cash returns on his campaigns. When he finally saw the wisdom of aiming for a long-term development of a brand profile, and patiently associating a product and its producers with carefully chosen ideals and principles, he made it his life's work and the secret to his success. Your Web site will be competing for attention with a riot of "direct-mail" sites, and they will only make your responsibility to provide an alternative that more acute.

A truly distinctive site is governed by a well-developed aesthetic, but it does not pop up in full flower overnight. One recently instituted is Sin City, an umbrella site for friends and fans of magicians Penn & Teller. This is really an aggregate of two separate fan pages, plus a Usenet FAQ (list of common questions) and a repository for professional and casual writings by the pair. Collaborators reside in the U.S., England, and Germany, who each have their own pages in their respective countries. The performers were impressed enough by their fans' individual efforts to offer to pay the storage fees for all of them, so the projects were promptly relocated to one server. This collection is at once completely unforced and masterfully calculated softcore publicity for these two human logos for hire. Art and adverts are all the same to these guys, so you will find video clips of their station identification spots for Comedy Central alongside a photo tour of Penn's house with reports from the architect, and the original drafts of Teller's articles for *The Washington Post, Atlantic* and *The New Yorker.* Full-motion versions of their notorious recreation of the Kennedy assassination (with melons standing in for the President's head) demonstrate simple physics and promote their book, *How To Play With Your Food,* at the same time. If you're really in a self-reflective mood, you may notice how offline media, especially that new market of newsstand magazines devoted to personal computers, use these guys and their Web site as softcore promotion for Net access itself!

There's a fine line between mutual backwashing and empty gladhanding, but this new variation on the skin game (slang for con job) tries to open up a social setting in which content design can take place according to a new paradigm. The Web is more than an electronic Gutenberg press for the twenty-first century; it is not a one-way content-delivery system. Overall, the Net has felt some ugly growing pains in the past few years as hundreds of thousands of new users stressed it to the utmost. Growth in fits and starts will most likely continue in the near future. We all have to keep each other entertained and in good spirits while we tend to the often tedious chore of testing the Web's constant stream of updated hardware, software and system protocols.

Choose or Lose

The crucial challenge for the Web designer is to balance the tradeoff of bandwidth and standards of quality. The term bandwidth refers to the total capability of the Net and its components to allow a flow of information — not just your individual computer or your access provider. Only so much information can travel at any given time through the phone lines, but more traffic on those lines makes a slow job even more boring.

A Web site is not accessed through local memory as a CD-ROM would be. The protocols of software/hardware make it so that you reach a server — the hardware that "houses" Web sites — through a relay of phone lines rooted at your access provider. When it arrives at your site destination, your browser must request every single element on the page residing on that server — first the text, then each picture file one by one. If you access a media file, your browser must cache it on your system, then retrieve a playback screen. Only after you press "play" on that screen will it actually let you see or hear the final product. Even pages that contain too much text will overload your browser and kick you out of the program or even off your Internet provider account. Larger sites at massive corporate servers can store entire movie trailers with soundtracks, for downloading. The average personal or small business site cannot afford to take up so much memory. Moreover, the average user could only download even a compressed file of a three-minute film with sound in the middle of the night, if at all, for reasons of traffic and bandwidth.

What follows is an outline of the media options available on the Web right now. More details will follow in separate sections on text, image and animation.

Text on the Web

The Web began as a text-based medium, when Tim Berners-Lee invented the HTML language at CERN, the particle physics lab in Geneva considered the birthplace of all Web technology. A great number of documents, especially those produced and hosted at educational (.edu) sites, are pure hypertext. A certain amount of control can be exercised over textual elements because codes exist to arrange text into lists, outlines and banner headlines. Centering, italics and other formatting niceties are also possible. Real typographic fonts are presentable only as image files, and browsers specific to an alphabet, such as Cyrillic or Kanji, cannot recognize other alphabets. Languages that use the Roman alphabet can be presented with indigenous characters, such as the umlaud or grave accent, as long as proper coding allows browsers to represent them symbolically. These languages include Icelandic, German, French and Spanish. Berners-Lee posted his own style guide online in 1995, and typically it refers only to the structure and layout of text documents. He even mentions at one point that his editor was so outdated that for a long while his own Web pages did not even include icons!

Pictures on the Web

Images were the first breakthrough on the Web, when the graphical user interface was made possible by NCSA's invention of the Mosaic browser. By 1993, this browser could be run on the major PC platforms, Mac and Windows. Mosaic is all but dead now, as it has not been developed beyond its original hypertext/image display functions. However, many Web pages still rely on this formula as the happy medium between those with the very latest beta of Netscape, and those who rely on text-based Lynx because they need the speed.

Such decorative or elaborative elements are still best presented sparingly, in a format that won't crowd the user's screen. Thumbnails or miniatures are recommended, to stand in as links to larger versions or close-ups of selected images. Layout is becoming more easily controlled with newer versions of HTML standards, and a variety of software tricks can make your illustrations load faster without rendering them unintelligible. Stills can have an interactive feel when programmed as an image map — an invisible interactive hotspot around an image — but these often must be so large (in order to be intelligible) that they take too long to load.

The “progressive” .gif (.gif being a graphic file format standing for Graphics Interchange Format, one of the electronic formats for images) is a new twist on the old standby of the static icon. Abbreviated, attention-getting motions can be introduced without placing too heavy a burden on the user’s browser. The technique involves building the .gif in layers so that it is downloaded and displayed in sections. As long as the .gif is not programmed to loop indefinitely, this can draw attention to a certain area of the screen without leaving the user wondering why the page never finishes loading. As they do for HTML editing, shareware or freeware programs can make building a progressive .gif automatic.

Animation on the Web

Online animation recalls the earliest stop-motion films from the nickelodeon era. A set of picture files are drawn upon to provide the visuals in the page. An actual online flipbook can be produced in a few ways: Perl (a specific programming language) programming can result in two kinds of animation: server push and client pull. In the former situation, the server sends continually changing information to the user (client), in the latter, the client is continually “requesting” this changing info from the server, even if he or she is unaware of it. Also, a Java script can be attached as an applet to the HTML in the page’s programming and can actually draw images on demand, rather than just loading a premade series of pictures.

Each of these tricks have their own drawbacks depending upon the strain put on the user’s computer. Certain plug-ins, or browser attachments, can make these flipbooks look much more impressive. Macromedia’s celebrated Shockwave technology has been a boon, allowing users to enjoy animated, interactive “movies” on the Web. Unfortunately, it also has a tendency to destabilize the accessing computer and browser by demanding more memory as the plug-in is loaded. Innovation has its price, and bugs are the most common side effect of evolving online software devoted to multimedia.

Sound on the Web

Streamed, real time, synchronized audio/video is not yet possible on the Web, though streamed audio is now accessible for those with a RealAudio server (explained below). Many Web pages still package their audio and video separately. Video must be compressed even within the tiny 160x120-pixel-size format. This can be accomplished with shareware tools, and you can get up to 75 percent compression (or better) without ugly picture degradation becoming too obvious.

RealAudio, which is a proprietary technique for playing "streams" of highly-compressed audio files in real time — can be used to your advantage even if you or your site hardware is not equipped with a RealAudio server. The browser and compression package are free, and the 10:1 compression ratio offered by the .ra format is unrivalled. RealAudio is not the only means of achieving live audio broadcasts, but the one thing that can be said about all these competing schemes is, they all wind up transmitting something that sounds like bad AM radio. At least the dancing bear now has a backup band. True A/V transmission is something that's still possible only on the M-Bone, an experimental transmission link that the average Web user only reads about in the news.

Dividing the Screen

Frames are an oddity. They were introduced as a means of dividing the browser's window into something akin to separate browsers. In this fashion, a user could presumably conduct two kinds of transactions at once: surfing and chatting, or logging onto a remote site while keeping the old one in view. The problem with implementation was that only the cleverest HTML programmers could make frames do anything useful enough (allow temporary note-taking in one subdivision for instance) to counterbalance the increased download time required to accommodate the piggybacked windows. Even Netscape, which instituted frames, has at this writing suspended use of that programming on their pages. Users found it disorienting when they tried to press their browser's back button to retrace a step in one subdivision, only to find themselves thrown back an entire level in their navigational history instead. Frames are of interest because they are still promising, and their inventors have pledged to go back to the drawing board.

Interactivity on the Web

Interactive programming is now done in all sorts of programming languages, including the ones typically used for ROM interfaces. The most common and simple to implement are done in Perlscript or CGIscript. Perl and CGI (Common Gateway Interface) scripts are code fragments that allow specific interactions in real time. Basically, they allow a user to deliver a message or fill out a text form online and file it so that you can retrieve the input directly from your server. The most common uses are the "mailto" or automatic e-mail collector; automated order forms, and the online demographic questionnaire. Although the hot new programming language Java is most obviously associated with the interactive application, Java is not the only platform-independent option out there. For instance, an upstart company called WorldWired announced a variation on the Tudor language licensed from Carnegie Mellon, called CT Professional and marketed as part of the Smartband Authoring System. President Dr. David Stone presents this package as an alternative that even interfaces with Windows 3.1, a still widely used operating system Java can't handle. The cross-platform language can, like Java, create WWW applications that work on the user's browser. Stone does not expect to take on the marketing heavies that now champion Java, however, but will instead reach out to the academic market.

Other difficulties are faced by Java: It is many times slower than and not as optimized as C++, which is a robust and highly-popular programming language. Additionally, Java byte codes can be stolen with the help of a cracker's technique called reverse-engineering, which means its source codes may as well be public domain until this problem is addressed. Old reliables such as C and Unix can still do the job as well, though programs written with these must be accessed and run at the server. Visual Basic can be called upon if you feel the need, but its compatibility is the most restricted: to Microsoft browsers only. Different interactions are possible, from online coloring to shoot-em-up gaming. A sort of poor man's interactivity can be had with cleverly formatted hypertext and image maps, but most users fall into one of two camps: those who want high-impact action and those who can do without it altogether. Know your audiences and try to direct them to the proper areas (low and high bandwidth) on your site from your front page.

Chat on the Web

Live chat was originally implemented as a text-only construction. At first, the Web versions could not hold a candle to the gawky, but still more responsive, versions offered by online services such as AOL. Constant, incremental improvements have by now made it possible for live chat — still text-only — to be embedded into VR (Virtual Reality) environments. In these areas on conglomerate Web sites, run by the likes of Sony, participants are represented for all to see by a chosen icon known as an "avatar." "Virtual Vegas" gained notoriety for having an interactive VR environment so taxing that you would need a top-notch Pentium with 16 megabytes of RAM just to access it! CU-SeeMe, which is a rudimentary (though still evolving) videoconferencing technology for the Web, has gotten some press coverage, and ABC even incorporated the feature into its national overnight newscast for a time. This technology is still a curiosity more than a practical option, though. The video feed is jerky, perhaps one or two frames per second, and lags behind the audio stream.

As mentioned earlier, further details along with pointers on how to learn more about this wide variety of features are forthcoming. But "first things first" calls for planning stages. Once again, bandwidth limits and the radically random nature of the Web will make your site a headache for the new user or accidental tourist, unless you take certain precautions. The following recommendations are taken from the hypertextual strategies of fixed interactive media, with some bets hedged along the way to adapt them to Web usage.

Drawing the Blueprints

The ever-present considerations of time and budget come to the fore in Web design in terms of an incremental investment over the long term. Flexibility and recognizability can be juggled only if you, a volunteer or a consultant, maintain a regular update schedule. Overall costs are determined by this requirement, which is a more taxing version of the update schedule for fixed multimedia products, over and above the start-up investment. Planning will have to be even more detailed for a project intended to undergo constant change, in order to deepen and widen your repeat visitor's next online session.

Oddly enough, the use of storyboards so common in commercial film and television production appears to be a relative novelty to interactive and online designers. The initial planning seems to be more typically along the lines of programming, with hierarchical trees and flow charts predominating. The best of both worlds would map out a visual grasp of the experience of navigating a site, in tandem with some logical progression of information, presented within a total sequence. A global hierarchy radiates from the home page while links from page to page offer a variety of means to access sections of your presentation. Finally, navigation on any individual page will depend upon programming shortcuts and responsible captioning that allow access to media or footnotes without disorienting the reader. Task flow charts are helpful in predicting how someone might navigate from any one "back" page to the home page, or from one section to another.

Some essential features

Given the current state of Web activity, some global standards of form are advised. Embedded help documents, such as a site FAQ or company profile, will help identify your work and its goals, for instance. You may need to make these accessible from every .html or master document on your site. Also, a collection of such files may branch from a separate index page, referenced at your global navigational bar or icons. Certain elements would best appear on every .html file in addition to correct coding, such as hidden or footnoted author and "last updated" notices. These items all aid in orienting the viewer at any time.

Sections of your site may be devoted to different themes or take advantage of a variety of media artifacts. The flexibility of HTML allows you to incorporate these sections into independently navigable groups according to subject matter or style. This idea is known as ring formation, and the tactic is already used to sequentially link disparate home pages that may not be given high priority on corporate search mechanisms such as Yahoo!. The programming for external rings is more sophisticated, usually originating at the programmer's site. For example, the Ringmaster at Webring hosts a number of such formations. Each is set into place with an ID, password, Ring Name and main URL address maintained on an index page at the Webring server. After prospective members of any ring fill in an online form, a program automatically indexes their home page into the collection. You may wind up planning your site or a subsection of it as part of one of these rings, or merely adapt the concept to your site's infrastructure.

Making good plans

These considerations, and many other important ones, can be hashed out with diagrams. If your resulting collection of paperwork shows anything, it will at least clearly indicate how ambitious your plans are. At this point there comes a choice between trying to do it all yourself, handing much of the work over to a professional, attracting collaborators or lowering your expectations. . . maybe a little of all of those!

A Web site team can be broken down along the lines of an editorial board, or some other press or broadcasting model. However, the pressures of tailoring a Web site and maintaining it daily, weekly, or monthly, however you choose, may well call for another breakdown. Try to isolate which services you will offer and how often they will need to be maintained according to your plans.

If you want an autobot attached to your e-mail form, so be it; if you want to provide individual answers to questions, you may want to fix a schedule you can live with and let people know when they can expect to hear from you.

An emphasis on communications will take having someone online to chat with newcomers or e-mail back a human response rather than just a canned acknowledgement. You may want to operate a bilingual or multilingual site, and will need as many knowledgeable speakers to handle incoming transmissions. If you do want a flashy front page, you'll need a "head candy" dispenser, slang for a front end clever enough to randomize elements and refresh animations and illustrations without so radically redesigning updates that regular visitors are caught offguard. If your multimedia acts as illustrations for a solid textual base, you'll need a copywriter who can update the documentation as needed. Interactive elements still require serious programming and some ingenuity. Stealing the latest (and, consequently, most common) Java script won't cut it. Databases also need to be compact, easy to access and yet rewarding to use.

Getting help

On the periphery of your plans will be means of implementing the soft-sell approach outlined above. Think towards attracting prospective online volunteers. They may not be immediately forthcoming, but at least it will help define your goals and streamline your methods to imagine the kind of visitors you would like to engage and how they might contribute. A less appreciated but most critical role is to be played by someone who may have nothing to do with your actual site.

For example, a Net Hound is someone who will network for you by arranging link trades, posting to Usenet or mailing lists as a site or group rep; and otherwise garner nontraditional publicity for your site, without alienating Netizens with unvarnished sales pitches. If you cannot do this yourself, getting someone trustworthy to stand in for you will guarantee your site an auspicious launch and continued success. The Picture Palace (Figure 5-7) operated from the beginning on the precept of offering content of specific use to educational sites. The proprietors are quick to point out that of all the Web sites devoted to their trade, PicPal is the only one linked from sites as varied as MIT and an individual's master list of art history pages. Their range of subject-oriented pages have elicited e-mail about everything from author Charles Bukowski to the proper diet for hedgehogs; and they routinely field messages in Portuguese and Spanish about their South American Cinema feature.

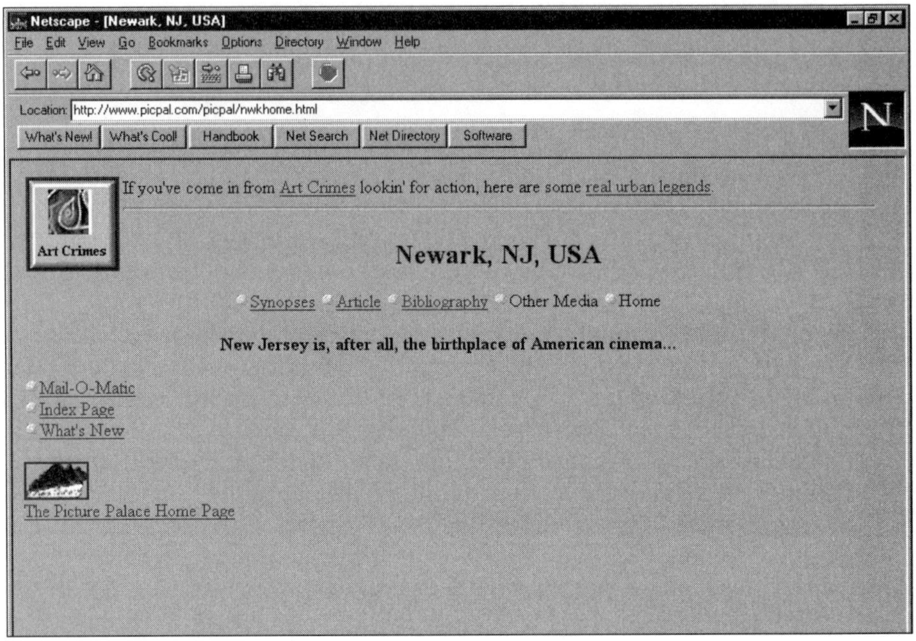

Figure 5-7: PicPal's feature on Newark, NJ covers everything from the invention of celluloid film stock and homegrown movie stars like Jerry Lewis and Ice-T to a gallery of local graffiti art (`http://www.picpal.com/picpal/`).

After you settle on a skeleton crew and an outline of your site's architecture, you may be relieved to note that you already have a motherlode of advice, tutorials, product reviews, tools and the like at your disposal. A growing number of resources offer late-breaking news on tips and technology for Web design and maintenance. The longstanding collection of online documents by relative old-timers, such as those by Tim Berners-Lee, have been supplemented even by print magazines, such as Web Developer and Web Techniques. The institution of a trade magazine called WebWeek is indicative of exactly how much activity has stepped up in just over a year since the Pre-Cambrian Explosion of early 1995. Do not limit yourself to material that promises specifically to apply to WWW authoring, however. The following two examples are of writers that have watched the Web take precedence over older forms of interactive software.

Deborah Mayhew is one name you may run across as you investigate Web media-authoring strategies. She is famous for her systems analytic approach to software interface design. She has written books and hosts workshops on the subject, and of course, she hosts a company Web page. Her methods apply cost/benefit analysis to the human factors involved in interface design. Testing for usability and efficiently weeding out design options by keeping to a set of objective, goal-oriented standards is her master plan. Information gathering during the testing phase is kept to a minimum without sacrificing applicability.

Just because your Web site is not a "product" per se does not exempt it from the testing criteria used in any other software production. Remember, Web interfaces have a stronger interpersonal aspect than ROMs or kiosks. Testing will be covered in more detail later in this chapter, but as with any other multimedia project, you will save yourself a lot of grief by pre-testing during the planning stages. Additionally, far too many surfers have been burned by sites announced with great fanfare for no apparent reason. The fact that setting up shop on the Web is so easy has only sabotaged the unprepared and the inconsiderate, leaving a bad taste in everyone's mouth. After you stretch a skin over your wireframe model, there's no reason that you can't announce minor experiments on at least an intermittent basis. If you present a new feature as an option and ask for feedback, a daily stream of users will be welcome to test and critique. Then your interface will be tailored to user needs gently over time.

Darrell Sand is known as one of the star programmers at Sun Microsystems, and his book on Web interfaces for corporate sites is actually misleadingly titled. His advice would be useful to any designer; his sense of unity and tasteful yet practical guidelines are sorely needed in this new, anarchic means of communication. He is fond of tables, an HTML formatting device not supported by all browsers, but he depends upon them to present a visual standard. This is his orientation strategy, and he applies it across top level pages, and all others down the hierarchy. All the rules for interface design in classic multimedia formats apply, but are complicated by considerations of 1) heterogeneous browsers; 2) an international audience and 3) multiple starting points on the site. His model is the printed page, which has limited appeal when viewed through a browser window shaped more like a miniature movie theater screen. Nonetheless, most users respond to these design standards as familiar, so they form a comfort zone that can serve you well.

Clever designers, whether scientifically justified or not, prey upon certain habits of seeing influenced by our reading habits. Our eyes will be caught by the largest and most colorful item on the page and advance clockwise around the viewing area from there, or read diagonals from left and then right alternately. These basic rules will hold even when specifics are altered for online consumption. Not all your options may be dictated by traditional media. Some niceties of the print trade, such as rules, bleeds and handfuls of typefaces, have either insufficient counterparts on the Web or none at all.

When you think deeply about your motivations and the interests of your prospective visitors, you may go about collecting the bits and pieces to cobble together for your site. Just be careful!

As Mom always said

Saying “please” and “thank you” is never a bad idea, after all. It’s especially called for on the Web. In cyberspace, no one can hear that you “mean well.” A grand collection of sites post loads of giveaways, free advice, outreach services, and other intangibles. This is true not only for content but also for novel uses of technology and the truly unique (they’re out there, really) subject-specific link lists. These elements can set an entrepreneurial Webmaster apart from the rest of the herd. Some designers post images for use in layouts or as backgrounds, though you will need to look for fine print about whether the author intends the offered decorations for nonprofit use only, as opposed to commercial pages. Shareware and freeware programs are uploaded to publicize the authors, or more ingenious designers anchor their programs at their sites in order to serve as the origin point for many Web link-ups. Many ways exist to acknowledge, share, benefit from or just steal elements from these pages.

The entire means of transmission is so new that issues of copyright can hang in the balance without quite being settled. For instance, HTML, as you’ll keep hearing in this chapter, is a simple programming language that doesn’t need to be compiled or debugged with any sense of urgency. So, if someone copies your format by using the View/Source option on their browser, have they infringed your copyright? Have they really siphoned off the sweat of your brow? Or can no one afford to copyright HTML, even the man who invented it in the first place? You’d be amazed at the arguments pro and con. Stealing, or “getting inspiration” is a grand tradition in art and design, after all, and the Web has simply made us all into would-be Picassos.

Information Wants to Be Free?

In a way, you will appropriate another's site as soon as you link to it as a reference or referral, but certain sites that act as databases should not be presented as your own or "brought to you by" your munificent self (hey, it's been done). Framing is a way of appropriating another site without the user actually logging directly into that remote host. If any reason exists to explain the premature fad in framing, that reason may well be the promise of corralling a user into staying. Mirroring — creating a "mirror image" of a site — takes some cooperation, so this is usually done above board. Yet outright copying is — thanks once again to the technology — almost impossible to trace if a Webmaster does not specifically relegate sensitive material to a protected directory at the server.

Online scripts, samples, browser plug-ins and other goodies are usually distributed on the honor system, with or without those handy little nag screens that may pop up and remind you to register with the distributor. You may run across an icon you like on someone's page, and it may save you a step or two to check at the bottom of that page for a credit with source link. Artists will offer their online libraries for use in exchange for such free publicity. True copyrighted images are usually plastered with the requisite warning labels.

The furthest shore of ownership of online content can be found on collaborative hypermedia sites, which accept text input from anyone and post the input automatically and permanently. You can help Clive Barker finish a short story at Kaleidospace, or keep up a running detective story called "The Doomsday Brunette." These textual automata range from the studied postmodernism of WAXweb, set up by an avant garde filmmaker on an .edu site, to the cheerfully shameless exploitation of Troma, a New Jersey film studio so notoriously cheap it will let you direct their next movie . . . as long as you do it for free and provide your own equipment! They've offered to pay $50 to each of 40 prizewinners to collaborate, two pages each, on Class of Nuke'em High IV: Battle of the Bikini Subhumanoids. That would make an 80-page script, but then they get to keep all the other submissions for free, thanks to a release clause in the directions. Whatta steal — I mean deal! No one has yet sued anyone over any of these group efforts, but it will be fun to see what happens to Troma's patchwork film script after it gets on film.

Exploitation is a matter of subtler interpretations when you have a preexisting community on the Net suddenly having to accommodate the rampant influx of corporate commercialism. A trip through the old-boy hacker network, made up of online zines such as "Phrack" and "2600," will give you a sense of the outrage felt when a Hollywood studio tried not only to employ the hacker underground as a backdrop for its newest teenybopper flick, but actually paid some design firm to post a Web site devoted to it. The company had appropriated not material per se, but rather an entire esthetic, and hackers took great exception to this commercial hegemony. In fact they made their opinion known in no uncertain terms, and the outcome of that escapade is stored for all to see. Seek and ye shall find a defaced commercial Web site home page . . .

Finally, you may find offline libraries of photos and artwork, sound effects, and movie clips that are advertised in terms of Web use, but in turn may or may not contain disclaimers involving the distinction between "home and office use" and Web posting. Matters are further complicated by the issue of public domain: If the company itself does not hold copyright, then using their material is at your discretion. Web-friendly companies such as Macromedia allow you to use their software as long as you post their logo online as well. Other than reading all the fine print and keeping on your toes, the best advice is to ask around if you are unsure about an appropriated media element. You may find life simpler if you just whip up your own from scratch.

Following Protocol

Following protocol can get confusing. The Web alone is an alphabet soup of acronyms, and additional developments such as VRML only adds more cooks to it. However, it may help to know the basics of how the machines that Websurfers use routinely work together as the whole called the Internet.

The old-fashioned method of information access was rooted in the ungainly mainframe computer. To get anything out of it you had to find a connected terminal and begin your search there. Not only was it not particularly user friendly, it was comparatively slow and inefficient. The client/server model is a standard of two-way interaction based on a certain communications protocol. Unlike older terminal/mainframe programming methods, this protocol is more flexible and less likely to crash at the site of a capitalization or some other context-specific requirements violation.

Display of the information called up is handled on the client's side, so the burden of supporting many simultaneous user queries is taken off of the server. TCP (Transmission Control Protocol) connections keep a Web system from overloading with users by applying HTTP as a stateless protocol, one that demands that every time another bit of information is needed a new connection must be made, transacted and closed down before another can begin. Now you know why you keep reading that "waiting for response" message over and over at every Web page.

This relationship worked very well in pre-Web days with Telnet. This allowed a remote user to access a library's in-house database by acting as a "virtual terminal." In the instance of a Gopher (search) access, you can harness a Gopher as a client, and make it in turn act as a client to another Gopher across the Internet. Most older forms of Net communications, including e-mail, take advantage of this increased efficiency. This virtual terminal connection is supported by TCP/IP core protocols. The digital taxonomy at use is the IP address, a four-section set of numbers that is given a name as well for conveniences sake. (So if your Internet provider is blah-blah.com, its IP address is anything from 0.0.0.0 to 255.255.255.255, even though you may never read those numbers.)

Both the numerical and the alphabetic names carry their own hierarchical information. The IP (Internet Provider) numbers outline a set of network connections, between the network and the host, that must be accessed in order to reach that host computer. Domain names are allotted with the maximum divisions applicable to an educational institution: sections refer to the host computer, the appropriate department, the institution's name, and its domain class. Because mainframes are no longer required, host computers can take the form of workstations and the high-end models of personal computer. (You can now buy an outfit server-ready for about $10,000 complete with bundled design software.)

The Web ties all these TCP/IP protocols together under the umbrella of its Hypertext Transfer Protocol, the HTTP that precedes all URL addresses on the Web. All older Net resources are addressed by their name as a prefix: WAIS, news (Usenet), gopher, telnet, ftp, and so on and accessible by hyperlinks in that fashion. A URL breaks down into a section that sets the protocol (http://), identifies the host computer (blah.blah.edu) with an optional port section (:80 or :70 in the simplest cases up to a string of UNIX code for the more obscure gophers) to guide proper connection and then a file name (/file.html or .txt, and so on) to retrieve via a GET request. “Root” refers to the default index page for a site, so even if you type only up to the path section of the address, you will get the home page traditionally marked “index.html” for consistency’s sake.

Access

Means of access are also developing in terms of convenience and ingenuity. SLIP (Serial Line Internet Protocol) or PPP (Point to Point Protocol) access provides drivers that work with TCP/IP software to hook up to a temporary IP address or a permanent one from anywhere without directly hooking into the Net. A permanent direct line of access can be leased from the phone company in three major classes, T1 being the fastest. Companies with LANs (Local Area Networks) that wish to provide constant access to the Net can feed their T1 into a service provider, then configure their operating system’s TCP/IP drivers. This is enough to make their entire LAN part of the Internet. It winds up being their choice if they want to make all the files on their network shared or if they want to leave some protected. ISDN (Integrated Services Digital Network) lines are digital and do not utilize standard modems; additionally, they may prove to be more an expense than they are worth.

Existing university and government sites often allow access and storage, as do the larger providers and online services. Smaller providers are getting into the act as well by promising to store your Web page as part of your access package. As your options widen, so does the range of features you may depend upon or, conversely, not really need. You may or may not covet a domain name of your own. You may prefer to maintain your own site but draw the line at upkeep of the server hardware for the sake of safety and economic convenience. These points will have to be negotiated with a prospective access provider. You can try the low-maintenance approach and then progress to updating your own site as you gain experience and confidence. The Kramers had to pull their site from a provider, because the people responsible for upkeep agreed to a weekly schedule and then proceeded to ignore it. PicPal’s current host allows the site’s Webmasters a certain amount of control over password-protected directories, CGI and Perl files, and the freedom to update his pages when they choose, via FTP (File Transfer Protocol, a common upload/download solution).

John Faherty sees another revolution in Net connections coming soon. In his opinion, the bandwidth problem can no longer be addressed in terms of compressing the information. Within the standards of 160x120 video windows, 16-bit RGB resolution and other audio/video components in a typical desktop, compression is an envelope that has been pushed to its limits. Adequate quality is now the watchword, and bandwidth will be supplemented by ventures such as that proposed by the MCI/British Telecom alliance. This, in combination with a new generation of speedier modems, will ease that cramped feeling you may now get online. Faherty downplays the possibility that cable operations might contribute as well. After all, the cable now laid has no means of providing two-way packet delivery — an enormous investment but all for naught in terms of the Net's client/server protocol.

Operating Systems

No longer are you required to conform to the UNIX hardware/software configuration to run a Web site. All platforms, including Mac, Win and PC clones, even Amigas, can now perform a host's duties. A server is needed even for local area networks, which act as mini-Webs without necessarily being linked to the Internet.

The original Web server was known as the CERN server for the obvious reasons. This prototype had been thought up by Tim Berners-Lee as part of his Web-specific client/server model. After prospective Webmasters got wind of the idea that they could use their own favorite machines as host computers, the demand increased for platform-specific servers. With clever enough programming, you can host a live chat at your laptop, so using a Windows compatible machine or a Mac will not present problems outside of their usual quirks.

Nowadays, manuals are sold that carry with them all the programming you need to set things up yourself. Your only real concern is to reserve sufficient memory and dedicate a backup to the machine, which will require being left on 24 hours a day. Despite the hype about "secure" servers, all the main servers have experienced their share of loopholes and bugs. As usual, the Mac is generally more reliable in terms of supporting a server, because it does not have a command shell or allow remote logins. This disables a potential hacker from coming in to the rest of the system at the usual points.

Other means to commit mischief on the Mac include causing the server to crash or attaching AppleScript commands to existing CGI scripts. Perl and CGI are the most common cause for worry, because CGI-bin and batch files can be latched onto and used to execute more insidious Perl commands that might do things such as wipe all the files off your server.

MIME (Multipurpose Internet Mail Extensions) is another crucial bit of programming that needs to be set into place to allow transfer of nontext files. This often needs to be adjusted whenever a new multimedia file extension calls for a different MIME type. Now you can imagine why someone would pay a provider to tend to server security; it's a 24-hour job! You can rent a server for as little as $75 a month, and many competitive services also throw in an FTP server to call your own, Infobot auto-responders, 24-hour technical support . . . even money-back guarantees.

Getting Hardware

If you do want to reserve complete control over your destiny, brace yourself for a long round of comparison shopping. The recommended minimum hardware requirements for running your own server include a 486 or Pentium processor, 16 MB of RAM, 5 MB of free hard disk space, and at least one 14.4 modem if you don't yet have a 28.8Kbps to dedicate. Others believe even a 56k leased line will suffer if your accesses top 20,000 a day. Setting up will be easy or hard depending on whether you pick UNIX and, if so, whether you know what you're getting into. On the other hand, some outfits are getting more automatic and even more luxurious: Dell's Power Edge comes with a Netscape server preinstalled and preconfigured. Silicon Graphics' WebFORCE Indy includes such party favors as a CCD Color Video Camera along with its 32MB of RAM; plus a GUI to guide you through configuration and administration. The Digital AlphaServer 1000 promises to be scalable and to run either Windows NT or UNIX as you see fit. O'Reilly WebSite Professional adds two encryption protocols and Cold Fusion, a feature for adding live content.

A popular setting for your server of choice could be the Windows NT, seen as a professional-level operating system. OS/2 and plain vanilla Windows are also possibilities, though the classic model is still some flavor of UNIX, such as AIX, run on a Sun Sparc or SunStation. Dozens of servers exist for these setups: the most popular being WebStar or MacHTTP for the Mac; EMWACS/ Purveyor, WebSite NT or the Netscape Communications Server for NT; IBM Internet Connection Secure Server for OS/2 and OS/2-Warp; O'Reilly WebSite or Microsoft IIS for Win95; and the old guard NCSA httpd, Apache, the still-unblemished CERN for UNIX. Even one for the AmigaOS has been spotted!

When you commit to a server, you will have to keep your nose in the air for news of holes and their patches, usually concocted by the software publishers and posted at their respective company sites. Netscape's much-touted Secure Commerce Server was found to have a seriously insufficient encryption device that had to be replaced. It employed a random number generator that turned out to be too predictable to be safe from a cracker for very long. The necessary update was made, but users with old browsers may have allowed that security hole to stay open longer than necessary. Other weaknesses have been reported in different servers; after all, these are all the work of human hands. Some have yet to display any shortcomings, but that doesn't mean they are infallible. You may not have to worry about protecting monetary transactions specifically, but the more interactive you allow your site to be the more open it may become to sabotage. In the long run, protecting your server will boil down to checking on it regularly. Something as simple as a mail form can be overstuffed by a ninja mailbot if you leave your site unattended too long.

If you do operate your own server, you will also be responsible for setting up an intelligent file hierarchy that keeps your media files, .html files, and scripts segregated into their own directory branches for safety and convenience. Log files will have to be generated as reports by appropriate software in order to keep track of accesses and traffic patterns on your homepage. Backups should be run every time the site is updated, or daily if your business is tied to homepage activities. These are all things that can be done for hire, so the decision to do them depends on whether you prefer to save the money and gain the experience or chuck all that and concentrate on your art. Finally, if you have access to a university or FreeNet account, you may be able to get such aid without having to pay much money or any at all.

Getting an Address

Registering your domain name (Web address) must be done through InterNIC or your site will have to be accessed by its numerical identification or the domain of your hired server. Right now the initial fee stands at $100 for two years' protection. Web fever and even the cause of a boyish prank or two led to a run on certain domain names that sound like registered trademark or brand names. This speculation forced Network Solutions, Inc., originally trusted by the National Science Foundation, with the responsibility for the major commercial and nonprofit domains, to require that a name be put into use within a reasonable period of time or be forfeited. Nevertheless, battles over the most generic names flare up intermittently, and many sites are differentiated from soundalikes by hyphens or a different domain extension. Some controversies will have to be settled in court according to a new law against "trademark dilution" caused by copycat registrations. You can have a hired server file for a domain name on your behalf, but if you plan to make it your business, you would do best to do a trademark search and establish that precedent, for safety's sake.

Lay It Down, Mark It Up, And Post It: A Tagging Primer

Sometimes it's easy to forget that putting a document into HTML, the Hyper Text Markup Language, actually qualifies as programming. This can be perceived as both a good thing and a bad thing. For people who are comfortable with computer programming, HTML is a simple language, easily grasped by even laypersons. But for the rest of us, programming in HTML is a fairly unnatural act.

This section should by no means be construed as a "complete" guide to HTML authoring. Excellent books are available on the subject, some of which are mentioned in the appendix at the end of this book. If you want to be a Webmaster or work with one, you'll have to know HTML. Maybe just a little, or maybe a lot. But you can't get around it. Period.

A wide range of tools exists for creating HTML documents. These range from simple text editors (which is really all you absolutely need to write HTML) to sophisticated programs that try to shield you (as much as possible) from the intimidation factor of hand-writing code. The methodology in those programs is to offer the same kind of drag-and-drop simplicity and graphical interface that computer users are accustomed to from their other applications. What's essential for the layman is often an annoyance to the expert, and vice versa, so HTML tools should be chosen on two important criteria — does it support a lot of HTML protocols and extensions, and is it comfortable to use? Luckily, many of these programs are available in demo form on the Web. You can try them out there, or, check out some of the demos that have been included on the CD-ROM that's bundled with this book.

Adobe PageMill

At the time of this writing, PageMill (for Macintosh, soon Windows) is a first-generation product that may hold major implications for the future of Web authoring. The concept here is that the interface is very much the same as a typical word processor. Rather than write HTML codes to perform such tasks as making text bold or italics, or inserting pictures and forms into the Web page, PageMill lets the user simply import text and pictures — the process of formatting it for the Web is largely automated. Besides this big news, PageMill is a true WYSIWYG program — you can actually see your finished HTML page as it's being formatted, right from the application. You don't need to open a browser as a concurrent application and evaluate the work separately.

Creating linked pages in PageMill can be as simple as dragging one page's icon on top of another page's highlighted text. Commonly used features such as text boxes, text areas, radio buttons and check boxes are also extremely simple to work. The limitations of the program are significant, though. For one thing, the program doesn't support the latest HTML protocols, which means that you can't do tables or elaborate spacing. These drawbacks are expected to be resolved by the time version 2.0 of this product arrives, which should be happening by the time this book comes out. See what I mean about being up-to-date?

HotDog, HotDog Pro

These Windows-based programs also use a familiar word processing interface, in which the user simply selects a feature and clicks it to create the desired effect. By using buttons, even an inexperienced programmer can integrate text, tables, graphics and sound on web pages.

HotDog has the advantage over PageMill of supporting all the latest HTML 3 tags, including tables. The program features a table builder that lets you construct a prototype of the page before you fill in the data, be it text, graphics or dynamic media. Pop-up menus display all the HTML attributes you might want to apply to your materials. The program is downloadable for a 30-day evaluation at `http://www.sausage.com`.

HoTMetaL, HoTMetaLPro

These programs are available for both Windows and Macintosh, and come from SoftQuad, a Canadian company with much experience in markup language. Both programs give you the ability to read and write files, and add markup tags with familiar menu bars and commands. A built-in browser lets you look at your work in progress, though you can't actually edit code when you're seeing the work in this view. The programs also have a spell checker and a thesaurus, which some people will find indispensable and others will complain that it bloats the program unnecessarily. You can download HoTMetaL (the "lite" version of the program) from several Web sites, including `http://www.sq.com`.

GoLive

This is a sophisticated HTML editor for the Macintosh, developed in Germany. It features a true WSIWYG interface, allows direct previewing of HTML pages, works with frames, can convert .gifs to "transparent" .gifs for more elaborate graphic effects, and is compatible with all Netscape plug-ins, including Shockwave. One particularly useful feature is that it allows the user to save a "gallery" of frequently used materials, which saves time when creating thematically-linked pages for a single site. A demo of the program can be found at `http://www.golive.com`.

It's Easy — Really!

Most of the standard HTML codes are in bracketed "open and close" commands that read in English much like their activity or subject. A paragraph marker is even simpler, merely a "chevroned" capital letter P — <P>. The most basic elements that make a page Web ready can be saved in your word processing program of choice as a template. You can cut and paste what you need from older pages or those written by others. Even an entire page saved from the WWW in View/Source mode can be emptied of its content and reused. If you're really lazy, you can buy or download one or many editing programs that will format text as you write it, or offer "wizards" to guide you. This is truly programming for the masses.

Especially if you are just getting your feet wet, you will likely branch off any of your media elements from a textual page. Each page must have a certain integrity, rather than just being a blind continuation of something you presume the reader has just seen, but may have not. Each page has a right and wrong way to explain to a visitor what is waiting under any glowing hyperlink. If you have been on the Web at all, you have quite likely seen the wrong way.

How Much Decoration?

Exceptions are always around to prove the rule, even on the Web. Certain subjects do not lend themselves to multimedia. One intriguing bare-bones site is known simply as "The Cemetery" (Figure 5-8). Wendel A. White of Stockton State College in New Jersey collected the last known relics of a local ghost town. It had once been home to a few dozen African Americans, relocated from the South during the turn of the century. Only a few wills, death certificates, and gravestones remain to piece together a social history of Port Republic and its fortunes. The resulting exhibit is presented as a ring of pages in a linear progression, with text and one or two illustrations per .html. No flashy compositions or decorations here.

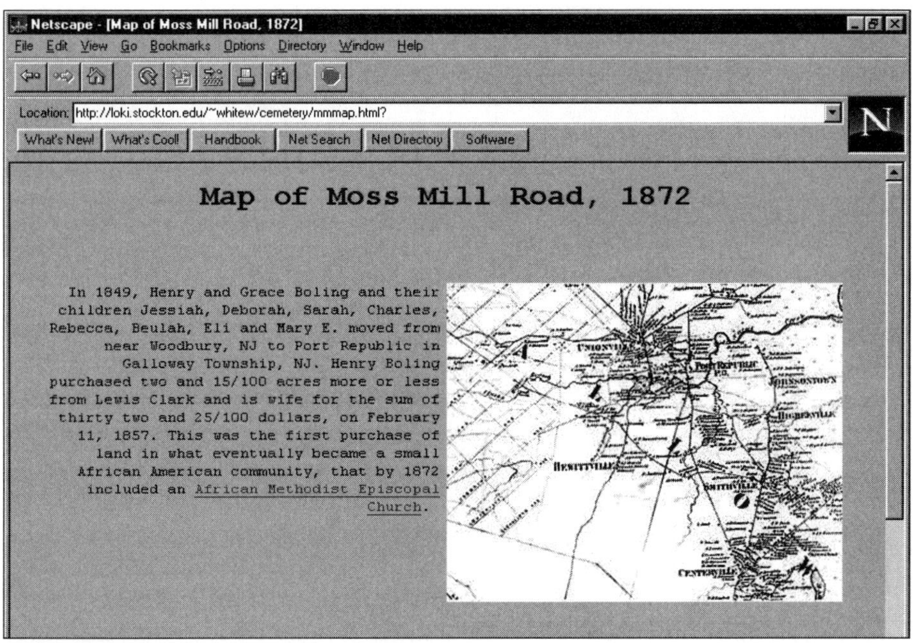

Figure 5-8: The Cemetery is part of Wendel White's ongoing project Small Towns, Black Lives (`http://loki.stockton.edu/~whitew/cemetery/cemetery.html`).

Such a compelling and rare topic deserves the dignity of an unadorned presentation. The download is a bit of a wait, but these black and white photos of worn and torn artifacts would not be intelligible after being subjected to the usual electronic compression tactics.

Personal touches can be as boring as anyone's home movies or vacation slides, but if you find something that conveys an arresting idea it won't matter too much if the element is not professional quality. An outpouring of fervent patriotism and intellectual idealism greeted the 1996 legislation to censor the Net. The shared goal of embarrassing those U.S. politicians responsible for the blunder of the failed Communications Decency Act lent a certain poignancy to the simple testimonials, recollections and mementos that soon peppered individual's Web sites. Jennifer Kramer marked off a little section of her commercial site for such a page, and illustrated it with a childhood photo of herself. The usual badly focused scrapbook shot had been taken when she was four years old, and enrolled in an early reading program at her hometown library. Cutesy in any other context, during the anti-censorship campaign it took on a political dimension that outweighed its limitations.

As if HTML weren't simple enough, several authoring tools, such as Adobe PageMill and DeltaPoint's QuickSite, promise that you won't even have to learn that! OCR (Optical Character Recognition) and other programs that translate or compile text are now being fitted with modules that automatically affix formatting codes to whatever you feed into them. This must be simple enough, considering that HTML files themselves are text-only (ASCII) documents. All you have to do is save them initially as "text only with line breaks" .txt extensions. Editing software for these files are generally called WYSIWYG, short for what you see is what you get and pronounced "wizzywig."

The bracketed commands in HTML are known collectively as tags. They generally come in pairs to open and close an instruction such as header, table or list formations. These two look almost identical, except the "close quote" or end tag contains a forward slash (/). Command elements may include attributes or internal stylistic commands. These fit into the BODY, IMAGE and other main decorative tags. The language is case-insensitive, but it would be beneficial to keep with standards as you learn. Browsers that don't recognize newer commands are supposed to ignore them, but you can never be too sure about that. The minimum number of commands, which must be present in order to be itemized by Web-crawlers and accessed by browsers, are presented here with capitalization for emphasis:

```
<html>
<head>
<TITLE>DOCUMENT TITLE</TITLE>
</head>
<body>
<H1>THIS IS THE LARGEST HEADLINE SETTING</H1>
Here's a paragraph that ends now.<P>
Plus another so you get the point.<P>
</body>
</html>
```

You will have to eventually save and post your .html or .htm files depending on whether you have software that allows four-digit extensions on files or only three. The <html> specifies that your document is in the HTML code. The <head> notifies the browser of an upcoming title command. You can use the title area to identify your site, yourself and/or what you have to offer on the page, as well as some indication of theme. As long as you don't make this item gargantuan, it will go a long way towards making it easy for people to locate the document as something that might interest them, even from a global search.

The minimum <body> tag must be present, though you can detail a lot of attribute information in that line of text, as follows:

```
<BODY BGCOLOR=#RGB BACKGROUND=[insert image command]
      TEXT=#RGB ALINK=#RGB VLINK=#RGB>.
```

Headline tags range from H1 to H6, with 1 the largest size and 6 the smallest. <P> commands insert a return in the page, though a <BR> can also affect a smaller line break. These should be used for paragraph separation, because word wrapping happens automatically otherwise. You cannot put two <P> commands in a row because only one at a time is recognized. If you use <P> with </P> you can frame a paragraph with the open and close tags and also add attribute information such as <P ALIGN=CENTER>. Three kinds of lists can be constructed: unnumbered or bulleted lists, numbered lists or definition lists. Bulleted ones are the boldest and most common:

```
<UL>
<LI>one thing
<LI>another thing
<LI>the last thing
</UL>
```

Some additional tags do their best to standardize font size throughout. Instead of using double <P> commands, the <PRE> and </PRE> tags cause the browser to overemphasize spaces, lines and tabs. A WIDTH attribute must also be entered into PRE tags. <BLOCKQUOTE> and </BLOCKQUOTE> also serve much the same purpose. <FONT=#> and </FONT> can also specify a single digit size for capital letters. Another formatting element that can have a set size is the horizontal rule or <HR>, which can also be rendered <HR SIZE=# WIDTH=#%>. Notice how the width is set in percent, whereas the height is set in a single digit number.

Other tags help vary the text for emphasis. These include <STRONG>, <EM>, and <B>, all for varying degrees of boldfaced text, <I> for italics, <TT> for fixed-width text and <CODE> for computer programming items, each of which frames the text so altered with their respective close quotes in forward slash repeat form.

Not all of these commands allow use of attributes, and some commands must be written in specially devised code so as not to interfere with the language code elements of open and close brackets. The following list is of certain punctuations and non-English letters that need specific formulations.

Making HyperLinks

Linking is the most crucial code, and creates a glowing hyperlink in your color of choice. That command format is as follows:

```
<A HREF="http://domain/path/file.extension">Hypertexted word
      or phrase</A>.
```

Remember to surround the URL address you want to link to in quotation marks or the link will be broken. Links can also be made between pages on your server, in which case you do not need the domain and path elements of the URL if both connected documents are stored in the same area on the hierarchical tree. Within a single page, linking is handled with the following variation:

```
<A NAME="anchor word fragment">Hypertexted word or phrase</
      A> instead.
```

A combination of the two is possible with

```
<A HREF="filename.extension#anchor word fragment">Hypertexted
      word or phrase</A>.
```

To link to an e-mail address, you use

```
<A HREF="mailto:address@host.domain">Person's name</A>.
```

Inline images are most simply displayed with <IMG SRC=image.extension> with the URL of the file you need. You can nest this command if you want to use a thumbnail of an image to lead to a full-sized reproduction, as so:

```
<A HREF="http://domain/path/file.extension"><IMG
      SRC=image.extension></A>.
```

Further attributes can set screen size of the image in pixels as HEIGHT=### WIDTH=###; just place these commands after the file name in the IMG SRC notation. Alignment is indicated by ALIGN=TOP, and so on with the following options available: LEFT, RIGHT, TOP, MIDDLE, or BOTTOM; and according to the surrounding text TEXTTOP, ABSMIDDLE, BASELINE, and ABSBOTTOM. To make images intelligible to those users without GUI (Graphical User Interface) browsers, ALT instructions allow you to embed a substitute caption: <IMG SRC="file.extension" ALT="Description">. To perform more efficient text wraparounds, include a <BR CLEAR=LEFT/RIGHT/ALL> depending on your layout preferences.

Tables are popular and follow this skeleton, which may be added to by rows and columns of elements:

```
<TABLE BORDER>
<TR><TD>Item 1<P></TD><TD>Item 2<P></TD></TR>
<TR><TD>Item 3<P></TD><TD>Item 4<P></TD></TR>
</TABLE>
```

In the preceding example, paragraph markers are put in, though redundant, so table-resistant browsers will at least be able to recreate the table to some extent with spacing.

These are all the basics you need for layout, though announcements are always made through Netscape and other sources about new codes. New additions to HTML 3.0 extensions promise sub and superscript commands, but these are not yet widely used. A fairly new command that is useful for Web-crawlers and other indexing mechanisms is called the meta tag. `<META name="description in keywords" content="simple sentence about host site">` after the body tag is all you need.

Now for Some Real Canned Code

If you haven't been completely befuddled or intimidated by the preceding section, you're ready to move on to CGI. CGI stands for Common Gateway Interface, and its long name indicates how it can be a security risk if it is not stored properly on your server. A CGI script is a mini-program that outputs dynamic information by sending a Web daemon to a database engine, submitting information, getting a result and then displaying it to the client. As long as you don't place related Perl scripts in your CGI-bin directory and make your CGI-bin password protected, you should be fine.

Many useful scripts have already been made in C or C++, Fortran, Unix, VB, AppleScript and most often Perl. These are openly available on the Web and do not have to be compiled. ACTION, METHOD, GET and POST are all common commands. Within the <FORM> . . . </FORM> various inputs are standardized as text, password, check box, radio, submit and reset. CHECKED means that a button or box will be activated by default. For fill-in boxes, TEXTAREA will set how large a message can be typed in according to rows and columns so you do not have someone filling up your storage space with huge documents. Current implementations of CGI are fill-out forms, even multiple independent ones in a single document; simple questionnaires with "radio-button"-type yes/no type responses; password entry forms, pull-down option menus, or scrollable lists and activated online image maps.

CGIs can also be used to create Server Side Includes or SSI scripts, to perform what is known as server "parsing." This is necessary to do housework such as create counter mechanisms and generate access logs. If you rent space on another server, SSIs may not be allowed, or may be tailored to the specific server's UNIX syntax. This sort of thing is, again, done for security reasons. An SSI creates an HTTP access file in a top-level public .html directory, and server parsing is accomplished by adding a line of code to that file, creating a new MIME type that attaches to all files on the site ending in .html.

Those who run your remote server may let you perform this operation only on a special set of .shtml or secure .html files. In either case, a command will call either a CGI program or UNIX shell command to in turn insert the results of access logging into the document as it is displayed. The Net offers various tutorials about the ins and outs of these programs, as well as in the newer Web-specific glossies at your local newsstand.

Error Codes

No matter how careful you are with your code, a visitor may see one of the following access error codes. They can be called up because the Net as a whole or your server is down, or experiencing heavy traffic at the moment — not necessarily because you did something wrong. As you surf the Web, you may run across them as well. Below are some all-too-common error codes you're likely to see as you surf the Web:

ACCESS ERROR CODES:

302 - Redirect

400 - Bad Request

401 - Authorization Required

403 - Access Forbidden

404 - Not Found

500 - Server Error

501 - Not Implemented

Hyper, Shocked, Stuttering, and Buzzed

The running joke about the Web is that it's the proverbial dancing bear; but the constant barrage of new additions, programming gizmos, and abuses of same make the "dancing" look more like stage-diving. Some old faves such as Webcams have really started to date badly, though this may have been more a function of chosen subject matter you never watch in real life, such as coffee perking or some empty company lunchroom. Even the ULM Model Railroad, a set of toy trains you could activate remotely, has been temporarily dismantled. The push towards instant response and in-depth viewing explorations has unleashed a horde of competing software items with varying levels of corporate support.

Java

Few technologies can boast a higher hype factor than the Web itself, but Java may be one of them. This simple programming language, an evolution of C++ programming, has been hailed as everything from the cause of a second Web revolution to the harbinger of a new computing standard, for which applications are replaced by smaller programs called "applets" — programmed in Java, or course. Many of these claims are drenched in hype, but the uneasy truth here is that the claims may actually be true. Java may be the first step in a new computing paradigm. But that day is far off. For now, it's an excellent way to throw some flash into your Web site.

Java is actually a group of technologies rather than a single entity. First and foremost, it's a language for creating applications — applets. Then, it's also the architecture for running these applications, and finally, it's a group of tools that allow for the creation of Java materials.

One of Java's most attractive qualities is its portablility; — that is, it can run on any machine that has the Java interpreter running. These days, that capability is built into the Web browsers themselves, which effectively makes Java a completely platform-neutral technology. Windows, Mac, SGI, Sun — it doesn't matter. If the software in use can run Java, the Java applets will perform the same on any of these machines, minus the particulars of the specific machine's modem, graphics display, and so on.

What can you do with Java? Virtually anything that you can program as an application. According to the people who designed it (a team that branched out from Sun Microsystems), Java applets can become word processors, spreadsheets, self-running animated movies, and, when bandwidth issues are solved, real-time video and VRML clips. One of the most interesting potential uses of Java is as an intelligent "agent." This means that Java applets can be programmed, for example, to search the Web for specific information or files; sort of an automated library search.

Java capability is currently offered through two main Web browsers; Netscape Navigator and Microsoft Explorer. Undoubtedly, by the time you read this, other browsers will be Java-capable. With the plethora of programmers creating Java applets and scripts, and the widespread appropriation of the resultant code by the millions of interested users on the Web, it seems likely that Java will be with us for quite a while. Whether it becomes the "next wave" that its developers envision remains to be seen. In the meantime, many books on Java programming have already flooded the market, and an active user base exists in many spots on the Web. This technology is well worth exploring — as long as you understand that the technology is still in its infancy and doesn't always work as advertised, and that not everyone who visits your site will be able to play Java material.

Shockwave

Shockwave is a technolgy developed by Macromedia, makers of popular multimedia authoring tools such as Director and Authorware. The idea here is that interactive multimedia and animations are authored as they would be for any other medium, and saved as a self-running "movie." But a Director movie is much too big to play on the Web — even the simplest presentation can be several megabytes large.

In order to counteract this problem, Macromedia devised a compression scheme called "AfterBurner," which dramatically reduces the size of the movies and makes them small enough to play in real-time on the Web. Virtually anything that you can put into a Macromedia movie — including the proprietary scripting language called "Lingo" that is a staple of Macromedia authoring — can be compressed through AfterBurner and used as a Shockwave movie.

When the end user encounters a Shockwave movie on your site, several procedures automatically go into motion. First, the browser sees that a Shockwave movie has been requested by the client, so it begins to load the Shockwave "plug-in." This accessory is loaded only when it's needed to play a Shockwave movie — otherwise, much RAM would be unneccesarily gobbled up. Macromedia recommends that at least 8 megabytes of RAM be allocated in order to see Shockwave on the Web. The reasons for that are not so much that the plug-in is large, but that no way exists to determine how big the requested movie will be. You need enough memory to play it. After the plug-in has been loaded, the Shockwave movie begins to download, just as a normal .gif or .jpeg picture would. When the movie is downloaded, the user can interact with it, just as easily as they would with a CD-ROM.

It sounds amazing, and in its way, it is. True interactive presentations are now possible on the Web in real time. Naturally, though, some caveats need to be mentioned. Obviously, having an audience with a Shockwave-capable browser is the first consideration. But in particular, the size of the file is still an important factor. Even when heavily compressed during the AfterBurner process, a serious interactive file (even a small one!) can take up dozens or hundreds of kilobytes of space. Because of this limitation, special authoring techniques for Shockwave are already making the rounds on the Web. Some basic ideas include using dramatically reduced color palettes, smaller pictures, low-res graphics and shortened sound samples.

The best Shockwave library on the Web is at the Macromedia site itself, which can be accessed at `http://www.macromedia.com`.

VRML

VRML (pronounced "ver-mul") is the most comprehensive of these novelties because it is a markup language like HTML, with its own evolving library of standards and protocols. Virtual Reality, like all 3-D modeling, will demand an attitude adjustment if you have been long acclimated to 2-D orientation and navigation. As usual, the young find that transition easier than their adult counterparts. John Faherty held a birthday party not too long ago for his youngest son, and left some authoring software running on a desktop for those who might want to amuse themselves that way. The VR program loaded was an early version of what's now called Fountain, available for free at the Caligari Website. While John's back was turned, his son and a young friend produced an environment (Figure 5-9) without training or supervision!

His explanation for this feat compares VR-building to Legos, because you connect blocks of mathematically defined space together to make structures on the 3-D stage. As far as the kids were concerned, they were doing something familiar, rather than something alien and disconcerting.

Tim Berners-Lee is as central to VRML as he was to all previous WWW standards. In 1994, CERN hosted the first international Web conference, and there Berners-Lee interested Mark Pesce, a hypermedia designer and MIT dropout, in nudging the 2-D experience of surfing towards 3-D options. By 1995, The World Wide Web Consortium had a set of standards in place, and VRML fly-bys were already operational. Currently some rivalries are building between Moving Worlds, submitted to the VRML Architecture Group by Silicon Graphics, and Microsoft's counterproposal of ActiveVRML. Will one beat out the other? Will Sun's HoloWeb or IBM's World win out after all? Will Microsoft implement its proposal in its own software regardless?

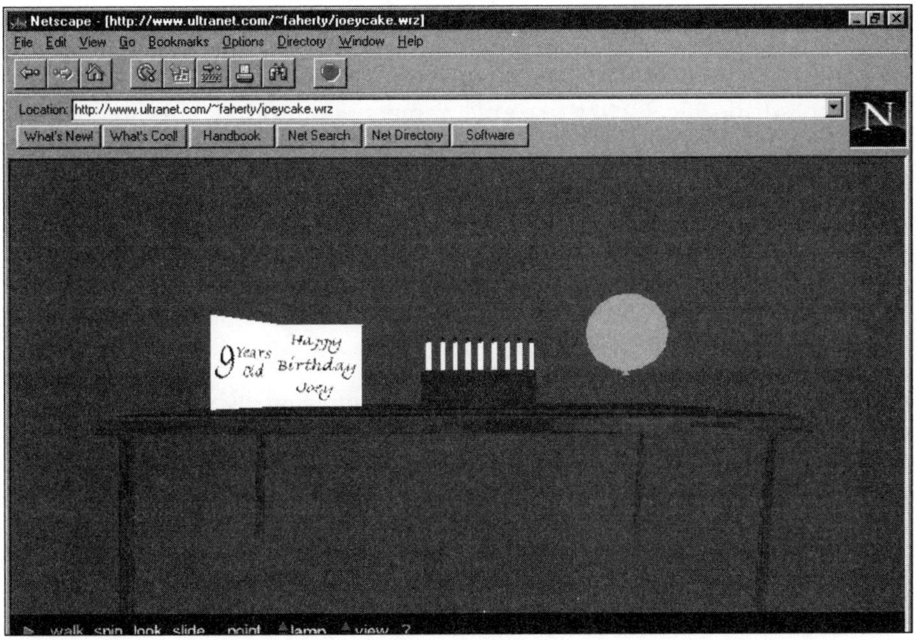

Figure 5-9: Joey Faherty began making VR worlds at his ninth birthday party (`http://www.ultranet.com/~faherty/joeycake.wrz`).

As with HTML, a VRML file is an ASCII text file saved in its unique extension for posting. Imagery is set forth in polygons, described by texture map files that suggest color and shading. Overall protocol is broken down into action-related areas called "nodes." The WWW Anchor node is the equivalent in VR of a textual hyperlink. WWW Inline embeds 3-D images. VRML 2.0 will include nodes related to 3-D modeling, so you can draw simpler objects within your VR project, as well as importing 3-D objects from higher resolution programs such as Macromedia's Extreme 3-D. Background, fog effects and doppler effect noises will add realistic detail to environments. Certain behavioral norms will be programmable with sensors that will force the user's mouse to activate only certain types of navigational movement such as rolling or spinning, and also allow the designer to embed "motion detectors" to trigger events when a user passes over a certain area in the total design.

The actual size in terms of memory for the sum of all texture files in a VRML world may only be 25KB, but it's the sheer number you have to worry about being called up as you navigate the virtual interior. Browsers are being adapted specifically to these environments. Authoring tools are proliferating for Windows systems, but oddly no Mac outfits are forthcoming as yet. Other more general complications will weed out only the most dedicated designers, including the fact that VRML 2.0 is not backwards-compatible with its previous incarnation.

Interactive Programming

Interactivity can be as straightforward as allowing visitors to search for words or phrases on your site instead of having to search the entire Web with a spider at some other location, saving them time and the annoyance of wading through long lists of found files. SWISH is short for Simple Web Indexing System for Humans. This was the first Web-specific indexing program to improve on the WAIS (a relic of the Gopher Age), that allowed you to install your own search mechanism at your site. It was simplified to not look for variations or synonyms of entered words, and modified to give higher priority to information stored in certain code brackets in .html pages. It was written in C and needed compiling before it could be installed in your executable path. Now, as with many such programming innovations, high-profile companies are giving away their own plug-and-play versions for free in return for a link.

Previously, Web programmers have tried to introduce motion to their sites by relying on what's called illegal code. "Stuttering" titles and background colors were forced by repeating an HTML code many times when it is supposed to appear only once. This, in the long run, wreaked havoc with user's browsers and only kept visitors from the programmers' sites rather than drawing them in. Now, better options are at hand that don't (it is hoped) have such fundamental drawbacks, yet also don't take up massive amounts of room or require special browser plug-ins.

Animation sequences of a somewhat more impressive sort are possible with client-pull or server-push programs and .gif animation or "progressive .gifs." The client-pull strategy is to get the server to prompt the browser to ask for a series of pictures after the user mouse-clicks for the first one. Server-push sends down an entire multipart media element with its own MIME type with the help of a CGI script, such as the one available for free at Matt Wright's Script Archives. Both of these tie up a browser into a comparatively long-term commitment for a mouse click!

A GIF89 construction by contrast seems like manna from heaven. The Gif Construction Set from Alchemy Mindworks can be downloaded as shareware and used within minutes in Windows, or you can try HexEdit on your Macintosh. Just get a series of .gifs that match up as a flipbook — from, say, a Director animation file with appropriate fades — and fit into the same size area. Compose them in the shareware program as a multiple .gif and the finished product is no bigger a file than your run-of-the-mill pushbutton icon! The only word of warning is to refrain from looping the .gif so that it does not appear that the entire download is being held up.

Cool Stuff on the Cheap

Another low-rent tactic with upmarket appeal is the fake image map. Two kinds of formal image maps exist that break down along the lines of client-side or server-side. They both require a programming investment (CGIs to the rescue again) and produce a result that shows a blank face to the user. A mouse poised over a formal image map cannot retrieve link information as with common HREF links. Icons, logos or messages may indicate a screen hotspot, but sometimes you can't really tell what you'll get if you access the map definition file and thereby the underlying HTML page. The CGI can really slow down what could otherwise be simple and quick. David Lawrence, writing in Web Developer, undercuts all that with icons of nonstandard size and shape that are stacked into interesting shapes. His Web Developer $10,000 Pyramid (with apologies to the game show) indicates that an amusing interface is above all a matter of innovative solutions, not just programming.

Get Small

Many issues in Web media, such as technical standards and other practical considerations, carry over from desktop media production, only more so. Modems still choke information transfer to the detriment of multimedia, and Shockwave's recent innovation of allowing background sound during a video transmission is cold comfort to those whose teeth were cut on TV and the movies.

Miniaturization is an ideal for Webmasters who actually surf the Net with the sort of access and equipment the average person has. Although this is not quite the nanotechnology of building a fully functional car that can cruise along the perimeter of a penny and park over Lincoln's face, it can be stressful for someone who is used to eating up memory on a ROM without concern for the hazards of remote access. The average screen resolution presented to a user will likely be between 72 and 96 dpi, so your best bet is to compress and anti-alias until you have an experience that will not be lost on your viewer, yet does not truly degrade the image. For a still image, 25K is a good ballpark figure to aim for as a final size. In video, the standard in order to reproduce the source's presentation ratio is 160x120 pixels.

Dynamic Media

A/V and VR files all have their own extensions and require their own MIME types: MIDI (mid), RealAudio (ra, ram), AIFF (aif, aiff), and StreamWorks (xdm) are the dominant sound files; MPEG (mpe, mpeg, mpg, mpv), and QuickTime (mov) are MIME types for video; plus you can find new, experimental or specialized files such as VRML (wrl) or Talker, a speech-text format (spc, talk).

In graphics, grayscale vs. 8-bit or higher color modes, dithering, raster vs. Vector images, drawing or importing scanned images are all options for Web visuals. Bitmaps are the rule, so their drawbacks of aliasing and resistance to resizing will have to be wrestled with continually. It becomes even more important to choose your own palette of colors and stick with it, so when you reduce the number of colors in the name of compression, you are not made to pay the price for dithering an image too heavily. Lossless and lossy image compression reduces the actual number of pixels without (with luck) degrading the image too much. Both of these operations can be performed in your favorite graphics program or with compression aids such as DeBabelizer for Macs or L-view and PC Graphics Workshop/Alchemy Mindworks. The same rules apply to video, but the software changes to titles such as MovieShop or Movie Cleaner Pro. For a more thorough discussion of these tools and techniques, see the next chapter.

One way to bypass the issue of bandwidth for visuals is to fall back on "vector" type imagery for certain effects. Unlike a "bitmapped" graphic, a vector image is mostly a set of instructions, rather than drawn pixels on a screen. You can tackle this, especially in Java, only if you approach drawing in terms of mathematics: plotting polygons, radians, and sine waves and combining them with presentation algorithms for real-time animations.

Audio Formats

Sound has its own turf on the Web, consisting of sites devoted to music and related technology such as MIDI. They are not necessarily one-trick-pony sites: One devoted to Vietnamese music (Figure 5-10) has an enticing page with animation loops and full color pictures. MIDI arrangement files, .au files, and RealAudio clips are joined by an experimental MOD format set for those who do not have MIDI synthesizers attached to their PCs. The link list connects to related pages in Denmark, Japan, and Norway with biographies, pop music news, karaoke and pointers to MIDI resources online.

The variety of formats allows you to choose the easiest download depending on how completely your PC has been outfitted for MIDI playback. MIDI loops may seem clever until you realize that you have no way to stop the loop short of leaving the page. RealAudio is making news, but it requires special server software and the streaming cuts down the number of people you can actually connect with simultaneously. For a real-time clip, you're looking at a 22KHz, 8 or 16 bit .aiff or .au file that you will then encode and otherwise

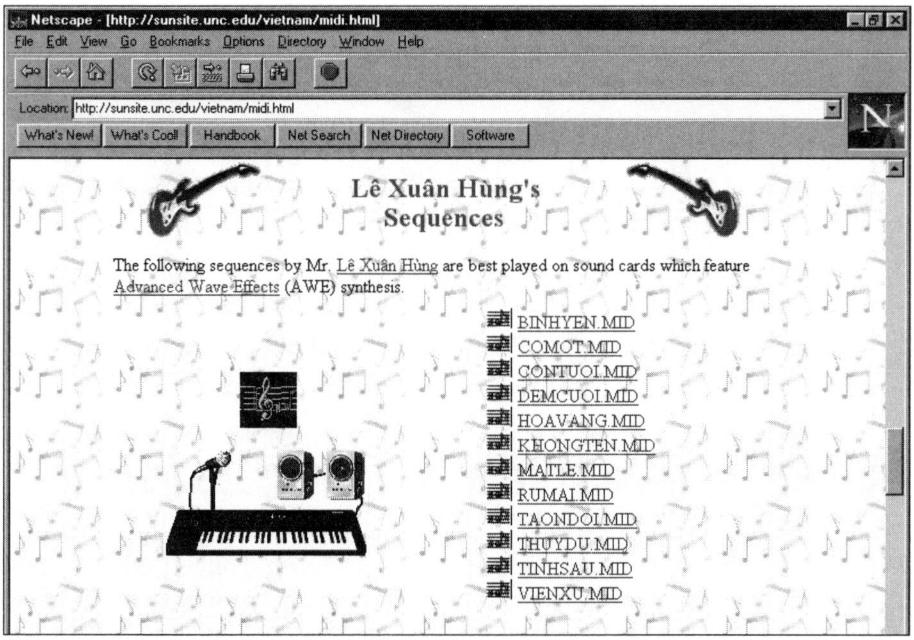

Figure 5-10: MIDI arrangements, title translations, online animations and international links have been collected by `lam@cptca.neep.wisc.edu`, who also posts audio clips of Vietnamese poetry on another page (`http://sunsite.unc.edu/vietnam/midi.html`).

process into another file with a RealAudio extension. The file will then be packeted and fed to your users' system continually. This is fully possible only if you can afford the server and software package, though you can use the compression technology separately and for free.

Other Stuff

Video is a continuing difficulty, considering that MPEG is still not a universal format, and the others, such as .avi files, are still comparatively huge (300K and up) for clips of only a few seconds. Compression takes an ugly postage-stamp-sized image and compromises it even further.

Video with sound can be attempted, but you will need to apply separate compression schemes to the audio portion, as with SoundEdit 16 by Macromedia. This will take a QuickTime file and bring the audio track down to 4:1 of its original size. This is the smallest size a soundtrack can be without sacrificing intelligibility.

Virtual Reality has its own standards of what makes a big or small file. Images for VR are built out of polygons, so the total number will dictate how long your download will be. A total of 10,000 for a scene is considered the upper limit for an optimally sized file. On the other hand, the resolution of VR files, compared to equivalent image files, is less taxing. So, you may find yourself being able to represent a fairly detailed 3-D image that would take too precise a rendering in 2-D to be an advisable illustration. VRML files can also be compressed themselves, up to 20 percent.

In all cases, it is a matter of netiquette to post accompanying information on the size of your media files so that a user can make an informed choice as to whether they can wait, or their system can handle the burden of your download.

R U GQ? Or Are You Just Overdressed?

Producing for the Web world is not just about splashy images and slick interface design. It's about welcoming your guests. Think of what it may be like for your visitors at a given moment. They may be looking for something in vain and getting steamed about it. They could be thinking, "If I see one more copy of this [clever gizmo flavor of the month], I'll jump out the window!" Don't just go for the obvious attractions when you could challenge yourself by giving a 3-D effect with a layered 2-D design, or breaking a larger video clip into sections within a text-based frame story sequence or MUD (Multi-User-Dimension) environment. The things that turn off surfers in any great number have less to do with your high-bandwidth development than they do with showing consideration for users and trying to contribute to or at least help them along on their latest outing.

That being said, here's a list of things you *don't* want to do:

The 10 Most Hideous Mistakes Made On Obscenely Expensive Commercial Sites

1. A really huge picture with a logo on it — and nothing else.
2. A really huge picture bearing a legend that promises the most comprehensive site in the universe — with no details or due date or indication of human presence whatsoever.
3. A really huge image map that doesn't respond or lead anywhere.
4. A really huge image map that, when you click on it, loads itself.
5. A really huge image map that leads to a series of pages all marked "Under Construction," with no details or due date or indication of human presence whatsoever.
6. An address announced to the public that leads to a promotional demo for internal use, dotted with little notes that say things such as, "What would you like us to do on this page?" or "Item # and box cover here."
7. A front page bearing a list of demands and links to places to get all required browser plug-ins, and no link to anything on your site for which the plug-ins are useful.
8. A site touting your big new release that links to a site selling bootlegged copies of your big new release.
9. A mailto form linked to a robot that coughs up the same vague or even completely inappropriate response in less than three seconds — with still no indication of human presence whatsoever.
10. A front page that pleads, "We haven't posted anything yet, but please come back every week to check if we've made good on our promise!"

Think I'm kidding? Surf the Web and see.

Using Color

This is not to suggest that you shouldn't exploit decorative elements or even indulge in an attention-getting device or two. If you keep one eye on your site's overall personality you will be able to extend and explore design innovations without throwing repeat visitors off balance. The reservation to keep in mind here is that HTML codes, as they are, set up a certain range of design options, and on some levels, you cannot break out of those limitations. One example of a simple yet pervasive design element is color. Once a simple issue of standards set on browsers as default modes, color coding has turned into a free-for-all of combinations that attract Webmasters because they take up no memory and take no time to load.

RGB (red-green-blue) codes, like HTML itself, are another set of programming commands that are simple to understand. The code consists of six slots for information, and each slot is taken up by letters or numbers. This shorthand is called hexadecimal notation, or just "hex." Instead of using a cycle called base 2, which is the binary code used by computers or base 10, used in our monetary system, it has a radix of 16 with any number over 9 represented by letters.

This way, a command that would otherwise take a huge string of 1s and 0s can be written or copied more easily. Each two slots in the sequence represent the amount of red, green, and blue that make up the total hue. As is true of additive color theory, white is the sum of all possible elements. Therefore, equal amounts of red, green and blue will make white. Notice below how red, green and blue are coded separately. Then see how they are each represented by FF in the sequence that indicates white. Black is the point zero, with no color information in its code sequence.

red - #FF0000

green - #00FF00

blue - #0000FF

white - #FFFFFF

black - #000000

All other colors are mid-range combinations using letters from A to F and numbers from 0 to 9 incrementally. You can get the exact color you want in one of two ways: either use a color menu, available as a separate piece of software or in newer HTML editors; or refer to a list of predetermined arrays. A color mixer was an early feature in HotDogPro, a popular editor, which allowed you to fine tune the six-unit codes to get shades of the basic rainbow and neutrals such as grey and brown. Because this color spectrum is modeled after the additive model applied in photographic and screen printing, the secondary colors are magenta, cyan, and yellow. Notice how they mix red and blue, green and blue, and red and green FF sequences, respectively:

magenta - #FF00FF

cyan - #00FFFF

yellow - #FFFF00

After you crack the code, you can also just throw in numbers and letters to see what you get. Certain more detailed combinations are required to get light/bright or dark variations. The drawback to midrange combinations is the risk that the user's screen may not register such subtleties, and merely default to some predetermined color closest to your code. Here are some generic shades of primary and secondary colors:

Dark Brown #855E42

Dark Green #215E21

Dark Purple #871F78

Dark Blue #6B238E

Dark Red #4E2F2F

Dark Grey #2F4F4F

Dark Orange #FF2400

Dark Yellow #D9D919

Light Blue	#C0D9D9
Light Green	#8FBC8F
Light Brown	#EBC79E
Light Purple	#DB70DB
Light Pink	#BC8F8F
Light Grey	#A8A8A8
Light Orange	#E47833
Light Yellow	#EAEAAE

Be Creative, but Don't Go Overboard

An even more pressing issue is no less than a retread of the desktop publishing revolution of the '80s. Did anyone ever want to see neon pink resume paper or kaleidoscopic flyers? Like it or not, we all had to bear the brunt of poor taste . . . and now it's followed us onto the WWW! Certainly if you already have experience with multimedia design, you know that a headache-inducing interface will not be engaging. The new twist on that caveat regards the realities of widespread Web access: Some users have higher or lower resolution screens than you, or laptops screens that don't operate like desktop monitors, and, furthermore, some have black and white monitors with even poorer displays!

Your best strategy would be to fall back on the print designer's status quo: layouts that are bold enough to assert themselves in shades of grey as well as full-color. High contrast is the key. The challenge comes from the fact that currently you can set RGB codes for up to four separate HTML commands: one for the background, the main text, the visited and the unvisited links (as determined by the access history in your browser's cache file). Your overall layout may be complicated if you use both a background color and a background image, in which case the background color will show through your <HR> hard returns as bands across the page rather than subtle indentations.

In this environment of a small handful of colors that may reverberate, disappear into each other, or read as different tones in combination, the simple guidelines of "difference by contrast" can save you time. Pale colors frame, but strong ones can overpower. Dark backgrounds or black outlines will make inset elements look brighter, light or white ones render them comparatively darker. A large area of warm color will intensify a spot of cool color and vice versa. Direct complements such as green and red will "buzz" like an optical illusion if small areas are interspersed in a design, adjacent to one another.

One person's style may be another's petty annoyance, so it will be up to you to try and perhaps fail to innovate at your site. How cutting-edge you can afford to be depends upon how responsive you can be to feedback and how well you keep ahead of the Jones' media tools. Now Fractal Design's Painter 4 includes Net Painter, a feature that intends to make it easier for artists to collaborate online. WebSuite 1.0 is a quirky Website builder that specifically intends to keep you from choosing design elements from its library that clash on the page. Microsoft's Internet Explorer is trying to circumvent the whole "noisy background" problem online by instituting Watermarks and presenting them frozen in place while you scroll text over them onscreen. Enterprise has a Color Browser to simplify palette setting. Other major and minor refinements will aid your decision-making process and allow you more options in the future.

Overall, your personal iconography, novel as it could be, may leave the overseas visitor cold, or a more sedate personality just baffled. Try to introduce elements of your site, especially the wackier ones, as part of a series of navigational choices. This approach recognizes the simplest interactive mode on the Web, that of a surfer making decisions and taking chances according to his or her tastes. Many stylistic considerations for home pages (especially the index page of your site) are holdovers from multimedia screen design: keep text to a minimum; design color and resolution for 16- or 8-bit viewer systems; choose arrangements and elements for readability rather than flash and dash.

Testing, Testing, 1-2-3 (and 4, and 5)

Testing how your pages look and work online is made tedious by the range of browsers available. They all do something differently; many do not support the newer HTML commands or other programming extensions, but all have their users. Some problems are caused by sheer lack of support on the part of those who offer the software. Especially, the flagging fortunes of the commercial online services have left their respective proprietary browsers in limbo. Those who run Netcom, the largest of the new breed of access providers, have at this writing simply refused to update their browser to do any more than an old version of Mosaic could handle. The software used by Netcom subscribers as of 1996 cuts you out of any site that uses tables or frames. It also refuses to ignore Java applets as commanded, and simply loads the first couple of lines of programming but nothing more. You can't override this bug. Your worry as a Webmaster is keeping up on news about such difficulties.

Why? Because otherwise you run the risk of a neophyte user blaming your site for some glitch really attributable to the browser. You cannot bend to the whim of every browser out there, but a three-step plan will help you minimize the damage. First, you must test through at least one browser. Second, after you fix what you can, you can leave a text note on your front page or FAQ alerting users with certain browsers that a feature will not work. Last of all, you must provide a range of options or alternate pathways like the popular "text only" alternative. Just don't make your text-centered users wait for a rat's nest of picture files to download before you offer them their own section! If you have to make two or even three "front" pages to choose from, this extra work will garner you a measure of goodwill.

A variety of page creators promise to help you standardize your output. HTML Assistant PRO 2 promises you will be able to test against all browsers with it, though the online services' proprietary browsers are the hardest to judge and are most likely represented only according to the category they most resemble: Mosaic or Netscape. Adobe PageMill for the Mac offers image tools that can convert JPEGs to GIF and create interlaced images that can be loaded more conveniently. Some authoring tools do not support multiple simultaneous browsers, so comparisons can be difficult to make. More arcane considerations of dead or broken links and overall page organization are left to programs such as WebAnalyzer.

A Word About Browsers

The major browsers are still Netscape, Internet Explorer, Lynx, and Mosaic, along with some minor browsers designed for Macs and other non-PC platforms. They will always be out of step with each other and, to a certain extent, with newly adopted or proposed HTML extensions. Sometimes you will just have to bite the bullet with some browsers and hope that users will take text-only or other options you offer them.

A more niggling consideration is of user-set preferences. Sometimes folks have their default color combinations set in their browser and those will override yours. They will set their windows at the minimum size and not open them for your more ambitious layouts. If they are using their provider's proprietary browser and the company has not cached your site, it cannot come up at all, or just be unreadable. Your only option is to respond quickly to anyone who registers an odd complaint about how your site looks, and hope you can get someone to make adjustments based on the advice.

Your test sequence can double check as you bring pages nearer to public view. Testing offline is possible with editors or by accessing your files locally with your own copy of the Netscape browser, for instance. This will weed out the more egregious syntax and spelling errors, and give you a chance to adjust your compositions. If you have a standard setup, with a low-end modem, you can log how long it takes to access your site and certain media elements at different times of the day and use that timetable to judge how much memory any one element can take. Though you can use standard timetables that are broken down according to modem speeds, these do not take into account influence such as time of day and other external bandwidth considerations.

If you have friends or employees on different online services, or who own a range of platforms, they may be able to let you know if something looks out of place. After you load new pages onto your server, you can access them as .htm files to test one more time, then change the extensions or replace the older pages with the newer ones so that the public can see them. Every once in a while, touring your site with a text-only browser to see how it might look to a new visitor would be useful. The visually impaired hook up text browsers to devices that "recite" sites for them, for instance, so if you have lots of code without "alt tag" captions, they may just hear so much gibberish.

Inclusion as an ideal refers to more than designing for a range of browsers — it's really for a range of users beyond these browsers. Workstations have been designed for people with motion or sensory impairments, and these people can also surf the Web with the help of tailored equipment. Various experimental interfaces have been given coverage on the Web, and organizations and hospitals have designed pages devoted to specific concerns. The simplest guidelines for socially inclusive pages were mentioned above, but interventionary technology can be of particular interest to multimedia authors. Items originally intended to ease a disability can be explored for potential media applications.

Deaf participants are now collaborating on systems intended to aid those using or learning Sign as a first or second language. Notation and transcription for the sign language used by the deaf is a unique challenge that is best approached with multimedia applications. Robotic attachments are also being devised to act out finger spelling at deaf/blind user workstations.

Peter B. L. Meijer, working at a Philips research lab in The Netherlands, is testing an innovation he calls vOICe, that produces soundscapes for the blind. Originally intended as a sort of echolocation device for blind travelers, it can also be used in the virtual world of the Web. If all goes well, his WWW site for the technology will integrate an online program of some sort, to allow interaction on the part of sighted visitors. You will be able to draw something online in a 16-tone greyscale palette; then produce a corresponding "soundscape" for it with the online program.

Meijer already has soundscapes stored as .wav files that can be downloaded. He believes that this technology can allow the blind to experience mathematical progressions in graph form, as with transforming a plotted curve into a time-varying tone. The conversion process can be integrated into browsers as a performance option, so .wav files do not have to be premade and stored. Then any image or even VR constructions can be broken down by vOICe on contact. Meijer is awaiting funds to field test the equipment as a mobility aid. Meanwhile, his Web site publicizes his work and provides food for thought, and maybe even inspiration!

Predictions du Jour

Webmastering in the immediate future will take flexibility and sensitivity. Sheer traffic and amounts of new material and means to access it all are increasing at an explosive rate. John Faherty reports that more and more members of his social circle are getting online, if only through a service such as AOL. The Picture Palace was suddenly flooded during the spring of '96 with messages and requests filed at their site; double the rate previously experienced. Many countries are experiencing a peak in Net mania for the first time, such as Germany and Japan. The Faherty Family site even got e-mail from a Korean housewife, who had read about them in her local newspaper! You will never be able to keep everyone happy; but you can try to take advantage of this rare and, with luck, not-so-fleeting opportunity by offering your own positive contribution to the nascent Net culture. The currency on the Web is still word of mouth, though now there's ever more of it, circulating at a faster rate and in arenas such as entire conventions devoted to Web use, Webmastering and even specific elements such as Java programming.

No wonder American politicians found it all so intimidating that they tried to put a lid on it by tacking the Communications Decency Act onto a deregulation bill passed in early '96. Americans on the Web, especially new media artists, were so up in arms that at first they did not recognize the irony of calling for federal control of an international network. The legislation was declared unconstitutional in a matter of months, but the episode provides a working example of how fully ignorant folks who have their own Web sites (including members of The White House, individual politicians and political action committees) can be about the very medium they seek to capitalize on for personal gain. No mechanism exists to enforce such laws. The humor of the situation did not escape John Faherty, who wrote and posted a satirical essay set in the early 21st century, evoking a world in which all the promise of the Web has already been taxed and regulated out of existence. Little did he know his passing reference to taxing packets (of information) would come true as proposed legislation, despite the fact that monitoring the packets as they whiz down our phone lines would be practically unfeasible!

Faherty does see hope for the future, even if the politicians remain loathe to cooperate. Corporations may invoke netiquette as a public relations strategy much the way they adopted environmentally friendly policies in the 1980s. VR may also become more widely available and easier to use, so individuals can set up virtual living spaces instead of just posting "home" pages. These personal spaces can be linked into communities, and advertisements can be packaged into the environments in such a way as to be unobtrusive. Instead of being forced to look at a print-style banner ad on a page, he suggests, you can have a virtual TV in the corner of the room that you can choose to turn on and off. More bandwidth, more user-friendly software and a more diverse pool of access providers may combine to produce a fertile environment for a later influx of new users.

Meanwhile, your experience as a Webmaster and any contributions to Web media you might make will take place in a constantly shifting experimental laboratory. You may find satisfaction in creating the newest of new media, or you may be able to apply what you learn to offline multimedia projects. You may get caught up in social experiences unavailable to you otherwise. Most critically, you will be at the source of technological and methodological innovations. If you have the stamina and patience to handle these developments in their embryonic stage, you will learn, do and see more than any of your offline counterparts.

CHAPTER 6

Tools and Resources

✦ An incredibly wide range of software and hardware tools is used to create multimedia, ranging from simplified beginner software to professional production "farms" that link many computers together.

✦ The layperson can create multimedia using nonprofessional tools. The advantages of using more sophisticated tools are flexibility, precision, and speed.

✦ Better tools cost more money. In the case of software, the difference is usually recouped by increased productivity. In the case of hardware, more discretion is necessary.

✦ Tools are only a means to an end, and production value is not a substitute for good content. That said, good production value is important, and good tools make it easier to achieve.

What Do You Need to Make Multimedia?

Although it's fair to say that brainpower and money are the two most important things to have when beginning a multimedia venture, neither amounts to anything without the tools and skills with which to create a title. In this chapter, I provide an overview of the many different types of hardware and software tools you'll need to produce multimedia content.

Unfortunately, there's no way to offer a complete overview of all the available hardware and software tools for multimedia production — that subject alone would encompass several entire books in itself. Why? First, there are thousands of different pieces of hardware that can be used in a production environment, ranging from consumer VCRs with a simple "pause" button on the remote control, to dedicated special effects systems for big-budget films that cost more than a house. There are multimedia titles that use audio from home cassette decks, and there are others that use full-blown recording studios that cost hundreds of dollars per hour. Multimedia is produced from floppy disks to terabyte storage systems, and from $1,000 PCs to million-dollar multiprocessor supercomputers. And that's just the hardware. Beyond that, there are tens of thousands of programs to run on that range of computer systems, from freeware that costs nothing, except some download time, to custom applications that can cost more than $100,000.

Of course, you don't need all that stuff to produce multimedia, or even most of it; though I'll be honest and say that, budget allowing, it would be nice to have. Generally, the more expensive gear lets you work faster and more efficiently with higher-quality output, but compelling multimedia titles have been produced on a single black-and-white computer system with a couple of applications. In this chapter, I try to present a range of systems and options for different budgets and give you an idea of the kind of work you can be expected to produce with them.

Another problem in discussing tools and techniques for multimedia is that many of these tools are very complex — computer programming languages, for example, can require years of specialized training for full mastery — and can't be adequately explained in this format. In this chapter, I offer an overview of what some of these specialized tools do, some of the pros and cons of using them, and whether or not they make sense within the context of your particular production. In the final chapter on information sources, I recommend a few good books on programming and other multimedia techniques — besides this one, of course!

What's current today is often outdated tomorrow

Hardware, and especially software, products are being constantly revised and updated by manufacturers, both to provide new features and functions and to fix the problems discovered in previous versions. By the time this book reaches the editors, the printing house, the distributors, the retailers, and then the reader, many of these programs will have been revised, updated, or maybe even discontinued. No hard-copy book can be completely up-to-date on this topic, so when you read about a program here, understand that the commerically available version of that program may have changed between now and then.

Beyond that, there are some programs that, because of their open architecture (their ability to accept plug-ins and other modifications from third-party developers), get updated even when the original manufacturer hasn't changed anything. So, inevitably, some of the tools that I discuss here will be out-of-date or superseded by newer, better tools by the time you read this. The goal here is to give you the current information on popular multimedia production tools and techniques. Probably the most up-to-date news is available in the online world, and especially the World Wide Web, where information is often updated daily. So, following are some sources for current multimedia information, both in stand-alone online services and on the Internet. Most of these Web sites have extensive links to other multimedia sites. Again, see the chapter on "Sources" for more information on how to access these information sites.

A platform to stand on

One of the first and most important issues a CD-ROM developer must face is which platform — computer system — to develop for. The reality is that consumers with "Wintel" (Windows operating software running on Intel-based PCs) computers represent more than 70 percent of the CD-ROM market, with Macintoshes accounting for most of the remaining sales. A handful of less popular platforms, such as the Commodore Amiga, represent a negligible part of this market. When developing CD-ROM content, this crucial decision can be solved in one of two ways. Some producers create titles that are designed to run on a single platform. The advantage here is that the work can be optimized for a particular playback medium. The disadvantage is that in order to not ignore one platform at the expense of the other, a second pltaform-specific version of the title is often created, which means extra work, budget, and marketing effort.

There are titles that will run on both Wintel and Mac platforms; these are called "hybrid" or "cross-platform" discs. What essentially happens here is that two versions of the same title, or two versions of the application that runs the title, are present on a single disc. This is more effort in terms of development and especially testing, but it's a great selling point for the title, and ensures the widest possible audience.

In the videogame world, titles are always released to run on a specific platform, be it Sega, Nintendo, Atari, and so on. But relegating your title to a single platform is bad marketing strategy, so most producers who create content for this market end up "porting" content from one platform to another — essentially releasing multiple versions of the title so as to satisfy each sector of the potential buying public.

On the Web, cross-platform issues aren't nearly as critical as they are for fixed media. The most important files that are downloaded to the user — text files and graphic files — generally work with consistency no matter what the platform. To be sure, certain formatting of these files, along with other screen enhancements like tables, charts and animations, are technology-specific. But this doesn't mean platform-specific — it means that certain Web browsers can use these enhancements, whereas others won't support them. These issues are looked at in detail in the chapter on Webmastering. Other online multimedia, such as content prepared for the commercial online services, is usually platform-specific, which is why the major commercial services, with the obvious exception of the Microsoft Network, release versions of their software for both Wintel and Macintosh.

Choosing a development platform

According to a 1996 poll in *New Media* magazine, more than 90 percent of respondents reported that they use the Macintosh as their primary development platform for audio, graphics, animation, and video, and expect to still be Mac-specific two years from now. This presents us with the first irony of multimedia development: when it comes to making multimedia, the Mac platform is still the preferred platform. When it comes to delivering it, most people still use Wintel.

So, faced with economic realities, most developers decide to release their products in Windows formats; many produce for Windows only. Others will release separate Mac and Windows versions, with the attendant difficulties of tracking two versions of the same product. It has become much more feasible, though, in the last year or so, to produce reliable cross-platform CDs that will run on both Windows and Macs, and this trend will continue to grow. The most common stand-alone authoring tools, such as Macromedia Director, can create cross-platform compatible applications that will run on Mac and Windows with little modification necessary. Even Apple recognizes the dominance of the Wintel platform, and so its Apple Media Tool produces cross-platform code.

As previously stated, one realm in which the Macintosh does dominate is graphics and audio, and that has led to the Mac's much higher penetration in multimedia production studios. A recent estimate stated that about 65 percent of all multi-media content is produced on Macintoshes. Many of the best multimedia production tools, such as Adobe After Effects and Equilibrium's DeBabelizer, are available only on the Mac at this time. If you seem to detect a pro-Macintosh bias in this guide at times, there's a reason — the Mac generally has a better selection of high-quality production tools than the Wintel platform, although that gap has been closing lately.

Authoring

The process of making multimedia requires many different kinds of digital creations. Some are simple, such as scanned photographs or digitized music. Others are more complex, such as the actual computer instructions that are written into a software program to execute the movement and interactivity of the multimedia production. The process of laying out these instructions is called authoring.

In order to author multimedia, two things are necessary: a computer to develop on, and a software program that facilitates the gathering of the multimedia elements (graphics, text, sound, and so on) into a single, cohesive digital file or group of files. The software programs that allow you to make this cohesive product are extremely varied. The technology can range from a simple program containing preformatted interactivity scripts to computer languages that build every aspect of the production from the ground up. Naturally, the level of authoring has an effect on the sophistication of the project. However, it is possible to author highly effective and compelling mulitmedia with simple, user-friendly authoring tools that even a layperson can quickly master. The key to the process of authoring is not so much in the tools as in the logic of the person using those tools. Many of the most important authoring decisions are made before booting a program. But which program to boot after those decisions is made is, obviously, another key decision. There are many choices of actual products, but they usually fall into one of two categories: programming languages or authoring software.

A word about programming languages

Although there are many programming languages around the world, the dominant language for development of fixed multimedia is C. Developed as an offshoot of technology from Bell Laboratories (called, appropriately enough, "B") for the purpose of designing the world-standard UNIX computer language, C and its later incarnations, C+ and C++ are the core technology of Windows (and OS/2). This makes for a pool of talent worldwide that is familiar with this powerful method of programming.

There are advantages to working from the ground up with a language such as C. For one thing, there are few limitations, as you'd find to one degree or another in a multimedia authoring package. Whatever you want the presentation to do can be programmed in C, within the limitations of the development machine and, more important, the target machines on which the multimedia will play. Also, because C is so popular, there are great many versions of it and a generous variety of associated compilers and other tools. More important, working in a language such as C means that you can make almost anything on a computer — applications as well as multimedia titles. One can even contain the other.

That being said, there are some disadvantages. The primary one is that computer programming such as C isn't learned overnight. It takes patience and discipline to learn it, and the results aren't tangible until all the code is compiled — which is the process of assembling and checking the code to make sure that there are no bugs. This takes much of the excitement out of working on the project, because progress doesn't look as immediate to the producer (and the investors!) as it would on an authoring program.

A thorough discussion of any programming language would be foolish to attempt in a single chapter, much less a single chapter heading. Any guide worth its salt on C or a related language would easily be the size of this entire book. The decision to work with these tools is one that the producer needs to make, but the knowledge to be able to work with them is highly specialized. If you see yourself in that role, you've got a lot of studying to do.

Rapid application development

Halfway between the ground-up approach of programming language and the "user shell" of authoring programs lie rapid application development, or RAD, tools. These allow for a certain level of immediacy and convenience that you don't get with C, but with (usually) more flexibility than you find in authoring programs. Rather than perform their tasks simply with lines of code, these programs let you import multimedia elements, choose them from a menu, and drop them into the presentation. There are a variety of these on the market, and although most of their afficianados are in the business sector, where adherence to established standards for databases is necessary, some of them have found more acceptance than others.

One of the most popular of these programs is Visual Basic by Microsoft, which is the official programming language of Windows. Using Visual Basic, you can author multimedia in a drag-and-drop metaphor, using pull-down menus, buttons, icons and the like. Because Visual Basic is so common to the majority of desktop computers, working in this medium ensures a large, compatible target audience. Call it machine-level programming with a smiling face.

Authoring programs

Because there are many people wishing to make multimedia but who aren't computer programmers, there are applications called authoring programs. These packages essentially put a "shell" around the actual programming component, allowing the user to accomplish his or her goals through simplified means. These means include preprogrammed "scripts" that the author can drop into the presentation, which will make things happen — black out a screen, begin an animation, move to the next screen, and so on. The idea here is to make the process of authoring more friendly and intuitive, though different programs succeed at different levels.

Authoring programs first found favor in simple "presentation" applications that were used as a business communication tool. These allowed for the creation of colored slides and charts, and some of the more advanced ones eventually offered rudimentary animations for moving bar charts and the like. These eventually morphed into the basis of today's more simplified authoring packages. Although these beginner's tools provide a good place to learn the basics, none of them is really adept for commercial multimedia production, which typically includes more elements and requires a greater degree of allowable user interactivity.

A number of capable authoring tools are available to developers on both major PC platforms. The advantages of one over the other may be profound or merely a matter of taste — virtually every multimedia author has a favorite tool from which he or she is loath to stray. This comfort level is important to the production — new tools mean a new learning curve, which means time lost, which means money lost.

Choosing an authoring program needn't be a long-term decision. A particular package may be suitable for one job but insufficient for a larger one, or even overkill for a smaller one. Many authoring packages excel in one area, such as animation or interactivity, but fall short elsewhere. Others are completely capable, but require a longer learning curve than many individuals may be willing to undertake. The best way to find out about them is to jump in and try to use them yourself. Rather than present you with a checklist of all the available authoring programs on the market (there are dozens), I'll take a look at some of the more popular authoring tools that have a proven track record of user satisfaction. Demonstrations of several of these authoring programs are available for your perusal on the CD-ROM that accompanies this book.

Macromedia Director

Director is one of the most popular authoring programs on the market, and has one of the longest histories, going back to the late 1980s when the company was called Macromind. Originally, Director was mostly used as an animation program, and the program still retains formidable animation features. Eventually, it grew to include interactive scripts through a built-in language called "Lingo," and was able to apply those scripts to a variety of multimedia elements, such as pictures, text, elementary sounds, and control of external devices such as CD-ROM drives, through associated Director components called "X-objects."

Director has come a long way since then, and because it was one of the first major packages to offer cross-platform delivery for both Macintosh and Windows (the program originated on the Mac), it rapidly gained acceptance with multimedia developers. Today, Director is in version 5.0, and not only remains a comfortable standard for hundreds of thousands of developers, but is now beginning to form a large presence online through an associated technology called "Shockwave," which plays Director "movies" in real time on the Web. For more on Shockwave, see Chapter 5.

The gist of Director is that it lays elements down in a "timeline" structure. A horizontal row of "cells" represents events in time, from left to right. Each row of cells becomes one "channel," much like the layout on a video editor's log or a sound recordist's track sheet. Each channel contains multimedia elements, such as pictures, sounds and text, that are arranged for however long a time the author desires by filling up the appropriate number of cells in a track. Subsequent tracks are overlaid onto each other, with more and more multimedia elements added until the title is built. When the authoring is finished, the final file is compiled into what Macromedia calls a "movie." This final movie is distributed to users via a play-only technology called a "projector." Director projectors can be built for either Macintosh or Windows delivery, and versions of the program are available for both platforms.

Probably the major reason that Director has become so popular is because of its self-contained scripting language, Lingo. Lingo code attempts to allow authoring through English words and phrases, as opposed to the cryptic keywords one might find in a C or UNIX environment. Many of these Lingo scripts are pre-written for the author's convenience, and can simply be dropped into the timeline as another element, just like a picture or sound. For example, if the author wants to create a "pause" button for an animation, the button can be assigned a Lingo script that says "on mouseUp, pause." Obviously, not all interactivity is this simple, though Director attempts to make it so.

This emphasis on simplicity of execution extends to the rest of the program. Animations, for example, can be simplified by creating "key frames" instead of the entire animation. Click a few buttons, and Director will create the "in-between" animation for you. In its latest incarnation, Director has also greatly expanded its text-handling capabilities, for years one of the most consistent complaints with the program. That being said, there's little that needs to be accomplished in a multimedia project that can't be done in Director.

Macromedia Authorware

Some authors not only prefer more elaborate production software, they prefer icon-based authoring, as opposed to the popular timeline paradigm. Macromedia offers a more professionally oriented authoring program that fits this bill called "Authorware," which, at the time of this writing, is in version 3.0.

The advantage to icon-based authoring is that some developers find it more convenient to "see" the entire flow of production at one time, as opposed to the rows of otherwise indistinguishable events that one sees in a program based on a timeline. In Authorware, you create multimedia by dragging icons onto a flowchart, which Macromedia calls a flowline. Parameters are assigned to these icons, which are divided into 13 basic types. One type of icon might send a message to begin an animation, or to perform a calculation. Although this is conceptually similar to the Lingo events used in Director, the possibilites are more open ended in Authorware.

One thing that Authorware does offer over its less capable sibling is the ability to form frameworks for programs and events to which the developer finds him or herself returning. For example, a text box that gets used over and over again in the presentation, only with different text, can be saved as a template and reused; this is a great timesaver. Another impressive feature is a customizable debugging routine that lets you track individual components of the production from start to finish. This allows for a quicker debugging process, as the program will hunt for errors only in the areas the author specifies.

Probably Authorware's greatest selling point is that it is a highly cross-platform development tool. It is available in versions for both Windows and Macintosh, and can deliver final runtime applications on both platforms. These "packages" can be distributed royalty free. By being this cross-platform compliant, Authorware can perform some neat tricks. It can convert Windows files to Macintosh and vice versa, a feature unique to programs of this sort.

Though this program does come close to being truly transparent between platforms, a truly cross-platform title must be checked and rechecked because of issues that are essentially at odds between the two platforms, such as font issues and screen resolution.

Authorware is a significantly bigger program than Director, and significantly higher in cost. But despite the increased power, the learning curve isn't substantially steeper, and many of the routines are precustomized, saving valuable production time. For now, this program can rightfully claim status as king of the hill, at least in terms of authoring programs on the Macintosh side. On the Windows side, there's significantly more competition.

Allen Communications Quest

Quest is another icon-based authoring package, and although it is similar to Authorware in terms of power and flexibility, it takes a different approach to the authoring process. The best metaphor here might be the "storyboard," where small pictorial representations of the desired screens are represented by icons, and these are labeled by smaller on-screen symbols (smaller icons) that signify what is happening in the storyboard. This does make it easier to see what's happening to any given multimedia element at any given time.

Like Authorware, Quest includes a library of preprogrammed elements that can be quickly added to the presentation. These include screen layouts, buttons, menus, borders, and yes/no queries for the user. Because these have been preprogrammed, they can often be used in their original state, though obviously it's possible to edit the characteristics of any of these elements or events to fit your specific application. Quest also comes with a library of clip media to quickly facilitate new elements and tools with which to generate clip media, such as drawing and text. There is also an ample collection of special effects that can be easily applied to the elements, thus quickly facilitating animation or any number of other effects.

One of Quest's most powerful selling points is that the scripting language is close to C, and when the built-in scripts can't be customized to the exact application that the author desires, C language can be used directly. Of course, this assumes that the author has proficiency in C. If that's not the case, Quest offers a "C-coach" that helps the author customize various elements offered inside the program.

The only real downside to Quest is that it can deliver multimedia only to the Windows platform, which may or may not be a hindrance, depending on the marketing plans of your multimedia production. However, in a group situation, the visual layout of Quest might prove a great advantage, in that members of the team who are not programmers can quickly grasp where the production is and where it's heading.

Apple Media Tool

Figure 6-1 is a fairly recent release that is actually two different products. Apple Media Tool (AMT) proper is an object-based graphical interactive authoring environment that requires no coding to produce applications. It includes RunTimeMaker, which lets you create self-contained, double-clickable applications. The Apple Media Tool Programming Environment (AMPTE) uses Apple Media Language (AML), an object-oriented language similar to C++, to extend and add functionality to AMT. You'll need to be a programmer to work with AMTPE.

AMT is an object-based authoring environment that lets you connect objects and behaviors visually by drag-and-drop into a project map.You start a project by creating an empty map, then importing the media elements you want to use into the Media window, which is a storage bin for media files. You then create your first screen by clicking with the screen tool in the map window, and drag media elements, or objects, to the screen to add them to the project. From there, the Browser window lets you double-click objects to assign events and actions to them. After you've created several screens, you connect them with "patchcords" in the map window to set up interactivity paths and branching.

With a completely graphical interface, it's easy to quickly create prototypes and proof-of-concept applications, and AMT doesn't require knowledge of a programming language to create a reasonable interactive experience. Some other advantages of AMT are its support for irregularly shaped hotspots and "magic wand" hotspots, where selected colors in a scene become interactive. Beyond that, AMT handles large numbers of media files of all types, and it's simple to globally replace or reuse media elements. Non-programmer designers should find AMT pretty easy to learn and use.

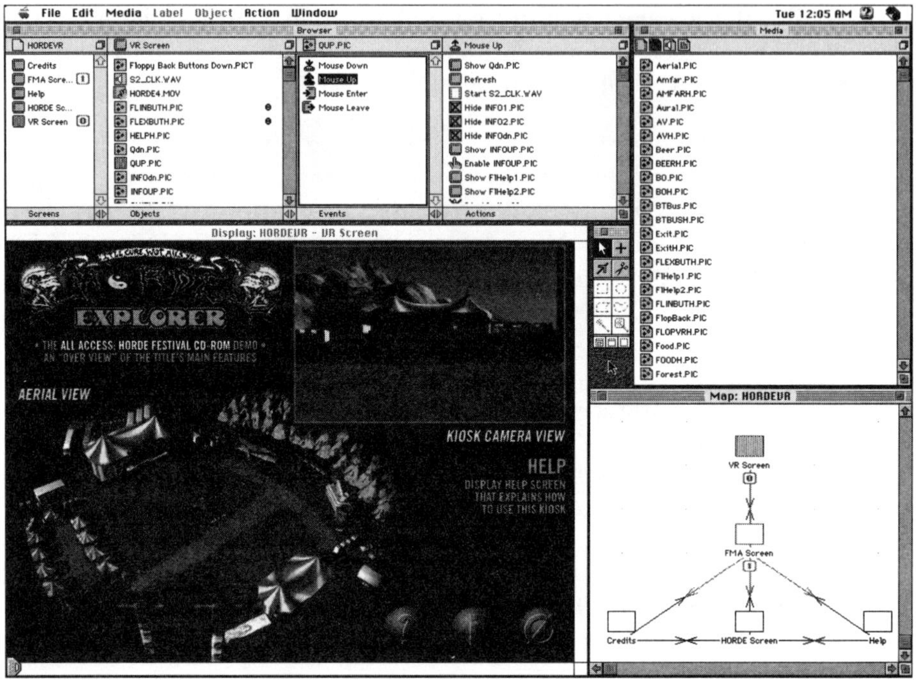

Figure 6-1: AMT's graphics interface is based on a map metaphor.

AMT's ease of use is paradoxically also one of its main disadvantages. A graphic programming interface can sometimes be limiting to productivity, particularly when doing many repetitive tasks that would be much faster to handle through a script. Beyond that, creating an application with complex interactivity or links to a database will require working in AMTPE, and you'll need to develop (or hire) advanced programming skills for that.

mFactory mTropolis

mFactory's mTropolis (Figure 6-2) is a brand-new, high-end graphic authoring environment. Designed for professional developers, it's the first in next-generation development tools, and future versions could well establish it as the preeminent desktop authoring program, although at the time of this writing, it's not quite there yet.

Like Apple Media tool, mTropolis is an object-oriented interactive authoring environment in which you can create complex, highly interactive games and applications with little or no coding. In mTropolis, every object is either an element or a modifier; modifiers are attached to elements and change their behavior. mTropolis uses an outline structure as its metaphor, in which objects below a level become children of the object in the level above, as shown in the Structure window. You can use this structure window to change the hierarchy of elements in the project, or arrange them graphically in the Layout window.

In mTropolis, you start by importing media into the Assets palette, then dragging media to the layout window to assign them to a scene. You then select from a huge library of modifiers and drag it onto the element to assign the modifier to it. You can attach unlimited numbers of modifiers to an element; you can also create aliases of elements or modifiers, which lets you easily make global changes to either. Double-clicking a modifier lets you configure it for your particular use.

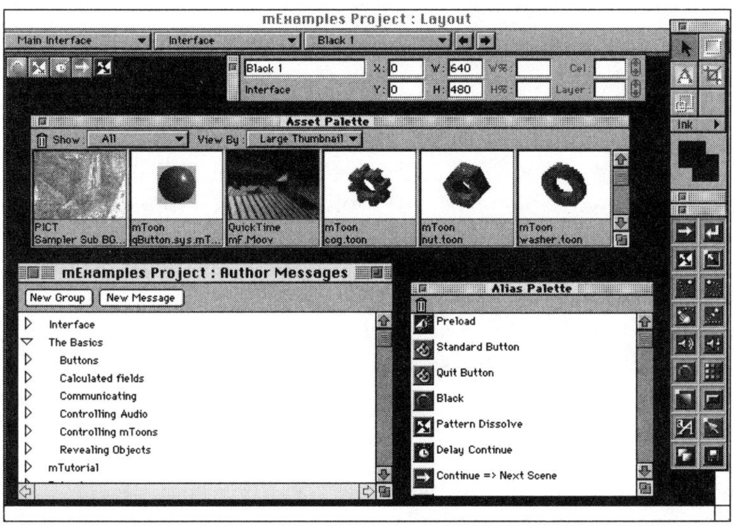

Figure 6-2: mFactory's mTropolis lets you develop your product with minimal coding.

Modifiers include MiniScript, a programming language for custom interactivity, messages (which cascade down the hierarchy to all child objects below it), if/then, keyboard input, variables, and actions (including links, paths, auto buttons, sound, and graphics). You can also create custom modifiers. Some of the unique modifiers in mTropolis that will be of special interest to game developers include boundaries, which constrain an element within a specified area, and collision detection, so that objects will be aware of and bounce off each other. These would let you program an entire interactive basketball game, for example, without any scripting or coding at all.

mTropolis is incredibly powerful for a graphic programming environment. You can go much further here before having to write code than you can in any other program mentioned in this chapter. In many cases, you can create complete, complex interactive games or other entertainment titles without scripting at all. mTropolis' strongest suit is game development, in fact; its text-handling capabilities are a little weak at this point, so it might not be the best choice for text-heavy applications. Still, except for its cost, it's probably the best choice for nonprogrammers who want a powerful interactive development tool without many of the limitations of other object-based graphic programming.

AimTech IconAuthor

One of the veteran programs of multimedia authoring, IconAuthor, at the time of this writing, is in version 7.0. The feel is similar to Authorware, in that icons are dropped into an on-screen environment and connected via events to other multimedia elements, controlled by time or user interactivity. The difference here is that IconAuthor is compliant on many different platforms. Besides being available in versions for Windows, UNIX, and IBM's fast-fading OS/2 operating system, IconAuthor can deliver finished multimedia to all these platforms, plus the Macintosh. This flexibility extends into the program's acquisition capabilities, too — IconAuthor supports a generous selection of multimedia file formats.

For multimedia development that has an eye on the Web, IconAuthor is an attractive choice. The program has the ability to create bidirectional links with Web browsers, and can integrate HTML documents into the presentations. This allows IconAuthor to interact not only with the Web, but with the small-scale "intranets" that are popping up all over in the corporate world.

Although authoring the presentation to take advantage of these capabilities is a skill that isn't learned overnight, the program can be remarkably automated after the process is understood. IconAuthor can handle an entire online transaction — logging on, connecting to a server, and moving elements to the server. Of course, this process is fraught with hazards, though that's more a result of limited phone-line technology than anything else. Because a modem moves data much slower than a CD-ROM, it's unreasonable to expect full transference capabilities between these two mediums. That means that multimedia-rich content, such as video and audio clips as well as larger animations, aren't always practical in real use. Smaller files work better, as they always do with Web material.

Because of its compliance with many different operating systems and its ability to work with so many file formats, as well as its savvy toward the Internet, IconAuthor is a flexible tool that is capable of virtually any authoring situation. It may not be the easiest program to learn, but it has, by virtue of its robust implementation and years of fine-tuning, become a favorite for many multimedia authors.

Oracle Media Objects

Oracle is a company better known for its database technologies than authoring programs, but it does offer a powerful package called Media Objects. Because of the company's interest in expanded media integration, particularly through networks and the Internet, Media Objects is an authoring tool with a flexible delivery approach. Projects created with Media Objects can be delivered not only to Windows and Macintosh computers, but also on the proprietary "set-top box" technologies that everyone from cable companies to huge telecommunications giants are heralding as the next big thing.

The authoring procedure in Media Objects consists of what the company calls "stacks" — groups of events that signify a segment of the presentation, such as an animation. Each stack consists of a number of "cards" that make up the individual components of the stack. Each card contains its own graphical layer, as well as other multimedia elements such as sound and text that are controlled by a scripting language called Media Talk. The stacks, and hence the cards that comprise them, are activated and manipulated by events, which are either determined by code written into the presentation or by interaction from the user.

In order to make the authoring process painless, Media Objects includes a selection of prefabricated objects that can be customized or, in the case of simple interactive events, used as is. These include buttons, fields, color palettes, timers, data sheets (text in tabular form — another holdover from the company's database expertise) — and a unique "pick list" feature that represents an easy way for the end user to choose from many segments of text in a multimedia project.

One of Media Objects's strengths is that virtually every aspect of the program is customizable. For example, characteristics of the tool set can be tweaked to the author's particular needs, as can virtually any of the functions, and even the screen environment. Because virtually everything that happens in Media Objects is under some form of script control, customizing the workplace is just a matter of tweaking the scripts, which, like Lingo, are an attempt to graft plain English onto computer syntax.

For situations in which the multimedia developer needs to be aware of future technologies, such as set-top boxes, Media Objects offers an authoring package that can allow for the porting of multimedia content to these evolving technologies, with little modification. Media Objects may not be the most flexibile of the authoring programs during actual production, but when the project is finished, there's very little work involved in bringing that project to widely divergent platforms.

2-D Graphics and Animation

One of the most important, indeed fundamental, skills needed for multimedia development is the production of 2-D graphics. Nearly every CD-ROM ever made incorporates some kind of 2-D graphics, illustrations, or animation. Many titles require hundreds of custom screens, buttons, backgrounds, and sprites.

First of all, what do I mean by 2-D graphics? In the multimedia world, images are categorized more by how and where they were created than by what their final format is. This is because anything displayed on a computer screen is, by definition, a flat grid of pixels — a 2-D, *bitmapped,* image, no matter where it came from. Such an image is also sometimes called a *rasterized* image. A raster is the grid of pixels that defines your computer screen; a rasterized image is one which has been converted from some other format to pixels so that it can be displayed on-screen.

You'll notice that I referred to bitmapped images previously. There are two main types of graphics files produced on the computer — bitmapped and *vector*, or *outline*, graphics. A bitmapped graphic is a collection of pixels, as mentioned. Because the computer has access to the smallest detail in pixels, bitmapped graphics tend to reproduce shades better, as in scanned photographs or captured video clips. However, the level of detail in a bitmapped graphic is limited by the number of pixels in the image; to get more detail, you have to add more pixels, which increases the file size. Common bitmapped file formats include PICT, BMP, GIF, TIFF, QuickTime movies, AVI movies, and JPEG, with PICT and QuickTime being the standards for cross-platform development. Programs that work with bitmapped images are often called *paint* programs.

Vector graphics, typically produced by programs such as Adobe Illustrator or Corel's CorelDRAW!, are created with curves and other mathematical shapes instead of pixels. Because a mathematical curve always stays smooth no matter how closely you look at it, vector graphics always print at the highest smoothness level, and the graphic's file size remains small. For print, the most common type of vector graphic language is PostScript, which is a cross-platform standard for manipulating, storing, and printing vector graphics, including fonts. Programs that work with vector graphics are usually referred to as *illustration* or *draw* programs.

Vector graphics don't reproduce photographic detail well, however, and most authoring programs can't handle them anyway. For multimedia purposes, 2-D images are almost always in bitmapped format. Any vector graphic illustrations you may produce for your CD-ROM need to be rasterized into bitmaps before they can be used. One of the most common vector file formats is EPS, for Encapsulated PostScript.

So, in terms of sources, a scanned photograph or drawing, an original Photoshop or Painter image, a rasterized Illustrator or EPS file, an animated Director sprite, or any captured video image or sequence, are all examples of 2-D imagery. Images created by 3-D programs, even though their final format is a 2-D image, are called 3-D. I get to 3-D software a little further on.

A visual glossary

I need to define some of the terminology before I go any further. As we've mentioned, any image shown on a computer screen is by definition a bitmapped graphic — that is, an image defined as a specific arrangement of pixels. How many pixels are squeezed into a linear inch, and how many pixels there are in total, define the *resolution* of the image. The size of an image can be expressed strictly as the horizontal and vertical dimensions in pixels; so, you'll often hear people speak of a "640 by 480" image, meaning 640 pixels wide by 480 pixels tall. Images can also be described in inches and pixels per inch (ppi), as in an 8-1/2 by 11 inch image at 300 ppi. Most computer screens have a resolution of around 72 ppi (which is actually fairly low; most color printing is at 300 ppi or more). A standard 14-inch monitor usually displays 640 x 480 pixels at 72 ppi, so this resolution has become the standard for a "full-screen" image. This is also the standard desktop video resolution for full-frame video.

Each pixel in an image can be at least black or white; depending on the hardware capabilities of the system you're viewing an image on, a pixel may be able to display any one of 256, 32,000, or 16,000,000 colors at any one time. Each of the preceding values is derived from the number of bits used to express colors, and that number is called the *bit-depth* of the image or the display system. A purely black-and-white image (with no grays) can be expressed with just a single bit; so, black-and-white images are sometimes called *1-bit*. A 1-bit display system, like the first Macintoshes, can display only purely black-and-white images, with no shades of gray.

Eight bits can describe up to 256 different colors or shades of gray; *8-bit* is a common multimedia image and hardware display standard. 8-bit color is also sometimes referred to as *indexed* color. *16-bit* color gives you around 32 thousand different colors to work with; *24-bit* gives you more than 16 million. 24-bit color is also called photorealistic. 256 different colors usually aren't enough to accurately show all the hues and shades in a color photograph, which results in a *dithered* image (although there are ways to improve this situation, as you'll see). 16-bit color is a fair compromise between 8-bit and 24-bit, and works well for displaying captured video.

Dithering is a very important concept that deserves a closer look. Dithering, in general, is a process the computer uses to convert a piece of data from a higher bit-depth to a lower bit-depth. This applies to audio as well as images, as you'll see later. In graphics, dithering results when you permanently convert a 16- or 24-bit image to 8 bits or lower, or when you display a higher bit-depth image on a monitor that can show only a lower number of bits. What happens is that the computer assigns a number to every color in an image. If the computer is capable of displaying only 256 colors at once, and the image to be displayed contains more colors than that, the computer will then simply change the colors it can't display to the nearest equivalent colors it can display. The computer has to do this as quickly as possible for real-time display, so it has little time to search for the best color matches. This generally results in a blotchy or spotty image, with subtle shades and gradations reduced to bands of solid colors or patches of dots.

So, why ever use 8-bit color? The most important reason is that many multimedia computers can display only 8-bit images, a result of inexpensive graphics displays or monitors. So, it's often a waste of time and resources to include higher-quality images. Also, because a 24-bit image contains three times as much data as an 8-bit image, the 24-bit image takes up three times as much disc space on your CD-ROM, and also takes longer to open and display on most computers. Many developers compromise somewhat in image quality in favor of faster response times and being able to include more assets on the disc. Whenever you're developing for either CD-ROMs or the Web, 8-bit color should be your final destination for graphics files, though it's preferable to begin your work with 24-bit source material, so that you can begin work with the highest possible quality.

As mentioned, however, it's possible to improve the look of lower bit-depth images with *optimized palettes*. A palette is simply the group of colors the computer uses to display an image with fewer than 24 bits of color. Because an 8-bit system can display only 256 colors out of more than 16 million (for 24-bit color), the computer has a wide range of colors to choose from for its 8-bit display. Most computer systems have a default 8-bit color set that they use for standard display; this is often called the *system palette*. The system palette is generally optimized for displaying icons and windows, which have few colors; if you look at the colors in a typical system palette, you'll see many different ranges of colors (blues, reds, and so on) but few intermediary shades of those colors (so, you see only a couple of different shades of blues and reds.)

What this means is that the system palette is not well suited for displaying the tones and shades in an image of a human face, for example. When the computer tries to display a 24-bit image of a face with its system palette, you'll see a lot of dithering in the flesh tones, as the system tries to *map* (find the nearest neighbor of) the colors in the original image to the system palette colors. In the example of a head-and-shoulders shot of a Caucasian woman's face with dark hair, you need a wide range of pinks and browns to accurately display the face, whereas greens and yellows are used less. A typical system palette won't have that many different pinks and browns available, so all those different shades will be mapped to only a few close colors, resulting in the "Barbie-doll effect" — a flat, plastic, blotchy image. The computer can't help it; it has only the system palette to work with.

To improve this situation, you need to provide the computer with a better palette. An optimized palette is just that — a customized, limited group of colors designed to improve the lower bit-depth display of an image or collection of images. The best way to create an optimized palette is to run the image or images through a program that analyzes the colors in the image and produces the best possible palette for your target bit-depth. Right now, the best program for that is Equilibrium's DeBabelizer Toolbox, which I get into later. For now, all you need to know is that DeBabelizer can create the optimized palette and automatically attach it to the image, so that when you display this image in 8 bits, the system loads and uses the improved palette, and the 8-bit image will look much more like the original image. You'll still see some dithering, but if the palette is well made, the dithering will be hardly noticeable.

You can use this optimized palette technique with full 24-bit images; in this case, the optimized palette is attached to the image, but isn't used when displaying the image in a 24-bit system, so you get the full range of photorealistic color in the image. When this image is displayed with 8 bits, the system loads the optimized palette and displays the dithered image with the best possible colors. You can also create an optimized palette and then use that palette to permanently dither the image down to 8 bits, thereby reducing its size on disk. In this case, though, the 8-bit image won't look any better in a 24-bit system. As I've said from the beginning of this book, multimedia production is nothing but a string of compromises.

One thing to watch out for when authoring with optimized palettes for 8-bit displays is *palette flashing*, which is what happens when you load a new palette into your program while still displaying elements on-screen that use the previous palette. As soon as the new palette loads, everything on-screen immediately changes to the new colors, often with hideous results. There are several ways to avoid this. One is to use only one palette and never change it; this, however, may be too limiting if you have a wide range of material to display. Another is to fade to black or clear the screen before switching palettes. This may not always be possible, of course.

One of the best ways to avoid palette flashing is to create palettes that have some common colors, such as a limited color set you always use for on-screen navigation and interface elements, leaving a relatively large set of colors that can change from palette to palette. You can then optimize your palettes to always include the common set and use the remaining available colors to best display the image or animation. It's a little tricky doing this, but it's possible.

An important topic that's related to dithering is called *antialiasing*. Antialiasing is a process the computer uses to display images with an apparently higher resolution than they actually have. The result is that images on-screen have apparently cleaner, less jagged edges than they would otherwise. Remember, resolution is the size of the image in pixels, as well as the number of pixels in an inch. In a typical full-color magazine, images are usually printed at around 300 ppi. At 300 dots to an inch, most readers can't see individual dots in an image, and so visually the dots fuse together at normal viewing distance to create the illusion of continuous color. (You've probably seen the optical effect created by printing Lincoln's head as a collection of large pixels. At arm's length, you can't make the features, but when viewed from across the room, the pixels resolve together to form a recognizable image. It's the same idea.)

On a computer monitor, however, the image resolution is much lower, usually between 70-80 ppi. This isn't a high enough resolution to blend the pixels together as well as a printed page can. (This is one reason that screen shots of computer images tend to look jaggy when printed.) This jaggy, *aliased* effect on screen is particularly evident at the edges of images or at the transitions between foreground and background elements. Antialiasing is one way around this problem, and helps to create smoother-looking images on-screen.

Antialiasing

Antialiasing works by creating transition pixels between the edges of foreground and background that are a blend between the two. Take a look at Figure 6-3. This shows a 3-D-rendered sphere with aliased edges. Figure 6-4 is a zoomed-in view of the same image. You'll see that the edges are jaggy or stair-stepped; even when this image is zoomed-out to its normal viewing size, you still see these jagged edges.

Figure 6-3: A spherical object rendered without antialiasing has visible jagged lines.

Figure 6-4: The larger the magnification, the more jagged the lines appear.

Figure 6-5 shows this same image zoomed out and rendered with *antialiased* edges. Note that it appears significantly smoother, even though it's the same resolution as the previous image. Figure 6-6 shows how this effect is achieved. You'll note that the edge has been smoothed by the addition of extra pixels that are different blends of the foreground and background colors.

Figure 6-5: Antialiased spheres look perfect from a distance.

Figure 6-6: Extra pixels help smooth the surface.

Antialiasing is a function of the program that renders the images onscreen. Most 3-D applications allow for variable antialiasing, so you can control how smooth or jagged the edges are; generally, because of the methods used for antialiasing, the higher the antialiasing, the longer it takes to render the image. Some applications can render certain on-screen elements with antialiasing on the fly, although this usually requires a faster-than-average computer for best results. For example, the new version (5.0) of Macromedia Director can render antialiased text on the fly, which greatly improves the appearance of text on-screen.

The last topics about color that I need to address before moving on are *RGB channels* and *alpha channels*. 24-bit color in the computer is usually handled as RGB information; this means that colors are expressed as varying proportions of red, green, and blue. (RGB color is an *additive* color system, by the way; red, green, and blue create white when added together at full intensity.) With a total of 24 bits of information to express the whole color palette, each channel uses 8 bits, or 256 different values, to define a level for that channel, which, when added to the other channels, produces the final color. (With each pixel in a 24-bit image able to have any one of 16.7 million different colors, you can see we're talking about a lot of data here.) 24-bit images are often referred to simply as RGB images.

An *alpha channel* is an additional 8-bit layer of grayscale information that is used to define a transparency level for the image. An RGB image with an alpha channel, sometimes called an RGBA image, carries 32 bits of data for each pixel (making it a third larger on disk than a straight RGB file). The image is all a lot easier to show than describe, so take a look at Figure 6-7. The image is a simple checkerboard, which will be your background layer. Figure 6-8 is a rendered sphere, and Figure 6-9 is the same sphere layered on top of the checkerboard.

Figure 6-10 shows the alpha channel of the original sphere. Normally, you don't see the alpha channel by itself; I've separated it here for clarity. As stated earlier, an alpha channel is simply shades of gray that define transparency; the darker the shade of gray, the more transparent the image will be when layered on top of another image. Figure 6-10 (the alpha channel for Figure 6-8) is pure black and white.

Figure 6-7: The checkerboard alone, as background.

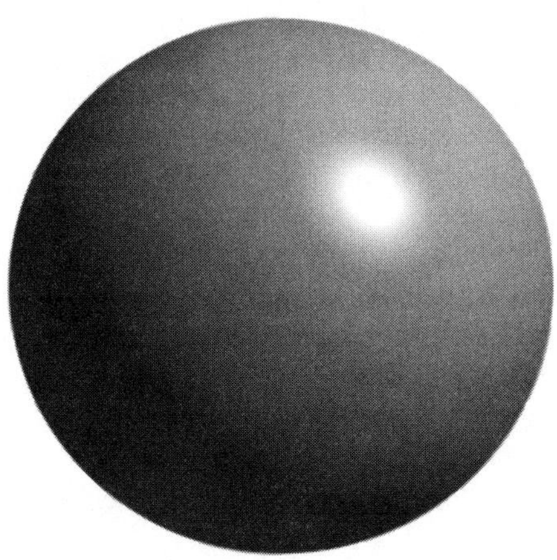

Figure 6-8: The sphere has a background that you want to make disappear.

Figure 6-9: When the two objects overlap, the visual is seamless.

When you layer, or *composite,* Figure 6-8 on top of Figure 6-7 — and tell the compositing program to use the alpha channel for transparency — everything that is pure white in the alpha channel will be completely opaque. The white area, which is exactly aligned with the sphere, blocks out the background and lets the sphere appear over it. (This alpha channel was created automatically when you rendered the sphere in a 3-D program.) The black area of the alpha channel will make those parts of Figure 6-8 completely transparent, allowing the background (Figure 6-10) to show through.

My original alpha channel was pure black and white; what happens when the alpha channel contains shades of gray? Figure 6-11 is a modified alpha channel for Figure 6-7; as you see, it shades from pure white at the center continuously through gray to black at the edges of the sphere. When you use this alpha channel for transparency, what you get is Figure 6-12. You can see that the sphere is solid at the center, but gets more and more transparent out to its edges.

Figure 6-10: The alpha channels have allowed "light" to pass in appropriate measures.

Figure 6-11: A modified alpha channel allows selective shading.

Figure 6-12: The resulting images are blended through this information.

Alpha channels, also called *mattes*, are especially useful for compositing 3-D rendered elements into 2-D scenes, as you've seen. Most 3-D programs will render alpha channels automatically, which makes it really easy to composite these renders with other images. Alpha channels can also be used to composite 2-D elements, such as actors on film or video, with rendered 3-D backgrounds — a very common multimedia production technique.

Hardware tools

You don't need too much fancy gear to produce 2-D graphics for multimedia. Besides the computer (which should have a 24-bit color graphics display system that can also run in 8-bit mode), you'll want a CD-ROM drive, a scanner, and a pressure-sensitive graphics tablet.

The CD-ROM is essential because of all the great clip art and other software you can get these days — literally thousands of discs full of stock photos, fonts, buttons, backgrounds, sounds, movies, and so on. They're a powerful resource for multimedia producers. You'll see some examples on the CD-ROM that came bundled with this book. There is so much digitized art already available that it may not be necessary for you to get a scanner. Even if you have original photography that needs to be digitized, you can avoid the cost of a scanner by having the film converted to Photo CD format and reading the images into your computer directly.

The most common type of scanner is a flatbed scanner, designed for scanning relatively large, flat prints and pages. Some flatbed scanners can also scan slides or other transparencies; however, if you need to scan a lot of slides, a dedicated slide scanner is usually faster and provides cleaner, higher-resolution scans. Scanners are usually SCSI devices, and tend to be somewhat finicky; they usually work best at the end of the SCSI chain. Flatbed scanners have gotten a lot cheaper lately, and a good quality, 24-bit, 600-ppi scanner can be had for around $500. Scanners create bitmapped images; look for one that interfaces directly with an image-editing program such as Adobe Photoshop. This lets you scan directly into Photoshop and have its superb image-editing tools available immediately.

Besides being useful for acquiring photographs and textures for backgrounds and 3-D models, scanners can also be used for *optical character recognition*, or *OCR*. Many scanners come bundled with OCR software, which lets you scan a printed page of text and turn it into digital text, ready for word processing. This is particularly useful for multimedia producers who need to input large amounts of printed historical text and turn it into searchable data. Even the best OCR programs have an accuracy of no more than 98 percent, so you'll still have to go back into the text to proof and correct it all. This definitely beats having to type all that text yourself, though.

A pressure-sensitive graphics tablet is also a useful tool for multimedia production. Most consist of a thin tablet or pad connected to your computer's serial port, ranging in size from 4 by 5 inches up to 24 inches square or more, and an electronic pen, which may be cabled or cordless. The cordless models are generally easier to use. If you're a traditional artist, a pressure-sensitive pen is essential. This, coupled with software that supports pressure, such as Adobe Photoshop or Fractal Design Painter, lets you create amazingly realistic natural-media artwork completely digitally. Even if you can't draw or paint, a graphics tablet is still useful for modifying photos by smudging or cloning and for creating original textures for backgrounds and 3-D elements. Wacom's series of tablets and cordless pens, including new pens with digital erasers, are among the most popular and flexible models.

Software tools

For multimedia producers, software tools for 2-D graphics can be divided into four broad categories: utilities for image acquisition, conversion, and compression; fundamental tools; special effects; and animation. I consider 3-D and video-editing software as separate categories, even though the end result is 2-D. A number of programs straddle categories, such as Adobe After Effects, which is both an animation and video-editing application; I note these programs as they appear.

Bear in mind that I can't cover every graphics application and will perforce skip over many useful tools. The tools that I will cover, however, can handle all the basic tasks for 2-D production, and most are extensible enough with third-party add-ons and plug-ins to handle every conceivable task. I'll be looking at many of these plug-ins for graphics programs. In fact, the concept of third-party additions to existing programs has really taken off in the graphics world.

Utilities: image capture and conversion

First, of course, you have to get the artwork into your computer before you can do anything with it. This may involve scanning it, importing it from a CD, or pulling it over a network from a machine with a different operating system. This network could well be the Internet; more and more software is being distributed via the World Wide Web. In this case, handling the graphic might require decompressing it from some exotic format and converting it to something your software can use. I look at the software that does each of these things in turn.

Scanning a piece of artwork (a photo, say) requires controlling the scanner from your computer with some kind of software, which also handles transferring the digital data from the scanner to your hard drive. Some scanners have their own proprietary applications; these may range from very simple one-button programs to the full-featured (and expensive) custom applications required to run high-end scanners. Many manufacturers, however, just write a simple Adobe Photoshop plug-in to interface their hardware and the computer, and bundle Photoshop with the hardware. The scanner can then be controlled from within Photoshop, with the scans opening directly into the program ready for editing. This is one of the best solutions, as no standalone scanning program has all the features and power of Photoshop (or an equivalent image-manipulation program). This kind of plug-in is called an acquire module, and needs to be installed in Photoshop's plug-ins folder before launching Photoshop to be accessible.

Most scanners accommodate a wide range of resolutions: from 72 ppi (or lower) up to as high as 2400 ppi or more for slide scanners. As a rule, you shouldn't scan at much higher resolution than you need for your final output, as it just wastes disk space. For example, final-processed images to be viewed on the World Wide Web should never be higher than screen resolution (72 or 80 ppi), as they can only be viewed at this resolution, and higher resolutions require much longer download times, which tends to turn off your potential surfers. Sometimes, in order to yield a better quality scan, it's worthwhile to scan your artwork at a higher resolution — say, double the screen resolution — and then reduce the ppi to screen resolution. You should yield final artwork only at higher-than screen resolution if you need to zoom into the image in an animation, for instance.

On the other hand, you should always scan at the highest possible bit-depth, 24-bit if at all possible, even if your final output will be 8-bit. This is so that when you create optimized palettes, you always have the largest and most realistic range of colors to sample. An optimized palette created from a full 24-bit image will be more accurate than one created from an image scanned at a lower bit depth.

Beyond allowing you to scan directly into it, Photoshop (and most other image-editing programs) lets you open and convert to and from a wide variety of image formats, including all standard Mac, Windows, and UNIX formats, as well as many proprietary file types. You can also save compressed JPEG files from Photoshop, including the new progressive JPEG format designed for the World Wide Web. Many times, Photoshop will be the only program you need. But if you have to open and convert a lot of different files, or need to perform a series of operations to a set of images, Photoshop may not be the best choice. For these kinds of operations, Equilibrium Technologies DeBabelizer Toolbox is the ideal choice. In fact, of all the graphics tools that I mention here, DeBabelizer is possibly the single most important tool for multimedia producers.

DeBabelizer

As you'll see from the demo version located on the CD-ROM that's been bundled with this book, DeBabelizer is, basically, a *scriptable* batch processor for graphics files. By scriptable, I mean that you can assign processing instructions to a batch of files, and the program will run that script — the processing instructions — across all the files in the batch. You can use DeBabelizer to open and convert to nearly every known graphics file format created on nearly every computer platform, including exotic graphics hardware systems, as well as animation formats such as QuickTime. Equilibrium regularly adds new file support and can create custom import/export modules if needed. This alone makes it a must-have for cross-platform developers and producers who need to convert many different types of graphics to a common format.

DeBabelizer's real power, however, lies in all the different types of image processing you can apply to your imported images, although much of this power is hidden away in obscure dialog boxes. DeBabelizer has a superb color-reduction routine, for example, that produces great-looking 8-bit (or lower) images from higher bit-depths with optimized palettes, and can even make a SuperPalette, which is a single optimized palette made from a series of images or video frames. You can use DeBabelizer to run Photoshop filters on an image, or apply DeBabelizer's own brightness and contrast, rotation and scaling, and blurring functions to it. DeBabelizer can composite images based on alpha channels, crop the edges of images based on a background color or alpha channel, or let you modify the color channels directly. In fact, just about anything you can think of to do to an image you can do in DeBabelizer; not only that, but because these processes can be scripted, you can automatically apply them to batch lists of images and run the scripts on them, automatically processing potentially thousands of images.

For example, suppose that you had created a 3-D animation on a Silicon Graphics computer that you need to convert to small 8-bit PICT files for a Director animation on the Mac. First, you need to network the machines or transfer the files to the Mac via removable media; networking with Ethernet is usually the most efficient method, if not the fastest. Then, in DeBabelizer, you batch open the files; DeBabelizer can read the SGI RGB format directly. Then you tell DeBabelizer to apply the script you've created to each image in the batch. In this case, the script might include cropping the edges of the image slightly and scaling it to 320x240, and then dithering the image to an 8-bit System palette and saving it as a numbered PICT file. You can make a script by entering functions in a list or by simply having DeBabelizer record your actions into a *macro*, or a routine of keyboard instructions. Finally, you batch save the images and walk away while the computer goes to work. Hundreds of images could be processed this way overnight, whereas it might a week to do all this by hand in an image editor.

Unfortunately, at this time DeBabelizer is available only for Macintosh. It's so useful, however, and will save you so much time, that it's worth it for non-Mac shops to buy a lower-end PowerMac just to run DeBabelizer. For about two grand, you can get a reasonably fast Mac and DeBabelizer; just think of it as a $2,000 program that comes with free hardware. It's that useful. One other thing to remember is that DeBabelizer deals only with bitmapped images; any EPS files you want to work with must be rasterized first.

Utilities: compression

Compression, or data reduction, is an important aspect of image production, and with the recent explosion of the World Wide Web, has become even more significant. The highest theoretical throughput of a standard 28.8 kilobaud modem is 3.6 kilobytes per second; it's rarely that high. Contrast that with the 300 kilobytes per second available from a double-speed CD-ROM drive, and you'll see that graphics delivered over the Web need to be tiny compared to CD-ROM graphics, if you don't want to lose your viewers. There are several ways to do this, the first being, of course, to make your images smaller. Another very common practice is to reduce the bit-depth of your images, dithering them down to 8 bits or less. For Web delivery, you generally cannot use custom palettes because most browsers don't support them, so you have to dither with System palettes. Beyond that, there's *data compression* and *image compression*.

Data compression involves removing or restructuring redundant file data, which usually turns out to be error-correction data. This does not affect the image quality itself; only nonimage data is altered. Data compression requires a dedicated compression program, such as Aladdin System's Stuffit Deluxe, which supports all the standard compression types used on the Internet. Because most of the information in a graphics files is image data, though, data compression can reduce the file size only so far. The amount of compression applied to the file is called the *compression ratio*; data compression usually is no greater than a 2:1 ratio. In the graphics world, data compression is sometimes called *lossless*, because all the original data can be reconstructed. Another common compression PC compression program is PKZip, which performs many of the same functions as Stuffit while specializing in files meant for the Windows platform.

On the other hand, image compression removes redundant pixels in an image, so that graphics are visibly altered to some degree. Compression ratios using image compression can be 50:1 or greater, meaning that the final compressed file takes up only 2 percent of the disk space that the original, uncompressed file took up. There's a price to pay, though: this type of compression is sometimes referred to as *lossy*, because some original data does get discarded. The more compression, naturally, the more visible *artifacting* you'll see in the image. Artifacts are abberations in the picture, which are visible as color smudges, misplaced pixels, blurring of detail and pixellation, or a "blocky" visual quality.

One of the most common image-compression types is JPEG, which compares neighboring pixels and averages them together. JPEG, which stands for the Joint Photographic Experts Group, is a worldwide standard for image compression, and has been in use since the early 1990s. With this compression standard, good-quality images can be expressed in a fraction of the original filesize, especially if the compression ratio used is conservative, say at less than 5:1. JPEG artifacts, when they do appear, are usually blocky or patchy areas, especially at the edges of foreground elements or in text.

A new subset of JPEG, the Progressive JPEG format, is in use on a lot of Web pages. A progressive JPEG image is drawn as an entire image, but a very low resolution. The image is then redrawn at progressively higher resolutions until all the detail is visible. Many people find the wait for progressive images to be fully redrawn less frustrating than waiting for high-resolution graphics to be drawn in one line at a time. Another JPEG variation, M-JPEG or motion JPEG, is most commonly used with dedicated hardware video capture cards such as Truevision's Targa 2000 or Avid's turnkey video editing systems. M-JPEG is especially useful for real-time, high-data-rate video capture and output.

Another important compression standard for video and audio is called MPEG, which is an acronym for the Moving Picture Experts Group. MPEG comes in several different flavors, and is designed for high-quality, low-data-rate delivery such as CD-ROMs and video on networks. MPEG requires hardware assistance in order to work — which is why you see many new PCs today being touted for including an MPEG card. That card simply means that the computer is capable of decoding MPEG-encoded data.

MPEG is a highly *asymmetric* compression scheme, meaning that it takes much longer to compress the video stream than to decompress it for playback. Beyond that, because MPEG uses a complex compression scheme based on comparing many different frames against each other, getting the highest quality output depends on tweaking a lot of obscure parameters. As a result, MPEG production systems tend to be expensive and usually require trained operators, called *compressionists*, to get the best final product.

There are also several software compression routines, called *codecs* (for compressor/decompressor), built into Apple's QuickTime system software, as well as the competing AVI (Audio/Video Interleaf) software for the Windows platform. Any QuickTime-aware program — QuickTime is available for both Windows and Macintosh — can access these codecs, allowing you to include video clips with database programs and so on. Built-in QuickTime codecs include Photo JPEG (for still images), Animation (for high-quality 3-D or video footage), and Cinepak, which provides very high-compression ratios for video playback from CD-ROM. The differences between these codecs, to the naked eye, is the amount of compression and final-image quality. Because QuickTime is a cross-platform standard, Cinepak is probably the most common video compression codec currently used for multimedia production. I take a closer look at some of these compression issues in the animation and video sections later.

It's common for Internet delivery to apply several layers of image and data compression to a graphic file. This is okay, as long as you're careful to not apply more than one layer of image compression. This results in what's called *concatenated compression*, in which two or more different compression schemes interfere with each other, causing severe image degradation. (Concatenation is a problem you need to watch out for with digital video, too.) Also be aware that applying data compression to a file that has already been image-compressed usually doesn't result in much space savings; most of the redundant data has already been squeezed from the file. You may save only five percent or so.

Fundamental imaging tools

The single most powerful tool for 2-D graphics creation is one I've mentioned many times already — Adobe Photoshop (Figure 6-13). DeBabelizer is great for processing images, but you can't create artwork from scratch with it, or retouch pixels in an image, except in a very crude way. Every multimedia developer should have Photoshop. Photoshop is the premiere desktop photo editing program, can import and export many different file types, and is also invaluable as a paint program — many developers create their interfaces exclusively in Photoshop, including 3-D elements. Photoshop's new layering capabilities — available on version 3.0 and up — are especially useful for interface design. For example, you can keep every button variant in a control panel on its own layer against a constant background, and simply turn the button layers on and off to create different interface screens.

Other applications worth mentioning as image creation and editing tools are CorelDRAW! for Windows, Live Picture's Live Picture for Macintosh and SGI, and Macromedia Xres for Mac and Windows. These programs are particularly useful for creating, manipulating, and layering high-resolution images. Each works by essentially creating low-resolution proxies of the elements to be composited, keeping a record of all operations performed on the proxies, and applying them to the high-resolution image at the end of the

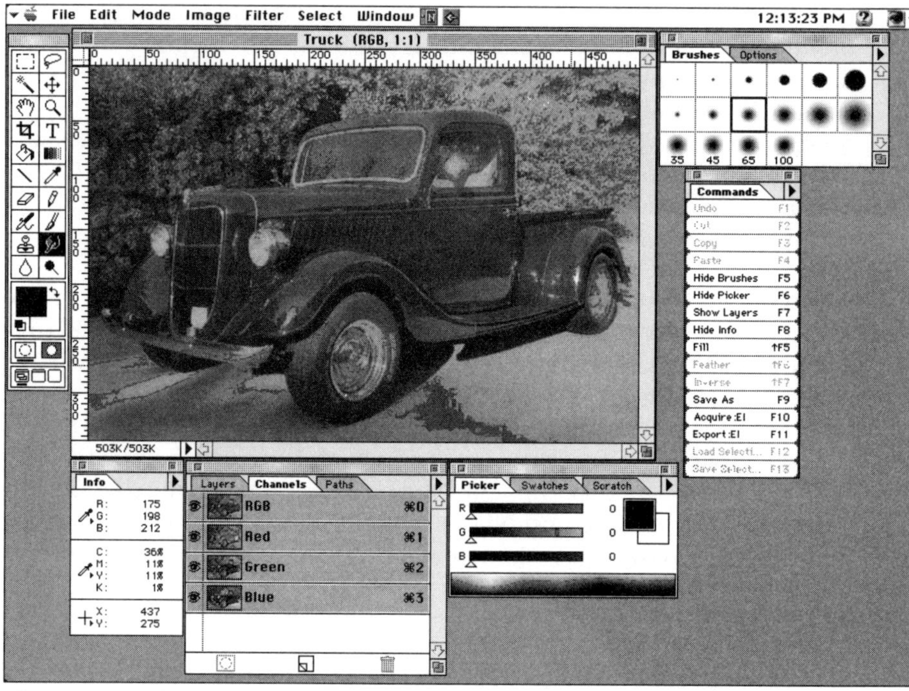

Figure 6-13: Photoshop features comprehensive image-manipulation tools.

session. By dealing only with the low-res proxies, the applications respond much faster to the artist. For high-resolution output, these programs can process images much faster than Photoshop, which works on all elements at their full resolutions and so can bog down with high-res files. Live Picture, the more sophisticated (and expensive) of the two, is particularly good at compositing very high-resolution photographic images. However, Live Picture and XRes lack Photoshop's precise and powerful pixel-level editing tools and brushes, and their high-res processing power is less useful for typical multimedia resolutions.

Photoshop, because of its open architecture and wide adoption by graphic artists, has engendered a large third-party market in *plug-ins* — pieces of software that add some particular function to a program. Some Photoshop plug-ins perform utility functions, such as the scanner plug-ins that I mentioned previously; some add support for particular types of files, such as the plug-in Adobe recently released to import and export GIF89, a new Web-standard image format with transparent backgrounds and interlaced rendering.

Other plug-ins are more effects-oriented, and I take a closer look at some of these. Best-known of this crop of plug-ins is MetaTools' Kai's Power Tools, now at version 3.0. Kai's Power Tools is actually a collection of plug-ins, some of which are straight image processors (blurs, noise, smudging, and so on) and others of which create psychedelic tiled or gradient patterns, fractals, and organic textures. As with all image applications designed by MetaTools' Kai Krause, Kai's Power Tools sports an unconventional, innovative interface (Figure 6-14).

Figure 6-14: The interface in Kai's Power Tools lets you see things in a different way.

The Black Box, a filter set from Alien Skin Software, has a number of useful effects for multimedia designers. With one filter setup, you can create automatic drop shadows, 3-D bevels or cutouts, glowing edges around selections, and photographic motion blur effects. More than one interface screen that looks like a 3-D rendering was actually created with The Black Box (Figure 6-15).

Xaos Tools' Terrazzo creates kaleidoscopic patterns from bitmapped images (Figure 6-16). You simply choose your image, open Terrazzo, select a symmetry type, and resize and drag the tile area around in the image until you find a pattern you like. This is a great way to create complementary backgrounds and textures that are related to your original image. Here's a Terrazzo Tip: Because images created with Terrazzo are by definition tileable (terrazzo means "tile" in Italian), you can use it to make background GIF images for Web pages that will automatically tile at any page size. Just find a suitable foreground element in your Web page design, run it through Terrazzo, and you'll have an infinitely tileable browser background derived from the foreground element.

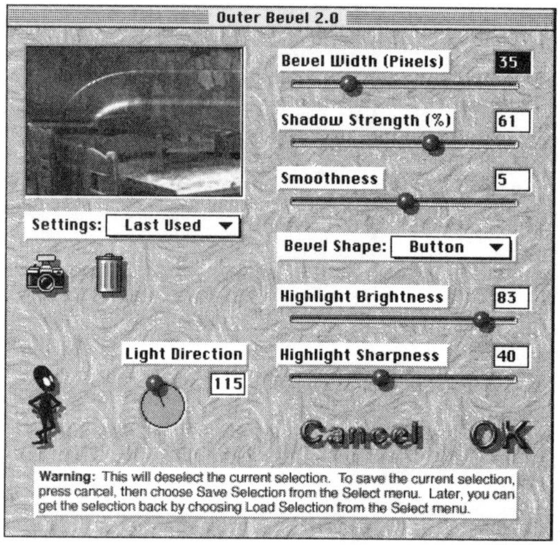

Figure 6-15: The Black Box filters can be a handy visual "Swiss Army knife."

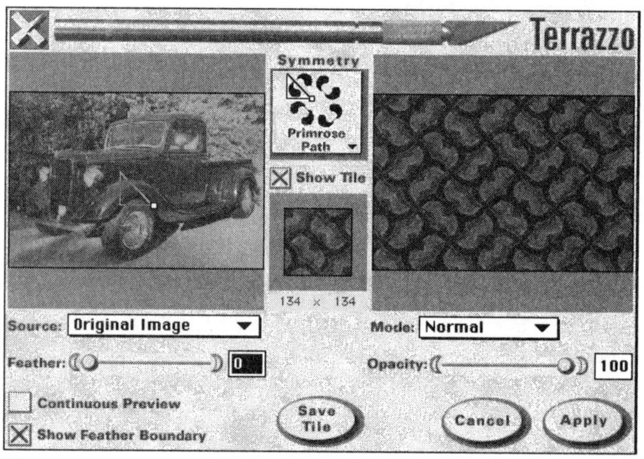

Figure 6-16: Terrazzo's tiling option is especially useful for Web site backgrounds.

Typecaster, also from Xaos, is another useful multimedia tool. It lets you create true 3-D text within Photoshop, and gives you a number of controls for modifying 3-D parameters such as angle and position, lighting, surface attributes, and textures (Figure 6-17). Although you can't create animations

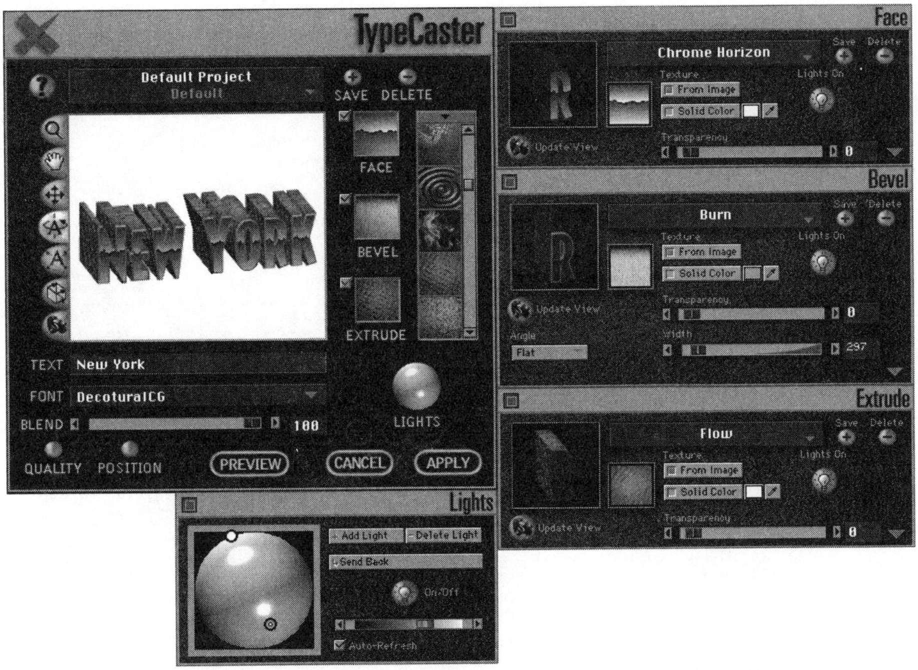

Figure 6-17: Typecaster is a good introduction to 3-D effects in Photoshop.

yet, Typecaster is a good introduction to 3-D for Photoshop users. Andromeda Software's Filter Series 2 is another 3-D filter set, allowing you to map Photoshop textures onto cubes, cones, and so on. With Black Box, Typecaster, and Series 2, you can do a lot of basic 3-D design without having to learn a 3-D program at all.

Photoshop's plug-in format has become something of a standard in the graphics world, and many other programs can now use plug-ins originally written for Photoshop. These include DeBabelizer, Fractal Design's Painter, and Adobe's own After Effects, Illustrator, and Premiere. After Effects and Premiere, motion graphics programs, which I cover in greater depth later, let you animate some Photoshop filters to create moving brushstrokes and other effects.

Speaking of Painter, Fractal Design's "natural media" paint program for PC and Mac is a powerful, though underutilized, resource (Figure 6-18). Painter can simulate the look of painting or sketching on paper and other media better than any other program, and really shines when used with a pressure-sensitive tablet. Even if you can't draw, though, you can still scribble, right?

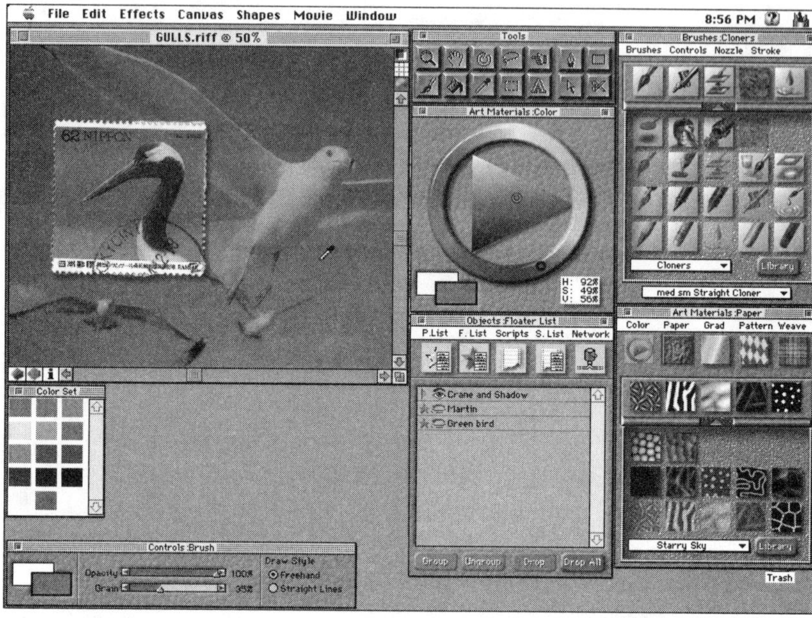

Figure 6-18: Fractal Design's Painter program emulates natural art media.

Figure 6-19: A photographic image prior to manipulation in Painter.

Figure 6-20: Suddenly, the photograph resembles a painting.

Nonartists may find Painter particularly useful for processing existing photographic or 3-D imagery and making it look hand-rendered. You can open a photograph or 3-D image and massage it with a wide variety of texture and brush tools to create a unique image (Figures 6-19 and 6-20).

Illustration

As I mentioned, illustration programs deal with vector graphics, although a current trend in illustration development is the addition of bitmapped tools and layers that let you incorporate paint elements in the illustration. Generally, though, illustration programs use vectors to produce resolution-independent PostScript graphics. In an illustration program, you typically work by drawing a curve, manipulating its outline with special tools, and filling it with color. You can create very complex illustrations this way, although it's hard to get a photographic look with illustration tools. The big advantage of illustration graphics is their small file size compared to their potential resolution.

Most authoring programs, however, for CD-ROM or for the Web, can work only with bitmapped graphics, and most viewing engines and browsers have the same limitation. (One exception is Macromedia, developer of Freehand, a long-standing and popular illustration application, which has released a version of Shockwave that can display Freehand files. This is a special and proprietary case, though.) So, even if you're a whiz with CorelDRAW! and can't produce graphics any other way, you'll have to rasterize the vector file into a bitmap to display it with a viewer or browser. Still, illustration programs are often the best choice for things such as setting type and creating charts. Corel's CorelDRAW! is probably the best-known and most popular illustration program; until recently, it was available for PC only. The new version for Mac (and PC) includes a paint application and a 3-D program, and comes with a huge collection of clip art and fonts.

Adobe Illustrator (Figure 6-21) was one of the first of several illustration programs for the Mac, and the current version is probably the most powerful and full-featured of the lot. Macromedia's Freehand and Deneba's Canvas are some others. The latest Illustrator can use Photoshop filters to process images, and its superb text-handling and drawing tools have long made it a favorite with print designers. Some of these designers who have made the transition to Web design still use Illustrator to lay out interactive pages.

2-D Animation and Special Effects

2-D animation differs from 3-D animation not so much in its final form, because in each case you're producing a QuickTime or AVI movie or a series a numbered, sequenced image files, but in how it's produced. First of all, I'll distinguish between traditional animation and computer animation. Traditional or *cel* animation goes back to the beginnings of film and is still how most animation is produced today. In cel animation, the master artist draws the *keyframes,* or points of important action, according to the *exposure sheet,* which is a master list of all shots, camera moves, layers, and timings of the animation. *In-betweeners* create all the hundreds of intermediary drawings that fill in the action between keyframes. *Ink-and-paint* artists clean up and color in the drawings, *backgrounders* paint static background scenes, and then the animation components are layered on top of the background, with each individual component on its own cel, or transparent plastic sheet. Each layer is positioned and exposed, one frame at a time, for a specific number of frames of film to create the final animation. As you see, it's a labor-intensive process.

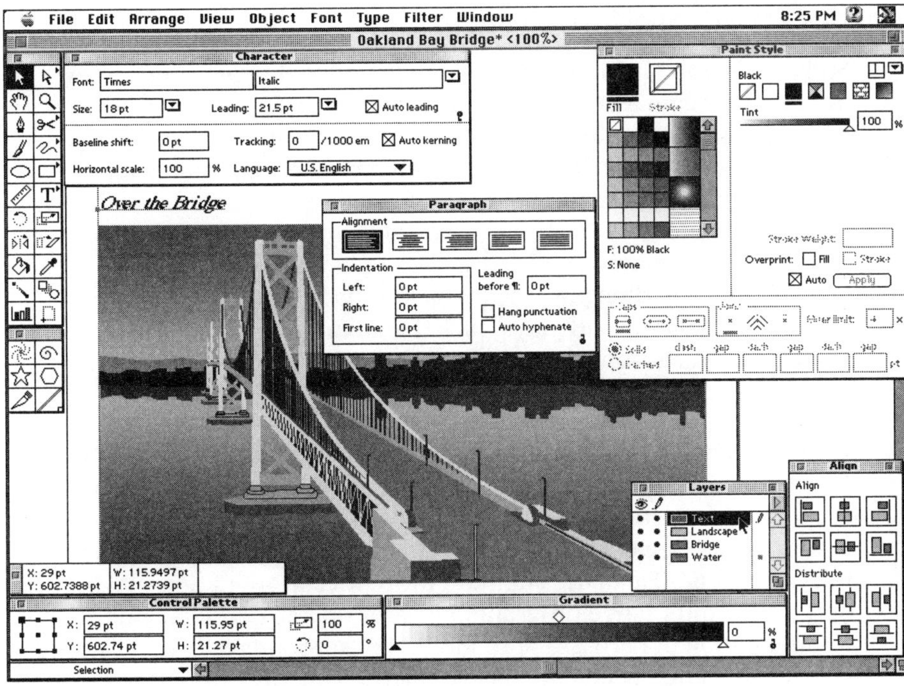

Figure 6-21: Adobe Illustrator is one of the most popular vector-based illustration programs.

Computer animation reduces much of the labor in the animation process by eliminating some of the steps and automating many of the others. And, not only can you use computers to produce the kind of slick 3-D graphics that first come to mind when you think of computer animation, but programs are available now to produce professional traditional cel-type animation, as well as video graphics animation, in a completely digital environment. These kinds of programs are classified as 2-D because their original sources are flat images, rather than 3-D geometry. A 2-D program can move images only along the horizontal and vertical axes; a 3-D program understands and can move objects or its camera along the Z axis, or depth axis, as well. Some 2-D programs can simulate Z-axis motion, as in a video animation program such as Adobe After Effects, which can tilt and move an image in pseudo 3-D space; these programs are sometimes called "21/2-D" applications. After Effects in particular can already create many common 3-D effects that used to require a dedicated 3-D application. Adding more powerful and sophisticated 3-D capabilities is a growing trend with 2-D animation developers. I'll further refine my definitions here. In multimedia production, there are two types of 2-D animation commonly in use: *sprite animation* and *rendered animation.*

Sprite animation

Sprite animation, which is the type most authoring programs work with, involves using an animation engine that controls sprites, or individual screen objects, directly, and renders to the screen in (more or less) real time. In Macromedia Director, for example, you animate a ball bouncing across the screen by importing a picture of a ball, making it a cast member (thereby making it a sprite), and setting important position keyframes. Director then figures out the in-between frames, so you don't have to animate every frame individually. You then play the animation back, and Director renders it to the screen immediately and plays back the animation. In this way of working, you would animate a woman waving by cutting her arm out of her image, making the arm a separate sprite, and animating that.

Sprite animation was the first type of animation used in interactive authoring, mostly because it makes lower demands on the computer than playing rendered animations does. Director, one of the best-known authoring programs, in fact began life as a sprite animation program long before the release of QuickTime, the standard for rendered animation playback, and only added interactive programming later on. Most video-game animation is a combination of fairly static rendered backgrounds and active sprite foreground elements, which are usually driven by a proprietary or custom-coded animation engine.

Some other advantages of sprite animation are that sprites can be made interactive, allowing you to create clickable moving objects or sprites that can interact with each other. Sprites can also have irregular outlines — they don't need to be rectangular, as rendered images do. Also, because the animation is being rendered in real time, the actual animation file is rather small, because it contains just the sprites and the code that moves the sprites. This small file size is the key to Macromedia's Shockwave technology for the Web, by the way. A Shockwave file is a highly compressed Director animation that plays within a browser, using a *runtime engine* built into the Shockwave plug-in. A runtime engine is a self-contained playback module created by an authoring program that contains all the code necessary to play a particular animation. This lets you make interactive animations that are self-contained, launchable applications that don't require any other software to work. I talk more about Shockwave and other proprietary Web animation schemes in the chapter on Web design.

To be sure, there are some disadvantages to sprite animation. Because the animation is rendered real time, the quality and speed of the animation is dependent on the power of the computer it's being played on. For example, animated sprites usually have jagged edges, because antialiasing is too complex to compute on the fly. You also can't make objects partially transparent or fade them in and out for the same reason. Beyond that, the more sprites or layers you have moving on screen, the more power it takes to move them around, and usually your animation speed suffers as a result. In general, sprite animation is best used for simple motion in relatively limited scenes that require interactivity.

As mentioned, most authoring and presentation packages have some form of sprite animation, be it simple screen transitions and chart animations, such as Adobe Persuasion or Microsoft PowerPoint, or reasonably sophisticated timeline and path controls such as Director or mTropolis' mFactory.

Rendered animation

Rendered animation is essentially motion graphics that have previously been created in an animation program and saved as a linked series of finished images. These images may be in the form of sequentially numbered and named PICT or TIFF files, a QuickTime or AVI movie, or any one of a large number of proprietary formats. The frame size may vary from postage stamp to 4000 pixels square or more for film resolutions; frame ratios are often, though not always, 4:3 in the standard television proportions. For multimedia, a common frame size is 320x240 pixels, which is 1/4 of the accepted desktop video full-screen resolution of 640x480 pixels.

Rendered animations need to be rendered because they can't be created in real time; it may take several hours to process a single frame of a dense 2-D animation with many layers and effects. The advantage over sprite animation, of course, is that a rendered animation can be much more complex, with antialiasing, transparencies, blurring, smooth motion, multiple layers, and so on. However, a rendered animation is a series of complete frames that can't be altered except by re-rendering, so elements within an animation can't be controlled or manipulated directly as they can in a sprite animation. So, to summarize, sprite animations are generally a collection of commands and objects driven by those commands, with, on average, lower image quality but greater interactivity; rendered animations are image files only, with better image quality but no interactivity (other than start and stop).

Apple Computer's QuickTime is the most common cross-platform format for rendered animations. Microsoft's Video for Windows is close behind, but isn't cross-platform compatible. QuickTime is usually perceived as a video format, but digitized video is just another bitmap, and QuickTime supports rendered animation of any type. QuickTime runs on Macs, PCs, and SGIs, and can support any resolution, color-depth, or aspect ratio. It also incorporates multiple synchronized audio tracks, text tracks, and copyright information. One of its most important features is that it has a variety of graphics compression schemes built in, and is designed to be able to accept third-party codecs.

A codec primer

Every codec has variable compression, so you can adjust image compression for your target data rate. The most important built-in codecs for animators are Animation and Cinepak. The Animation codec is intended for, as you probably guessed, animation files — that is, files that are comprised of digitally-created flat artwork, rather than photographs or video. At its highest-quality setting (that is, the least amount of compression), Animation is lossless, and is an excellent choice for producing first-generation graphics. Because Animation at its highest setting does perform data compression on the file, it reduces the overall file size by about half, so it makes more sense to use Animation than to save your files completely uncompressed.

By contrast, Cinepak is a highly lossy codec. Cinepak compression ratios may be 50:1 or more, and you generally see some degree of artifacting in a Cinepak image. Cinepak compression is also highly asymmetric; on a Pentium PC or a PowerMac, it may take an hour to Cinepak-compress a minute of video. Cinepak's big plus, of course, is that it looks reasonably good at very low data rates, like those available from CD-ROM drives, so it's very commonly used for video on CD-ROM. The coming of DVD — the new Digital Video Disc — may soon change that. DVD uses MPEG-2 compression (explained later in this chapter), which yields both excellent data compression and terrific image quality. At the time of this writing, DVD is scheduled for a public debut in time for the Christmas selling season, 1996.

Back to existing technologies. Generally speaking, you should save your first-generation renders from an animation program without image compression, rather than render directly to a lossy codec such as Cinepak. Even though it may require a lot more disk space to store the files, rendering to a lossless codec gives you much more flexibility down the road in terms of recompressing the file to different compression types. For example, suppose that you render an animation in Cinepak format for CD-ROM. Your producer decides that you're going to try Truemotion S for playback instead. If you try to recompress the Cinepak version to Truemotion, it will look awful, because of the concatenated compression problem that I mentioned earlier. Your only choice would be to go back to the original materials and re-render from scratch.

Instead, if you had rendered to lossless Animation, you could easily recompress from that to any other lossy format without concatenation artifacts. In fact, in almost all cases, making any kind of significant change in an animation file, such as resizing it or adding titles or even a sound track, requires re-rendering and re-compressing the file. If you keep your files in a lossless format all through the process until the very last step, you'll avoid any intermediary image degradation.

Animation applications

One of the best 2-D animation programs available is Adobe After Effects, currently for the Mac only, but coming soon for Windows NT (Figure 6-22). After Effects began as a video graphics program that took a frame-based approach to video design, rather than the timeline-based style of Avid's Composer and Adobe's own Premiere. It also was the first video graphics program to implement high-quality subpixel positioning, for ultra-smooth motion. Currently at version 3.1, After Effects has proved invaluable for many multimedia producers for its superior bluescreen compositing, versatile special effects, and excellent Cinepak compression.

After Effects supports unlimited layering, direct import of Illustrator and Photoshop files; Photoshop files with layers can be imported with each layer as a separate video layer. After Effects also sports a wide variety of plug-ins, including MetaTools' Final Effects, an advanced suite of software tools that provide sophisticated pseudo 3-D motion graphics, many different types of particle systems, and unique, psychedelic special effects (Figure 6-23).

Speaking of special effects, warping and morphing remain useful additions to an animator's tool set. *Warping,* the distortion of images within controlled parameters, and *morphing,* the warping of one still or moving image into another, are the domain of specialized applications such as Avid's Elastic Reality, the Valis Group's Flo and MovieFlo, and Gryphon's Morph, one of the first morphing programs for the desktop.

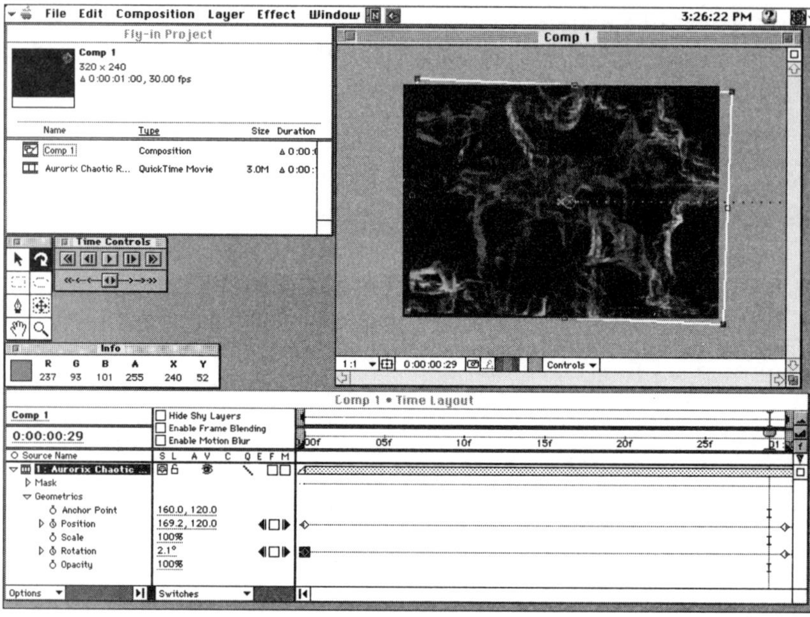

Figure 6-22: After Effects is an exceptionally useful tool for animation and video applications.

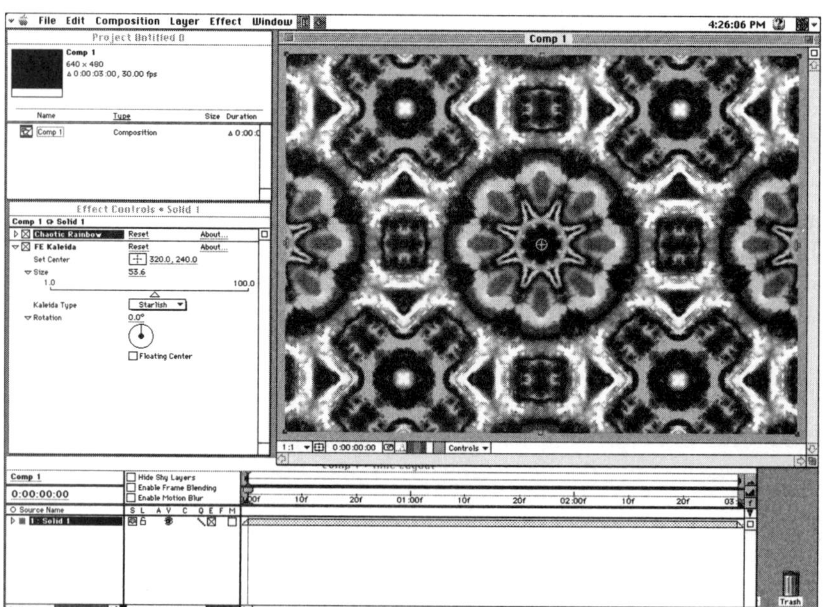

Figure 6-23: The lines between video and digital artwork can be effectively blurred.

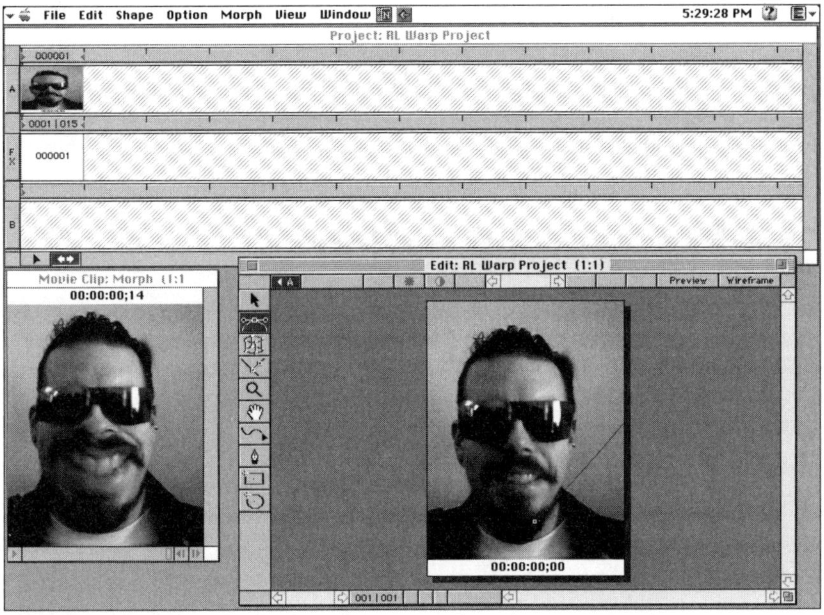

Figure 6-24: Elastic Reality is an apt name for what you can do with this program.

Elastic Reality (Figure 6-24) for SGI, PC, and Mac, is perhaps the most powerful of the desktop programs. The basic procedure for warping an image is to define an area or shape to be warped and then distorting the shape into the final form; the program then animates the in-between states. Elastic Reality defines its shapes as bezier splines, allowing for very precise placement and control over the warp. A *bezier spline* (named, perhaps not too creatively, after a man named Bezier) is a curve with digital "handles" on it. These handles allow you to move, stretch, or otherwise manipulate the curve by simply dragging it. This allows you to do things such as animate a filmed character's mouth to lip-sync with new dialog, a technique used to good effect in the film *Forrest Gump;* the effect was done with Elastic Reality on Silicon Graphics machines.

I close this section with a mention of some specialized 2-D animation applications designed for digital cel animation. Cambridge Systems Animo (for SGI and Windows NT) and Linker Systems Animation Stand (for Mac, NT, and SGI) let skilled cel animators assemble complete productions digitally in the computer. Both feature exposure sheets, direct painting with tablet support, scanned artwork management, pencil test modes, ink and paint modules, and variable resolution rendering to a wide variety of file formats. Because these programs are modeled on the traditional animator's way of working, animators without traditional training will probably find them difficult to learn and use. However, animators with traditional cel and drawing experience will probably love them.

3-D Graphics and Animation

In the dim and distant past, all of 15 years ago, 3-D animation was so expensive and complicated to produce that its use was reserved exclusively for feature films and network television. Back then, computer animation systems cost hundreds of thousands or even millions of dollars, with the software not much cheaper, and usually required on-site programmers to get them to work at all. A little later, desktop workstations with more or less off-the-shelf software began to replace the old closed systems; these workstations and their programs could be had for as little as $100,000 — chump change. Somewhere along the way, personal computers began to get more powerful, and 3-D animation capabilities began to filter down to ordinary mortals. Recently, we've begun to see reasonably priced desktop systems that can do nearly all that the workstations could do, at a fraction of the price.

At the same time that computers and 3-D software have been getting cheaper and easier to use, there's been a corresponding explosion of 3-D production for multimedia. It seems as if every new CD-ROM title and Web site these days features an elaborately rendered 3-D environment, or at least 3-D interface elements. Each phenomenon feeds the other, so there's an increasing need for reasonably priced, full-featured 3-D applications and the people to use them.

3-D graphics is a broad topic, and there are least three different disciplines you need to master to produce professional results: modeling, animation, and rendering. Modeling, the process of creating 3-D objects in the computer, is akin to sculpting, but you use software tools. Here, you may start with basic shapes (cubes, spheres, and so on) and combine them in various ways to build up the model from smaller components. Another common modeling technique is *extrusion*, where you begin with a 2-D outline and "push" it into 3-D space. Yet another standard technique is *skinning* or *lofting*, in which you create a series of 2-D profiles that define the skeleton of a shape (the ribs of a ship, for example) and stitch a geometric skin over the profiles in order to create the solid shape.

Modeling

Modeling is often the most labor-intensive step of the 3-D process. As a result, an active market in third-party, preconstructed models has sprung up to support those too busy (or too unskilled) to make their own models. Viewpoint Datalabs is one of the largest and best known, and can supply custom models to any specification. Their models are typically available in several different resolutions, ranging from simple, low-detail objects designed for video games and virtual reality applications, to exact and highly detailed planes, cars, and buildings for film production.

Animation

Animation, making things move around, is another skill set entirely. Here, the animator isn't so much concerned with the realism and detail of his or her models as in making them move in a convincing manner, whether it's realistic motion or exaggerated cartoon antics. The standard 3-D animation program is based on keyframes, which I discussed in the 2-D animation section, although some of the newer physics-based animation types don't implement keyframes. Again, as with models, it's possible to buy prefab motion data sets, such as all the keyframes necessary to animate a golf swing, which can not only recreate the motion convincingly but serve as good material for analysis by the animator. These data sets aren't as widely available as prefabricated models, though.

Rendering

Rendering, which includes skills such as texture mapping and lighting, is the last step in the 3-D graphics process. During the rendering stage, the renderer assigns surface materials to models, lights the scene in question to create the desired mood or effect, and sets up camera angles and moves. Finally, the renderer sets up the rendering parameters and lets the computer crank out the frames. Rendering can take between seconds and days per frame (and remember, I'm talking about 24 or 30 frames to make one second of animation), depending on the complexity, number of lights and textures, and size of the final image, and is often the most technical step of the process.

As you can see, there's a lot to do to produce 3-D animation, and the tasks are often divided up among specialists for maximum efficiency, especially in big, expensive productions. Also, it's rare to find 3-D artists who are equally accomplished in modeling, animation, and rendering. So, in the credits for a

3-D adventure game, for example, you'll often see separate modelers, animators, texture mappers, and even lighting and camera operators, all working on the same project.

3-D programs cover a wide range of platforms and price points, ranging from $100 to $100,000. Of course, for more money you get more features, although in general, the prices of 3-D applications are going down as their performance and capabilities go up. I take a closer look at some popular 3-D applications for multimedia on the PC and Mac platforms, and close with a quick overview of some higher-end platforms and programs.

Before I go on, I'll define some other 3-D terms that I use as I discuss these programs. Specifically, I cover exotica such as polygonal geometry, spline geometry, Phong shading, ray-tracing, Boolean modeling, deformations, particle systems, and inverse kinematics.

Until recently, almost all 3-D modeling programs worked with polygonal geometry exclusively. This means that all object surfaces are described as finite groups of two-dimensional flat planes — usually triangles or quadrangles, but sometimes more complex shapes. The math required to describe a shape as polygons is pretty simple, which is why polygonal geometry is so popular, but flat shapes don't lend themselves well to describing curved shapes, as you can imagine. A cube is easily defined as six planes, but approximating a sphere requires many small polygons arranged to simulate the spherical shape. The more polygons you use to describe the sphere, the closer you can approximate its shape, but you can never truly create a smooth curve with polygons. The closer you get to such a shape, the more obvious its straight edges become. And, of course, the more you increase the resolution of your shape by increasing its polygon count, the more memory and CPU power required to push those polygons around.

Splines

Splines (variable curves) are a relatively new way to describe complex, organic geometry that define curves as mathematical formulas rather than a collection of small shapes. NURBS (Non-Uniform Rational B-Splines) are a refinement of basic splines that are used in a number of newer modeling programs. Because a NURBS shape is a formula, it has infinite resolution and is always smooth at any zoom factor. Spline math is considerably more complex than polygon math, so splines are less used at this time, although their acceptance is increasing in the 3-D world. Of course, if you send a spline-based model from one program to another, the second program needs to understand the spline math to correctly handle the model.

This is all somewhat analogous to the difference between a paint program, such as Adobe Photoshop, and a draw program, such as Adobe Illustrator. Photoshop uses finite bitmapped pixels (the equivalent of polygons) to define an image; you can zoom into such an image only so far before seeing the individual pixels and losing the quality of the overall picture. Illustrator uses 2-D Postscript splines (very much like NURBS) to create an image at any desired resolution, but your output device needs to understand Postscript to render the Illustrator file.

Phong shading

Phong shading renders the shading of a surface by calculating the color of an individual polygon based on its surface textures and lighting parameters, and then smoothes the surfaces of adjacent polygons together to create the final image. Phong rendering can create very realistic images when set up correctly, and generally renders much faster than ray-tracing. Phong's main limitations are that it cannot calculate reflections and refraction, which is the bending and distortion of light as it passes through transparent objects. To create these effects with a Phong renderer, you have to fake them with texture maps.

Ray-tracing

Ray-tracing is a completely different procedure, based on the physics of light, in which surfaces are calculated by tracking virtual rays of light throughout a scene as they bounce off objects (reflected) or pass through objects (refracted), depending on the objects' surface characteristics. The advantage of ray-tracing is that shadows, reflections, and refractions are calculated automatically as part of the process, so it's generally easier to create photo-realistic images with ray-tracing than with Phong shading. The disadvantage of ray-tracing is that the computer has to calculate potentially millions of virtual light rays bouncing around in the scene, so ray-tracing is usually much slower than Phong shading.

Boolean modeling

Boolean modeling is a powerful technique based on logical operations performed on the intersections of models. That is, Boolean modeling lets you take two spheres, for example, position them so that they overlap, and then cut away the first sphere in the shape of the second sphere where they intersect, leaving a dimple in the side of the first sphere. It's ideal for cutting holes and tunnels in simple or complex objects, and in the hands of a skilled artist it becomes a powerful sculptural tool. True Boolean modeling is difficult to implement in software, and so relatively few programs support it.

Deformations are pretty much what they sound like: the ability to bend, twist, bulge, or otherwise warp an object's geometry into new shapes. Most programs featuring deformations will let you animate these changes over time, which lets you create the kind of "squash and stretch" animation made popular by Warner Brothers cartoons and seen today in commercials with dancing cars and cereal boxes.

Particle animation

Particle systems are a special animation effect causing hundreds or thousands of points to spray from a surface, each one following specified behaviors but with randomness built in. You set up the basic parameters, such as gravity, initial direction, and velocity, and the program calculates the rest, without the need to individually animate all those points. With the correct tweaks, particle systems can simulate water, smoke, fire, and other natural phenomena as convincing 3-D graphics.

Inverse Kinematics, or IK, sets up hierarchies of motion between parent and children models (models attached to parents) so that you can more easily simulate natural movement. Basically, IK lets models lower in a hierarchy affect models higher in the hierarchy. A correctly configured IK link will let you pull on a figure's foot, for example, and have the lower and upper legs follow along naturally so that you don't need to individually animate the leg components. IK is an important addition to the animator's arsenal, but isn't necessary or even desirable for convincing movement. Pixar's phenomenally successful 3-D movie, *Toy Story,* for instance, was created without IK.

Macintosh Programs

Strata StudioPro is an integrated modeling/animation program, an earlier version of which was used to created the hugely successful CD-ROM game *Myst.* It has a high-quality ray-tracing rendering engine and extensive modeling tools including Booleans, deformations, and particle systems.

Electric Image Animation System is the premiere animation application for the Mac. It also used to be the most expensive, at $7,500, but its price has recently dropped under pressure from SoftImage for NT and 3-D Studio Max, both for Windows. It features one of the fastest renderers on any platform, superior anti-aliasing, and many special effects previously found only in workstation-class applications. It does not include a modeler, so models must be created in another application and imported into Electric Image. AutoDesSys formZ, one of the best modeling programs around for Mac and Windows NT, is often used as a modeling front end for Electric Image.

Fractal Design's Poser is an interesting one-trick pony that generates natural or fantastic human body models in correct anatomical positions for rendering in other 3-D programs. It lets you define the body type that you want to create (male, female, child, superhero) and then implements *inverse kinematics* to let you put the body model into any pose you like. Inverse kinematics is a relatively new system for 3-D animation that lets you constrain a model's joints to only the positions a human being (or any other creature) could assume. You then set up hierarchical links between the various joints in the model, linking a finger to its hand, the hand to an arm, and so on.

Special mention should be made here of MetaTools' KPT Bryce 2, which is optimized to create spectacular realistic (or fantastic) 3-D landscapes, complete with skies, mountains, and water. The current version can import models created elsewhere, but it's difficult to create environments other than landscapes in Bryce. It has found some popularity in the game world for producing alien planets and exotic skyscapes.

3-D Programs for the PC

Although it took a while for Wintel-based machines to catch up to the Mac in terms of good graphics applications, the gap has narrowed considerably over time, and there are excellent new tools available for Windows, particularly for Windows NT.

Autodesk's 3-D Studio, for example is a hugely popular program that has actually been around since the bad old DOS days. The newest version, 3-D Studo Max, is designed to run under Windows NT. In it, 3-D modeling, rendering and animation are accomplished in a single-screen environment. The program will work with hardware that's running multiple processors, which dramatically speeds rendering time. Other noteworthy features include a "history" feature that lets you go back and reverse edits, an animation timeline for precise motion control, and editing functions for source or imported materials.

Lightwave 3-D is a program originally developed by NewTek for the Amiga platform, but it has now been ported to PC in a 32-bit version that will run under Windows. The program is capable of particle animation, several different types of image mapping, and morphing effects, which means that one effect can melt into another.

Softimage, which is a product now controlled by Microsoft, is an extremely powerful program for 3-D modeling, rendering, and especially animation. Originally designed for UNIX-based hardware, Softimage not only features some of the most advanced animation capabilities in the field, it also includes a number of surprising effects, such as a randomize feature, a "bump map" feature that can create organic surfaces from smooth geometry, and numerous animation "helpers" that let the software do much of the work of bringing the 3-D shapes to life.

Extreme 3-D from Macromedia (also available for Mac) is a spline-based program that also does animation. It straddles the line between too-basic 3-D programs and the powerhouses such as Electric Image and Softimage, which makes it an appropriate choice for a novice that intends to take 3-D seriously at some point. There is an excellent selection of texture-mapping features, and the program comes bundled with many preformed textures that can be applied to newly created files. A demo of Extreme 3-D is available on the CD-ROM that's been bundled with this book.

Advanced 3-D Graphics Workstations

Macs and PCs have improved significantly in speed, power, and memory in the last few years, and are beginning to rival the capabilities of higher-end graphics workstations. Workstations represent the next level in performance beyond general-purpose desktop machines; some of Sun Computers' and Silicon Graphics' top-end graphics machines have power rivaling the supercomputers of a few years ago. In general, a graphics workstation consists of one or more RISC processors, lots of memory and drive space, hardware graphics acceleration, and an unfriendly operating system, usually UNIX. Naturally, you pay a premium for this kind of power. Whereas a capable Pentium or PowerPC-based machine capable of multimedia production can sell for as little as $2,000, UNIX graphics workstations cost from $10,000 to $100,000 or more.

Workstation applications tend to be expensive and difficult to learn, but have great power and flexibility. Because of these programs' expense and steep learning curves, it's usual to only run one or two applications on a workstation so that most workstations become dedicated to a single task. In exchange for these steep learning curves, workstation applications provide the user with features and performance far beyond the usual desktop applications.

Alias | Wavefront, now owned by Silicon Graphics, has a number of programs used by the higher-end multimedia developers, with PowerAnimator a clear favorite among 3-D animators. Other UNIX graphics programs include RenderMan from Pixar, which is not so much a program as a programmable rendering language. RenderMan was used to render everything in *Toy Story*, Pixar's highly successful 3-D animated feature film. SoftImage, now owned by Microsoft, and ElectroGig, Vertigo, and Side Effects are some other companies developing high-end 3-D programs for workstations.

An interesting recent development has been the purchase of SoftImage, long one of the premiere workstation 3-D programs, by Microsoft. Microsoft has since ported SoftImage to Windows NT, Microsoft's workstation-level operating system. Computer manufacturers such as Intergraph have responded with a variety of NT-based workstations featuring multiprocessors and graphics accelerators, which offer speed and power comparable to UNIX workstations at much lower prices. SoftImage, with its superior character animation tools, is often the tool of choice among game developers. Expect to see other major graphics applications of all types ported to or developed for Windows NT in the near future.

Audio Tools and Resources

Audio (and I include music in that category) is an important but often-overlooked aspect of multimedia production. Yet, an effective sound track can mean the difference between success or failure in a multimedia title. It's often a subtle addition such as an interesting sound effect while screens are loading, but it can also be a star as in any number of multimedia projects that are scored like a film or a music video.

Fortunately, desktop audio production tools have come a long way since their inception, and it's possible to produce fully professional audio for multimedia without an enormous investment in hardware. In this section, I discuss some basic concepts of sound, take a look at audio hardware and how it works, and finish up with an overview of digital audio production techniques and tools.

Basic concepts

Sound is a physical vibration in the air that moves your eardrums; nerves attached to your eardrums send information to your brain, which is then interpreted as a particular audio event. This means that, in essence, sound is *mechanical;* that is, it requires the movement of a physical medium. Without that physical medium (air, water, or some other substance), there is no sound, which is why there is no sound in space, *Star Wars* notwithstanding. We hear periodic vibrations as pitches; aperiodic or random vibrations as noise. Natural sounds almost always contain some mixture of each type, which gives each sound its unique character.

The faster the rate of a periodic vibration, the higher the pitch we hear. Human beings can't hear the entire range of possible vibrations; our range of hearing is about 20 vibrations per second, or 20 Hz (Hertz, the standard unit for sound frequencies), to 20 thousand vibrations per second, or 20 kHz (kiloHertz). Actually, many people can't hear much above 15 kHz or so; many multimedia speaker systems can't reproduce frequencies below 100 Hz or even higher, and many computer systems can't reproduce sounds higher than 11 kHz. I get into more detail about this later, because you need to be aware of these limitations when you design your own audio tracks.

As mentioned, natural sounds consist of some combination of pitch and noise; even relatively pure-pitched sounds, such as flutes, contain breath noise and a complex mix of pitched tones. These tones, called *harmonics* or *overtones*, are usually not individually audible but combine together to form a sound's distinctive tone color, or *timbre*.

Seeing sound

Any sound, no matter how complex, can be represented as a *waveform*, which is a pictorial graph of changes in loudness, or *amplitude*, over time. Take a look at Figure 6-25, which is a graphic representation of a digital sound file as shown in an audio editing program. What you see is a waveform representing the sound of a plucked string. Amplitude is the vertical axis, time is the horizontal. You'll notice that the sound starts out with a fairly sharp onset, or attack, representing the initial plucking of the string, and then fades away, or decays, slowly. Figure 6-26 shows a few beats of a drumkit phrase in stereo; you see an individual track for each channel of the stereo signal. Note that you can clearly see the main beats of the music. Here, the attacks are sharper and the decays much faster than the plucked string, as you would expect with drum sounds. It takes a little practice to get used to reading these waveforms graphs, but you'll find that skill invaluable when you start editing digital audio. The ability to identify beats in music is especially useful for music video editors.

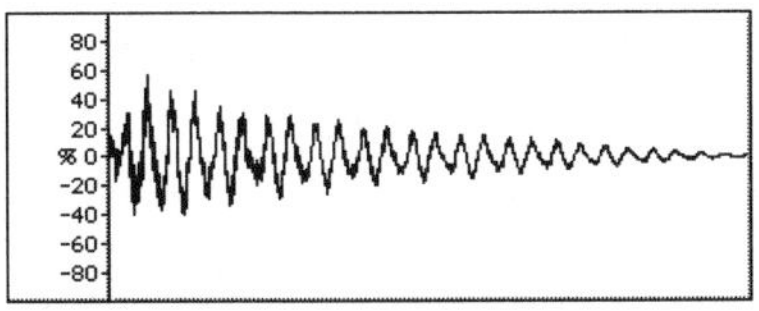

Figure 6-25: As you can see from this visual representation, the waveform of a plucked string eventually decays to nothing.

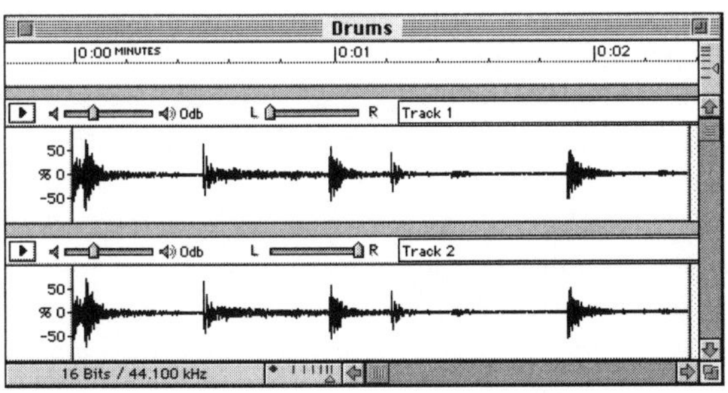

Figure 6-26: If you follow the amplitude "spikes," you can follow the drum beat.

Multimedia is digital, but sound isn't

Acoustic sound is inherently an analog signal; that is, it changes continuously over time. In order to record and manipulate acoustic sound, it needs to be converted into an electronic signal so that electronic audio equipment can work with it. Turning an acoustic signal into an analog electronic signal is called *transduction*, which means the conversion of one form of energy into another. A device that transduces is called a *transducer* (duh); microphones and speakers are the most basic types of transducers.

Microphones

A microphone converts acoustic energy into electrical energy, whereas a speaker (or headphone set) converts electrical energy back into acoustic energy. Both are essential pieces of gear for an audio producer, especially the speakers. A microphone (or mic) works a lot like your ears; a thin diaphragm contained in the mic housing is attached to a wire, which is surrounded by a magnetic field. Sound makes the diaphragm move back and forth, and the movement of the wire in the field generates an electronic signal that mimics the movement of the air that produced the sound. This type of microphone is called a *dynamic* mic, and is the cheapest and most common type. They're often used in live sound applications because they're relatively sturdy and fool-proof, and can withstand very high sound levels.

Another common type of microphone is the *condenser* mic. These are usually much more expensive and more sensitive than dynamic mics, and are a good choice for recording voices or acoustic instruments in a studio setting. In a condenser mic, two thin charged plates, one fixed and one movable, are placed close to each other. The movable plate serves as the diaphragm. As it moves back and forth in relation to the fixed plate, the changing distance between the two generates an electrical signal. Because the plates need to be continuously charged, a condenser mic needs an internal or external power supply to work. Most recording studios will have both dynamic and condenser mics on hand for different uses.

The signal coming from a mic is usually very low amplitude and needs to be *preamplified* to bring it up to a high enough level to be processed in an analog or digital environment. By contrast, signals coming from most electronic audio equipment — "line level" signals, as opposed to "mic level" signals — are "hot" enough to not require preamplification.

A typical speaker or headphone set works exactly the opposite of a dynamic mic. A variable electrical signal causes the speaker diaphragm to move back and forth, displacing the air in sound waves. Because the electrical signal from a piece of audio gear such as a mixer or computer isn't strong enough to push the speaker diaphragm by itself, an amplifier is necessary to amplify the signal to the point where it can push the speaker. The more power the power amp supplies, the louder the sound (until the speaker blows up, that is).

The recording process

An analog tape deck like the familiar cassette recorder is another common type of transducer. Here, the electrical signal from a mic preamp, for example, gets converted into magnetic energy that displaces metal particles on a piece of recording tape. This displacement is more or less permanent, so the tape can store the transduced audio signal for playback at a later time by reversing the recording procedure and turning the magnetic patterns back into an electrical signal.

Multitrack tape recorders take this concept a step further and allow you to record tracks — individual parts of the sound — separately while listening to previous takes. This way, a single producer can assemble a piece of music by recording each part individually and mixing them in a final *mixdown* to produce the finished master recording. In fact, this is a very common technique in all phases of modern music and audio production.

Mixing down the individual tape tracks to a stereo master requires running the tracks through a *mixer*, as you might guess. A mixer basically consists of multiple individual inputs, each with its own volume, stereo placement, and effects controls, all running into a final (usually) stereo output. The mixer is usually the centerpiece of a recording studio, because it's used to route and control every audio source in the studio. The mixer's stereo output is typically split into two pairs, one feeding a power amp and pair of speakers or headphones, the other connected to a two-track mastering deck, DAT tape recorder, or CD-A (audio CD) burner.

Most professional mixers have some sort of *equalization* controls for each input. Equalization, or EQ, is the emphasis or suppression of selected frequencies in a sound. The familiar bass and treble controls on your stereo are the most basic form of EQ. Turning the treble down engages an electronic filter that reduces high frequencies while leaving lower frequencies alone. The bass control reduces or increases lower frequencies while letting higher ones pass. More sophisticated EQs, like those found on quality audio mixers, let you control middle frequencies or several different bands, or let you adjust the high- and low-pass filters cutoff frequencies. The purpose of EQ is to let you change the tonal colors of sounds so that they will blend better (or stand out more) in a mix, to compensate for shrill or muffled recordings, and for special effects.

Recorded sound is never perfect

As you can imagine, these various conversions and transductions of the original sound mean that the final recorded results are unlike the original. Every time the sound energy gets translated into another form, or gets patched through another piece of audio gear, some change happens to the original sound — elements of the sound are lost, and new elements are introduced. A multimillion dollar audio industry has sprung up around trying to minimize that change, and now analog audio gear is so good that at the highest levels of the industry, the changes are inaudible to all but the most sensitive ears.

In the last few years, however, the audio industry has largely moved to digital audio formats, and that move has opened up audio production to the use of the computer and software-based production tools, which in turn has led to the desktop audio revolution. It's now possible for musicians (and multimedia producers) to produce fully professional audio in home studios for a fraction of what it used to cost in recording studios, and without the need for specialized, and expensive, technicians. That's not to say that analog audio is dead — we still need to deal with acoustic sound, so mics and speakers will be with us for a while yet. Digital tools and techniques are definitely taking over the audio world, though, and multimedia producers are members of the digital vanguard.

Digital audio concepts

Like all digital information created and processed in the computer, digital audio consists of bits of data — ones and zeros. An analog or acoustic sound needs to first be *digitized*, or converted to digital data, before it can be worked on in the computer. The hardware that does this is called an *analog to digital converter*, or *A-to-D*. Many multimedia computers now have A-to-Ds built in, enabling you to record via a microphone directly onto the computer's hard drive, or have the computer recognize your spoken commands.

Unlike analog sound, which varies continuously, digital sound always consists of discrete steps. The fineness of these steps, and consequently the accuracy of the reproduction of your sound, is determined by the *sample rate* and *bit-depth* used during the digitizing process. The higher the sample rate, the higher the frequencies you can record, and the more of the sound's natural brightness you'll be able to retain. The higher the bit-depth, the more detail and dynamic range in the sound will be preserved. CD-quality stereo audio is sampled at 16 bits, 44.1 kHz, in two interleaved tracks. (This represents a data rate of about 150 Kilobytes per second.) Multimedia audio is often 8 bit, 22.05 kHz, mono or stereo. Sometimes you'll come across lower sample rates, such as 11 or even 8 kHz, on the Web, but rarely lower than 8-bit resolution.

How digital audio works

What does this all mean? Something called the Nyquist Theorem states that a digital signal can't reproduce any frequencies higher than one-half its sample rate. Stated another way, audio sampled at 44.1 kHz can't contain overtones higher than 22 kHz (half of 44.1). Audio sampled at 22 kHz can't contain overtones higher than 11 kHz (half of 22). You'll recall that the upper limit of human hearing is about 20 kHz, so it seems that you would always want to sample at 44.1 or higher for the most realistic sound. In fact, multimedia projects for which audio is critical should always be produced at 44/16.

However, because there is relatively little meaningful sound information above 10 kHz, and most multimedia speaker systems won't play that high anyway, the audio team can often get away with non-CD-quality sound. With careful management, you can still have perfectly usable sound for most projects recorded at 22 kHz, with half the data rates and disc space required for 44.1 audio. With the right software tools, you can even get acceptable 11 kHz audio, perfect for tight-bandwidth Web delivery.

Equally important in determining the quality of your final sound is its bit-depth. A sound sampled at 16 bits of resolution has 32,768 different amplitude levels with which to accurately reproduce a sound. An 8-bit sound, by contrast, has only 256 different amplitude levels. As you can see, an 8-bit is going to be much coarser and less able to capture the details of a sound. Of course, 16-bit sound takes up twice as much space as 8-bit, and many multimedia machines can reproduce only 8-bit sound anyway, so sometimes you have no choice. Luckily, there are some good software tools for making decent 8-bit audio, and this seems like a good time to introduce the best.

Waves' WaveConvert for Mac and PC (Figure 6-27) is an essential tool for multimedia audio producers. It lets you batch process audio conversions, has superior sample-rate and bit-depth conversion algorithms, makes cross-platform compatible files, will let you optimize QuickTime audio tracks in place, and is pretty cheap besides. WaveConvert can even make decent-sounding files at very low sample rates for Web delivery, better than any other software tool at this time. It's highly recommended.

Software Tools for Multimedia Audio

Software digital audio tools have come a long way in the last ten years. Fully professional applications with a wide range of "plug-ins" allow the desktop producer to record in a full multitrack environment with completely nonlinear access, synthesize unique sounds, design sound effects, and edit music, voice, and video tracks all on the desktop. These tools divide into four broad categories: digital audio editors, multitrack recorders, MIDI sequencers with digital audio capabilities, and audio-for-video tools.

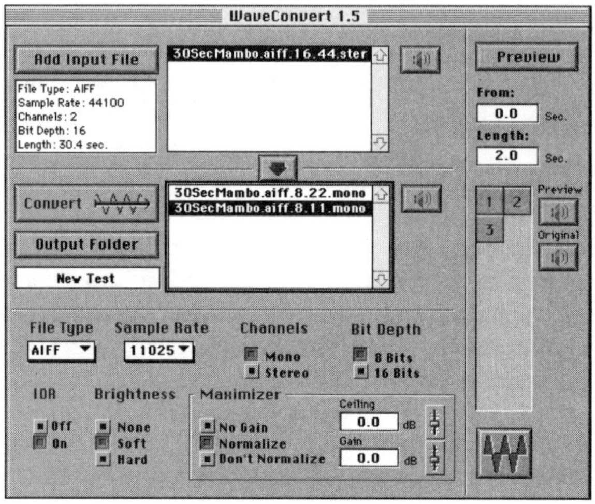

Figure 6-27: WaveConvert lets you do batch processing on a chosen group of sound files.

Digital audio editing tools

Every multimedia producer at some point finds himself having to edit a digital audio track — to cut a breath out of a narration or substitute one word for another, to make a music bed twice as long, or to create a seamless loop for a multimedia wait state. Fortunately, there are some good tools on different platforms available to do all these things and more. Computer-based graphic editing makes it easy to locate the offending breath, for example, by playing the track, stopping playback when you hear it, selecting it with the cursor, and deleting it with a keystroke or replace it with a sound that you've copied and pasted from another file.

Macromedia SoundEdit

SoundEdit was one of the first software-only audio editors available on any desktop platform. It was initially developed for the Macintosh and used the Mac's barely adequate audio hardware for output. It always had decent audio editing tools, though, and has since matured into a powerful application equally at home editing QuickTime audio, CD-quality tracks, and low-res multimedia audio. With the current version, SoundEdit 16 2.0 (Figure 6-28), you can record and edit multiple tracks, edit QuickTime audio tracks, apply a

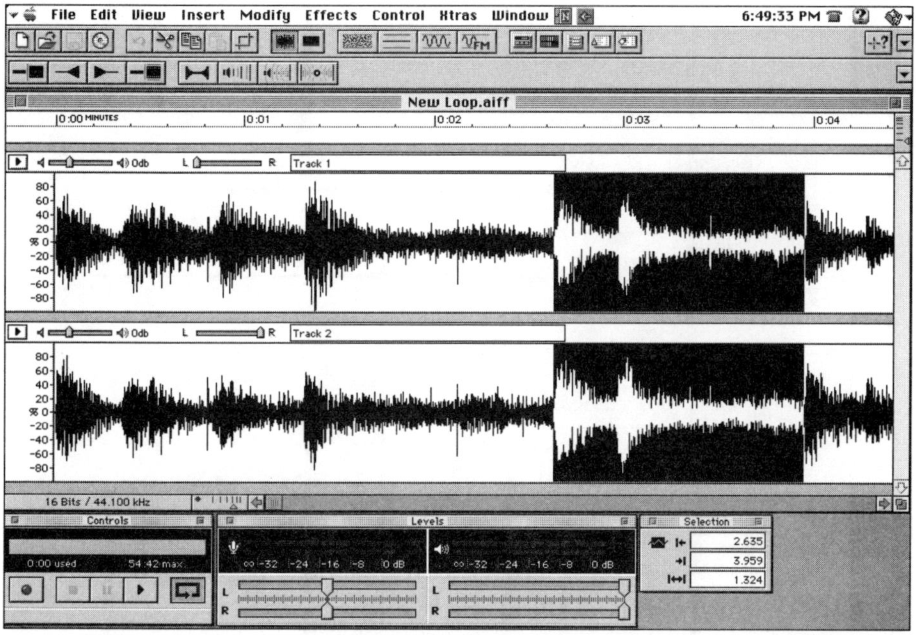

Figure 6-28: Macromedia's SoundEdit 16 offers multitrack digital audio capability.

variety of special effects to the audio, and output to a wide range of files types and formats. You can also easily create loops for multimedia backgrounds tracks; SoundEdit lets you save 44/16 audio in the new high-quality IMA compression format, whose 4:1 compression gives you CD-quality audio in the space of 8/22 audio.

Digidesign Sound Designer

Sound Designer (Figure 6-29) was the one tool that can claim credit for the Mac's ascendance as the platform of choice for professional digital audio production. The original Sound Designer, intended for interfacing with sampling keyboards, also proved valuable for editing digital master recordings for CD. More powerful auxiliary hardware allowed more record and playback tracks, and third-party developers began to produce plug-ins for the Sound Designer environment, such as Waves' S1/L1/Q10/C1 series of professional signal-processing tools (Figure 6-30).

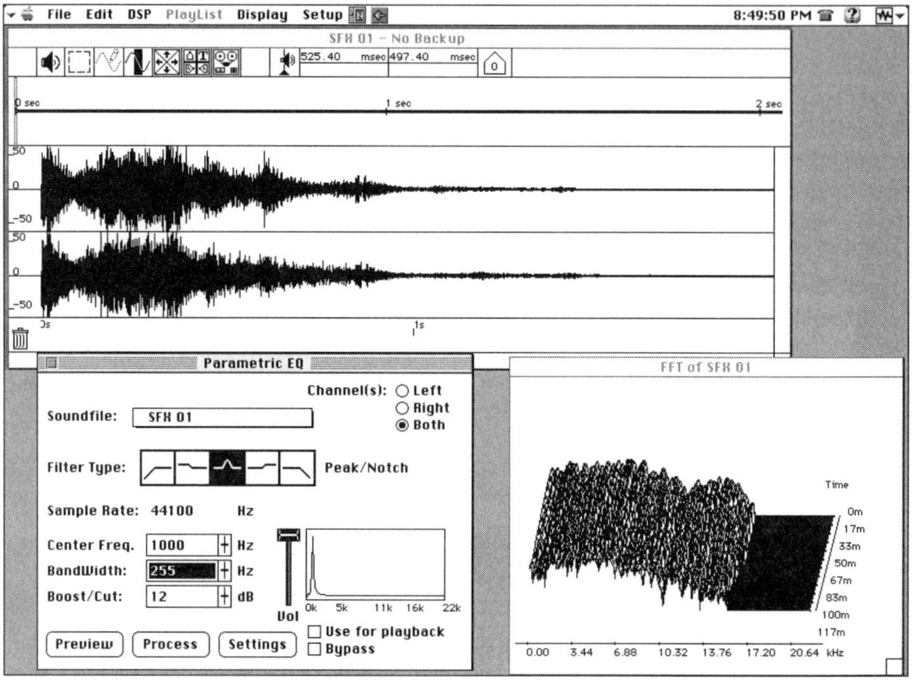

Figure 6-29: Digidesign's Sound Designer can rightfully claim to be an industry standard.

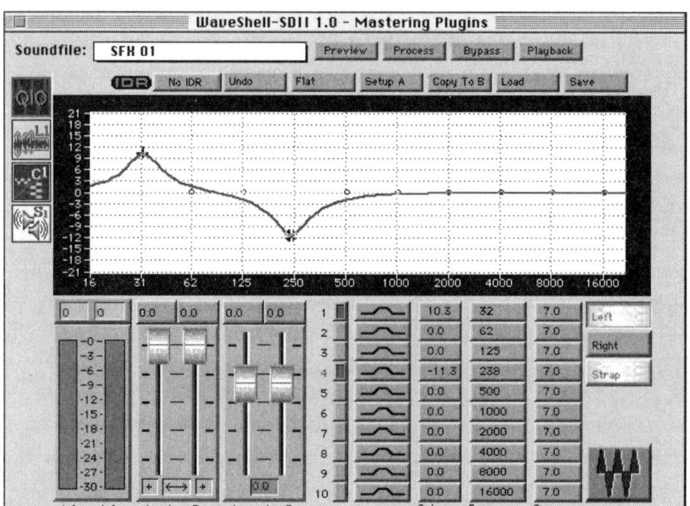

Figure 6-30: Plug-ins for Sound Designer (such as these by Waves) are common.

Sound Designer features extremely precise and flexible editing tools, with markers, memory locations, and multiple loop support. Digidesign later introduced the highly successful ProTools hard-disk based multitrack recording and editing environment, which is in use in many recording and audio-for-video studios. Another venerable Mac editing application is Passport Design's Alchemy, favored by some sound designers for its unique special effects.

Sonic Foundry Sound Forge

On the Windows side, Sonic Foundry's SoundForge is a good choice for multimedia audio production. It has many of the same editing features as SoundEdit, such as graphic selection, cut, copy and paste, normalizing, and equalization, and includes a wide range of special effects such as reverb, delays, flanging, and so on. It works with a wide variety of sound cards, including the standard Sound Blaster-compatibles as well as higher-end products such as Turtle Beach's Tahiti and Digital Audio Lab's CardD systems. It's also available for Windows NT.

Multitrack recording software: the Mac still rules

One recent breakthrough in desktop audio production has been the introduction of computer-based multitrack recording systems. These allow for full random access to all audio tracks and much more flexible editing than tape-based systems can provide. The first versions of these systems were from Digidesign and eventually developed into their industry-standard ProTools product line. ProTools and other related systems require specialized and relatively expensive computer audio hardware installed in your system; without this hardware, essentially audio accelerator cards, the software is useless. With the hardware (and fast hard drives — a minute of 44/16 stereo audio requires 10MB of disk space), you're guaranteed glitch-free playback with real-time signal processing and special effects, as well as top-quality analog and digital audio I/O.

Recently, though, desktop computers and hard-drive systems have become fast enough to allow multitrack recording and playback without the need for additional hardware. Such systems currently exist for the Mac and SGI platforms, both of which have their own built-in 44/16 audio systems. The PC still requires at least a basic audio card, so some additional expenditure is necessary for these systems. The amazing thing is that most of this new crop of multitrack software is quite cheap — between $200 and $500, as compared to $1,500 to $8,000 or more for hardware-based systems.

Macromedia Deck II

One of the first software multitrackers was Deck II, currently at version 2.5 for the Macintosh (Figure 6-31) and soon to be available for Windows. On the fastest PowerMac with an accelerated hard drive, Deck can play back 32 tracks of 44/16 digital audio with real-time mixing. Deck has sophisticated real-time EQ and special effects built in, and can accept third-party Adobe Premiere-compatible audio plug-ins. These, however, need to be applied to a track and rendered — they can't be used for real-time playback. Deck's only real drawback is that the Mac's audio outputs, except on the most recent machines, are fairly lo-fi stereo mini plugs, rather than the more professional-style RCA or XLR balanced audio connectors. The most recent PCI PowerMacs at least have RCA I/O but lack any kind of digital audio output, so even if your audio sources are entirely digital, you have to output in an analog format for your final recording, thereby losing a little quality. Fortunately, some inexpensive add-on cards are on the way from Apple and other manufacturers; these will allow for digital audio I/O using the Mac's native audio processing.

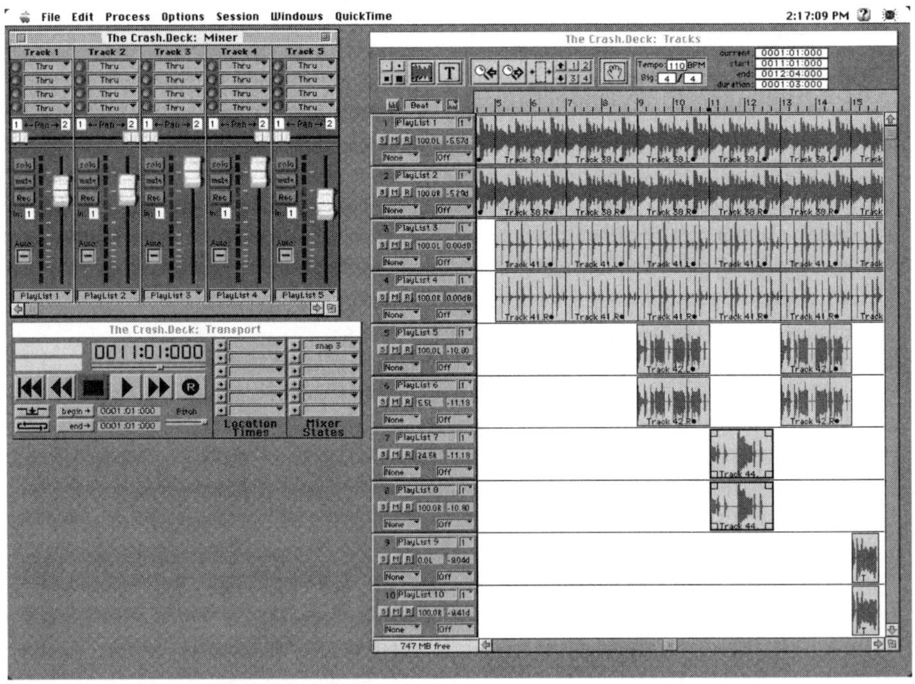

Figure 6-31: Deck offers elaborate multitrack possibilities without additional hardware.

Digidesign Session

Another powerful software multitrack recorder is Digidesign's Session Software, which provides 16 tracks of playback with real-time mixing and EQ on PowerMacs with no extra hardware (Figure 6-32). It's available for Windows too, but requires a sound card; when used in conjunction with Digidesign's Audiomedia III PCI audio card, 8 tracks of real-time audio with digital audio I/O is possible. Innovative Quality Software's SAW Plus is a popular Windows-only multitrack application that works with most standard Windows-compatible audio cards and provides more playback tracks than any other Windows multitrack program. SEK'D's Samplitude Studio, also exclusively for Windows, can give you up to 16 monophonic audio tracks on a Pentium-level PC with a fast hard drive and standard audio card.

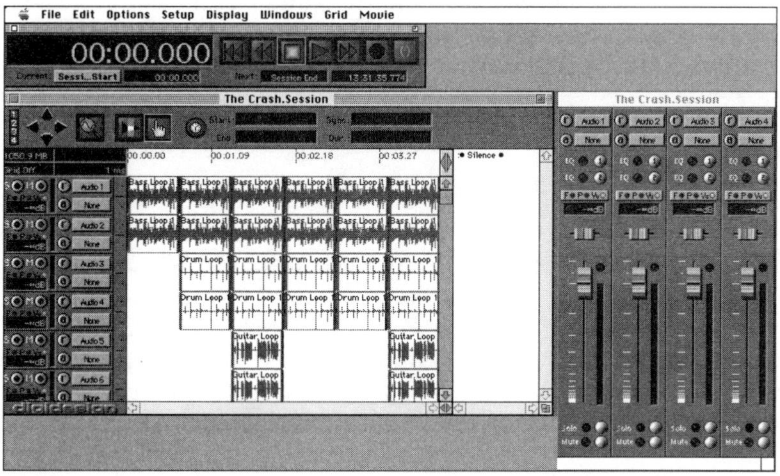

Figure 6-32: Session brings powerful multitrack audio to the Windows platform.

Digital audio for Windows

Because a Wintel computer needs to be equipped with additional hardware in order to work with audio, most audio professionals still prefer the Macintosh as their production platform of choice. But there is excellent software for the PC platform as well. S.A.W., from Innovative Quality Software, is a good one. It can record up to 16 stereo tracks simultaneously, while being able to mix and match tracks recorded at different bit-depths and sample rates. It also comes bundled with an effective set of DSP plug-ins, including a parametric equalizer, echo effects, and a compressor/limiter.

Sounspiration's Samplitude Studio is another powerful Windows-based digital audio program for multitrack work. It can record up to eight stereo tracks, which can be output from up to four sound cards simultaneously.

Audio for Silicon Graphics

If you're working with a Silicon Graphics platform, especially the Indy, TimeLine's MediaSound software is about the only choice for editing and multitrack recording. The Indy features both analog and digital audio I/O built in, making it the only current desktop platform that doesn't require extra hardware for all-digital production. MediaSound gives you a full graphic interface, eight real-time audio tracks in playback, unlimited virtual tracks (which must be mixed down to one or more of the eight live tracks before they can be heard), extensive cut-and-paste editing, and basic EQ. Because of the speed of the SGI's RISC processor and its subsystems, MediaSound is a particularly fast and responsive editor.

Intro to MIDI

The development of MIDI (Musical Instrument Digital Interface) was the main reason computers infiltrated recording studios in the first place and changed the music business forever. MIDI was originally intended as a standard control language to allow electronic music synthesizers from different manufacturers to interface with and control each other. Because MIDI is a digital protocol, it soon became evident that personal computers could be used to control synthesizers, and the first MIDI sequencing programs appeared.

The great advantage of MIDI over live recording is that MIDI is a control language — it contains only instructions on how to play sounds, not the sounds themselves. The sounds themselves are created externally, in synthesizers. This makes MIDI a much more compact way to record music than recording audio tracks. And because it's purely digital data, MIDI can be manipulated in the computer just like text or graphics — cutting, pasting, duplicating, inverting, and so on. A MIDI sequencer is a kind of word processor for music, allowing a single performer to record unlimited virtual tracks and create perfect takes with simple editing techniques, or even construct complete performances note by note.

Of course, because MIDI doesn't make any sound on its own, you need synthesizers to hear MIDI music. Literally hundreds of different synths are available, in all price ranges. The number of sounds and voices available in a synth, and its overall sound quality, will determine the final quality of the MIDI score being played by the sequencer. It is not uncommon to see a small project studio with a dozen or more synths and special effects boxes, all MIDI controllable. With MIDI, it is possible for an individual to create a convincing music score with synthesizers only; in fact, many multimedia soundtracks are composed just this way, with the final output being a digital audio file.

MIDI for PC sound cards

On the PC platform, another way MIDI is used is in soundtracks, especially for games, designed to be played by the on-board synth in a standard PC audio card. As mentioned, MIDI's compact file size frees up disk space for graphics, and MIDI can also be programmed to higher levels of interactivity than digital audio can at this point.

Because most multimedia PCs for the Wintel platform include a MIDI-capable sound card with a synthesizer or sample player built into the card, many multimedia programmers compose their soundtracks as MIDI data to be outputted through that sound card. It's an elegant solution — it allows small file sizes, and there's even an agreed-upon standard for which MIDI notes will equal which musical "instrument" being played back on an appropriate sound card.

But there are some disadvantages of the on-board MIDI approach. First and foremost, the composer is at the mercy of the MIDI sounds in whatever sound board the user has (and they vary widely in quality), and MIDI cannot reproduce human voices well without a lot of expensive sample playback gear. Plus, the method of synthesis used on these sound cards aren't standardized at all, and a "flute" sound on one sound card can sound more like a bassoon — or a nasal whine — on another. As multimedia computers get more powerful, expect to see MIDI soundtracks begin to disappear in favor of digital audio soundtracks. In the meantime, MIDI for multimedia soundtracks on the Windows platform makes a lot of sense.

MIDI and digital audio

There are many MIDI sequencing programs available for the amateur or professional musician, but of particular interest to those producing multimedia audio are sequencers that combine digital audio recording and playback capabilities with the standard MIDI features. Opcode's StudioVision for Mac and Windows is one of the more capable (Figure 6-33). StudioVision

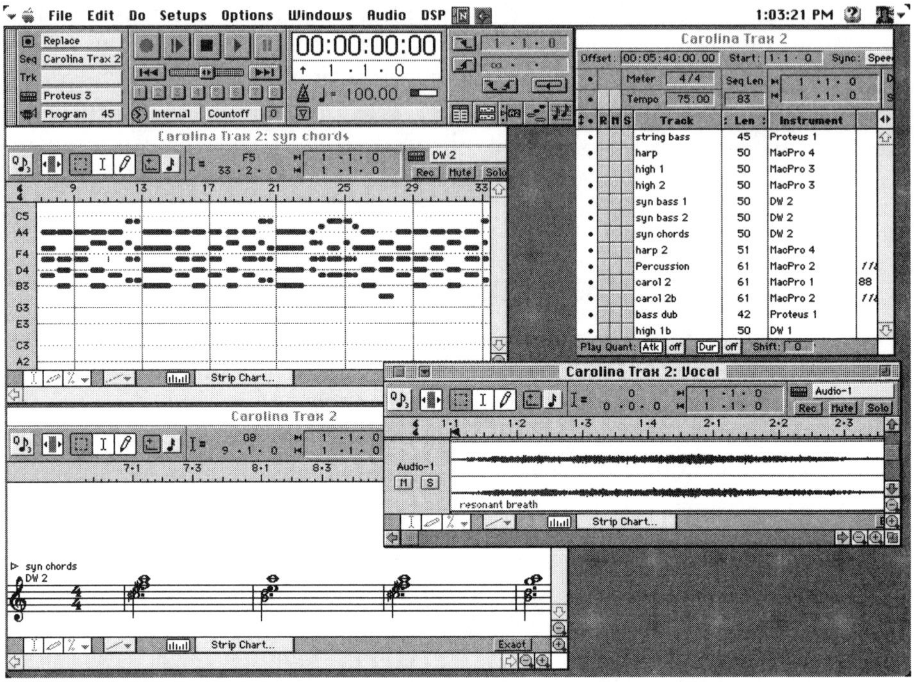

Figure 6-33: Opcode's StudioVision combines digital audio with MIDI.

lets you view MIDI data tracks as text for easy editing, in a piano-roll format, and as music notation. It features unlimited tracks, rules-based editing (being able to make selections and perform operations based on criteria you set), and integration with Galaxy, Opcode's universal management program for synthesizer voices.

Beyond that, StudioVision can record, play back, and edit up to 16 tracks of digital audio, depending on the capabilities of your hardware. This capability makes it easy to sync audio tracks, such as voiceovers or live instrumental tracks, with your MIDI tracks. StudioVision also features some remarkable DSP (digital signal processing) functions, such as the ability to turn digital audio into the equivalent of MIDI data (which lets you edit it with all the standard MIDI editing tools such as quantization) and back again.

Some other capable MIDI sequencers with digital audio capabilities for Mac and PC: Mark of the Unicorn's Digital Performer, Steinberg's Cubase Audio, Voyetra's Digital Orchestrator Plus, Cakewalk's Cakewalk Pro Audio, and Emagic's Logic Audio.

Audio-for-video applications

Many standard desktop video editing applications have surprisingly good audio editing capabilities, and should not be overlooked by multimedia producers. An outstanding example is Adobe Premiere (Figure 6-34), shown here in audio editing mode. You can use Premiere to record audio directly into your computer from an external mic, tape, or CD, and save it as an audio-only QuickTime movie or in the standard AIFF audio file format. After you've captured or imported your audio files, you can layer up to 99 tracks of mono or stereo audio, mix their levels with flexible graphic "rubber-band" controls, apply a variety of effects to any file, and even set keyframes to have the effect automatically change over time, and output the whole thing in a variety of sample rates and file formats.

Premiere features some decent sample rate conversion algorithms, so you can use it to optimize audio for low-res QuickTime playback. Adobe has developed an open plug-in standard for Premiere, and some interesting third-party plug-ins have appeared, including CyberSound FX from Invision and versions of Waves' Sound Designer plug-ins. One highly recommended Waves plug-in is AudioTrack 1.0 (Figure 6-35). This plug-in features Waves' professional-level graphics EQ, compression, and noise gate algorithms found in their much more expensive ProTools plug-ins, all in one reasonably priced program. AudioTrack is invaluable for removing hiss and rumble from raw video tracks, as well as emphasizing voice-overs and punching up music beds.

Recording audio for multimedia

Most multimedia producers coming to digital audio via the computer don't have the traditional analog recording studio background that you find in many audio engineers. In fact, in many projects (particularly those whose time hasn't been well budgeted), a graphics producer suddenly gets an order from on high to "throw some sound effects and music in there, and don't forget the voice-over." Needless to say, this is a recipe for instant stress. In an effort to relieve this stress, here's a highly condensed primer on recording audio in the computer environment, especially when using a computer's built-in audio. I use the Mac as an example platform, but most of what I discuss translates just as well to the PC.

You need good speakers

First, there are some basic hardware issues to address. You need a decent audio-monitoring system so that you can hear what you're editing. At the least, this should include a compact mixer and a pair of powered speakers.

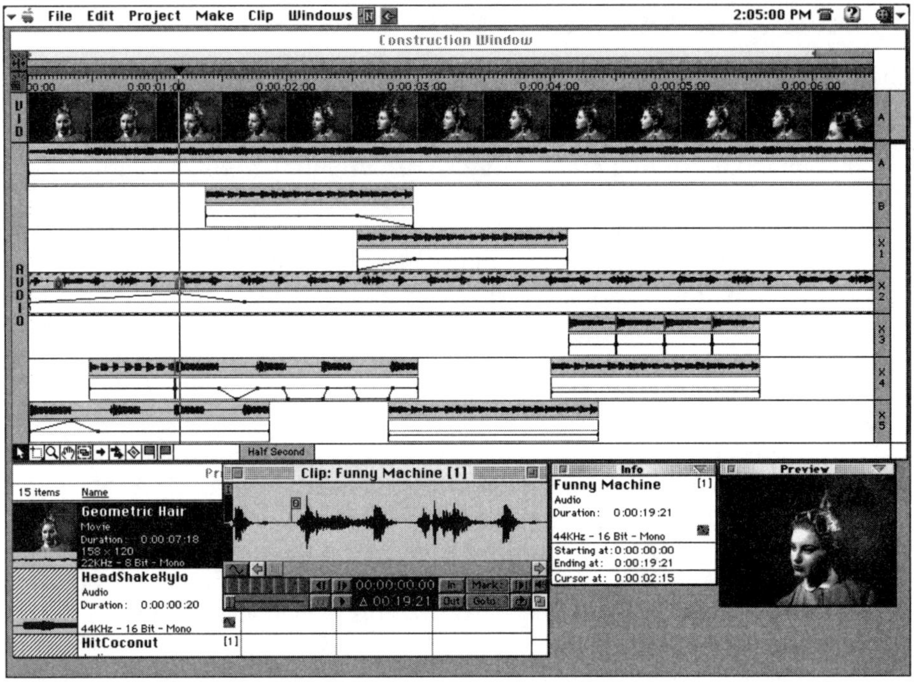

Figure 6-34: Although Premiere is more noted as an application for editing video, it's also a capable audio editor.

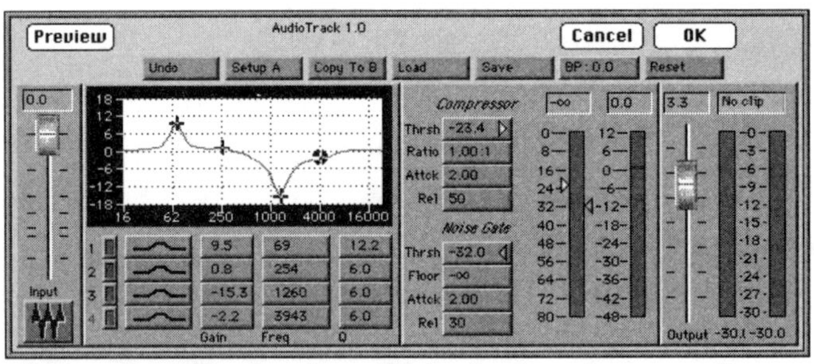

Figure 6-35: Waves makes plug-ins for Premiere as well as Sound Designer.

A number of companies, including Apple, Yamaha, Bose, Altec, and Acoustic Research make stereo-powered speakers designed for computer use. These speakers are magnetically shielded, so you can place them near your computer monitor without distorting its image, and have the right connectors to plug directly into your CPU. The amplifiers in these speakers tend to be a little weak, however, so that increased distortion at higher listening levels becomes a problem.

A better solution is separate, studio-quality, near-field monitors (designed for close listening at relatively low volume levels) and a power amp to drive them. Yamaha NS-10s are a common studio standard; Tannoy and JBL near-fields are also popular. Any studio-grade power amp of at least 100 watts RMS per channel is a good match for these. Professional-quality speakers such as these are important for detailed sound editing and music production, but you should have a pair of multimedia speakers on hand as well to test your mixes, because this is what many multimedia users will be using. For the same reason, you should listen to your mixes through the computer's built-in speaker as well. (Music industry professionals typically mix on expensive professional studio monitors, but most test and adjust their mixes on boom boxes and car stereos before final release, based on where they feel the music is most likely to be heard.)

You need a good mixer

At least as important as good monitor speakers is a clean, high-quality compact mixer to preamplify, mix, and route your audio signals. Many audio producers overlook this crucial piece of gear, even though a good one can be had for $300 or so. One of the best for multimedia is Mackie's 1202 VLZ. It features 12 input channels, can amplify microphone signals and supply power for those mics that need it, an extremely clean sound, and, perhaps most important, has multiple busses for routing audio to different locations. At the higher end, but still under $2,000, is Yamaha's Pro-Mix 01 digital mixer. This is a 16-channel, MIDI-controllable mixer with moving faders and an all-digital internal signal path. It has two built-in digital effects processors, 8 mic preamps, internal memory to record mixer states, and is an excellent choice for those who want to create a totally automated studio.

A mixer bus is simply a discrete signal path. A multiple bus mixer lets you switch an input or group of inputs to any output or combination of outputs while controlling the levels of those outputs independently. This is important because any audio you deal with usually has to go to at least two different places — the monitor speakers and the record input. The record input itself might be the computer's audio input, a cassette or DAT deck, a video deck, or any combination of these. Without a multiple bus mixer, you'll constantly have to repatch inputs and outputs or use clumsy splitter cables to route your audio, and you still won't have independent level control.

Another advantage in running all your audio through a mixer is that the mixer will give you much finer input level control than is usually available in the computer itself. The Mac, for instance, has only seven different audio input levels in its built-in hardware. Seven levels is just too coarse a resolution to properly set input levels. Why is this important? Because when you record, you usually want to get the hottest possible signal on disk without distortion, and sometimes you need to set the input in between the Mac's allowable levels to get the best recording. (More on this later.) An analog mixer, with its continuously variable controls, lets you tweak the inputs to your heart's content for the best results.

You need a good microphone (or two)

Another essential piece of gear is at least one good microphone for recording acoustic sources. Unfortunately, there is no single mic available that is ideal for every purpose, and there are hundreds of different models to choose from, but I can narrow the choices down a little. Probably the most common type of acoustic recording for multimedia is voice-over or narration reading, most often of a single voice. For this, you'll want a professional large-diaphragm condenser mic, such as the classic Neumann condensers. These mics aren't cheap (in fact, they range up to several thousand dollars, although a decent one can be had for well under $1,000), but if you're doing a lot of voice recording, it's an investment that will really pay off in the much higher audio quality that these mics provide. They're also excellent for recording sound effects and acoustic instruments, although their large size and extreme sensitivity make them less suitable for field recording and amplified instruments.

Be aware that any microphone you use will need to be preamplified before you can record from it into the computer. The signal from a microphone is actually very low — too low to be directly registered by most recording devices, in fact. Most recording devices, be they CPU, video deck, or tape machine, expect a line-level source — that is, of a certain minimum voltage level. (There are actually two standards for line-level signals, professional and consumer, but I won't get into that now.) The direct mic output is much less than line-level, so it needs to be preamplified before the recorder can sense it. The Mackie mixer mentioned previously has nice clean mic preamps built in, which is another reason that it's a good choice for multimedia production.

You need a quiet space

If you do find yourself recording a lot of voice-overs in-house, another important consideration is acoustic isolation. Obviously, you don't want a lot of traffic noise going on in the background of your narration track, but even a quiet space has a certain amount of ambient noise, and that goes double for computer rooms. Hard drives and their cooling fans tend to make a lot of noise, some monitors emit high-pitched frequencies, and even keyboard clicking and disk insertions can ruin a good take. So, whenever possible, you'll want to isolate the voice artist in a quiet room with as little ambient sound as possible, and ideally with some added acoustic isolation. This can be as simple as a closet with a door (although your voice talent may not be too thrilled with it), or as elaborate as an installed isolation booth with its own lighting and ventilation.

Acoustic isolation, by the way, is not simply a matter of slapping some egg cartons up on a storage room's walls, contrary to popular belief. Egg cartons and their more sophisticated counterparts, acoustic foam panels such as Sonex, do very little to block external noise. Their only function is to reduce high-frequency reflections from interior walls, which cuts down on the reverberation in a room and gives it a "deader" sound, which gives the recording engineer more flexibility in controlling the reverberation ambience of the final mix. To truly cut down on external sound leakage, your space needs to be as air-tight as possible and have walls as massive as possible. The more mass in the walls, the greater the sound blockage. So, if you're thinking of turning a spare storage room into an isolation booth, an air-tight door and an extra layer of wallboard inside will be a much better investment than covering the walls with foam (although you'll probably want to do that too, if you can).

An alternative to a built-in isolation booth that might be worth looking into is a portable isolation booth, essentially a closet on wheels. The more elaborate portable booths have their own lighting and ventilation, with easy access for cabling in and out, and can be a good solution when modifying an existing space or building a new one aren't possible.

Don't forget good wires

A final important hardware consideration is good cabling. Avoid cheap, thin cabling — heavier cabling means heavier shielding, which cuts down possible noise interference. By the same token, look for heavy-duty metal connectors, with one important exception. The input connection on most Macs is a stereo mini-jack that is recessed on the back panel behind a plastic housing. Only thin-profile mini plugs will snap fully into the mini plug jack; if you seem to only get one input channel, check this connection. Happily, the newest higher-end Macs have more professional RCA jacks for audio I/O, and more and more Windows sound cards are going to these higher-quality connection points.

Okay, on to the actual recording

If at all possible, it's usually better to record acoustic audio to a high-quality tape system first, such as DAT or a multitrack digital audio machine such as Tascam's DA-88, than directly to hard disk. There are several reasons for this. One is that tape is much cheaper than drive space, and you can record essentially unlimited versions or takes by just switching tapes. If you take notes as you record, and you should, you can easily find the good take and just record that one to the drive. Beyond that, a desktop computer-based hard-disk recording system is inherently less stable than the average tape environment, and there is unfortunately a much greater chance of losing the perfect take to a hard-disk crash or weird system error.

The most important reason for recording to tape first is that it provides much more control over your input levels than recording directly to hard disk. Most software recording systems have pretty inaccurate input meters, which makes it all too easy to record a signal too hot or too low. Recording too low is bad; to get a usable signal level, you usually have to destructively edit the audio file by amplifying it in software, which also increases the background noise.

If recording too low is bad, recording too hot is murder. If you try to push the digital recording environment past its highest levels, the signal gets clipped off, resulting in horrendous digital distortion. Refer to Figures 6-36 and 6-37 to see what I mean. Figure 6-36 is a correctly recorded vocal phrase; note that its highest peak is near, but not over, 100 percent. Figure 6-37 shows the same phrase with the first section clipped. The audio effect of this clipping is a disgusting crackling or crunching sound that completely obliterates the original signal. If any of your tracks look like this, throw them out and start over — they can't be repaired.

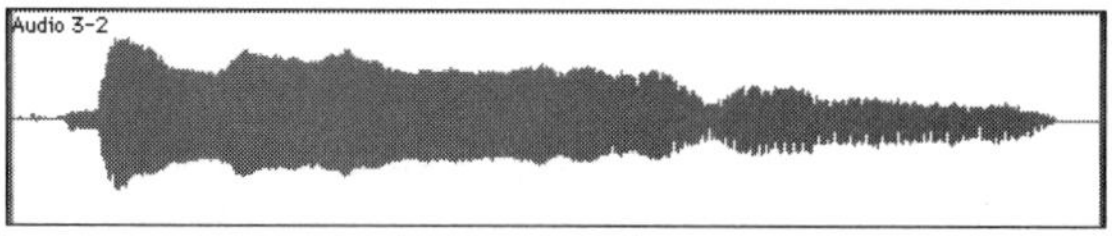

Figure 6-36: A properly recorded vocal phrase shows a clean waveform.

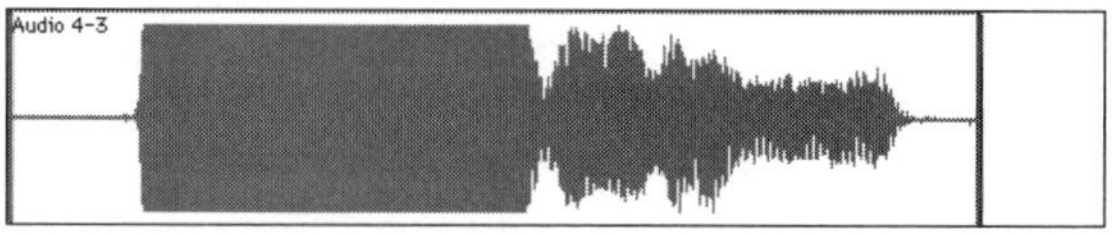

Figure 6-37: The clipping is clearly apparent on this overloaded sound file.

It's all too easy, in the heat of a live recording, to speak, sing, or play louder than you did in rehearsals or even the previous recording, possibly overloading the input and ruining the track. By recording to tape first, you can isolate the desired take, play it all the way through before recording, set your levels interactively for the best possible signal, and then rewind and record. If you set it too hot, just reset and re-record; it's much less stressful than trying to record live into the computer.

The right levels

However you decide to record, live or from tape, you'll need to set the Mac's hardware input level to 0 or 1 before setting the input level on your recording software. This is because the Mac's audio input is actually a microphone input and has its own, rather inadequate, preamp. On the PowerMac, the input level in the Sound control panel should be set to 0 (zero); this doesn't actually disable the input, but does bypass the mic preamp and bring the signal straight in at line level. On AV Macs, setting the Sound input to 1 does essentially the same thing. Because your mixer output is line level, you want the audio input to be as close to line level as possible. Otherwise, it will be much too easy to overload the input and cause that nasty digital distortion. (By the same token, an output level of 1 is also line level, which is what you want if you're going back out to the mixer.)

After you've set the hardware input correctly, you can adjust the recording level with the software's input controls, if it has them, or the external hardware mixer. Again, because of the hardware mixer's greater sensitivity, adjusting externally is usually better. In many programs, the software input meters are inaccurate, to say the least; it's a good idea to record some test tracks at different input levels until you find where distortion occurs.

After you've recorded your tracks, inspect them visually to find any clipped areas. A slight amount of clipping may not be audible, so give a test listen to any clipped tracks. If you're satisfied with the results, you might want to *normalize* any tracks that don't hit 100 percent. Normalizing searches the audio file and looks for the highest peak, and then amplifies the entire file so that peak hits 100 percent. The relative levels between different parts of the track remain the same, so this isn't an audio compression function. Because no peak is over 100 percent, no distortion occurs, and you've got the hottest possible signal to work with. Normalizing is most effective with tracks whose peaks are relatively close to 100 percent; if you normalize a very low-level track, you run the risk of dramatically increasing the noise level in the track. It's better in that case to re-record the track.

Normalizing is especially important for 8-bit output. 8-bit audio has such a limited dynamic range compared to 16-bit that any low-level 8-bit signal usually gets lost in general background noise; you'll want to crank it up as much as you can get away with.

Finally, be aware that mixing tracks adds the levels of the various tracks together. This may seem painfully obvious, but what isn't so obvious is that many relatively low-level tracks mixed together can add up to a clipped final mix, especially if you have many virtual tracks in your mix that you can't play back live to hear the results. And, most programs can't figure out what's going to happen before you mix down; they can't warn you about clipped output. In this case, it's probably best to look through your aggregate tracks and try to identify areas where clipping might occur, and then select just those areas and do test mixes of them.

Video Tools and Resources

Video production used to be the exclusive domain of large teams of highly trained professionals in multimillion dollar studios. Each piece of equipment in that studio usually performed only one function, however well it did it. And everything was analog, with analog's inherent generation loss and signal interference problems. Gradually, digital video gear began to appear in production studios. These were still one-purpose boxes, for the most part, and fabulously expensive, but allowed for a new flexibility in editing and particularly for special effects.

QuickTime

Along the way, Apple introduced its QuickTime system architecture and brought digital video to the desktop, first for Macs and later for Windows. (Microsoft followed later with its Video for Windows architecture, since superseded by the as-yet unproved ActiveX.) Initially, because of the relatively slow speed of the CPUs of the time, QuickTime video playback was limited to postage-stamp sized windows and low-res audio, and so was seen as no threat to traditional video production techniques. However, QuickTime itself had no limitations on frame rates or sizes, and as hardware improved, QuickTime came closer and closer to broadcast quality standards.

With QuickTime, desktop applications now had a consistent, standard way to handle digital video, and a number of ground-breaking QuickTime-based programs appeared, including editing and video graphics applications such as Adobe Premiere and COSA (now Adobe) After Effects, and special effects programs such as Gryphon's Morph, Avid's Elastic Reality, and Strata's MediaPaint. Most of these programs are available for both Mac and Windows. These tools, in turn, helped fuel the explosion in QuickTime video production for CD-ROMs.

With QuickTime, CD-ROM developers now had a way to integrate live video footage with other interactive content. Further developments such as QuickTime VR, which allows for interactive panoramas of real or computer-generated scenes and objects, have increased the usage of QuickTime-based content in CD-ROM and, to some extent, on the Web. In the rest of this section, I overview digital video basics, especially on the computer, and look closer at some indispensable QuickTime production tools for multimedia.

Digital video basics

Digital video has already become a popular alternative to traditional analog video production. Although this medium is still quite young, many of the basic ideas are based on technology that's more than half a century old.

NTSC

The broadcast and home VCR video with which we're all familiar is in *NTSC* format, NTSC being the National Television Standards Committee. Among other things, the NTSC standard states that color video should be transmitted at almost, but not exactly, 30 frames per second, that the transmission be *interlaced*, that it be *overscanned*, that colors must fall within certain limits, and that all the brightness and color information be carried in one signal. I'll discuss each of these in detail, and then compare NTSC to computer video.

First, you should understand that video displayed on a cathode ray tube monitor (the standard CRT monitor in TVs and computers) is drawn in horizontally rendered scan lines. That is, a phosphor dot starts at the top of the picture tube, draws a line across the screen from left to right, snaps down to the beginning of the next line, and so fills in the screen. This happens fast enough so that you don't see the individual lines being drawn, but only the complete picture. One full screen is called a *frame*.

Originally, black-and-white NTSC video was transmitted at exactly 30 frames per second (fps). When color television was introduced, for technical reasons, the frame transmission rate needed to be slowed slightly to 29.97 frames per second. Either way, approximately 30 fps is not fast enough for the eye to see an image without flicker. Technical limitations did not allow for higher transmission speeds, so to create the illusion of a higher frame rate, the single video frame is split into two interlaced *fields*. The first field, consisting of the odd-numbered lines in the frame, is drawn in 1/60th of a second; while that first field is still glowing on the screen, the second field of even-numbered lines is drawn. Then the first field of the next frame is drawn, and so on. Because at least half of the screen is being redrawn every 60th of a second, it looks like a faster rate than 30 fps. A full-frame NTSC picture consists of 525 of these lines, one under the other.

Overscanning means that the video image is drawn past the edges of the visible frame, so that the picture completely fills the screen. This means that you can't see the extreme edges of an NTSC picture because the monitor's *bezel* (which holds the picture tube in the cabinet) wraps around the edge of the frame. Because there is no NTSC standard for how much the bezel can wrap around, a videographics designer can't be sure exactly where the edges of the video image will be cut off. Most bezels don't obscure more than 5 percent of the screen, so you can be sure that any movement which stays within the center 95 percent of the screen will be visible. This area is called *action safe.* No bezel obscures more than 10 percent of a screen, so text confined to the middle 90 percent of the screen will always be completely visible. This is called *title safe*.

Other technical issues limit NTSC colors to a narrower palette than the typical computer is able to produce. Because of the distortion of the picture caused by transmitting too-saturated colors, a station can theoretically have its license revoked for broadcasting these colors as part of its signal. That's why this limited color palette is called *NTSC-legal* in digital video production.

Video signal formats

Video travels along signal paths in several different incarnations. Some of those forms are better than others, but you won't always have the choice of which one to work with.

Composite video

When standard NTSC video is transmitted, the color and brightness information in the picture is combined in a single signal flow called the *composite* video format. This allows the transmission of color video with a single signal, but, inevitably, the encoding process causes smearing and other color distortions in the picture, because the separate signals for brightness and color information tend to interfere with each other when combined through a single wire. Your standard VCR records and plays back composite video (with two or more audio tracks encoded and recorded on separate tracks); composite is usually the lowest-quality video format. Some older high-end editing systems are composite only, and though they feature a much higher image quality than consumer VCRs, in general you should avoid capturing video from composite sources if at all possible.

S-Video

The next best video format is *S-video* (sometimes referred to as Y/C). This format is commonly found on Hi-8 and S-VHS (Super-VHS) decks, as well as higher-quality machines. S-Video actually stands for "super-video," which is an extended bandwidth format that results in higher picture quality than standard video recording. The extra quality on these super-video decks, like the aforementioned S-VHS and Hi-8, necessitated a better way of sending the signals through a wire, so the S-Video connection was born. In S-video, the color and brightness information are carried on separate wires in a single S-video cable. This reduces the color distortion found in the composite format. The S-video cable carries only video information, by the way; it's a common misconception that the S-video cable also carries audio.

Component video

The highest-quality analog video format is *component* video, found on Beta-SP decks and other high-end analog editing machines. In component video, color and brightness are broken out into three separate elements, each on its own wire. This minimizes color distortion and allows for many generations of editing. Beyond component video is a wide variety of digital video formats that I look at later on.

It's important to understand the difference between video formats such as composite and component, and tape formats such as VHS and Beta-SP. Video formats are output formats, and a video deck may have more than one type of output. Hi-8 and S-VHS decks usually have both composite and S-video outputs; Beta-SP decks usually have all three formats. Although you can record compatible video signals from one type of deck to another, you can't interchange their tapes. Beta-SP has the widest bandwidth of the different tape formats, so the S-video output of a Beta SP deck usually looks better than S-video from Hi-8 or S-VHS. So, even if you're working with an S-video capture system, capture from the highest-quality tape format you can get your footage in.

Computer video

By contrast to all that, computer video is a completely different format. Video in the computer is processed and displayed as *RGB* information, meaning that every pixel in a video frame is defined as separate red, green, and blue components, or *channels*, rather than the brightness and color of the NTSC system. It's worth knowing that NTSC was designed for the colors in natural scenes, so it's easy to produce color combinations on the computer that NTSC doesn't handle well. This includes nonlegal colors as well as bright color fields next to each other, which tend to vibrate and "buzz" on a television monitor. Most digital video graphics programs include some kind of NTSC-legal filter; if your final output is going to be for broadcast, it's a good idea to run one of these filters before final output, especially if you can't preview it on an NTSC monitor.

Digitized video must be converted, or *transcoded*, from NTSC to RGB before it can be processed in the computer. If you're using a video capture card, the transcoder is built into the hardware. An animator producing all-digital files for video needs to use a transcoding video output card or transcoder software before the RGB files are usable as video.

Another difference between computer and NTSC video is that computer video is *progressive*, meaning that each scan line is drawn in order, instead of the odd/even interlaced display method. Computer frame rates are higher than NTSC, too. Computer displays vary between 60 and 80 frames per second or higher, fast enough to conceal all flicker. Computer monitors also display in *underscan* format, so that you see all edges of the screen image.

Finally, most computer monitors have a higher resolution than NTSC, so a computer monitor can display much more detail with less color distortion than an NTSC system. A full NTSC frame in most desktop video systems is captured and displayed at a resolution of 640 pixels wide by 480 pixels tall. (Note that systems designed for D1 digital video format, which uses nonsquare pixels, display a video frame at 720 by 486 pixels.) Most computer monitors display at 800 by 600 pixels or higher.

What this all means is that producing NTSC video on the computer requires an awareness of the differences in the two systems, so that you can compensate for those differences and get the best possible results. The easiest way to avoid color problems is to design and edit your video footage while displaying it on an NTSC monitor, so you can see any problems as they arise. If that isn't possible, use an NTSC-legal filter on the footage before outputting it. Even if it is possible, using this filter is always a good idea.

Issues to consider

Designing interlaced graphics on a progressive display is more difficult than an interlaced one. The problem is that with interlaced video, each field consists of alternate scan lines, each line one pixel wide, and a field is on the screen only half the time. So, a one-pixel-wide horizontal line that displays perfectly on an RGB monitor will flicker like mad on an NTSC monitor, because the line is on-screen only half the time. This applies not only to lines but to any thin graphic element, including serifs on fonts. This is why most text used for NTSC video display is sans-serif. To avoid interlace flicker, don't use serif fonts or thin lines in video frames.

You also need to watch out for action and title safe when designing for video, to avoid clipping your video unnecessarily. Fortunately, most video editing and special-effects programs let you display markers for the safe areas in your video window. In general, just remember that video on the computer screen will generally look better than it will on an NTSC monitor, so scale your expectations accordingly. If it's any consolation, NTSC video eventually will be replaced by a higher-quality digital television standard, and these design problems will go away.

If, however, you're designing video for QuickTime or a similar multimedia format, and it's going to be displayed on a computer monitor, then you're all set. You needn't worry about title safe, interlace artifacts, or other NTSC issues. You will need to worry about things such as frame size, frame rate, compression ratios, and so on, all of which I discuss in the compression section.

Compression for Video and Motion Graphics

There is one inescapable fact about real-time digital video on computers, at least for the near future — compression. The amount of information per second a video clip requires for real-time playback is called its *data rate*. A single frame of full-color video (for now, I define that as 640 x 480 pixels) requires about 900K of disk space. At 30 frames per second, that's a data rate of 27 megabytes a second that need to be retrieved from the hard drive, processed through the system, and thrown up on the screen. Only the biggest, fastest, most expensive computers these days can handle those kinds of data rates; no desktop machine can at this time. So, for digital video to be viable at all, you need to compress any video that you want to use in real time on the computer.

Digital video the old way

For years, people have been producing broadcast, or even film-quality, video and animation on desktop computers. Until recently, though, this was not a real-time process. The standard procedure was to render full-resolution files without compression, or with lossless compression, and output them to a video deck or laser disk recorder one frame at a time. Usually, this means that you need a video frame buffer or output card, an animation controller (hardware that precisely controls the recorder to record single frames), and a video recorder with external edit control. The animation controller cues the recorder up, rolls the tape, and puts the deck into record at exactly the right moment to record the frame. It then repeats this a zillion times to record the full animation.

Not only does all this take a long time, but it stresses the video recorder because the deck is constantly shuttling back and forth to record each frame. More significantly, the videographer or animator never gets to see a full-motion render of the creation until after everything has been recorded to tape. Then, if there are any problems, you have to go back to the top and re-render and re-record everything to make the changes. This lack of immediate feedback really puts a kink in the creative process, and is one of the reasons tape-based editing is still so widespread. However, you do get the best possible image this way, because no compression is involved.

Digital video the new way

More recently, though, fast, hardware-assisted compression systems have been developed that allow for more realistic data rates with decent image quality. The first and probably best-known company to make a practical nonlinear editing system that integrated real-time video compression with a desktop computer was Avid Systems. This first system could capture and playback only 15 frames per second (fps) and so was suitable only for off-line editing. The technology has steadily become better, and now Avid systems, and many others like it, are used to create broadcast-quality video directly on the desktop. Real-time compression allows for real-time feedback, so the editing process is much more efficient and productive — at least in theory.

Motion JPEG compression

The most common compression format for desktop digital video is M-JPEG (motion-JPEG), which I mentioned in the image compression section previously. This is usually implemented by dedicated chips on a video capture/display card, which allows for real-time digitizing of incoming video with low compression ratios. High data rates like this usually require accelerated hard drives or even arrays for capture and playback without dropped frames. M-JPEG doesn't look very good under high compression ratios, so it's not appropriate for low data rate delivery systems such as CD-ROM, and at any rate, M-JPEG playback almost always requires the same hardware used for capture, so it's inappropriate for mass-market delivery. For that, software-only codecs such as Cinepak, Truemotion, or Indeo are called for.

As I mentioned earlier, JPEG (and M-JPEG) compresses an image by looking for and discarding redundant or at least similar pixels in a frame. Each frame is treated separately and does not depend on other frames for decompression. This makes the format ideal for nonlinear editing, because you can freely cut and paste frames without affecting other frames.

MPEG compression

Unlike M-JPEG, MPEG and MPEG-2 (confused yet?) are optimized for low data rates with good image quality; MPEG-2 is the compression scheme used in the upcoming DVD format. MPEG compression works by removing redundant pixels, but also by a process called *frame differencing*. In frame differencing, the codec looks at a particular reference frame (the "I" frame), encodes it, looks at the next frame, and encodes only the differences between the second frame and the first. This process continues, with new frames referencing the master frame, until the scene radically changes — the camera moves, lighting changes, or the video or film cuts to a new scene.

MPEG-2 takes this concept a step further by not only looking forward to reference frames (called predictive frames or P frames), but looking backwards as well (B frames). This helps to reduce data rates even further, but increases the complexity of the encoding process. Establishing I, P, and B frames and tweaking other parameters for the possible image is a black art, and the compressionists who do it are highly paid. MPEG also takes a long time to compress, so you want the fastest computer you can get for this kind of work.

As you can see, using MPEG compression for nonlinear editing is difficult at best, not only because high-quality MPEG capture isn't real time, but the relationships between the frames force you to make cuts only on P or B frames, severely limiting the editing process. If you cut an I frame, you've removed the master reference for the P and B frames, and all those related frames will have to be cut, too. So, most developers producing video for MPEG will edit in a high-quality M-JPEG format, and recompress to MPEG after the edit is complete.

MPEG playback for the most part still requires additional hardware, although there are some software-only MPEG schemes in the works. So, it isn't ideal for CD-ROM distribution, unless you know your target audience has the necessary hardware. This is changing to some degree, with more and more multimedia PCs being bundled with built-in MPEG cards. This will all change again with the advent of DVD computer peripherals.

Other methods

There are some other compression formats you may come across, including wavelets and fractal compression. These are usually used in a closed editing system, so the files must stay within that environment to be played. Eventually, though, you can expect these proprietary systems to fade away in favor of more open standardized desktop tools. For desktop editing systems, the ultimate goal is being able to work with uncompressed digital video, and as computers get faster and more powerful, this is inevitable.

The next big thing on the digital video horizon, though, is the new DV format currently available in camcorders, with editing decks and computer interfaces on the way. The DV format features an all-digital signal path, variable compression ratios, high-quality digital audio, and a universal connector and transmission format for maximum compatibility. In theory, at least, you should soon be able to shoot footage with a digital camcorder (which has better picture specifications than Beta-SP) and dump it directly onto your computer's hard drive for editing and special-effects processing with your familiar software tools, and then output it back to a DV deck for playback, all in the digital domain and without recompression artifacts.

Video I/O Notes

In the meantime, though, desktop video production still involves capturing footage with compression and recompressing it for output. I'll go over some notes for maximizing your video capture quality and optimizing video for computer playback.

Getting video into the computer

Generally, capturing video with a desktop system requires a video capture/display card with hardware compression, usually M-JPEG; a fast CPU with subsystems capable of high throughput; and an accelerated hard drive. The limiting factor in capturing with the least compression and the highest quality is almost always the hard drive. A drive for capturing video has to be able to sustain high data rates without glitching, which results in dropped frames. One of the chief causes of frame-dropping in earlier desktop systems was thermal recalibration, or *t-cal*. This is a diagnostic routine that hard drives go through to compensate for changes in the drive structure due to heat, and normally is a good thing. However, most drives perform t-cal automatically, and while the drive is recalibrating, it can't read or write anything. If this happens during a capture, you lose frames.

Most current drives designed for video use intelligent recalibration, waiting until the drive isn't in use to perform the t-cal. These drives are commonly called AV drives. An AV drive is a good choice for video capture, especially because the internal drives shipped with most computers are definitely not AV drives. Neither are they particularly fast; and a drive containing the operating system will always have more overhead from background activity and other system operations than a dedicated capture drive. Some computer systems even use IDE internal drives instead of the faster and more flexible standard SCSI drives, which makes them even less useful for video capture.

More about AV hard drives

As mentioned previously, the higher the data rate your drive can sustain, the less compression you can use and the better your captured video will look. On most current desktop systems, an unaccelerated AV drive's data rate will top out at about 2.5MB a second. (With most capture cards, broadcast quality requires data rates of 5MB/sec or above.) The next step up from a single external AV capture disk in terms of speed is a software *RAID* system.

RAID (redundant array of independent disks) is a standard for controlling individual drives so that they work together as a single virtual drive. Some RAID systems are designed so that one drive mirrors another; if one drive fails, the other serves as an instant backup. RAID Level 0 is of particular interest to desktop producers; this specifies that two or more drives be *striped* together, so that data is written in turn to every drive in the array. Data can be written at least twice as fast this way, depending on the number and speed of the individual drives in the array.

Arrays

A software array is one that uses the dual built-in SCSI busses available in higher-end Macintoshes, some Windows workstations, and Silicon Graphics computers, rather than a dedicated controller card. Although less efficient than a dedicated accelerated SCSI bus on its own card, a software array should be able to sustain data rates of 4 to 5MB/sec.

A hard-drive accelerator card attached to a single fast AV drive can achieve data rates as high as a software array. If you already have a fast external drive, getting an accelerator card such as ATTO's Silicon Express or FWB's JackHammer might be a better investment than an additional drive.

Providing higher data rates than either a software array or a single drive on an accelerator is the hardware array, which combines two or more drives with a single-channel SCSI accelerator. The latest SCSI Fast & Wide systems, with twice the bandwidth and twice the speed of standard SCSI, can sustain data rates above 10MB/sec with fast hard drives. The fastest SCSI system of all is a multiple-channel accelerator with striped drives; in this configuration, each drive is assigned its own dedicated accelerated bus. These drives, like the Micronet Data Dock with an ATTO MC Express card, can hit data rates as high as 20 MB/sec, allowing for compression ratios as low as 2:1.

The poor man's solution

Super-speed hard drives aren't always necessary for capturing high-quality video, especially for multimedia. First, if your QuickTime video is going to be displayed in a quarter-size window at a data rate of 150 Kbps, you're better off capturing at the quarter-frame size to start with, if your capture system permits it. A few M-JPEG cards let you resize the video before capture, including the Radius VideoVision, a favorite with multimedia producers. By discarding three-quarters of the data before compression, a compression data rate of 1.25 MB/sec will give you the same overall video quality as a data rate of 5 MB/sec with a full size frame. By the same token, try to capture your audio at its final sample rate and bit depth, both to save disk space and capture bandwidth and to minimize resampling artifacts.

After you've captured your clips, you'll need to edit them and compress them for final output, say as QuickTime video on a CD-ROM. If you're developing a cross-platform disk, one critical thing to be aware of is that because of the way Windows systems handle audio, QuickTime movies with audio will not play as well on Windows computers as on Macs. On a Mac with a double-speed drive, you can expect to be able to play a QuickTime movie with a data rate of 250 Kbps without choking; an equivalent Windows system will need to have the data rate reduced to 150 Kbps to play without skipping. If you need cross-platform compatibility, be sure to compress to the lower data rate for best results.

Digital Video Software Tools

There are two main types of applications designed for digital video production: those that require specific or proprietary hardware, or closed systems, and those that can work with a variety of hardware, or open systems. Closed systems can consist of one or more dedicated black boxes that run a unique operating system, or can just be a certain board set and its software that you plug into your own computer. In either case, the advantages of a closed system are that they're usually more efficient or faster than an open system, because the closed environment can be tweaked for maximum performance. Examples of these systems include Avid's Media Composer line, Data Translation's Media 100 system, the ImMix VideoCube, and D-Vision's DVision system.

Open systems can work with a variety of hardware and software and are usually QuickTime-based. Open systems include Radius VideoVision, Truevision's Targa 2000, Data Translation's Media 100qx, and even Intergraph's StudioZ Windows NT D1 video workstation, all of which use Adobe Premiere as their front end. Premiere was one of the first QuickTime video editing tools, and has evolved into a powerful and full-featured digital video production system. It is easily the widest-used application of its type, and so deserves a closer look.

Adobe Premiere

Premiere (Figure 6-38), currently at version 4.2 for Mac and Windows (including Windows NT), is the best all-around production tool for multimedia video. You can capture video and audio in a variety of formats, using any QuickTime-compatible hardware; edit, layer, and effect up to 99 tracks of video and up to 99 tracks of mono or stereo audio; apply a huge variety of built-in and third-party special effects filters to any video or audio track; work with sophisticated motion effects to superimpose and fly-in video tracks or still graphics; work at low resolution for off-line editing, and recapture high-res video later or output an edit decision list for online editing; work at resolutions of up to 4000 by 4000 pixels for HDTV or film output; and render the final output in a wide variety of formats suitable for broadcast, desktop, CD-ROM, or Web delivery.

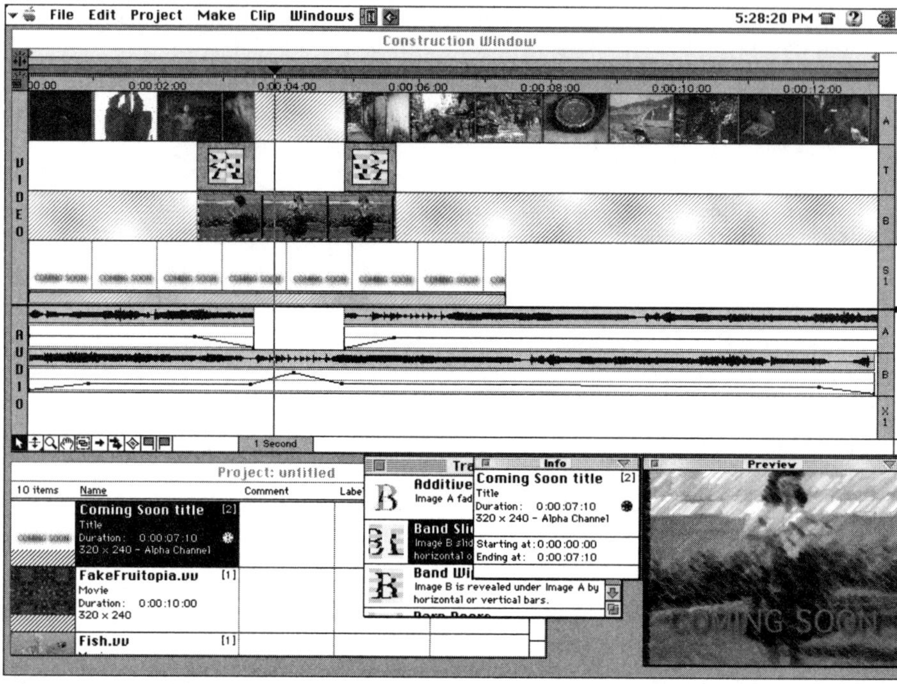

Figure 6-38: Adobe's Premiere has become as important to digital video production as Photoshop is to digital imaging.

Premiere is useful for blue-screen compositing of live action footage into 3-D or otherwise artificial scenes, and includes a sophisticated title generator and almost 100 transitions. Premiere is also an excellent audio editor, especially of sound effects and music for video. Beyond that, the latest Premiere features the CD-ROM MovieMaker plug-in, with reasonably complete controls for creating optimized Cinepak movies for CD-ROM. Its graphic capabilities may not be as powerful as Adobe's other important video software, called After Effects, and it may not compress to the Cinepak codec quite as well as Movie Cleaner Pro, but Premiere does everything a multimedia producer needs to do for most projects, is easy to learn, and is reasonably priced. Everyone working with digital video on the desktop should at least be familiar with it.

Movie Cleaner Pro

A long-standing problem in multimedia production has been how to make the best-quality Cinepak movies for CD-ROM, especially at low data rates, and how to compress a lot of them at once. You can Cinepak-compress captured video with almost any QuickTime-capable application, but this allows very little control over how the movie will be compressed and generally won't give you the best possible results. Premiere or After Effects give you a little more control, but until very recently, neither had batch processing — the ability to process multiple files simultaneously.

Apple's MovieShop, included with the QuickTime Developer's CD releases, was the first (and for years, the only) program that let you tweak compression parameters and batch-compress more than one movie. However, this was never a commercial product and so has no tech support, is hard for anyone other than licensed developers to get, and has a difficult interface that only a programmer could love. It also hasn't been updated in over two years. Fortunately, Movie Cleaner Pro from Terran Interactive for Macs and Windows is an ideal solution to the problem.

Movie Cleaner is a small, easy-to-use utility for optimizing QuickTime movies (Figure 6-39). It has many powerful features for tweaking the compression process, but is also designed to make it easy for beginning multimedia producers to output the best possible QuickTime movies. Movie Cleaner's compression routines arguably produce the cleanest Cinepak movies of any application, especially at low data rates.

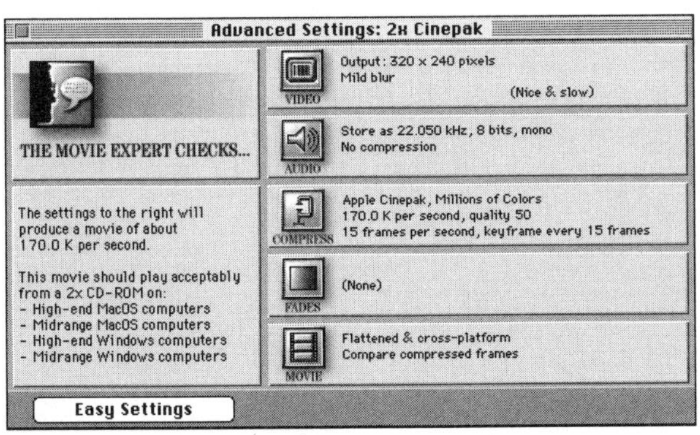

Figure 6-39: Movie Cleaner is a superb post-processing tool for digital video files.

Movie Cleaner operates in two different modes — Easy and Advanced. Easy mode asks questions about the kind of movie you want to produce, including anticipated CD-ROM playback speed, platform, and sound compatibility, and then sets the compression parameters accordingly. More experienced users can go into Advanced mode and set specific values for parameters to get the maximum amount of control over the final output. Movie Cleaner is highly recommended for anyone producing QuickTime content for CD-ROM.

As you can see, there are hundreds of tools and thousands of techniques for creating multimedia. A thorough discussion of all of them would take up a library or a career, rather than a single chapter in a book. The gratifying news is that mastering these tools and techniques is usually just a matter of experience. The more you record, the better your recordings sound; the more you animate, the less time you need to do good work. Although nobody can expect to master the art of production in no time, the tools are becoming sophisticated enough so that generalists, as well as specialists, can produce good work.

Delivering the Goods

PART

In This Part

CHAPTER 7

The Road to Completion

✦ The testing period is as important to the project as the production process. Without adequate testing, even the best project may be flawed.

✦ Preliminary testing should commence as soon as the production team can start delivering segments in progress.

✦ A thorough testing regimen may be expensive and time consuming, but in comparison to angry users and flooded phone lines, it's worth it.

✦ Testing should concentrate on the technical aspects of the production. Other issues such as attractiveness and content are immaterial to the tester.

When the production finally comes to the point at which the release date is looking like light at the end of the tunnel, attention starts turning toward the last part of the technical process and the first part of the distribution and marketing process — the testing period. Vigorous testing of any multimedia product is absolutely essential if there's to be any pretense of a satisfying user experience. It's extremely important to make sure that your product is as bug free as possible, and that it has been tested for usability by people who are representative of your target audience.

Note that I said "as possible." Anyone who uses personal computers understands to one degree or another that software often does things that you don't want it to. Glitches do happen, even if the glitch isn't necessarily a bug within the product that you release. Different users have different platforms, operating systems, graphics cards, sound cards, system extensions, and other configuration variables.

The job of testing is to try to simulate those variables before the product is actually released, and get the product as bulletproof as possible within those varying conditions. When the final multimedia product is fixed media such as CD-ROM, the chances for total success are better, because there are fewer user variables compared to a Web site. When the production is an online project, there are the additional considerations of the different browsers, all of which deliver a different experience. Beyond that, users configure their browsers in many different ways, have different fonts, platforms, operating systems, and so on. It's a fact of digital life — computers sometimes give you things that you don't want.

Still, you have to make sure that they don't. At least not on *your* product.

Stages of Product Development

The terms *alpha* and *beta* are used to describe the stages of product development when your project is near completion and is ready for testing. Alpha releases are generally for internal circulation only, and are distributed to a small group of select users. These versions of the product are most often the first working drafts of your project. The alpha version is expected to have problems, and is typically incomplete. Beta releases, which follow the alpha releases, are sent to a larger audience, usually external to the company.

Although the alpha release is expected to have bugs, the beta release represents an effort to not have bugs. Beyond that, the beta release is intended to be a fair representation of how your product will look, perform, and feel. Feedback is an essential element from your beta product, and as the beta release nears completion (soon-to-be release version), you should already have a pretty good idea of how well the product is meeting your intended goals with the people who are going to experience it.

Alpha testing and delivery

The alpha date is a milestone in your product's life, a sort of a birthday. For one thing, the alpha is usually the first point in the production at which your product is far enough along that you will be able to send it to someone and let that user have the experience on his or her own, without someone from the production team running it for the user. All the features of the product should be showcased, though at this point you will probably not have all of the content integrated. Second, the alpha data is often the proof of delivery that warrants a percentage of payment by the client or publisher. At this point, the client really gets to see what you have created for him or her.

For better or worse, it's also early enough in the project's life that it gives the client a last opportunity to make substantial changes to the project — even, in some cases, a redesign. This unfortunate circumstance happens more than any of us would like to think, although when it does, it should obviously be for only the most compelling and persuasive of reasons.

Depending on the size and complexity of the project, you should expect the alpha stage to happen approximately 6 to 8 weeks before the completion of the fixed-media production. This leaves enough time for there to be initial feedback from the alpha and a reasonable testing period for the beta versions. For an online project, the situation is more fluid. Web sites commonly put beta versions online for months at a time, with unfulfilled content sections and features labeled "under construction." In many of these cases, user feedback from the test versions actually determine the direction of the beta releases, and, ultimately, the finished site.

As you consider the comments of your alpha testers, try to keep an open mind. They are seeing your project with new eyes, and may find that they are having trouble with your interface or design. One of the most interesting aspects of multimedia design is that different people approach an interactive experience in many different ways. What seems an illogical navigation path to the programmers and the team designers may come absolutely naturally to the very first outside person who looks at the alpha version. Criticism from the alpha testers is a subject for more than just the testing and quality assurance team. Because this is the first look-and-feel experience that anyone outside the team has had with the project, everyone, especially the producer, should be curious as to the feedback.

Even if the feedback is critical, the knowledge gained from early impressions can be extremely useful in making a clearer or more exciting product. Even with tedious planning, you will still likely uncover things that you have overlooked, and will have to revisit some concepts. For this select group of first impressions, the testing department should use a few people who are not friends or acquaintances of the production itself. Outside impressions are most useful, because they will be least susceptible to user preconceptions, which people friendly or unfriendly to the production will always have to one degree or another. Unbiased information should be the overriding goal of the alpha test period, though leavening the first impressions with some from people who are familiar with the goals and talents of the production can also be a useful addition.

Beta delivery

As you are preparing your data, whether on CD-ROM, the Web, floppy, or hard disk, the dream of the first beta version is that it will be your last version. Most likely, it won't be, but it's a nice fantasy that's well worth shooting for.

The beta version of a multimedia project is one that's deemed ready for the public to look at — at least in a limited way. In the case of CD-ROM, the beta period is finite, usually limited to a low number of beta testers so as not to give too much away to the public before the product is actually marketed. In the case of a Web site, the beta period can go on for much longer, with succeeding versions of the beta supplanting existing versions and sometimes existing as an indefinite stand-alone product. The Netscape Navigator Web browsing software, for example, is available as more or less constant beta versions, in addition to existing release versions.

You will likely go through several iterations of beta testing before ironing out all of the problems. Because the beta version is the final testing stage for your project, all of your content and functionality should be in place and (to your knowledge) completely operational. This is a chance to see whether people like and can use your product, so it doesn't make sense to release incomplete versions that aren't representative, unless the missing features are clearly cordoned off from the rest of the functioning beta. Having incomplete content is more forgivable than having buggy functionality; likewise, having incomplete content is forgivable if the content that is present is functional.

The role of beta testers

The people in the beta test group should be representative of the real users of your product, with a similar level of experience and a reasonable representation of the kind of hardware setup a target user is likely to have. As previously mentioned, you want to avoid having a significant measure of the beta testing performed by friends of the production or the company, because of preconceptions and predisposition. In order to eliminate this problem, you may want to consider hiring an outside firm to do the beta testing for you. It can provide assurance of proper test user screening, and may offer the added benefit of test users who have had experience with similar software packages that may be your competition.

Outside testing firms may also offer other added services that may be advantageous for your production, freeing up time for other work that goes on in the background during the beta test period. This vendor will also have experience managing the user feedback and data, which is a critical component in alpha or beta testing. If you do not properly integrate and analyze this data, then the beta test will be a failure, and a waste of time and money. Accepting feedback and information from an objective source such as this is something for the producer to take extremely seriously.

Again, fixing the bugs found in your product may be enough of a goal, especially if the multimedia project is "locked" in terms of an approach because of content or a studio's style. But it stands to reason that if you can also integrate any good suggestions from the beta testers on the usability of the multimedia product, you will increase the likelihood of the production being a success. Test marketing is a valuable way to get information before offering *anything* to the public, and although the beta tester's main responsibility is to help fix problems, personal opinions on the quality of the title and whether it lives up to expectations can sometimes yield surprisingly good input.

Quality assurance

Quality Assurance (QA) is essentially the formal name for the process of beta testing. When the producer releases a beta version and begins to test its functionality, the QA process has formally begun.

As discussed in the previous section, the beta testers are basically trying — with your encouragement — to break your product. They will be checking possible paths of navigation, and logging all events that strike them as unusual. In addition, they will be doing things that you hope most users will *not* do — pointless, ill-informed, or confused user actions such as multiple mouse-clicking, dragging things around, and entering unneeded keystrokes. The object is to go through every possible permutation of an actual user experience and look for things that don't work. It takes a certain thoroughness of approach and nitpicky nature to be a good beta tester, because you're looking for someone else's mistakes. Then again, some people really enjoy this.

When the next beta version of your product comes to the testers, they will have to do everything again. Not only must the testers make sure that you fixed one bug that they reported, they must also make sure that you did not birth another when you did it. If you are very formal about the QA process, your testers will also be checking for content inconsistencies. They'll be checking for overall content flow and will compare content in all sections of your product, making sure that everything that's supposed to relate from one thing to another actually does. This means following navigational paths up and down, and then re-tracing the steps to make sure that every possible combination of mouse, joystick, or keyboard responses actually turns up the content that the product has been designed to deliver.

Where does the testing take place?

At some point, you have to decide whether you have the resources to do all this testing in-house, or you want to source out the job to a professional lab, or release the product to the public, or a combination of all three. Naturally, the widest range of beta testers is always the best, unless product secrecy is an issue, in which case the controlled environment of a professional test lab may be the only reasonably effective recourse.

In a serious QA lab, the multimedia production will be tested on multiple platforms in multiple environments, which is exactly the situation you're paying for, if the production goes this route. If the testing is to be done in-house, it's essential to have an adequate number of machines on which to test, to reflect with some accuracy the wide range of hardware gear that a target audience might be using. It's a given that there are innumerable variations on both major PC platforms, with hundreds of different models and manufacturers' products, many of which may be old, slow, or otherwise constricted in terms of the ability to run multimedia. Who knows whether your product will work on an old 386 machine with 4 megabytes of RAM, or an old Macintosh 68020 with a monochrome monitor? Worse, the internal components on even current Wintel machines represent a universe of hardware possibilities. Who knows whether the product will be compatible with a graphics card by ACME computer or sonically effective through an old-technology soundcard? The QA process is about finding this out.

Very often, if you are creating a title for an established multimedia publisher, the publisher will have access to a QA lab that it generally uses, or may even have one in-house. You can expect the beta process to last approximately 4–6 weeks for a fixed-media project — depending, of course, on the size and scope of the title — under optimal conditions. More likely, you will be under pressure to deliver the final product and will have less time to go through this process. If this is the case, the beta testers and programmers will be very tired when they are finished. In a Web environment, in which the decision has already been made to allow beta to go on for an unspecified period, the rules are obviously much looser. Still, even in this ongoing vein, an end to the beta period and an official release or launch is only fair to the end user.

Testing procedures

The most widely used testing procedures present a methodical approach to finding things wrong with the multimedia title. Just as building multimedia is a step-by-step, cumulative process, the process of tearing it down is similarly logical. This is mostly true, though, in the case of a professional testing site, for which an established set of approaches and techniques is in place for discerning errors in software. In the less rigid situation of informal or public beta testing, people will approach the multimedia in the way that's comfortable for them, and report bugs that they find along the way. It obviously takes longer to find all the bugs in these situations, not only because of the haphazard nature through which these different people will approach the process, but also because the process of logical elimination undertaken by a professional test site is usually more efficient and thorough. But that's why professionals cost money and unpaid beta testers take a long time to give thorough feedback.

Compatibility testing

This process evaluates the compatibility of your product with specific categories of external computer components. The general rules of compatibility should correspond to the minimum system requirements envisioned by the producer and the production team. Within those requirements, the variables that are examined under the process of compatibility testing are such components as video and sound cards, operating systems, system extensions, network cards, modems, and other common (or uncommon) hardware and software variables.

Functionality testing

This aspect of the testing process evaluates the product and any potential problems — such as crashes — by analyzing its functionality and by systematically checking each feature of the product. Functionality testing is the fundamental step, the building block of the testing process. If the product or an important part of the product is nonfunctional, then there is no use for any of the other tests. A project that looks great and that has fantastic content still relies on working links to get to any of the parts of the program. During the functionality testing, the testers are looking for glitches that are hidden beneath the "look" of the piece; the functionality is not generally a visible occurrence.

Functional localization testing

This process evaluates whether the product can be well understood by multiple cultures, and checks for potential language translation issues. Much of the language of multimedia is expressed with icons and other visual shorthand, and as a result, the associations that the user makes during the interactive experience are supposed to be more intuitive than intellectual. But different cultures, and sometimes even different regions from within a culture, interpret these visual cues differently. As an example, a culture that reads its language from right to left won't always interpret the right-pointing "forward" arrow so familiar to English-speaking audiences as a forward button, because to them that arrow signifies moving backward.

Install testing

This process evaluates the compatibility of the installation procedure with multiple system configurations. This process is extremely important, because without an adequate installation program (if one is required), the user has no access to the production at all. Again, the parameters have already been laid out in terms of the minimum hardware and system requirements, but the installation program must work under a variety of conditions.

Performance testing

This process evaluates performance of the product under various system configurations. The product is measured for speed, and is also tested against competitive products. Just because an animation has been programmed to run at one speed doesn't mean it'll do it on every machine. Dynamic media such as audio, video, and animation are the most taxing on the hardware that the end user will be working with. During this part of the testing, the minimum system requirements should be looked at closely, and if necessary, revised.

Stress load testing

This process evaluates the product under challenging usage conditions. Stress testing is functionality testing under extreme and maximum conditions, which, ironically, can come from the least potent hardware. This part of the testing procedure is mostly concerned with "what if?". Although it can be assumed that most users probably won't subject the title to this kind of rigor, it cannot be assumed that some won't.

Load testing

This is a combination of stress testing and performance testing. Load testing focuses on timing under large data loads and can be applied to networking and multiuser situations. Until recently, this was a minor part of the test, and for many titles, not particularly relevant. Still, more and more end users are using multimedia in work situations in which their PCs may be networked to a server or many other machines. It's a reality that can't be ignored anymore, and should be part of the testing regimen.

Advantages of sourcing out QA

There are many advantages to using an external QA lab. You can be sure that they will have multiple configurations of several computer platforms, as well as many types of external and internal hardware that can be cost prohibitive to invest in for the producer or the production house. Their engineers have most likely evaluated and solved hundreds of problems on various types of software products, and will be able to anticipate common problems that plague software developers. They will probably even have solutions, or at least be able to give direction, to help the team solve these problems.

In addition, a professional test site will also have experience in drawing out the important information from the beta testers, and can supply the information the developer needs to know. The people at this site will be diligent and comprehensive; their reputation as a testing lab rides on their performance as much as the production team's rides on the final product. Because the QA process executes at the end of the production, the team will be in a crunch as it is — an external resource can be very helpful in keeping the project moving to avoid the extra internal pressure to test the product. This is especially true for in-house testing, because finding too many bugs or flaws can be demoralizing to the team and can easily slow down the work flow.

QA on a budget

For situations in which doing the QA testing internally makes more sense, you should keep a few things in mind. First of all, the producer and test team have to make sure that everyone understands what the customer is looking for. It is important to have a clear vision of standards for what "quality" is to the target audience members. What is the value of the product for them? What do they like about competitive products? What needs do they have that these products don't meet? Someone must make an effort to properly represent the target audience and its needs — a user advocate.

If the product is innovative and exciting, it will be easy to get people to be beta testers. Try to find people who will not only resemble the end users but might actually become them — people who will have an ongoing use for your product. They will give you some valuable information concerning the long-term value. Make sure that you are responsive to the testers' feedback. Let them know that you want as much information as they can give, and make sure that the development team is briefed on the information in a timely fashion so that the appropriate fixes and changes can be made.

It's also a good idea to start your QA process as early as possible, and sometimes that can happen even before the betas are distributed to the testers. As a producer, what issues and problems have you run up against in previous projects? What can be done to prevent them from happening again?

The installer application

One of the last forms of QA testing to be considered is installation testing. However, this is one of the most important testing procedures that must be performed. Consider that the first impression of your product is your install routine. As with the cover of a book, the customers' first real glimpse of your product is the splash screen of your installation program. In addition, the first impression of functionality is how well your installation program performs and its ease of use. If the customer has a difficult time with the installation program, his/her impression of your product will already be colored.

Windows installation

Most Windows installation programs work on the principle of having an Install.exe file that installs the applications using a file called install.inf or intall.cfg to provide the information that tells the .EXE file — the executable — what to do. The installation program will prompt the user, modify any .INI files in the system if necessary, create program manger group icons, copy the application and support files, create directories, and display Readme.txt files. They can also install custom icon files and display bitmaps (you have probably seen a few sales pitches and some product propaganda) that can be shown during the installation process.

Microsoft provides developers with an advanced tool for creating an installation program with its software product. Microsoft's Setup Toolkit for Windows is a powerful and flexible tool for creating an installation process. This tool is very scripting intensive, and it is necessary to spend a significant amount of time (using an advanced programmer) to create the install. This utility is really for the developer who needs access to system-level information for determining complex installation procedures. For most developers, though, a quick, easy-to-build installation utility is preferable and often more appropriate.

20/20's PC Install and Win Install

Other install programs require very little programming and can be used right out of the box so that end users can copy and set up applications on their system according to your instructions. Win-Install and PC Install are programs released by 20/20 Software that create installation programs for Windows and MS-DOS, respectively. PC Install and Win Install have two components: Install.exe and Install.cfg. The first is the installation program, and the second is the configuration file that you create, which then defines the installation procedure that is to be used for a specific installation. Install.cfg is an ASCII (text) file that contains a set of instructions that the executable file, Install.exe, follows. When files are shipped to the end users, a copy of Install.exe is included, along with an Install.cfg that tells the installation program what to do.

Creating a configuration file is not difficult. An ASCII file can be created with any file editor, such as Edit from DOS or Notepad in Windows. 20/20 includes basic installation templates for the software, which allows you to easily customize them to your needs.

Macintosh installation

Installation on the Macintosh is usually simpler than on the PC, when it is necessary at all. Generally there is an Installation program called "Install <name of software here>." Some programs use a support configuration text file similar to the PC's install.inf. Other programs have the install script built into the application.

Apple, like Microsoft, provides installer software that is consistent with the Macintosh interface. If you have ever installed any software on a Mac, you have probably used this program. The only drawback is that you need to have some — if not some advanced — programming skills to create the installation script. Some of the features of Apple's install program are

- ✦ **Easy install.** The user can click one button to start the installation. The developer can predetermine the appropriate installation based on system analysis.
- ✦ **Custom install.** The user can customize his/her install based on predetermined components by the developer.
- ✦ **Network install.** Allows the user to install the software over a network connection.
- ✦ **Installation from multiple disks.** Allows the developer the ability to put the software on multiple floppies and multiple folders.

Some third-party developers have created installation programs that use the Apple interface but do not require scripting expertise. These programs do the scripting for you and then bundle your software into an application program with the same installation features as Apple's installer.

MindVision's Developer Vise

One such product is Developer Vise from MindVision Software. No scripting is needed; Developer Vise uses a point-and-click interface that allows the developer to choose the software to install, and then choose where it should be installed. The software features integrated compression, and assembles all of the software into one package that can be split among floppies or placed on a CD-ROM or hard drive. The software will also allow you to check system configurations and the existence of particular expansions and their creation dates so that the appropriate software will be installed.

Like Apple's installer utility, there is a choice for the end user to do a standard install or a custom install. The standard install will check the user's system and place the appropriate software in the correct locations automatically. Custom install will allow the user to install components that have been predetermined by the developer.

And Now, on to Completion . . .

One of the more difficult questions that the producer must answer is a simple one: When is the product actually done? At what point is the beta stage over; when do you have to stop and call an end to it? Unless there's a client with a drop-dead date, it is easy to get trapped in the "we'll just fix this and then we're done" stage. There will always be ways to make your product a little better, but that's what software updates and new revisions are for. If you're releasing a product with only one version — for example, a video game — when do you release the final version for duplication?

The best way to answer this is to determine what the real deadlines are — the drop-dead date by which, if the product isn't released, significant opportunities will be lost, such as a holiday selling season or back-to-school rush. After the "real" deadline is determined, what are the arbitrary deadlines, the ones the team would like to hit as opposed to need to hit? What features would you like to have? Which ones are mandatory and which ones are optional? What features does the user advocate who works among the in-house testers consider essential for a successful product? Is that feature there? If not, is there time, budget, and motivation enough to keep fixing things up until those features are real?

Second, you must decide which bugs must be fixed and which are not as important. Your product will probably always have something wrong with it; most software releases have many known bugs in them (sometimes hundreds). A Web site will often have bugs in the browser, which may or may not directly affect the functionality of your created multimedia. It's essential to know which ones are important to the success of the product and which ones are not. This prioritization will help you facilitate the release. Generally, after all elements have been thoroughly tested, everything is functional, and the critical bugs have been fixed, you are ready for the final version.

The project that never ends

The producer and production team can sometimes find themselves in a situation in which they have no control over the closure of the project. This will usually happen when you are doing the job for a client that's either confused about its goals, or accustomed to large budgets and tolerant of capricious decisions.

Horror stories about the never-ending project from hell are legion, and virtually every experienced multimedia professional has a good one. In the CD-ROM world, there are tales of projects that took so long to complete that entire platform operating systems passed it by, and in order to optimize the title for the most current machines, additional programming had to be undertaken. There are Web sites that took so long to beta test that the Netscape browser they were designed for underwent two significant advancements before the producers decided to scrap the beta and redesign the site for the HMTL enhancements afforded by the new browser software.

Clearly, there are a number of client issues that may come up that make a drop-dead completion date problematic for the producer to call. Very often, the client has multiple layers of bureaucracy to go through before approval of even the simplest of changes. This can significantly slow up the production process, as the producer waits for reliable client feedback before assigning out further work for the changes.

Probably the most chilling force to be reckoned with along these lines is the executive from the client side who comes in to approve things at the end of the project. This person very often does not understand the process that the production team has gone through, and may want to make changes of significant proportion — thinking that these changes will be easy to implement. What seems like a small change in narration to this individual can be a nightmare of additional studio time, programming time, and QA time, not to mention the materials and budget necessary to implement it. The preventive for this situation is unpleasant but sometimes necessary: a contract stating that no changes to design, content, and functionality may be made after a certain date in the production calendar unless there is a financial renegotiation.

Particularly when dealing with corporate clients, the producer will often be faced with content changes up to the last possible moment. This is particularly common when creating presentations and Web sites. In these situations, it's an intelligent move to actually plan for a way to change the content easily, by making segments of the beta test modular. This can save a lot of headaches as the project nears completion. When given a chance, a client will almost always have a tendency to add a little bit more, and to continue to finesse the content. The producer will have to make the decision when enough is enough. Knowing how fast the team can work and understanding the scope of the changes should be the factors to consider when deciding on a point at which to stop. The producer needs to be adamant about a date or a time when these changes can no longer be processed. When push comes to shove, the client will generally understand when you say no.

Another situation that may delay the release of your product is the availabilty of shelf space in the marketplace. The stores that would stock the completed multimedia product may not have any shelf space available. These are considerations that in theory should have been taken on by the marketing team in the first place, though delays of all stripes can prevent this goal from actually being reached with any reliability. In general, this is one of the crucial parameters for a real release deadline: a marketing initiative must find shelf space for the product well in advance. If the market becomes saturated, or the deal falls through even temporarily, for reasons of test delays, production cycles, or budget, the production may not make it to the shelf.

Preparing a final version

When the project is truly completed and thoroughly tested, the producer is ready to prepare the information for final release — the deliverable. Whether the project is going to be delivered on a CD-ROM, over the Web, on a floppy or a hard drive, there needs to be an accurate list of which files make the up the actual finished product. It is very helpful to create a checklist that can be referred to whenever the materials need to be copied, for reasons of security or additional deliverables. This list should include file names and the directory structure within which they exist.

Preparing for CD-ROM

When you're ready to prepare the final elements for your CD-ROM project, there are a number of things to consider. For one thing, it's important to arrange your information in a way that will be very self-explanatory for your end user. One of the best ways to work is from a single hard drive that has been created with the appropriate path names and folder nests that reflect the final version of the project. The supervisor for this process will want to make sure that all the appropriate files have been collected together — and will also want to check to make sure that any additional work files and unused files are removed from the disk that will serve as the source for the premaster disc.

Performance

Because of the nature of how CD-ROMs work, the less files that you have on the disc, the better the performance. The seek time of the CD-ROM is affected by the number of files and the size of the files on the actual disc. For example: if the application is looking for a specific file in a specific directory, and there are five hundred files that it must take a look through in order to figure out where the requested file is on the CD — and then has to physically move to the correct sector — the user ends up waiting. This can significantly impact the performance of your CD by delaying and increasing load times, and degrading the user experience. After you have stripped down the show to the smallest, most efficient number of needed files (but have made sure to back up the original materials), it's important to arrange your information in a logical way. The software that's used for creating CD-ROMs have their own individual ways of working, but all of them lean toward a layout that's logical and efficient for the CD-ROM drive's laser to search.

Additional software

If there's additional software that needs to be installed, such as QuickTime or AVI, these need to be prepared for inclusion. Many developers creating software for the Macintosh either place these items in a folder named "Place Contents in System Folder" or have them installed as part of the installation program. Developers will generally make any installation of system files for the PC software a part of the installation program. If the CD-ROM makes use of any video codecs or system functions that the user may not have installed, it is good practice to include them on the disc, as it will ensure compatibility with the product.

If the CD-ROM needs any support files such as external bitmaps, sounds, or video files that you do not want the user to see, or simply don't want to have cluttering the window, you have two choices. One is to hide the information out of view of the main window so that the user would have to scroll down to view the file. Or, it's possible to make these files invisible on the CD. If you choose to make them invisible, you have to make sure that the application is capable of finding invisible file information. If the plan is to make a hybrid disc, external files have to be shared between both the Mac and PC applications; the latter is not a choice. PCs will not recognize invisible files.

Correct path names

If you have made a copy of your original working directory, or have changed the location of the working files, it's important to make sure that the correct path names have been embedded in the application and that all your links have been updated. Remember that if the CD-ROM requires cross-platform files, the Mac and PC look at file directory structures in different ways. The files must be properly coded to take this into account, which saves not only trouble but time and money as well. Nothing is more frustrating than believing that the final CD has been created and then finding that the application returned an error because it could not find a particular file. Paying special attention to this issue is worthwhile because it happens often and is easy to overlook.

When all this information is set up, and you are sure that your path structures are okay, you have your master hard disk! You will probably want to make a backup of the disk now, especially if you plan to have the gold disc, or duplicable master, created by an outside vendor.

Premastering

Now that all of the elements have been set up, the time has come to burn your master CD-ROM. This CD will serve as a test disc, and will let you see how well your product works at the low data rates of CD-ROM players, as opposed to the faster performance that the title enjoys on a standard PC hard drive.

At this point, the decision is reached as to whether the master disc will be burned in-house or out-sourced to an external service bureau. There are advantages to both ways. If the plans for the producer and the company include burning many discs, and there are more CD-ROM projects in the future, it will probably be cost effective to purchase an actual CD-ROM burner. Just a couple of years ago, you would have to pay $5000 or more to purchase a single-speed CD burner. Now, it's possible to buy a double-speed burner for less than $1000. A software package is usually included, making it fairly simple to make just about any type of CD-ROM. Actual CD-WORM (write-once, read-many) media have dropped below $10 per disc, and can be purchased at many software and electronics stores.

Of course, if the budget doesn't include a CD-ROM burner, or you plan to cut only a handful of discs, using a service bureau probably makes more sense. Plenty of them are out there now; take a look in some of the leading multimedia trades, as well as the final chapter of this book, and you will easily find several. Preparing the data for the service bureau is fairly simple, but creating a list of parameters to which the vendor can refer is a good idea.

First, there should be a backup of your final setup — who knows what could happen on your way to the service bureau — something not so funny. If the material is mailed out or sent via courier service, there may happen to be a giant magnet in the next box, or the truck delivering it may find its way into a highly magnetically charged alien spaceship. Don't assume safe passage for anything until there's the secure knowledge of redundant backups in hand. Equally important, don't assume that the service bureau will have the same external media device that can play the files that are being sent. Be sure to find out what media the service bureau will take — Syquests, Jaz, ZIP, opticals or one of the other proprietary formats. In some unfortunate cases, the actual hard drive containing the files must be sent to the service.

One very clear way of showing a service bureau how you want to have your icons set up on the disc is to create print-outs of the desktop. One should show an example of how the window setup should look for the CD. The second should show all of the files and folders at the root level of the disc. If the plan is to create a hybrid disc, you may want to circle files that are to be included in the Mac partition, underline the files that are to be included in the ISO partition, and highlight the files or folders that should be shared between the two. The vendor will generally charge you a set price for premastering (formatting the data) and the first burn, and will have a lower price for duplicates.

Testing

This is the fun part: everyone gets to see how well the application works under low throughput situations. It won't be surprising if there are significant performance differences in the application now that it is on CD-ROM, or if there are a few files with incorrect path names. This is fairly common for the first one-off. But that's why a test disc is created in the first place. The test parties will want to do a complete run-through of the product. Check for bad links, misplaced files, and significant performance degradation. If a miracle happens and everything works exactly as planned, please write me! I will hire you!

There may be some changes that are obvious and have to be made before sending the disc off for replication. At this point, additional time may be spent creating a new version of the product with all of the appropriate fixes. It's not unusual to go through this process two or three times before everyone is comfortable with the performance of the disc. There are many unforeseen issues that will pop up — and things that probably should work fine on CD often won't. When you are comfortable with the fixes, it is time to show the client. If the multimedia product is for internal purposes, the producer may want to do some more user testing. Get several people on different speed machines to try to break your product. They will probably find things that you wish they hadn't.

Replication

Most replication facilities will accept a CD-ROM gold disc as a master. Now that everyone is sure that the product is ready to go, and that everything is running the way it's supposed to, it is time to send out the disc for replication.

If all that's required of a title is a small run, the producer needs to check with the replication company on what their minimum number of replicates per job is. A service bureau may accept jobs of only 300 discs or more. Some replication companies will go as low as 100 CDs, but usually will not press any less than that. If all that's needed is a quantity of 1–100, most often the product will have to go through a CD-ROM one-off service, unless the disk is burned in-house. However, cost is an issue that's interactive with quantity. Pressing a hundred discs at $25 a piece at a one-off service will end up costing more than a thousand discs made through mass replication. Obviously, replicating quantities of these small numbers is not cost effective for anyone, which is why service bureaus have stringent rules about minimum runs and why manufacturers are able to sell CD-ROM burners. Keep in mind that, as with most industries, the last four months of the year are very busy for replication plants. If the plan to press discs is around this time and there needs to be a product available for the Christmas season, make sure that the replication is scheduled well in advance. One- to two-month (as opposed to two-week) turnarounds at this time of the year are not uncommon.

Getting Technical: What Is a CD-ROM?

In 1986, Philips and Sony introduced compact disc technology to the consumer market as a way to deliver audio information in digital format. The compact disc (CD) is a thin piece of clear polycarbonate plastic with a metal layer, covered with a protective layer of lacquer, with the aluminum layer measuring 120mm in diameter. There are nearly three miles of pits (the spaces between the pits are called *lands*) that wind in a spiral from the center of the CD to the edge. These pits measure from 1 to 3 microns long and are about 1/10 micron deep and 1/2 micron wide. A laser in the CD player reflects off the aluminum as the disc spins. The laser focus is affected by the pits, and this difference in focus is interpreted into a series of 0s and 1s, making up the binary information of the digital audio samples.

The primary logical unit of data storage on a CD is a sector. Each sector is 1/75 second in length and contains 2352 bytes of data. There is an additional 882 bytes following each sector that consists of timing control data and two layers of error-detecting/correcting information. This means that a CD actually requires 3234 bytes to store 2352 bytes of data. This error-correction process allows damaged sectors to be reconstructed by software interpretation, which will usually keep the audio from dropping out, even in the presence of errors. The timing codes are used to display the track and time location of the CD on your LED readout.

The disc spins at a constant linear velocity, which means that the rotational speed of the disc may vary from 530 rpm when it is reading near the center of the disc, to about 200 rpm when it is reading near the outside of the disc. This allows the data to be read at a sustained data rate of 150K per second. This is sufficient for 16-bit 44.1 stereo audio, but is not sufficient for reading large computer data files. There are now CD-ROM players that read information up to 8 times this speed (1200K per second), and that will probably continue to increase in speed.

This first standard for CDs, which was for audio playback, was named Red Book. The Red Book standard, officially known as the Compact Disc Digital Audio Standard, defines the format for CDs available in music stores today. Red Book Audio discs can provide up to 80 minutes of playing time. There can be up to 99 separate tracks on an audio CD. Each track of the CD may contain different types of information.

Several other standards have been created to meet various digital information needs. These include: Orange Book (for write-once, read many (WORM), Yellow Book (standard CD-ROMs), Green Book (CD-I), White Book (digital video in MPEG1 format), and Blue Book (CD Plus).Within each standard there are modes, forms, and levels. These variations define the way the player reads the information and how the information in the sector is formatted.

A CD track can be made up of one of the following: CD Audio, CD-ROM Mode 1, CD-ROM Mode 2,CD-ROM XA, or CD-I. When there is more than one type of these data formats on the CD, the disc is called a mixed mode disc. The CD-ROM/XA (extended architecture) format requires additional hardware from the user, and uses additional subheader information that tells the software what type of data to expect in that sector. This data type will either be audio with interleaved video, or it will be computer data. As a result of the increased complexity and demand on the part of the user, this format has proved to be relatively unpopular in the consumer marketplace.

Other standards

Because development of optical media has advanced so rapidly in the years that it's been available, there are (unfortunately) numerous other technical standards that developers should be aware of. Not all of them are germane to most mainstream multimedia projects, but you never know what a client will one day ask for.

Yellow Book

The Yellow Book was developed by Sony and Philips to provide an established standard for data retrieval and storage. Yellow Book provides an additional layer for error checking that accommodates the reliability required of computer data. It also provides two modes, one for compressed audio and video data, and one for computer data. The most common CD format used for CD-ROM evolved from the Yellow Book, with Microsoft contributing as a collaborator, and has been approved by the International Standards Organization as ISO-9660.

Other standards for these types of data purposes were developed later to primarily deal with user requirements, such as synchronized interleaving of compressed audio and visual information in interactive digital movies (Green Book) and with formats for one-off and magneto-optical CD technologies (Orange Book).

White Book

The White Book specification is a new technology that allows you to play linear video material from a compact disc. This specification is commonly referred to as "Video CD." The interleaved video and audio streams are stored in the MPEG1 format. MPEG1 is an international video compression technology that allows for more than 70 minutes of VHS-quality video material to be stored on a standard compact disc.

Video CD has the ability to be played back on multiple platforms. This ensures a large installed base of devices on which Video CD titles will play. Video will allow the delivery of music videos, movies, and training applications. Video CD is independent of all broadcast standards (NTSC, SECAM, and PAL), and a single disc plays on any Video CD platform worldwide. Target platforms for Video CD discs are specially configured computer systems (you must have an MPEG1 decoding card), dedicated Video CD players, and CD-I players with Digital Video cartridges.

Blue Book

In June 1995, Sony, Philips, Apple, and Microsoft formally announced the new specifications for enhanced multisession CDs called the Blue Book, and defined the data formats that can be included on an enhanced multisession CD. What's enhanced about the CD is that it's a mixed-mode disc that actually enjoys the possibility of wide consumer compatibility. The enhanced CD is believed to be compatible with most CD-ROM drives and needs only updated CD drivers to play on Windows and Macintosh computers.

This technology allows for stamped multisession discs so that a CD-ROM can contain two separate sessions on the same CD. The first session is Red Book CD Audio, and the second session contains computer data. An audio CD player will play the disc as a normal consumer audio CD. A CD-ROM drive will find the second session and mount the CD-ROM portion. This standard alleviates the danger of an audio CD player accidentally playing the data track, which is a most unpleasant sound and potentially damaging to the audio playback system that's unfortunate enough to have this happen to it.

ISO-9660

ISO-9660 is the most widely used format for storing and delivering digital data on CDs. The naming standard convention follows the MS-DOS style of eight characters, a period, and three extender characters as a suffix. Directory names are limited to eight characters. Acceptable characters for names are the capital letters A–Z, the digits 0–9, and the underscore character. An executable program designed for the PC will not run on a Macintosh (and vice versa). It is possible, however, to access all files on a CD from either platform. However, on the Mac you will need the Apple CD-ROM extension, the files' names, and software extensions for both foreign file access and ISO 9660 File access must be in the system folder.

On MS-DOS computers, a device driver supplied by the player manufacturer must be called from the Config.sys files, and the file MSCDEX.exe or the equivalent (Corel's .CDX extension, for example) must be run during bootup. Many developers place both Mac and PC files on the same CD in a hybrid format, letting the user launch the proper applications from the appropriate platform.

HFS

Apple's method for managing files and folders on the Macintosh Desktop is the Hierarchal File system (HFS). Apple has developed its own drivers for Yellow Book Mode 1 CDs, and the HFS driver for CD-ROMs provided the Macintosh users with the expected comfort and face the familiar Apple desktop, complete with the 32-character mixed-case file names. HFS does not comply with international ISO-9660 standards. If the ROM is designed only for Macs, this is the preferred choice.

CD-ROM/XA

XA (extended architecture) is an extension to the Yellow Book standard. XA defines a new sector format to allow computer data (Form 1), as well as compressed audio data and video image information (Form 2), to be read and played back simultaneously. Computer data can be interleaved, or mixed with audio and images. In effect, XA provided audio synchronization, similar to the more modern variants of this idea, such as Quicktime and AVI. Special enabling hardware is required on board a CD-ROM/XA player because the audio must be separated from the interleaved data, decompressed, and then output to speakers, while the computer data is sent onward to the computer. XA audio can be played back at two quality levels, though it falls short of Red Book quality. Production of a CD-ROM/XA requires extensive premastering because the data and audio/video information must be properly interleaved from the original material.

Photo CD

In 1992, Eastman Kodak Company pioneered a well-planned and heavily financed effort to establish an early market share in worldwide electronic photo-imaging systems for consumers. Designed to protect Kodak's investment in the photoprocessing industry and its vast sales and technology infrastructure, and to allow gradual consumer transition from film-based cameras to digital cameras over the next decades, the new technology is a merginge of silver halide wet processing and digital processing and display techniques. Kodak has named this venture Photo CD.

Customers present an exposed 35mm roll of color film for wet processing, and purchase a Photo CD for an additional charge. The source images are then processed by a technician who scans each image at an imaging workstation. The images (a session) are written onto Photo CD write-once media, a color index of thumbnails (photographers know this as a contact sheet) of all the images is printed, and the photo CD is returned to the consumer in a CD jewel case with the index inserted as an attractive cover.

The customer can later return that same photo CD to have more images written on it, creating a multisession disc. A photo CD can contain 125 or more high-resolution images. Photo CD images may be viewed using a dedicated Kodak Photo CD player connected to a television at the customer's home or business. That player can also play Red Book consumer audio CDs as well as Red Book tracks that may be associated with any Photo CD image. In addition, the capability of playing Photo CD images is now standard fare for most current CD-ROM drives.

Green Book

Published in 1988, Philips CD-I (Compact Disc-Interactive) specifies an Extended Architecture format and real-time operating system (CD-RTOS) for this proprietary multimedia environment. Like Photo CD, CD-I discs are designed to play on a consumer grade player connected to a television set. To prevent the users from playing a CD-I track on an audio player (which is a sound that you do not want to experience), the CD-I tracks are not listed on the table of contents. CD-I uses XA Form 1 and Form 2 data formats. CD-I ready discs are Red Book Audio discs with special information stored just ahead of track 1, in an area called the pregap. These discs are designed specifically to work with Philips CD-I players allowing special pictures and text to be loaded into the player's memory before the Red Book Audio tracks begin to play. The disc can also be played on a Standard CD-Audio player without interference from the additional information stored on the disc.

The Glass Master

The master disk for a CD-ROM is made in what is generally called a family process. The glass master is made using the well-developed photolithographic techniques created by the microchip industry: First, an optically ground glass disc is coated with a layer of photoresist material 1/10 micron thick. A laser exposes a pattern of pits onto the surface of the chemical layer of the material. The disc is then developed (the exposed areas are washed away) and is silvered, resulting in the actual pit structure of the finished master disc.

The master is then electroplated with layers of nickel that are one molecule thick, one layer at a time, until the desired thickness is reached. Finally, the nickel layer is separated from the glass disc and forms the metal negative, or father. In cases in which low runs of just a few discs are required, the father is used to make the actual discs. Most projects, however, require several mothers, or positives, to be made by plating the surface of the father.

In a third stage, sons, or stampers, are made from the mother and these are the parts that are used in the injection molding machines. Plastic pellets are heated and injected in the mold or stamper, forming the disc with the pits in it. The plastic disc is coated with a thin aluminum layer for reflectance and lacquer for protection, and then given a silk-screened label for marketing and packaged for delivery.

These activities should occur in a particle-free cleanroom because many hours of work can be ruined by one speck of dust. The mastering process alone can take around 12 hours. CDs produced in this manner typically cost less than 2 dollars apiece, depending on the size of the run. Masters typically run between $500 and $1500. Additional expenses might include premastering, if you are not supplying a gold disc, a silk-screen setup for around $400, and packaging at $0.25 per disc in jewel case, shrink-wrapped and ready to be shipped.

Additional materials

If the completed multimedia project will be delivered to an audience that will consist of many different types of computers, it's necessary to prepare the files so that they can be easily installed onto the various platforms. Simply copying the application and support files to the user's hard drive most often is not effective. For the proper installation, you will probably need to install special system and runtime files.

It may be necessary to provide a single program that acts as an installation routine so that the end users can easily set up the application on their own computers. It is important to include exceptional documentation explaining the installation process so that users have a clear step-by-step procedure to follow. This documentation must include a discussion of potential problems and issues relating to all potential target platforms.

Documentation

In most cases, you, the producer, will not have any control over the end user's computer platform and specifications. It is important to include specifications and warnings regarding the minimum requirements for proper performance of the application. The more detailed this description is, the less likely you are to have people calling and asking questions. Technical support for your product can be an expensive, excruciating process, as you'll see in Chapter 8. The more attention paid to detail now, the fewer headaches the future will bring.

These system requirements and other specifications should be listed on the packaging and in a file generally referred to as the Readme file. This explanatory addendum to the user manual should be presented as an ASCII text file, allowing users to read it with just about any word processing program. Developers will generally include information in the Readme file that was not able to be printed in the documentation, for reasons of time or last-minute revisions.

Readme files

Some people will tend to open up a software package and use it before ever consulting the documentation. But there is a source for information on the product that should be read (though most users don't bother), called the Readme file.This file generally includes information on known incompatibilities, tips, and tricks and an overall product summary. There will often be last minute instructions, the latest bug reports, and new feature implementations that did not make the printed documentation before it went to press. Contact information for technical support and e-mail addresses for registration are conveniences that aren't always found on the Readme, but they are excellent ways to facilitate communication with your customers. Of course, there are Readme files just so that the author can pontificate on how great the software really is and how it beats the socks off any product that dares to compete with it.

It's good practice to include written instructions on the CD packaging, especially if it's going to a wide audience, or to an audience that may include users with very little computer experience. As a general rule, this must always include the minimum machine requirements necessary to run the multimedia title, including memory and graphic requirements, processor speed, the speed of the CD-ROM drive, compatibility with sound cards, and other peripherals. Most multimedia titles today have nearly identical specifications.

Installation instructions should be basic and, except for complex exceptions such as titles that need to work across networks or over modem lines, are generally fairly straightforward. They typically consist of launching a setup application with which most users are familiar. If the installation program is well designed, the process will be self-explanatory. In cases such as this, when the execution of the installer program is elegant, installation instructions can be brief enough to fit on the back of the CD insert.

It's also important to be aware of any licensing requirements when using outside tools or system extensions that are used to author or run the multimedia title. For example, if you are creating a project with Macromedia Director, and you will be selling the product commercially, you must include Macromedia Director's logo on the packaging and it must be embedded electronically in your software package. There is also a requirement from Apple computer that the Quicktime logo be displayed on the package if the title uses this technology. Be sure to read the licensing agreements for any external software needed for your application.

Packaging and assembly

When creating the packaging for a consumer product, keep in mind that the design will, in many cases, determine whether someone picks up your product over another from a shelf full of titles. There must be something that is an excellent representation of the product's function and content, and that is also very attractive so that people will be drawn to it. Packaging can make or break a title the way a jacket can sell a book or a poster can sell a movie.

The title of the product should obviously be prominent, along with strategic placement of the company logo. It's usually a good idea to put the title on the lower half of the box; the top can often be hidden or blocked by overhanging shelves in a retail environment. The title should also be on the spine of the packaging, in case the software is stocked and displayed with the spine out instead of face out. Crowded software stores, unfortunately, often resort to half-hearted sales displays such as this when the shelves become too crowded with competing titles.

If the product is MPC-approved — in other words, it lives up to the standards of the Multimedia PC council, which sets minimum standards for multimedia playback on the PC — the MPC label should be displayed on the bottom-right corner of the front of the packaging; also next to the system requirements on the back, and on the jewel box spine. Stickers on the package can also be a big help, as you'll see in the next chapter. Many developers will print product ratings or use holograms on these stickers — anything to attract attention and perhaps a potential buyer.

Unusual box design can be very intriguing to potential customers. But before undertaking this route, be aware that retail stores have specific types of shelves and a certain amount of shelf space to sell, and packaging of an unusual size or shape is never appreciated for very long. This type of packaging can be hard to stack and can decrease the number of products that the store can display. The idea is to be visually appealing while still giving the retailer a fighting chance to sell the product.

Gatefold packaging offers an interesting option because it often piques a potential customer's curiosity, especially a child's. People like to think that they are getting something extra, so when you grab their attention with more information outside and more stuff inside, they feel that they are getting more value for their money. It's a gimmick, but it works. Packaging information for schools and libraries requires a slightly different approach, because the information is not usually purchased from the shelf, but rather through catalogs. Money is better spent on catalog space and layout because the packaging is not really seen by the buyer, and will probably be thrown out on delivery anyway.

Because many consumers tend to relate the packaging of a product to its quality and price, the larger, heavier, and more decorative the package is, the higher its perceived value. So, even if the package contains small items such as software, user's guide registration card, quick reference, and some collateral materials, it can appear more significant depending upon how it is packaged. Air-filled plastic materials, open cell foam, and compartmental containers can be utilized to hold items in place and allow vendors more flexibility when setting the price.

Shipping considerations

Basic shipping options through a packaging specialist include the user manual and disk shrink-wrapped together, a cardboard envelope with disks and manuals inside, a cardboard box with disks and manual inside (with or without air filler to make the box bigger) shrink-wrapped. The cardbox as described here is enclosed with a slipcover and shrink-wrapped. Other options include an open-ended cardboard box with sliding tray insert containing manuals and disks with or without a slipcover, or an open-ended cardboard box with a ring binder containing manuals and disks. Packaging costs can range from about $5 per unit for simple shrink-wrapping (including printing costs for manual and floppy disk) to more than $50 for elaborate boxes and materials.

It may sound petty, but it's important to know how much the product is going to weigh when the packaging is being created. There may be a significant difference in price for shipping if the weight of the product is even slightly reduced. Decide whether the customer-perceived added value for a heavier package is applicable to your product, and whether this is potentially important as a marketing ploy to increase sales.

The MPC standard

The MPC standard, in addition to creating hardware and software standards for multimedia products, has also created a packaging design standard. The MPC guidelines recommend the following:

Standard software boxes should have a width between 6.75 and 6.85 inches. The height should be 9 to 9.5 inches tall. The depth of the box is dependent on the product and its documentation. This size of packaging will fit on most retail shelves, and will generally allow 6 or more boxes to be faced out on the shelves.

In less specific terms, the height of a standard CD audio case is 4.875 inches. Short CD boxes are 9 to 9.75 inches tall, which is approximately the same height as the software box. The short CD box width is 5.75 to 6 inches.

Information titles for education, and software priced at $59.95 or more, should use standard software boxes. Any software priced at less than $59.95 should be in CD boxes. Any software title that costs more than $200 is usually packaged in a way that's at least two inches deep. This may sound like an arbitrary decision, but again, the perception of value is important to instill in a potential customer.

Printing CD-ROM materials

The disc replication facility will usually handle the printing for the CD-ROM project. There are three elements that the production team needs to prepare in advance of the actual disc printing. First, the artwork for the CD-ROM itself will be silkscreened onto the face of your discs. The replication costs for CDs usually include two-color printing on the disc face. Additional colors vary in price. Some manufacturers are able to print on the entire disc. For readability, it is a general rule not to use type under 6 points.

The inlay card is the piece of cardboard on the back of the disc's jewel box. It is folded on one side to create the spine of the disc. There is usually no printing on the inside of the inlay, but it is becoming popular to use clear plastic for the CD trays, allowing the customer to see this part of the inlay.

The third part of the printed materials is the booklet, which slips into the inside of the cover of the jewel case. The thickness of the book should not be any more than 1.5 mm when it is closed. You will find that many manufacturers suggest the use of 100-pound, coated text paper. This book should open to the left. The front cover is what people will see when they view the disc, so your product and company name should be prominent.

Corporate packaging

Corporate packaging can be very similar to retail, with a few exceptions. For one, the marketing team should not have to worry about packaging the product with large, flashy boxes. The target audience will probably not be influenced by a larger or heavier box — these are not the elements that will create the perception of added value for a corporate client. In this context, packaging should be elegantly and efficiently — as opposed to flashily — designed. Visual appeal should be tight, attractive, and informative, making clear to the user exactly what the product is and how it will benefit them.

More often than not, the corporate multimedia product will be a part of a larger presentation package, or will be part of a mailer. Here, it's worthwhile to examine the possibility of just using a shrink-wrapped jewel case, or even a cardboard mailer or jewel case. Obviously, make sure that the system requirements for the product are printed on the back. Most computers in the corporate environment that have a CD-ROM drive will at least meet the MPC2 standard specification. But it's clearly to the producer's benefit, as well as the user's, to make the minimum system requirements clear. There is nothing worse for a company than to send out a demo disc of its work and have the potential client not be able to get it to run.

Ready, willing, and able?

Now that the team has got a great product out there, what happens when people start calling with technical support questions? How will you support your calls? Will you need technical support available for only eight hours a day, or 24 hours? Do you need to cover the time differences between east coast and west coast consumers? Will the product need international support? What call volume do you expect? What kinds of questions may be asked, and how will you properly prepare and train your technical support people?

Consider the costs of hiring one full-time support person to sit by the phone and answer e-mail questions. Will one person cover all the tech support needs, or will a larger support staff be necessary? There are companies that specialize in technical support for software products. These companies can be a great help in the expectation of a large amount of support calls. That situation generally arises with a product of unusual complexity, or a product that's been rushed to market. As with the professional beta-testing service, a professional customer support service will have people already set up with the proper equipment, and will have experience dealing with customers. There are many other options here, including electronic and phone support, faxback services, and a general questions/answers voice recording. The benefit to the publisher is the customer's view of the quality and reliability of your company. If a customer who has a technical problem calls your support number and speaks with someone who is helpful and tries to find a solution, he or she will very likely be a second-time customer. A good experience will increase the perceived value and quality of your product, meaning that customers will be more likely to buy another title by your company.

If customers have a bad experience, they will very likely consider buying another company's product the next time they go software shopping. Technical support is a hard cost to the company and is figured into the total costs of production. It is a cost that is not directly justifiable in the sense that it must be implemented at a specific cost, even when there is very little knowledge of actual sales. In the absence of this investment, however, reviewers and customers who do not get support from the start will spread the word. And that's not good.

Online support can be an expensive venture as well. There still needs to be someone operating and managing the online support site, as it will need to be updated regularly. If the company already has a computer server, the cost of online support startup will be manageable. If not, this can be a significant investment. Even if that equipment is in place, and even though many, if not most, users will find an online support site useful, many users will still need one-on-one hand-holding to get used to the product. You can learn more about customer support in Chapter 9.

Product registration

By creating a scheme for product registration, the producer can create a useful database of information on customers and will make it simple to inform them on upgrades so that they can purchase more software from the company in the future. Be aware that people do not want to spend a long period of time filling out these forms. Decide which information is important and tailor the form to allow the user to submit this information with the least amount of effort. Most people will supply information on their address, computer type, or anything they feel is directly applicable to your understanding of how their system is set up. Do not expect handwritten notes with detailed information; check boxes are enough. Make it as easy as possible, and also include postage. People are less likely to register if they have to spend money on the process, unless it is a very expensive package. Include a phone number. Some people will call in to register, epecially if they also have questions. A fax option for registration is also a convenience and encourages people to actually register the product.

Some publishers have increased the number of people who register by creating electronic registration. An online registration application can be created and included with the software so that if the customer has an online connection, the application will connect the user to your server. This registration information can be sent directly to the company without the cost of postage and will allow the information to be placed directly into a database rather than keyed in by company personnel, which is tedious, time consuming, and expensive.

There are several direct benefits of registration. First of all, it creates a direct sales list for the company. You now have a list of the people most likely to use your software. These lists can also be sold to data management organizations and research companies, unless the registration gives the registrant the option of being left off these lists. Other multimedia and software/hardware companies are always looking for statistical information on sales and demographics of the purchasers. You will also have a rough idea of the number of people who actually purchased your software, which is a useful thing to know when trying to pitch future projects. Unfortunately, registration cards aren't an absolutely accurate measure, because nobody knows the exact percentage of buyers who actually fill out and mail registration forms. But any sales data is better than no sales data.

Some software packages have free technical support for a period of time and then switch over to payment technical support, so having a list of product owners can help you sell this service. It's also advantageous to begin user groups and newsletter mailing through the registration client list. By creating communication between users, you may help to steer some of the technical questions away from precious intellectual resources from within the company, and will also create a group that might be able to tell you a few things you didn't know about the product.

And, if you create an incentive program, you may get even more responses from user registration. If users can receive a free newsletter, product support, or magazines, they will be more likely to take the time to fill out the form and may even be willing to put their own stamp on the postcard. After a user has done so, you'll know you have a paying customer.

Okay, so now the project is completed, tested, and declared ready by the production team. It's now time to figure out how you can get it out to where people can use it and enjoy it. Next, you'll take a look at marketing and publishing your multimedia.

CHAPTER 8

Marketing and Publishing

✦ Even the best multimedia project is only as good as the reception it gets. Proper marketing makes sure that it gets the right reception.

✦ It's largely impossible to sell a multimedia product if you've picked the wrong market, though many companies go broke trying.

✦ Picking the right publishers and partners is key not only to the project, but to the long-term viability of the entire production company.

✦ Marketing for CD-ROM is a known animal. Marketing for the Web is a barely known animal. New methods of outreach are being devised for both formats.

Although most producers concern themselves with the creation and development of the best possible products, many multimedia and Web producers have expanded their role to include some aspects of marketing and publishing. As expressed so many times in this book, unless your multimedia creation is distributed to an audience that can enjoy it, it's a labor of love more than a commercial venture. Although there's nothing wrong with that, most producers would like to profit from their work. This not only allows them to feed themselves and loved ones, but affords the opportunity to begin new projects, which is what every multimedia professional really wants.

The multimedia world has several types of publishing and several types of markets. This chapter begins with a rundown on the types of publishing and the markets they serve.

Where Do You Buy Multimedia?

When consumers shop for multimedia software, they most often visit a retail store. CD-ROMs are sold through several types of retail stores, notably computer hardware and software superstores (such as Computer City and CompUSA), software superstores (such as Media Play, whose selection also includes books, music, video, and videogames), software specialty stores (such as Software, ETC.), consumer electronics stores (such as Best Buy and Circuit City), office superstores (such as OfficeMax and STAPLES), and mass merchandise discounters (such as Wal-Mart). Some bookstores also sell software. Barnes & Noble and Borders, for example, stock hundreds of multimedia titles. Between 75 and 90 percent of consumer software is sold through retail stores. Competition for shelf space in these stores is fierce, and many publishers, even those with well-regarded titles, may not be able to secure shelf space for their products. Most of the remaining 20 percent is sold through direct mail catalogs, such as PC/Mac Connection, PC Warehouse, and MacMALL.

With few exceptions, consumer publishing on the Web is not yet a "profitable" business. Although this platform is extremely promising, and although some Web publishers have great strategies for the best possible combination of subscriptions, advertising, and transactions (consumer purchases, for example), this business is still in its infancy. Most successful Web sites are used for promotion of non-Web products and services. In the current era, revenues are generated by advertising or subscriptions, not by transactions. As digital money becomes more commonplace, more software (and other products) will be sold through Web stores.

Consumers Aren't the Only Consumers

Although consumer publishing is by far the most visible type of digital publishing, consumers are not the only market for CD-ROMs and Web multimedia products. In fact, many companies have developed successful businesses by concentrating on vertical markets, such as medical publishing. A wide range of educational software, for students as young as preschoolers and as old as graduate students, also occupies a significant niche in computer publishing.

In addition, many software products are sold by one business to another (hence the term "business-to-business" marketing). Most business-to-business titles are not multimedia products. Instead, they are tools, such as word processors, graphics programs, and database managers. The channels can be less distinct. Many CD-ROM titles are produced specifically for internal use by one corporation, or department. These titles are, by and large, training tools. On the Web, business-to-business publishing is most often used for technical support and product information such as catalogs.

Consumer CD-ROM Publishing

There are hundreds of CD-ROM publishers in the U.S., plus hundreds more in other countries throughout the world. Regardless of their size or location, all of these companies share two challenges: comparatively high product development costs, and limited availability retail shelf space for their products. This is a tough combination. A small number of well-established publishers sell an extremely high percentage of commercially-accepted CD-ROM products, leaving their competitors with expensive publishing programs that are often difficult to justify to shareholders or other financial interests because of the small number of units sold.

Although some new companies have entered the market within the past few years, the most successful publishers have been selling software for well over a decade. They enjoy long-established relationships with the buyers who choose products for retail chains, and they've learned, often by trial and error, how to successfully launch a new product. They know how much to spend on development, how to price and package a product, how to present the product to retail buyers, how to get good reviews in magazines that generate good word-of-mouth, and so on. The right combination of knowledge, experience, and the appropriate products has eluded nearly every large media company, and a vast number of 1990s start-up companies besides.

Many of the successful software publishers began as small-scale start-ups in the 1980s, selling their wares on 5¼-inch floppy disks (and, in some cases, on audiocassettes, which preceded disks) to a small number of tiny computer retailers. Often, these retailers shared the same sensibility as the software publishers ("nerd" is the word that comes to mind most often, though it is a stereotype). As the business became more sophisticated, the publishers adapted and grew. Microsoft began this way, and so did Broderbund, Sierra, Interplay, Mindscape, Voyager, and Electronic Arts. On the children's side, Davidson, MECC, and The Learning Company developed classroom products that became popular with parents as well.

Not many large companies have succeeded in software, but there are notable exceptions, including Disney, Virgin, and GTE. On the other hand, Paramount, IBM, CBS, and HarperCollins have struggled to find their way. Simon & Schuster, Random House, and Houghton Mifflin are among the book publishers with operational software groups; apart from Random House's joint interest with Broderbund in Living Books and some other investments, these companies' impact has been less impressive than the work done by smaller, more focused firms.

Toy and amusement companies have jumped into the fray as well. Hasbro recently entered the field with a line of titles based on well-known games such as *Monopoly, Trivial Pursuit,* and *Battleship;* Mattel is also finding a place for itself with multimedia products based on *Barbie* and *Hot Wheels*. Will these established toy companies succeed where Parker Brothers tried, and gave up the fight, a few years back? Was LEGO smart when the company licensed its valuable brand name (to Mindscape) rather than investing in its own start-up software group? The market is unpredictable. In fact, some of the biggest hits come from unexpected companies. There is always room for a new company; the success of GT Interactive and its *DOOM* product is an outstanding example of this phenomenon (GT grew out of a home-video distributor).

At retail, where all of these companies' products are sold and compete directly with one another, consumers don't know much about brand names or company history. Consumers buy products that are familiar because of reviews, friends' comments, advertisements, recommendations from teachers, and a wide range of other reasons beyond the direct control of even the most savvy publisher. Successful retail sell-in (to the buyers) and sell-through (to consumers) is an ongoing challenge for all but the largest companies.

Consumer CD-ROM Publishing, Step by Step

The first step in launching a CD-ROM publishing program is the development of a strategy. With so many CD-ROM publishers in the marketplace, and so many notable failures, an effective strategy has become critically important.

One aspect of the strategy, unfortunately, is usually rapid return on investment. Whether the CD-ROM publishing operation is backed by a large company or private investors, the first product line must earn back the initial investment within the first year or two. Investors have become very, very impatient with CD-ROM publishers who do not earn back investments. Great products that don't sell well do not, as a rule, provide sufficient impetus for a new company to succeed.

This pressure is not an especially healthy addition to the wealth of challenges faced by a new business venture, but it is reality. It must be acknowledged, but should not be the guiding factor behind the product strategy.

What will sell?

There is no guarantee that any product or product line will be successful, but the odds of success are greatly increased if many of the following statements are true:

- The product or product line does not compete in the same category as well-established products from top brands.
- The product line is based upon absolutely bullet-proof content from other media.
- The product line consists of at least three related products.
- The product line is competently produced.
- The product is competently marketed.
- The pricing is fair, and in line with current industry trends.
- The product and product line are widely reviewed in consumer magazines — and receive positive reviews.
- The product is competently distributed by a firm that regularly does business with a wide range of important retail buyers.
- The publisher is perceived as a "keeper," a company that will supply a continuous stream of successful products.
- The product is published by a company whose principal business is CD-ROM publishing.

In the following sections, I look at these statements one at a time.

Competition within Product Categories

CD-ROM publishing is a category business. Software is racked by category in retail specialty stores and sold by category in mail order catalogs. Some categories are dominated by products that have consistently sold, year after year, giving retail buyers and consumers no reason to look further than the existing titles. The children's geography education category, for example, is "owned" by Broderbund's *Where in the World is Carmen Sandiego?*. The math category is dominated by products from Broderbund, MECC, Davidson, and The Learning Company, all well-established players with products for every age range and every level of ability. The same can be said about learn-to-read products for children. Edmark has solidified its position in preschool software, sharing the market with top-selling storybook and activity products based on *Pocahontas* and other Disney films. Some product categories are not entirely dominated by one product. Science and foreign language education, for example, are not dominated by category killers.

A visit to a well-stocked children's software specialty store, such as Zany Brainy in the mid-Atlantic states, will provide up-to-date information about current products and trends. (Make friends with a salesperson who knows the category, and if possible, try to make friends with the buyer for kids' software.)

Children's software is one of three principal multimedia categories. The other two are games and reference. To say this another way, the vast majority of multimedia CD-ROMs are children's products, games, or reference software. If a CD-ROM does not fit into one of these categories, the buyer may have concerns about its potential for success.

Games

The game business is a "hits" business. Hits are nearly impossible to forecast. Some games look promising but sell poorly. Other games unexpectedly capture the attention of consumers and become huge successes. In a world in which game products cost $500,000 to $1,500,000 to produce and usually just as much to market, a more secure means of forecasting success is obviously desirable. In the game business, success is more likely for games that are designed by people or teams who have developed hits in the past.

Consumers buy new games based on reviews and on word of mouth. Both are more likely to be positive on a new game from a trusted designer or design team. A publisher that has succeeded in games is also a desirable. A new designer and new publisher will have a tough time in the marketplace — some stores will stock the product, but in smallish quantities; some will "test" the product by placing it only in some stores (and potentially missing the big selling season); and most will simply wait to see how the product sells in other stores.

Reference

Reference products have evolved in an entirely different way. Most successful reference CD-ROMs are multimedia encyclopedias. The most successful CD-ROM encyclopedia is Microsoft *Encarta,* followed by similar products from Compton and Grolier. These are large-scale ventures by big, well-established companies. Microsoft established its market leadership by bundling their encyclopedia with new home computers — that is, it gave the disc away for free, in hopes of igniting a consumer appetite for updated editions. Grolier and Compton pursued a similar strategy. Each of these companies has developed other reference products, generally with mixed results.

Bullet-Proof Content

This test is an especially tough one. Bullet-proof content is a new Disney-animated feature, such as *The Hunchback of Notre Dame,* or a book that has dominated every best seller list for a year or more, such as those in the *Goosebumps* or *The Magic School Bus* series. It's the nation's top TV series, or a band whose singles or albums have been top ten for a year. In other words, the best of the best.

Most content does not meet this criteria. There's plenty of material that's well known or well regarded by a particular audience. Book publishers, for example, have placed their bets on titles that have routinely sold well in print form, only to be disappointed by only so-so performance on CD-ROM. Many promising movie licenses have resulted in very short-term successes on the CD-ROM front, followed by a sharp decline in sales after the movie has peaked in the theaters. Even the most aware computer user is only vaguely aware of most CD-ROM titles, so most titles based upon top movies (and TV series, and so on) go unnoticed by their potential customers. The software must develop its own popularity, as the Disney Animated Storybooks have done. When a new Disney film is released, consumers now know that they should visit the local computer store to buy the software. Few other media properties have generated this kind of consumer behavior.

Some titles come with a built-in marketing program. If the author (in the writerly sense) of a multimedia title regularly lectures, or keeps in touch with his or her readers via e-mail, then the target customers can be made aware of the new CD-ROM product, and, presumably, the product can be sold via direct marketing as well. These situations are relatively uncommon, however. Most products are sold at retail, where A-minus and B-plus content licenses are common — and many of these underperform.

Most successful software publishers have avoided the purchase of expensive licenses in favor of their own concoctions. In fact, the majority of successful software titles available in stores today are *not* based upon licenses from other media.

Of course, a great many of the titles available in retail stores are not built with bullet-proof content. They've managed to find their way to the stores because their launch timing was good, and they've managed to sell a consistent, if not huge, number of units. There are many such categories, and these represent real opportunities for risk-taking entrepreneurs.

Test preparation software, for example, is an example of a category in which at least a half-dozen companies are fighting it out (test preparation products help high school students to improve their SAT scores and scores on other tests). Some companies are well known in the test prep field (The Princeton Review, Kaplan Interactive), some are strong educational software publishers (Davidson & Associates, The Learning Company), and some are entrepreneurial software companies with a good idea and some marketing strengths (SWFTE). In this category, and in many others, bullet-proof content simply isn't available in any form; there is no recognized "best" in the test prep business, but only a group of licenses and companies who are recognized as generally competent. So companies fight it out, some win, most lose, and in time, a small number of companies control most of the category's shelf space and the potential customer's mind share.

Products vs. Product Lines

To understand the importance of a product line, it's best to view the software business from the retail buyer's perspective.

A retail buyer receives materials and sits through sales calls from hundreds of publishers each year. Most of the products are not well thought out; others are not backed by any serious marketing effort. Some companies have a reputation for faulty products, which results in unhappy customers and returned merchandise. In short, the buyer often wastes a great deal of time on companies that are not serious competitors — hoping to discover a small number of companies and product lines with real sales potential.

One quick way for the buyer to identify a company that does not understand the marketplace is to identify a one-product company. Usually, the one-product company is a small operation, incapable of dealing with customer service issues, and easily swamped if large numbers of orders suddenly materialize.

Like any other sales-oriented business, software retailing is based upon relationships. A company representative who breezes in with a great story about a single product will be asked, inevitably, about the company's plans for a product line. If there is no good answer, then the representative had better know a great deal about the company's extraordinarily clever and well-funded plans for marketing and advertising this single product. That's one path. The other, which wears thin quickly, is a request to carry the product as a favor to the salesperson or rep. (A relationship will stand only so many favors that don't pan out, though.)

The right way to prepare a product line is to focus on a single target market. Two products are not generally perceived as a product line, unless another two are planned to follow in a matter of a month or two. Three products make up a product line, as do four, five, or six. More than six makes a full-blown publishing program (these are general guidelines, not absolute definitions). All (three) products should be planned to be sold in the same section of the store: three action games, three preschool products, three foreign language products (Spanish, French, Japanese), and so on. Again, the actual number of releases will vary, but the objective, which should be taken seriously, is to demonstrate a long-term understanding of the retail buyer's needs — and then, to deliver as promised.

Competent Production

The software business moves very quickly. Product development schedules are often delayed in their early phases (the deal is taking longer than planned, the contract requires four drafts before it's right, the publisher's funding sources are getting nervous, the publisher's internal development staff is overworked and can't get things together to start a new project, and so on). All too often, the early stages of production do not begin on time — but the ship date does not change. As a result, many developers are very busy in June and July, rushing to make their dates for products that must be duplicated and packaged in August and September for release in time for the holiday season. This kind of pressure is reality in the competitive CD-ROM marketplace, pressure that is often turned a few notches higher at public companies, where revenues need to be shown before the end of a particular quarter.

This kind of schedule is difficult to manage for any venture, but it's especially tricky in the software business, in which the product developer is, often, a contractor to the publisher. That is, the publisher does not exercise any direct control over the producer, the artists, the programmers, or the staff that is actually building the product. The publisher supervises these efforts and may control many of the key creative decisions, but, ultimately, the developer is responsible for delivering a product acceptable to the publisher. On time. And on budget.

Trust, then, becomes the single most important component in the publisher's choice of developer. That is: the publisher must feel absolutely certain of the producer's ability to deliver a gold master disc on or before the specified date. New developers may find it difficult to convince a publisher of their reliability; as a result, many publishers rely upon established production houses for the bulk of their work. Meeting deadlines is so important, in fact, that the primary role of a publisher's in-house producer is, usually, the assurance of on-time delivery (other factors, such as on-budget delivery, creative wonder, marketability, product features, even technical perfection, are usually secondary).

Of course, this situation creates some tension. When the original product specification is written and approved, the product's budget is based upon a series of features and assumptions. As the on-time delivery demon enters the picture, typically a month or two before an alpha version, the trade-offs begin. Features may be dropped or simplified. What was to be animated may now become flat art. A complicated music soundtrack may be reduced to a smaller number of sound files. Problems with game and interactive elements that do not play properly may be fixed by redesigning the game in a way that compromises the overall product's impact.

Between alpha and beta, a long list of technical changes almost always overwhelms the available resources. Many of these changes are functional — to make the product work more effectively. Some are editorial and artistic changes — to make the product look "right," or at least, consistent with license requirements or an overall vision. And then, there are the bugs, the technical problems that must be fixed before the product is released. The in-house producer's job is to set priorities, to help the developer sort through a loose-leaf notebook filled with bugs and other changes, and still, get that product out on time and on budget. Some changes will not be made in time for the release date. Experienced developers talk about the balance between product features that do not work perfectly and the resulting consumer dissatisfaction versus the likelihood of tech support calls and product returns. The release date rules; it is almost never changed, or slipped, for more than a week or so.

Through all of this, the product must work properly. Although there may be some technical glitches — fixed by offering either a download from the company's Web site or an updated disc — the overall user experience must be satisfactory. In fact, it must be more than satisfactory in today's marketplace. It must be superior. So good, in fact, that the user will want to buy a follow-up product in the line.

Competent Marketing

When a product is under consideration for publication, the marketing department should have a strong say as to whether the product should be published. If things work as they should, the marketers will understand how best to position the product, how to package it, and how to build the product so that it will reach its target customer most effectively.

About a year before the product is launched, the product development and marketing people should get together, preferably with the developer, to set strategy and discuss key product features. The product development team then works with the developer to get things moving.

About nine months before a product is launched, the marketing group should get together with the developer for a rundown on product features. At this stage, features can be emphasized or de-emphasized, but no major changes can be made in the overall product design. If the product is set for release in September — the majority of multimedia products are released in August, September and October, in time for the holiday selling season — then these meetings will occur in January.

Bundling — packing the disc in a Hewlett-Packard or Compaq box to encourage word of mouth — generally requires at least six months of lead time. Time ahead of this schedule must be allowed in order to make the deal and work out the logistics.

Four or five months before the product is launched, the marketing department should be fully involved. This springtime activity is likely to involve the development of box art, a catalog sheet, and, perhaps, an interactive demo for use at conventions (the E3 convention, for example, is held in June). If the product is an important one, then it should be shown, in demo form, to long-lead magazines (that is, publications whose lead time for editorial coverage is 90 days or more).

A Catalog Sheet

The catalog sheet (or "one sheet" or "selling sheet" or "sales literature") should be a single, two-sided color sheet. The basic box art, logotype, and several screen shots should be featured, along with basic product specifications and a list of key features. The catalog sheet may be prepared a month or two ahead of the box deadline, but the front of the box may need to be designed at this time in order to complete the catalog sheet.

An Interactive Demo

The interactive demo need not be robust or full featured. It should provide a sample of several functional features and show some flashy artwork and animation. This demo is used for sales purposes; it rarely gets more than five or ten minutes of attention from busy buyers. A demo should be done, but it need not be elaborate or comprehensive.

Communicating image vs. communicating features

Although product features play an important role in product reviews and actual day-to-day usage, a product's image is equally important. Disney's Animated Storybook line, the Living Books line, many of the Voyager CD-ROM products, MECC's *Oregon Trail* and other trail-type products, the Metatools line, and various Adobe products sell largely because of the company's brand — its reputation and its image in the marketplace. Of course, the fact (or belief) that these are consistently good products is the underlying reason why the reputation and image exist. But established companies are often wise to develop packaging and advertising art with a particular branded image in mind.

Fractal Design has done a terrific job with this approach, going so far as to sell its Painter 4 package in a paint can. From the start, Claris has sold its products in clean, modern-looking packages, with very carefully selected type styles and elegant use of white space. If you look carefully, you'll notice that most companies build their packaging, and overall marketing communications strategy, on the basis of a strong design philosophy. The approach is most likely to contribute to sales if the company is already successful with at least one recognizable product, but the overall strategy should inform all discussions about every piece of printed and screen communication — from box art to press releases to mailing labels.

The box

About two or three months before the launch, the box must be finalized. The design of the box is critical. In fact, some firms (such as Woods + Woods in San Francisco) specialize in package design for software products. It's a specialized field.

The front of the box must communicate not only the title and basic content, but a mood, a sensibility that's likely to draw some attention from a busy retail customer. The name of the product must be clearly visible at a distance of ten or twenty feet. Single large illustrations are better than clusters of smaller ones; fine artwork gets lost on crowded retail shelves.

The back of the box should be used for about three screen shots, shown as large as possible and selected to highlight both product features and captivating visual presentations. Bullet points should highlight the product's most exciting features.

The sides of the box are also important because "spine out" display is more common, in many stores, than front-face display. That is, more people will see the spine of the product than the artwork on the front of the box. The name of the product, in logotype, should dominate both side panels. Product requirements, such as amount of memory or disk space needed, should be placed either at the bottom of one side panel, or on the bottom of the box. The top should not be left blank; it should also display the product's logotype. Bar code can be placed anywhere. Copyright and company information can also be placed anywhere, but a distinctive publisher's banner or logo is desirable, particularly if the brand name is familiar to consumers. Suggested age group and rating (for violence and so on) should be prominent as well, especially if the intended users are children.

Given appropriate time and budget, it's wise to develop several box designs, and test them. This can be done informally, by simply creating prototypes and then showing them to friends and family. A more formal approach, which is costlier, is focus groups, in which potential customers comment on the package designs in a guided conversation. An in-store test is even better. Several prototype boxes are placed on the shelves, and consumer behavior is observed under strict test conditions. In general, good results can be attained through informal testing — provided that the tester is diligent and asks the right questions about cover art, type size, logo design, product features, and overall impact to at least a few dozen potential customers.

The press kit

About two months before launch, the press kit should go into production. Every product should be announced to the press with a 1-2 page press release describing product features and detailing the publisher's plans for selling the product and reaching the target audience. Pricing, platform, and availability information should be included in this release. The release should be accompanied by a B/W or color screen shot, preferably one that's designed to capture the attention of a writer or reviewer who receives well over fifty such packages every week. A catalog sheet should be included. An up-to-date list of products and a company backgrounder should be included as well.

About a month before release, the press kits should go out to key members of the press. This activity requires the involvement of an experienced, well-respected public relations professional. This PR pro will know how to reach all of the important writers and publications. He or she will also know which writers and publications should receive product review copies, who should receive pre-release beta versions, and who should receive press releases but not products. If the product is ready for review more than a month prior to street date, key publications should receive advance copies. These copies may increase the odds of a review within a few weeks of the street date.

Advertisements

Advertisements in key publications are also important. Two advertising programs should run in parallel. One is the consumer ad campaign. Ads should run about a week ahead of street date, and for a month or two or three afterwards. Ads should be placed in computer magazines that target the right customers: for kids' products, the right magazines are *Family PC* and *Family Computing;* for games, the right magazines are *PC Gamer* and similar publications. Ads in noncomputer magazines don't reach a sufficiently high percentage of potential customers to justify the expense.

The other advertising campaign is never seen by consumers. It's the trade campaign, and its intended impressions are made on retail buyers, store owners, and, ultimately, analysts and other industry professionals.

Promotions

Promotions are also important. Large retail accounts offer promotional opportunities in their own stores, and in their ads and catalogs. A percentage of the marketing budget should be held in anticipation of these opportunities. In some cases, your team will want to put a professional promotion agency or representative to work. This is obviously a significant added expense — such agencies typically cost several thousand dollars per month of activity. But these professionals know how to generate excitement and positive buzz about your product.

Post-launch

After the product is launched, ongoing promotions and publicity keep the title in front of consumers and retailers. Most products live or die within their first eight weeks (sometimes ten or twelve, sometimes as few as six weeks). Still, a good publisher will continue to "work" a title, doing everything possible to encourage sales. Awards competitions are one way to keep a product alive — when a product wins an award, that's an excuse for a new press mailing and a sticker on the already finished, shrink-wrapped package. If the product hasn't sold well, then excess inventory should be used for contests, for buy-one-get-one-free promotions, and so on. Anything that can get attention should be attempted.

Ideally (from the developer's perspective), a publisher should continue to work a product for two years or more. From the publisher's perspective, however, it's more important to listen to the marketplace. Products that sell well can be supported to sell even more units and to become the basis for promotions that sell other products. Products that don't sell well should, by and large, be forgotten. Not every product succeeds. Although publishers can affect the outcome either by doing the marketing job right or by diverting resources, they must place their bets on products that are most likely to generate significant returns on investment. This can be frustrating for developers, licensees, and retail buyers, but it is the reality of the marketplace — not just in software, but also in the record, book, and video businesses, too.

Reasonable pricing

As a rule, the range of choices available for any given product category is limited. Children's software, for example, rarely costs less than $25.95 and rarely costs more than $44.95. Lower-priced products are generally mature; they're well-established, but they may be based upon older platforms. Publishers can afford to sell these products for less than $30 because the products have already earned back their investments.

Pricing for children's products

Most new children's products are sold at retail for $30-40, so this is the range in which most publishers place their bets. Higher prices are desirable if they produce a greater return or larger market share, but competition often drives pricing below $35. Products that sell for more than $40 are usually newer, enhanced versions of classic products.

Pricing for games

In the game area, pricing is more flexible. Most games sell for $35 to $60. The higher price points are reasonable in the gaming community, where videogame CDs and cartridges often cost more than $50. Pricing is often affected by the size of the project, but not always. For example, it makes sense for a publisher to try for a higher list price on a CD-ROM title that features three discs instead of one. But the consumer rarely cares what it took to get the title out, and doesn't care at all what the developer's expenses were.

Developing a pricing strategy

Because most multimedia CD-ROM products are either games or children's products, setting prices for other types of products requires some educated guesswork. The analysis should begin by visiting several types of stores, presumably stores that would be likely to carry the new product. Identify ten products that are similar to the proposed product or product line, preferably products that are widely distributed. Then, visit a Wal-Mart, a Borders, a Computer City, a Software ETC., and a handful of other stores, and then, find the products in three or four direct mail catalogs. Write down the pricing for each product on your list. Chances are, you'll find only about half of the products on your list at more than a few stores or catalogs. Work out the average, mean, and median pricing and you'll see some significant patterns (if you don't remember what average, mean, and median are all about, consult your spreadsheet's help files!).

If you're a new company, or you're launching a product into a new category or channel, you should strive for pricing that's right in the center of the marketplace. Don't go too high or too low, and try not to buck the trend — unless you've got plenty of available cash to encourage and then support your desired change in retail buyer and consumer behavior.

The Importance of Positive Reviews and Word-of-Mouth

Hundreds, perhaps even thousands, of new CD-ROM products are released each year. Most of them go unnoticed, here and there receiving a review but never reaching any serious level of distribution.

Some products — notably those deemed as worthy of special attention by larger publishers, and a special subset of really cool new products from smaller publishers — get most of the attention. The press has a great deal to do with generating this buzz.

A truly innovative product, or one in which a large publisher has invested heavily, usually becomes the primary focus for the public relations person or department. They're excited, and they get members of the press excited. The press publishes teasers about an innovative product set for release later in the year. Advance copies are sent out to key members of the press. If the reaction is good, then reviews are written to encourage consumers to buy the product (certainly, this hype can backfire!).

Most consumers don't read reviews, though. Instead, they ask knowledgeable friends what to buy. Since these friends either read the reviews or know others who follow the software biz, this achieves the same end result. Retailers pick up on the excitement and display the product more prominently in anticipation of strong sales. The buzz begins. It's tough to get this buzz going and tougher still to keep it going, but in some instances, and for some products, the story catches on and generates strong sales.

In most cases, the product is simply shipped to reviewers and followed by a polite phone call to remind a busy reviewer to pay attention to a particular box (one that's inevitably buried with dozens of other new releases). Some products are perceived as important by editors — and these are the ones that get most of the ink.

Online demos

One way to encourage a buzz is to give part of the product away, at no charge, to potential customers. This was certainly a key to the success of the game *DOOM*, and it has helped the sales of other products, too. Consumers will usually tolerate about fifteen or twenty minutes of download time. With a 14.4 modem, that's about a megabyte. Some publishers include demos of a variety of products on the otherwise empty space on a CD-ROM.

Competent distribution

For many producers, distribution is a concept that's shrouded in mystery. Essentially, distribution begins as the product leaves the hands of the publisher, and ends when the product arrives at the retail store.

Several large distributors, such as Ingram Micro or Baker & Taylor, serve a percentage of retail accounts and handle products from most important publishers. Retailers order specific numbers of each product from Ingram, which passes the orders on to the publisher, whose warehouse fills the order, and ships to Ingram, which in turn ships to the retailer. Most retailers work with a central ordering, warehousing, and inventory system, but some operate regional centers, and all routinely encourage small orders from individual stores. The distributor typically charges a percentage of the wholesale price in exchange for services rendered.

In large discount stores, the distributor may play an even larger role — that of a rack jobber. Here, the distributor selects the products to be sold to each store under contract, and arranges the merchandise on a special rack that is serviced exclusively by this distributor. Rack jobbers typically sell only products that sell themselves — top twenty titles, for example, or products that show a great deal of promise because of the publisher's or license's success with past software titles.

Some publishers distribute products to large accounts directly, without the involvement of a distributor. One reason to do this is tradition: when the retailer and the publisher were smaller, they worked together, and the pattern has never changed. Another reason is the nurturing and protection of a valuable relationship. A third reason is servicing special needs: the publisher may, for example, supply specially packaged products for a high-volume retailer. A fourth reason is fill-ins. When a publisher runs out of inventory on a particular product, stores look to the distributors' warehouses for more supply. (This happens often because it's so difficult to forecast sales volume, particularly on a newer product.)

Larger distributors are more likely to be more successful in collecting monies from accounts, and more consistent in paying publishers on time. If you're setting things up for the first time, don't hesitate to call some medium-sized software publishing companies. Ask for the person in charge of distribution, and ask for contact names and numbers for distributors who are reliable and relatively problem-free. This is not generally regarded as a trade secret. In fact, a publisher who introduces a successful new line to a distributor will enhance its own reputation. Most publishers work with more than one distributor.

Affiliate label deals

Small publishers often require assistance in the marketing and distribution areas. They often benefit from the long-standing distribution relationships available through an affiliate label program with Electronic Arts, Broderbund,

Sierra, or other companies who sell small publishers' products along with their own. An affiliate label is sold by the larger company's sales force for a commission. Many medium-sized publishers began as affiliate labels. MAXIS, publisher of SimCity, for example, began as a label affiliated with Broderbund. Nowadays, MAXIS is independent, and strong enough to sponsor today's emerging publishers.

Publisher as a "keeper" – a serious CD-ROM publisher

In many cases, a product line costs well over a million dollars to launch. As a result, most publishers enter the business and leave in just one season. This is true not only of small companies, who simply run out of money or find it difficult to raise second-year funding after a tough year one, but of large media companies, too. Many well-regarded media companies have tried the CD-ROM multimedia business. Some have merged, some have given it up for strategic reasons, some have sold their operations, and some have simply closed them down. A big media company's logo does not fill a retail buyer's heart with glee: for every serious contender, such as Disney or Simon & Schuster, there are dozens more that have disappeared. Retailers and distributors strongly prefer companies who are in the CD-ROM publishing business for the long term. Too much time and energy is wasted on dabblers — and in today's competitive software business, big media companies who launch CD-ROM lines are frequently perceived as dabblers. Despite promises, despite claims about strong management commitments and more than sufficient financing, valuable licenses, and other assets, and despite real experience in publishing, marketing, and distributing media products, most of these companies are not keepers. For this reason, a small, well-funded software publisher, particularly one launched from an established affiliate label program, may be taken more seriously than a label that expands the reach of a very large book or magazine publisher, or cable network.

Running the Numbers

Every software company shares the same fundamental objective: to sell enough units to cover the costs of product development, marketing, and overhead — and to make a profit.

Few commercial CD-ROM products cost less than $200,000 in development costs, and many cost over $500,000. Marketing costs typically add at least 10-20 percent, and sometimes this number can go to 100 percent and more. Without burdening the package with the complexities of overhead, internal vs. external development, and other such issues, it's time to look at a sample multimedia model based on a $200K product with a $25K marketing budget.

A Sample Product

Say that the product will be a CD-ROM based upon a successful self-help book. The author will speak directly to the user through video clips. The product will also include plenty of self tests whose results will be automatically scored. The author will then comment on every answer. This will be a straightforward product with an author who is reasonably well known, at least to her readers. Over five years, her book has sold about 250,000 copies, an average of about 50,000 units per year, generally at about $15 per book.

How many of these people will buy the author's software? What percentage of these readers own the necessary equipment, such as a CD-ROM drive, or a newish computer with enough power and memory? Most software is sold in computer retail stores — do these people ever go into computer retail stores? If not, how will they ever find the product? For most products, these answers are unavailable because there is no market research available for this level of specific behavior. (Unfortunately, predictive market research has not proven successful in the software business.) Although the subject matter may differ, the situation is essentially similar with most non-game software. When reliable research data is available, new technology often foils even the best attempts at mapping old data on a new product's projections.

Having considered these issues, go back to the numbers, and, so far, a blank spreadsheet.

Costs

We begin with costs. There are two cost categories. The first is fixed costs: these are monies that must be spent in order to make the product. The second is variable costs: these costs are based on a per-unit estimate.

Production costs

The estimate of fixed costs begins with a production budget, an estimate that includes both external and internal costs. If the product is based upon a license, and involves the acquisition of rights, these costs must be shown as part of the budget (royalty expenses are handled elsewhere). Assume product development costs of $250,000, including beta testing and mastering (see Chapter 7).

Packaging costs

The product requires packaging. This packaging must be designed and prepared for the printer. If the package is to include a book of instructions or other ancillary materials, these must be designed and produced as well. The one-time costs of designing and preparing these materials are carried here; printing costs are variable, so they're listed elsewhere. Assume $15,000 for art and design, including printer preparation.

Other marketing costs

The next line item is marketing costs. These are often related to the preparation of sales materials, such as demo disks, color catalog sheets, press kits, and the product box. Costs related to preparation, development, and production are carried here; printing, duplication, and distribution are variable costs because they are dependent upon the number of units. Some large retailers also require promotional fees, catalog fees, and/or shelving fees. These all amount to the same thing: the publisher pays the retailer to carry the product, or to place the product in a prominent position in the store and in advertisements. Assume $10,000 for the marketing materials and another $10,000 for store promotional costs, for a total of $20,000. Variable costs are calculated in the pricing model (described shortly).

To review: product development will cost $250,000; marketing will cost $20,000. The total investment: $270,000. To be realistic, at least $30,000 in company overhead should be earned back, too. So, you're looking at total costs of $300,000.

Revenues

Now, you turn to the revenues side. If things work out, you want to see no less than $300,000 in revenues at the end of year one, and the potential to earn no less than another $300,000 over the life of the product.

Pricing

It's best to build a separate spreadsheet as a pricing model. Say that you want to sell the product at retail for $30. Most large retailers require a discount of approximately 50 percent, so the wholesale price of this product will be about $15. On a strictly constructed model, costs would be deducted from this $15 in "gross publishers' revenues." The first cost will be some items related to doing business: returns, for example, often affect revenues by as much as 20 percent. Assume a total of 25 percent in similar costs. Next are royalties. The product is based upon the work of a successful author. People in this position often receive a combination of up-front payment for their time, and back-end, or royalty, payments for the value of their name and reputation. A royalty in the 7 to 10 percent range is not unusual; I'll use a 10 percent royalty to keep the example simple. On a $15 gross, you deduct $3 for returns and $1.50 for royalties. The net is $10.50.

Cost of goods sold

Now, look at the variable costs. The first cost is the "cost of goods," or "COG" (sometimes, "COGs" for "cost of goods sold"). Because the incremental pieces in a software package are produced by the thousand, or tens of thousands, you may have to do some dividing in order to figure out the actual cost of each individual piece. Try an example.

The CD-ROM itself costs about 50 to 75 cents to press if you do it in large enough quantity and find a good price; say, 60 cents for this example. Add a few cents for silk-screening artwork on one side, bringing the total up to 65 cents. Each CD needs a cardboard sleeve or a plastic jewel box; say that you add 20 cents for a jewel box. Now you're up to 85 cents per unit. A printed instruction book adds another 50 cents, and the box itself costs, say, $1 including the assembly of these parts. The total COG: $2.35. With greater quantities, or a simpler package (no instruction book, plain vanilla CD sleeve without any printing, and so on), the costs could probably be reduced to about $2 per unit. For the sake of this example, if the initial run is 15,000 units, then the variable costs total $30,000.

Justifying the numbers

Okay, now for the dramatic end of act one. You need $300,000. You earn $8.50 per unit. So: how many units must you sell in order to reach the goal? The answer: 35,294.

A walk over to the sales department brings the bad news. They've done some checking on similar products, and looked at the company's recent history. It's unlikely that this product will sell more than 20,000 units in year one. Act two begins.

The biggest cost is the cost of production. So, you go back to the producer and production company and ask for a reduced budget. This will mean tradeoffs: less animation, the elimination of some favorite elements, less profit for the producer (perhaps balanced by a promise of future royalties). The producer may become grouchy, but cost reductions are necessary — otherwise, this project will not move ahead. The producer reduces the budget to $200,000. Marketing costs probably shouldn't be touched. The contribution to overhead is reduced from $30,000 to $25,000.

Now, the hard part. Right now, you're looking at a $30 retail price. If you increase the price to $35, will you lose sales volume? A trip to several retail stores shows similar products in the $35-40 range. For now, see whether you can keep the price as low as $35.

We go back into the model. You need to balance the budget at $275,000. With a $35 retail price, and a $17.50 publisher's gross, minus 20 percent for returns ($3.50), and 10 percent for royalties ($1.75), and an unchanged $2 cost of goods, you net out at $10.25, about $2 better than before. You recalculate based on $275,000, and need to sell 26,829 units in year one. You're getting better, but you're not there yet.

One option is to increase the sales estimates. Producers like this approach — especially if the sales people are held to their estimates, and are expected to generate sales to meet their budgeted estimates. Another is to reduce costs. What started as a $250,000 project becomes a $175,000 project, with a contribution to overhead of just $15,000 and a total marketing budget of $10,000. You're now trying to earn back $195,000. Working with the same $10.25 net, you can make the numbers work with sales of about 19,000 units. Before anybody looks too closely at these numbers, you can reduce the production budget to $180,000 — and give the project a green light!

Low-Priced Software Packages

Several companies, including KidSoft, Essex Interactive, and SoftKey, sell CD-ROM products for as little as $12.99. Assuming the same 50 percent discount to retailers, the publisher's gross is only $6.50 per unit. In order to earn significant money in this game, the publisher must acquire the product at a very low cost, or sell very large numbers of units.

The KidSoft example is instructive. KidSoft does not produce products for its $12.99 spinner rack (which you can see in Toys R Us and other large retail stores). Instead, KidSoft acquires completed products from other publishers. These products are often top-quality products that did not sell well in the past. So, the acquisition cost is low. KidSoft also keeps its cost of goods low by selling the products in plastic jewel boxes — there are no cardboard boxes. Titles are not sold to the retailers one by one. Instead, dozens of titles are sold at one time, so all products share the marketing costs.

Sires' software's approach is ultimately similar, though the products appear in a very different form. The Sires 10-pack offers ten CD-ROMs in a single consumer package. Once again, individual titles are not produced, but acquired, often at a low cost per unit. One physical package is used for ten CDs (the package is a kind of fold-out wallet). Titles are not individually marketed or advertised; the products sell themselves because of the low cost and high value to consumers.

The producers of the original products in these low-cost publishing programs earn only a few cents per unit. In the software business, low-cost publishing is one way to pick up a few extra dollars on a product that is no longer in the stores, or no longer selling in any meaningful quantities.

Further Thoughts on the Economics of CD-ROM Publishing

As I've noted, CD-ROM publishing is a high-risk business. The ugly truth is that most commercial CD-ROM titles do not earn back their investments. Although CD-ROM is an enormously appealing format for multimedia producers, consumer acceptance has been limited. Only one in four or five home computing households currently owns a CD-ROM drive. Few of these households purchase more than one title every month or two — and many purchase fewer than six titles per year. The business is dominated by publishing companies that have been deeply entrenched for a decade or more. And, to make matters even worse, it's difficult to produce a multimedia CD-ROM title of any quality for less than about $250,000 (if you really cut corners, or keep the product simple, you may be able to do the job for about $150,000).

Take heart, though — despite the odds, it is possible to succeed, and succeed in a big way. CD-ROM publishing is now an established business, and a blockbuster product will be carried by every retailer, even if the publisher is unknown. Consumer demand will cause this to happen. Of course, this scenario is precisely the one that has put CD-ROM investors, and many big media companies, into the hole for millions of dollars.

CD-ROM publishing is going to change, and this technological blip could cause a big mess for CD-ROM publishers. Currently, a CD-ROM can store up to 660MB in data (video, animation, sound files, applications program, and so on — all considered data here). The new DVD CD-ROM, which is months away at the time of this writing, will hold at least eight times as much data — and, according to some estimates, about thirty times as much data. Game publishers, always thirsty for more storage space for graphics, will push consumer acceptance. But right now, *nobody* owns a DVD-ROM drive. Next year, thousands of new computer users will become confused — should they buy a standard CD-ROM drive, or wait for prices to drop on the new DVD-ROMs? Most people will buy standard (4X or 6X) CD-ROM drives because they'll have no choice — these drives will come as part of their new computers. As DVD-ROM takes shape, and becomes popular with gamers, the marketplace will become cloudy and muddled.

Finally, the whole idea of computer publishing on tangible, permanent media is beginning to change. As Shockwave and other Web publishing tools become more robust, home computer manufacturers are desperately trying to get their prices down below $1,000. On the way to this price point, the CD-ROM drive could become an accessory. Home computing may become much more Web-centric, and may, in the long-term, not involve a CD-ROM at all.

But that's the future. For the present, CD-ROMs are the very best way to distribute fixed multimedia content to large numbers of consumers.

Self-Publishing

The best-known multimedia titles are sold by larger companies. These companies command shelf space, advertise their wares, and employ public relations professionals to promote and market their brands and products.

There is, however, a tradition in software publishing that runs contrary to this approach. It's called "self-publishing" and it has some interesting parallels in the record business, the book business, and even in the film business.

The basic idea is quite simple: one or more people develop a product and then do everything they can to sell the product on their own, without the help or resources of a large company. This is the equivalent of small, independent record labels, and similar to the many self-published, how-to books that have sold tens, and even hundreds, of thousands of copies — despite large publishers' claims that the market for such-and-such a book is too small to matter. In software, the tradition of self-publishing and online distribution (which has almost no costs associated with distribution) apply more successfully to simple software tools and mini-apps than full-scale multimedia projects, but... well, read on!

Most self-publishing companies don't make much money. Some lose a bit of money; some don't. Here and there, a company or product succeeds beyond the inventor's wildest dreams. Most often, the product does just well enough for the mini-entrepreneur to keep the small business open. Here's how it works.

This story most often begins with a programmer or a producer with a "great idea." Well, the idea may be great, but the expenditure of time and money may be hard to justify without a marketing and publishing plan. This plan should provide honest, real-world answers to the following questions:

1. **How much will the product cost to produce?** Can a high percentage of these costs be covered by sweat equity, favors from friends and family, and so on? (Ventures that require large amounts of cash should be very carefully scrutinized because most lose money.)
2. **How will the product reach its target customer?** There are two related questions buried in this apparently simple question. The first is related to marketing communications — how will target customers find out about the product? (That is, will the product be advertised, promoted, aggressively publicized by a well-connected, diligent public relations professional?) The second is related to distribution — how will the product physically make its way to customers?
3. **Which format is most reasonable?** For most multimedia products, the answer will be "Web publishing." There are some good reasons why. Web publishing requires no inventory. Web-published products can be ordered and distributed in real time. Conversely, CD-ROM products must be duplicated, so there's a cost of building inventory before the product can be put into the hands of distributors or customers. Unfortunately, most Web publishers have not yet figured out how to make money (see Chapter 5).

4. **Can the cost be justified?** The product may not earn back its investment, but there may be other reasons to proceed. A good product, for example, can establish a new company and show off capabilities. It can do the same for an individual. If most of the work can be done without spending much cash, the product may be worth producing, just to gain experience and marketplace savvy.

For any self-publishing project, it's wise to prepare a publisher's profit-and-loss statement, or P&L. Even if the project is being done without any serious intention to earn money, a P&L will provide far more focus than simply proceeding in a haphazard way.

Shareware

Since the beginning of the PC revolution, avid amateur programmers have written small application programs for use by other enthusiasts. Many of these shareware programs have been distributed via BBSes, the online services, and now, on the Web (a large store of shareware programs can be found at `www.cnet.com`).

A shareware programmer typically writes the application with only the vaguest hopes of earning any money. An address is typically printed in the documentation, along with a request to send $15, $25, maybe as much as $50 to the programmer — but only if you actually use the program. It's a wonderful idea, one that has made a handful of programmers some serious money. Of course, most people never pay the shareware cost (despite the best of intentions). Some shareware has become commercially available.

Shareware is ideally suited for smaller programs, such as specialized calculators, some kinds of games, and system enhancements. Shareware is not ideally suited to multimedia applications. There are two reasons why. First, most multimedia applications weigh in at a few megabytes or more, a costly download. Second, plug-ins like Shockwave notwithstanding, a small-sized multimedia application is, typically, a yawn.

There's one notable exception: the distribution of music on the Web. Some bands now circumvent the traditional system of record company distribution, and offer samples of their music directly to connected fans. As bandwidth increases, these files will move more quickly, and may someday change the record business. For today, this is an interesting use of the Web, and, perhaps, an entrepreneurial opportunity. For now, this system is used mostly for sound files; in time, video will be a regular feature, too.

Freeware

Some multimedia applications are provided at no charge to customers. Most such applications are promotional. Several movie studios, for example, now produce mini-applications to promote major motion pictures. Downloadable freeware may include movie clips, games, star pictures and bios, and so on. These packages are often lavishly produced, sometimes at a cost of $100,000 or more. As the Web develops, these applications are less likely to appear as downloadables, and more often as the basis for Web sites themselves, complete with Shockwave, Java, and so on.

Distribution of free multimedia CD-ROMs has been limited. Sometimes, a magazine will produce an advertiser-supported multimedia CD-ROM, but Web publishing has largely eclipsed these activities because the Web offers lower costs (that is, lower costs of production, no inventory costs, and no mailing or shipping costs), more immediacy, and a larger number of potential customers.

School and Library Publishing

Although these two concepts are often grouped together, the phrase actually includes the K-12 market, which consists of 105,000 elementary schools, middle schools, and high schools. There are two types of libraries: 11,000 public libraries and their branches, plus libraries in many, but not all schools. Start with the school market, by far the largest part of the school-and-library market. This gets a bit confusing, as school librarians are becoming school media librarians (some are full-time professional librarians, some are not).

In the 1980s, when a relatively small number of households owned computers, Apple Computer concentrated a long-term marketing effort on hardware sales to elementary schools, high schools, and colleges. As a result, a large percentage of school computers are Apple computers; unfortunately, Apple built its market based on Apple II machines, and the schools invested heavily in a platform that Apple abandoned (about 1 in 3 school computers are not Apple Macs but Apple II machines!). About half of the computers in schools are Apple, the other half are IBM compatibles. But they're not all Windows machines, not by a long shot. Change comes slowly to this market, and as many as 25 percent of the current classroom computers are DOS, with processors incapable of running Windows. Pretty frustrating! On the development side, most of the coolest new software for kids can't be sold to most schools. And on the school side, they want better computers, but theirs won't keep up with the technology!

In any case, Apple worked closely with the emerging software development community — good software was a strong incentive for hardware purchases. After a few years, both Apple and small companies such as MECC, Broderbund, The Learning Company, and Davidson & Associates were well established in the elementary school classrooms of America. When parents asked schoolteachers which software to buy for their home computers, they heard about *Number Munchers, Where in the World is Carmen Sandiego?, Reader Rabbit,* and *Oregon Trail* — software that continues to sell, ten years later, to both the school and consumer markets. (This form of guerrilla advertising is a big reason why certain publishers concentrate on schools.) Each of these software publishers maintains a strong school marketing department. The relationships run deep, and although other companies have made inroads, these companies have maintained a respectable market share in the elementary school market.

Several other companies, with roots in filmstrips, video, laserdiscs, and other supplementary classroom products, have focused almost entirely upon schools, with only scant or no attention to the more competitive and less predictable consumer market. Tom Snyder Productions, for example, briefly entered the consumer software market in the 1980s, and has returned to its roots, publishing only for schools. Jostens Learning has experimented with the consumer market, but maintains a strong position as a school software publisher. Some school textbook publishers have also established themselves in software.

Anxious to take some of Apple's market share, several large makers of Windows computers, such as Compaq (in alliance with Microsoft), Dell, and IBM EduQuest have been aggressive in marketing hardware to schools.

Products for the School Market

In general, products sold to the school market are most likely to succeed if they link directly to a particular curriculum, or if they are tools, such as *KidPix* or *Print Shop* or *Children's Writing and Publishing Center*. One of the reasons that MECC's *Oregon Trail* succeeds, for example, is because it simulates life in the American wilderness more effectively than a textbook or lecture. Broderbund's *Where in the World is Carmen Sandiego?* succeeds for a slightly different reason — it brings geography, sometimes a dry, uninvolving subject, to life. MECC's *Storybook Weaver* succeeds because it provides a kid-friendly collection of tools that can be used to produce an original, illustrated storybook.

Many consumer products are bought directly by schools, in retail stores, with no change in packaging or pricing. As the market has gained purchasing sophistication, school editions, "Lab Packs," site licenses, and network versions are more common. Typically, a school edition contains multiple copies of the software, perhaps ten copies of the CD-ROM, along with a specially prepared teacher's guide and, in some cases, some bulletin board materials or handouts. A school edition does not sit on a retail shelf, so the external packaging need not be elaborate. In fact, many school editions are sold in nothing more than a loose-leaf notebook in a corrugated cardboard box — teachers never see the packaging until after they see the product (there's no need for the publisher to spend money on fancy packaging). As schools move toward networked computers, a school edition may contain a network version of the software in place of individual discs.

School sales, marketing, and distribution are managed by a separate department, a small part of a big publishing operation. Catalogs such as Educational Resources (owned by Davidson), Learning Services, and Fast Track are direct marketing catalogs for the school market; educators buy from these companies, primarily attracted by low prices. Additionally, there are catalogs that are subject-matter specific, such as Carolina Biological, which sells everything from earthworms to fetal pigs to microscopes to software and CD-ROM products related to the science curriculum. Also, there are regional companies that sell products to schools. Every technology coordinator in the Baltimore region, for example, knows Kunz, a local distributor that does everything from wiring the school for the Internet to helping a teacher develop a classroom library.

Exhibits and conventions are also important — such as the National Education Computer Conference, held each June, plus state conferences, regional conferences, and subject specialty conventions, such as the National Council of Teachers of English, where a new poetry product might be shown.

Of course, many teachers simply purchase single boxes of consumer software. According to educational marketing consultant and former VP, Education Sales and Marketing for Broderbund, Marylyn Rosenblum, "Teachers and schools consistently account for 15 percent of retail sales for any successful children's educational product."

Most school software is sold to a single teacher who supervises computer education for one or more schools within a district. In some schools, this teacher is not a traditional classroom teacher, but the school librarian. More and more school libraries are becoming resource centers — multiple media centers with computers, software, access to online services and the Internet, as well as books, magazines, and other traditional school library wares. Therefore, school library marketing and school marketing, for the purposes of the software industry, are more or less identical.

Several pricing theories apply to school marketing. One is a variation on the basic consumer pricing model: products are sold to teachers at the same price as they are sold to other consumers. If a teacher buys more than, say, ten or twelve copies, then a small discount (perhaps 10 percent) may apply. Another applies to lab packs. Because per-unit costs are low, the teacher may be able to buy ten or twelve copies of the software, in a single box, for only three or four times the cost of a single product. Some publishers consider school software to be more of an institutional sale; that is, special products are developed for a special market. This theory justifies high prices for certain types of products: a software product that has been designed specifically for use with an interactive textbook, for example. Each of these approaches is valid and currently in use.

Some publishers operate school sales divisions, selling not only their own products but also products from other publishers.

Products for the Library Market

Some public libraries buy computer software, but many do not. The price per title is considerably higher than the cost of a book, but only about one in six library "customers" can benefit from the purchase. The most promising public libraries are those in affluent areas, where a higher percentage of computing households may help to justify the purchase. Still, libraries often work with limited budgets, and, given the choice between computer software and, say, videos, most libraries choose videos (they cost less, serve more people, and aren't affected by changes in hardware platforms).

Compatibility is also an issue. Most librarians don't want to know a whole lot about sound cards, processors, hard disk space, Windows 95 vs. Windows 3.1 — what a mess!

Libraries that purchase software may do so through a local store, but most buy through catalogs that specialize in library products. A software publisher who feels strongly about the library market should take the time to attend the American Library Association convention, held late each Spring, for a better understanding of current buying patterns. There is also a convention for school librarians.

Corporate and Institutional Publishing

Just about every company, association, and institution buys a large amount of software every year. Most of the products sold to these organizations are tools, such as Microsoft Word or Lotus 1-2-3. So far, multimedia publishing has not had a big impact on this market. There is one exception, of course: software tools that are used to produce in-house multimedia products. Most corporate multimedia production departments own multiple copies of Macromedia Director, Adobe Photoshop, and related tools.

Many multimedia products are made for corporations and institutions. Although the range of these products is both wide and deep, several types of products dominate. For example, interactive demos that promote or demonstrate features of a particular type of product, such as an automobile, are often used in malls, showrooms, and trade shows. Typical delivery for these kinds of productions is through a kiosk setup.

Multimedia is often used in employee training, most often for sales training but also in training for safety, manufacturing procedures, and more specialized topics. Some industries, such as the health and medical field, use multimedia and other computer capabilities as tools within broader areas such as visualization and telecommunications. Financial services firms also make use of multimedia to instruct potential customers about the benefits of particular investment strategies.

Multimedia is also used for in-house company magazines and digital newsletters. Some CD-ROM discs are used to expand an existing business franchise. The entertainment industry trade magazine *Variety*, for example, now publishes a quarterly disc for subscribers. The disc includes some film clips and several databases. One database is filled with information about shooting movies on location in each of the fifty states. Another database contains information about Los Angeles restaurants.

Most multimedia software for corporate and institutional use is custom made. A small number of products are made for sale to multiple companies with common needs. Several multimedia products designed to teach Windows 95 were successfully sold to a broad range of corporations, for example. Some titles in the sales training realm have also been successfully marketed to a wide range of companies. This business has its roots in the sales and rental of training films and video, with products growing out of marketplace needs, not from "great ideas" generated from the product development perspective.

Site-Specific Publishing

Many multimedia projects are developed for use in one location or in a limited number of locations. These projects are typically developed for museums, corporate headquarters, trade shows, and entertainment attractions.

These projects do not follow any standard economic model. In fact, they are rarely developed with any notion of "return on investment." These projects are funded from special budgets, and many cost well over $1 million. The scale of these projects is often well beyond the capabilities of consumer publishing platforms. Enormous storage capacity and sophisticated telecommunications or networking systems are often required to support these ventures. Some involve laserdiscs; the newer installations connect PCs to digital video playback systems.

These are extraordinary projects, living on their own timetables and in their own worlds, often without much regard for consumer or business marketplace factors. Still, there are several publishing-like aspects to their operation. First, they must be promoted. If the setup is part of a museum, for example, then the museum's publicity and advertising department must be coordinated so that the right people get the information they need, or, to take a more aggressive tack, these marketing communications groups may need to be pushed to promote the setup as a kind of special event.

A variation on "distribution" also needs to be considered. Often, these multimedia setups are built to accommodate only a limited number of users per event or per hour. The flow of people through the event, the average amount of time spent, the number of work stations required — all of these are distribution-type issues for the single-site multimedia operator. At a trade show or fair, there may be many kiosks and each may require its own independent soundproof station or headphone (otherwise, users will hear one another's soundtracks). At some stand-alone information displays, such as airport kiosks featuring travel information, a touch-screen may be a more sensible input system than a standard keyboard. Each of these factors must be considered as a part of an on-site multimedia "publication."

If you keep your eyes open, you will notice these setups in a surprising number of places. Most amusement parks and museums have multimedia installations (science museums, in particular, tend to showcase a variety of technologies and multimedia approaches). More scholarly museum installations, such as the Wexner Learning Center at the Holocaust Museum in

Washington, D.C., are a superb example of multimedia's power to communicate and inform. As corporations build museums to tell their own stories (a growing trend), multimedia is a powerful way to bring together photographs, advertisements, text, data, and archive film footage.

Online Publishing

The idea of online publishing is not new. In fact, the idea is about twenty years old. Online publishers, such as LEXIS/NEXIS, have provided subscribers with access to libraries of printed articles, searchable databases filled with useful business, legal, or business information.

The online services added sophistication in several ways. CompuServe contracted with "SYSOPS" to manage communities of interest known as "forums." These forums contain message boards, downloadable files, and chat rooms. Some sysops developed their forums as online magazines, even going so far as to cover sporting events — with coverage by other CompuServe members who were active in that particular forum. America Online brought large numbers of information providers from other media, such as *Scholastic, INC.* magazine, *Stereo Review* magazine, *ABC,* and *Family PC.* These organizations brought editorial sophistication, and, frequently, impressive graphic presentations. Meanwhile, Prodigy developed and published thousands of screens filled with graphics and text.

To this day, only a small percentage of these offerings involve multimedia. Until recently — not more than a year or so ago — online multimedia was a dream. Aside from some downloadable files, multimedia was not, generally, a term associated with online media.

The Web, of course, changed all of that. Although the idea is still relatively new, multimedia is now very much a part of just about every Web publisher's plans. Shockwave is one of several plug-ins that can transform an ordinary Web site into a multimedia publication. Although Shockwave is currently available, it is not yet in widespread use. Shockwave is available as a plug-in that must be installed by the user; the next step, in which Shockwave and similar software are incorporated into the browser, is likely to increase the installed base by a considerable margin.

With Shockwave, online multimedia publishing becomes technically viable. Technical viability is only part of the online publishing story, however.

Building a Business Based upon Consumer Behavior

There are many issues here. In general, they are related to the behavior of end users, and the ways in which this behavior can be harnessed to build a successful business.

Some consumers have demonstrated a willingness to read and interact with online information. Although these consumers represent a small minority of the overall population (most of whom still strongly prefer TV, magazines, books, and newspapers), the question about whether people will read from the screen seems largely resolved. After some initial reluctance, most people do become comfortable with on-screen journalism and other text, provided that the material is concise and to-the-point. Stories tend to be shorter. Stories are best when there's a linear spine and a variety of sidebars presented as optional material. Pictures add a lot. Multimedia adds even more — the more the Web looks like television, in fact, the happier many users seem to be. It would probably be fair to say that interactive television will finally become a reality...perhaps on the Web.

Consumers who use the Web are notoriously fickle. They visit a site regularly for a while, and then their interest fades and they stop visiting. With so many new sites arriving weekly, it's hard to imagine people behaving any other way. So far, the Web is not about developing regular habits — it's about exploration. When sites are promoted, usage predictably increases, but normal usage is rarely counted in more than the tens of thousands. In order to keep these users happy, new material must be posted on the site weekly, or, if possible, daily. Because multimedia projects are very demanding in terms of time, money, and staff, most new postings are either text files or pictures; multimedia takes longer to build, so new material appears less often.

The Web as a Marketing Tool

Most Web sites are provided to users at no charge. This is consistent with the philosophy of the Web — plenty of interesting information, presented in an entertaining way, provided free to anybody willing to click on a link or type in a URL. As the cliché goes, "information wants to be free."

Of course, somebody's got to pay for the time spent by producers, programmers, editors, illustrators, and other personnel, as well as telecommunications and equipment costs. If the users don't pay, then the next place to look for the money is a company that's interested in communicating with those users. This company might be interested in promoting its own marketing programs — and original content might encourage people to visit the site. This is a clean, straightforward approach, one that keeps the content and the financial backing very close together (on the Web, there is less of a separation between church — the editorial team — and state — the publisher and advertising sales group.)

Unfortunately, this approach is uncommon. Most marketers treat their sites strictly as online brochures and catalogs, and then wonder why usage is lower than expected. There's an interesting question here: should a car manufacturer's Web site deliver roughly the same content as the brochures available in the showroom, or should the manufacturer's site also include other content, such as reviews from car magazines, stories from people who drive the car, dealer listings (with maps that automatically plot the best route from the user's office to the showroom), comparative pricing information, company history, results of user surveys, pictures of the company's classic cars from the past, the company's annual report, perhaps even downloadable clips from the company's old TV commercials?

The addition of information and entertainment content, perhaps enhanced with some ephemera, along with an imaginative presentation, is probably likely to increase the number of users, the frequency of each user's visits, and the amount of time spent during each visit. Would more people visit Chevy's Web site if it included pictures of every past Chevy, a downloadable library of past commercial jingles, and a contest every once in a while? Seems likely, doesn't it?

The Web as an Advertising Medium

Advertising is a promising avenue for Web sites. Because the Web is a new medium, with new user habits, the physical form of these advertisements is still being developed. On TV and radio, advertisements fit neatly into breaks that pace the linear storylines, or run between one program and the next. In print, advertisements appear on pages next to editorial content. Again, the approach is linear, with breaks for advertisements. On the Web, the tradition is both linear and nonlinear.

One common linear type of advertising is the "banner," an advertisement in the shape of a bumper sticker or highway billboard. It usually appears at the top of a content page, and includes not only a logo and slogan but also a button leading to the advertiser's own site. Most people see the banner but don't press the button.

The game site called `www.riddler.com` takes a more aggressive approach. The user chooses a game to play, but before the Start button is shown on the screen, the user sees a full-page advertisement. The Start button appears at the bottom, below the ad. Riddler goes a step further by including advertisers' logos on the pogs that users collect as they win the site's games.

As frames — separate, defined fields on a single Web page (see Chapter 5) — become more common, Web pages will begin to resemble magazine pages, with quarter, third, and half pages sold to advertisers.

Each of these schemes can be varied in some interesting ways. In the print and broadcast world, the frequency of an ad's appearance is largely determined by the number of linear slots it fills in the broadcast schedule or on pages over a series of printed issues. Web advertisements can be smarter. A smart Web site, for example, can collect information about users and then choose to show certain ads to certain users, the selection being made on the basis of user interests, demographics, geographic region, and other criteria.

According to Webtrack Adspend/Jupiter, Infoseek sold about $3 million in advertising in the first quarter of 1996, followed by three other search sites: Lycos at $2.6 million, Yahoo! at $2.1 million, and Netscape at $1.9 million. Among content companies, c\net took in $1.3 million and ZDNet sold $1.1 million, as did ESPNet SportsZone. Time Warner's Pathfinder took in just under $1 million. It should be no surprise that the top advertisers were nearly all technology companies: IBM, Microsoft, Netscape, c\net, AT&T, NYNEX, and MCI. Saturn, the car maker, was the only nontechnology company on the top ten list; American Airlines and MasterCard International, top ten advertisers from the fourth quarter of 1995, were no longer in the top ten in early 1996. First-quarter expenditures by each of the top ten companies was in the $400,000 – $1.5 million range, with the greatest concentration in the $500,000–$600,000 mark.

Web advertising is evolving very quickly. The best way to learn more about Web advertising and its effects on the user experience is to get on the Web regularly and explore for yourself. Also, read magazines such as *Advertising Age* to learn more about clever Web-based advertising and marketing programs.

The Web as a Subscription Medium

Sooner or later, most Web publishers consider the possibility of charging users for the privilege of entering their site. Some have acted on this plan, but far more have simply worked on the mechanics: collecting information about users and assigning each user a unique name and password. It won't be long before a large number of Web sites look to their users for some revenues; look for requests for credit card numbers coming soon to your favorite Web site. Most publishers are still working on their pricing models: the objective is to keep the subscription price as low as possible, and to generate as much as possible through advertising. There's a seesaw problem here: advertisers want lots of qualified users, but only a high percentage of potentially qualified users will be turned off by the request for the credit card information.

How much should a Web subscription cost? Most national magazines are available for $15–20 per year, or about $1.50 per monthly issue. With a subscription base of around 200,000 – 500,000 (some higher, many lower) and a publisher's net of about $10 per subscriber, that's $2–5 million. (Deduct mailing costs of 50 cents to $1 per subscriber per month, and you begin to understand that it's advertising, not subscriptions, that keep magazines alive).

With no costs of distribution (aside from minimal costs related to server and telecommunications), a higher percentage of subscription revenues goes to the Web publisher's bottom line. Over time, this will be a good thing. Short term, however, it's tough to get people to subscribe to a Web site — there are so many sites available at no charge, it seems "unfair" for a publisher to charge for its goods (never mind whether it's "fair" for a user to expect to receive quality content at no charge).

So: how much should a Web publisher charge for a monthly or annual subscription? It's tough to justify much more than a consumer magazine, so $20, maybe $25 is the ouch point. That's less than $2 per month per subscriber, but a community of 50,000 subscribers, each paying $2 per month, or even $1 per month, will generate more than enough in revenues to pay for a small, well-managed Web site. Higher pricing just doesn't make sense in this marketplace, though a $5-10 per month price point might be acceptable for some types of specialized content for special audiences. Electric Library, from Infonautics, provides access to an enormous database of articles and books for just under $10 per month. By comparison, access to a full-scale online service, which comes with endless content, e-mail, news, chat, message boards, and lots of other stuff, costs only about $15 per month, or less than $200 per year.

The Web as a Transaction Medium

Online media in general, and the Web in particular, have also been used as a cross between a self-service store and a direct-marketing catalog. The basic idea: the consumer has instant access to product information, makes the decision either on the spot or at some point in the future, and completes the purchase by entering credit card and shipping data into his or her computer. This unaided transaction is ideal for certain types of merchandise, such as books, computer software, compact discs, travel reservations, even some kinds of apparel (Land's End, for example, has been selling clothing and other soft goods online for years).

This is a trend that's bound to grow. It's convenient for consumers and cost effective for marketers. Right now, there's a problem with the security of these transactions — savvy hackers can gain access to personal credit card information — but the credit card companies are working hard to assure secure credit card transactions on the Web.

After transactions are secure, look for major retailers to develop online stores, and large numbers of consumers making purchases at home or at the office. The Web's upscale, educated users will be sought-after consumers. As the Web becomes accessible to greater numbers of households — through add-on devices that connect to TV sets, and Net-only computers that cost less than $1,000 — the market for Net shopping is likely to grow.

For the Web publisher, this will create another potential source of revenues. When combined with marketing and advertising, and subscriptions, the Web should eventually support a large number of publishing businesses. The role of multimedia in this world seems assured, as merchandise is more likely to sell when it's presented with more than just words and pictures. Once again, the visions of interactive TV take shape on the Web: a sweater is not just shown, it's modeled by an actress who will describe the merchandise if you click on her mouth. This is not wildly futuristic. Instead, it's possible now (though not entirely practical) with Shockwave and Java technology.

The Bottom Line on Web Publishing

Forrester Research, a leading trend forecaster, recently developed a model for Web economics. According to *Inter@ctive Week* (June 17, 1996), "An average Web site can expect to generate $170,000 in revenues from advertising, subscriptions and transactions this year." Although these figures sound impressive, the costs of operating a Web site are often much greater.

Although some sites will leap ahead of the pack, earning very large revenues, most will not. What can be done with $170,000 in revenues? The short answer is: as much as two full-time people can do during a work week. Add a third salary and the formula falls apart. Add too much multimedia content, which is time consuming and costly, and the numbers don't work. That team of two people has to do all of the design work, all of the writing, most of the programming (it's okay to hire a programmer, but revenues won't support one working full time). What about subscriber marketing, advertising sales, and special promotions? There are a few possibilities. One is to off-line this work, using an outside ad sales rep. Another is to hire just one person to produce the entire site and use the other salary for marketing. Not a great idea, either.

So, there's a dilemma. The Web is ideally suited for small-scale publishers, but small-scale publishers can't get the advertising support needed to make the machine work. Big media companies can sell the advertising, so they're the most likely candidates for successful Web publishing. Or so says the common logic. But there's one thing about the whole Web experience and its development — there is nothing common about it, and there's nothing logical about it, either.

So, what does it all mean? And how can you make money publishing on the Web? Only a few companies have figured out the answer to these questions. Many more will fail trying. Then, the answer will materialize. The marketplace, supply and demand, big companies with money, small companies with ideas, consumers with their emerging habits — all of these will help to shape

Web publishing. Despite the best efforts of every forecaster, business analyst, entrepreneur, business development executive, and visionary, only time in the marketplace will provide the answer. Unfortunately for many new technology companies who have promised the sun, the moon, and the stars to their investors, time is the one commodity that's in very, very short supply.

A longer-term view will prevail. As it always does.

CHAPTER 9

Continuing Support and Revisions

✦ A publisher's outreach strategy aims to build a positive relationship with customers or clients over time.

✦ Customer service and technical support are best taken into account from the earliest stages of any project, not just for troubleshooting.

✦ Various ways to keep lines of communication open with the public are becoming more accessible to the individual entrepreneur.

✦ Upgrading your multimedia product will be influenced by factors peculiar to computer hardware and software, as well as conditions that exist for most consumer goods.

Customer Support

In the multimedia world, three major goals constitute customer satisfaction: ease of installation, ease of use, and convenient documentation. Unfortunately, the task of achieving all three of them perfectly is impossible. The cause of this impossibility stems from the nature of a much larger industry than multimedia — the electronics industry.

Many consumer electronics products exist that run multimedia in the home. Included are hundreds of different personal computers and sound cards, controllers, and display devices. Also found are dozens of Web browsers, half a dozen different types of CD-ROM drives, and an incalculable number of differently configured user systems. The task of creating a product that's flawless is impossible. No one has yet. Television is more than fifty years old, and even this medium has problems with total technical satisfaction for the user. Multimedia is much younger and much, much more complicated. Technical problems are a fact of digital life. As a producer, the aim for the happy medium is designing a product for the largest number of people in a target market and staying prepared for any difficulties that may arise during the life of the product.

Customer support is more than troubleshooting during the first few weeks or months of a new release. However, that's the time when the project is going to need it most. A well-organized team that attends to customer questions and concerns over the long term can carry the new release into a successful upgrade or second edition of an existing product, or a new and perhaps more accomplished multimedia venture.

Technical Problems Aren't Always Your Fault

Many technical problems will be the fault of the production team. The technical problems that cause an unwanted event on someone's machine, or fail to enact a wanted one, are called "bugs." Killing them is important. The best way to reduce customer support costs is to have a good product that works properly. Bug killing, however, may not be the biggest problem.

Many outside factors, from both a technological and marketing perspective, can cause technical problems that are squarely out of the producer's control. These factors can set the project's plans back by months because the critical time period after the project's delivery date is spent chasing problems that escaped attention in development, rather than in more productive after-market strategies. Perhaps a beta period may have not been long enough, resulting in a lack of adequate feedback from the testers, or in the case of a Web site, the target users.

Other factors come to light only after the product is out in the marketplace vying for consumer dollars. The chosen format, such as the CD-ROM, may bear the weight of a number of past difficulties, inconsistencies, and outright disappointments felt industry-wide. Many CD-ROM drives exist that are slow and inconsistent. Amazingly, these are the best ones! The more inferior CD-ROM drives barely play many modern multimedia titles, although, to be fair, this usually applies only to the older drives. The delicate question for customer support is how to avoid the prospect of a buyer blaming the product, or company, or even computer technology when faced with a relatively minor and unavoidable difficulty, especially during installation.

The response to these situations is actually a larger calling than simply servicing the product. The producer's chosen methods of outreach can have a small or far-reaching effect on the prospects of consumer electronics, cyberspace, and multimedia as a true mass market medium for the long run. Whatever can be done to demystify the process of buying, installing, and using a product specifically will serve to demystify computers in general. Such outreach methods help the entire multimedia world.

Who Are These People?

In a burgeoning industry such as multimedia, and in an increasingly more technology-oriented, global economy, customer relations is an interesting new skill that attracts employees from diverse backgrounds. To service a product, an understanding of the product is required. Because multimedia is so many different things at the same time, a customer-support person is usually multifaceted, too. Broken is the old corporate mold of strict delineations between marketing, sales, customer service, and other staff divisions. The multimedia team gains strength from these people because they have the ability to interpret the product for themselves, yet they can also understand a user's interpretation. This is the most valuable feedback about the product that the multimedia producer can get.

The people who fill these jobs often come from interesting backgrounds. The apparent oxymoron of "technical writer" offers a new career path for experienced computer professionals whose companies may well have been downsized or humanities majors who might otherwise quail at the prospect of graduating into an uncertain job market. Customer support personnel ranges from guru-like product experts to twenty-somethings seeking employment. Job titles in customer support are just as wide-ranging as they are in the rest of the multimedia world. On a smaller project, a technical sales consultant might be a basic envoy between customers and the product. In a larger corporate context, a moniker might exist as imposing as Process Leader of Product Information, or Technical Support in Telerelations!

Good Support Builds Good Customers

Tailoring a support crew to managerial requirements and/or budgetary constraints, and then preparing it to meet all imaginable needs of the projected customer base, is a huge task best taken on as soon as a project begins to be outlined. However, after that crew is in action, a skillful performance on its part can help or hinder fragile relationships with new clients or customers. Sufficient customer support is a means by which to ensure that customers are reassured as soon as they call and hear a recognizable, authoritative voice, or when they read their e-mail and notice a quickly delivered, clear, and courteous response. The production's, and by extension, the producer's, fortunes lie in this subtle yet palpable difference. This is the kind of difference that builds customer and client loyalty over time, and sets successful companies apart from their competitors.

Variations on this theme of sufficient support come into play depending upon the nature of the project and the standards invoked in the project's contract, either with the client or the more subtle contract with the public. This is true even if the responsibility for product support eventually leaves your hands. If one is a freelancer, or associated with a small or medium-sized company, and is contracted by a publisher who will shoulder the burden of providing support, other considerations will arise besides the potential of a forthcoming project. Even when hired to provide a finished product and deliver it to a third party for maintenance, certain responsibilities remain to the client and those who finally use an item. An individual's reputation rides on those responsibilities. The producer's best interests are served in knowing at what point those responsibilities end, so as to free attentions to another client with the next new challenge.

What Is Customer Support?

Support, as a generic term, is really a three-tiered structure involving quality assurance, customer service, and consumer education. Each has its own bearing on the fate of the project in particular and a business concern in general. Ascertaining that the venture doesn't fall prey to the weaknesses that impede far too many new product launches is essential. Such pitfalls include shallow or incomplete market research, unforeseen design flaws, faulty engineering, expenses that were underestimated or that escalated during an emergency, bad timing, cutting corners, or rushing the project to completion before its time, such as for the Christmas shopping season. That's just a partial list, of course. Completely avoiding all these distractions or disasters may not be possible, but adjusting to a sudden development can salvage a reputation for quality. That adjustment takes a commitment to customer service that applies consumer education to each instance of a problem — whether real or perceived — that comes as a complaint or question.

Quality assurance as a goal reaches back to the earliest steps in the project, implying that the interface and code designers, engineers, and testers will have already done what they could. To further that original commitment into an overall maintenance program, the people who take over the project at the delivery date will ideally call on the same methods of communication, cooperation, and methods of self-analysis that followed the project during its development.

The software industry refers to initial quality assurance endeavors as "requirements capture." This phrase emphasizes fulfilling contractual demands, and for better or worse, that's the only perspective that many companies use in regarding customer support. Usually, this process involves finding the technical and design formula to create a user-friendly task flow and interface, to add on automatic or semi-automatic modes of operation (when possible or appropriate), and to provide a seamless integration of hardware and software for an "idiot-proof" stand-alone product, if that's the intention. To quote Dr. Einstein, "Everything should be made as simple as possible, but not simpler."

Certain details within these goals may prove elusive to designers. Why? Why ask why? Multimedia workmanship must be accomplished with an ever-changing kaleidoscope of platforms and other hardware, new techniques in programming that force an old hand to unlearn old coding habits, and other inconsistencies and uncertainties that would leave any lay bystander in complete oblivion. Will that bystander be one of a company's customers or clients?

Worst cases are really bad

The worst risks posed by quality-assurance problems that persist after delivery can be truly devastating, perhaps going so far as client litigation for breach of contract regarding faulty or inoperative product, late delivery, or other promises unkept. Obviously, this is an unwanted outcome. In the case of dissatisfactions from the mass market, complaints regarding faulty or inoperative products or claims of misleading advertising may be filed with the Better Business Bureau or other watchdog organizations. Such complaints are not desired, either. Disparaging word of mouth can be especially virulent and of immediate impact.

The assumption stands that everything possible will be done to prevent any such outcomes, but a grain of salt can be found in the possibility that a consumer may go to the BBB if a sufficient explanation of difficulties and options for their solution is not offered. This responsibility will be borne by support services rather than designers, programmers, or engineers. If the company is so small that even these roles are all taken on by the same people, remember that many people wear many hats. The producer must emphasize preventative measures during the development process and during the customer support phase, including regular self-analysis and attention to details such as low response time.

Customer service refers to instances of direct contact with those who have bought a product or announce an intention to do so. The immediate issues that come to the foreground in this branch of support strategy fall under the category of interpersonal communications, dealing with various complaint styles, and learning to deal effectively with the public, perhaps an angry public. The emphasis is on immediate problem-solving, defusing tension, and maintaining a profile that inspires trust and fosters customer loyalty. Customer service is truly provided by anyone in the organization who elects to answer queries. This concept demonstrates that each staff member becomes part of one team. Sales representatives take pre-sales inquiries; the marketing team may have to provide answers to common questions posed to retailers; technical questions may be relayed from a service representative on the phone to someone in engineering if a customer demands to talk to someone "in the know." A manager may field a phone call to placate a particularly irate consumer. The possible combinations depend on the size of the organization, the type of project undertaken and, of course, the intended audience or market.

The goal of consumer education presents a mistier horizon, but the product and the long-term business prospects may die on the vine if the unsophisticated users, or the "newbies," in your customer base are neglected. After all, today's newbie is tomorrow's choice demographic. If a producer or company is unwilling to help grow the overall market for new media, those parties might find themselves out in the cold one day, with a lot of unhappy company. Venues for such outreach are multiplying most quickly on the Internet and the surviving on-line services such as America Online and CompuServe. If the prospect of straightening the learning curve for a whole demographic proves to be a bit overwhelming, it is a pleasant relief to find that the greater Net society is full of folks willing to lighten the load. They may even have a thing or two to teach!

The relationship with clients and customers

Before the methods of outreach are tackled, the open-ended nature of maintaining relations is worth a few words. The producer's goal is not only to tend to existing relations, but to also keep open the possibility of additional customer or client relationships at any time. This goal begins to overlap with information in those chapters on product testing and marketing, and reaches into plans for any company's future growth.

For a refreshing take on this age-old dilemma of juggling old customers while enticing new ones, a look to the Internet is warranted. Delivery over the Net has its own effects on standard categories of publisher, distributor, customer, client, and audience. Multimedia on the World Wide Web is so radically new and compelling that it demands its own chapter in this book (plus, the publisher demanded one!). Yet the sheer state of flux experienced on the Internet gives rise to instances in which support becomes negotiable or even impossible, while opportunities to establish public relations multiply at an unprecedented rate. The polyglot nature of the content, delivery infrastructure, and audience participation on the Web make it a good sample environment for customer relations information pertinent to this chapter.

The WWW is a loose network of programs and stored files designed to be accessed by tailored software packages known as "browsers." These stored items are housed by host computers linked together to form the entity known collectively as the Internet. Browsers and their customized extensions can be obtained from many different programmers and are configured by the user to suit personal tastes and applications. This can prove to be a nightmare for the developer looking for user uniformity. Accessed multimedia files can also prove to have been cobbled together with programs and media elements from various sources. These ingredients can be commissioned, obtained from the public domain, or a mix of both types.

Precisely because his work is not strictly commercial, Clifford Pickover's approach to public relations offers a wealth of unique examples. Mr. Pickover runs the gamut of outreach activities possible for a cutting-edge researcher. Most appropriately, he can be described as a quintessential multimedia figure. The fractal that bears his name, the Pickover Attractor, is a stochastically recursive mathematical pattern that can be sounded out as it is visualized. Stochastic is an adjective that refers to an element of chance, and the recursive properties allow these chances to be recombined; in this case, in an infinite number of ways. Pickover's vast output has been published in venues ranging from print magazines to the World Wide Web.

Pickover's public home page, hosted by the University of Wisconsin at Madison, is a fun and pretty place to see and play with puzzles, animations, and interactive pattern generators. Some early work in the new Java programming language has been posted at the site. In addition to a personal biography, an awesome curriculum vitae, and an imposing schedule of past, current, and upcoming publications, Pickover features articles that give mathematical formulae or short programs in the programming languages of C or BASIC. When users learn something of these languages, they can feed these formulas into their computers to create mathematical animations. These online tutorials are straightforward and brief, although they are no substitute for training.

Pickover will take evaluative e-mail through an on-site forum. He will even answer simple questions if a questionnaire is answered in return. The questionnaire usually regards some intriguing subject such as alien IQ tests to provide material for one of his whimsical magazine columns. Of course, he cannot teach anyone the language C. After his prodigious output has been sampled, imposing on his time might be too intimidating, anyway!

Pickover is also part of an intranet at IBM that confers with colleagues on works in progress. The internal web he uses for this nascent research looks and acts like the WWW, but is not accessible from the Internet. When Pickover switched groups at this job, his interests shifted to doing high-powered graphics on personal computers equipped with graphics accelerators. This, in turn, affected the goals and methods of his experiments. He wound up abandoning Java for an even newer language called "OpenGL" because it can make flashy 3-D and photorealistic images, and also takes advantage of hardware acceleration. Pickover may or may not transfer OpenGL work for publication on his external Web site, as he sees fit. Such decisions will be influenced by whether he feels he can begin to develop a market for such material or derivative works by posting to his public site, or whether he decides that the average cybersurfer will not yet be able to access or appreciate it.

Overall, his internal and external networks synergize his research, his educational outreach, and his public relations. Pickover was clever enough to realize that the best way to play to a wide variety of markets, paying and nonpaying, is to target no one in particular. After all, today's schoolchild is tomorrow's fellow researcher; today's curiosity seeker is tomorrow's programmer. His site is designed to whet a new visitor's appetite for his publications at the same time that it spurs the interests of those who already buy and use his work.

The lesson here is that even with exceptionally difficult content material, such as Pickover's, it's possible to have a friendly, open-ended approach to customer satisfaction (see Figure 9-1). Attitude matters greatly, as does knowing your client base. The tacit assumption in Pickover's site is that people who are savvy enough to be on the Web and who will look at his work are technologically sophisticated, although not necessarily sophisticated enough to work easily with his material. He'll help and he'll answer, but there's an open-ended quality that encourages, not forces, the user to seek his or her own solutions to technical questions. It's akin to answering a question with more questions, which is not always the best answer to give. In this case, however, it works.

Customer service includes technical support

Cross training isn't just for health nuts anymore! Customer service and technical support may have to double for each other in a pinch or the populations may even overlap, as mentioned before. An entire organization may also supplement an existing support bureaucracy as well. True technical support (direct answers to direct user queries) may enter into this mix at any time. Existing companies have been swaying with the ebb and flow of demand and also the shifting politics of the retail market in multimedia for years. They've continued to rely on old-fashioned methods even as they apply new-found communications technologies to their advantage. Their histories best describe how technical support fits into the grand scheme of consumer outreach from project to project.

David Foley's entire company offers convertible support services. He began Foley Hi-Tech (see Figure 9-2) while in graduate school, and began a Game Factory division in 1990. "Hyperware" is the name of another offshoot: FHT's shareware label. His company offers a Web FAQ (frequently asked questions) file on its products. Support staff can be contacted through a mailing address or at phone, fax, and BBS numbers. Files posted on FHT's BBS also have the capability of being downloaded from the Web site and through FTP access. E-mail is taken through a CompuServe address as well as at CompuServe's Forum CIS. Support for each of its software projects, including new games and upgrades for older ones, plus utility products and authoring tools, is approached with different publishing and marketing realities in mind. Items with target markets can be supported solely by FHT. Games done for hire sometimes call for FHT to step in as the second line of defense, to absorb the overflow when a publisher cannot immediately respond to all technical support queries. In this instance, the publisher's staff takes the role of customer service by screening all incoming calls and rerouting some at the staff's discretion, to keep response time as brief as possible and to prevent lost calls during periods of heavy traffic or intense consultation.

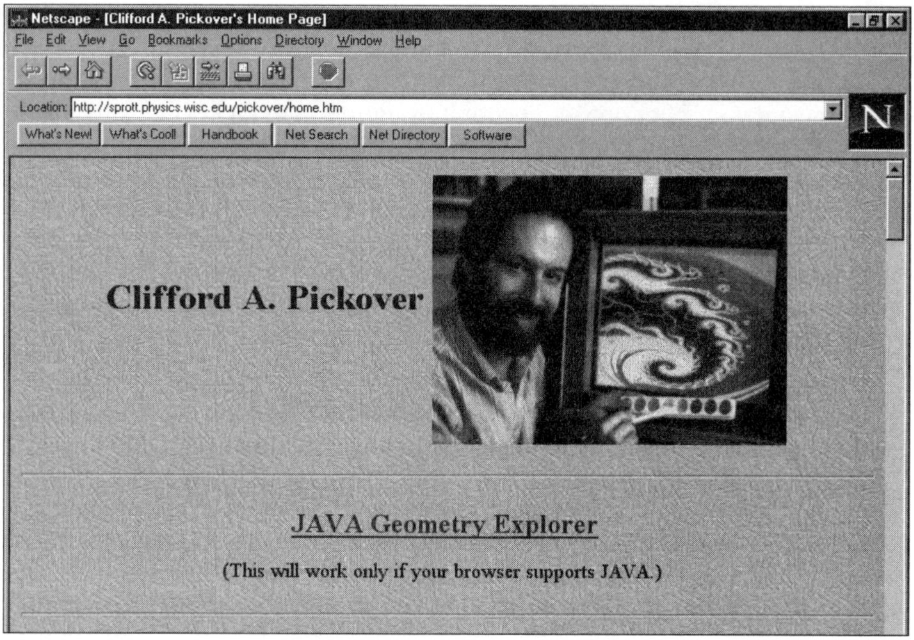

Figure 9-1: A witty self-portrait crowns Clifford Pickover's public home page, designed to appeal to researchers, artists, and cybersurfers alike.

Figure 9-2: Foley Hi-Tech juggles many works in progress (`http://www.fht.com/gamefactory.html`).

Customer service also addresses nontechnical issues

Nontechnical aspects of customer relations are directly or indirectly affected by the delivery of prompt and coherent technical support. Confusion may arise not only if the product's packaging is nonstandard or presents incomplete specifications, but also if the advertisements are cryptic or too vague. These may be misinterpreted no matter what is done. Confusion over packaging can be a simple, and simply handled, problem. David Foley's company Web site explains Foley Hi-Tech's nonstandard packaging. Those who may first think they've been mistakenly sent a CD will open the jewel case and find the floppy disk they ordered instead.

As the electronics industry opens new markets, it reaches into areas populated by those who use computers at work and even own personal computers, yet typically underutilize them. To many consumers, and unfortunately to many manufacturers and retailers, a desktop computer is often considered to be essentially indistinguishable from other big-ticket appliances such as a sophisticated stereo system or a noiseless dishwasher. Sometimes, the cards seem completely stacked against the user's having a painless multimedia experience.

Another population that may prove to be a source of trouble is the sophomore computer user who has begun to modify a home system without fully understanding that either a piece of software that compresses stored files on a hard drive or a nonstandard sound card might render a new CD-ROM inoperable. If a market of neophytes is reached, will it expect that the software's sale price will include the hardware on which to run it as well? Will the advertising be misinterpreted and consequently judged to be misleading? If detected signs of unrest are not directly addressed, how should those signs be countered without appearing confrontational?

The fundamentals addressed by customer support

The scenarios just discussed are really various examples of the same fundamental need that can, if insufficiently or carelessly tended, give rise to what's been nicknamed The FUD Factor: fear, uncertainty, and doubt. Now that purchase decisions are made by consumers according to how much technical information is printed on the retail packaging, new difficulties often arise from inconsistent terms. What does "full-screen video" really promise? What does "full-motion video" really promise? Industry standards, formats, and platforms, plus their attendant compatibility risks, add up to a witches' brew of worries.

There's no need for gloom and doom, however! Serving the needs of those who use a product can also be dictated by the style and substance of that product's presentation. A unique insight on the potential that makes multimedia such an invigorating new field is provided by the following medical aid title, and the support strategy devised by its project director, a multimedia producer, and scholar.

A case study

Alan Van Biervliet, Ph.D., of the University of Arkansas for Medical Sciences, decided to push the envelope of support to include therapy and peer consultation with "Take Control: A Multimedia Guide to Spinal Cord Injury." Prior to the compilation of this CD-ROM, a patient guide, called "Yes, You Can," was used internationally as part of a series of classes hosted by health care centers that catered to victims of spinal trauma. This paper document was copyrighted by the Paralyzed Veterans of America's Spinal Cord Injury Training Committee. Two factors influenced the decision to convert the pre-existing document and its classroom methods into a more comprehensive and convenient resource. A sea change in the medical industry over a five-year period led to a shift in focus, growing from a handful of dedicated centers across the country to a range of hospitals offering such services as subdivisions of their general care programs. In Arkansas alone, hospitals serving the newly injured grew from 3 to 13. Meanwhile, the number of staff that could be devoted to outpatient classroom instruction was spreading thin.

With the co-sponsorship of the University and the Department of Veterans Affairs, Van Biervliet and a team of colleagues widened the original document to include interactive options that could be customized, videotaped interviews, and in-depth medical illustrations. Van Biervliet, a professor and director of research at the Department of Physical Medicine and Rehabilitation, solicited modules from authors around the country much the way he would call for book chapters from fellow academicians. "Challenge Activities," such as quizzes, puzzles, and a sequential atlas of the nervous system, "The Dermatome Explorer," can be opened anytime by the user. Advice covers every aspect of daily life from breathing to skin care. Peer guides are embedded into the interface as virtual hosts, as well taking part in the interview sections. Van Biervliet, who was experimenting with multimedia since the introduction of Hypercard during the '70s, knew that making "Take Control" a stand-alone application in a durable form, such as a CD-ROM, would minimize problems. Authoring tools used were the sort available to consumers on the open market. No bugs were reported during in-house tests and in-field research conducted at a national convention. Demonstration discs were sent to 33 sites in North America, but no negative feedback resulted. However, differences in industry standards, and the prospect of orienting new users to CD-ROM technology, made support a necessity. Help was planned to become available after the August 1996 delivery date, via phone, fax, and e-mail at a site operated by the Arkansas Spinal Cord Commission.

The support crew was envisioned as part of this overall experiment in collaborative instruction. "Take Control" stands as a one-of-a-kind experience for both its publisher, an international medical textbook company, and its distributor, the Arkansas Spinal Cord Commission. Consequently, neither was prepared to offer direct phone bank support so common in the world of computer software. Instead, the proposal was made that a staff be drawn from the vocational training programs already implemented by the Commission and state vocational services. Standard retraining for the injured who cannot continue their previous careers has often placed them in industries that rely heavily on computers. In this case, the support staff of "Take Control" would not only explain the usual installation glitches, cross-platform difficulties, and other specifications, but would also double as live peer guides (see Figure 9-3). In return, staff members could gain experience regarding a growth field within the computing industry.

Exceptions and limits

As mentioned earlier, there is an upper limit to the support to be provided for a finished product, and many instances arise in both the nonprofit and commercial sectors of the multimedia world in which support is rendered impossible or unnecessary from the beginning, or eventually becomes untenable, or is simply left to history. Support is an especially touchy subject when it hinges on the eventual fate of new electronic storage formats. This is no more apparent than with CD-ROMs destined for libraries.

Leslie Jarmon of the University of Texas became one of the first Ph.D. candidates ever to submit a doctoral dissertation on CD-ROM. Her subject matter was perfect for multimedia because her specialty is kinesics, or nonverbal communication. Most of her research material consisted of taped studies of infants fussing and adults or children using gestures and preverbal utterances during normal speech. At one time, this unwritten language of sorts had to be painstakingly transcribed with a unique set of symbols — a tedious gestural version of Labanotation, a graphic technique once used in fine arts to record choreography on paper. Even though University Microfilms, Inc. has pledged to publish and store this format along with its library of microfiche, the long-term viability of current laser formats presented librarians with a headache rivaling those caused by high-acid paper and glued bindings in books. Jarmon herself, however, couldn't be expected to deal with such issues directly. She took the chance that her thesis may be unreadable in mere decades in order to explore the full range of new techniques in multimedia communications. The moral of the story is that there are no sure survivors in the world of multimedia formats. CD-ROM and the

Figure 9-3: Peer guides not only appear in this patient care CD-ROM for accident victims, they also make up its support staff.

Web will be around for a long time, but in what form? The first CD- ROM drives were capable of only 25 percent of the performance of today's mainstream drives. In a year or two, improvements to on-line technology will make many of today's advanced programming techniques unnecessary or obsolete. The multimedia producer must be aware of evolving technologies, yet, at some point, must work with the present and not the long-term future.

Artist Stewart McSherry is another exception. As Silicon Graphics' first artist-in-residence, McSherry produces work with the newest of new high-powered hardware. When the Technology Museum of Innovation in California staged its exhibit, "Virtual Worlds: Multimedia and the Internet," its hardware was donated from the biggest names in the industry: Apple, Cirrus, IBM, Pacific Bell, and McSherry's benefactor, Silicon Graphics. The remote sensing and virtual reality technology was not going to pose a long-term maintenance problem for anyone considering the experimental status of the works' host computers.

Sometimes, it makes sense to work with a lesser technology, with the expectation that it's at least proven technology, and that it may well be serviceable until the next wave of reliable technology comes forth. David Karam of Post Tool in California comments that kiosks are designed to be idiot-proof and free-standing, and that his small company has never been called upon to upgrade or re-purpose a kiosk of its own, or another's, design. Post Tool's installation for the Rock-and-Roll Hall of Fame in Cleveland utilized CD-I technology because the presentation relied heavily on full-screen video. This marginal laser format could be chosen for the sake of video compression because upgrades were not in the plan. Karam observes that, in general, these items are sturdy enough to be used to the point of exhaustion just in time to be replaced by a completely different technological innovation.

The situation is much the same for commercial installations such as interactive sales training programs, ordering systems, information kiosks, and convention directories for corporate use. Post-delivery maintenance for the kiosk maker is such a nonissue that the mere mention of "tech support" drew a complete blank from a new media project coordinator for Edwin Schlossberg, Inc., a specialized company active in the kiosk industry for many years.

Similar to kiosks, interactive Web designs made for hire get turned over for day-to-day maintenance provided by the server staff or a hired Webmaster. The contractor's involvement ends upon delivery of the finished product, typically a fully functional set of media files, CGI, or Perl programs and a framework of Web pages codified in HTML. Thereafter, the client's online representatives provide support to their paying (or more often nonpaying) audience of Net surfers.

An exception exists for this norm that can illuminate how a support strategy may combine flexibility with consistency in order to adapt to a multiplicity of clients in a changing environment. Diversified companies that lease Internet access, operate servers, build multimedia Web sites for a package fee, and store prefabricated ones on a subscription basis consequently play to more than one market at any given time.

For example, InteleCom Data Systems in Rhode Island was the first dial-up access provider to grant subscribers full access to the Internet. This occurred in 1989 when even Gophers did not exist. However, the onset of a graphical environment provided by World Wide Web programming and software obliterated the company's original status as a dedicated BBS. Steve Babigian, head of technical support at IDS, started as part of a three-person Web services division. He admits that the need quickly became apparent for departmental breakdowns in service, but the complexities of server/browser interactions ruled out any dependency on specialists. Today, the day crew consists of a customer support group that screens calls of more simple or generic problems. This customer support group is supported by a tech crew devoted to troubleshooting. Even those who field telephones queries are well versed in Net technology so that they can provide clear, if only partial, initial responses. The night shift is handled by a smaller group with more diversified skill sets. Employees are drawn from area colleges, and even high schools, because these demographics provide the required expertise base for support staff.

IDS leases commercial Web space to customers who maintain their own sites while administering full service to others. At the same time, they are under pressure to keep pace with a variety of multimedia "plug-ins," which visitors to these sites might have attached to their Web browsers. Full-paying customers do not have to worry about staying on the cutting edge at all times, because IDS staff will update their sites as contracted. On the other hand, Babigian sees no reason to begrudge customers self-administered sites. Customized functionality is at issue. When a Webmaster "soups up" a page stored by IDS, this creativity helps showcase new technology and reflects well on the company. Babigian draws the line at writing or installing scripts without a fee, but IDS will provide indirect aid on a case-by-case basis.

Such facilitation was required in the case of Macromedia's Shockwave, a compression scheme that allowed the Netscape browser to access animated clips faster than ever. Although IDS regularly beta tests many new programs and products, in this case, someone leasing space on its server beat them to a beta of Shockwave. The customer placed an inquiry, perplexed that his browser was not responding to a "shocked" clip he had just carefully installed. Technical support realized that they must add a MIME type to the server's configuration to force the host computer to be able to deliver the compressed video file to a visitor's appropriately customized browser. This alteration of the server's basic internal programming had to be administered by an IDS employee.

Although IDS creates, installs, and hosts multimedia for many clients, its support strategy aims to cover all paying customers and the worldwide audience of Web users under its umbrella without taxing its staff unfairly. Functional groups within the company's subdivisions cross-pollinate their knowledge and skills, and integrate approaches to marketing and technology into an adaptive whole. This keeps the support staff prepared for the challenges presented by the steady flow of new media appearing on their server.

Support can also be diluted, if not fully abandoned, to accommodate the ground-breaking experiments in multimedia authoring on the WWW. Chris Skinner is co-founder and Vice President of Information Technology for Websys, Inc., an interactive multimedia company based in Virginia. He gained Net fame as the designer of the animated "meteor shower" logo, placed top right on the revamped Netscape browser. Skinner is one of the many pioneers in Java programming, an endeavor that involves a new coding language and a new approach to how the user's computer interacts with any host server. Java can not only animate any pictorial element of a Web page but can also, in the manner of an arcade game, produce an animated response to input provided by the user. On his own Web site, Skinner refers to his public domain efforts by the common, diminutive nickname "applet," or even "code fragment." Such items are not so much full-blown programs as they are portable experiments in real-time animation.

One of Skinner's shiny new toys will force a scrolling line of text, whatever input desired, to loop from right to left as long as a Netscape user stays at a Web page. The "Scrollit" applet can be copied from Skinner's or any other site and applied to a commercial or noncommercial Net site free-of-charge.

The price paid for such a bargain is twofold. First, the internal copyright and liability notice must be retained. Notice how the disclaimer appears between a /* and another /* mark, embedded in the program code to follow. The star-slash marks notify the Netscape browser to ignore the comments between them. The applet is not necessarily rigged to prevent removal of the copyright notice, but these programs are so ticklish that unless they are used in their entirety, they are more likely not to work after being edited. Here's the HTML:

```
<BODY
        onLoad="timerONE=window.setTimeout('scrollit_r2l(100)',500);"
<p>
<br>

<br><script><!— Beginning of JavaScript Applet ----------

/* Copyright (C)1996 Web Integration Systems, Inc. DBA
        Websys, Inc.
   All Rights Reserved.

   This applet can be re-used or modified, if credit is given
        in the source code.

   We will not be held responsible for any unwanted effects
        due to the
   usage of this applet or any derivative. No warrantees for
        usability
```

```
   for any specific application are given or implied.

   Chris Skinner, January 30th, 1996.

   Hacked for CNNfn by RD, Jan. 31, 1996
*/

function scrollit_r21(seed)
{
        var m1  = "Our fun, new";
        var m2  = "scroooooling";
        var m3  = "billboard-type";
        var m4  = "whachacallit!";

        var msg=m1+m2+m3+m4;
        var out = "If you thought blink tags were annoying,
       how's about:";
        var c   = 1;

        if (seed > 100) {
                seed--;
                var cmd="scrollit_r21(" + seed + ")";
                timerTwo=window.setTimeout(cmd,100);
        }
        else if (seed <= 100 && seed > 0) {
                for (c=0 ; c < seed ; c++) {
                        out+=" ";
                }
                out+=msg;
                seed--;
                var cmd="scrollit_r21(" + seed + ")";
                    window.status=out;
                timerTwo=window.setTimeout(cmd,100);
        }
        else if (seed <= 0) {
                if (-seed < msg.length) {
                        out+=msg.substring(-seed,msg.length);
                        seed--;
                        var cmd="scrollit_r21(" + seed + ")";
                        window.status=out;
                        timerTwo=window.setTimeout(cmd,100);
                }
                else {
                        window.status=" ";
           timerTwo=window.setTimeout("scrollit_r21(100)",75);
                }
        }
}
// -- End of JavaScript code ------- --></script></p>
```

Skinner's second demand is to eschew the support obligated a paying customer. Dozens of Web site customers installed Scrollit on their home pages soon after its debut, disclaimer intact. That number soon grew into the hundreds. Professionals and amateurs alike simply used their browsers' copy-and-paste tools to post a scrolling message on their own site. If Skinner himself were to service every one of these experimenters, he would obviously never have time to do anything else!

The home site of Websys, Inc. does post a nontechnical FAQ for Scrollit and other Java giveaways, along with installation documents. The company has its own mailing list for aspiring Java programmers. Skinner himself is also active in collaborative third-party venues, such as comp.lang.java, to ease the learning curve for as many folks as possible. However, Websys, Inc. cannot make individual replies to visitor mail. If Scrollit will not perform on a Web page, diagnostics must be addressed individually.

The "gold rush" atmosphere frenzy during 1995 could only cloud predictions of the future of multimedia on the Net. Post Tool's David Karam experienced a sudden, radical shift in demand from kiosk projects to Web applications in that period. Determining whether this shift signaled a merely fashionable trend or a fundamental shift in communications is impossible. Java programs may become the new delivery method for multimedia by the time this book is printed, or perhaps retain their tentative public-domain status for a time. New paradigms of communicator/audience and contractor/client relations are being shaped on the Internet at the whim of its freakishly mutating technology. All questions pertaining to "how," "when," and "among whom," will remain at large until the "whats" take care of themselves. Issues specific to ongoing support for established formats are already being handled with novel Web-based approaches, as will be delineated in the following section on technical support.

The Meat and Potatoes of Technical Support

Technical support is a subdivision of customer service that most typically steps into the breach created as a consumer encounters a roadblock during installation, or some other immediately apparent difficulty not alluded to in support documents. The technical support staff is required again when upgrades must be installed, or in the meantime, if the software apparently fails or does not operate according to the user's expectation. This paradigm is borrowed from the old guard in the mass market computer software industry. The phrase "technical support" may seem painfully transparent to readers with a background in computer software. Surprising is the fact that even the biggest corporations can drop the ball on technical support for multimedia.

When called upon to provide technical support, guidelines are to be followed that apply to any product launch. Testing and tech support groups, or other company sectors, may share members, or a wealth of responsibilities may be handled by the same people. Such an allocation of human resources is accomplished by treating this overlap as a strength rather than a weakness. As long as enough staff is provided to handle the heaviest flow of incoming queries, or automated communications aids can be relied upon, this tactic can work in technical support's favor. Personnel issues include maintaining proper communications between customer service and technical support, and keeping in contact with engineering, marketing, and sales representatives.

Hiring specifications for these individuals should be tailored to a company's needs, with an emphasis on basic skills in phone communication, conflict resolution, information gathering, and software troubleshooting. Of benefit is attracting people who are also well versed in the subjects, themes, or techniques involved in the project, so that they can share your customers' enthusiasm. More sophisticated skills will be required to log reports on customer feedback patterns, troubleshooting, and verification of program bugs, and to turn raw data into useful analysis of support operations. Trickier characteristics to find in a prospective tech support employee include patience, a pleasant voice, and an engaging phone personality. These skills become more than cosmetic attributes if tech staff members ever find themselves handling a temporary overflow of incoming calls, or if any staff members come across a particularly truculent, unsatisfied customer.

The list of trouble spots in a personal computer that may raise a red flag for technical support is fairly lengthy. The recommended installation procedure may simply seem not to work. Sound or video cards may not respond. The mouse may not activate what it clicks on, or a cursor may not appear on-screen. The operating system may develop instabilities. External devices such as speakers may not transmit random access memory, or "buffer," and they may buckle under the pressure after the user tries to access something.

The list of combinations of these elements that might be employed by any user borders on the mind-boggling. "Swapped-out" or "souped-up" parts make Frankensteins out of desktop computers, indicating a first time for every variation. Despite the fact that a brand of operating system has just been upgraded, not everyone will have rushed to purchase it. Well-equipped developers test their works in progress on dozens of brands of hardware architecture, operating systems, and mice, plus memory and media components, all of different configurations. A knowledge of a battery of common problems and their probable causes is the best preparation. Forewarned is forearmed, as the saying goes, but caution must be applied to what may lie ahead.

Even if a division cannot be staffed precisely for such testing, the possibility exists to secure an independent contractor or to run limited tests with the help of a technical staff. The bigger the budget is and the more high-tech the product is, the greater the challenge for long-term quality assurance. The testing process may need to be expanded into the post-date period, especially if handling technical support in-house and planning on developing successive upgrades is proposed.

Make it possible for customers/clients to use the product

The simplest goal in technical support is to make installation and use as painless for the user as possible. With this in mind, the first line of defense is not posed by the customer service staff, but rather by the documentation supplied with the product. Prose, even of computer industry support documents, still calls for good, old-fashioned writing skills. Think of a projected support document not just as a technical manual but as a marketing tool, a form of community outreach, or even a theatrical experience that users could be willing to purchase separately. Now, a hint of the brave new world of consumer support will appear.

Document varieties include tutorials, "quick reference" or "shortcut" cards, installation instructions, and electronic or online help files. As with any technical writing, support documents are rendered most effective by organized, concise text and clear sentence structures, simply articulated ideas, a logical task flow, unobtrusive graphic enhancements, and well-positioned illustrations. They can also contain modified sections for beginning and advanced users. Support documents can reflect the bugs left undetected until far into the developmental process, which indicate supplements such as electronic help files and "read me" files.

An unusual case study

Origin is a successful game design and manufacturing outfit that has produced a clutch of highly touted, role-playing and action/adventure series such as Wing Commander. Origin's three-pronged aim for its documentation divides into: 1) post-date marketing; 2) scaled tech support that aids use of the product without giving away the game; and 3) an ancillary revenue stream. Origin's support may pave the way for another marketing push, or may even be its own ancillary market.

Although some game producers leave strategy books to the publisher, or only provide hints and cheats to the writers, Origin maintains a separate division to produce all its documentation. Initially, its designers wrote their own materials, but this became an untenable situation when development took up increasing amounts of time and energy. The company's high output rate of ten products per year, including major upgrades and platform variations, also influenced its decision to devote full-time staff to writing instructional and supplemental materials. To prevent a compromise in quality, the company began hiring writers such as Melissa Tyler for its "Wing Commander" series.

For Wing Commander III and IV, documents broke down into four subgroups: a "keystroke" or shortcut reference card; an installation guide; a play guide; and an oversized manual that doubles as a work of fiction. Origin's installation manuals may include notes that alert the user to disable a product called "Smart Drive," which may interfere with one or more of its games. As Origin's upgrades become more demanding, its documentation will more likely offer remedial advice or make other adjustments to accommodate late-breaking news.

Game documentation may cause another round of complaints that are sometimes unavoidable. For the sake of Origin's production schedule, a writer is assigned to create an installation manual and a book of hints and techniques during the last two months of a project. The first step is to interview the designers, but because the book is due before the game is generally finalized, vague information may substitute for explicit advice. This sort of fudging sometimes riles those suffering from a manual dependency, but these complaints are preferable to what might result from completely erroneous details in an unalterable and widely distributed a form such as an oversized paperback.

Beyond Documentation

The use of a product can be stymied by a host of difficulties, each of which must be diagnosed upon first encounter. Those not dealt with in documentation will be addressed through customer service. Some problems will pertain more to the user's tastes or computing habits. Others may be caused by bugs that flew under troubleshooting's radar. Still others may result from an incompatible device or program in the user's computer. The task of the representative is to divine those usage difficulties, and to decide whether they must be removed or disabled for the intended multimedia experience to unfold smoothly.

Confusing or incomplete search mechanisms or interface designs should be repaired during initial quality control or beta testing, but defining "confusing" or "difficult" is just as often a matter of taste. Conversely, the support team may be called upon to explain why an executable file doesn't quit upon command, or why video playback stutters or freezes at either random or specific points. A certain area in a virtual world may seem corrupted, and call up the same error message from the operating system. Other mysterious series of events may lead to the users' removal from a game, or from their operating systems altogether. Sound and visuals may not synchronize.

Run-throughs and simulations are some of the "war games" used to train customer and technical support staff members during development and beta phases. This training will presumably prepare a team for those critical weeks after the product hits the open market. The realizations that many open options exist for providing support, and that a selection of those are becoming more cost effective and easier to use, are comforting thoughts.

Tech Support Comes in Different Flavors

HomeStyles is a publisher of floor plans that grew from a small Portland company to a network of designers based in Minneapolis during the 1980s. This company's commitment to new media led it to embrace video tapes and eventually CD-ROMs, as well as books and magazines. Subjects integrated by this firm's multimedia presentations range from real estate to building construction to home decorating. The corporate Web site of HomeStyles offers a comprehensive model of existing outreach methods as outlined in this chapter. The company's CD-ROM for Windows, HomeDesigns, is distributed by another company to retail and other outlets across the country. However, HomeStyles supports all its major products with the help of what is termed a "telerelations" staff. Contact information is posted for all members of the company and its associates. E-mail can be sent to the HomeStyles product information team from the site, or the team may be contacted through its 800 telephone number.

The most salient feature of this company is a seven-question, online form that features pull-down lists and check boxes for those diagnosing certain technical problems. A user will be asked to choose or provide:

1. What version of the product is being used
2. Which operating system is utilized
3. A HomeStyles error message number

4. Reproduction of the problem, if possible
5. A pattern of occurrence of the problem
6. Any other error messages, such as General Protection Faults
7. A preferred method of reply, plus contact information

This online questionnaire reproduces a step-by-step interview technique of a technical support representative. When the user presses the Send button, the information is filed automatically on the HomeStyles server. This process ensures the saving of time when the service representative examines the user's problem.

Additionally, clever monthly features and new announcements maintain a flow of information that enrich the user's experience and quietly promote the HomeStyles network of associates (see Figure 9-4). The company's "Blueprint FAQ" includes explanations for all of the visual shorthand appearing in a typical floor plan. An article posted for May of 1995, "Light Up Your Life! Finding the Perfect Fireplace for Your New Home," was illustrated with an example provided by a designer, installer, or manufacturer. The article "Tips on Narrow Lot Homes" presents advice from a HomeStyles architect on maintaining privacy when building a house between two existing structures. These services support more than a certain software. They enable a company to embrace the whole activity for which the product was intended.

Types of Support

The following options are the vehicles currently available providing technical support. Speculations on future developments will also be detailed.

In-bound telephone service center

Upgrade Corporation of America is a service center for hire, and has proved to be a popular choice with large software corporations such as Microsoft. Individual staff members are instructed to answer the phones as if they were employees of the represented publisher, despite the fact that they are not in the offices of that publisher. The company is paid by commissions calculated on a scale that depends upon their turnover rate. The more quickly a given problem is solved during a toll call, the higher the payoff is. Many such companies act as fulfillment houses, providing telemarketing and related services. These companies are most often used by major software companies or other big companies in the manufacturing industry.

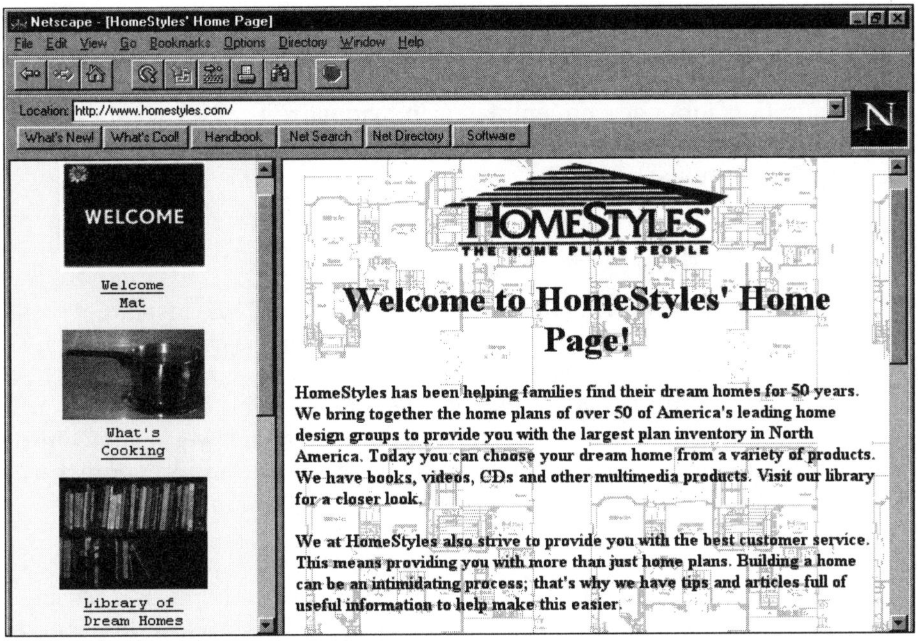

Figure 9-4: HomeStyles' customer service methods are diversified and are given prominence on its Web page.

Such an in-bound service center can be established with sufficient funds to rent space, hire full-time staff, and lease business telephone lines. Such a major undertaking would depend upon limitations on cash flow and capital investment, and faith in the long-term growth of the business.

Automated help desks

Another option for the customer support team is to automate these services as much as possible. This agenda has been served in many business arenas by the "help desk" industry. These software designers provide a single package that stores the kind of statistical information a support staff would have needed to record by hand. CATS is the acronym for the Corrective Action Tracking System, invented by Intuitive Data Solutions in California. Costing just over one thousand dollars, a system can be purchased that will accommodate up to five users. It promises to be compatible with all DOS and Windows networks, and offers automatic updating, an automatic mail system — mailbot — and self-monitoring capabilities. The software can be customized and can also generate statistical reports on long-term trends, patterns of nonconformance queries, and preventative or ameliorative actions. Other help desks are intended to computerize the service centers of any manufacturer. Features available include: in-house tracking and logging of calls; a diagnostic information database with importing features; report generation; input screen templates; individualized call assignation; and optional beeper and e-mail hookups. Such capabilities could amount to price tags in the thousands of dollars.

Voice mail

Relying on an answering machine is an option available instead of employing a help desk program, but the drawbacks could outweigh the savings. The help desk programs outlined previously protect against the risks of dependence upon a potentially unreliable machine left unattended for hours at a time. Some people balk at leaving messages on an answering machine. An unwanted impression could be perceived of a lone entrepreneur who may be here today and gone tomorrow.

Voice mail is an attractive option when humans cannot be dedicated to the task of fielding customer calls. Merlin Legend, for example, is a package of services available from AT&T that can cost as little as a few thousand dollars and as much as nearly $50,000 for a multiyear contract. Voice mail with automatically triggered, prerecorded prompts can be provided for more than a dozen phone lines maintained by AT&T's local service representatives. The company will track lost calls and act as a fulfillment house. The infrastructure remains the telco's responsibility. This prevents being laden with an outdated phone system in a few short years, and lack of access capabilities. Obsolete and broken equipment will not create an extra burden.

Telephone technical support service, even with 24-hour-a-day access, is not the ideal of a convenience anymore. If a company's technical support is free, yet a telephone query involves a long distance charge, this may be enough to discourage users. Those who do call and are placed on hold may be outright annoyed!

Fax-back, mailbot, Web, FTP, or Usenet FAQS

Update alert or notification services can be rendered automatically with the correct software, and delivered by fax or e-mail. The contact information is notated for those who would like to subscribe to regular updates on the status of a product, or a completely robotic service can be used that will only return the same message when prompted by e-mail to a dedicated address.

As seen in the case of HomeStyles and Foley Hi-Tech previously, a gaggle of Internet sources can be utilized and itemized on a World Wide Web page. This is convenient but also risky. What occurs when those provided with Internet access by Prodigy, for example, cannot see the page with the company's proprietary browser because it was never cached in their system properly?

A bulletin board service, or BBS, is the old-fashioned way to reach customers but presents a challenge akin to setting up a Web server instead of renting space on another's. At least one computer and telephone line must be dedicated to the BBS and its software configured to handle incoming calls and act as an open message service. When customers make contact through a BBS, it will be costly in the manner of a toll call, and as taxing as being put on hold if they encounter connection trouble. The benefits of a BBS arise from it being its own universe. Such features as lively user input, downloadable files, message threads, and direct contact with a system administrator, or sysop, who either represents or actually is the publisher or the producer, add up to a social experience of total immersion. Would demand for a product be widespread and passionate enough that users would go through the trouble of calling the terminal?

The long-term promise held by desktop organizing and operating software such as Windows, in relation to telephony, is that magic moment when telephone and computer are finally one. Then, all the attributes listed previously will be obtainable in a compact plug-and-play system someday. Currently, Windows can be successfully adapted to achieve capabilities similar to an inbound service desk or BBS, but the challenge remains to provide the modifications. Time can be invested solving this challenge, or monies can be paid, perhaps developing a debilitating dependence upon an independent consultant. The most serious warning to keep in mind regarding this option is that the more automated a PC-based voice mail or phone system is, the more taxing it will be on the computer's memory.

An e-mail system to solve specific customer/client problems

Even those who take the darkest view of the future of the Internet agree that e-mail is its long-standing "killer app." Those who don't use the Net for anything else will at least subscribe to an online service for e-mail capability. CompuServe is the granddaddy of all online services for warehousing vendor or product-specific forums. A vendor support team or volunteer sysops maintain areas devoted to a product or suite of products.

To create a forum, a contract must be made with an online service as if a business were a content provider. If this area proves popular enough to inflate subscribers' monthly bills, the terms of the contract could be loosened. More likely, a set fee will be charged. The benefits are similar to those listed previously for a BBS because the major online services are all essentially overgrown bulletin board systems. Online service forums are generally more carefully monitored than the free-for-all message boards on Usenet. Additionally, the more clever services make off-line "readers" available to subscribers who do not want to be charged too much for browsing. However, such forums have classically been restricted to subscribers of the services. The services as a segment of the online industry are becoming more obsolete. Some of the older companies have either suspended operations or tried to marry their infrastructure with the WWW as much as possible. The option of forums may become even more limited in scope or even disappear in the next few years.

Demos with interactive or hypertext Readme files

Those last-minute updates tacked onto support documents can be housed in Readme files bundled with executable files, or added into a demo or shareware version of the software. This option is best for games and programs distributed on floppy disks. Shareware has a long history in the computer business. BBSes and smaller retail outlets have traditionally offered distribution venues, but they are slowly being taken over by more convenient Net delivery methods such as FTP, Usenet, and Web sites. Here is where efforts at outreach can be aided by other entrepreneurs and interested amateurs.

Ancillary support and third-party providers

A thriving example of Web-based ancillary support is known as Happy Puppy (see Figure 9-5). This gargantuan set of pages, chat area, and file collections was begun in 1995 by game-design freelancers Jennifer Diane Reitz, Stephen P. Lepisto, and Sandra Woodruff. They originally intended that their Web site promote their self-administered shareware distribution scheme. That intention soon dissolved in an ensuing deluge of outside demos, code fragment "patches," and user comments. They are now committed to supporting other retail and shareware efforts. Their high-traffic Web site hosts tens, and even hundreds, of thousands of visitors per week. The trio has discovered that these visitors will make purchasing decisions based on information and product samples downloaded from Happy Puppy pages. These three freelancers are open to news items, editorials, demos, walk-throughs, editors, patches, and animation samples. They are supported by traditional banner, or billboard, style ads on their front page, and are able to charge their rates on the strength of their market influence. More important in terms of support, their chat groups and message sections set the stage for users to contribute to a customer service agenda by trading tips and reviews, and informing ongoing technical support by sharing common problems.

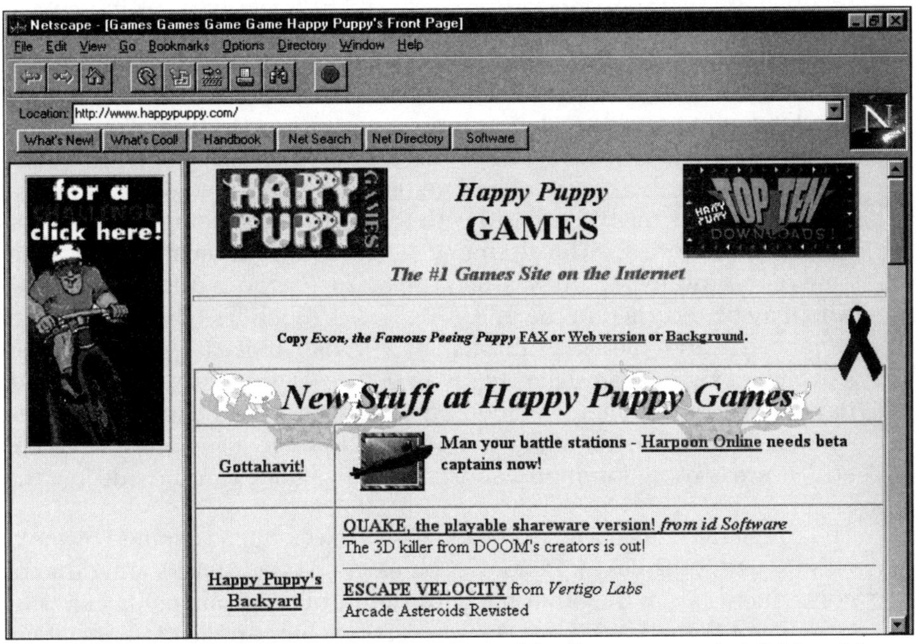

Figure 9-5: Happy Puppy serves as promo central for the game market (`http://www.happypuppy.com/`).

The question may arise of the effort involved in attempting to register a forum through an online service compared with the installation and maintenance of a Usenet-style message board with a free program from Matt Wright of Matt's Script Archives. Why not run a personalized Happy Puppy? The major drawback is the novelty status of the Web, a reality easily forgotten by someone acclimated to the online world. Many people with personal computers who are perfectly capable of buying, installing, and enjoying multimedia are not affiliated with any online service. Online subscribers themselves have only recently been granted access to the "Wild, Wild Web," and many are not used to the idea that Web sites are housed on remote computers. Otherwise intelligent people may not be able to log on to a page sometime for reasons beyond anyone's control, and they will infer that the page no longer exists and that the business is gone! If third parties are willing to maintain the sites and build their Web pages into popular destinations for a target demographic, there is much to lose by trying to strike out independently. If commitment can be made to maintain a Web page, an online directory of services will supplement other networking activities.

As mentioned previously, Web, Usenet, and BBS conduits attract interested parties such as other more-experienced users. Independent conversations develop in open forums such as Usenet and Internet Relay Chat, whether or not they are being monitored! The catch phrase "active learning" is not really a redundancy, considering the energy being expended by various gurus and experts in the online community. The greatest enemies and allies lurk together in this shadowy world of internationally transmitted, erasable graffiti. Sleepless nights might be saved with the realization that these messages will not be stored forever. The attempt can be made to dedicate at least one part-time representative to prowl around online for signs of a disgruntled customer who may be returned to the fold. This task is much less daunting now that advanced search mechanisms such as AltaVista make it possible to perform a live word search through roughly 15,000 news-groups any minute of the day. As long as comments on computer Usenet groups can end with a line such as, "There are not many companies as well-focused on their customers," there is room for improvement. Such vigilance can provide just that.

The bright light of consumers helping themselves can be dimmed by violations of Netiquette, the easy spread of urban-legend-type rumors and other sneaky consequences. On the other hand, the spirit of one-upmanship can work in one's favor sometimes. One user of a 3-D graphics application posted a complaint about a woman who answered his telephone call by stating, "Tech support," when she was not a member of the crew. Another user retorted that she may have answered the line when no one else was nearby so as not to lose the call. Even customers can clarify this situation so common to customer service, that of trying to hit an ever-shifting target. No matter how few and far between they may be, they aid all fellow software producers.

Those who post in Usenet message boards usually ask for fairly explicit aid. Folks can publicly request support service contact information. A typical technical pre-sales question consists of the opening gambit: "I'm thinking of buying [whatever]. Any bad or good stories?" Although an interested party may get "flamed" for contributing a public post so as to hype his own product or credentials, bonus points will be scored if a personal response is offered to any query. Common subject lines for flames include "STUPID [brand name] TECH SUPPORT" and "[brand name] TECH SUPPORT SUCKS."

An even newer venue for third-party support is coming to a storefront near all! The cyber cafe, a hybrid of the once wildly popular coffee houses and video game arcades, and a little of a computer retail outlet thrown in for good measure, is gaining ground as the hip meeting place for new media and its potential users. Habitués who tire of purely online networking can have their electronic cake and eat it, too — and then wash it down with a double espresso. People who find computer warehouses intimidating and uninspiring can satisfy their curiosity with the help of specially trained personnel.

Another Unusual Case Study

Tomas Wise actively promotes his Cyber Café in New York, among other locations, as a testing ground for new products. Wise feels that even beta or prerelease versions of The Next Big Thing are a thrill for his clientele, who typically express strong interest in advanced technology and new media. Windows 95, Netscape and other Internet software, various ROM games, and digital cameras have been tested or have made their debut at the café. Facilities are also rented for special events and press conferences.

During normal business hours, one technician is on duty weekdays, and two handle the weekend crowds. The manager is on hand to assist if demand temporarily surges during high-traffic hours. Part-time staff members are scheduled to conduct private lessons by the café's Director of Educational Services. The director also oversees classes for larger groups and hosts seminars.

For product launches, café management may call upon more than half a dozen extra staff members to assist party guests. Cyber Café's manager, assistant manager, and both partners also stand by. This dramatis personae depends upon two crucial variables: 1) the complexity of the product being demonstrated; and 2) the amount of money the client is willing to set aside for technical support in addition to basic party expenses. More complex operations, such as multicasting, video-conferencing, and installing reflectors or satellite uplinks, call for a network specialist. An in-house software developer may assume these responsibilities, or management may "outsource" a freelancer. Any software and hardware required by a particular event will routinely be installed during the week prior to the scheduled date. Various tests are conducted to search for weak spots in the set-up. Finally, a dry run is held the day before to ascertain that transitions and dramatic high points progress smoothly and professionally.

Developers and publishers are drawn to the concentrated market posed by Cyber Café's thousands of weekly visitors. They are further reassured by continuous on-site technical support from a professional staff that can act as a safety net during a critical event. The minimum of capital investment required for this public exposure in a protected environment makes for a relative bargain. Usually, contracts are negotiated directly through the manufacturer's representatives or marketing department heads. However, events have occasionally been staged for smaller public relations or consulting firms.

Eric A. Zarko, an enterprising computer science major, began seeking backers for a small chain of cyber cafés in the mid-1990s. His business model capitalizes on a Web-like interface for multiplayer gaming, and ordering at terminals. The wait staff will be trained extensively in all software implemented for customer use, although automatic ordering would not completely replace traditional food service. Local user group meetings could be held in reserved meeting rooms that would offer a more relaxed F2F (face-to-face) experience for those who feel limited by online chats or message boards. Zarko is committed to making his first café into a catalyst for the local art scene. His moderately appointed facility would be within the financial means of a start-up company, an artists' collective, or an independent developer.

When to Upgrade to a New Software Version

Planning a new version of a multimedia product is far more daunting than it is with any other form of computer software. Often the original project adapts to the choice of format and other determining factors while under development. An upgrade may call for an entire re-purposing task, so as to take advantage of the benefits and avoid the pitfalls of some new authoring software package or another recording medium. If the desire is to make an educational resource more compelling with a game-like interface, this may require a new programming language or another technique of access and retrieval. If live-action video and 3-D graphics are added to an interactive CD-ROM, how can excessive demands from a user's home computer be eliminated?

More than technical considerations come into play. The classic marketing paradigm will rule the product like any other as it fights for consumer interest against its closest competitor. No matter how fancy, or cutting-edge, or unique the product is, a limit exists as to how much money or interest the average person will surrender to a purchase of a CD-ROM. Can that goal be achieved even after an additional layout of capital for an upgrade? Will the improvements be worth the additional expense asked from the existing customer base? Will those new improvements open the market to those who did not elect to buy the first version?

When an update is needed immediately

Conditions that call for an immediate update may or may not be easily addressed. If the software is delivered on floppy disks, "fix" patches and supplements can be provided. This option is not available for laser media, such as CD-ROM. If the limits of the chosen format become apparent in short order, the only thing to do may be to retrench and start again — if redressing the miscalculation can be afforded.

Republic Pictures' Home Video Catalog 2.1 on CD-ROM offers many details crucial to its products' distributors and retailers. Yet even the newest, corrected version arrived too out-of-date to be useful as a ready reference. Should companies in the home entertainment industry, which literally produces hundreds of new releases and retires dozens of older ones on a monthly basis, abandon CD-ROM technology altogether? Should updates come on floppies between versions, or should another type of storage be considered altogether? It's their move.

Serious Technical Flaws or Bugs

A passing reference was made earlier in this chapter to established publishing entities that fumble technical support when they try to make the move from traditional media to multimedia without laying the groundwork. The star example of this pitfall is the Disney empire's marketing fiasco, "The Lion King" on CD-ROM. Disney's problem was, paradoxically, a direct result of its unprecedented success. The conglomerate's unrivaled brand-name recognition broke into that virgin marketing territory presented by thousands of families with dormant CD-ROM drives. Disney capitalized on its biggest theatrical success to date. On Christmas Day, 1994, those who had bought a personal computer finally had a reason to play a CD-ROM on it. Unfortunately, many of those consumers owned equipment already outdated by the standards applied during product development. They were also not in a position to divine whether the problems were inherent to the CD-ROM and its programming, or a matter of hardware incompatibility.

Frazzled parents of disappointed children swamped the developer's phone lines with complaints, to no avail. In frustration, they began contacting Disney's own customer support division, without realizing that those employees had not been trained or even been expected to respond to technical support complaints. Disney fell into the classic trap that can clamp down on any product launch by ignoring quality assurance issues specific to interactive software. If Disney's idea was to market multimedia as just another entertainment medium, it ignored the fact that no one should have to install a book or wonder whether they might not be getting everything out of their videotape that they should be. The only thing that prevents the marketing world from forgiving this event as a complete fiasco is Disney's refusal to admit that it blundered.

Minor Technical Bugs and Glitches That Affect Product (and Publisher) Reputation

Less serious bugs or glitches can be handled by a competent staff. There will always be incompatibilities, errors in documentation, and other trouble spots listed previously. Additionally, an ounce of prevention can go a long way toward expecting calls from people using the software who find that it no longer works after they install an upgrade of a media-related, memory-saving, or operating system program from another manufacturer. As soon as a new product is heard of that may affect an existing product, testers may have to be called upon to determine a way to counteract such influences. Even if an issue cannot yet be updated, an attempt can be made to discover a countermeasure to recommend.

The situation for a product can turn serious when entire platforms are involved, as opposed to an operating system or media software. An update may be required within a year if the target market has migrated from one playback system to another. If platforms are switched, be careful what is chosen! CD variants already include the Kodak's Photo CD, Philips' CD-I, the "enhanced" CD, and the CD-ROM. It is of little consequence that at heart they are all the same thing. The fact that some can operate only on certain playback equipment may have left average consumers ready to pick up their marbles (read "dollars") and go home. A price could be paid in the long run for a hardware manufacturer's miscalculation without having done anything to deserve being pushed out of a retail market. With luck and the choice of appropriate hardware, golden are the chances of success. Without these two elements, financing may be required to handle a redesign.

Technical Advancements and New Media Opportunities

Technology "push" comes to "shove" in a more gentle manner when it does not force the abandonment of one hardware setup for another. Melissa Tyler reports that Origin programmers act as their own focus groups, and perform what is tantamount to technical and marketing research in their down time. They are game fans to the core, and if they notice a catchy use of gameware by a competitor, chances are good that they will leap back to the drawing board. If an impressive new sound card appears, the programmers will often adjust their design around it if their gut instinct tells them it will be worth the risks.

"Hardware wars" are always being staged by competitors, demanding that the only way to respond to the pressure is to be ready for it rather than wait to react to it. At Origin, if the engine — the programming infrastructure — is rewritten during a series, then a whole new set of adjustments must be made that may or may not hamper the user's gaming experience.

The overall speed of a game is a function of its code. Therefore, a new first-person emphasis or drastic changes in the central characters, room layouts, and so on may demand a different structural approach. In the case of two early versions of Wing Commander, Part II was a cartoonish arcade environment, whereas Part III offered a video interface using live actors. These improvements affected the respective play-guides less than the installation manuals. The demands of the Part III upgrade relied upon a user's hardware, with separate adjustments made to setups on a Mac, versus a PC or PC clone. Interface changes between Parts III and IV also took advantage of new add-ons that designers felt would be put in place by members of their target market by projected release dates. In the long run, Origin was following the industry trend toward more realistic interfaces, game play, and keeping pace with its competition.

Market Conditions Versus Company Advancement, Diversification, and So On

Success with such educated predictions is a matter of quick thinking. Not only development operations but the health and wealth of the company affect the ability to turn a clever commodity into an ongoing revenue generator. Sometimes, "product pull," such as a company's cachet or a designer's reputation, will affect market research. The existing client or customer base may want more of what is offered, and be willing to pay more for an advanced product. Pertinent questions at this stage regard the status of operations and certain financial realities that apply to all business endeavors. Can the outfit diversify or change course? Are there more entities financially involved at this stage? Is debt mounting? Conversely, can an initial investor be bought out?

These economic questions affect the outlook for the product and its successors. Melissa Tyler claims that if Origin introduced a fully new interface or game design that ran counter to the reputation it has already built among action game fans, then that situation would likely call for inventing a new label or product "imprint." This option would prevent confusion, or perhaps lessen the aftershock of a marketing disaster if this situation developed.

The decision may be made to expand production to include such new imprints or foreign language versions for overseas sales. Origin's document translations are done in-house to avoid gross language mistranslations: the "bite the wax tadpole" syndrome. Tyler admits, however, that the games themselves are another prospect. Dubbing for major actors such as Malcolm McDowell is relegated to the same specific voice-over providers overseas. This maintains some semblance of a consistent persona. McDowell's German counterpart had to be hired to perform for the German edition through a native company, and selective editing was also employed to bring the game into line with that country's censorship policies. This sort of transatlantic negotiation is advisedly taken on when armed to tackle overseas markets, to reach out to the societies that host these markets, and to engage overtures to an unfamiliar group of would-be clients or consumers.

General economic considerations may be highlighted by a more offbeat example of what could be interpreted as multimedia, despite its traditional lineage. Kevin McCurdy is someone who draws attention at his industry's trade shows, although he will not been seen on the cover of any new media magazine. His specialty is categorized with amusements and attractions, yet his haunted houses are legendary, and his business model incorporates updates along the lines of an interactive game. Productions interlace live actors with light and real-time or recorded special effects, animatronics, music, and ambient sound. Tools range from Macs and video recorders to old-fashioned mirrors and performers in fright wigs.

According to Ron Levine, a representative of McCurdy's company Imaginart, every initial pitch includes plans for at least one or two yearly revampings. Exceptions may include special cases in which a haunting is intended as a one-shot fund-raising effort or special event. Revamps are incorporated or abandoned according to the client's needs, business prospects, and certain physical realities.

The king and queen of any such undertaking are named Time and Budget. Upkeep is negotiable regarding other aspects, including how much heavy machinery and robotics are incorporated into the attraction and the complexity of their interactions in terms of preprogrammed or recorded effects. Geographic location is also a factor, because Imaginart is stationed in New York but its representatives travel the East Coast for remote installations.

Levine likened the state of the "haunted house" specialty industry in the mid-'90s to the video game industry of the '80s. Many competitors decide to pounce on a fad, hoping to ride it like a wave, only to find it has already crested. Nevertheless, the product in such an industry is pure novelty and sensation, so "product pull" in this case indicates the need to scare regular attendees by varying the scale, style, and pace of a permanent attraction. Clients who do not fully appreciate the demands of this market can return the next year in panic, claiming, "Our numbers are down!" Because Imaginart's reputation is drawn from the response of a client's audience, its responsibility is to prevent its novelties from turning stale. To give an indication of the company's long-term strategy, Imaginart's own permanent installation in Poughkeepsie is revamped every year, with a two-year lead time budgeted for planning stages.

Existing Conditions for Most Multimedia Products

Multimedia is a more subtle novelty, but a leaf can be taken from Imaginart's book at a time when radical commentators are pronouncing the written word extinct. Some rules — in business, entertainment, and other old-time disciplines — still apply.

Knowledge of marketing will be tested here at the school of hard knocks. Has initial demand been underestimated or has the future market size been overestimated? Has distribution been handled inefficiently or inappropriately by management? Did a company target an unfamiliar market or a market unfamiliar with its type of product? Was unawareness of the competition so keen that a response could not be made to a countermarketing tactic that nudged a product off retailers' shelves? Did the product arrive at planned obsolescence ahead of the schedule drawn for it? Was a market surge capitalized too early or too late? Was a debt assumed for the venture without a fallback plan, or was deficit financing obtained in a pinch? Has the company finally found itself undercapitalized at a crucial moment, or did it invest too early in nonliquid assets and was unable to regroup under pressure? Was the attempt made to extend the existing business into the world of multimedia while still insecure about other ventures? Has a business staff slowly realized that its members all have different business styles, standards regarding quality assurance, or goals for the product? These questions all factor into the decision to extend or drop an enterprise.

Is a New Version Justified?

Every product has a life cycle, and although some breakaway consumer goods seem to have nine lives, they are subject to the same market forces as all others. It may be discovered that eventually a product has come to the end of its journey. It may be better for a developing business to relegate its game or CD-ROM to the cutout bin and try something new. After a number of such semi-retired products is accumulated, a whole new market can be reached by bundling them and selling them all for a radically lower price. Economies of scale can work in a positive direction for only so long, or the admission will have to be made that they will never kick in.

David Foley is reticent regarding the chances for any new game, especially one funded by a small outfit. His impression of the E3 trade show of 1996 was literally of thousands of top-grade games underwritten by major publishers. His estimation of the average development contract for an A-title game surpasses one million dollars, with an additional two million reserved for marketing. Foley's personal experience in that high-pressure market obliged him to grow his small company from 14 to 32, employees just to stay competitive during pitches for big-budget deals with major publishers.

Not everyone can risk the investment required to compete in that level of the market. This is true for major label releases by old hands in the computer game world. The following example traces the short and fairly lackluster history of a CD-format interactive game that gambled on a niche market and apparently lost.

Comics Penn & Teller, sometimes described as magic's own Beavis and Butthead, treated members of the Video Software Dealers Association to a free, albeit truncated, stage show at the organization's 1994 convention in Las Vegas. They appeared courtesy of Sega, sponsor of the duo's proposed interactive game suite. The title announced was "Penn & Teller's Smoke & Mirrors," or P & T's S & M for short. The intended format was the Sega CD, designed for play on the Sega CDX addition to the company's Genesis system. The project's development team at Absolute Entertainment were faced with the challenge of packing an even more shortened version of the pair's stage show into a medium designed for 16- and 32-bit video game players. The original completion date was targeted for the Christmas season of 1994.

What followed was a series of delays, revised delivery dates, and more missed deadlines. Demos were distributed and reviewed in magazines, but adjustments were made to the schedule quarter after quarter. Eventually, a key launch date was announced that fit the performers' image perfectly: April Fool's Day of 1995. As a perfect April Fool's joke, interviews published at the time announced a product that still didn't exist. Delivery was rescheduled for April 15 and promoted on America OnLine with a live chat and downloadable clips. During the frenzy of income tax filing deadlines, consumers were probably too distracted to notice that the product was still unreleased. It actually came out eventually, but over the next year, talk of 3DO and CD-ROM versions dwindled to nothing.

Some speculations about this promotional odyssey can be made even without exact knowledge of the challenges faced by the design team. To the developers' credit, no difficulties were reported, and the games (including Desert Bus, during which almost nothing happens for eight solid hours) were lauded as clever, if unexciting. However, it appears that Penn & Teller played out their auto-hype over nearly a year, and could no longer exploit the notion of two self-described "bad boys of magic" turning arcade game conventions inside out. If game fans couldn't really "get with" the magicians' postmodern program, and even more loyal P & T fans were not willing to purchase a Sega Genesis system just for the sake of one product, Smoke & Mirrors was bound to wind up in the wrong area of that demographic Venn diagram — out of reach of both target markets.

Herein lies an example of a slow loss of consumer interest and confidence. The impression of an uphill battle, implied by quality assurance delays, may be cause enough. Even if no real problem exists, potential customers may wonder enough regarding what might go wrong to question the wisdom of buying a product, investing in a certain type of playback equipment, or abandoning one format for another. If the FUD factor can derail even Penn and Teller's usually reliable formula of rubber gorilla heads, fake blood, and nose-thumbing, imagine what it could do to any other venture.

The overall rule appears to be that only "star" products get revised. Others languish or disappear. Market considerations for upgrades and new editions are not purely technical, but rather involve the industry-wide context of technical and economic competition. When more money must be charged for a fancy upgrade, will it be found that the closest competitor's variation on a product's theme suddenly looks like a bargain by comparison?

Even "star" markets seem to exert influence on the fates of individual products. Reportedly, the early difficulties with Windows 95 left its users unwilling to buy items designed for that upgraded desktop environment. If a new edition is planned around next year's hot software, will it be hot enough to light a fire under consumers and get them in the stores for a specific product?

The challenge, when the decision is made to drop a product or retire an upgrade, is to phase out support without alarming or alienating the existing customer base. Certain tactics, such as charging for support after a certain period of time, requiring customers with older product versions to make a toll call, and demanding demographic information, may work for certain kinds of computer software sold by larger companies. "Nag" screens and versions rigged to expire after a set number of hours in use are becoming popular, especially for unregistered shareware. A consumer may have invested a lot of money on an item, and taken a chance on a small or new company. Will rescaling customer service be worth jeopardizing that newborn customer loyalty? Or will it damage a reputation?

This is not to say that a new, updated product cannot be developed and supported on a modest scale! Lawrence Harbin was featured in the magazine *Black Enterprise* on the strength of his one-man success with an African-themed screen saver called "Art in the Dark." His recipe for support combines an e-mail address at a commercial online service with an 800 telephone number accessible for at least a few hours a day. Although Harbin's product was still in its initial release at the time of his interview, his skeletal arrangement of options can be emulated and easily modified to support upgrades and older versions concurrently.

Make Intelligent Decisions

The rule of thumb to remember is to consider overall capital investment, yet avoid a money pit. There is no more succinct working example of a fixed capital investment than a haunted attraction. From the consumer's perception, there is but one copy of this interactive game of sorts, and it must be exciting enough to draw people out of their house to the attraction. McCurdy and his crew emphasize as much recycling as possible in order to protect a client's initial capital investment from year to year. Even wooden planks are torn down and re-used. Expensive equipment is relocated on the site. With all four core members sharing a background in stage magic, Imaginart can apply its fixed crew and a flexible support staff to any revamping or rescaling of an existing site. If the attraction will be rededicated as a fund-raiser, for instance, an evocative yet efficient setup can be simple to operate even if a volunteer or two fails to materialize at the last minute.

The company does all it can to protect the interests of its clients, but sometimes a client doesn't appreciate the favor. Ron Levine admits that his company was once approached by someone who had just squandered a lot of money on high-tech hardware and demanded that he and his team mix it all in a bowl and cook up an attraction. The nightmare of being forced to use every bit of equipment in the absence of a chosen theme, budget outline, or marketing plan was the company's only inspiration to produce something spooky. He and his team may have undertaken the job, but they never considered for a second that it was a wise business choice.

If a number of people have been depended upon to fund, develop, produce, market, and support the first version of a multimedia project, they are owed a careful judgment at the crossroads presented by the option to upgrade or downshift. Objective market evaluations are more crucial at this time than any other because wishful thinking may tempt a search for a rainbow over the next hill. Protecting the investment of cold cash and hot sweat donated by backers and collaborators is important. A time to cut losses must also be decided, and that judgment must be made.

PART IV

Making a Living

✦ ✦ ✦ ✦

In This Part

✦ ✦ ✦ ✦

CHAPTER 10

Developing Your Career

- Multimedia is a literacy as well as an industry. Individuals who are fluent in digital communications will be able to find work in this business.
- Multimedia is a lifestyle as well as an industry. The hours are long, and sometimes you'll have no life. Families and friends don't always like that.
- Multimedia is an industry in which people make a living, not a fortune. But there are worse things than making a living doing work that you love.
- Multimedia is a generalist's art, but good specialists are always in demand, both by producers and employers.

The biggest question that everyone asks of multimedia is, "Yeah, but how do you make money?" Although good answers to that question are more sporadic than you might hope, better answers exist for the second most frequent question: "How do I get a job in multimedia?" As with many exploding industries, much work is available in the multimedia business, perhaps more work than money. But if money were all you were interested in, you'd be reading a book about Wall Street, right?

Developing CD-ROMs, Web sites, and other interactive media is a team sport. Although a sole creator can come up with a fully realized project, more typically, no one person develops a full-scale interactive title. Individual expertise matters, and personal career growth matters, but this kind of work forces those kinds of issues into the background. The fun, and the reason that everyone's working so hard, is to make multimedia magic.

This chapter provides a comprehensive overview of careers and career development in the multimedia fields. It begins with an overview of the opportunities, including how to prepare yourself for a career in multimedia, and how to determine where you want to work and what you want your job to be. Then, the chapter looks at the individual departments involved in multimedia and Web production. This chapter also follows typical career paths common to the following:

✦ Artists and designers

✦ Software engineers and programmers

✦ Editors, writers, content experts

✦ Musicians, project managers, and other production personnel

✦ Managers and executives

These career paths describe available jobs and the routes to and from these jobs. The chapter's mid-section deals with finding the right job, résumés, portfolios, interviewing, salary negotiations, and other topics related to finding and landing a specific job. Finally, the chapter addresses the choices faced by most career professionals, such as moving up the management ladder vs. forming a new company. If you're serious about forming your own company, you'll find information on that topic in the next chapter.

Do Your Homework

Before you even consider a career in multimedia, before you make the first phone call, and before you write one word on your résumé, you must do your homework.

People who work in multimedia are motivated. They enjoy working at the cutting edge of technology, and they enjoy the workplace camaraderie of other professionals who are interested in building the future. To communicate on a professional basis with these people, you should be fascinated with the rapid developments in Web and multimedia technology, and you should be up-to-date. To keep current, you must develop and maintain a working knowledge of the hardware, software, and infrastructure development that makes new media such an exciting field.

Nobody expects you to know what's inside every shrink-wrapped CD-ROM. They will expect you to know what a *Living Book* is, what *DOOM* is, what some of the other popular titles are, how new developments like Shockwave and Java are likely to change Web-based communication, and where the business seems to be going. You can do this most effectively by visiting important sites on the Web such as *c|net*, by checking out Cool sites on Yahoo! and other Web browsers, and by attending conventions such as the annual E3 show held each May. Most cities support local multimedia users groups; if you attend their monthly meetings, you'll see demos. If you're just starting out, you might be able to get a job at a store that specializes in software. The task of keeping current might not be the most creatively satisfying, but you might get to see and try lots of software. Of course, consumer magazines cover the most interesting titles. A subscription to *Family PC, Computer Life, MacUser, MacWorld, PC* magazine, and any number of Internet magazines will help you track the latest news and the latest products. The annual *Newsweek Editor's Choice Awards* CD-ROM disc is a good source of demos for children's titles. If you poke around online, you'll find plenty of demos— small versions of CD-ROM products that you can use for free on your home computer.

The best way to become familiar with technologies, trends, and actual job openings is to read the trade magazines. *Inter@ctive Age* is a weekly trade magazine that covers the Web and related developments; this magazine is free to qualified subscribers (you fill out a survey and the publisher determines whether you would be of interest to advertisers). If you don't qualify for a subscription on your own, a friend may be able to supply back issues. Monthly subscription magazines of note include *Multimedia Producer*, *Interactivity*, and *New Media*. On America Online, use the keyword "SIMBA" to see daily news about the media and new technologies.

No shortage of books about computer topics is encountered. Whether the subject is Java or Shockwave, C++ or Director, you will find books written for every level of expertise at any well-stocked bookstore. If you're lacking in technical expertise, books provide the right kind of education. Most new computer books are filled with illustrations and examples, and many come with a CD-ROM that contains demos of sample products that utilize a particular technology.

Knowing what's happening on the Web is also important. This knowledge is best obtained by spending hours surfing, checking out the most interesting sites. Cool sites are identified in special listings on Yahoo!, but the best way to find the most-talked-about sites is to explore on your own. You'll find a great many sites that seem to exist for no reason other than to point to other sites of interest. This pastime can occupy days, or even weeks; to keep up, you really need to spend at least an hour a day just surfing. Fortunately, there's no shortage of news coverage about Web sites. Many daily newspapers and monthly magazines now publish information about interesting Web sites. Other people are a great source; everyone in this industry shares information about cool Web sites. When you find someone who seems to know what he or she is talking about, jot down the URLs of every promising site; keep a list in your Wizard or your Day Runner or on paper, if you insist on being fashionably low-tech. When you find an interesting site, send an e-mail to other people who might care about it, too. Encourage friends and business associates to do the same for you.

At first, the amount of effort expended to stay current may seem like an overwhelming amount of work. The hope that this overwhelming feeling eventually goes away will not come true. Keeping up with current trends takes a lot of time and energy. If you're genuinely interested in this new medium, you will find the time to stay current. If you find yourself less than fascinated by what you're reading or learning, then you might consider another line of work. Consider this carefully — multimedia is a fast-paced, competitive business that requires outrageous amounts of time and dedication. If you're just not into it, find something else to do with your time.

One final note that might make you feel a little better about that overwhelmed feeling is that such an emotion is perfectly normal. Nobody in this business really has the time to follow every trend, explore every Web page, and read every magazine. Simply put, multimedia is so multifaceted as to prove almost impossible for one person to be completely fluent in every aspect of it. Do the best you can, ask lots of questions, help others get started, take time at home to explore Web sites, and try out friends' CD-ROMs. These efforts are all the right steps. Ultimately, your knowledge of things cyber is not the determining factor in career success. Your enthusiasm, your pleasant personality, your ability to get things done, and your ease in working as part of a team will be the determining factors. These reasons are why media people succeed.

Start by Learning about the Job

Before you start looking for a job, identify two or three people who have a job that you honestly believe you could do. Write a letter to each of them, requesting a half-hour meeting. Make your intent clear that you are not requesting a job interview. Instead, you want to know what they do on their job, how they spend their time, what parts of the job they do and don't like, and where they see the job and the business going.

What you are doing is called an "informational interview," a technique made popular by Richard Bolles in his essential guide to career development, *What Color Is Your Parachute?* (Ten Speed Press, updated annually). For a time, informational interviewing was so popular that people in popular jobs hated to hear the words "informational interview." The attitudes toward these informal interviews has mellowed, and if you politely ask for the interview during a slower part of the production cycle, you are likely to be granted the interview. Buying lunch always helps.

The best way to ask for the interview is by mail. Send a brief, pleasant letter explaining what you want to know, and why. E-mails can be tricky. Many busy people are overwhelmed by e-mails, and if your e-mail happens to arrive on the same in-box list as 79 others, it might get a quick "no." On the other hand, e-mail is quick, efficient, and demonstrates that you know how to communicate in the multimedia world. Faxes, however, are an inappropriate way to request information. A fax demands immediate attention. If the fax does not contain something of immediate interest to the recipient, then it is likely to be tossed.

Before the meeting, do some planning. Prepare a list of questions in a logical, reasonable order. Use these questions as a guide and checklist, not as a script.

If you just ask question after question, you will get some pat answers, but you'll never really establish communications, and you won't make much of an impression. You also won't hear what's unsaid; connotation carries a lot of meaning, and interrogation almost always obscures connotation. You're seeking deeper information. You also want to know the real stories: how this person got her job, whether she intends to continue on her current path, and what she would consider to be a reasonable next job. You will not get these answers without first developing rapport. Your challenge is to develop the formal conversation into a give-and-take session that results in this kind of conversation. In other words, you can't just sit back and listen. You must take an active part in the conversation, showing that you are sincerely interested in what your potential mentor has to say about herself, her business, her industry, and the world at large. Take notes. Don't ask to record the conversation; most people will not be candid if there's a tape recorder in the room.

As you're asking questions, consider the medium. Do you want to work in: fixed media, such as CD-ROMs; or online, perhaps designing Web sites; or in a more public forum, such as interactive exhibits? At this moment, Web sites are the most prominent aspect of interactive computing. Last year, the buzz was on CD-ROMs, and that buzz might return as higher-capacity CDs go into production. It's wise to gain experience in several domains; this world changes quickly, and you don't want to be pigeon-holed. Use your informational interviewing to evaluate your options.

When the interview is done, *avoid the temptation* to ask for a job. Don't go anywhere near, "Are there any openings around here?" Such a query breaches the intent of the meeting and the nature of the relationship. You said you were coming in to learn about the job. Stick with your promise.

That night, and no later than the following morning, send a brief thank-you note. Again, just thank the person for the time and personal attention. Do not suggest that you will contact the person for a job, or for contacts, at some time in the future. Just say "thank you."

Looking for work is something most people don't do very effectively. Instead of actively searching for a job that will satisfy their personal creative needs, many people settle into a job that pays a salary but doesn't move the career ahead. The "what you want to do" part breaks down, rather tidily, into a few components: the kind of medium, the kind of company, and the kind of job.

Learn About Companies

When you have a sense of what you want to do, you need to determine where you want to do it. There are two parts to this question. You need to determine something about the type of company and the type of culture that makes sense for you, your personality, and the way you prefer to interact with people. Then, you need to determine the region or city where you are most likely to feel comfortable, and where you are most likely to succeed.

Most multimedia companies employ fewer than 100 people, and many employ only a dozen or so. Newer companies are often fun, free-form environments without the standard work cubicles, policies, and structures that more mature companies seem to adopt regardless of their roots. Some people find this informality ideal, but others find the lack of structure (and the long, long hours often associated with this environment) frustrating.

Larger companies are involved in multimedia, of course, but most often as a sideline. Many magazines and direct marketing operations, for example, have one or two people in charge of a Web operation. Most large corporations employ a staff of media specialists, sometimes as an extension of a corporate video or corporate communications function. Few large companies operate with multimedia at their center. The exceptions are companies that specialize in games, such as SEGA, and in application software, such as Microsoft.

The company's culture is terribly important, but its culture is not easy to understand unless you spend time with the people on a daily basis. Internships are the very best way to do this: you are working, but without any real long-term commitment. Freelance and temporary work is another approach, certainly more suitable for those who are already in the workforce. Again, the best way to learn what's right for you is to try to spend time working at your company of choice.

Although this plan may seem unlikely, it's actually a pretty reasonable approach. Offer your services for free. That's right — offer to work at no charge as a kind of intern. Most companies, especially smaller ones who aren't yet bound by employee policies, will welcome the extra help.

A larger company will probably be harder to crack. One way to get involved with a big company is to befriend a busy multimedia producer and simply make the offer. If the producer is resourceful, likes you, and is need of help, you could score a small-scale freelance assignment. Another way to get in is to find a big company racing to make a deadline on a big project. Extra hands are often welcome.

Working part-time or as an intern may not assure future employment, but it can increase your odds. The more people you know, the greater the likelihood that someone will call you when a job is open. If you're not currently working, or if you're a student with some free time, internships and no-pay work are both good ways to get started, make friends, and learn something about the places you might work someday.

What you learn about a company this year may turn out to be quite different from next year's reality. Multimedia is not a stable business. Multimedia changes often. The best way to keep up with these big changes is to read the business section of the important multimedia newspapers such as the *San Francisco Chronicle,* the *New York Times* (on Mondays), or the *San Jose Mercury News* (also see their Web sites: `www.nytimes.com and www.sjmercury.com`). The Web site for the trade magazine's *Inter@ctive Week's* is also a good source of current information (`www.zdnet.com/intweek`). Most of the information is generated by the companies themselves, so it's shaped for media consumption.

A Look at Career Paths in Multimedia

Although the computer software business is about twenty years old (longer still, depending upon how you count), the current structure of the multimedia business is fairly new, and in the case of the Web, it's still taking shape.

This part of the chapter is organized by department: art and design; technical and programming; content and editorial; production; project management; and management and executive. Admittedly, you will notice overlap. This overlap should encourage artists to read the technical sections, managers to read the design section, and so forth. Each section starts from the beginning with the positions lower on the multimedia totem pole. The sections then work up to slots that offer a better view and more money, but, often, less hands-on involvement in the creative elements.

A Typical Career Path in Art and Design

Although the multimedia business is relatively new, art and design schools have been extremely attentive to new media. As a result, many of the better design schools are also accomplished in new media design.

Art school and internships

Natural ability, talent, a good eye, and dependable work habits are essential to the success of any working artist. A good education can complement these virtues, providing a young artist with a superior design sense, a better understanding of typography, an improved sensitivity to the effect of color, and a wide-ranging introduction to styles and techniques. The basic training at a respected art/design school, such as the Pratt Institute or the Parsons School of Design (among many others), also provides a young artist with a deep sense of community shared with other people whose talent is just beginning to emerge. Students who attend the better art schools tend to develop a strong network of working artists and art directors: a network of contacts for freelance assignments and longer-term career advice, recommendations, and references. Will a better school make you a better artist? Do the best artists attend the best schools? Such blanket statements are difficult to make, but an impressive number of high-visibility artists are alumni of the best schools.

The years in art school are devoted to technique, and deeper understanding and appreciation. In practical and professional terms, those years are most immediately useful because the classroom output can be packaged as a first portfolio. The good news here is that assignments are generally varied, forcing the artist into a variety of projects that he or she might not have otherwise attempted. The bad news is that a student portfolio almost always looks like a student portfolio. Still, a student portfolio is a start, and you can begin replacing student work as soon as you get your first job.

Demand for screen artists and extra hands in the multimedia process is great, particularly in the San Francisco Bay area, New York City, and other multimedia centers. Many companies employ interns — some pay very little, some pay nothing, and some pay expenses. Every serious design student should try to arrange several internships over the course of a college education. Although the temptation to intern only at multimedia and Web firms may be great, much can be said for an internship at a package goods firm and another at a print magazine. What you learn in one situation will almost certainly transfer, perhaps in some unexpected way, into another domain. While you're in school, take the time to experiment. You might even decide that you like package design better than multimedia! (Hey, you won't know unless you try.)

Regardless of the internship site, interns rarely get the opportunity to design at the macro scale. Instead, they focus on menial tasks. However, a great deal can be learned by simply hanging around a professional environment and picking up tasks as needed, even when the tasks require minimal (if any) real creativity. The informal structure that you may find at a smaller company may also allow you, as an intern, to take on larger tasks. To put this another way, if you intern at Pixar, you probably won't be asked to design for *Toy Story, Part Two*. The point to remember is that a multimedia internship offers a serious introduction to the technical and production sides of the business.

If you select the target companies carefully, arranging an internship is not difficult. Large, high-visibility companies are frequently overwhelmed with internship requests, but the multimedia business is dominated by small companies with big projects and big ideas. The trick is to find them, and this is easily done by reading the multimedia trade magazines, as well as the art and design magazines such as *HOW* (1507 Dana Ave., Cincinnati, OH 45207) and *Computer Pictures* (701 Westchester Ave., White Plains, NY 10604).

A final note on internships: an internship will be your first professional experience. You will meet other people who are starting their careers. The ones who continue in multimedia will probably contact you early in your career as they become involved in new projects and new companies. More senior people are constantly moving from one company or project to another and are often in need of staff. Take the internship(s) seriously. The people you meet during a few college internships could keep you working for the next five or ten years.

Just out of school: where to find work

Finding a job is difficult for everyone, and in the creative professions, the search can be daunting. The process requires a high level of confidence in yourself and your abilities, a thick skin, perseverance, and the maintenance of a high standard for your work and where you intend to have it seen.

This scenario is much, much easier to bear if you are not desperate for cash, which is an unfortunate Catch-22. Living at home is one way to avoid accepting just any job because you need the money. Freelancing is another: you can work on projects on nights, weekends, and in-between times while you concentrate on finding work during regular business hours. Working part-time is a reasonable idea, but part-time work really should be directly related to your career. If you lose time working in a retail store or restaurant through your early years, you'll probably find it difficult to catch up later on. Stick with the job search and hold on to the dream of becoming a designer. Seek out friends in similar situations and share ideas (and miseries and horror stories about awful interviews, dreadful companies, jobs you should have gotten but didn't, and so on.). Find whatever freelance work you can, and pursue the job search for twenty, thirty, or even forty hours weekly until you find what you want. Don't give up. This credo is important enough to say again. Don't give up. Just keep reading!

Working as a design assistant

If you are just out of school, you're likely to do whatever work is assigned. Most newcomers simply "help" — converting files, in-betweening on animations, fixing color errors, downloading images from a database, creating backgrounds, manipulating type, or manufacturing buttons. Over the course of even a single project, however, production needs often change. A novice who can illustrate, for example, may well find himself or herself creating a large number of illustrations by the time the project is complete.

Life as a design assistant should be looked upon as an opportunity to learn. Education should go beyond the basic skills required for the task at hand. At first, learning the basics is best, including software, or operating different kinds of hardware, such as scanners, platforms, capture boards, and so on. When these basics come naturally, then learn more about jobs done by other people. Learn about production management processes, about how procedures are built and tweaked, and about how one department interacts with another. If you're good, this education should take about six to nine months.

One of the more ideal situations for a young designer is a busy shop. Look for a shop that hires plenty of freelancers and always seems to be slightly over capacity. Take note of how quickly designers have moved from entry-level jobs to more meaningful responsibilities. If you're talented, willing to work hard, and don't make people uncomfortable with nasty habits or bad behavior, you can move up quickly. In some cases, you can progress very quickly. By the one-year mark, you should have demonstrated a high level of competence in one or several areas. These areas might include interface design, typography, clever use of existing art and photos, and so forth. Each is a step toward an designer slot.

Working as a designer

A designer is a working artist. He or she is responsible for the on-screen design of pages, screens, buttons, logos, and other visual treatments. Designers typically work on full projects, with more or less complete responsibility for the details of the work. The art director, described later, maintains the higher-level view.

Most CD-ROM and large-scale multimedia projects depend upon visualization, so the designer is often a senior member of the development team. Most designers quickly learn that design is not well understood by other members of the team, and find themselves teaching the fundamentals of good design, color, typography, and others. Some people on the team will "get it," but others will simply nod and act as though they understand. Appreciating good design is not something that comes to most people naturally. Most people miss the fine points. Michael Pinto of NYC's Vanguard Media, a multimedia design firm, explains, "An icon on a button is not a logo and it's not an illustration. It's just a picture that helps you to understand what happens when you press the button." Pinto has developed this explanation after many meetings with people who want to put a complicated illustration into the tiny space allotted to a button.

In multimedia, a designer must have a working knowledge of technical details. Plenty of work is done at odd hours when the technical person with the answers may not be available, because perhaps that person is asleep for the night. Waiting until the next day is rarely an option. Multimedia deadlines come up fast, and, because of the number of dependent steps in a project, no one can miss a step or slow down the process.

Most working hours are spent at the screen, grinding out work. Some time is spent planning, and a great deal of time is spent reworking art that needed to be changed. These changes may be necessary because of insufficient interdepartmental communication, modifications in the project, deadlines that require the project to be simplified, or random creative ideas that someone in power latches onto when it's far too late to be thinking about such things. Changes can be frustrating, particularly when facing tight deadlines and when staff and other resources are limited; however, they are a reality. How the designer faces these problems and deals with them may have a greater impact on future work with other team members than the quality of the art itself. Given two designers of comparable talent, the one with the superior people skills will get the job every time. In fact, most producers are willing to give up some creative quality in exchange for some sanity during a tough production cycle.

To put this another way, a good designer must possess a combination of design skills and people skills. The design skills are evident in the finished product. The people skills are reflected in the attitude of the staff members and their willingness to work together in the future.

In this business, long hours are a reality. Many designers achieve the balance between long hours required for these tasks and some sort of personal life. Others become workhorses.

A workhorse is someone who puts out tons of material and dependably gets the job done, regardless of the hours and personal sacrifices involved. Danger is involved in such a situation. The workhorse who comes to the office every weekend can get the job done correctly, but this pattern can quickly become the normal course of events. This person's long hours become essential to the process. The workhorse often hands in an assignment of a superior effort because it's been done without a zillion interruptions, a natural consequence of working off-hours. In the course of such dedicated effort, the workhorse unfortunately misses out on the interpersonal relationships that are part of every project and venture. One possible side effect can surface when the managers are considering people for advancement: the workhorse may be passed over. Someone else (sometimes less qualified or talented, for example) becomes assistant art director. The workhorse remains a workhorse while others move ahead, despite the fact that they haven't worked nearly as hard or contributed as much!

The morals of this story:

- ✦ Don't work too hard (just kidding).
- ✦ Work really hard and get the work done, but remember that relationships are as important as the work itself. Having a life is even more important than work.

Working as an art director

The art director manages the design department. Working in tandem with the producer, he or she typically sets the vision, hires the artists, works out the storyboards, and assigns the work to individual designers. Because most art directors are former designers, these processes are often comfortable and familiar.

The supervision of designers, however, may be unfamiliar. In fact, an art director will often experience difficulty in supervising the work of a designer without imposing his or her personal style. A designer should be more than a pair of hands that executes the art director's work. An art director should also do more than set an overall vision and walk away until the project is complete.

People skills are vital to such situations, often in a major way. A designer, who has essentially worked with a screen every day for years, may encounter difficulty in moving away from that task into one in which people, not images, are the primary concern. With a good art director as a model or mentor, many designers make the transition with relative ease. Some people never make the transition, either by their own decision or because they lack the necessary people skills to manage others effectively.

The title of art director is meaningful, as are the credentials and the money. If you are considering a career transition in that direction, focus on the people skills. Take courses and read books about employee management. Spend time at other studios, and watch successful art directors do their work. Befriend art directors in other media businesses such as advertising, package design, and television, and you'll find that their issues are similar.

Working as a creative director

Although an art director generally takes responsibility for a single project, a creative director's responsibility is frequently more wide-ranging, taking charge of multiple projects or the company's entire creative output.

Whereas sheer talent and people skills are the stock-in-trade of designers and art directors, the creative director often operates at a higher level. A creative director may be hired for one of two reasons. Trust is usually the major reason: the firm can trust the creative director to make the project happen on time, on budget, and with a creative flair. Talent is the other, and this is the intangible reason. A company might hire a new creative director to "make magic," always a dangerous expectation.

Contrary to the implications that this title and hierarchy convey, a creative director is not necessarily someone who has been an designer and an art director. The term is borrowed from advertising, in which a creative director supervises both artists and writers. Management prowess, not creative skills, may be the key component on the creative director's résumé.

Unlike the art director, whose time is spent managing lower organizational levels, the creative director may spend as much, or more, time managing a cross-section of the organization as well as senior management. Everything that goes into a multimedia project requires some visualization, so the design team is often affected by many departments. The creative director is the person who makes these interdepartmental relationships work.

Moving further up the ladder

With so much exposure to other aspects of multimedia production, many designers, art directors, and creative directors have crossed departmental lines and joined the production team. Many producers have found their design backgrounds to be very useful. Consequently, in some companies, design has become something of a training ground for producers and other production personnel. Another interesting development has begun to take shape. Creative people, now recognized to be the core of some cyberbusinesses, are carving out a new kind of senior management role. This role is titled chief creative officer. In a handful of companies, working alongside the chief technical officer (CTO), chief executive officer (CEO), chief information officer (CIO), or chief operating officer (COO), you'll find a CCO, too. The hope is that this trend gains momentum!

A Typical Technical Career Path

Despite their great numbers, good programmers, software engineers, and software architects are always in short supply. There are many, many opportunities for clever, fresh-thinking programmers, and not just in the Silicon Valley.

Many programmers start with a hobby in high school. The impetus may be a high school course or time spent with a friend who knows how to program, or, more often than not, sitting down at the computer and learning on your own. Many programmers are self-taught, but few learned without help. For many, a series of books provides the necessary education.

A serious programmer typically pursues a degree in computer science, engineering, mathematics, or a similar field. A minor in a content-oriented liberal arts field such as film, television, journalism, education, or English can be an asset. Coursework or a minor in design, marketing, or business can also expand the value of a résumé, and provide some basis for understanding how and why other departments work. These courses may also prove useful as the programmer seeks new challenges beyond programming. This preparation for an unknown, and often unforeseen, future can prove enormously useful.

Technology and programming languages change very quickly. During a four-year college experience, the entire world of computing can change several times. College is the time to become proficient as a programmer, but the majority of courses should not be devoted to learning how to program. You can learn this skill on your own or by working as part of a team. Instead, college should teach you to concentrate on the discipline and structure of learning, the basics of how languages function, and the fundamentals of a variety of common languages.

A broad-based college education is essential because the industry changes so much faster than the curriculum. Also, the teachers who manage that curriculum are often out of the mainstream because they spend their time teaching, not writing cutting-edge code. Ultimately, college is not about learning how to program at all; it's about the maturity and the refined thinking that a superior college education can provide. A college experience can also provide a network of potential future contacts and the opportunities for mentors and internships, even for the genius programmer who can earn a respectable livelihood at age 17. Learning as much programming as possible throughout this period is supposed to be the cake, but is often just the icing.

Unlike designers and production personnel, new programmers can start their careers by either being paid for projects, or by working as interns for top-notch firms. These specialized internships are not easily arranged, and there is competition for slots at the best companies. Working on an innovative project or learning from a top-notch team, are significant reasons to choose an internship, perhaps over paid programming work, during the early stages of your career.

Try to start working part-time while you're still in school. Part-time and project work can be found via networking and by answering advertisements. A regular search through message boards on AOL, CompuServe, newsgroups, and Web sites usually results in a list of opportunities, full-time and freelance, from all over the country. Visits with local firms, particularly those who specialize in multimedia and Web applications, can also result in part-time and project work.

Working as an assistant programmer

Large programming projects are often broken into smaller components. The senior software engineer, or senior programmer, writes much of the code but depends upon contributors to write certain sections of the overall application. These tasks are typically handed to lower-level programmers. This organizational structure frees the programmer's time for more important tasks while training the next generation of talent.

Becoming a programmer or software engineer

Even within a sophisticated organization, the day-to-day work of a programmer is, to nontechnical types, akin to alchemy. Of course, within the software community, the tasks are not only comprehensible, they can become routine. Most programmers enter the software business in general, and the multimedia business specifically, because of the inherent creative challenges. In today's world, these challenges are rarely handled personally by individual "genius" programmers. One person may serve as project architect, but the bulk of the work is done by teams of programmers who attack specific aspects of a project.

Often with schedules that are both unreasonable and aligned with marketing decisions that may seem incomprehensible to the working programmer, the teams move toward milestones on a project manager's chart through long hours, weekends, and too many late nights. The programmer must succeed not only with workable code, but also with code that both meshes with the work of other team members, and that operates quickly and efficiently, even on the most mundane hardware. This need to succeed often results in exceedingly long work days and extreme pressure; regardless, a great deal of thoughtful patience is required as elusive errors manifest themselves in unexpected ways.

Many multimedia programming tasks are large-scale and complex. Management of the process is often handled, therefore, by a professional project manager and/or a manager of software development. This person manages the complexities of the software's component parts while dealing with interdepartmental concerns.

Working as a senior programmer

The main difference between a programmer and a senior programmer is perspective. A programmer works on specific tasks: parts of programs that must interact successfully with other components. A senior programmer sees the project from a different perspective, focusing not so much on individual components, but rather upon the integration of components. A senior programmer is also expected to take on the large challenges, to set the most promising course for the most difficult pieces of the program, and sometimes to write the code for these components. In addition, most senior programmers write or rewrite code, often under harsh deadlines, that other members of the team did not do properly, or were unable to do properly because of changes in the deliverable.

Although some people work their way up through the ranks to the level of senior programmer, others possess the magical combination of talent and sheer ability that propels them past the crowd. “Awe” and “resentment” are two of the many words that programmers use to describe their feelings toward fast-moving senior programmers. Personality plays a big role here, and so does the senior programmer’s ability to deliver on promises.

Working as a senior software engineer/ senior software architect

Different companies hire programmers with different titles. A senior programmer at one company may have the responsibilities associated with software architecture. However, a senior software architect at another company may, in fact, have less impact on the overall project and how it is completed, instead offering a technical “guru” perspective. Clearly, in the best of circumstances, the senior software engineer or architect is responsible for planning the programming project and for supervising its construction.

A Typical Content or Editorial Career Path

For its first twenty years, the computer software business was dominated by technical people, such as programmers. Some programmers developed games which were sold to other computer-savvy amateurs. The consumer software business began in the early 1980s, and after a few false starts, started to assume its present, more mainstream form later in the decade.

In that beginning, most software products were application programs, such as word processors, database managers, and spreadsheets. Some were strategy, action, and role-playing games. Some games were based on editorial content. *Where in the World Is Carmen Sandiego?,* published by Broderbund, was an early example; players answered multiple-choice questions about geography in order to catch an elusive criminal. MECC's *Oregon Trail* is another early example; players managed limited resources in order to make their way across the wilderness. In time, Grolier published its first CD-ROM encyclopedia, CompuServe and America Online began to add content in large amounts, and people began to think of the computer as a kind of information appliance.

In the broad context of the computer industry, content remains a relatively new addition. Few individuals possess deep, long-term credentials in the development and production of content for digital media, but this situation is changing. In the past two years, Web sites have become a significant training ground for content editors, writers, and online journalists in which to explore new editorial territory. Although this territory will eventually contain truly interactive content, most online content is currently "static" — re-purposed magazine or newspaper articles available through keyword searches or various types of menus. Also, much of the current content on the Web is promotional in nature, not entertainment nor journalism in the traditional sense. As those with Web sites figure out how to make money (most are still experimenting with shaky combinations of advertising and subscription revenues), Web journalism will mature, with luck, will result in fascinating new ventures that nourish the next generation of writers, editors, and other journalists.

Working as a researcher

One of the best ways to learn about multimedia content is to provide services as a researcher or fact-checker. An ideal role for those making the transition from print media, fact-checking is firmly grounded in traditional media, yet it's very much a part of new media.

What kinds of projects might be assigned to a multimedia researcher? No one answer is standard; the range could extend from something mundane to research projects of Herculean proportions. The following list includes a sampling of possible projects:

- ✦ Identify twenty Greek gods and explain their roles in language that children would understand.
- ✦ Find at least five hundred photographs or paintings of American Indians at work and play, and write a description for each.

✦ Scour every available archive and private collection in search of visuals on a famous jazz musician; secure clearances so that these images can be used on a CD-ROM and a Web site.

The actual work varies from one project to another, but most research tasks fall into these categories: find and clear art work, footage, or sound; dig through books and other reference materials to provide raw material for a writer's script; and check facts in an existing script or one that's currently being written. If this job doesn't sound easy, that's because it isn't. However, research is a great place to start out.

Becoming a Content Expert

Many content experts have combined their deep understanding of a particular subject with a significant professional involvement in new media. The situation is quite common in children's software, in which educators have traditionally experimented with every new medium in order to reach new generations of children.

Jan Davidson is the president and founder of Davidson & Associates, a leading publisher of children's educational software. She started her career as a teacher and then founded a nonprofit educational tutoring service. At that company, Davidson realized that computers could be valuable learning tools for students. This was in the early 1980s, the beginning of the children's software industry. The details may vary, but this kind of scenario plays out time and again. A teacher, or another content expert, sees the potential in new media and moves from one career to another. Davidson is a market leader, one who's helping to change the way that children learn to read. In her own way, Jan Davidson is still teaching, although no longer based in the classroom.

Working as a multimedia writer

Writers have been involved in creating digital content for well over twenty years: devising scenarios, writing text adventures, creating questions for trivia games, and developing characters for children's products, as well as the production of role playing games, corporate training tools, health and medical instruction, among others. The role of the writer continues to expand. Writers now play a significant role in many software titles and on every Web page. Interactive storytelling may redefine the writer's role in new media as video, animation, and similar forms offer greater potential for visualization and interactivity.

Writing is more art than craft, but you can teach yourself a great deal by simply writing on your own. Keep a journal. Write articles for small local newspapers; write book reviews for a newsletter; write letters to friends. Find every conceivable reason to express thoughts and ideas in words. The media, the frequency, and the time spent may vary, but writers learn how to write by writing. If you write more often, you will definitely become a better writer.

College is a good training ground. Coursework in English or journalism can be supplemented by work at the college newspaper: preferably, both writing and editing, so that you can work with other writers' material. Most colleges sponsor student Web pages, offering direct, hands-on involvement with a medium that offers a worldwide audience.

Early in your writing career, focus on the basics: paragraphs that organize ideas into reasonable spaces; sentences that are action packed and neither too long nor too short; words that accurately convey intended meaning; techniques that improve clarity and mood; story structure; character development; and dialogue that sounds real and helps to build understanding of character. A great deal can be learned by writing, and rewriting, and rewriting again, preferably with the guidance of a skillful writing teacher and a peer group of promising writers, if possible. Time spent reading and analyzing the work of different kinds of writers is also meaningful. At this stage, don't worry too much about interactive storytelling, unless it happens to be a form that you really enjoy.

In college or after, a writer's group can help to sharpen your skills. Most cities and towns support at least one writer's group. These groups usually meet once a month, allowing members sufficient time to write and rewrite before each meeting. Members share their work, comment, criticize, and provide emotional support. If you're a working nonfiction writer with an interest in storytelling, a writer's group may be the right kind of bridge to new work.

You might also attend a writer's workshop. This is a more formal gathering of "wannabe" writers, some published writers, and, sometimes, editors and agents. The idea behind attending a workshop is to meet other writers, share experiences, attend classes, and offer your work for critique.

One way to learn to write, or to learn to write more skillfully, is to read the work of others. Other writers are your best source of material. Reading books about writing is also a step in the right direction. Some suggested titles include *On Writing Well* by William Zinsser, *The Writing Life* by Anne Dillard, and the broad range of writing how-to titles published by Writer's Digest Books. You'll find a shelf or two filled with writing how-to books at most bookstores. Some writers also find the magazine *Writer's Digest* helpful; it's available at well-stocked newsstands.

After you've mastered the basics, you need to know more about multimedia writing. Fortunately, this is an easy area to study. Exploring Web sites doesn't cost much. For 20 dollars a month, you can spend an unlimited amount of time on the Web. If money is a problem, just subscribe for a month or two, or glom onto a friend's account, offering to pay for telephone charges. Although you may find vast numbers of interesting sites, for this exercise, you should concentrate on sites that feature good writing for this interactive medium. Sites with repurposed print content may contain good writing, but these won't teach you much about new media. Look at the original stories written for the Web, and look at e-zine sites, which are sites built as Web magazines, typically without print counterparts.

On the CD-ROM side, study magazine reviews for information about the latest story titles. If you can't afford to buy the magazines regularly, do the research in local stores that rent CD-ROMs. You can also get in touch with the editor of every computer and game magazine on the newsstand, and offer your services as a reviewer. If you can establish yourself as a writer of reviews, some publishers will send you every product they release. Other publishers will send you press releases with the name and number of a contact person who will send you individual titles upon request. Reviewing titles is one of the very best ways to learn about titles, and about the industry.

Of course, most people don't go to this extent of effort. Instead, they may network, or respond to the occasional advertisement, or send sample material that may or may not get read by the right person for the right project; somehow, these people will find the right opportunities. Nobody's quite sure how or why this approach works, but things do happen. The random factor leaves plenty of free time to think, pursue other interests, and wonder how you're going to pay the rent.

Working as a multimedia musician

Music and sound effects are significant components on CD-ROMs, but music and sound effects in the online environment are a few steps behind. This lag has already started to change, in fact, with the addition of Real Audio and other innovations.

Music is more than central to some CD-ROMs. *Pete Townsend Presents Tommy, The Interactive Adventure Then and Now* (published by Interplay for Windows; MacPlay for Macintosh), *The Residents' Freak Show* (published by Voyager), and *XPLORA1: Peter Gabriel's Secret World* (Interplay/MacPlay) are very different from one another. Each is an exploration of the CD-ROM as a rock medium. Microsoft's Musical Instruments is an encyclopedia of instruments from around the world. The same publisher has experimented with symphonies; the scores of these works appear on the computer screen in synchronization with the music. Most CD-ROMs use music as a kind of audio wallpaper, appropriate to the overall design, yet none too prominent. Much of the music heard on CD-ROMs comes from music libraries that produce and license music in bulk. The producer pays a very low fee for use of the music library.

Original music allows more creative flexibility, an audio track that is more ideally suited to the visuals and the interactivity, and in the end, a better product.

When original music is composed, performed, and produced for a CD-ROM or another electronic media presentation, all of the work is usually done by one person working in a small studio. The composer/musician/producer is paid a flat fee for unlimited use of the music, and typically the sound effects that accompany each button click as well. Musicians who work in these situations typically produce music for television, radio, commercials, and other media. Some setups are quite modest — little more than a keyboard and a digital recorder. Others are far more complex, with huge racks of MIDI equipment and enough hardware to make even the most wizened programmer jealous.

A great deal of work is also done by small music production firms. Most medium-sized cities support several such firms. These companies stay afloat by producing music for commercials, corporate events, interactive media, and just about anything else that comes their way. Jobs at these companies are often hard to find; the workload is sufficient for the owners and a small staff, but not for many extra hands. Larger cities such as New York, Chicago, Boston, San Francisco, and Los Angeles support more music production firms, including some larger ones where apprentice and staff jobs become available from time to time. Commercial work and corporate work provide the revenues. Interactive media typically contributes a small percentage of the work.

The career path for a musician or composer is not at all straightforward. The best way to learn the craft is to intern, apprentice, or simply hang around a studio where this work is being done. Another way to learn is to do a small project on your own, or to work in a more traditional production role and simply offer to "do the music" on your own time at home. In time, the work should come, but interactive media will not, in all likelihood, support you. You can expand your focus to other kinds of music work, which leads toward musical direction for larger projects, perhaps in advertising, TV, or film. Alternatively, you can focus on interactive production work, becoming a producer or another senior member of the team, offering to package music as part of your range of services.

Working as a production assistant

One of the most common routes into the multimedia production business is a short-term, low-paying job as a production assistant. The role here, as the title suggests, is to assist the producers, the associate producers, and other production personnel. The actual work ranges from fact-checking to making copies (on paper, or copying files) to distributing files and other information. Other responsibilities could include making phone calls on Sunday afternoon at 4:30 p.m. to locate a store willing to stay open past 5:00 p.m. that sells a 2GB drive, taking food orders, and researching photos from a database. Some production assistants are assigned to specific people: a project manager, for example. Other production assistants are available, as a kind of pool, for any task that might come up.

Although some of the labor is truly menial, the work is done in exchange for the opportunity to learn. Just by hanging around a busy production site, a good production assistant will find the right things to do, and will be helpful and get noticed at the same time. Ingratiate yourself so that you will become part of the team, and so that you will be hired for the next project, perhaps in a more significant role.

Talented production assistants are always difficult to find. When an associate producer or producer finds a dependable, bright, hard-working production assistant, he or she keeps the name around, either for his or her own use, or for recommendations to friends who are building staffs. Time spent as a production assistant is a great investment in future relationships.

Working as an associate producer

The associate producer occupies the important space between the production assistant and the producer. The difficult aspects of production are accomplished by this position: the planning, the details, and the coordination. The associate producer's job varies with every project, but the ability to manage details is a constant throughout almost every project.

The role of associate producer is neither an entry-level position nor a permanent stopping place. If the associate producer role does not lead to producer, for whatever reasons, then the next step is either a parallel move (perhaps to production management, or to another department, such as marketing), or a move to another part of the industry or to another industry entirely.

Working as a production coordinator

Similar to movies and television, the multimedia business is famous for inventing titles to suit particular situations. The title of production coordinator sounds like such an invention. In some companies, this might be the case because the title more or less hangs between associate producer, which is a middle manager role, and production assistant, which is entry level.

A good production coordinator can be quite valuable. He or she worries about the conventions of file labeling, makes certain that everyone's hard drive contains only the most recent versions of files (a chronic problem on complicated productions), solves minor computer problems, and tracks the small steps toward progress that eventually appear as the project manager's macro view of the production schedule.

Similar to the associate producer's taskload, the production coordinator's workday is filled with details. An associate producer will manage those details, essentially making certain that every member of the staff is doing what needs to be done. The production coordinator, or PC, is actually handling those details on a computer screen, relabeling names of files, moving files into proper folders, and organizing every asset so that it's properly and consistently tagged and backed up, and can be found later.

These tasks may seem trivial, and taken one at a time, they may well be. Multimedia production is not about individual tasks. The coordination of hundreds, and often thousands, of tiny tasks and details must work perfectly if the multimedia production is to be bug-free.

Working as a director

In complicated multimedia productions, a director may be employed to supervise some or all of the creative aspects. Certainly, a director is essential for a video shoot with live actors and actresses, and may be helpful for voice-over work, too. Some directors have made the transition from television or film animation to the creative supervision of videogame and software animation. Recently, the role of the director has begun to expand. With visual storytelling through animation, live actors, video, special effects, and other techniques, the role of the multimedia director is quickly evolving into a visual storyteller. The writer prepares the script, and the designers put together the look and feel of a production, but the director is ultimately responsible for telling the story. Along with this responsibility comes creative control over design, performers, and some aspects of programming.

How does one become a multimedia director? One route is to direct TV, film, and commercials, and to migrate to the new medium. Another route is to write for multimedia. If you persevere as a multimedia writer, you'll get a chance to direct as well. Not many people understand interactive storytelling yet, so writers have a unique advantage. The same can be said for multimedia designers and for animators. Another route is to work your way up from a production assistant to an assistant for a busy director. Then, as a result of your apprenticeship, make the move into directing your own projects.

Some college programs plan to offer multimedia storytelling and directing coursework. To reiterate, the best way to learn is to work in a company or on a project where you can observe a skillful and talented multimedia director at work.

Becoming a multimedia editor — or producer

Much confusion exists as to whether to call a senior product developer by the editor title, or by the producer title. Some companies prefer "editor," which suggests wisdom and care, as well as an understanding of the content material; this may the right answer for Web sites. Other companies prefer the "producer" title because it connotes creativity, the ability to get the job done, and a certain amount of technical ability. These characteristics make sense on a CD-ROM. In fact, a great deal of logic will not be evident in this confusion of titles. These titles are often created at the whim of the person doing the hiring, either by personal preference or in accordance with a company's traditions, whether they happen to make sense or not. Because multimedia combines aspects of both print and electronic media, it deserves either a hybrid title or something entirely new. At the moment, there is no real industry-wide distinction between the titles. Some differences may exist, however, at the company or project level.

Either way, the editor or producer is responsible for some or for all content-related aspects of a project, or a part of a project. That phrase — "content-related aspects" — can be the cause of confusion. Although a multimedia project's content is central to the user's experience, the content department (producers, editors, and related personnel) must balance priorities with software development and marketing. Unlike a television program, in which the producer of the content is more or less left to his or her own judgment on most content matters, multimedia content demands far more interaction between departments.

A successful editor or producer will possess, or will develop, a keen understanding of the technical aspects of multimedia production, and if possible, an appreciation of marketing considerations as well.

Deep down, the process of multimedia content editing and/or producing is not fundamentally different from the worlds of books, magazines, newspapers, radio, and television. The editor and producer make creative decisions, and then package information and entertainment through a combination of words and images. The primary differences are of scale: available budget dollars (less than TV, usually more than print); delivery schedules (which vary widely, depending upon the project); the need to keep up with the latest technology; and the high level of co-dependent relationships between departments.

Television and radio are more dynamic media; changes can be made even after the audio and video master tapes are delivered. With print, changes may complicate the production process, causing concern about reserved press time and other deadlines; however, individual changes along the way are possible and common. Digital media can be changed, but the process is usually more complicated than it is in audio or video. Changing even a single icon can affect dozens of graphic screens as well as aspects of the program itself. For this reason, many producers and editors are surprised by the lack of creative flexibility in CD-ROM production. Web production is more flexible; changes made on the fly are relatively easy. Why are these differences mentioned in a chapter about careers? The fact is that some people find themselves well suited to media that are more dynamic (Web pages, TV news, radio), whereas others find more comfort in the successful completion of a truly finished product (CD-ROM, motion picture, book). The philosophy of professional satisfaction is not a trivial judgment.

Becoming an executive producer/editor-in-chief

The executive producer is the person entrusted with the successful development, production, and delivery of a multimedia project. He or she must possess management and creative skills. Once again, a clear understanding of the technical, production, and marketing issues is a definite asset.

An editor-in-chief occupies a similar role. Multimedia requires close integration between departments, and a successful editor-in-chief will protect and nurture the editorial agenda while making way for the mission to succeed with the cooperation of other departments. In the best of all possible worlds, the executive producer and editor-in-chief roles would be filled by people who have worked their way up, either within the company or the industry. The requisite knowledge, and relationships, will help this senior person to succeed.

In the real world, multimedia producers and editors are frequently imported from other media, or from other departments. Such a background is acceptable for someone responsible for specific aspects of a project, but the executive producer and editor-in-chief should possess a clear, deeply-rooted understanding of the interactive world and its realities. For those who have spent ten years or more in book publishing, for example, the transition to digital media can be uneven.

Wearing all of these hats and more: becoming a Webmaster

The Webmaster's position has been saved for last, because in many cases, the position of Webmaster encompasses all of the aforementioned jobs. Many Web sites are small-scale operations, and the entire infrastructure and upkeep might fall to one or two people. Some Webmasters do it all: creative endeavors, production, programming, quality assurance, and responding to e-mails. Such comprehensive task-managing is becoming less common, though. As Web sites become larger and more complicated, the Webmaster's role is becoming more of a technical and an operational position.

A Webmaster is the person responsible for daily operations of a Web site. Part editor, part producer, part software wizard, and part project manager, the Webmaster has both the charge for smooth operations and the responsibility for implementing the details.

How does one become a Webmaster? There is no single route. Some Webmasters develop their own web sites, and then offer their services to manage other Web sites. Some are company managers who taught themselves how to build a Web site, and now maintain it. Others are company employees who worked on the site as a sideline to other work, and are now responsible for Web operations. The title and the role aren't more than a few years old. For a more considered approach of what life might be like as a Webmaster, see Chapter 5.

A Typical Career Path in Project Management

A simple multimedia project is not a single entity. With the combination of text, graphics, audio, video, and programming, one person must be assigned to the management of the schedule, assets, and deliverables. With or without the official title, this is the job of the project manager.

In some companies, the role of project manager is clear from the start. In others, the role is buried within the responsibilities of a producer, associate producer, or another staff member.

Multimedia project management requires a unique combination of skills. These skills include budgeting, managing a schedule, managing people, managing every file and backup, interdepartmental coordination, and problem solving. Some people are well suited to this variety of tasks; creative people may find them daunting and even overwhelming. Experience helps immensely. For example, when a situation flares up in which the designer and the senior programmer are fighting, the "been there, done that" factor can work in the project manager's favor. He or she can look to past experiences for a solution to a common problem. This depth of experience, along with the sort of personality that's well suited to solving problems like these, can be polished by a mentor.

One of the project manager's most important roles is budgeting. The term "budgeting" breaks down into smaller components. The first is the preparation of the budget estimate, a preliminary budget based on early assumptions about the project. This step usually requires the preparation of a schedule that is used to determine salaries, equipment and office rentals, overhead, milestone deliveries, and many other variables. Few projects move ahead with just one budget and schedule pass, so the project manager must possess a unique combination of patience and a resourceful style because the budget often needs to be trimmed without changing the project in any substantial way.

After the budget is approved, the project manager tracks and reports expenses to the client, the producer, the production company, or some other supervisor. A budget report should be prepared no less than once weekly, and twice, per week if possible. This dictates timely entry of every incoming invoice. This attention to detail is a nontrivial aspect of multimedia production. Over the course of even a modest project, several hundred invoices will pass through the hands of a project manager. With so many invoices to be tracked and passed on for payment, the project manager must be meticulous.

Help, in the form of a bookkeeper, is nearly essential. If bills are paid late, important vendors and other contractors can become cranky. The project manager's job is to keep these people happy and to keep the project moving, even if the checking account is empty and payments are delayed because the deliverable is delayed.

Few projects proceed without the threat of going over budget, so the project manager must be constantly aware of potential overages as well as any potential savings. This balancing act is tricky, one that must be performed with the cooperation of the other senior people in the project. Often, the project manager is the messenger — the one with the bad news. A skillful and talented project manager will work with the team to solve these potential problems.

The project manager serves a similar function in the tracking of overall progress. At the start of the project, he or she typically prepares a detailed schedule, a chart of tasks and milestones. These milestones, and the ultimate delivery date, are generally based upon the project manager's own experience, and upon detailed conversations with every department. The interdependencies between departments are a significant factor here: "We can't get the programming done until the revised art is delivered," for example. The project manager must understand the functions and intricate details of every department. A good project manager can negotiate compromises that will keep multiple departments happy, and keep the overall project on schedule.

No school or formal education teaches project managers how to do their jobs. Project management software and college coursework are avenues of education, but experience is the best teacher. Apprenticeship with a project manager is also a good idea, as is a mentoring relationship with someone who can help to solve problems, or at least discuss possible solutions.

A capable project manager is likely to succeed in middle management. As someone who can deliver projects on time and on budget, with a minimum of bother, a project manager can move beyond individual projects, and move on to a more senior role within a company as well.

A Typical Career Path in Management

Management is a necessary evil, or so says the rest of the team. Good management is a desirable goal, or so say the producers. Poor management will derail projects and cripple a company's potential — so says history.

Working in product development management

The head of product development, often called director or vice president of product development, supervises all aspects of the development and production cycle. On a day-to-day basis, this supervision typically includes involvement in conceiving and structuring the project, budgeting, scheduling, and assembling the team. Other responsibilities are staff supervision, project management, client relations (and/or interdepartmental relations), and input or deeper involvement in marketing. These tasks generally require broad familiarity with technology and with creative trends, such as the latest in interface design and in graphic look and feel. A great deal of senior management time is spent in this arena as well. Senior management often operates as part of a small group setting company direction, and makes the tough decisions: which projects to do, and which ones not to do; or how many staff members to hire, or release, during tough times. Interaction with third parties, such as outside suppliers, strategic partners, and owners of intellectual property (or their representatives) is also part of the job.

A product development chief typically comes to a multimedia organization with five to ten years experience, in multimedia, software, videogames, or in a related field. Finding someone in this job who began in book publishing or television is not unusual. Commonly, this person worked in the medium of print, and then founded some form of electronic magazine on CD-ROM or on the Web, for example. Perhaps the new medium presented more opportunity or the chance to become involved in something new. Some people have made similar transitions from the television and motion picture industries.

The head of product development is often a producer who has worked his or her way through executive producer and now supervises all aspects of CD-ROMs, and Web activities.

In entrepreneurial concerns, which are common in multimedia, the head of product development may simply be the person on the start-up team who is best, or most reasonably, suited to the task. Gaps may occur, and these are generally filled by hiring people with particular expertise, as money allows.

Further up the ladder: senior management

No clear plan is outlined for the growth of the multimedia business. A few years ago, CD-ROMs showed great promise as the next big thing, but supply outpaced demand. Now, CD-ROM development and production is a far less tantalizing business, at least from a purely business perspective, than it might have seemed in the early 1990s. As of this writing, the Web is showing itself as the next big thing, but only a small number of Web-page publishers have figured out how to turn their ventures into money-makers. In the future, possibilities include: ordinary TV sets used to receive Web pages; faster modems connected to cable TV lines; faster modems connected to ISDN lines; and higher-capacity CD-ROMs that display full-motion video. Each of these advancements could dramatically change the way in which large numbers of people use their computers or watch TV.

Although the development of a deep understanding and technical expertise in each new medium is possible, specific expertise is not the key to success at a more senior level. Instead, being a generalist is better: A generalist is someone who understands that technological change is a reality of the multimedia business. This person will also know how to manage through the chaos of changing operating systems, unpredictable consumer demand, overproduction by CD-ROM producers, and the constant potential for serious competition posed by companies that did not exist only the year prior.

Most multimedia production people never ascend to the level of senior management. The pressures are different in this level. The pressure is no longer a struggle to please a client with an offbeat creative approach or to get an artist to submit her work on schedule. The pressure in this level is to get the whole company and organization to move forward. Often, this movement accomplished by solving problems that impede growth. Such problems include moving people from one department to another, and adding bodies to tasks that were not previously deemed important. Other areas of attention are setting up systems so that progress can be accounted and reported to senior management or a board of directors, setting up responsible legal and financial procedures, recruiting and interviewing, and, ultimately, growing the company. Growth is rarely accomplished by improving the status quo. More often, growth requires bold steps in new directions, investments in new technologies, additions of new staff members, and starting on new projects.

Often, these tasks are more closely related to management than to multimedia production. For those who have struggled through all-nighters because a disk drive crashed, management may seem like the more reasonable way to live one's life. For others who enjoy the hands-on process of making things, management may not be the answer. Instead, career growth might be found with a company doing more exciting projects, or perhaps starting an entirely new company, which will be discussed in another chapter.

Moving from One Step to the Next

A touch of the "kid in a candy shop" syndrome is intrinsic to multimedia. With so many interesting aspects of work in this industry, and so many new technologies, wandering toward the most exciting ones is easy. Losing focus on the most productive steps for your own career is also a caution.

For example, suppose that you're a screen artist, a good one. You move up to art director, and you become curious about 3-D animation. You also become curious about producing. Being motivated, you work late and you work weekends, teaching yourself about 3-D animation. You also produce some small projects (demos, perhaps) on your own.

Although you've introduced the possibility of moving up the line, you've also confused the potential employer. Are you still a viable screen artist, one who will remain interested in the current project, or are you a producer or animator without enough experience to effectively complete the job? These confusions are not unique to multimedia, but the pace of change in this business, and the opportunities created as a result of that change, create more complexity in the hiring process than one might find in other businesses.

The Job Search

Looking for a new job can raise all sorts of complicated issues. Money is certainly one; everyone prefers to earn more money at a new job than at a previous one. Self-worth is another issue. The new title and the new menu of responsibilities should be more challenging, more engaging, and generally more impressive than the previous one. Personal growth is also important: the flow from the first job to the second to the third should demonstrate professional progress.

None of these issues is very important to the person doing the hiring. He or she would like to hire you for the same amount that you earned before. In theory, this amount is how much you "cost." A modest increase should, in the minds of most employers, provide sufficient enticement. Most companies have no real interest in promoting your career. If the employer hires you, he or she is doing so because you can do the job. Your desire for personal growth is fine, and the employer may acknowledge this desire, but your growth is not especially important to the person doing the hiring. One exception exists for this general rule: if you're not sufficiently challenged, you might leave the company too soon.

If the employer lacks the funds to hire a sufficiently senior person, then the notion of personal growth might come into play as a means of convincing the candidate that he or she can grow into an opportunity for which the candidate's actual experience is somewhat lacking. To put a more positive spin on this, some employers hire people with more potential but less experience, saving some money along the way, in hopes of nurturing the candidate's talents. Most candidates don't exactly have this idea in mind when they hear the phrase "personal growth," but this reality is as close as most people get.

For the employer, hiring the proper people is the key to success. Hiring even one "wrong" person can really mess things up. The hiring process begins in one of two ways. First, someone who previously had the job is leaving, or has left. The cause might be internal, as when an employee moves up or to another department, or external, when a company decides to leave town — or even leave the industry. The second way, extremely common in multimedia, is that the job is a new hire. These positions often reflect a dedicated effort on the part of the hiring manager. Keeping permanent "head count" low is important to managing company finances, especially for start-up companies who must manage cash with extreme care. Each new hire pushes profitability another 50 thousand dollars or more into the distance.

Regardless of how the opening was created, word about the available job spreads. If someone within the department, or a nearby department, seems capable of doing the job, he or she will usually get the job. Such as internal promotion is easier for the manager than going through a time-consuming recruitment process. In a larger company, the job is officially posted. This posting may occur weeks after the job became available, so those who see the internal posting may be the last to know. The job may be advertised, but most multimedia jobs are not. Instead, people find out about them through word of mouth. The hiring manager tells everyone he or she knows that the job is open, and slowly, résumés start to come in.

If you're looking for a job, knowledge of available jobs at any given company may be unobtainable. In-house postings are late, if done at all. If you happen to know "someone who knows someone," and at an opportune time, you could get in for the interview. Consider, however, the odds against a manager who has a job opening and a capable candidate who wants that job. The most valuable commodity in this whole process is luck. In truth, a combination of your ability to do the job, your pleasant manner in dealing with the hiring manager or human resources department, and your perseverance must all work together in an idealized combination. The manager, working alone or with a human resources department, aggressively spreads the word, does lots of interviewing, and eventually finds one or more candidates.

For most people, in most job searches, a certain random factor prevails. Luck will play a part. For example, you happened to talk to someone who knows a manager who's hiring, or who knows that of a new venture starting up. If you're seriously job hunting, you must increase the odds of becoming lucky. You can do this by meeting more people, finding out about more jobs, and letting more people know that you're looking for a new job.

Networking

The word "networking" may be hated, but the process needs a name, and this one works. The idea is to build a network of people who know you are looking for a job. Don't be obnoxious about this network development; don't talk to every person you know and ask everyone for three names that may or may not be of value. Do, however, be diligent. Go to the trade shows and shake a lot of hands. Tell people your skills; find out who, at each company, might be intrigued by those skills. Try to develop mini-relationships, the kinds of brief friendships that a quick lunch or a cup of coffee at a convention can bring. These conversations should be very focused, but they should also be balanced. Establishing what each party can offer the other either immediately or in the near future is the essence of networking, though, happily, not all human relations.

Don't be shy. Try to impress the other person without appearing overzealous. Manage your expectations because only a small percentage of these conversations result in even a follow-up phone call. You'll need to take the action on your own by writing a letter to recap the conversation; e-mail can be used for this communication. Later, make a phone call to proceed a bit further. Do this with care; you don't want to hamper a new relationship by pushing too hard. Also, don't treat these encounters as one-time-only events.

If you're a part of this business, you will run into people time and again, especially at conventions. As you attend some of the same dinners, parties, screenings, and other events, you may hang out together and become acquaintances, or perhaps friends or business associates.

Outside the free-ranging convention or trade show environment, things are more buttoned up. People are more concerned about their available time, and they're unlikely to give time to you rather than their family, friends, or leisure pursuits. Still, a brief lunch date, or an occasional phone call — or, best of all, a periodic e-mail mentioning some fact of mutual interest — can keep the relationship going.

Networking is not defined by connecting with one person who can lead you to three more. Networking includes developing relationships with individuals: people who you can help, and those who can help you, too. Networking also involves doing favors without even thinking about whether they will be returned. For all of those in this sloppy, disorganized, incredible, strange, hard-to-understand multimedia, interactive, Web, CD-ROM business together, a concerted effort is warranted to make it as easy as possible for one another.

A word of caution should be noted: a relationship is easily damaged, especially one born of networking. If your primary objective in meeting "person A" is to meet "person B," that's not easy to disguise. The first person might not have a positive feeling about being used, and might say something negative to the second person. Now, as a result of networking, you've found two people who can affect your career in a negative way. Once again, networking is not meeting lots of people who can help you. Instead, networking is being part of a community of people who truly enjoy helping one another. A big difference should be obvious.

Responding to an advertisement

On the west coast, the *Los Angeles Times*, *San Francisco Chronicle,* and *San Jose Mercury News* are fruitful sources of employment advertising for multimedia specialists. On the east coast, the best sources are probably the *Boston Globe* and *The New York Times*. None of these are great sources; you could go for weeks without seeing an ad that's even remotely suitable. Among newspapers, however, these are among the best sources for employment advertisements. These ads are far more useful for CFOs, and for sales and marketing VPs and directors.

You will find some ads in trade publications, notably *MacWeek* and *Inter@ctive Week*. From time to time, ads will also appear in trade publications for related industries: television (*Electronic Media, Variety, Broadcasting & Cable*), newspaper publishing (*Editor & Publisher*), book publishing (*Publishers Weekly*), and advertising (*Advertising Age, ADWEEK*). If you're looking for a job, check these publications regularly. You'll find current and back issues in many large public libraries, and the majority of college libraries.

The appropriate response to an advertisement is a cover letter and a résumé. Keep the cover letter brief, but use it to do some self-promotion, highlighting the most exciting and/or relevant parts of the attached résumé. Do not use the cover letter to explain why you want to leave your current job, or for any reason suggesting that you might be a risky hire. Keep the tone positive, upbeat, and brief. Limit your e-mail communications. You want your personality to come through, both on the telephone and in person. Allowing your personality to shine via e-mail is difficult. Letters are better. Send a fax only if the ad specifically requests faxes.

If the ad asks for salary information, you're faced with a predicament. Ideally, you want to know the potential employer better before you tell anyone how much money you earn; you will find that some ads don't list the employer. When the employer asks your salary requirements, your answer should be honest. Ideally, the employer should tell you how much the job pays; then, you should agree if the salary for the job is within your range, citing a similar salary paid for your most recent job. Usually, this process works the other way around. Because the employer is the one with the money, avoiding "naming a figure first" is tough. You should do what you can to find out the employer's plans before you volunteer too much about yourself and your present situation.

The role of executive search firms

Executive search firms, also called head hunters or recruiters, play a role in the multimedia field. They find senior executives, but they also find producers, designers, and programmers.

When a search firm is retained by a company, the company agrees to pay a commission to the firm in exchange for services rendered. That commission is typically 20 to 30 percent of the salary, paid from company funds. Restated, search firms are paid by employers. They are never paid by employees.

The search firm typically begins by contacting people with credentials that suggest a potential match with the employer's needs. The courtship begins with an innocent-sounding phone call. "Hello, this is (name of recruiter), with (name of search firm). We are conducting a search for (name of job), and wondered if you would know somebody who would be suitable?" Note the phrase, "if you would know somebody who would be suitable?" This message is masked. The question that the recruiter poses translates as, "Would *you* be interested?" This approach is too direct, and may place a well-positioned person in an awkward position. Instead, the dance continues with the potential employee asking for more information. The recruiter then paints a broad picture of the company doing the hiring, and a general idea of the job description. The recruiter rarely mentions the company by name, but often provides more than enough meaningful clues by which to guess the company's identity. As the dance proceeds, the prospect is encouraged to send a résumé or biography to the recruiter. If the match looks promising, the recruiter then discusses the candidate with the hiring manager, and meets the candidate.

The meeting with the recruiter is a job interview, albeit one with someone who will know only a limited amount about the company and the job. Ask whatever questions you consider appropriate, but go in with the idea of presenting yourself, and selling yourself, as effectively as possible. A good meeting with the recruiter will often result in a meeting with the employer. At that point, you're conducting a standard job interview.

The recruiter will keep in close touch with the promising candidate. He or she may take a personal interest in the candidate, and encourage the employer to focus on the candidate's most promising attributes. At this point, the recruiter wants the employer to hire the best person, but also wants to close the deal.

How to write a résumé

From a candidate's perspective, a résumé is a pronouncement of great skills and abilities. A résumé is a list of personal accomplishments set forth in such a way that no sensible employer would refuse a job to the person it represents.

From the employer's perspective, résumés that match the available jobs are extremely difficult to find. Most résumés get less than a minute's attention, and often far less than that. A typical résumé review session starts with approximately 20 résumés, and ends with one or two; on a great day, three résumés with any potential at all will remain for consideration. Weeding résumés can become quite a mess.

The object of this game is to not be eliminated. Your résumé should encourage an employer to interview and hire you. In many cases, because the résumé doesn't communicate the potential match clearly and quickly, it gets sorted out. Some people unintentionally hurt their chances by making inappropriate choices as they prepare the résumé. Here are some tips. Read them before you write your next résumé. Use this checklist, once again, just before the résumé is ready to be copied.

- Spell everything correctly.
- Make your résumé easy to navigate, with easy-to-read job titles and company names.
- Don't lie.
- Keep the résumé to a page or two. Let the employer request more information.
- Print the résumé on 8½-by-11-inch vertical sheets. Use light-colored paper with black type. Good résumés are copied, and if yours won't copy easily, your odds worsen.
- Don't include your salary. Most likely, you'll be too high or too low.
- Don't waste valuable space on references.

Start the résumé with your name, address, and telephone number. A fax number is unnecessary; during the hiring process, nobody is going to send you anything by fax. An e-mail address is a convenience, and although its presence demonstrates that you have some understanding of cyberspace, remember that you'll mainly be communicating by telephone and in person. The inclusion of a work objective, once considered an appropriate flourish, now seems trite. If you have something great to say about yourself, include it. If not, then move on to the section of work experience.

Résumé books offer all sorts of creative presentations. The presentation that most people use, and the one most employers tend to prefer, is the straight chronological list of job descriptions. Start with the most recent job title, the name of the company, and the city in which you were employed. Then, briefly describe your role by delineating your responsibilities and principal accomplishments. Because résumés are more often browsed than read (at least in the early stages), key points may be better than full paragraphs. Mention specific products and brands, especially if well known. Impressive sales figures can be meaningful; just be sure you aren't publishing confidential information. You should mention awards, too.

Ideally, you will demonstrate consistent growth from one job to the next, creating a spectacular unbroken line from your choice of college major to your current position. In the real world, very few people can present that sort of résumé. Most people have gaps. If you spent time in an unrelated endeavor, mention this, but briefly. If the unrelated endeavor involved related skills, highlight those skills. Take care not to stretch the truth, and don't work too hard for relevant connections.

After listing five or six jobs, the résumé may appear too long. If you've had several jobs — because you enjoy a variety of experiences, or for whatever reason — provide details on the most relevant jobs, and keep the other descriptions brief. Freelance assignments can be listed either as jobs, if they lasted more than a few months, or in a tidy list of additional assignments at the end of the résumé. If freelancing was your principal occupation, then your job title becomes "freelance designer." The projects become the core of your job description.

Be careful about being too clever. Conversely, you don't want your résumé to look the same as everybody else's. You don't want to submit a résumé that's not kept because it's not special. Maybe the quality of the experience on the résumé doesn't communicate the depth of experience and talent possessed by the person behind the résumé. Maybe the targeted organization is well known for doing crazy things, so a crazy résumé will fit right in. Maybe the boss, or the human resources department, is looking for an original thinker. Many "maybes" are factors.

Should you do something crazy? Such a gamble is a measured risk. The advantage is that you'll get noticed. If nothing else crazy comes in the same time that your résumé does, you could stand out. However, if your amazingly creative piece arrives a half-hour after some guy dressed like a Zip drive, you could be out of luck.

A word about interactive résumés

A trend is developing for multimedia professionals to distribute their résumés in some interactive format, such as a floppy disk, a CD-ROM, or a personal Web site. As with everything else connected to multimedia, pros and cons must be weighed.

On the positive side, an interactive résumé clearly shows that you're fluent in the medium. For example, a designer can fit an entire digital portfolio on a single disc, which could be easily distributed by the potential employer. No separate trip is required to see the work because the person who's hiring already has it. Similarly, a programmer could show off his or her skills easily in an interactive format, and a potential Webmaster could certainly do worse than showing off a great site as a portfolio piece.

Definite drawbacks can be encountered when your résumé is sent in an interactive format. For a diskette or a CD-ROM, you'd obviously have some technical challenges; namely, the disc would have to be playable on any potential machine at a potential employer. This dictates a cross-platform disc or bust. Worse, this situation makes two grand assumptions. The first assumption is that the prospective employer actually has a conveniently located CD-ROM drive on which to play your résumé. Second, the assumption is made the employer has either the time or inclination to actually play it. Neither of these assumptions should be counted on, by any stretch of the imagination.

Although well-executed interactive résumés can be an enormously impressive way to showcase your value as a potential employee, they should not be regarded as a substitute for the old-fashioned paper résumé. As an addendum, they're fine. To repeat a point of emphasis, prospective employers are usually busy; in the time it takes for them to boot up your CD-ROM or URL, they could have read through several résumés. That's what they'd rather be doing.

What a résumé is — and what's it's not

A résumé is a document that hopefully gets filed in a folder marked "Promising Candidates," or something similar. Copies of the résumé are made for either the hiring manager or for the human resources department. In a large company, your résumé may be scanned and stored in a database for later keyword searches. After the résumé is scanned, the paper is thrown away. True, the résumé is a kind of advertisement for yourself and your skills, but it may never reach your intended customer — the manager with an open slot to fill and the power to hire you. As a direct marketing device, résumés don't usually do too well. As a specific answer to the question, "Does your past experience suggest that you might be able to do this job?", a résumé is an adequate place to start the process of getting to know the candidates by telephone and in person.

Résumés should be customized. Unlike the success of a direct marketing piece, defined when three percent of recipients respond, a résumé must succeed with a better response rate. For this reason, following the current fashions is generally best. This approach will provide the information that the potential employer needs, and will afford a variety of subtle ways to demonstrate skills and creativity.

Preparing for interviews

An interview should be a balanced conversation between a potential employer and a potential employee. Most job interviews, however, don't follow this ideal. Each side should provide background and expectations, and each side should be forthcoming with details that could affect a future relationship.

In fact, this balance rarely happens. Once again, because the employer is the one with the money, the candidate typically operates at a disadvantage. Part of the reason for the disparity is numbers. A bona fide company has the resources to advertise for positions, and also enjoys the benefit of having a staff (perhaps a dedicated staff) responsible for seeking and sorting out potential employees. The candidate, on the other hand, is less experienced, and possesses fewer resources. Additionally, he or she probably needs the money that an employer can provide.

The scales are not tipped entirely in favor of the employer, though. The candidate possesses two assets that the employer needs: the ability to get work done, and talent.

Few employers take these assets at face value. The purpose of the interview — and your résumé and your portfolio — is to prove that you really possess these assets.

One measure of your ability to get work done is your appearance, or personal style. If you arrive for an interview in attire that's too casual, such as a tee-shirt and ripped jeans), the employer will probably express concern about your understanding of the workplace. If you show up for a job as an artist wearing a conservative suit, the employer may express similar concerns. A clean, well-groomed appearance is essential. Dressing well is also wise; dress better than you would for a typical day of work.

Your ability to communicate is also important. Eye contact is essential, and so is a smile. (This advice may sound trite, but if you don't do this, you will lose points). A good handshake is also a useful tool. Most important, you should go into the interview with three key points that you intend to communicate. Practice communicating these points so that you can express them clearly and concisely.

Interviews

Interviews are difficult. You may have as little as 15 or 20 minutes in which to: learn about the job; learn about the employer and the company and the current project(s); tell the employer about your background; and do some selling. Ideally, you'll meet with a manager who knows how to interview people and what questions to ask, how to magnify the résumé into a more complete profile of the person sitting across the desk or table, and how to evaluate previous experiences and to map them onto future needs. In the real world, most managers (and most people who hire other people), have never been trained to do the job. They ask random questions and hope that they're asking the right ones.

A well-organized interview should begin as the manager talks briefly about the company, his or her role, and what the job requires. This allows the candidate to frame his or her presentation within the context of the employer's needs. A skillful employer will then inquire about the recent jobs and responsibilities. The interviewer will make these inquiries not only to find out what the applicant did in a previous job but also to mine for specifics that tell more about the person and how he or she performs and behaves at work. Be prepared, for example, to talk about a specific activity related to each past job, or perhaps a problem and how you solved it. The actual solution doesn't matter as much as your thinking and your behavior in solving the problem. The employer is trying to understand how you evaluated the problem, how you determined what action to take, and how you modified your course in order to ensure success. He or she is looking for clues about your management style, about the ways in which you solve problems, about how deeply involved you become in the details, and about your relationships with associates.

Answer the questions you are asked, but listen carefully. Try to determine what the employer really wants to know; try to understand the concerns and challenges. Answer using specific examples of your own behavior to underline your potential value to the organization. Once again, use at least a few of these examples to show why you are special and why you are well suited to the job.

This probing is likely to go on for about a third of the interview. Toward the end of your meeting, the interviewer will either begin to conclude the interview or will ask more questions. The latter is usually a good sign. This is your opportunity to ask questions. This time also permits you to relax a bit, and to let your true self come through. Most important, this window of opportunity allows you to evaluate the following: what you have said so far, what still needs to be said, and, inevitably, what you have said that requires correction or clarification.

You can feel comfortable in probing for information about the organization and the reporting structure. You can also ask about recent projects, including how they have been received and how they might have been made better. Be careful not to interrogate the employer; even if the employer is asking you lots of questions, not asking too many yourself is best. Instead, try to draw the other person out in a friendly conversation. You'll learn more, and, if your personality and presentation are on target, the other person may be more candid. Remember that you are the one being interviewed, not the other way around.

Listening skills are extremely important. Don't just listen to the words. Watch the eyes. Watch the body language. Notice whether the employer changes his or her temperament when, for example, questions about reporting structure or recent project history are answered. Try to get a feeling for what's really going on. Sometimes, things are precisely as they seem; sometimes, an underlying story may prevail. If you sense that things are exactly right, pay close attention to what is being said and how the answers are phrased and presented.

You now want the conversation to move toward the future. You want the employer to begin thinking about how you might fit in. This kind of conversation is difficult to promote. If you force the conversation, you could ruin the interview's natural pace by trying to take control. The potential employer might then think that you are trying to take control, which is just as detrimental.

At this point, you want to know more about current projects, members of the team, deadlines, and deliverables: anything that's more specific than, "Gee, we might have a job here for the qualified candidate." When the interview progresses to this point, try to be quiet and listen! Stop selling! The employer is trying to determine how you could work within the current, or emerging, organization. Don't derail that line of thinking! Instead, answer questions briefly and stick to the point. Before you offer an example as proof of your capabilities or experience, ask yourself whether this example illuminates a new aspect of your working life. If the topic has been covered before, bring it up very casually, not in the kind of detail that might pull the focus away from the future-thinking employer's determination of your fit with his company.

Showing your work

If you're a designer or art director, or a producer or director, you will probably be asked to show your work. As a rule, packaging the samples in an oversized portfolio is best. Choose a portfolio that's large enough to show the work as color prints, but not so large that the employer must clear his or her desk before the portfolio can be opened. Portfolios are standard equipment for artists and designers. Producers should use them, too.

Although you may be proud of your work, and confident of its quality, you don't want to start the interview by opening your book. What you're selling is yourself, and the portfolio should support that sale. You are not, after all, selling the work in your book. You are selling a relationship, with the understanding that the book contains work that you have completed as a result of prior relationships.

Also, the style of the work in the book may be inconsistent with the needs of the employer. If you begin with your book, and your work doesn't match the employer's needs or expectations, the interview may be over. Starting with your own personal talents, skills, personality, and style allows you much more latitude. When you understand the employer and his or her needs, you can discuss your previous work in the context of the employer's current and future needs.

Some key concerns – for employers

When a new person comes into the office, the first impression is often strong. An opinion is easily formed based on the way a person looks, dresses, or talks. That opinion has another name: prejudice.

Start the interview by briefly reviewing the résumé. Ask questions about specific job experiences. Ask the candidate to provide detail on his role in the various companies listed, and to provide even greater detail on his involvement in specific projects. Look for verbs that suggest specific skills: managed, organized, produced, created, illustrated, wrote, edited, and coordinated. Pay particular attention to the way that the candidate presents his or her experiences. Notice how the candidate defines himself or herself as part of a working team, or as the team leader. Listen for statements regarding personal growth as the person moved from one job or project to the next. Look for internal motivations: did the person progress to make more money, or was there some other driving force? Listen for promises made, and goods delivered on time and on budget.

If time permits, try for a complete picture of the person. Asking about hobbies and about school experience is acceptable. Discussing family life, health, personal life, or family heritage is not permissible. If you stick to the parameters of the job, and the applicant's qualifications for the job, a problem will not arise. A degree of formality is more acceptable in the job interview than in other aspects of work in the software business; this artificial distance sometimes prevents any sort of personal discussion during the job interview.

Err on the side of a lighter book with perhaps ten or 12 carefully selected items in all. Be sure everything can be easily seen. Slides are not a good idea because they're hard to screen in an office. Web sites, although they're not inappropriate as a leave-behind, also require special effort on the part of the employer; chances are, he or she won't do that work. Go for medium-sized, high-quality color prints in a book that's 18 to 24 inches wide. This size is large enough to display the work in an impressive way, but not so large as to prove cumbersome.

If you're an artist, you probably know that people who are not artists can find difficulty in evaluating quality work. Most managers are not artists. In fact, few hiring managers can honestly say that they've done the job that they're recruiting someone to do. Therefore, you must help the manager to understand why the work in your book is special and unique. Present the projects as problems you have solved so that context becomes clear. In this way, the conversation also becomes more productive, and more of a two-way discussion than a presentation.

Still, the majority of employers will not take the time to evaluate every piece in the book. In many cases, the employer is likely to race through the portfolio. You should be ready, particularly with the first three pieces in the book, to tell a very brief story about each piece. The first piece should clearly demonstrate that you can do the job. The second piece should show some versatility, yet it should be closely related to the job at hand. The third piece should be "really, really good"; it should dazzle the potential employer. After number three, just be sure that no piece in the book will embarrass you, and that nothing looks like yet another student project. Because the work in this business is often done by people in their twenties, student projects are often supplied as demos.

Looking through the portfolio should occupy 10 or 15 minutes of the time allotted for the interview.

Demos and digital portfolios

An electronic presentation, although it may be consistent with the type of work you're seeking, can be a cumbersome addition to an already tense job interview. You don't want to make things harder on yourself by adding the possibility that a demo may not run on a particular machine. A solid production can work miracles. A carefully crafted presentation, involving some combination of graphics, music, video, and animation, can do far more to communicate than you can sitting there alone, ad-libbing, or recapping key points from memory.

Allow no more than ten minutes for your interactive demo. A demo length of five to seven minutes is best. Choose the elements with great care and vary them as much as possible. Demonstrate versatility; you never know what the employer wants to see. Keep the presentation simple and to the point, offering limited interactivity. You don't want to spend those valuable interview minutes explaining how to use the program. Take some creative chances, but be conservative unless you're certain that the job's demands are otherwise. If at all possible, tailor your presentation for each new interview. Build your demo in a modular way so that you can change it for each new potential employer. Keep your presentation up-to-date. Don't spend a fortune in time or money; the employer wants to see real projects, not sketches for future ideas (unless the presentation of those ideas is outrageously fabulous).

As stated earlier, some producers and some companies put presentation materials on a Web site. In theory, the selection of a site may seem like a good idea. In practice, problems may arise. The Web browser may be one problem. The potential employer may not have a working Web browser on his or her machine, or the LAN may be down, or there may be modem problems. Your work may not be optimized for the employer's Web browser. Graphics may not download properly. The server could go down. More important, Web pages are not the very best way to present on-screen graphics. On-screen text will not be read in the midst of a job interview.

A Zip disk, SyQuest, or CD-ROM can all be appropriate presentation vehicles, provided that you make certain that the necessary equipment is available. This confirmation requires a call to the employer prior to the interview. This call is not a very good idea if you've never met the person. You may ask questions that the employer may not be able to answer, thus creating an embarrassing situation for the employer, or a time-consuming one. The equipment must be available in the employer's office. You cannot, as a potential employee, request that the meeting be held in a well-equipped conference room. You could make the request, of course, but you would set yourself up for a very tough interview.

Another option is to bring your own equipment. Once again, proceed with caution. You don't want to be unpacking a 17-inch color monitor as you start an important job interview. A portable computer is not a bad idea, but be sure the demo is 100 percent flawless. If it crashes, you lose points. A larger color screen is a solid idea, as is an AC adapter because batteries die at the most embarrassing times.

If you take this path, you should probably bring along a demo that can be played on a desktop computer as well. Suppose that the employer likes the demo. Rather than ask you to bring the demo back a second time (bringing the computer back a second time, too), the employer may ask some associates to come in to his or her office to try it out. At this point, the small screen size of the portable becomes a disadvantage. If you have the demo in a variety of formats (Zip disk, CD-ROM, and whatever SyQuests may be available to you), bring them along. You never know what machines and peripherals you'll find in someone's office.

If the employer requests this kind of demo, ask for a 15-minute break to set up your equipment. Also secure a promise to complete the private interview after the demo viewed. Commit to a schedule for the next 30 to 60 minutes. Otherwise, you'll present the demo, but you may not get the attention that another interview candidate (one without a demo) would get under normal circumstances. In other words, showing the demo, powerful though it may be, could ultimately prove to be a distraction in the job interview process. If you experience technical problems — and you will, because computers truly enjoy misbehaving when the pressure is on — the employer's memory of your interview may be limited to, "Interesting person, but her demo didn't work."

The flip side: evaluating a presentation

As you hire your own staff, you will see plenty of presentations. Don't be too hard on them. People put these presentations together on their own time and with their own money. Try to look past the rudimentary presentation, and past the graphics that should have been done by a professional. Look for good organization of the material and ideas. Look for enthusiasm; observe how the candidate handles the presentation. Do apologies abound? Does he or she recognize what might be done better? Is the person dissatisfied with the changes imposed by past clients and employers? Has the person done the necessary homework? Does the program run bug-free? Is the program really, really, really, r-e-a-l-l-y slow, or has some effort been made toward optimization? How much of the work was actually done by the person you're thinking about hiring? Admittedly, these are nuances. During the presentation, those nuances are going to be more telling than the work itself, which was inevitably put together by a staff of people, not just by the individual sitting before you, wanting a job.

Completing the interview

The ideal interview lasts about forty-five minutes. The first half-hour is best used to discuss your background and the company's projects. If the interview is successful, the final 15 minutes should be a discussion about working together, and about the future.

Negotiating a fair salary

At this point, someone usually brings up the subject of salary. You should not be the person who begins this discussion because the employer will think you're interested in the job mainly for the money it pays. Wait for the employer to address the topic. If he or she doesn't mention money, let the subject pass. Perhaps the employer is not the person who negotiates salary. Conversely, the employer may not be interested in you as a future employee. You could also be one of several candidates, and the field needs to be narrowed before salary discussions begin. If any of these three hypotheticals is the reason why salary has not been discussed, which is likely, then asking the money question could cause you to lose a point or two, if for no other reason than lack of gentility.

As negotiating tactics go, you never want to be person who names the first figure. Wait for the other person. Wait patiently. Don't talk just to fill uncomfortable silences.

If the employer wants your answer first, and you feel the time is right, then answer the question simply and directly. If you feel as though the employer is fishing (trying to determine how much the job should pay, for example), or if you feel that there are other candidates yet to be interviewed, try to delay the salary conversation until you're more certain that you're the first choice for the position. This is tricky. If you're evasive, you may not get hired. If you're interviewed early in the process, and your request is a few thousand dollars too high, you may get crossed off the list, even if the final candidates cost a little more than originally anticipated.

Some people find negotiating by telephone to be easier. The sense of detachment makes them less nervous; they can be a bit more aggressive. Other people insist upon negotiating in person. The other party's eyes and body language communicate a great deal if you're practiced in nonverbal communications and know how to "read" what's being said.

Does a "fair" salary exist in the multimedia business? The quick answer is "no." General pay scales do exist, but these vary based on a variety of factors.

Newer companies, notably start-ups in the San Francisco Bay area, may offer employees a combination of current income (salary) and future potential income (options to buy stock at a low price, should the company be sold or go public). Flexible benefits are also common, at least in some companies. Work-at-home days, time off for personal (nonbusiness) pursuits, and flexible health plans are benefits increasingly common in small companies helping to invent the future of employment.

Salaries at larger, established companies are typically set by market rates. These rates are often a result of hiring practices at smaller companies. An artist who works for a smaller company would expect the same salary, or a higher one, if he or she moves to a larger organization.

How much should you be paid?

Ask your friends. Ask your business associates. Read the trade newspapers for the occasional article about salary surveys. These practices are precisely what companies use to set their salaries. Make lots of telephone calls and you'll find out what you need to know.

That said, there are some very general guidelines:

- An administrative assistant generally earns a salary of about 20 to 30 thousand dollars, depending upon the company and the level of responsibility. The same salary level applies to design assistants, editorial assistants, programming assistants, and similar jobs.
- The $30-to-40-thousand salary level is assigned to associate producers, lower-level programmers, junior designers, some screen artists, researchers, junior writers, and some editors: those people who contribute or manage parts of the process, but with limited responsibilities. Look for words such as "associate," and "coordinator" in the job titles.
- The $40-to-60 thousand salary level is middle management: producers, mid-level programmers, designers, most editors, and mid-level product development people. These employees get the job done and they take responsibility for what happens day-to-day. They do not, as a rule, establish direction or manage large-scale projects. The most common title in this level is "manager."
- The $60-to-90 thousand salary level is the next step up the ladder. A senior designer or senior art director, a managing editor, a product development manager with responsibility for one or more large product lines, or a truly talented senior programmer are the sorts of employees who earn money at this salary level. One job title common to this level is "director." You'll often see the word "senior" or "executive" attached to an editor's, producer's, or programmer's title at this level.
- New companies generally prefer to keep senior executive salaries in the $90-to-125 thousand salary range. This challenge can be difficult, because these same people can annually earn $125 to 150 thousand, or more, if they work for a larger company, or for one that has funds more

readily available. One way to keep the salary lower, and to keep the executive happy, is with a bonus. Fewer restrictions exist on bonuses than on salary, so the hiring manager often has more flexibility in working with bonus monies. Some bonuses are guaranteed; others are based on meeting goals. Some goals are specific and objective, whereas others are subjective, based on the boss' evaluation of work done within a given period.

- Salaries above $150 thousand are relatively unusual, but a premium may be paid for an individual contributor whose reputation and/or contacts may prove helpful in raising investment money, or in finding new customers.

Stock options

Stock options are another popular form of compensation. These options are most common for employees working at start-up companies, and for senior executives at larger companies. Start-up companies can attract top-notch employees by offering shares: the opportunity for wealth. Established companies offer stock options to senior executives who set direction and contribute, in a significant way, to the company's future.

A stock option is, essentially, the right to buy shares of company stock. For example, options might be granted to purchase stock on a specific date, at the price the shares were worth on that date. These shares can be purchased as the employee becomes "vested" (explained shortly). Typically, these shares cannot be sold until the company goes public, or until the company wants to repurchase its shares, or until a private investor wants to buy shares (many variations on these themes can be exercised).

Presumably, the value of the shares will increase. Shares that can be purchased at the old price and sold at the newer price should make money for the person who owns the options.

Most companies do not grant stock options to new employees without some strings attached. Stock options are one way that a company can encourage a valued employee to stay with the company. How? The employee's options do not become active — they do not "vest" — until the employee has been with the company for a period of years. In a start-up, the vesting period may be as brief as a year or two. In an established company, a senior executive may not be fully vested in his or her options for five years or more. Partial vesting is common. After the first year of employment, for example, an employee may be 25 percent vested in his or her shares. The employee, once vested, can now buy 25 percent of the shares under option.

The date that the options are granted is also important. Options granted early in the life of a start-up company may be issued with a very low "strike price" because the start-up company may have a very low valuation upon initial operation. Options granted later may have a higher price. Because the difference between the strike price and the selling price results in the seller's profit, employees want the strike price to be as low as possible.

Another hitch to stock options arises if the employee decides to leave. The option to purchase the shares ("to exercise the option") does not remain open forever. Typically, the former employee has a few months past his exit date to make the purchase at the current value established by the most recent large purchaser. The former employee now owns the shares, and may be out several thousand dollars. In a start-up, or a privately-held company, no guarantee is assured that those shares will ever be worth anything. If the start-up goes out of business, then the shares are certainly worthless. The company may take in additional funding, perhaps at a lower price per share. This reduces the value of the former employee's investment, on paper. In reality, the shares are still not worth anything until they can be sold, either to the company, or on the open market if and when the company goes public.

As you're negotiating, listen carefully, and take notes; if you're negotiating by telephone, this will be easier. The terms "options," "shares," and "stock" are sometimes used interchangeably. This interchange is misleading. "Options" are most often what is meant. A deal in which shares of stock are granted is an extremely unusual deal.

Stock options are sometimes granted as means to complete a compensation package. The current income figure may be reduced with the promise of earning several times as much in the future. You must stay with the company for several years, and the selling price may not, ultimately, be higher than the price you paid for the shares.

Other aspects of the deal: an employer is like a spouse

For most people, the "deal" consists of nothing more than determining the job title, the salary, and any stock options. Taking a closer look is wise.

A written job description is useful. The description should explain the job responsibilities and reporting structure in appropriate detail.

A discussion of company policies is also in order. Although you may be somewhat uncomfortable raising these issues, you should discuss vacation time, personal days, salary review periods, typical raises, opportunities for advancement, work schedules, status of current projects, and plans for projects that will begin within the next 6 to 12 months.

You should be clear on the company's policy regarding termination. If you leave, how much notice are you expected to give? If the company asks you to leave, for how many weeks do they normally pay a terminated employee? Try not to bring up every one of these issues or you'll frighten the potential employer. One way to find the answers is to ask to see an employee handbook before you are hired; in these handbooks you can look up the standard procedures regarding, for example, salary review periods. You can then address only your unanswered questions. The best time to find these answers is after you've negotiated a salary, but before you've agreed to take the position. Take notes. You may want to refer to them later on.

Managers and executives may have other issues. Because a senior person takes longer to find a new job, severance periods for senior managers may be longer. A consulting contract is not uncommon; the executive leaves a full-time position, yet remains available as a consultant in order to complete current projects, or to advise on others. Some agreements such as this limit work for competitors, vendors, and contractors; some do not.

How to Succeed in the Multimedia Business

Although success has no absolute formula, many successful people in the software business share common traits and working styles. Follow their lead, and your odds for success are likely to increase.

Work "hard" — and work "smart"

This concept supersedes just getting your work done. In any software organization, a vast amount of work must be done. If you work long hours, you will be recognized as someone who is either dedicated to the tasks and to the company, and/or someone who can't accomplish everything during normal business hours. If you consistently complete your tasks on time, and without working all night to get them done, then you will have time to help other people and to learn from them. Early in your career, when you're trying to establish yourself, these apprentice relationships can offer great meaning. When an associate producer rises to producer, or an associate editor becomes editor, you may move up with that person. When someone leaves the company for a better job, you may be invited to come along. More important than the immediate issues of advancement, though, is the expansion of your own skills. By doing more than you were hired to do, you will expand the range of your abilities.

Develop solid working habits. Start by making a daily task list. Be specific about what you must accomplish before you leave the office at the end of the day. If items linger from one day to the next, talk to other members of the team, or to your boss, and ask for help. Try to get out of the office for at least a half-hour every day. Even if you don't break for lunch or errands, then just take a walk. You will be amazed at how much better you will feel, and how few people take this time for themselves. Eat healthful foods. If you're sitting at a desk for most of the day and into the night, eating junk food is not eating sensibly. Get some fruit and veggies; snack on fruit juices; or have someone drive to a local bakery to buy some fresh bread (not donuts). If the company isn't feeding you (providing food during "crunch times" is common), chip in with others and ask a local supermarket to build a vegetable tray for you. Don't order from the same restaurant every day. Take off an hour and go shopping; get out of the office and buy everyone small, silly toys. It's funny how these small things matter. You'll have an easier time surviving the long hours and endless days if you follow at least some of this advice.

Produce solid work

Not much explanation is needed here. When you perform a job, take the time and be sure that you have the resources to do it properly. If the resources are unavailable, or the schedule does not permit you to put together the proper resources, then try to find a way to get the job done in acceptable way. Accomplishing this goal is easier to say than it is to do, but such obstacles are the reality of life in multimedia. The job must get done, and done properly, despite lack of time, staff, or money. Software budgets are usually too low to get everything done correctly; software schedules are usually too tight to move things along in a straightforward, reasonable, and well-planned way. You must learn how to work within the system, get things done, make little noise or create minor disturbance, and still deliver quality work on time and on schedule.

The realization comes quickly that the work must come from within you and your close allies. External resources are difficult to manage on a tight schedule; often, money is not available to outsource all of the elements that should be outsourced. Such circumstances dictate learning Photoshop and DeBabelizer yourself, learning about the use of type, learning some simple

HTML programming, and learning to get things done on your own. You must at least learn to handle small pieces of the whole, so that the master designer or programmer can keep the bigger chunks moving.

Work as part of a team

Software development is teamwork. In the old days, when two guys could clean out their garage and come up with a big-selling shoot-'em-up game, teams were small and simple. Today, when even the simplest software project involves a producer, art director, programmer, and a staff of helpers, successful interaction between every member of the staff is truly important. This interaction may not be immediately clear. When the project begins, everyone may be very concerned about getting his or her own area started. These individual concerns usually become evident after the first late night, or the first night when a problem or deadline forces everyone to miss dinner at home and work late. Everyone informally sits down, takes in a little pizza, and blows off a little pressure. You begin to learn about one another: what jobs each of the people does, where they were before, and why they chose to do this project or join this company. Slowly, bonding begins. From this point on (and this point usually happens within the first few weeks of production), people learn to watch out for one another. They pass information more freely, and they know when to visit other people and talk for a few minutes, or when to let other people alone to get their work done.

Group meetings begin. At first, people keep to themselves and their departments' issues. Then, as the key issues become evident, and interdepartmental cooperation becomes necessary, senior people express opinions and try to solve the most pressing problems. Gradually, more junior people feel sufficiently knowledgeable and learn to express themselves, too. Interaction is encouraged. The team is taking shape. Everyone starts to communicate.

Figure out what you do well, and what needs work

Everyone has strengths and weaknesses. Nobody does everything well. The strengths are often quite obvious: he or she is a master programmer, or a terrific designer, or a flawless producer who can deliver wonderfully creative work ahead of schedule, and for less than the budgeted amount. Weaknesses are not always as obvious. Self-doubt is pretty common among creative people; moodiness is not uncommon. Some people don't handle pressure well; they snap at other people, or become frenzied, or work themselves to near exhaustion. Some are poorly organized, or let the small details of a project go unchecked until too late to do much about them. Some demand too much of themselves and others, pushing hard-working, dedicated people past their limit. Some people are argumentative. Others insist that things be done their way, and become harsh and judgmental when things are done differently. Some people, try as they might, never quite understand what needs to be done, or when. These patterns emerge, but they're not always consistent. You'll meet all of these characters, and more, as you move from one project and company to another.

Although these issues can become the team's problem, the best thing you can do is to focus on your own strengths and weaknesses. This advice seems obvious, but worth saying: you will increase your odds of success and future promotion if you apply for, and accept, jobs that emphasize your strengths.

If you're not entirely sure how to find those strengths, or how to identify the weaknesses, some easy ways are available to identify these characteristics in yourself. One is to visit a career counselor (or your company's human resources department) and ask to take the Myers-Briggs Type Indicator, a personality test that's great for identifying your most natural tendencies, your working strengths, and your weaknesses. You can get some of the same information by reading one of the books based on the MBTI. One of the best books is *Do What You Are* by Paul D. Tieger and Barbara Barron-Tieger (published by Little, Brown). A third way, great for some people and unimaginable for others, is to simply ask your friends to tell you what they think you do well and what you don't do well. Don't just ask one friend. Ask several friends and try to discern patterns. This self-portrait can help you to identify weaknesses. You can work on some weaknesses, and teach yourself either new ways to work or additional skills. Other weaknesses you can accept as part of yourself, and then adjust your tasks accordingly.

The importance of good references

A solid reference is paramount. Don't afford people a reason to give you a denigrating reference. If you work hard, show honest dedication and personal growth, and develop positive relationships, then you should do very well. You don't have to be a star. You simply have to do what you were hired to do, and not cause problems for people who work with you.

The software development industry is growing quickly, but the size of any given niche is relatively small. The odds are that the person who's thinking about hiring you for a new job will know, or can locate, a former workmate. References are easily checked. If you worked diligently, and performed your job, the reference will probably be positive.

You may run into situations that don't allow you to do your best work. You may not get along with a boss or a co-worker whose cooperation is essential. You may find yourself in the midst of a political intrigue. You may be accustomed to working a different pace, or with far more or fewer available resources. For whatever reasons, the job may have changed. These things happen. When they do, it's wise to put the best possible face on the situation, and to move on.

Figuring out what to do next

Some steps are easy, and some are not. When you're a writer, the head writer role beckons. When you're a production assistant, you want to move up to associate producer, and then, to producer. What happens when you are the head writer? The producer? The senior software architect? Where do you go from there?

The answer is found, once again, by talking to people whose jobs interest you. One effective way to find these people is attend a convention or trade show, and to make a point of meeting people in the appropriate positions at interesting companies. Honesty is the key: you want to be completely straight with the person who is giving you his time. You are conducting informational interviews to learn more about potential jobs. You are not looking for a job. You are not using trickery to transform a well-intentioned informational interview into a job interview. These two ideas are separate.

In this fast-paced industry, your targets may not have the time for informational interviewing. Busy managers, often under pressure, are willing to see only real candidates. A manager who must staff a project with ten or twenty people, and has only a few weeks to do so, wants to see the best and the brightest, and needs to making hiring decisions almost on the spot. These are not situations in which the hiring manager will take kindly to your touchy-feely questions about the next step in your career. Instead, he or she presents a job with a list of tasks, and wants to know whether your experience, working style, and personality will "fit." You must be ready with these answers, and do your personal planning elsewhere.

This situation is not impossible. Look to friends and industry associates for guidance on your next steps. Networking can be effective here, not only for contact names but also for a sense of the direction the industry is headed. You might also consider some freelance work, or developing your own projects on the side.

Choose your employers with care

A working relationship, regardless of its formal structure, is a partnership. The company has decided that you're the kind of person who should be a part of it, and you have decided to devote a portion of your life to the company's success. The company's choices, and your own choices, say a great deal about each respective party.

Employment with a big and successful company will, for better or for worse, cause your résumé to get a certain amount of attention, certainly more attention than a smaller company of lesser renown. By being a part of that company, you share in its glory. Conversely, if the company is known to be dreadful, you share in its crummy reputation.

At a "good" company, you will meet plenty of "good" people — people who possess strong work ethics, people who are internally motivated toward excellence, and people who enjoy working with one another. This type of work environment is valuable for several reasons, the most obvious ones being your own self-esteem and the company's positive motion toward success. This kind of environment also tends to attract people who are special: people who might become your friends or allies, and who might help you along in your own career.

These people will prove to be far more important than anticipated over a much longer time. Some of these relationships will span decades. The idea is simple: work beside people who are interested in the same things that interest you. Dream together. Come up with ideas for the company, or for yourselves, that will push you further. Talk about what people outside the company are doing. Look for opportunities within the company in which you can work together and gain some notoriety. Most important for your own career, make an effort to stay in touch with people who leave the company. Under the best of circumstances, this network of former co-workers, and the networks that they inevitably create in future situations, will be valuable to your own career. You are building a network. You will call on these people for references, for ideas when you build your own staffs, for information on potential employers, and for aid in teasing out the realities behind new technical developments. The list is quite long. These are among the most important professional relationships. Over the long term, they may be the most important relationships of all.

Mentors

Along the way, you will also meet managers, associates, and strong individual contributors who will become your mentors. These relationships will develop either directly by working for or with them, or indirectly by simply observing what they do well. A mentor relationship can last years, months, or even weeks, during a critical time when you need a smart person's help.

Mentors can be extremely valuable. Very few people can properly assess their own skills. A mentor is someone you respect, and who also respects you. A mentor can help you to think wisely, and in the best of circumstances, can help you understand how to best handle yourself in a changing environment.

Strangely, many people are put off by the idea that they can be someone else's mentor. Most potential mentors are too busy trying to figure out their own next steps, much less guide the steps someone else might take on their advice. Still, great strength can be gotten from a mentor. The mentor typically gains as well, in self-esteem and possible work in future ventures. Sometimes a mentor provides direct advice: suggesting when to leave a job, deciding which of two offers to take, or handling a particularly difficult employee or co-worker. More often, the wisdom is general, and runs deep. Direct advice might not be forthcoming, but the mentor's own actions and vision might help you to determine your own.

If you are employed at a company that's not working effectively, you may not meet as many people who can be helpful to you in your future endeavors. The managers may not teach you what you want, and need, to know. The company's overall management may not provide the daily lessons that you need to nurture your career.

All of these issues hold true not only for full-time, so-called permanent positions, but also for project work and consulting. In fact, these issues have an even sharper edge for those who go it alone. Great clients — clients who understand their businesses and manage them effectively — make good use of a consultant or contractor's skills. Companies that are poorly managed may not know what to "do" with a skilled consultant, thus driving up the number of days spent by "expensive" consultants because of internal disorganization, lack of focus, and related issues.

How long should you stay with one company?

The answer to this question depends upon you. If you're happy, earning a fair salary, working reasonable hours, and you're learning and advancing, then you should stay where you are. If any one of these factors is missing, it's a sign that you should at least consider the possibility of leaving. If two or more are problematic, then it's probably time to look for a new job.

Bearing in mind that multimedia is a fast-moving business, more accepting of shorter stints on a résumé than you might find in other industries, a jump every two years is not uncommon nor unreasonable. Balanced with some three-to-four-year stays, and the occasional one-year job, such a work history is a more or less ideal for a multimedia résumé. Five years is a long time in this business; if you're going to stay with a company for five years or more, the résumé should show steady growth, with a significant change in job title and responsibilities every 12 to 18 months.

If you leave a company after less than a year's service, this usually suggests that your tenure did not work out as planned. For better or worse, the reason for separation is thought to fall upon the employee. Do this once, and you demonstrate that you can take control of your own life. Do this more often, and you'll have some explaining to do at the next job interview. For those who are happier moving from job to job, freelancing may be a better way of working.

Making the move to management

You perform your job well. You get along with people. You get things done. You are a valued employee, and you love your job. Still, you want to succeed, and to have more of an impact. You've mastered your job and you're ready for the next challenge.

The answer may be management.

Management offers more money, greater control, the opportunity to influence people and events, and the chance to learn how a business operates.

On the other hand, management may necessitate saying goodbye to some of the tasks that you enjoy, and some tasks that you do well. An art director will do some design work, but spends more time guiding other artists and sitting in meetings. A software development manager doesn't write much code; he or she hires other people to do that work, and helps to solve their problems. There's more responsibility, and many people are willing to trade the joy of creation for the feeling of personal growth. Fewer people find a way to combine the two.

Some people naturally gravitate toward management. They truly enjoy supervising others, and provide a wonderful, nurturing environment in which everyone does their best work. There is great creative satisfaction in these activities, and the satisfaction in leading a creative team to a wonderful end result can be even more profound than the joy in doing a great job on your own.

Other people never quite get the hang of management. They're terrific working on their own, or as a significant leader and contributor on small teams. Their joy is derived from the work itself, not from guiding a team.

Most people can learn and succeed at managing through practical experience. Others require some education. This education can be obtained by: spending time with a successful manager and learning his or her ways; by more formal coursework available through human resources, local colleges, and private organizations; or by reading one of the hundreds of books about management style and technique. Some people are not well suited to managing other people. Once again, you'll be most effective if you can develop a clear picture of who you are, what you do well, and those areas in which you need improvement. Play to your strengths, do your best to improve upon weaknesses through every available type of education, and try your best to avoid situations in which the primary work requires you to do things that you don't do especially well.

Developing your own projects

Given some motivation, a powerful desktop computer, and enough time to experiment, most creative people will eventually put together their own projects. Sometimes they're simple, homegrown concoctions: a family tree, begun as a homework assignment for a son or daughter, has now grown way out of proportion with a professional design, unique interface, sound bites, and video clips. This is a pretty typical project. The material is familiar, the assets are available at no cost, and the audience is limited to people who will, probably, enjoy what they see and do. With no commercial potential, the opportunity, and perhaps a good reason, exist to try some ideas and to bring your own project to completion.

With children around, many adults have produced their own interactive storybooks. With the ease of drawing pictures into a computer, or scanning them, only a short step is needed to learn Macromedia Director or some other tool to create some simple animations and interactivity. To add sound effects and voices, you must learn something about multimedia sound, a good exercise for future professional projects. Developing an interface that's easy to understand, and intuitive for children, is also a worthwhile exercise.

Interactive résumés are another popular project. As an adjunct to your print résumé, a multimedia résumé can become a useful demo, something you might show as part of a job interview. Most likely, the electronic résumé will not get you the job. Producing an electronic résumé will put you through the paces of creating your own multimedia project, and this task will force you to think like a marketer. Thinking of yourself as a product is not easy, but that's just what you must do. You must determine how your CD-ROM, interactive package, or Web site should look, what it should communicate, how it will be distributed (by hand on floppy disk, by hand on SyQuest, as a direct mail piece on CD-ROM, or as a Web site), and how it will be produced. In this situation, you are likely to be the screen designer, producer, writer, and programmer. If you can't do all of these tasks, you're going to become proficient at asking favors and in the art of persuasion.

Developing a project as the start of a business venture is the next step. After you've honed your skills, and you're confident that the end result will be presentable and competitive with other demos, start the planning process. Determine what you can do on your own, and what you can ask friends to do for you, either at no charge or by promising they will be paid when (and if) the production is funded. You'll be pleasantly surprised to find that many people want to create their own projects, and to experiment just as you're doing, with an eye on future possibilities. For this reason, you should treat any development project in a businesslike way. Define the business relationships with care; are these people partners or are they simply friends, helping other friends to launch a project and/or business? Take the time to write simple agreements between yourself and every party who contributes ideas, money, other assets, and time. Be sure to clearly detail expectations, deliverables, and, most important for the long-term, who owns what.

Keep your costs down. Don't rent an office; work in your living room. Don't print business cards until you're ready to become a business and ready to talk with people calling the telephone number on the card. Don't hire people when you can do the work yourself, or have friends do it for a reduced fee. If you feel the need to invest cash — some people don't feel that the commitment is serious unless their checking account has a few thousand dollars in available funds — keep the amount limited, and make sure that you set rules regarding how this money can be spent. A double-signature checking account is a safeguard. Don't allow spending money to become too easy; every expense should be scrutinized! Assume that the project will go through several versions. These version changes could be true of the name of the project, its scale, its main characters, and its location, if applicable. Be careful of how you spend your limited funds.

Producing a homegrown product is easier than marketing and selling the product so that it becomes a money-maker. For this reason, producing part of the project or producing a demo is often a better idea than producing an entire project. The demo can be used to show off your skills, and it can be shown to investors and publishers who may be willing to fund the larger-scale production. The demo can be used, very effectively, to determine marketplace interest in the project, and to teach yourself about the changes that must be made in the product plan prior to full-scale production and release. If the demo goes nowhere (the unfortunate reality for most projects), the financial loss should not sting. These projects can be quite valuable in the development of personal skills, the people met along the way, and the general understanding of how products are produced and marketed.

The fact that many home projects do not make it to production and release does not doom your home brew to failure. Your project might make millions. Just don't get your hopes up. Instead, approach the homegrown project as a way to expand the depth and variety of your skills, and as a way to learn. If fate decrees that you learn how to make money along the way, wonderful! Go in with the understanding that the way to make a million dollars is, in all likelihood, found somewhere other than the long hours and late nights associated with an original multimedia project.

Broadening your view – and getting older

The multimedia business is dominated by young people. Many companies were built by people in their twenties. If you're in your thirties, you're middle aged. What happens when you reach your forties and fifties? Do you simply drop out of the business and find something else to do? Do you suddenly become transformed, and take a new shape as an investment banker, with ready money for younger people's projects?

Age should bring experience and wisdom. Experience is a valuable commodity in a business in which younger people dominate. Experience often brings an ability to perceive and solve problems based on a wide array of past successes and failures. Experience also provides a deeper understanding of what's going well and astray, and what steps must be taken. Wisdom is the advanced form of street smarts. Instinct will take you a long way in this business, but street smarts seasoned with the ability to see the forest, the trees, and the underlying ecosystem prove more valuable than street smarts alone.

The elements of the broad view, plus depth of experience and wisdom, can be significant aspects of a senior executive's portfolio. Not everybody, however, becomes a senior executive. Most people don't go that far up the ladder. Instead, they form their own companies, or find niches in which they can excel, consult, or teach. They play to their strengths, and after years of working diligently, priorities change. Working endless hours on someone else's project doesn't hold the kind of appeal that it once did; they want to spend time with their families. Working their way up the ladder no longer fits the plan; they want to do what they enjoy. The world outside the multimedia studio materializes. People abound who are happy, productive, and even wealthy; those people don't work 125 hours a week and don't become obsessed with the speed of the latest PowerMac or the shortcomings of some 21-inch monitor. In short, they become more focused on what's really important to them, and place their work in a more reasonable, whole-life perspective. This refocusing happens to everyone. Some people encounter it sooner than others, but you'll enter this phase of life eventually.

Freelancing

Freelance work is widely available throughout the multimedia industry. Some freelancers treat their assignments as a form of permanent employment. They effectively work for themselves, hiring out for the day, week, month, or project. Other freelancers are simply between full-time jobs, keeping themselves busy and learning about new tasks, technologies, and companies before settling into a more permanent job.

Freelancing has some big benefits. The biggest is the sense of personal accomplishment. A freelancer owns his or her time, and can choose to spend it as he or she sees fit. For some freelancers, the lack of conventional constraints is a reality. For others, the freedoms are a bit of a fantasy because of the constant need for income. The truth usually floats between the two. This free-spirited attitude can be a breath of very fresh air in a corporate environment, but it can also be a source of tension because freelancers may earn more, per day, than corporate employees doing the same work. Also, a freelancer may not perceived as fully committed, regardless of the hours or days spent working alongside permanent employees.

A successful freelancer, one who is well-suited to a variety of tasks, productive, pleasant to have around, and not terribly expensive, can find work on a more or less regular basis. Most freelancers are successful, but only to a degree. They live with the constant cycle of feast and famine. The feast arrives in a particular week, or month, when so much work is available that the freelancer must turn some of it away. The famine shows its face when nobody calls with work. Those who work as freelancers rarely sell their services throughout the year, and often find that they can make more money with a full-time job.

Freelance work is not necessarily a full-time endeavor. Many people freelance while working at full-time jobs. An illustrator, screen artist, interface designer, writer, video editor, composer, or musician will find relative ease in working from home on a freelance assignment. The work is done behind closed doors, on one's own time. Some employers frown upon freelance work; others acknowledge that creative people often freelance as a way of earning some extra money and exploring new creative forms. Some ask that work not be done for direct competitors; confidentiality may be an issue. Others ask that the work not be done on company premises, using company resources such as the telephone and computers. Some employers are vigilant in their restrictions, and frighten employees to a point that freelancing is simply not done; others establish a work environment in which the occasional freelance project is fine, but ongoing freelance work is contrary to the company's best interests. Even with a single company, policies, traditions, and attitudes may vary.

Notwithstanding the rules and restrictions, freelancing offers the individual three potentially important opportunities: to earn extra money, to meet and work with new people, and to experiment with new roles without committing to them for a livelihood.

Working at home

With so many people now working at home, rules can be difficult to understand and to apply. One person can work at home 100 percent of the time and be considered an employee. Another does similar work, as an independent contractor, in an office used daily which is supplied by the company. The difference between the two examples is that companies vary in their rules. The IRS, however, does not recognize these differences. That person working in the company's office, presumably under the company's direction and control, is in all likelihood an employee.

These similar, yet different, work situations are gray areas. If a person works in a series of company offices for a limited period of time, then the person is more likely to be considered an independent contractor. If the person works in a company office, but does not work under the direct control of a company supervisor, then he or she is probably a contractor. History plays into this, too. If the person's normal way of working is to travel from one facility to another, then independent contractor status is probably more accurate.

Take the example of an artist who is hired to work on a project. For the convenience of all, the artist works at a desk supplied by the company. Equipment is provided by the company. If the artist works the same regular hours as the rest of the staff, and works as part of the team within the same schedule of deliverables, then the independent contractor designation is shaky. If the artist works his or her own hours, and is generally responsible for delivery of items on deadline, then the independent contractor definition is more likely to apply. The differences are subtle. If the same artist works sporadically for a company, and also works at his or her own facility (thus generating regular income), then the independent contractor definition is more likely to apply. The most important factor in this definition is the status of a primary employment.

Benefits

For people who freelance, and who also work in full-time jobs occasionally, the benefits situation can become pretty messy. A freelancer should maintain his or her own health benefits. When that same person enters the world of a company that buys insurance for all employees, the freelancer may be reluctant to give up a long-term relationship with a health insurance provider. Because companies usually provide long-term places for employees to hang their digital hats, this choice creates a potential conflict at the time of hiring. If you're young, in your twenties, then choosing the company plan is probably the best idea. If you're older, in your forties, then staying with your independent plan might be a better choice. The second choice assures that if anything happens after you've left the company, you won't be left trying to apply for health insurance as an older newcomer.

Group health insurance is a good idea in theory, but is not easy to find for freelancers. Most apply on their own.

CHAPTER 11

Should You Form Your Own Company?

✦ Being an employee has its drawbacks, and being self-employed has its advantages. But the inverse is also true for both — choose carefully.

✦ Many multimedia professionals already *are* their own companies, even if they don't know it. Independent contractors count.

✦ Consider the pros and cons of various approaches to taxes and other laws before you form any corporation.

✦ Running your own business is time consuming. Running your own *multimedia* business is *extremely* time consuming.

Multimedia and Web businesses are moving and growing at an astonishing rate. The opportunities are vast; someone can be working at a mid-level programming job one year and end up on the front page of *The Wall Street Journal* a year later. Most people remain employees or go freelance. For a select few, a new company is the only way to go. That way, in addition to being an employee and a freelancer, they can take on the additional headaches of payrolls, taxes, legal considerations, and establishing a solid corporate foundation. Maybe it sounds daunting, but it's the American dream — your own business. And despite the travails of getting your own company going, you may find satisfactions that go far beyond mere dollars and cents. The ability to cast your own direction, plot your own future, and keep control over your professional destiny is a situation worth envying, despite the perceived downsides.

The multimedia and Internet have generated thousands of new companies. Some grow; here and there, a company makes a fortune. Most companies stay small, either by design or because of their leaders' limited business expertise. Others shoot up because of the vagaries of the investment community; according to Wall Street, multimedia and the Internet are hot. Of course, that's this week. Next week, someone will say the revolution is over, and investments will drop. The week after that, it's hot again, and the cycle begins anew.

People form companies because they see clear and present business opportunities. To put this another way, people form businesses because they can clearly see their customers (or, in the case of some Internet businesses, their investors). Companies may be built on ideas, but they succeed because they satisfy a particular customer need.

Getting Started

Building a company is not easy. Most people don't do it very effectively. In fact, most fail. A great many others make a mess of it, even if they have the wherewithal to keep their companies going through the inevitable thick and thin. In this business, a lot of the "traditional" rules just don't apply. You can have a great product, but the market for it can dry up literally overnight — even before you've finished developing it. You can bet the farm on a hot new technology that's being promised by major Japanese hardware makers, only to find that those same companies have decided to wait another fiscal year before releasing it, much to the chagrin of your newly assembled development team. You can author great products for an important online service, only to watch that service take an extreme veer in technology, rendering all your hard work virtually obsolete. In short, you can do everything right and still end up losing out.

There is no one "right way" to build a company. In fact, many companies have succeeded while doing everything "wrong" — at least according to the traditional rules that most success stories follow. The story typically begins with one, two, or three people who know their business. They identify a specific need, a gap in the marketplace, a way to do something differently, or better, or a new technology with some potential.

The next step is researching and prototyping.

Research, if the core business grows from technology, can take years, or, in the case of a marketing-driven venture, months. The race is to get something up and running, some sort of visible or tangible prototype, as quickly as possible, so potential customers, clients, and/or investors can gain a clear understanding of the business' offering. Often, this process requires multiple steps — the first prototype isn't right, didn't work, didn't take some marketplace force into consideration, didn't address some competitive issue — so more time and money must be applied in order to make it right. This process can strain even the best relationship. Start-ups are not for everyone. Most people give up or put the project aside. Some persevere.

For those who move ahead, the next step is gaining advocates. It's rare that one person, or even two or three people, can launch a new business. Gaps are filled with consultants, or part-time employees — at least until the company can support some salaries. Business cards, brochures, and promotional or prototypical Web sites are produced, often when the business has no money in the checking account.

You can get the money in one of three ways. One method is to jump-start the business by getting money from clients and/or customers. (This works only if the project is ready, or ready enough so that people will actually pay for it before final delivery.) Another approach is to sell the future of your venture as a way to raise money from investors, trading away parts of the project's ownership to pay current bills. A third way is to expand the business offering — provide some sort of consulting or project service based on expertise available from the company's members, or license a core technology or intellectual property asset. This strategy can distract from the primary goal, but it allows the company's founders to keep the venture alive.

If the purpose of the company is to provide services — to build Web sites, for example — then the process is a bit simpler. The company puts together an electronic brochure — typically a Web site and some print support materials — and then starts reaching out for customers by meeting people, advertising, and doing some public relations. Some of the most successful start-up companies have been based on this premise — a great-looking collection of start-up smoke-and-mirrors that get people excited enough to jump on as customers. On the Web, nobody sees the size of your staff, or cares about how many people are putting in how many hours. A great Web site, one that gets people so excited that perhaps your company can build just as great a Web site for them, is often enough of a sales pitch. A small company can have a big presence on the Web — which, in terms of publishing, is the great equalizer between big companies and small companies.

Thinking big

The key word is here is "proprietary." To build something big, you need something proprietary at the core of the business. This could be a proprietary technology, such as one that provides real-time audio on the Web. It could be a proprietary license to a valuable intellectual property — for example, *Sesame Street.* It could be proprietary or preemptive access to one or more marketing channels. If the product or service is well ahead of competitors, then timing itself can be a proprietary asset.

Short of these advantages, the next best solution is a great idea and a team with amazing credentials. Of course, that puts you in competition with about another million or so small multimedia companies who are selling the same thing, at least in their opinion. This industry is often likened to the California gold rush. There are a lot of prospectors out there, and if your major sales point is that you do what you do better than anyone else does, you should understand that a lot of your competition is making the same claim.

Great ideas don't just happen, of course. They begin as notions, and grow as they're tested, evaluated, modified, tested again, reconstructed, refined, and put together in a coherent way. The idea itself almost never stands on its own. The idea is important, but proper execution is, in some ways, even more important.

That's where the amazing team comes in. The four components to this amazing team can be stated in remarkably simple language: you need someone to make it, someone to sell it, someone to manage it, and someone to count.

Making it is the job of the development person, who is almost always a technical wizard or strong technical manager. This person is responsible for the implementation of the product, which in this business doesn't always count for everything. In a crowded market like multimedia, the quality of the product isn't always a guarantee of success — in fact, most often, it's not.

Selling it is the job of the marketer, someone who understands the marketplace and understands how the product or service will fit. This individual is probably the most important member of the company, because unless the product sells, there's no capital to produce another one. The manager in this group is responsible for making sure that the developer and the salesperson are doing their jobs. The person who needs to count it all up at the end of the day will be the final arbiter of whether the preceding three individuals did their jobs well.

The core management team

Finding a senior executive to manage a new company can be difficult. The founder, who has the overview, is often the first choice. He or she possesses the vision, the passion, and, often, an appropriate broad-based combination of skills to get things moving. These skills may well be the ones that the company most desperately needs to get started. They may not, however, be the skills required a year later. A surprisingly small percentage of founders remain with their companies as CEOs. Instead, the role is more often filled by a professional manager.

Many small companies put off the hiring of a professional financial manager until it's too late. It's far better to hire this person as soon as funds are available, even as a part-time position. The early hiring of a chief financial officer can be an extremely wise move. An effective bookkeeping and accounting system is essential for every company. You'll save yourself all sorts of headaches if you set things up properly from the start — and if you keep a professional involved in the day-to-day operations of the business. But that's only part of the story. An experienced CFO can work with banks and other financial institutions to arrange loans and lines of credit, and can work with potential investors with a far greater degree of sophistication than other members of the team. An effective CFO will also see problems long before they happen, and, you hope, suggest possible solutions.

Other members of the team can do at least some of this work. But one person, wholly dedicated to the financial aspects of company operations, can usually do the job better.

And, by the way: don't confuse the work of an internal CFO with the services provided by an outside accounting firm. Although the basic financial record keeping and reporting can be handled by either, only the CFO, who is with the company every day (or, if need be, several days each week), will truly understand the opportunities and the potential problems.

Finding good people

The idea for a business will take the venture only so far. Good people — people who are experienced, enthusiastic, capable, and easy to enjoy working with every working day — these are the resources that every business must have in place if it is to succeed. Finding the right people is not easy.

This process begins, of course, by paging through your own address book. Names of past employers, past employees, contractors, clients, and customers are a good place to begin. The best medium for the preliminary work is the telephone; recruiting is a very time-consuming process, one that requires plenty of time and dedication.

After you've spoken with your inner circle and contacted people who are likely to return your calls, start the e-mail campaign. E-mail is an enormously useful tool for recruiting; you send the job description to people in your address book, and if the message is enticing, they forward the description to dozens, and perhaps, hundreds of other people. The responses come quickly and from unexpected places. Resumes via e-mail are now commonplace, so you can get a reasonably complete picture of someone quickly.

Newspaper advertisements can be useful, but only for some jobs. Results can be hard to predict, but it's worth doing because ads don't cost much. Some ads pull, others don't. A better idea is to place advertisements in appropriate trade magazines. This not only ensures that you're communicating with the specific crowd that you want to reach, but that you'll be hearing from professionals who are savvy enough to be reading the appropriate trade magazines in the first place.

With all of this activity, you'll be generating names of potential employees. But even with all this electronic communication, the very best way to do the serious recruitment is by telephone, which is an essential step even if the basis of the phone call came from electronic correspondence. Call one person and ask for several more contacts. Call each of them and ask for more names. Start these chains early in the process, because they take shape over time.

Choosing the best location

Many people start new businesses from home. This is a wonderful idea because overhead is low, hours flexible, and comfort level high. This may also be a rotten idea because the environment is filled with distractions, the hours are so flexible that some people can spend every waking hour in the office, and home is not the place to meet with potential employees or investors. Still, the good usually outweighs the bad, and for the first few weeks or months, it's not unusual to see a business nurtured at home. According to the most recent statistics from the Electronic Industries Association, a trade group that keeps count of these things, there are now almost forty million Americans working out of their home, full- or part-time.

Working at home often makes sense for the founder, and, maybe, for one or two more people. When the company grows beyond this core, it's probably time for an office.

Ideally, the office should be selected so that it will satisfy the company's needs for the first two years. In the real world, the first office is usually rented because it's inexpensive and because it suits the company's current needs. If possible, try to rent a smaller space with the opportunity to expand into a larger one in the same building. This saves the company from a big (and disruptive!) move early on, allows the business cards and stationery to remain the same, keeps the same phone and fax numbers, and so on.

For a start-up, there's no reason to pay a premium for an impressive address. Rent functional space. Your company's reputation will grow based on accomplishment, not on your choice of office space. However, in this business it pays to be close to where the action is. Even though clients and employees can communicate and work through electronic means, there is definitely value in being part of a multimedia community. It may be cheaper to rent an office in the suburbs outside of major multimedia centers such as San Francisco, New York, and Los Angeles. But if you're too far away or otherwise inaccessible, you'll find that traffic into your office might be less heavy than you had hoped for. It's a trade-off — proximity versus economy — and each situation should be decided on its own individual merits.

Office side dishes add up to a main course

Consider security. You'll be bringing in plenty of expensive equipment, and either buying or leasing more over time. The equipment will be quite visible; people who live and work near your company will see the trucks, the deliveries. They will know that your company's offices contain expensive equipment. Is the equipment safe at your new office? More important, are the workers safe? An abandoned urban loft district might be a hip and trendy address to have on a business card, but trendiness can seem a very dim benefit when workers have to leave the office in a deserted neighborhood at odd hours of the night. Many multimedia companies open offices in these less-than-corporate locations, valuing the funk that these neighborhoods can provide. Exposed bricks and high ceilings are great, but the choice of neighborhood should be carefully evaluated. Employees and contractors will inevitably work late. They'll want meals brought in, often at odd hours. Safety is one consideration; access to services is another. A security system for the office is essential. So is secure access, with cards or keys. First-floor or basement offices can be especially vulnerable. Buildings without front entrance security can be vulnerable, too.

Power is another concern. Older buildings may look great, but you'll be operating new equipment that's sensitive to uneven power. A trusted electrician should evaluate the building's systems and explain the upgrade options. If you're working with a long-term lease, talk with the landlord about the possibility of a power upgrade. It may be worth the investment on your company's end to ensure reliable AC for the long nights ahead. And, of course, you haven't forgotten to figure in expenses for uninterruptable power supplies, have you?

The telecommunications situation should be evaluated, too. Multimedia and Internet businesses are highly dependent upon dependable telephone service, and upon special lines, such as ISDN, T1, and T3. Although these services are generally available, there are some situations that make installation or service more complicated. Some cities are served by more than one telephone system; if you're thinking about several locations, access to the best, most versatile, most forward-thinking telephone system can be a real advantage.

Satellite service and cable TV service can be considerations, too. With cable modems on the way, it's wise to check on the availability of cable service for the new company location, and to check on the local cable company's recent history with technological innovations. With the recent federal deregulations in the communications industry, these considerations aren't nearly as cut-and-dried as they were just a few months ago. But they're still a consideration to be aware of. Your first few company headquarters are likely to be rental facilities. Be sure to ask about telecommunications, cable TV, and related concerns before you sign a rental agreement.

This sampling of office rental issues related to multimedia and Internet businesses should provide only part of the list of considerations. A much longer list might include physical modifications to the property, availability of parking, distance to public transportation, length of the lease, option on additional space, and so on. All of these things can be translated into money, one way or another, and should be factored into any decisions about the office space that's made on financial grounds. For example, you might save several hundred dollars in monthly rent from location A to location B. But if you, your partners, or your workforce have to spend hundreds of dollars per month in commuting or parking costs, the savings don't seem quite so real. Convenience has a value, which becomes higher each time an employee has to wait for a bus at a deserted stop on a rainy night.

The best way to learn about these issues is to talk to other people who have started companies and helped them to grow. Employees and friends can be useful sources, but don't limit your exploration to this group. Talk to other people who own businesses in your intended rental site, and other people who have rented in the area. Find out what you can about the landlord, the rental agent, and the building. Make a decision based on your intellect, not necessarily your gut feeling. Caution is always an advantage, especially when negotiating a lease, and more so when establishing a corporate locale for your new business.

Setting Up the Office

It's probably reasonable to assume that the needs of most multimedia and Web-based businesses are similar. If the property is mainly intended for production, then a small reception area and a small conference room may be all that outside clients expect to see. Production facilities do not require elaborate interior design, matching desktops, custom furniture, and so on. Go for the functional, at least until you're profitable. Used furniture is fine. So are big tables purchased at STAPLES or Office Depot. (Don't scrimp on the file cabinets, though — the inexpensive ones will fall apart. Also, spend as much as you can on comfortable seating.)

When you start thinking seriously about the new space, try to estimate the number of offices you'll need for the first year or two. Offices can be relatively small, and they can be shared, but be sure you allow more than enough open space for storage, files, and meeting areas. One conference room is essential, two are better. Windows and proper lighting go a long way toward good morale (fluorescent lighting is discouraging; try for incandescent light, preferably bounced off a high ceiling, with desk lamps). Go for at least one-third more space than your most generous estimate seems to indicate; you will always need more space. (And, worst case, you can always sublet some of the unused space.)

Pre-wire everything before you move in. Hire an experienced person to work out cable runs; otherwise, you'll be tripping over cables and, possibly, knocking out your small computer network.

Virtual Offices

With telecommunications so central to this industry, it's only natural for some people to want to work at home, or in a remote location. For the individual, there are real benefits: less time spent commuting means more time available for work, time uninterrupted by meetings and questions from co-workers, work at one's own pace, and so on. For the company, this can be a wonderfully forward-looking approach to work, and a way to attract talented individual contributors.

The ideal candidate for a virtual office is someone who is responsible for specific deliverables, supplied on a regular basis. People who work with words, such as editors and writers, are ideal because the transfer of works in progress from one location to another is easy with e-mail. People who work with pictures, such as artists and art directors, are also well-suited, though high-speed lines or patience for overnight delivery of SyQuests or Zip disks may be part of the formula. Public relations people can work from home, at least part of the time, because they spend so much of their time on the telephone, and because press releases and press kits are easily prepared at home as well.

Key members of the management team can work at home, or in a remote location, but only if the supporting management structure is strong and well trained. In general, senior people are available in the office for at least a few days a week, or a few weeks each month. Any manager who works away from the office should employ a full-time administrative assistant who works at the main office all the time.

The Board of Directors

One of the best ways to expand the network of contacts available to a new company is to recruit a board of directors. The board, comprised of individuals who are charged with the guidance of the business venture, should be able to make things happen above and around the company itself. Board members should be experienced, well-connected business people who can provide the level of guidance necessary for a young company to grow strong. They should have a substantial personal investment in the company's success, or they should represent companies whose investments are more meaningful than just money. They should have a vested interest in the company's success, and be willing and able to bring a great deal of assistance as the result of a powerful telephone call or friendly meeting with an old friend.

The board of directors is responsible, ultimately, to the shareholders. They are responsible, therefore, for company operations. The senior executives report to the board. This means, in effect, that the CEO, President, COO, CFO, and the various VPs work for the board, despite what might be suggested by an organization chart. Active board members communicate regularly with the senior team, offering help when it's needed (not just at the monthly board meetings) and identifying potential problems and solutions.

A wise, street-smart board of directors can monitor company progress and institute changes as necessary. When smart, dedicated people work together, there is likely to be a variety of opinions. A successful board works through these opinions, and proceeds as a positive force. It is not unusual to find a board member who is at odds with the other members; properly harnessed, this, too, can be a positive force. When things are not going well, there is likely to be some friction between one or more board members and the senior management team. This friction is often healthy, but it can become a messy problem. In these situations, a few months of fear, anger, and long, long weekend phone calls usually results in a change of personnel — sometimes on the board, sometimes on the senior management team, and, most often, in both places. It's not a desirable scenario, but it is a natural one.

Trusted Advisors

When forming a partnership, corporation, or LLC (limited liability corporation), the services of an experienced attorney are essential. Although it is possible to form a corporation without an attorney (most bookstores sell at least a few books about forming your own corporation), the potential pitfalls are too great to justify the savings of a few thousand dollars. To do the job properly, hire a professional. A good attorney, one who is experienced in setting up new companies, will provide far more than advice on LLCs or C corporations. He or she will provide guidance and direction, point out potential problems, introduce your company to people who can help, and perhaps suggest possible members of the management team.

It's best to hire an attorney who specializes in the multimedia or Internet business. Even with the explosive growth of this industry, there aren't all that many of these attorneys around — yet. But this industry carries special considerations of all sorts, and experience on the legal end can save aggravation and money later on. Most of the attorneys who specialize in these fields are located in San Francisco, Los Angeles, and New York. If you work elsewhere, find a local company with similar issues (that is, a company that develops Web sites, and so on), and ask someone for a referral.

Attorney's fees are likely to be $150–250 per hour, plus minimal expenses. It costs about $1,000–$2,000 to form a corporation, sometimes more to form an LLC.

A good accountant can provide parallel services while rendering the official duties in the management of your new company's finances.

Business Formats

Strictly speaking, there is no such thing as a company. There are sole proprietorships, partnerships, corporations, and LLCs (a relatively new format called "Limited Liability Company").

When you first start out, you may decide to do business under your own name, as an independent contractor. This is fine, perfectly acceptable, and, as long as you pay your taxes and follow some other basic rules, you should not run into any problems.

Sole proprietorships

Some people feel that their own name is somehow inappropriate for business use. So they print up business cards and stationery, and call themselves by a company name: The Internet Bagel Company, or something along that line. There's nothing wrong with this approach, and it works for many companies. However, it's necessary to register this name with a local authority, because you are no longer doing business as an individual. You are now doing business as a company. Sometimes called a "DBA" (which is short for "Doing Business As"), this format is extremely common, especially among very small businesses. In most cases, you'll need a DBA certificate before you can open a business checking account in the company's name.

With a sole proprietorship, you can hire employees, and you must comply with a range of government regulations. You can take out a loan. But you must pay taxes as an individual. Once again: in a sole proprietorship, the individual must pay personal tax on the company's profits.

A sole proprietorship is ideal for the individual who wants to look and feel more like a company. With a few employees, however, the situation can become quite complicated.

Partnerships

If a company is owned by two or more parties, then it may be organized as a partnership.

There are two types of partnerships. In a general partnership, the partners are actively involved: they own and operate the business together. In a limited partnership, there's a general partner, who is responsible for day-to-day management and is liable for financial obligations, and one or more limited partners whose involvement is limited in that they do not participate in day-to-day operations, and whose liability is limited to the amount of money they have invested.

Partners do not have to be individuals. Partners can be corporations or just about any other kind of legal entity (even other partnerships).

A joint venture is a kind of partnership that's usually formed for a specific business venture, such as the development of several CD-ROMs. A joint venture may have broader applications, too. It's best to leave the distinctions for attorneys who specialize in these business formats.

Partnerships are usually good news/bad news situations. The good news is that there's more than one smart person in charge. The bad news is that there's more than one smart person in charge. Each partner has the right to obligate the other, both operationally and financially. Partners pay individual taxes on the company's profits; partnerships do not typically pay federal taxes on their income.

As a rule, media companies are not often organized as partnerships. Liability is one reason why. There are large amounts of money involved, and either partner could, in theory, spend that money unwisely and jeopardize the financial stability of the other partner. A corporation provides more security — but there is more paperwork, and, usually, there's a bigger tax preparation bill at the end of each year as well.

Corporations

There are three kinds of corporations. The older, more familiar C corporations and S corporations are covered here. The newer Limited Liability Corporation, or LLC, is covered in the next section.

A corporation is a legal entity that exists separately from its owners. People who own parts, or shares, of the company are called shareholders. These shareholders elect a board of directors, who are, in turn, responsible for the election of corporate officers, the approval of significant company operations (approving a large expenditure or a substantial loan, for example), and setting overall policy. All of this may sound overblown for a small company, but a corporation is often the appropriate choice for media companies.

Because a corporation is a separate legal entity, the people who own the corporation are shielded, to at least some degree, from third-party legal actions. Media companies who are sensitive to libel, slander, copyright infringement, and related issues are often advised to become corporations (thus providing at least some protection for the people who run the company). The corporation format also allows employees, and other people, to own shares, or to participate in a stock option plan. There are other issues related to pension and profit-sharing plans, and ownership of property in which a corporation can offer advantages; an experienced accountant can detail these advantages.

"C" and "S" Corporations

A "C" corporation is a standard corporation, one that pays federal taxes and generally operates as a separate legal entity.

An "S" corporation is a variation on the C corporation format, one that allows accountants and clients some special flexibility. With an S corporation, the company's profits and losses are passed on to the shareholders. The key here, in many situations, is not the profits but the losses. Some individuals can lessen their tax burden by showing a loss in an S corporation.

There are some significant limitations affecting C corporations. For one thing, a C corporation can be owned by no more than 35 shareholders. For another, none of the shareholders can be a corporation. On a related note, a C corporation cannot become a subsidiary of another corporation.

A corporation must be identified by "Corp.," "Inc.," or "Ltd." at the end of its name.

As a rule, if you're a small player and your profits may never amount to a large amount, then an S corporation could save you some money, if for nothing more than income tax preparation. If, however, you have plans for future growth, then a C corporation is probably the better choice.

Note: A *big* but: BUT! Every situation is different. And the rules and best possible advice change constantly. So: Consult your attorney and your accountant. Do not, under any circumstances, base your business decisions solely on what you've read in this book! The advice of an experienced legal counsel is not an option here, it is a necessity.

Limited Liability Company (LLC)

A new business format, one which combines some positive aspects of S corporations, partnerships, and C corporations, is the Limited Liability Company, or LLC. Like a partnership or S corporation, Federal taxes are not paid at the corporate level, but at the personal level instead. Like a C corporation, personal assets are protected, or shielded, by the presence of the corporate entity. Ownership is also more flexible, so the benefits of an S corporation are available — without the other problems associated with that business format.

While it is expensive, and somewhat complicated, to change a corporation or partnership over to an LLC, the formation of a new LLC is relatively uncomplicated. If you are forming a new company, be sure to ask your attorney, and your accountant, about an LLC.

A careful comparison between a sole proprietorship, S corporation, C corporation, LLC, and, if applicable, partnership, should be made before you make any final decision in starting your company. This comparison should consider present ownership, the possibility of future sale of shares in the company, the possibility of a future public offering, potential for personal liability, your interest in taking in partners, and, perhaps the most difficult to foresee, future company plans and directions.

A resource

Information about corporate entities varies from state to state. Still, many sources of information are available from your local bookstore or public library. You might also contact the accounting firm, Coopers & Lybrand, for a copy of "Choice of Entity," available from its National Tax Services group, located at 1800 M Street NW, Washington, DC 20077-5984.

Financing

When a new company is formed, financing becomes a primary concern. Many creative people simply expand their successful freelance careers into small production companies. The financing aspects of these companies are covered in this section.

To get a company started, you really don't need much more than business cards, a checking account, and the ability to sell potential clients on your company's plans and/or capabilities. There's no need for a full-scale office, for a serious investment in hardware or software, or for a Web site. All of these are reasonable investments, but they look a whole lot more reasonable after there's some money coming in.

In most cases, whatever early money you need, you will supply your own, or take in from friends and relatives. Banks will not be interested in loaning money, and venture capitalists won't even talk to you unless you've got a serious business plan that presents substantial short-term growth. So, for better or worse, the step many producers take is toward a production deal.

Production deals

Many software products and the majority of Web sites are produced by third parties: companies who specialize in product development. These companies are typically paid per project by publishers and other organizations for their creative work and for their technical expertise.

Project funding is not, typically, a way to grow a company. It is, however, a reasonable way to produce projects under the auspices of your own company. This process typically proceeds along two parallel paths.

On one path, a product development or marketing executive takes responsibility for the creation of a product or product line. He or she considers possible ways in which the work might get done: hiring an internal staff, hiring some key internal people but outsourcing some or all of the development and production work, or hiring an internal marketing and distribution staff, outsourcing nearly all product development. There is no single "right way" to do this; people have succeeded, and failed, with each approach.

On a parallel path, one or more talented producers, designers, writers, and/or programmers decide that the time is right to venture on their own. They put together a company, pool their resources to build an office, and set out in search of clients. They may decide to produce products for other companies, or to publish their own work, or they may decide to do both. Self-publishing usually requires a cash investment. Producing products for other companies requires some impressive prototyping and the ability to sell new clients on the company's capabilities. Most companies opt for the production route, mostly because it's an attainable goal.

The two companies get together and agree to work on a project together. They detail the project's specifications and agree to a schedule, deliverables, a budget, and a payment plan. Most projects are made on a work-for-hire basis; the company that funds the project owns all of the rights. Most projects are also made as a buy-out; the company that funds the project keeps all future revenues.

This is not an altogether gloomy scenario. There is a company where there was none before. The production budget includes money to pay some or all of the staff salaries during the production period, plus additional money to pay freelancers and other contractors (an outside design firm, for example).

Working for fees, if the projects are more or less continuous, is standard procedure for freelancers and other contractors. If the work is more or less continuous, then fees can provide a comfortable income. If the work comes in feast-and-famine cycles, which is more typical in the creative world, then operating a company with production fees can become troublesome. Also, the staff lines in a production budget are locked-in when the budget is approved. If the production requires more time — and this is often the case — then the budgeted amounts will not cover the total amounts paid in salaries and contractor fees. (In some cases, the funder will provide additional money, and this really does happen from time to time, but this, too, is tricky way to run a business.)

Royalties

Some projects offer the production company an opportunity for future monies, typically in the form of royalties.

Let's say the project is a children's CD-ROM. The project is budgeted at $125,000. If the project has been budgeted properly, it should cost between $100,000 and $110,000 to produce. The remaining $15,000–$25,000 should cover overhead and help to provide a profit to the producer. In some deals, this $125,000 is considered to be an advance against future royalties. Given a $25 retail product (a reasonable price for a children's CD-ROM), and an 8 percent royalty (equal to $2 per unit), the product would have to sell 62,500 units before the producer received any additional royalty income (because 62,500 units, multiplied by $2 per unit, equals $125,000). Not a great deal, because most children's CD-ROM products sell nowhere near 62,500 units. It would be better to ask for another $5,000–$10,000 up front and let the publisher keep all future revenues. Better still, it would be wise to negotiate a deal in which a percentage (preferably, a high percentage) of the upfront fee be paid as a production fee, having nothing to do with the royalty. The publisher simply pays to have the work made, and then the producer receives a royalty (perhaps the 8 percent, perhaps a bit less) on every unit sold. A publisher may complain about the risk and ask to recoup at least some of its investment before paying royalties. This, too, is reasonable. The publisher is likely to recoup after sales in the 10,000–15,000 unit range, at least on projects produced for budgets in the under-$250,000 range.

The same basic ideas apply to other kinds of projects. For the producer, it's generally best to get as much money upfront as possible — covering all costs is essential, and covering all costs with a reasonable profit is better still. After that issue has been resolved, then it's reasonable to proceed with further negotiations. If the work is highly dependent upon the producer's talents, or upon a unique technology, then the producer should receive a percentage of future revenues. If the product is more pedestrian and could be made by any of a large number of competing producers, or the publisher already publishes a substantial line of similar works, then it's more difficult for the producer to negotiate for participation.

Most production companies find themselves working from one project to the next, never really growing because they're so busy producing. They are dependent upon the relationships with publishers, they can handle only a limited number of projects at one time, and, perhaps most significant in terms of growth, they are largely dependent upon the 10-20 percent profit built into the production budgets. Most products do not generate any royalty income, and those that do tend to generate relatively small amounts over long periods of time.

For these reasons, most production companies find it difficult to grow. Unless, of course, they move into other businesses, the most obvious being self-publishing.

Development deals

In the motion picture business, a studio sometimes negotiates a contract with a successful producer or writer or director or performer. The studio pays a weekly or monthly fee in exchange for the right to develop the creative person's projects. The economics of the software business may eventually support this kind of relationship. In today's world, these kinds of development deals are very rare.

Loans

A loan must be repaid at a reasonable rate of interest within a specified period of time. A loan agreement must be signed by a company officer and by the person (or company) making the loan.

A new media company is not likely to get a loan from a bank or other financial institution. The business changes quickly, and is likely to seem unstable to conservative sources of money. A company in need of a loan is more likely to find interested parties in family, friends, and, in some cases, vendors or customers who see potential in the new venture.

Writing a Business Plan

Nothing can assure the success of a business. The odds favoring success can be increased by taking the time to write a business plan.

Business plans serve several purposes, nearly all of which are worthy of the time and trouble involved in the preparation of a top-notch plan. The most valuable aspect of the plan is probably internal — the preparation of a written plan forces the new business owner to clearly state the purpose of the business and to describe its operations and its potential for making money in a clear, well-thought-out language. This encourages thinking well beyond "Hey, we'll make a lot of money by making Web pages for other companies" or "We'll produce CD-ROMs for Spanish-speaking children."

Another purpose of the plan is related to recruitment. People who are experienced with start-ups know that these ventures can be wild rides. A carefully written business plan at least suggests the possibility that someone has given some thought to the structure of the business and its future. Recognizing that the plan is almost always obsolete, at least in part, before it comes back from the copy shop, a business plan acknowledges the need and presents some proof of planning.

The most common use of a business plan is for presentation to potential investors. For this reason, a healthy chunk of any business plan is filled with financial pages: assumptions, sales projections, operating budgets, and a balance sheet. At this stage, the business plan needs to be considerably more than broad strokes and dreams; it must be a responsible statement of the company's goals, opportunities, and financial state. Investors make their decisions based upon information provided in the plan, so it must be accurate and up-to-date.

Of course, the object of the game is not to write, rewrite, and revise the business plan over and over again. It's wise to write a preliminary plan when the business is just starting up (for proof of concept and, possibly, for recruitment), and to prepare a substantial revision when the company is in need of funding.

Structure of the business plan

The business plan is usually a stylized document adhering to certain communicative and structural conventions that will make it easy to read for potential investors who, in all likelihood, are busy with other matters — and probably other business plans. No matter how cutting-edge your business, no matter how unusual your approach, the business plan is best left as a formal document that sticks to the established rules. Not everyone who reads your business plan is going to read it from cover to cover — perhaps all they'll be interested in is your basic financial model, or your projections for the next three years. These people want to get to the information that they need, and get to it fast. An eccentric business plan (from a presentation standpoint) is probably a first strike against your company. That being said, there is a form to be followed, outlined in the next several sections.

The cover page

The cover page should name the business and provide a business address, telephone number, fax number, e-mail address, Web site address (if applicable), and a statement of confidentiality. Confidential information in the plan may include names of key executive staff who have not yet made their intentions public, market data commissioned for the plan, observations on market trends, details on proprietary products, and, of course, financial projections.

Statement of confidentiality

The confidentiality statement (which might appear on the page following the cover page, and/or might be a part of a separate confidentiality agreement) should identify the business plan as a confidential document, and should clearly state that the plan is distributed to a limited number of people, as designated by the owner of the plan. The plan cannot be distributed to unauthorized third parties, and it cannot be copied without written authorization. Some plans are individually numbered. This is a good idea because the plan is likely to change, and the company may want to replace older copies with newer ones, or to recall copies from parties who have not come through with financing.

A table of contents

A table of contents is next, preferably keyed to colored sections that make the whole plan easy to navigate. Again, try not to be fancy here. The reader wants efficiency, not style (in most cases).

The Executive Summary

The Executive Summary follows. It should run 2–3 pages. This summary should identify the business opportunity in concise terms, and then demonstrate how the new company will take advantage of that opportunity. This part of the document should be written for the average investor, taking the time to explain the industry and the nature of the business in sufficient detail, and with sufficient clarity, that there is no question about the nature of the investment. Investors like to see the opportunity in a quantified form: how many households currently have 28.8 modems and CD-ROMs and Windows 95; how many new Web sites were produced in the St. Louis area in 1996; how many independently owned and operated hardware stores will benefit from this new product information kiosk. Estimates are fine, but reliable sources behind those estimates, such as from trade groups and respected publications, are essential.

The summary should also include brief information about the company's history and development to date, a rundown on the key company strengths and the immediate competition, the amount of money needed and the plans for its use, and finally, an upbeat look at the future of the company. Most people read the executive summary very carefully, so it's important to get it right: to make certain that the language is clear, that there are no usage, grammatical, or spelling errors, that the numbers make logical sense, and so on. The executive summary should be followed by a chart showing financial highlights. These highlights summarize detailed financial information found later in the plan.

Put meat on the bones

The next few sections of the business plan are descriptive. They explain the market opportunity (often with charts and graphs to show moderate growth in the first year, real promise in the second, and, of course, astonishing industry growth after that). The market opportunity is often expressed as a kind of need — in order for children to successfully compete, each child's bedroom must be equipped with ISDN service; seniors need improved dental insurance and online access, so these services are most effectively marketed as a single package; college students are too busy partying to do their own work, so they must have a service that will do research and write papers for a low, low per-semester fee — and, of course, the new company will satisfy that need with its new offering. (The humor here is intentional — but will your new idea sound crazy, too? Has the idea been carefully researched, or is there a fatal flaw that any knowledgeable third party will recognize as a reason that the business is doomed?)

The contents of these descriptive sections will depend upon the nature of the business. Product descriptions often appear here, along with data about the target market's size and its anticipated behavior, a marketing plan, a distribution plan, and so on. The objective here is, obviously, selling the prospective investor, but the tone should be straightforward and business-like, with a minimum of hype. "Sober" describes the desired tone.

Forecast: sunny, of course

In the meetings that follow the submission of a business plan, the size of the current market and the potential for growth are almost always points of discussion. Multimedia and Internet businesses grow from a marketplace that is constantly changing. Change is brought about by unpredictable consumer interest, advances in technology, new entrepreneurial players, giant established players with the power to change the rules, unexpected acquisitions, and business combinations.

Given all of these variables, a business plan is still expected to present the best available data, as collected by one of several reliable sources (Infotech, DataQuest, and LINK Resources are three popular sources, though there are many others). Then, the plan is expected to present reasonable growth assumptions based upon the company's own expert understanding of its specialized market. These assumptions should be consistent with the forecasts of industry experts. In fact, industry experts are sometimes called upon to provide such forecasts, expressly for use within a business plan or other business model.

Although general market forecasts are interesting, the company's own forecast for market share is considerably more meaningful. Of course, these numbers are predictions, often based on changing market conditions and unforeseen events. Within that reality, the business plan must present some form of financial forecast for the next five years. The first two years of this forecast are significant, and the company will be expected to operate with these numbers as goals that can be achieved. Years three, four, and five are presented as a kind of general indication of where the business might be headed, based on a stated group of assumptions. Are these numbers "real?" Probably not. Do they represent the company's best estimate of future performance? That's the right question, and the answer, to the best of anybody's ability, should be a qualified "yes."

Revenue projections: the art of realistic optimism

The next section should explain, in clear and compelling terms, how the company will make money. In a direct-to-consumer Internet business, the answer is likely to combine subscriptions, advertising, and transactions (that is, direct sales of products or services to customers). In a business-to-business venture, this list might be amended to include production services, design services, marketing consulting, and so on. In a multimedia products business, revenues are likely to come from product sales and product licenses (the right to sell a particular product or product line in another country, or on a different platform, such as a video game system). In a multimedia services business, revenues will come from design, production, marketing, and other services rendered to business customers.

The descriptive portion of this section should be brief. The revenues section should begin with two or three pages of assumptions, and then move on to the numbers. Concise spreadsheets should summarize each of the company's business activities, and its anticipated five-year growth (these are, in turn, summarized in the financial summary that appeared immediately following the Executive Summary earlier in the document).

Each revenue stream should be identified. For example, in the case of a consumer Internet content provider, the principal revenue streams should be listed as subscriptions and advertising. Then, within the subscriptions heading, the chart should show the number of new subscribers per year, the number of subscribers who cancel, the number who renew, the amount that each type of subscriber pays, discounted rates for special subscription programs, and so on. Within the advertising heading, the chart might show four principal advertisers, each paying $5,000 per quarter; plus eight smaller advertisers, each paying $1,500 per quarter; plus one charter advertiser paying $10,000 for the year. Every situation is different, but this is the level of detail required.

Where will the revenue come from?

Revenue projections are affected, of course, by the amount of money it costs to operate the business. Using the example of subscriptions, for example, it's fine to say that 10,000 subscriptions will be generated in year one. But how much does it cost to generate those subscribers? And to maintain them?

New subscribers don't just show up. People don't just "hear" about some new subscription service and decide to pay a monthly or annual fee. Instead, they must be told about the service, typically through advertising. It's naive to assume that people who surf the Web will somehow find out about a particular Web site and decide to pay to see it again. A more likely scenario, borrowed from other media, is the need for a subscription marketing campaign. Magazine advertisements, a public relations campaign, perhaps a direct mail campaign (using snail mail, not e-mail) — these are the traditional ways to reach potential subscribers.

Each of these media costs serious money, even for a small campaign. When someone does decide to subscribe, people are needed to process the account and to answer the phone when the subscribers call with problems or questions. It is possible to outsource some, or all, of these activities. Whether they're handled in-house or out-of-house, they cost money. The cost of these services must be reflected in the operating budget and then compared with the value of each subscriber. Managing the cost per subscriber is an art in the print magazine business, one that hasn't made its way to the Web side just yet.

All of this is offered for the sake of example. This is a very preliminary level of thinking that must be applied and presented as part of the business plan. This is the big difference between simply having an idea for a product, and understanding how a product becomes the basis for a real, operating, promising business.

A full-scale operating budget closes out the business plan. To create this budget, you must estimate the costs and revenues associated with every aspect of the operation. To present this budget, only the headlines for each budget category are needed. In many cases, investors will request additional detail, but there's no reason to bog down the initial proposal with too many numbers — investors won't take the numbers seriously until they meet with you, anyway. Be ready, at that meeting, with a more detailed operating budget, and with more detail on the revenues side as well.

Concluding the business plan

Two more sections should be included in the plan, either as appendices or integrated into the main sections: biographies of the senior managers and a description of the competitive forces that may affect the business. The bios can be as brief as one or two paragraphs. Relevant key credits are all that anyone needs to see; the age of each senior manager is also standard. Competitors should be described in modest detail. The name of the company, its competitive product line or service(s), and its likely future impact should be addressed in one or two paragraphs. There's no reason to go into great detail; you are simply acknowledging the issue here. Subsequent meetings will address competitive concerns in detail.

Additional sections can address key proprietary technologies or licenses, unique marketplace advantages, operational superiority, and other selling points. These sections should be included if they strengthen the overall presentation. If they are not provided, they will not be missed in the early stages. Later, in meetings and perhaps in a revised version of the plan, they may be addressed and, if necessary, included in a revised document.

The next step: raising investment capital

Although the business press and trade magazines are full of stories about venture capital firms and large media corporations investing in small companies, most small companies find it difficult to raise money. Of course, the stories that appear in print are the successes. Stories rarely detail the tedious, time-consuming struggle that preceded the deal. And stories about companies who didn't get funding are uncommon. Most companies start on a shoestring and hobble along with insufficient capital until they're sufficiently stable to appeal to an investor.

Two or three guys working out of their living rooms aren't likely to get any money, regardless of the accomplishments on their resume. Those same guys, working in a small office with a small staff, are still not likely to get the money. Those same three guys — or, if you like, those same three women — aren't likely to see any investment money until they're much further down the road. A written business plan is one step, and a great sales pitch is another. A solid background in a substantial start-up operation, or corporate responsibility for an innovative, money-making success, takes the venture much closer to possible funding. A working prototype is a good idea, and a product in distribution or a service with real customers is even better.

Some new ventures chase their own tails: no funding means no prototype, and no prototype means no funding. This is one reason why so many companies begin with internal funding — or, to put this another way, funding provided by the people who started the company. There's another reason to take this approach: the ownership of the company, and its products, remains with the founders.

The next step up the ladder is funding from friends and relatives. If you've succeeded before, and all you need is some minimal seed capital to pay for a Web server or to hire a designer, then these are reasonable sources.

Like any other funding, these dollars can be provided either as an investment or as a loan.

Investments

For the person (or company) providing the money, an investment can be more risky. There is no requirement that the investment be paid back. There is also no strict rule about the rate of return, or the time period. In a general partnership, the investor can pay any negotiated amount in exchange for an operating role in the company. In a limited partnership, a limited partner can invest any amount approved by the partners, and can receive any negotiated return over any negotiated time period (there are rules regarding fair treatment of all limited partners; consult your advisor).

If the company is organized as a private corporation or LLC, then the investor will purchase shares of stock owned by the company. The value of the shares is determined by the company, or, in truth, as the result of a negotiation between the investor and the company. The Securities and Exchange Commission has very specific rules regarding the sale of corporate shares and the treatment of shareholders (again, consult your advisor).

Making a deal with a big company

For many new companies, this is one version of the big dream — the other is "going public," which is covered later.

Some large media companies maintain departments whose primary function is the acquisition of smaller companies, or, to be more accurate, the acquisition of stock in smaller companies. The Tribune Company, for example, owns television stations in New York City, Chicago, Los Angeles, and other large cities; radio stations; newspapers, including the *Chicago Tribune;* and the Chicago Cubs. It also owns a percentage of America Online, Peapod (a venture that allows people at home to shop for groceries via personal computer), iVillage (operates `www.parentsoup.com` and other large Web sites), and Starsight Telecast (another venture that displays TV schedules and other information on home TV sets).

Most large companies do not invest in small start-ups or even promising young companies. Some do, however, and these companies are often mentioned in the trade press (magazines such as *Inter@ctive Week*) and in consumer magazines that cover the software and Internet businesses (*WIRED*, *Upside*). As you might expect, these large companies are deluged with proposals from would-be deal makers. A personal introduction, at a high level, is nearly essential to get the attention of one of these companies. Although this might happen as a result of a telephone conversation, or a friend of a friend of a friend, it's more likely to happen as a result of a trusted business relationship.

A big company is likely to show its strength by offering the necessary funds and other resources (such as access to large-scale distribution), but these experienced deal makers are likely to demand a great deal. They may, for example, ask for a change in company management, substantial changes in the way in which the company operates, a big say in new ventures and the ways in which money is spent, and, typically, one or two seats on the board of directors.

These issues should be balanced with the potential benefits. The involvement of a big company can mean a great deal to one that's much smaller: Access to resources, high-level executive talent, experience in areas that the new company must enter, opportunities to expand or enter new businesses, access to technologies and/or intellectual property licenses, and cooperative ventures with other companies within the corporate family. Many ideas are discussed, but the actual benefits are, typically, access to the necessary funds, some useful advice and direction from the new board members, perhaps some new staffing and facilities, some access to other resources, and a smattering of operational help. In short, most big companies do the investment, but if the investment does not give them control of the company, they contribute what they can from the sidelines.

As the Internet world grows, it's not uncommon to find more than one big company involved in a smaller one. Hearst New Media and Ameritech, for example, are both larger investors in KidSoft LLC, a distributor of children's software. iVillage, the new media company responsible for Parent Soup on America Online and a similar Web site, `http://www.parentsoup.com`, obtained $12 million in venture capital from America Online, TCI Internet Services Inc., The Tribune Company, and Kleiner Perkins Caufield and Byers, a venture capital firm.

Venture capital

Venture capital is money invested in a comparatively high-risk business, such as the development of a new Internet or multimedia business, in anticipation of a high rate of return. Typically, the start-up begins with the entrepreneur funding the early stages of development, from his or her own money and from funds invested by friends and family. This pays for the prototype, some early fees, and other early start-up expenses. The next step usually involves the courtship of high-net-worth individuals, and, sometimes, individuals at venture capital firms who want to invest early, when less money will buy a greater number of shares (of course, at this stage, the risk is enormous). At this stage, the company will have raised up to about $1,000,000.

Now the company's future is becoming more clear. The key executives are in place, or they have been identified pending additional dollars to cover salaries. This is the time when a venture capital firm may take an interest — at a time when the risk is quite high but the potential for a large return is also evident (at least to the visionaries). William E. Wetzel, director emeritus of the Center for Venture Research at the University of New Hampshire, told *Business Week* in late 1995: the traditional venture-capital industry is "made up of more than 500 venture-capital funds that invest between $3 billion and $4 billion a year in some 3,000 companies," plus "the invisible venture-capital industry, drawn from some 2 million self-made high-net-worth individuals who conservatively invest between $10 billion and $20 billion a year in more than 30,000 ventures."

A venture capital firm typically invests with the intention of a high return within a few years. That goal, as high as 30 percent or more during the best periods, and as low as 20–25 percent during leaner times, requires the venture capital firm to be extremely selective about the opportunities it determines worthy of funding. Venture capital firms invest on behalf of wealthy individual investors, venture capital limited partnerships (a limited partnership created for the purpose of high-risk investments), and other financial institutions. In exchange for the investment, the venture capital firm will negotiate for a comparatively large percentage of the company's equity. (Over 50 percent is common, and, often, the figure is as high as 75 or 80 percent.) This much equity ownership effectively places control of the company in the hands of the venture capital firm.

One of the most popular ways for a venture capital firm to get a high return on its investment is to participate in an Initial Public Offering (IPO) of stock.

Going public

This is the much-publicized gold at the end of the rainbow. You come up with an original idea, build a small company and establish a splendid reputation, garner some interest from big companies and court the right people in influential venture capital firms such as Robertson, Stephens, and, a year or two later, you're preparing for your Initial Public Offering, selling a portion of the company for $25 a share. Because you bought your 250,000 shares at just 50 cents a share, you're going to make a fortune. And so will most of your employees. Happens every day — maybe it'll happen to your business, too.

Often, if there is a venture capital firm involved, there will be pressure to take the company public. This is a substantial task, one that will require about half of the waking hours for most members of the management team, and will cost a few hundred thousand dollars in legal, accounting, and other consulting fees. Because these people stand to gain a great deal, everyone puts forth the special effort. Typically, a percentage of the company's equity is sold as stock; the remainder of the equity stays in the hands of the private investors and other shareholders, as well as company employees with stock options. The amount of equity to be sold is determined by the amount of money needed to keep the company moving, and by the potential to earn the best possible return based on the timing of the IPO. (That is, if the shares are likely to be worth a great deal now, but because of competitive conditions, they may be worth considerably less later, more of the shares will be sold sooner.)

The value of the shares seems to be subjective, and, at least in the world of Inter-net companies, it doesn't seem to be based on anything except market demand. Netscape is one of many extreme examples of this phenomenon; in late April, 1996, based on sales of $1 million, the company was valued at over $275 million.

Final Thoughts

If you bought this book because you figured you'd make millions in multimedia, you probably bought the wrong book. It's possible, but for every tale that ends up on the cover of *Business Week,* there are thousands or tens of thousands of stories that the storytellers would rather forget. Multimedia can be a very profitable business. But that's certainly not always the case. It's an industry with many, many rewards, and monetary rewards are only a part of the picture. Many of the best sites on the Web are almost purely labors of love. Many of the most elaborate and expensive projects lose their shirts. A sense of realism is an advantage that lasts a lifetime in this business.

In the real world, most companies never go public. Most companies never capture the interest of venture capital firms. Most companies never get past the first few years of operation, and then, if they do, they begin to change. Most change to survive, perhaps not in a big way, but in a way that allows the owner(s) to earn a reasonable living and to insure that there's enough money to make payroll every other week.

In the scheme of things, that's not a bad place to be. As a result of your talent and dedication, you've made a company. You've made a living, breathing entity that provides meaningful work for maybe a dozen other people. With all of the hype and craziness surrounding this business, the fact that this is a wonderful accomplishment is easily overlooked. But this is precisely the sort of success that you can achieve, the kind of success that you should hope for and dream about. Think of it: a company, with people working hard doing what they love to do, making products that children adore or that adults find useful; a company that allows you to live your life on your own terms and pays you enough money so that you don't have to worry about your future. In American business life, how much better than that does it really get?

Appendixes

PART V

In This Part

APPENDIX A

Sources

Magazines

Anyone who's interested in being successful in multimedia needs to keep up with as much news as possible from this constantly shifting industry. Even printed magazines can be outdated by the time they reach the stands, but the ones listed here are an excellent source of information on business issues, technology news, and industry trends.

1. *Advertising Age*
   Crain Communications
   Detroit, MI
   800-678-9595
   Some of the most important trends in multimedia happen in the advertising industry. This magazine is one of the most influential publications in the business, and keeps a watchful eye on interactive trends.

2. *AV Video*
   Montage Publishing
   White Plains, NY
   914-328-9157
   Originally targeted to professional video producers, this magazine has expanded its coverage to multimedia development.

3. *Byte*
   MacGraw-Hill, Inc.
   Peterborough, NH
   800-257-9402
   A bit technical for the average user, but always full of good information and not too beholden to any one platform or technology.

4. *CD-ROM Professional*
   Pemberton Press Inc.
   Wilton, CT
   800-248-8466
   No glitz or whacked-out design — just simple, straightforward info on issues of critical importance to the CD-ROM developer or distributor.
5. *Computer Pictures*
   Montage Publishing
   White Plains, NY
   914-328-9157
   This magazine specializes in issues of interest to the computer graphics professional. Lots of interviews with graphic artists and software features.
6. *Desktop Video World*
   IDG Communications Publishing
   Peterborough, NH
   603-924-0100
   Yes, desktop video is an important enough field to warrant its own publication. This one covers both professional and semi-professional tools and techniques.
7. *DV*
   Active Media, Inc.
   San Francisco, CA
   800-998-0806
   As its initials suggest, this magazine originally concentrated on digital video, but has branched to include all aspects of multimedia production.
8. *Electronic Entertainment*
   Infotainment World
   San Mateo, CA
   415-349-4300
   Geared more toward the end user than the developer, this magazine is nonetheless an excellent barometer of which titles and trends are hot.
9. *Electronic Musician*
   Act III Publishing
   Emeryville, CA
   800-843-4086
   Superb coverage of all things MIDI, plus extensive how-to articles on production issues.

10. *Imaging*
    Telecom Library
    New York, NY
    800-999-0345
    Geared toward MIS-types, this magazine covers hardware and software for business presentations.

11. *Inter@ctive Week*
    Ziff-Davis Publishing
    Garden City, NY
    516-229-3700
    `http://www.interactive-week.com`
    Available only online, this "magazine" has quickly established itself as one of the most important sources of information in the online world.

12. *InterActivity*
    Miller Freeman Publishing
    San Mateo, CA
    800-467-7498
    An outstanding publication featuring much usable information on design, production, and marketing issues for the multimedia professional.

13. *Internet World*
    Meckler Media Publishing
    Westport, CT
    203-226-6967
    Most Net magazines are either too techie or too cutesy. This one straddles the line, with a wide outlook that covers human as well as technology issues.

14. *MacUser*
    Ziff-Davis Publishing
    Foster City, CA
    800-627-2247
    The monthly bible for acolytes of the Apple Macintosh platform, mostly geared toward the consumer.

15. *MacWeek*
    Ziff-Davis Publishing
    New York, NY
    609-786-8230
    A weekly trade journal for Mac people, with timely information on new products and trends for the Mac platform.

16. *Macworld*
    Macworld Communications
    San Francisco, CA
    800-288-6848
    Along with *MacUser*, this is the most important publication for devotees of the Macintosh platform.
17. *Mondo 2000*
    MONDO 2000
    Berkeley, CA
    510-845-9018
    Obtuse, over-designed, and leaden with attitude, this publication still hovers near the cutting edge of all issues relating to cyberculture.
18. *MultiMedia Merchandising*
    Eastman Media L.P.
    Santa Monica, CA
    310-458-3102
    Finally, a trade publication with strict emphasis on the business side of the multimedia industry. If you want to sell your titles, you need to read this.
19. *Multimedia Producer*
    Montage Publishing
    White Plains, NY
    914-328-9157
    A monthly journal of tips, tools, and issues of interest to the multimedia producer. A nice mix of business and technical coverage.
20. *Multimedia World*
    PC World Communications, Inc.
    San Francisco, CA
    415-281-8650
    A bit heavy on the gaming aspect of the business, but that's a reflection of the market. This colorful publication keeps you up-to-date on the latest titles.
21. *NewMedia*
    Hypermedia Communications, Inc.
    San Mateo, CA
    415-573-5170
    A superb monthly that covers virtually everything of importance to the multimedia professional. A subscription to this magazine is mandatory.

22. *PC Magazine*
    Ziff-Davis Publishing
    New York, NY
    800-289-0429
    The mother of all PC magazines. Comprehensive coverage of hardware and software for the PC platform, if you can ignore all the ads.

23. *PC Week*
    Ziff-Davis Publishing
    Riverton, NJ
    609-786-8230
    An important trade weekly that focuses on trends and business news from the Wintel juggernaut.

24. *Publish*
    Integrated Media, Inc.
    San Francisco, CA
    800-685-3435
    Mostly geared to print publishing, this magazine nonetheless features excellent coverage of design and output issues.

25. *Upside*
    Upside Publishing Company
    Foster City, CA
    619-745-2809
    The multimedia industry as seen from the eyes of investment professionals. Perhaps a bit myopic, but an influential publication nonetheless.

26. *Variety*
    Variety
    Los Angeles, CA
    800-323-4345
    This is the bible — sort of a *Wall Street Journal* for the entertainment industry. Multimedia isn't always covered, but when it is, it's from a perspective you need to know about.

27. *Web Developer*
    Meckler Media Publishing
    Westport, CT
    203-226-6967
    Slick monthly that covers all the issues of interest to a Webmaster. A bit technical, but good, specific information.

28. *WebMaster*
    IDG
    Framingham, MA
    800-788-4605
    A holistic view of running a site, with articles on the business, technology, and economic issues of your presence on the Web.

29. *Wired*
    Wired Ventures, Ltd.
    San Francisco, CA
    415-222-6200
    Where would cyberculture be without *Wired,* the *Rolling Stone* of the digital age? Articles range from exhilarating to infuriating, but always interesting.

Publishers

Finding a publisher for your multimedia title can take as much time as making the title itself. There are all sorts of publishers, both big and small, and the biggest ones aren't necessarily the best choice for every title. Still, the major publishers are the ones with marketing clout, and if you would like to see your title on the shelves of major retailers, you'll stand a good chance if you're working with an industry powerhouse. What follows is a very partial listing of important multimedia publishers. Good luck.

1. Aris Entertainment
   310 Washington Boulevard, Suite 100
   Marina del Ray, CA 90292
   310-821-0234

2. Baker & Taylor Software
   3850 Royal Avenue
   Simi Valley, CA 93063
   800-775-4100

3. Brøderbund Software, Inc.
   500 Redwood Boulevard
   Novato, CA 94948
   415-382-4617

4. Cambrix Publishing
   6269 Variel Avenue, Suite B
   Woodland Hills, CA 91367
   818-992-8484

5. Compton's New Media
   2320 Camino Vida Roble
   Carlsbad, CA 92009
   619-929-2500

6. Creative Multimedia Corporation
   514 N.W. 11th Avenue, Suite 203
   Portland, OR 97209
   503-241-4351

7. Discis Knowledge Research, Inc
   90 Sheppard Avenue East
   Willowdale, ON, Canada M2N 3A1
   800-567-4321

8. Disney Software
   500 South Buena Vista Street
   Burbank, CA 91521
   818-973-4015

9. Electronic Arts
   1450 Fashion Island Boulevard
   San Mateo, CA 94404
   415-571-7171

10. Educorp
    7434 Trade Street
    San Diego, CA 92121
    619-536-9999

11. Grolier Electronic Publishing
    Sherman Turnpike
    Danbury, CT 06816
    800-356-5590

12. Philips Interactive Media of America
    11111 Santa Monica Boulevard
    Los Angeles, CA 90025
    310-445-5000

13. Time Warner Interactive
    2210 West Olive Avenue
    Burbank, CA 91506
    818-955-9999

14. The Voyager Company
    578 Broadway
    New York, NY 10012
    212-431-5199

15. Wayzata Technology, Inc.
    2515 East Highway 2
    Grand Rapids, MN 55744
    800-735-7321

16. Xiphias
    8758 Venice Boulevard
    Los Angeles, CA 90034
    310-841-2790

CD-ROM Mastering and Replication

Striking the "gold disc" master is one of the most joyous moments in the entire production process. But unless you have a CD-ROM burner, you need someone to press the master, and even if you do, you'll need duplication services to make copies for mass distribution. The service houses listed here offer a comprehensive package of mastering and duplication services.

1. 21st Century Media
   883 Fourth Street
   San Rafael, CA 94901
   415-453-9407

2. American Multimedia Inc.
   2609 Tucker Street
   Burlington, NC 27215
   910-229-5554

3. CD-ROM Works
   2647 S E. 60
   Portland, OR 97206
   503-771-3398

4. Denon Digital Industries
   1380 Monticello Road
   Madison, GA 30650
   706-342-3032

5. Digital Audio Disc Corp.
   1800 N. Fruitridge Avenue
   Terre Haute, IN 47803-1788
   812-462-8100

6. Disc Makers
   7905 N. Route 130
   Pennsauken, NJ 08110
   800-468-9353

7. Disc Manufacturing
   1409 Foulk Road
   Wilmington, DE 19803
   302-479-2500

8. Image Management System, Inc.
   239 West 15 Street
   New York, NY 10011
   212-741-8765

9. Metatec Corp
   7001 Metatec Boulevard
   Dublin, OH 43017
   614-761-2000

10. Magnetech Corp.
    3941 SW 47 Avenue
    Ft. Lauderdale, FL 33314
    317-870-5700

11. Memcon Corp.
    2430 S 156 Circle
    Omaha, NE 68130
    402-333-3100

12. OneSource
    8-10 W. 19 Street
    New York, NY 10011
    212-727-1010

13. Optical Media International
    180 Knowles Drive
    Los Gatos, CA 95030
    408-376-3511

Conferences and Trade Shows

One of the key skills that any multimedia professional needs to master (or at least become competent with) is networking. Finding other people with similar skills and interests widens your professional circle and puts you in situations in which your work or your project can get noticed. The best place to network is at industry trade conventions, where many people just like you are gathered together — often for the sole purpose of networking. Following is a list of some of the most important trade shows, but there are many others that you'll find by perusing the magazines listed in this chapter.

January

1. Consumer Electronics Show (CES)
   Electronics Industries Association
   Las Vegas, NV
   703-907-7600
   The oldest and most respected of the electronics trade shows. A huge convention, with many workshops and exhibits of interest to the multimedia professional.

2. MacWorld Expo
   Mitch Hall Associates
   San Francisco, CA
   617-361-2001
   The Macintosh is king at this gathering of Mac professionals. Because most multimedia producers still develop on the Macintosh platform, this is an especially fertile ground for networking purposes.

3. MILIA
   Midem Organization
   Cannes, France
   212-689-4220
   A mixed bag, with television, film, and music industry professionals well represented. A good place to work out international deals, and if you can swing it, a trip to France is always nice.

February

1. Consumer Online Services
   Jupiter Communications
   New York, NY
   212-941-9252

Jupiter Communications is one of the most respected sources of information regarding the online world. This event attracts one of the highest concentrations of cyberprofessionals and MIS persons anywhere.

2. Digital Hollywood
   American Expositions
   Beverly Hills, CA
   212-226-4141
   Plenty of opportunities to network with the Hollywood set, but not all of the proceedings are geared to multimedia. There are also lots of special effects and post-production specialists.

3. Intermedia
   Reed Exhibitions
   San Francisco, CA
   203-840-4800
   One of the more established multimedia conferences, it offers a nice cross section of developers, publishers and marketing professionals.

March

1. Electronic Books International
   Mecklermedia
   London, UK
   203-226-6967
   Meckler is a strong presence in both the multimedia and online industries. This gathering brings in a mix of developers, publishers, and library professionals.

2. National Association of Broadcasters (NAB)
   Las Vegas, NV
   202-429-5346
   Strictly for the trade, but if you can get in, this is where you'll find the latest information on cutting-edge interactive technologies.

3. Software Publishers Association (SPA)
   San Diego, CA
   202-452-1600
   The SPA is the most important source of information on what's selling, what's being developed, and what's the latest on legal and technological issues.

April

1. Computer Game Developers Conference
   Computer Game Developers Association
   San Jose, CA
   415-948-2432
   From the heart of Silicon Valley, this gathering is a great place to meet developers. Bring a demo — there are lots of publishers here as well.
2. COMDEX Spring
   The Interface Group
   Atlanta, GA
   617-449-6600
   By the time you read this, this smaller version of the important COMDEX show will have merged with CES to form a new, hybrid "converging technologies" convention. In 1997, the show will be in Atlanta; for 10 years after, in Chicago.

May

1. Apple Worldwide Developer Conference
   Apple Computer, Inc.
   San Jose, CA
   408-974-4897
   If you develop multimedia on the Macintosh platform, this is a good place to network. Leave your Windows files at home.
2. Electronic Entertainment Expo (E3)
   Los Angeles, CA
   800-800-5474
   A huge convention of multimedia exhibitors, mostly from the gaming sector. Much flash and noise; lots of ponytailed executives looking for projects or distributors.
3. SGI Developer's Conference
   Silicon Graphics, Inc.
   Mountain View, CA
   415-960-1980
   Many developers are leaning toward workstations like the SGI for speedier production. If you're one of them, you'll find kindred spirits here.

June

1. American Booksellers Association (ABA)
   Chicago, IL
   203-840-4820
   This is the most important convention for the book industry, which now distributes multimedia product as well. Just don't expect everyone you meet here to understand or appreciate multimedia.

2. IICS Annual Conference
   International Interactive Communications Society
   Anaheim, CA
   503-579-4427
   The IICS has been around longer than CD-ROM or the Web. Some of the most knowledgeable and influential professionals in the industry attend this conference.

3. VISCOMM
   United Digital Artists
   San Francisco, CA
   212-777-7200
   Anything and everything for the visual communicator, including hardware and software exhibits, seminars, and workshops.

August

SIGGRAPH
Special Interest Group-Graphics
Association for Computing Machinery
312-644-6610
This convention gathers some of the most advanced professionals working in digital graphics, 3D, and computer animation.

September

Online Developers Conference
Jupiter Communications
San Francisco, CA
212-941-9252
Another convention by Jupiter, this one geared more toward the production end than the business end.

October

1. CD-ROM Expo
   Online
   San Francisco, CA
   203-761-1466
   A great place to meet developers, publishers, and marketing contacts. Less emphasis on games than the E3 expo, more on the industry as a whole.

2. Macromedia Developers Conference
   Reed Exhibition Companies
   San Francisco, CA
   203-352-8296
   If you use Macromedia tools to develop multimedia (and most producer do), this is a great place to network and learn the latest trends.

November

1. COMDEX Fall
   The Interface Group
   Las Vegas, NV
   617-449-6600
   The biggest computer show in the world. Heavy on the hardware exhibits, but a great place to meet other software developers and see the latest tools.

2. Virtual Reality Convention
   Mecklermedia
   New York, NY
   800-632-5537
   There are as many rumors as realities in this infant industry, but this is one of the best places to find out what's going to be real, and when.

Books

Despite the plethora of books on the market geared toward multimedia, most of them are written for the end user — how to hook up a CD-ROM drive, how to log onto the Internet, and so on. Outstanding books that are valuable to the multimedia professional are far less common, but the ones that do exist are well worth reading. Following is a list of recommendations:

1. *About Face: The Essentials of User Interface Design*
Alan Cooper
IDG Books
Good overview of the basics, but more emphasis on the intangibles, such as user expectation and mnemonics. A bit esoteric, but well worth reading.

2. *The Business of Multimedia*
Nina Schuyler
Allworth Press
Concise guide to the basics of putting together a development team, striking a production deal, finding capital, and striking a deal with a publisher.

3. *Careers in Multimedia*
Vivid Studios
Ziff-Davis Press
A no-nonsense guide to what jobs exist in the industry, how to train for them, how much they pay, and when to move on to another one.

4. *CD-ROM Handbook*
Chris Serman
McGraw-Hill
A comprehensive compendium of knowledge for the CD-ROM producer, mostly on the technical aspects.

5. *Computers as Theater*
Brenda Laurel
Addison-Wesley
Seminal work that argues for a paradigm of interactivity in which the screen is a stage, the developer the director, and the user the audience.

6. *Interactivity by Design*
Ray Kristof and Amy Satran
Adobe Press
Wonderful guide to the essentials of interface design, as well as useful basic information on color palettes, compression, and many other important topics.

7. *The Low Budget Video Bible*
Cliff Roth
Desktop Video Sytems
Newly updated, this volume is filled with useful tips on how to shoot, edit, and produce video with minimal production budgets.

8. *Making Money with Multimedia*
   David Rosen and Caryn Mladen
   Addison-Wesley
   A bit dated, but lots of timeless information on how to set up a business plan, how to talk to investors, and where to find potential publishers for your project.

9. *The Multimedia Casebook*
   Mary Mallenstein Herman and W.R. James
   Van Nostrand Reinhold
   Profiles of a dozen major multimedia projects, with interviews with the creators. An essential inside look at how this industry really works.

10. *Multimedia Law Handbook*
    Diane Brinson and Mark Radcliffe
    Ladera Press
    A legal primer for nonlegal specialists. Includes a floppy disk of sample legal contracts.

11. *The Musician's Home Recording Handbook*
    Ted Greenwald
    Miller Freeman
    A good way to familiarize yourself with the basics of audio recording, with good overviews and simple language.

12. *A Primer of Visual Literacy*
    Donis Dondis
    MIT Press
    An involved look at the issues involved in communicating with visual elements. This book puts into words what graphics people intuitively understand.

13. *Running a Perfect Web Site*
    David Chandler
    Que
    A bit dated (any book on this subject is out of date as soon as it's published), but still a good introduction to the vicissitudes of running a Web site.

14. *Software Development: A Legal Guide*
    Stephen Fishman
    Nolo Press
    There are few useful books available to the layman regarding the evolving legal issues of multimedia. This superb volume is one of them, and it's essential reading for anyone hoping to publish in this business.

15. *Techno Trends*
    Daniel Burrus
    Harper Business
    Geared toward the business sector, this book offers good insights on how corporate America perceives the digital revolution, and how you can keep up.
16. *World Wide Web Marketing*
    Jim Sterne
    John Wiley & Sons
    A great primer on how to make your Web site into a success, how to treat your visitors, and how to get more exposure.

Appendix B

CD-ROM

Adobe Photoshop

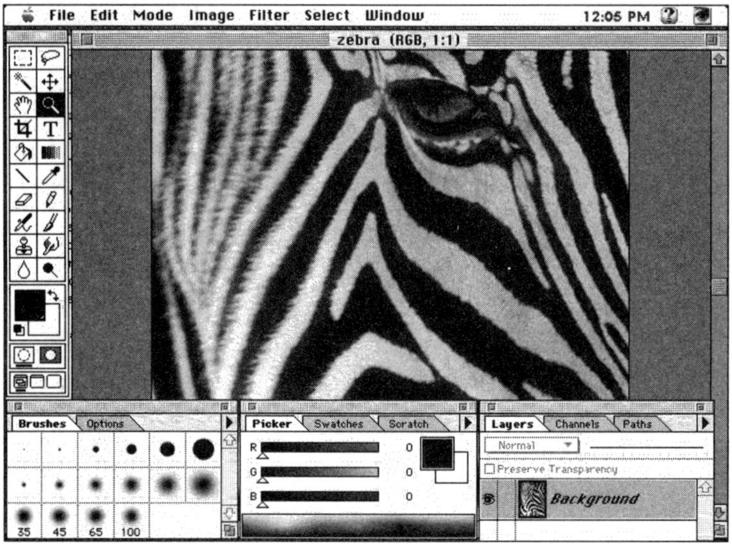

Where would the digital world be without Photoshop? It has come to define its own genre, with comprehensive features and applications for digital image manipulation. If you don't already own Photoshop, you've probably used it elsewhere, and if you haven't, this demo will convince you that you need it. Check out the tutorial files for a glimpse at how a single application can meet virtually any need in this vital multimedia area. On this CD-ROM, you find a demo for version 3.0.5, for both Windows and Macintosh.

Adobe Illustrator

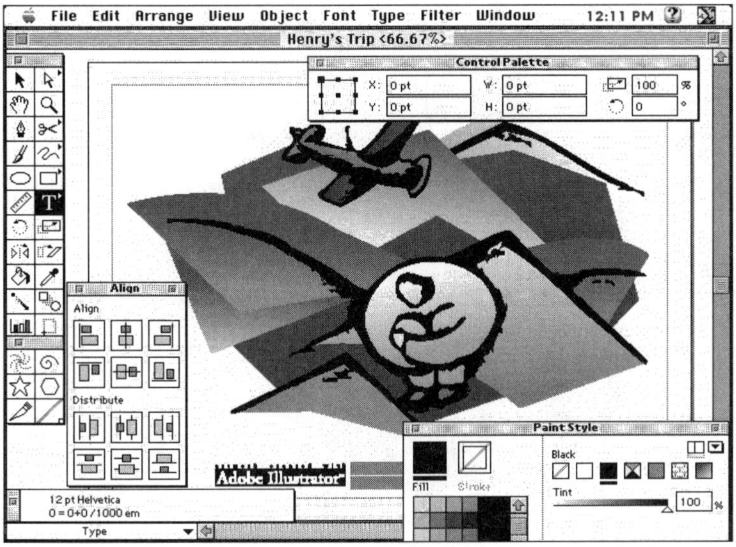

This tryout version of Adobe Illustrator, which is version 6.0 for the Macintosh, contains virtually all the features of the full program. Illustrator has established itself as one of the most important applications for vector-based image generation; files from Illustrator can be rasterized into bitmapped graphics. Illustrator is one of the most established and mature software tools on the market, and is invaluable not only for creating images for multimedia, but for print illustration as well.

Adobe After Effects

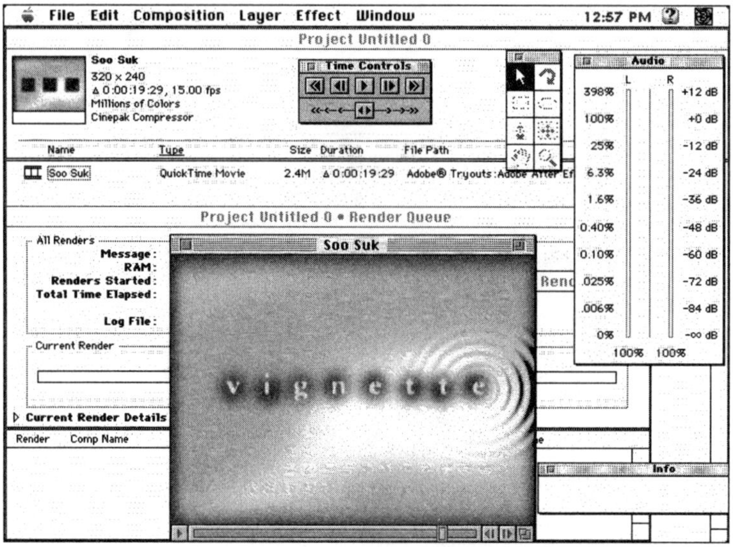

The demo of After Effects is version 3.0 for the Mac, though a version for Windows NT is coming soon. After Effects straddles the line between 2D and 3D animation, and takes a frame-based approach to digital video work. It offers a variety of effective bluescreen capabilities, versatile special effects, and excellent compression. You can import files from Photoshop and Illustrator to include in an After Effects. There is a Production Bundle available that further enhances productivity, as well as plug-in support for third party software.

Adobe Premiere

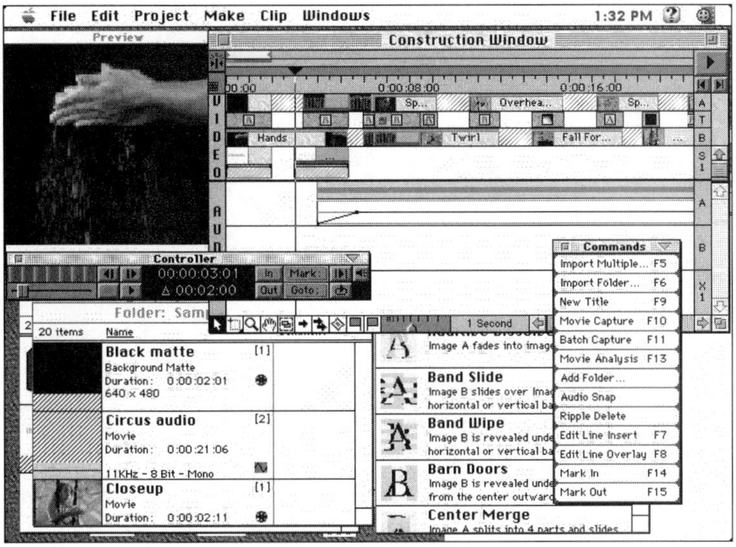

Premiere was the first important digital video editing software for desktop multimedia, and remains the most important today. The demo versions contained here are 4.2 for Windows and 4.2.1 for Macintosh. You can capture video and audio in a variety of formats, edit, layer, and effect up to 99 tracks each of video and audio, work in varying resolutions and sizes, take advantage of many third-party additions and finally render the final output in a wide variety of formats suitable for broadcast, desktop, CD-ROM, or Web delivery.

Adobe Dimensions

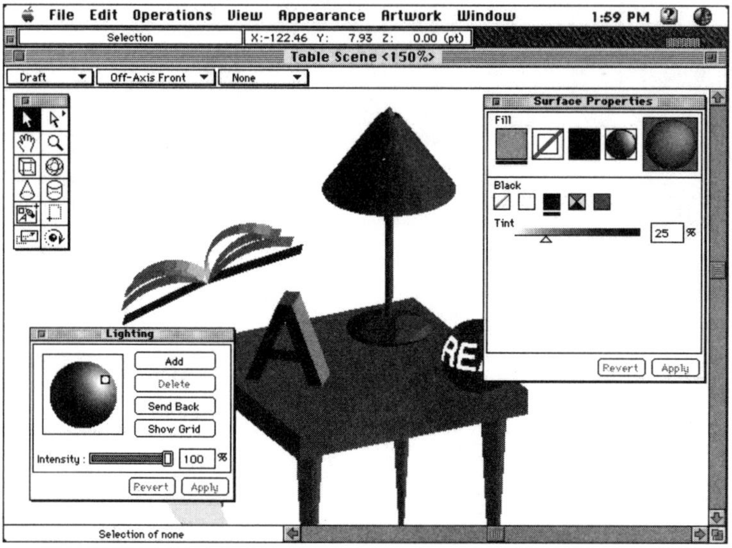

Dimensions (v2.0 for Macintosh) is a 3D program that allows non-experts to create, edit and render three-dimensional graphics without experience and a learning curve. It's a tool that adds depth, shading, and perspective to simple 2D images to transform them into 3D objects. In minutes you can create a 3D object that would have taken hours or days of work using a 2D illustration program. Artwork created in Dimensions is in PostScript language format, which is resolution-independent.

Adobe Streamline

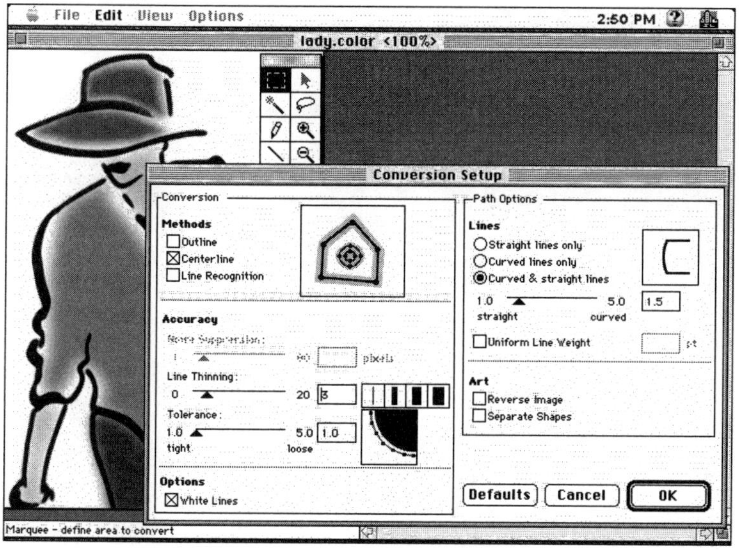

Streamline software is a companion to drawing programs such as Illustrator and FreeHand. Streamline provides a variety of tools and options for converting bit-mapped images into line art, which can then be edited in the illustration program. Source material can come from scanned photos or sketches, in any number of file formats. The images can be "prepared" prior to conversion via retouching tools that give control over highlights, shadows and midtones. This disc contains version 3.0 for Windows and 3.1 for Macintosh.

Adobe PageMill

This demo version of PageMill, which is 1.0 for the Macintosh, shows how you can create Web pages as easily as word processing documents. PageMill shields the user from most common HTML codes, allowing graphic and text elements to be imported and formatted with simple open, cut and paste commands. While this first version of PageMill doesn't offer comprehensive support for fancy HTML formatting, it can get a novice up and running very quickly, and let an experienced writer bang out quick pages almost on the fly.

Macromedia Director

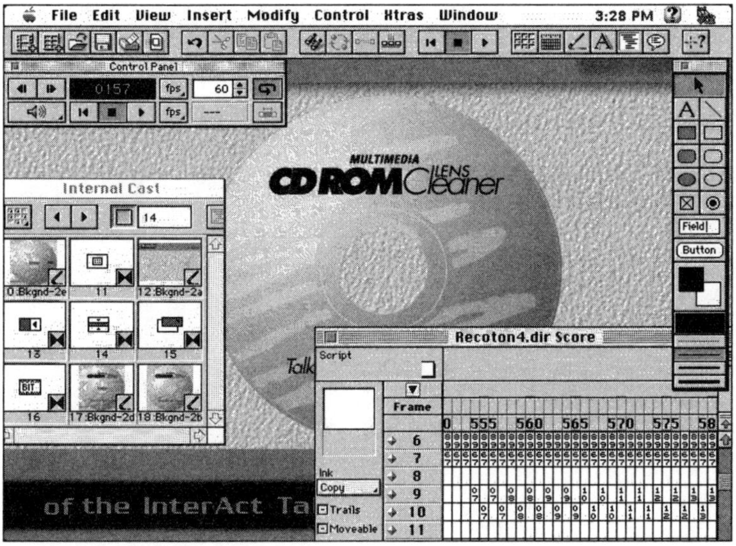

The Director Studio 5.0 is presented here in demo form for both Windows and Macintosh. The studio is a suite of programs for animation, 3D and 2D graphics, digital audio production and, of course, Director itself, which is a multimedia authoring program that puts these elements togeter. Version 5.0 includes support for Web work, particularly in the way of ShockWave. The ShockWave compression module, called "AfterBurner" is included in the gallery. Install the demo and watch thorough demonstrations of tools you need to create multimedia.

Macromedia Authorware

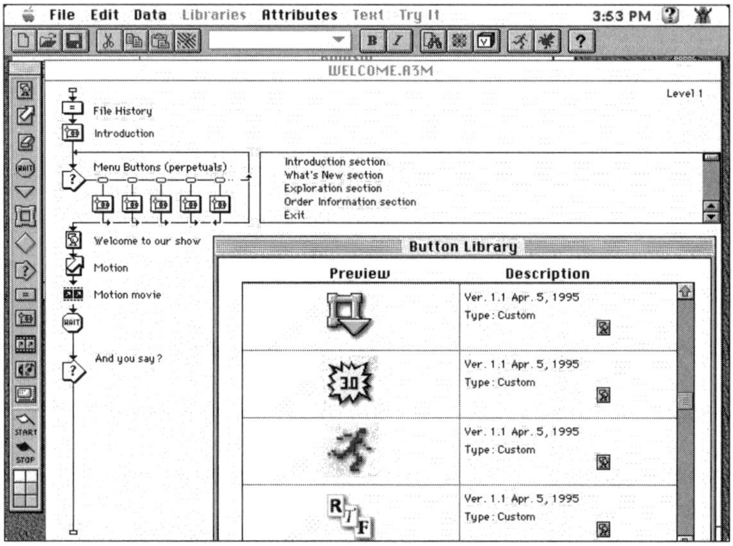

Authorware, shown here in version 3.0 for Windows and Macintosh, is an elaborate authoring program that not only contains powerful coding techniques for advanced users, but simplified programming icons for developers to get running quickly. As you can see from the screen shot, Authorware uses a flowchart metaphor, rather than a timeline. This version of Authorware can also import Director files, making it a natural step-up for the experienced Director author needing to work on more complex projects.

Macromedia SoundEdit 16

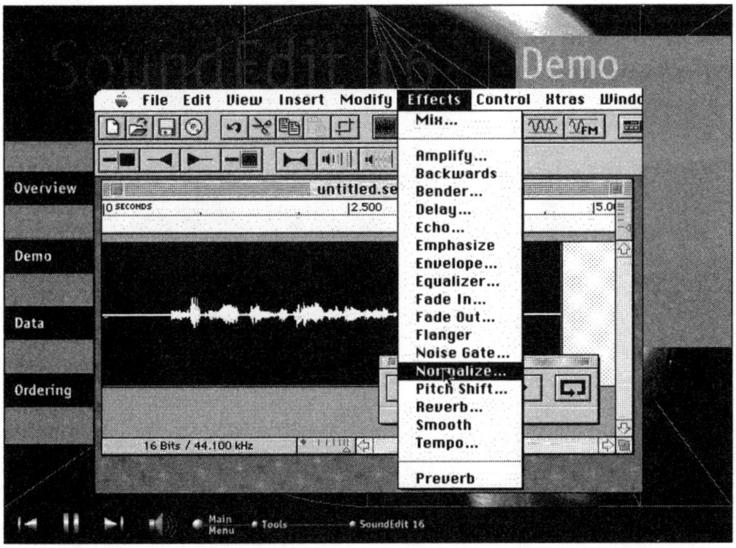

This demo (Macintosh, v2.0) is actually part of a two-way audio suite included in the Director Studio. SoundEdit 16 is a digital recording and editing tool, which can input and output digital audio files in a number of different formats, sample rates and bit depths. As you can see from the screen shot, a generous helping of effects can be applied to the files. The other part of the package is Deck II 2.0, which is multitracking software that turns your hard drive into a multitrack recorder with non-destructive editing.

Macromedia xRes

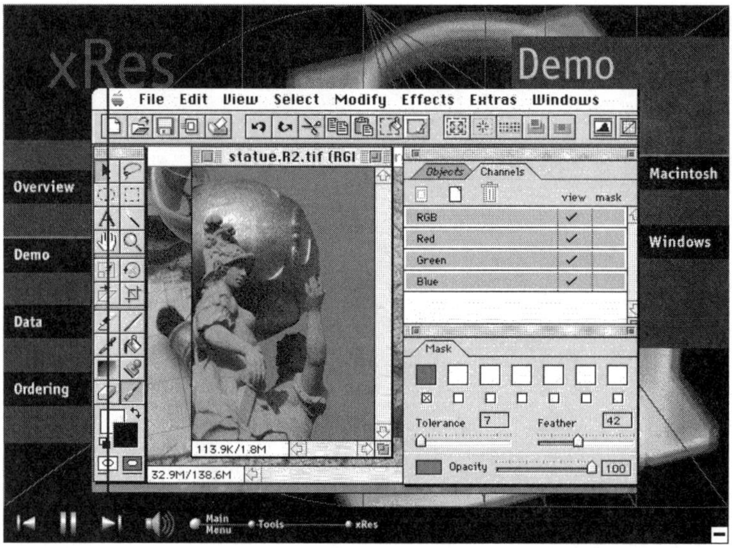

xRes, for both Windows and Macintosh, is an image manipulation program that can perform many of Photoshop's tricks and then some. It's greatest strengths are its batch-processing modes, which can alter large numbers of files automatically; a powerful set of undo commands, and the ability to display huge files quickly, thanks to a design that only renders the final layers and effects when you give the command.

Macromedia FreeHand

Along with Illustrator, FreeHand set the standards in the early days of desktop illustration. Over the years, it has not only retained a loyal following, but through various upgrades and enhancements gained new enthusiasts. The current implementation builds powerfully on some of the oldest ideas, such as the extensive undo flexibility. The program also integrates nicely into the rest of the Macromedia suite, including native file compliance with several programs.

Equilibrium DeBabelizer

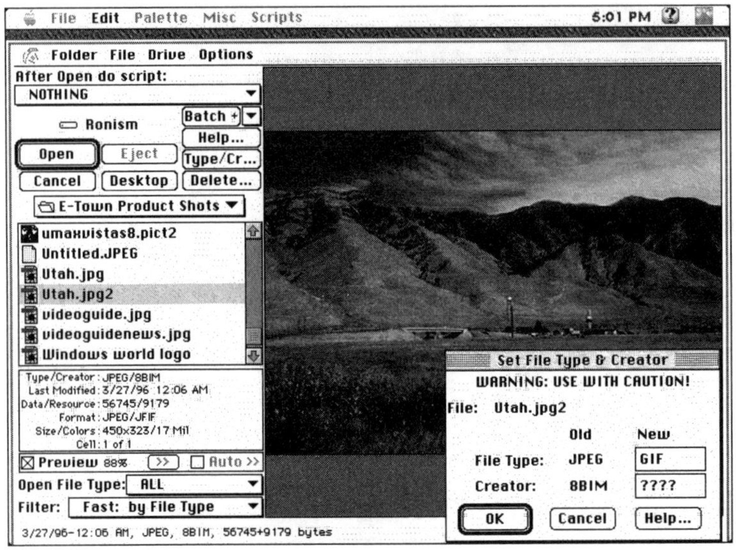

This Macintosh utility for graphics processing is so well-loved that some PC-based production companies will actually purchase a Mac just to run it. DeBabelizer is a swiss army knife for all kinds of digital graphics. It can perform good-quality bit conversions and file translations; generate custom palettes for efficient color use, and provide excellent compressed files that are of particular use to the Web developer. In addition, these tools can be scripted and written as batch-processing events — a great time saver.

Oracle MediaObjects

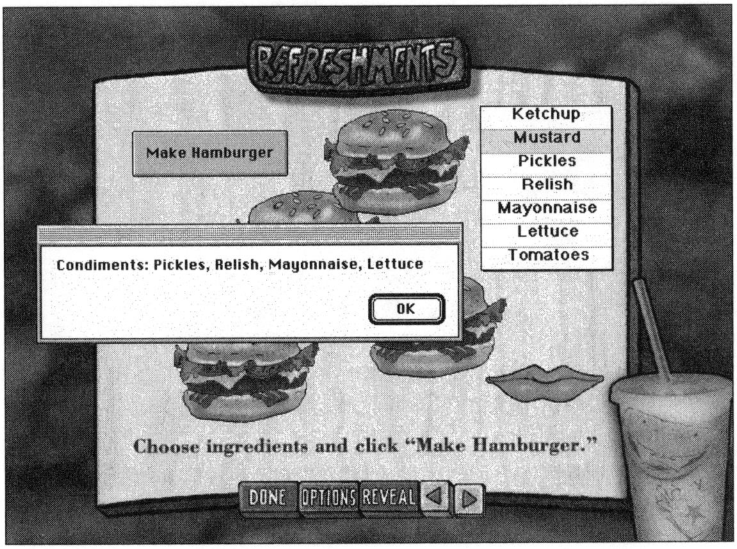

Oracle has developed MediaObjects as a solution to the widest variety of cross-platform applications — perhaps out of the PC environment itself. With technologies like consumer electronics, video game consoles and DBS broadcast merging with the multimedia world, an authoring program that works independent of hardware and operating system is an interesting idea worth checking into. OMO's authoring metaphor of cards and stacks will be familiar to experienced and intuitive to the uninitiated.

CorelDRAW! 6

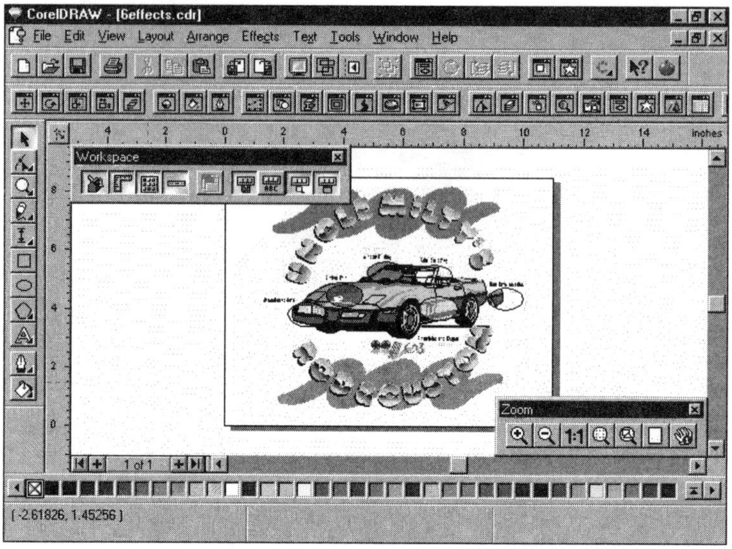

This suite of imaging tools is a complete solution to drawing, manipulating and processing 2D and 3D artwork. This demo of v6.0 is a 32-bit version which runs native on Windows 95. The drawing program is called Draw, which combines vector illustration with page layout; Photo-Paint is a bitmap editing program; CorelDream 3D offers spline-based 3D modeling with various shadings; Motion3D creates animated 3D artwork like logos, and there's also a presentation program which can create powerful multimedia for situations where user interactivity isn't warranted.

Appendix C

Cool Web Sites

AAIM Association for Applied Interactive Multimedia

`http://www.aaim.org`

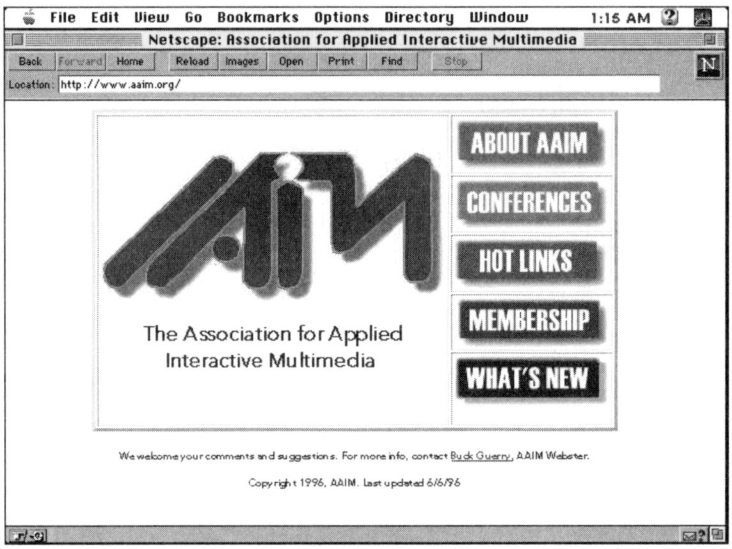

AAIM was created to support professionals using and developing multimedia. While the focus is on business and commercial projects, papers and seminars on a wide variety of related issues are presented.

Association for Multi-media International

http://www.ami.org

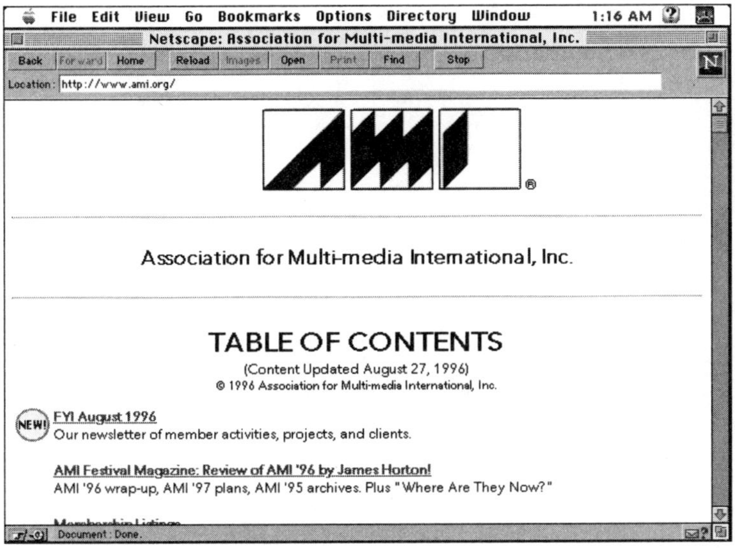

A non-profit, international association serving professionals who promote, produce and use all forms of media to communicate, educate, entertain, and persuade. A good place for professionals, both established and aspiring, to network.

Interactive Multimedia Association

http://www.ima.org

Exceptional source of knowledge for CD-ROM producers and other interactive professionals. Important developer forums, hardware and software news, and a sponsored trade exhibition.

Intermedia Professionals Association

http://www.his.com/~kara/ipa.html

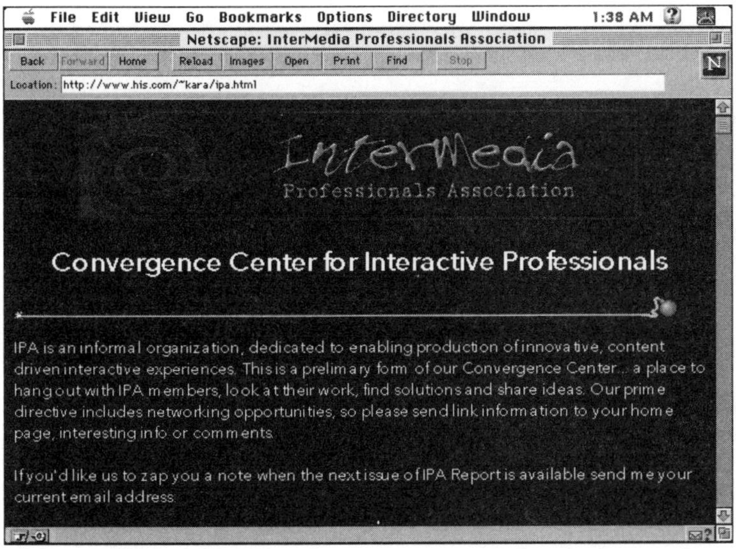

An informal organization dedicated to devising creative solutions and information sharing regarding multimedia experiences. They produce a newsletter and host live chats on America Online (Keyword MMM).

National Multimedia Association of America

http://www.nmaa.org/nmaa/grfxindx.html-ssi

A non-profit organization set up to exchange ideas on development and enabling technology for present and future multimedia. Job listings and useful links to utilities and FAQs are featured.

Lingo User's Journal

http://www.penworks.com/LUJ/home.html

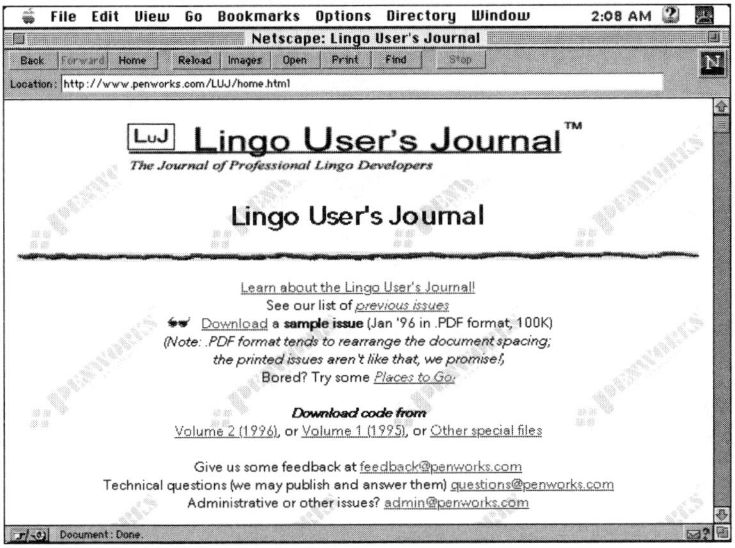

A site for programmers who work in Lingo code on Macromedia projects. A monthly printed or electronic newsletter is $42; various scripts and coding are available for download.

IEEE Multimedia

http://www.computer.org/pubs/multimed/multimed.htm

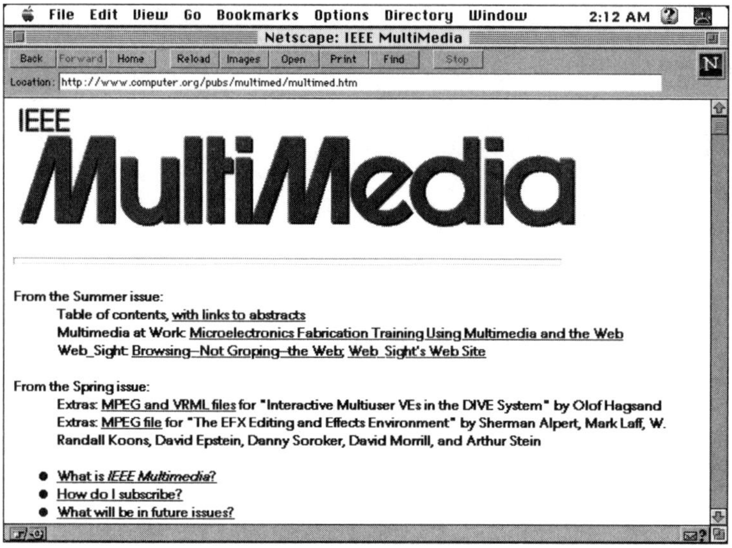

The home page for the Institute of Electrical and Electronics Engineers is an essential resource for comprehensive technical information on hardware and software issues relating to multimedia. In addition to various features and sub-publications, there are links to important related sites.

CNUCE IEI Page

`http://www.pianosa.cnuce.cnr.it/welcome.html`

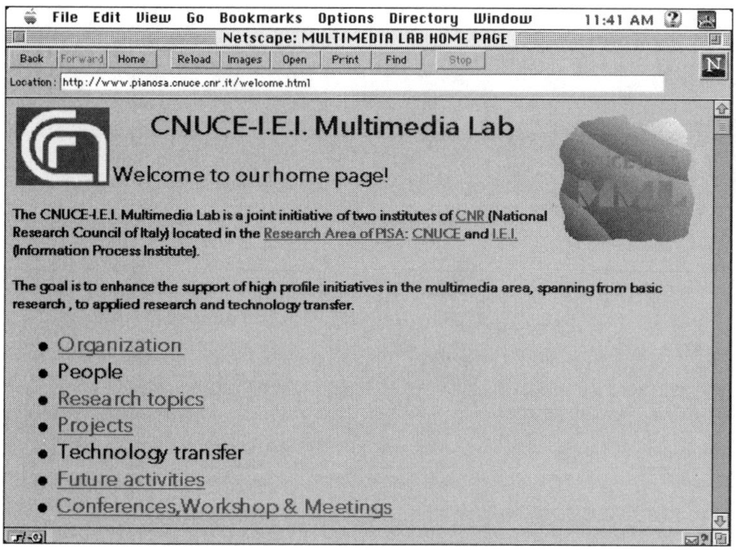

An organization from Italy serving an international audience of researchers and programmers engaged in high-level multimedia development. Interesting theoretical readings, and a source of provocative ideas.

SunSITE Japan Multimedia Page

http://sunsite.sut.ac.jp/multimed/

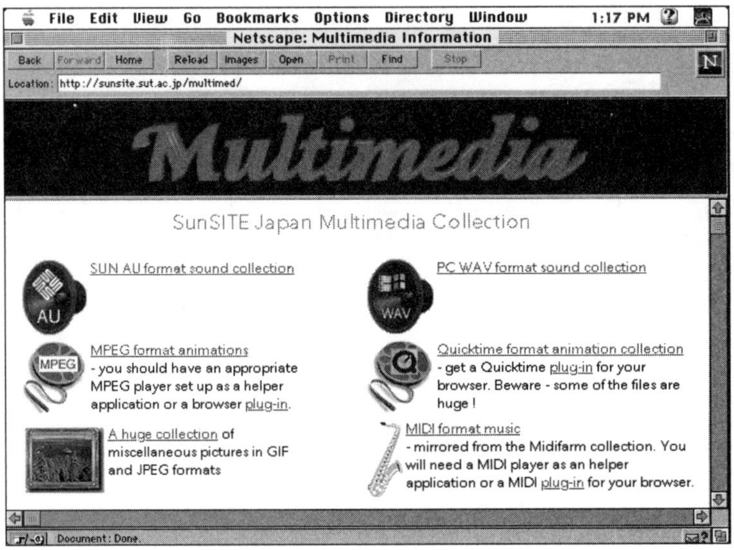

An generous collection of source material for multimedia developers, including MIDI files, WAV files, MPEG files and various pictures and animation.

Apple Developer Tools

```
http://www.devtools.apple.com/general/Guide2MacTools/
     multimedia.html
```

An exhaustive supply of tools, techniques, and tips for developers using the Apple Macintosh. Includes essential information about QuickTime and QuickTime VR.

Timestream Inc.

http://www.timestream.com/web/info/mmedu.html

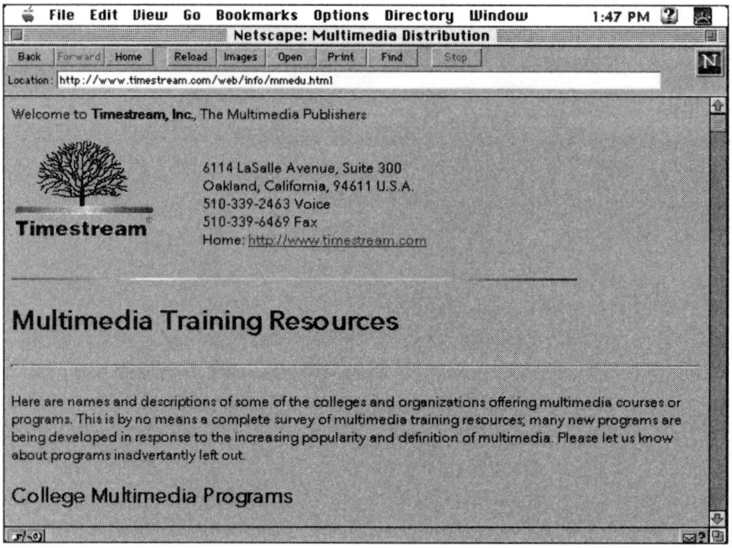

A site that focuses on training for careers in multimedia. Here you find a list of universities and independent programs that teach multimedia design and programming.

The MIDI Home Page

http://www.eeb.ele.tue.nl/midi/index.html

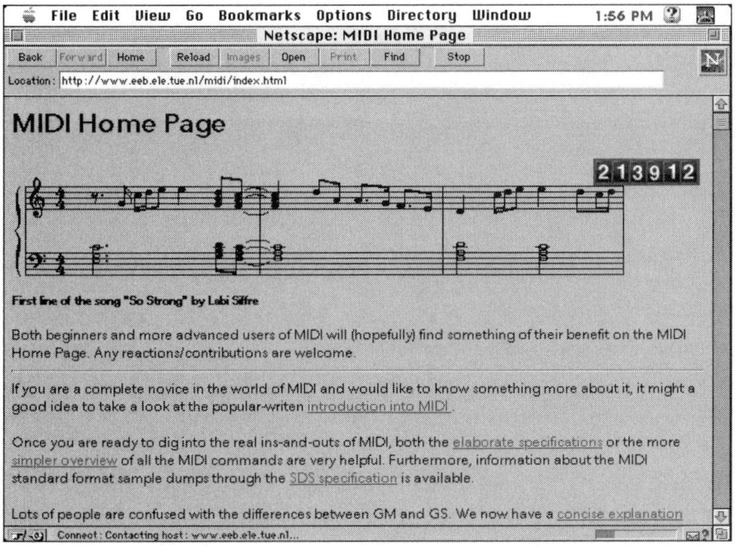

Everyone from beginners to advanced audio professionals can find something useful at this site dedicated to MIDI and digital audio techniques. The site includes a nice list of links to other MIDI pages.

The Multimedia Networking Group

http://minas.stanford.edu/

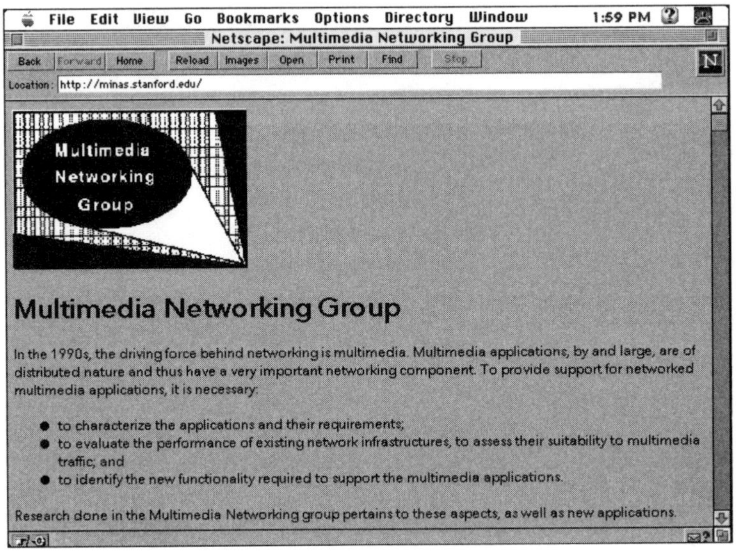

This site, out of Stanford University, focuses on the development and delivery of multimedia, with particular attention on research. Programmers will find this an excellent source for information sharing.

WWW Multimedia Law

http://www.batnet.com/oikoumene/index.html

An indispensable guide to the latest developments in intellectual property and copyright laws as they pertain to multimedia and other digital content. Articles, books, and newsletters are available.

CU-SeeMe

http://cu-seeme.cornell.edu/

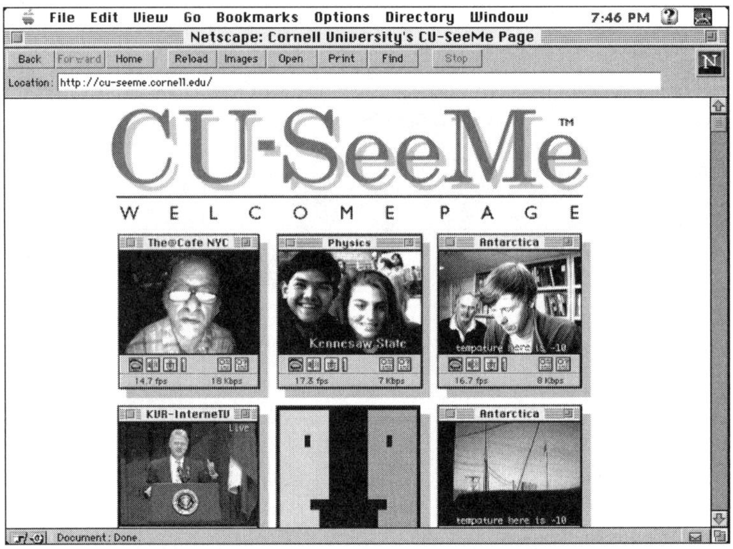

This company, centered at Cornell University, is pioneering video telephony and other forms of real-time multimedia.

RealAudio

`http://www.realaudio.com`

The home page for the popular audio plug-in for Web browsing. RealAudio allows for streamed audio files to be delivered during Web sessions.

EarthWeb's Gamelan Java Directory

http://www-b.gamelan.com/index.shtml

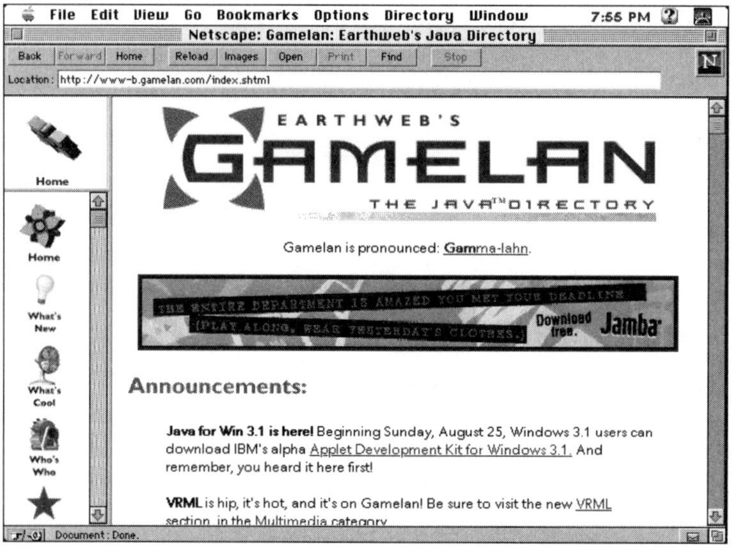

Here's where Java programmers can meet, exchange ideas or chat, and leave samples of their work for evaluation and comments. Contains interesting Java applets that can be downloaded.

WEBWEEK

`http://www.webweek.com/`

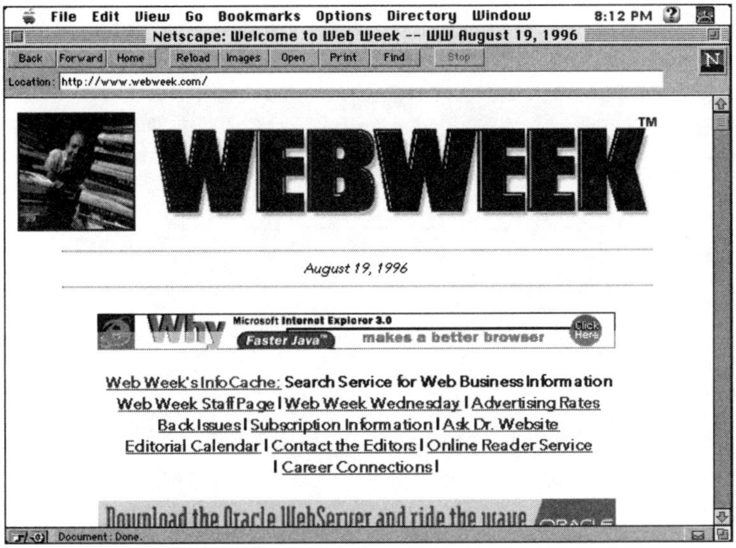

A timely, in-depth publication focusing on the business side of the WWW. A well-implemented search engine lets you sift back issues for topics of interest.

mmwire

`http://www.mmwire.com`

This division of Phillips Business Information delivers free weekly information via Web (including back issues) and a daily fax or e-mail newsletter for a subscription fee. Also contains good classifieds regarding jobs and projects.

SIGGRAPH Online

http://siggraph.org

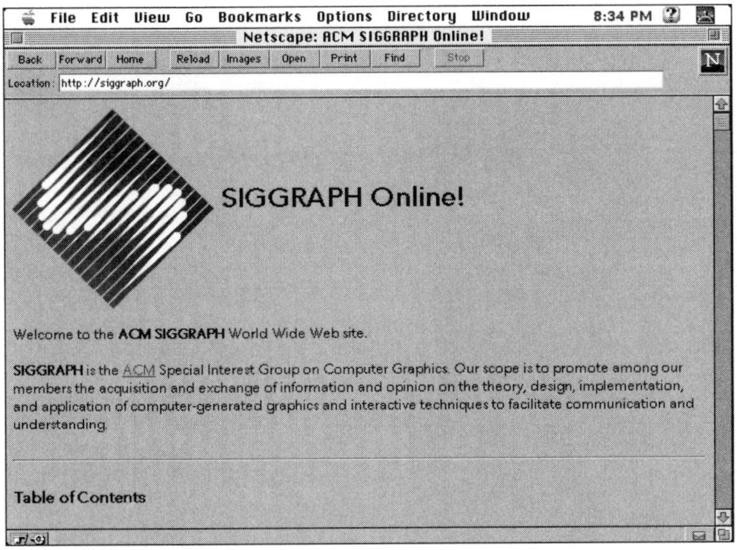

Don't let the plain-looking home page fool you — this is one of the best places to see the latest in computer-generated graphics. The mandate here is to promote techniques, talents, and advances in digital artwork.

Computer Games Developer Association

http://www.cgda.com

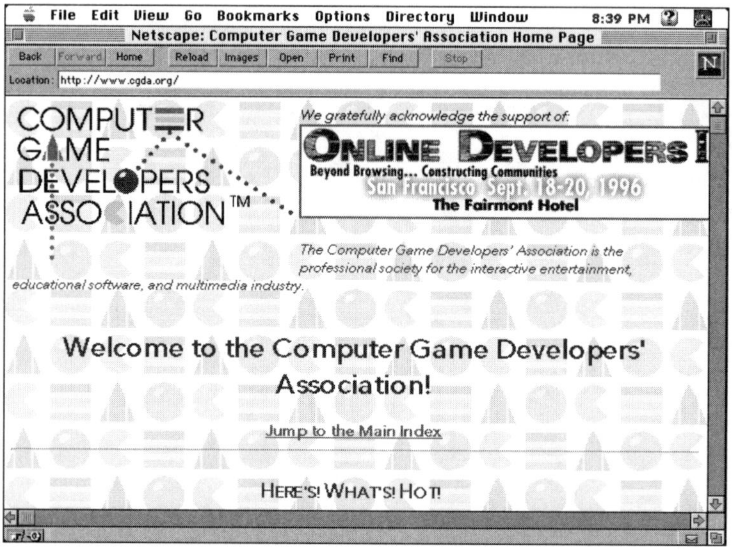

The site for this trade association is a valuable repository of knowledge for people who make video and computer games. The Association's site features business trends, hardware, software, and information sharing, with important links.

Multimedia Development Group

http://www.mdg.org

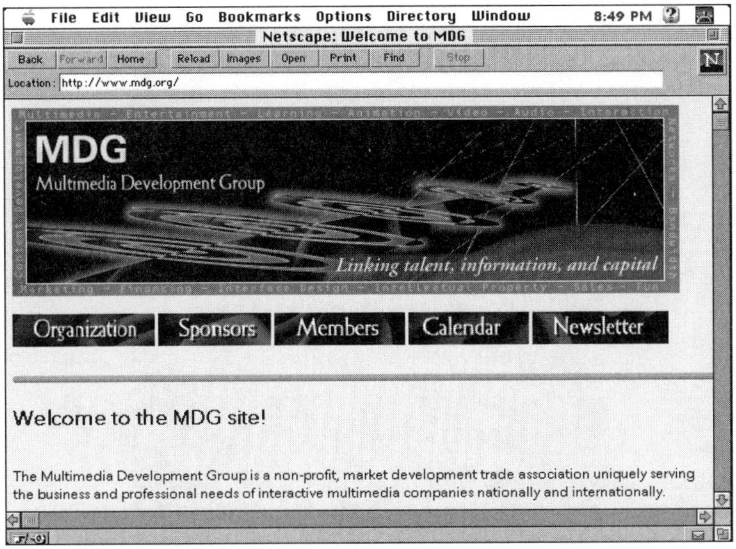

This San Francisco-based organization was set up to facilitate communication between developers, producers, infrastructure providers and government. A superb place for multimedia professionals to network.

Virtus

`http://www.virtus.com`

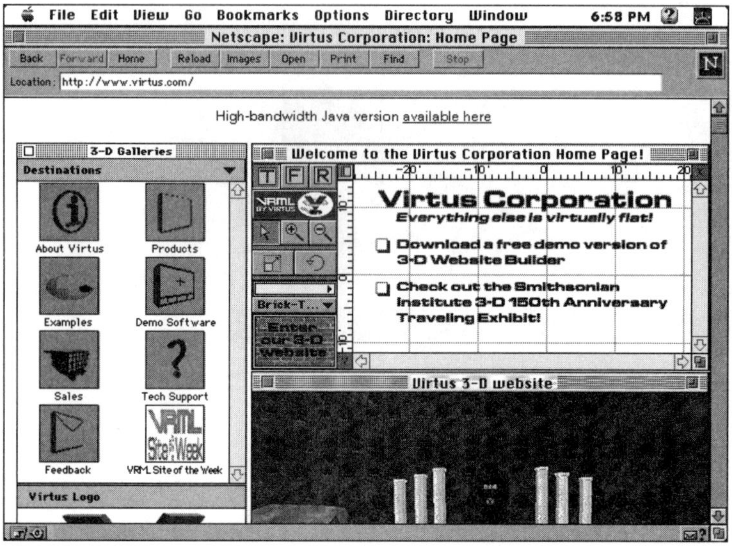

This company pioneered accessible 3D artwork and layout for digital media, and now has moved its focus to the Web. They have their own VRML protocol, which you can sample here.

The KIPI Page

http://www.kipinet.com

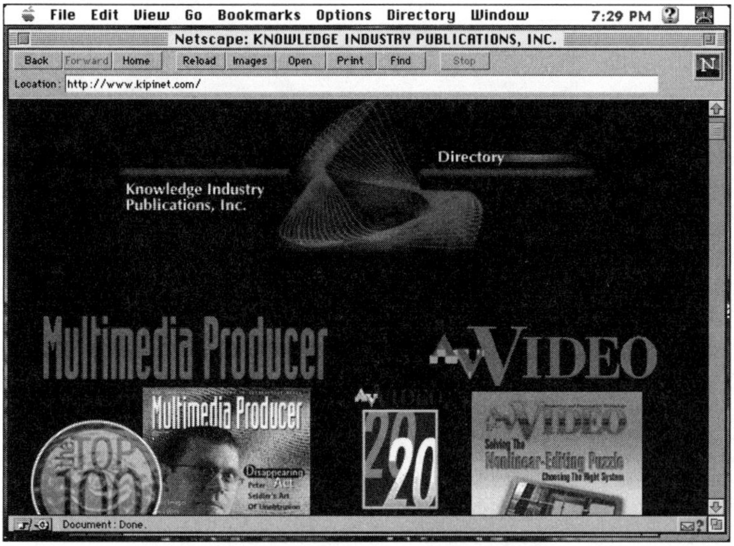

Knowledge Industries Publications is the source for several publications of importance to the multimedia producer. In addition to a magazine of that precise name, there are sub-sites for video and audio producers.

The CGI Page

```
http://www.yahoo.com/computers/world_wide_web/
      cgi_common_gateway_interface/index.html
```

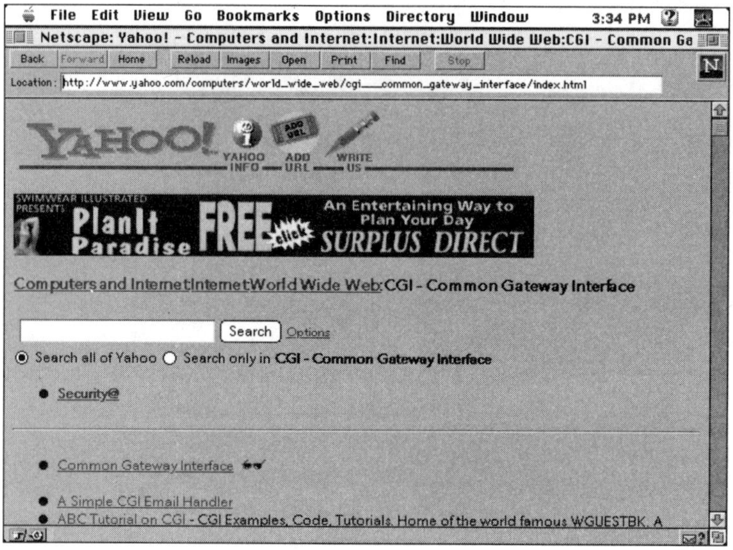

CGI scripts are useful for many Web applications, but programming them is a skill with a definite learning curve. On this directory page, you can take your pick from a variety of useful scripts ready for downloading.

G•WEB Home Page

`http://www.gweb.org`

This is a central exchange point for artists and animators who work in 3D. There are user forums, job listings, links to important sites, digital galleries, and trade exhibits listed here.

Electric Media

http://www.electricmedia.com

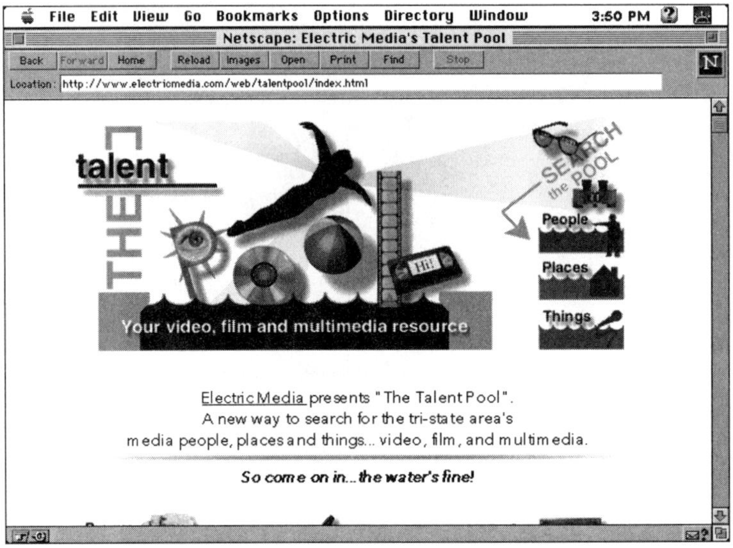

This site acts as a talent pool for multimedia professionals working in the New York tri-state metropolitan area. Sites like these blur the lines between networking, promotion, and marketing.

Control

http://www.musicpro.com/controline/aboutC.html

This is a unique resource for audio engineers interested in tools and techniques for digital audio production. In addition to the Web site, there's an interactive CD-ROM newsletter that actually demonstrates techniques and products.

CD-ROM Paradise

`http://www.cdrom-paradise.com`

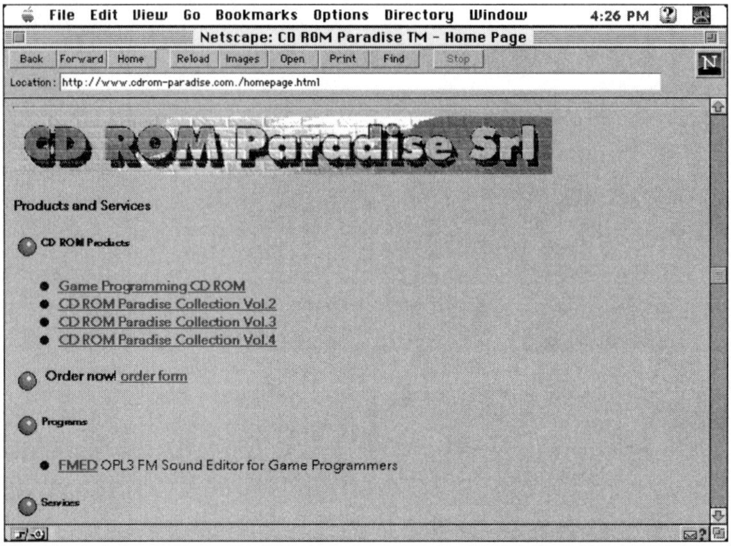

Game programmers are well-served by a series of CD-ROMs that outline advances and techniques. The company also offers utilities and culled shareware resources.

Media Links Free Graphics

http://www.erinet.com/cunning1/tiles.html

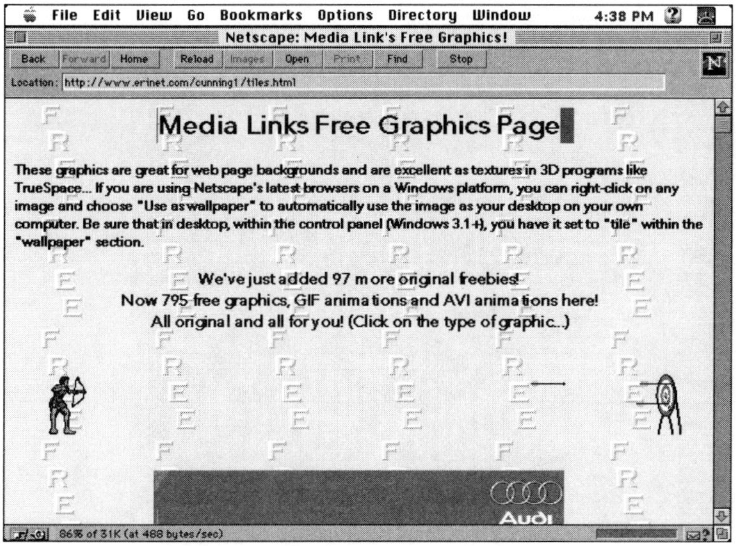

An excellent selection of graphic resources, such as 3D artwork, AVI files, GIFs, highlight lines, and background textures.

Jawai Interactive

http://www.jawai.com

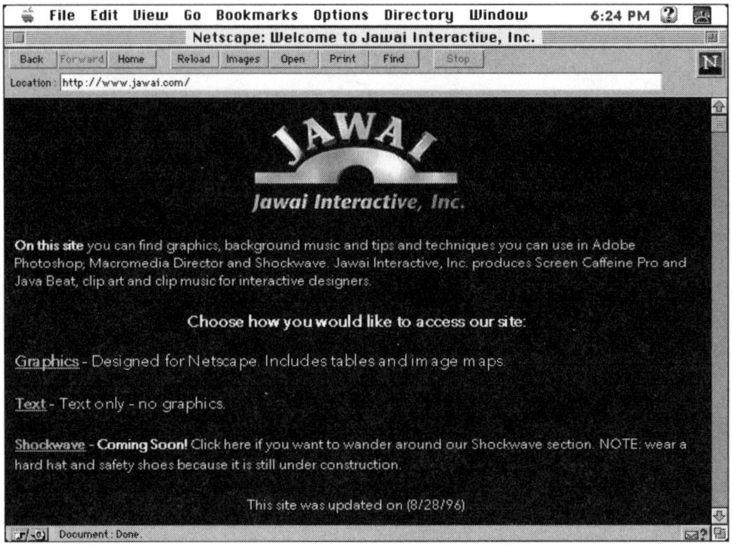

This is a group of digital artists who create tools for other digital artists. Makers of the “Screen Caffeine” series of backgrounds, buttons, and clickable scripts, they also offer files and tools for Photoshop and Shockwave.

Virtual Search's Online Center

`http://www.vsearch.com`

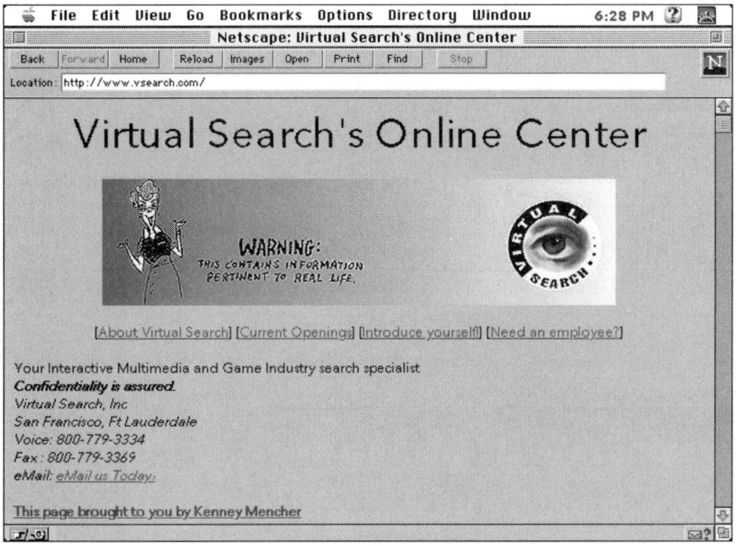

This online agency specializes in matching up multimedia talent with companies and projects on a commercial basis. They bill themselves as "researchers" rather than headhunters.

the Biz

`http://www.thebiz.co.uk/maraudmul.htm`

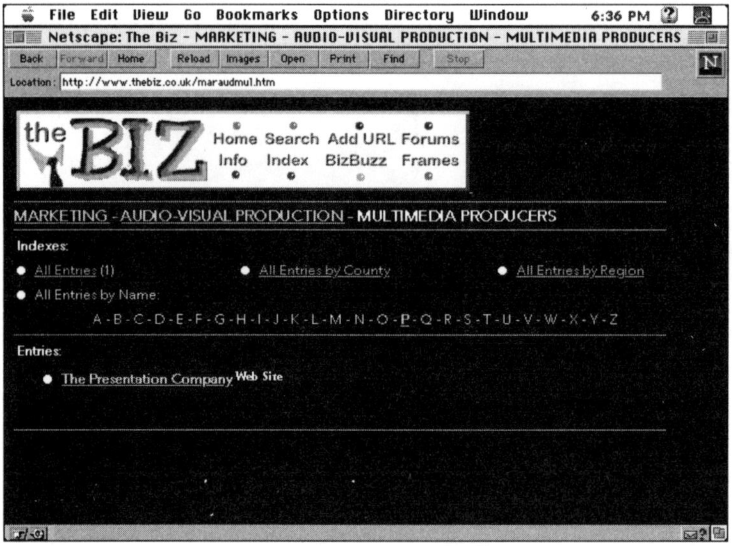

This British site serves as an information exchange to businesses in the UK that are looking for multimedia talent. But the good list of links to other design and technology groups are of wider interest.

IndexStock

http://www.indexstock.com/pages/whiteppr.htm

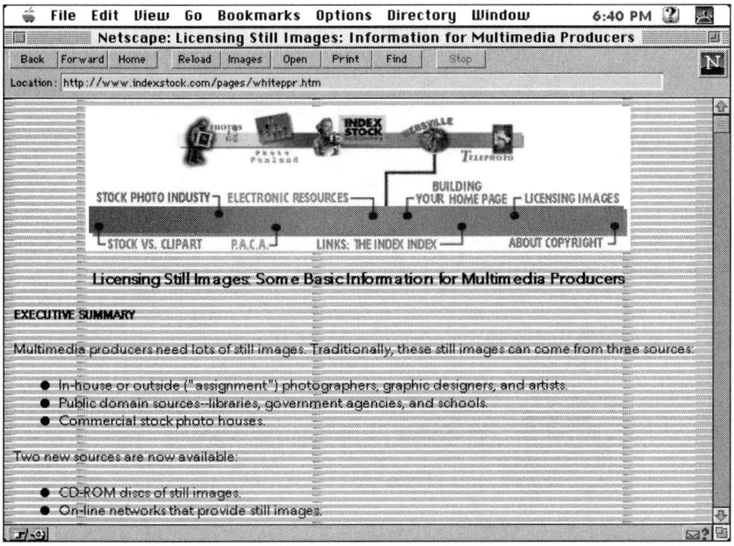

This page is a superb resource for information about acquiring and licensing images for multimedia productions. In addition to legal advice, there are links to stock agencies and other image services.

C/Net

```
http://www.cnet.com
```

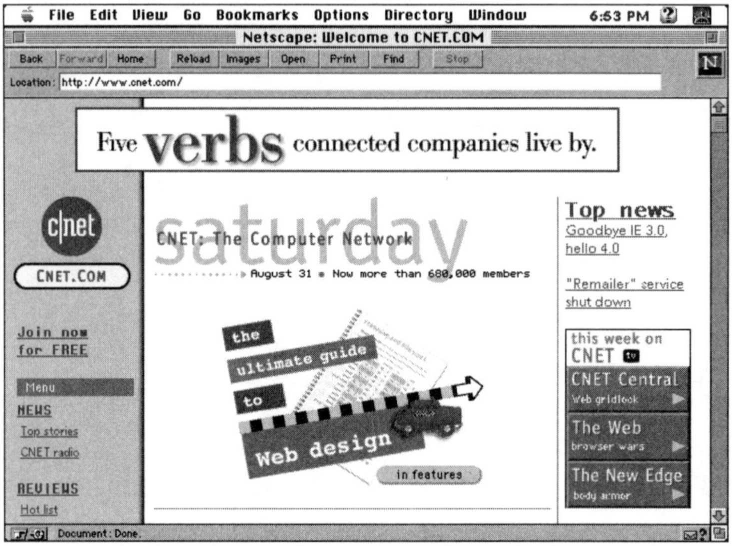

C/Net is the granddaddy of all digital-life publications. An enormous resource of news, opinion, entertainment and software. Any multimedia producer's browser should be bookmarked here.

E/town

http://www.e-town.com

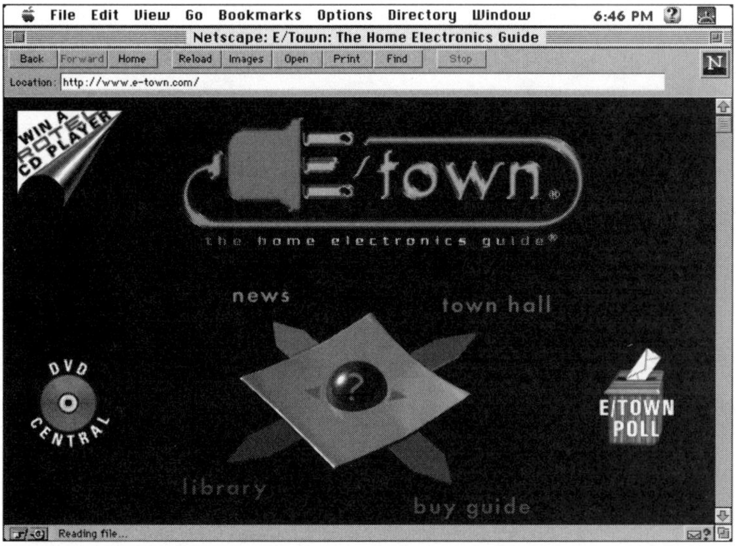

A comprehensive site dealing with consumer electronics and its convergence with multimedia. News, features, and public opinion regarding multimedia hardware and software in the home. And a shameless plug for the author!

Index

Special Characters

A

B

C

D

E

I

J

K

L

M

N

O

P

Q

R

S

T

U

V

W

X

Y

Z

ORDER FORM

IDG BOOKS WORLDWIDE

Order Center: **(800) 762-2974** *(8 a.m.–6 p.m., EST, weekdays)*

Quantity	ISBN	Title	Price	Total

Shipping & Handling Charges

	Description	First book	Each additional book	Total
Domestic	Normal	$4.50	$1.50	$
	Two Day Air	$8.50	$2.50	$
	Overnight	$18.00	$3.00	$
International	Surface	$8.00	$8.00	$
	Airmail	$16.00	$16.00	$
	DHL Air	$17.00	$17.00	$

*For large quantities call for shipping & handling charges.
**Prices are subject to change without notice.

Ship to:

Name ______________________

Company ______________________

Address ______________________

City/State/Zip ______________________

Daytime Phone ______________________

Payment: ☐ Check to IDG Books Worldwide (US Funds Only)
☐ VISA ☐ MasterCard ☐ American Express

Card # ______________________ Expires ____________

Signature ______________________

Subtotal ____________

CA residents add applicable sales tax ____________

IN, MA, and MD residents add 5% sales tax ____________

IL residents add 6.25% sales tax ____________

RI residents add 7% sales tax ____________

TX residents add 8.25% sales tax ____________

Shipping ____________

Total ____________

Please send this order form to:

IDG Books Worldwide, Inc.
Attn: Order Entry Dept.
7260 Shadeland Station, Suite 100
Indianapolis, IN 46256

Allow up to 3 weeks for delivery.
Thank you!

IDG BOOKS WORLDWIDE, INC.
END-USER LICENSE AGREEMENT

Read This. You should carefully read these terms and conditions before opening the software packet(s) included with this book ("Book"). This is a license agreement ("Agreement") between you and IDG Books Worldwide, Inc. ("IDGB"). By opening the accompanying software packet(s), you acknowledge that you have read and accept the following terms and conditions. If you do not agree and do not want to be bound by such terms and conditions, promptly return the Book and the unopened software packet(s) to the place you obtained them for a full refund.

1. License Grant. IDGB grants to you (either an individual or entity) a nonexclusive license to use one copy of the enclosed software program(s) (collectively, the "Software") solely for your own personal or business purposes on a single computer (whether a standard computer or a workstation component of a multiuser network). The Software is in use on a computer when it is loaded into temporary memory (i.e., RAM) or installed into permanent memory (e.g., hard disk, CD-ROM or other storage device). IDGB reserves all rights not expressly granted herein.

2. Ownership. IDGB is the owner of all rights, titles, and interests, including copyright, in and to the compilation of the Software recorded on the CD-ROM. Copyright to the individual programs on the CD-ROM is owned by the author or other authorized copyright owner of each program. Ownership of the Software and all proprietary rights relating thereto remain with IDGB and its licensors.

3. Restrictions on Use and Transfer.

(a) You may only (i) make one copy of the Software for backup or archival purposes, or (ii) transfer the Software to a single hard disk, provided that you keep the original for backup or archival purposes. You may not (i) rent or lease the Software, (ii) copy or reproduce the Software through a LAN or other network system or through any computer subscriber system or bulletin-board system, or (iii) modify, adapt, or create derivative works based on the Software.

(b) You may not reverse engineer, decompile, or disassemble the Software. You may transfer the Software and user documentation on a permanent basis, provided that the transferee agrees to accept the terms and conditions of this Agreement and you retain no copies. If the Software is an update or has been updated, any transfer must include the most recent update and all prior versions.

4. Restrictions on Use of Individual Programs. You must follow the individual requirements and restrictions detailed for each individual program in the CD-ROM of this Book. These limitations are contained in the individual license agreements recorded on the CD-ROM. These restrictions include a requirement that after using the program for the period of time specified in its text, the user must pay a registration fee or discontinue use. By opening the Software packet(s), you will be agreeing to abide by the licenses and restrictions for these individual programs. None of the material on this disk(s) or listed in this Book may ever be distributed, in original or modified form, for commercial purposes.

5. Limited Warranty.
(a) IDGB warrants that the Software and CD-ROM are free from defects in materials and workmanship under normal use for a period of sixty (60) days from the date of purchase of this Book. If IDGB receives notification within the warranty period of defects in materials or workmanship, IDGB will replace the defective CD-ROM.

(b) IDGB AND THE AUTHOR OF THE BOOK DISCLAIM ALL OTHER WARRANTIES, EXPRESS OR IMPLIED, INCLUDING WITHOUT LIMITATION IMPLIED WARRANTIES OF MERCHANTABILITY AND FITNESS FOR A PARTICULAR PURPOSE, WITH RESPECT TO THE SOFTWARE, THE PROGRAMS, THE SOURCE CODE CONTAINED THEREIN, AND/OR THE TECHNIQUES DESCRIBED IN THIS BOOK. IDGB DOES NOT WARRANT THAT THE FUNCTIONS CONTAINED IN THE SOFTWARE WILL MEET YOUR REQUIREMENTS OR THAT THE OPERATION OF THE SOFTWARE WILL BE ERROR FREE.

(c) This limited warranty gives you specific legal rights, and you may have other rights that vary from jurisdiction to jurisdiction.

6. Remedies.
(a) IDGB's entire liability and your exclusive remedy for defects in materials and workmanship shall be limited to replacement of the Software, which is returned to IDGB at the address set forth below with a copy of your receipt.

This Limited Warranty is void if failure of the Software has resulted from accident, abuse, or misapplication. Any replacement Software will be warranted for the remainder of the original warranty period or thirty (30) days, whichever is longer.

(b) In no event shall IDGB or the author be liable for any damages whatsoever (including without limitation damages for loss of business profits, business interruption, loss of business information, or any other pecuniary loss) arising out of the use of or inability to use the Book or the Software, even if IDGB has been advised of the possibility of such damages.

(c) Because some jurisdictions do not allow the exclusion or limitation of liability for consequential or incidental damages, the above limitation or exclusion may not apply to you.

7. U.S. Government Restricted Rights. Use, duplication, or disclosure of the Software by the U.S. Government is subject to restrictions stated in paragraph (c) (1) (ii) of the Rights in Technical Data and Computer Software clause of DFARS 252.227-7013, and in subparagraphs (a) through (d) of the Commercial Computer—Restricted Rights clause at FAR 52.227-19, and in similar clauses in the NASA FAR supplement, when applicable.

8. General. This Agreement constitutes the entire understanding of the parties, and revokes and supersedes all prior agreements, oral or written, between them and may not be modified or amended except in a writing signed by both parties hereto which specifically refers to this Agreement. This Agreement shall take precedence over any other documents that may be in conflict herewith. If any one or more provisions contained in this Agreement are held by any court or tribunal to be invalid, illegal or otherwise unenforceable, each and every other provision shall remain in full force and effect.

CD-ROM Installation

To use the attached CD-ROM, insert it into your computer's CD-ROM drive. Find the folder for the tool you want to try, and follow that program's installation instructions.